T0190392

Lecture Notes in Computer Science   14040

Founding Editors

Gerhard Goos
Juris Hartmanis

The series Lecture Notes in Computer Science (LNCS), including its subseries Lecture Notes in Artificial Intelligence (LNAI) and Lecture Notes in Bioinformatics (LNBI), has established itself as a medium for the publication of new developments in computer science and information technology research, teaching, and education.

LNCS enjoys close cooperation with the computer science R & D community, the series counts many renowned academics among its volume editors and paper authors, and collaborates with prestigious societies. Its mission is to serve this international community by providing an invaluable service, mainly focused on the publication of conference and workshop proceedings and postproceedings. LNCS commenced publication in 1973.

Panayiotis Zaphiris · Andri Ioannou
Editors

Learning and Collaboration Technologies

10th International Conference, LCT 2023
Held as Part of the 25th HCI International Conference, HCII 2023
Copenhagen, Denmark, July 23–28, 2023
Proceedings, Part I

 Springer

Editors
Panayiotis Zaphiris
Cyprus University of Technology
Limassol, Cyprus

Andri Ioannou (iD)
Cyprus University of Technology
Limassol, Cyprus

CYENS
Nicosia, Cyprus

ISSN 0302-9743   ISSN 1611-3349 (electronic)
Lecture Notes in Computer Science
ISBN 978-3-031-34410-7   ISBN 978-3-031-34411-4 (eBook)
https://doi.org/10.1007/978-3-031-34411-4

Foreword

Human-computer interaction (HCI) is acquiring an ever-increasing scientific and industrial importance, as well as having more impact on people's everyday lives, as an ever-growing number of human activities are progressively moving from the physical to the digital world. This process, which has been ongoing for some time now, was further accelerated during the acute period of the COVID-19 pandemic. The HCI International (HCII) conference series, held annually, aims to respond to the compelling need to advance the exchange of knowledge and research and development efforts on the human aspects of design and use of computing systems.

The 25th International Conference on Human-Computer Interaction, HCI International 2023 (HCII 2023), was held in the emerging post-pandemic era as a 'hybrid' event at the AC Bella Sky Hotel and Bella Center, Copenhagen, Denmark, during July 23–28, 2023. It incorporated the 21 thematic areas and affiliated conferences listed below.

A total of 7472 individuals from academia, research institutes, industry, and government agencies from 85 countries submitted contributions, and 1578 papers and 396 posters were included in the volumes of the proceedings that were published just before the start of the conference, these are listed below. The contributions thoroughly cover the entire field of human-computer interaction, addressing major advances in knowledge and effective use of computers in a variety of application areas. These papers provide academics, researchers, engineers, scientists, practitioners and students with state-of-the-art information on the most recent advances in HCI.

The HCI International (HCII) conference also offers the option of presenting 'Late Breaking Work', and this applies both for papers and posters, with corresponding volumes of proceedings that will be published after the conference. Full papers will be included in the 'HCII 2023 - Late Breaking Work - Papers' volumes of the proceedings to be published in the Springer LNCS series, while 'Poster Extended Abstracts' will be included as short research papers in the 'HCII 2023 - Late Breaking Work - Posters' volumes to be published in the Springer CCIS series.

I would like to thank the Program Board Chairs and the members of the Program Boards of all thematic areas and affiliated conferences for their contribution towards the high scientific quality and overall success of the HCI International 2023 conference. Their manifold support in terms of paper reviewing (single-blind review process, with a minimum of two reviews per submission), session organization and their willingness to act as goodwill ambassadors for the conference is most highly appreciated.

This conference would not have been possible without the continuous and unwavering support and advice of Gavriel Salvendy, founder, General Chair Emeritus, and Scientific Advisor. For his outstanding efforts, I would like to express my sincere appreciation to Abbas Moallem, Communications Chair and Editor of HCI International News.

July 2023   Constantine Stephanidis

HCI International 2023 Thematic Areas
and Affiliated Conferences

Thematic Areas

- HCI: Human-Computer Interaction
- HIMI: Human Interface and the Management of Information

Affiliated Conferences

- EPCE: 20th International Conference on Engineering Psychology and Cognitive Ergonomics
- AC: 17th International Conference on Augmented Cognition
- UAHCI: 17th International Conference on Universal Access in Human-Computer Interaction
- CCD: 15th International Conference on Cross-Cultural Design
- SCSM: 15th International Conference on Social Computing and Social Media
- VAMR: 15th International Conference on Virtual, Augmented and Mixed Reality
- DHM: 14th International Conference on Digital Human Modeling and Applications in Health, Safety, Ergonomics and Risk Management
- DUXU: 12th International Conference on Design, User Experience and Usability
- C&C: 11th International Conference on Culture and Computing
- DAPI: 11th International Conference on Distributed, Ambient and Pervasive Interactions
- HCIBGO: 10th International Conference on HCI in Business, Government and Organizations
- LCT: 10th International Conference on Learning and Collaboration Technologies
- ITAP: 9th International Conference on Human Aspects of IT for the Aged Population
- AIS: 5th International Conference on Adaptive Instructional Systems
- HCI-CPT: 5th International Conference on HCI for Cybersecurity, Privacy and Trust
- HCI-Games: 5th International Conference on HCI in Games
- MobiTAS: 5th International Conference on HCI in Mobility, Transport and Automotive Systems
- AI-HCI: 4th International Conference on Artificial Intelligence in HCI
- MOBILE: 4th International Conference on Design, Operation and Evaluation of Mobile Communications

List of Conference Proceedings Volumes Appearing Before the Conference

1. LNCS 14011, Human-Computer Interaction: Part I, edited by Masaaki Kurosu and Ayako Hashizume
2. LNCS 14012, Human-Computer Interaction: Part II, edited by Masaaki Kurosu and Ayako Hashizume
3. LNCS 14013, Human-Computer Interaction: Part III, edited by Masaaki Kurosu and Ayako Hashizume
4. LNCS 14014, Human-Computer Interaction: Part IV, edited by Masaaki Kurosu and Ayako Hashizume
5. LNCS 14015, Human Interface and the Management of Information: Part I, edited by Hirohiko Mori and Yumi Asahi
6. LNCS 14016, Human Interface and the Management of Information: Part II, edited by Hirohiko Mori and Yumi Asahi
7. LNAI 14017, Engineering Psychology and Cognitive Ergonomics: Part I, edited by Don Harris and Wen-Chin Li
8. LNAI 14018, Engineering Psychology and Cognitive Ergonomics: Part II, edited by Don Harris and Wen-Chin Li
9. LNAI 14019, Augmented Cognition, edited by Dylan D. Schmorrow and Cali M. Fidopiastis
10. LNCS 14020, Universal Access in Human-Computer Interaction: Part I, edited by Margherita Antona and Constantine Stephanidis
11. LNCS 14021, Universal Access in Human-Computer Interaction: Part II, edited by Margherita Antona and Constantine Stephanidis
12. LNCS 14022, Cross-Cultural Design: Part I, edited by Pei-Luen Patrick Rau
13. LNCS 14023, Cross-Cultural Design: Part II, edited by Pei-Luen Patrick Rau
14. LNCS 14024, Cross-Cultural Design: Part III, edited by Pei-Luen Patrick Rau
15. LNCS 14025, Social Computing and Social Media: Part I, edited by Adela Coman and Simona Vasilache
16. LNCS 14026, Social Computing and Social Media: Part II, edited by Adela Coman and Simona Vasilache
17. LNCS 14027, Virtual, Augmented and Mixed Reality, edited by Jessie Y. C. Chen and Gino Fragomeni
18. LNCS 14028, Digital Human Modeling and Applications in Health, Safety, Ergonomics and Risk Management: Part I, edited by Vincent G. Duffy
19. LNCS 14029, Digital Human Modeling and Applications in Health, Safety, Ergonomics and Risk Management: Part II, edited by Vincent G. Duffy
20. LNCS 14030, Design, User Experience, and Usability: Part I, edited by Aaron Marcus, Elizabeth Rosenzweig and Marcelo Soares
21. LNCS 14031, Design, User Experience, and Usability: Part II, edited by Aaron Marcus, Elizabeth Rosenzweig and Marcelo Soares

47. CCIS 1836, HCI International 2023 Posters - Part V, edited by Constantine Stephanidis, Margherita Antona, Stavroula Ntoa and Gavriel Salvendy

https://2023.hci.international/proceedings

Preface

In today's knowledge society, learning and collaboration are two fundamental and strictly interrelated aspects of knowledge acquisition and creation. Learning technology is the broad range of communication, information, and related technologies that can be used to support learning, teaching, and assessment, often in a collaborative way. Collaboration technology, on the other hand, is targeted to support individuals working in teams towards a common goal, which may be an educational one, by providing tools that aid communication and the management of activities as well as the process of problem solving. In this context, interactive technologies not only affect and improve the existing educational system but become a transformative force that can generate radically new ways of knowing, learning, and collaborating.

The 10th International Conference on Learning and Collaboration Technologies (LCT 2023), affiliated to HCI International 2023, addressed the theoretical foundations, design and implementation, and effectiveness and impact issues related to interactive technologies for learning and collaboration, including design methodologies, developments and tools, theoretical models, and learning design or learning experience (LX) design, as well as technology adoption and use in formal, non-formal, and informal educational contexts.

Learning and collaboration technologies are increasingly adopted in K-20 (kindergarten to higher education) classrooms and lifelong learning. Technology can support expansive forms of collaboration; deepened empathy; complex coordination of people, materials, and purposes; and development of skill sets that are increasingly important across workspaces in the 21st century. The general themes of the LCT conference aim to address challenges related to understanding how to design for better learning and collaboration with technology, support learners to develop relevant approaches and skills, and assess or evaluate gains and outcomes. To this end, topics such as extended reality (XR) learning, embodied and immersive learning, mobile learning and ubiquitous technologies, serious games and gamification, learning through design and making, educational robotics, educational chatbots, human-computer interfaces, and computer-supported collaborative learning, among others, are elaborated in the LCT conference proceedings. Learning (experience) design and user experience design remain a challenge in the arena of learning environments and collaboration technology. LCT aims to serve a continuous dialog while synthesizing current knowledge.

Two volumes of the HCII 2023 proceedings are dedicated to this year's edition of the LCT 2023 conference. Part I focuses on topics related to the design of learning environments, the learning experience, technology-supported teaching, and supporting creativity, while Part II covers XR and robotic technologies in learning, as well as virtual, blended, and hybrid learning.

Papers of these volumes are included for publication after a minimum of two single-blind reviews from the members of the LCT Program Board or, in some cases, from members of the Program Boards of other affiliated conferences. We would like to thank all of them for their invaluable contribution, support, and efforts.

July 2023   Panayiotis Zaphiris
                                                                    Andri Ioannou

10th International Conference on Learning and Collaboration Technologies (LCT 2023)

Program Board Chairs: **Panayiotis Zaphiris**, *Cyprus University of Technology, Cyprus* and **Andri Ioannou**, *Cyprus University of Technology and Research Center on Interactive Media, Smart Systems and Emerging Technologies (CYENS), Cyprus*

Program Board:

- Fisnik Dalipi, *Linnaeus University, Sweden*
- Camille Dickson-Deane, *University of Technology Sydney, Australia*
- David Fonseca Escudero, *La Salle Ramon Llull University, Spain*
- Francisco Jose García-Peñalvo, *University of Salamanca, Spain*
- Aleksandar Jevremovic, *Singidunum University, Serbia*
- Elis Kakoulli Constantinou, *Cyprus University of Technology, Cyprus*
- Tomaž Klobučar, *Jozef Stefan Institute, Slovenia*
- Birgy Lorenz, *Tallinn University of Technology, Estonia*
- Nicholas H. Müller, *University of Applied Sciences Würzburg-Schweinfurt, Germany*
- Anna Nicolaou, *Cyprus University of Technology, Cyprus*
- Antigoni Parmaxi, *Cyprus University of Technology, Cyprus*
- Dijana Plantak Vukovac, *University of Zagreb, Croatia*
- Maria-Victoria Soulé, *Cyprus University of Technology, Cyprus*
- Sonia Sousa, *Tallinn University, Estonia*
- Sara Villagrá-Sobrino, *Valladolid University, Spain*

The full list with the Program Board Chairs and the members of the Program Boards of all thematic areas and affiliated conferences of HCII2023 is available online at:

http://www.hci.international/board-members-2023.php

HCI International 2024 Conference

The 26th International Conference on Human-Computer Interaction, HCI International 2024, will be held jointly with the affiliated conferences at the Washington Hilton Hotel, Washington, DC, USA, June 29 – July 4, 2024. It will cover a broad spectrum of themes related to Human-Computer Interaction, including theoretical issues, methods, tools, processes, and case studies in HCI design, as well as novel interaction techniques, interfaces, and applications. The proceedings will be published by Springer. More information will be made available on the conference website: http://2024.hci.international/.

General Chair
Prof. Constantine Stephanidis
University of Crete and ICS-FORTH
Heraklion, Crete, Greece
Email: general_chair@hcii2024.org

https://2024.hci.international/

Contents – Part I

Understanding the Learning Experience

Technology-Supported Teaching

Supporting Creativity in Learning

Contents – Part II

Learning with Robots

Virtual, Blended and Hybrid Learning

Designing Learning Experiences

Security and Privacy in Academic Data Management at Schools: SPADATAS Project

Daniel Amo-Filva[1] , David Fonseca Escudero[1(✉)] ,
Mónica V. Sanchez-Sepulveda[1] , Alicia García-Holgado[2] ,
Lucía García-Holgado[2] , Francisco José García-Peñalvo[2] ,
Tihomir Orehovački[3] , Marjan Krašna[4] , Igor Pesek[4] , Emanuela Marchetti[5] ,
Andrea Valente[5] , Claus Witfelt[6] , Ivana Ružić[7] , Karim Elia Fraoua[8] ,
and Fernando Moreira[9,10]

[1] La Salle, Ramon Llull University, Barcelona, Spain
{daniel.amo,fonsi,monica.sanchez}@salle.url.edu
[2] GRIAL Research Group, Department of Computer Science and Automation, Universidad de Salamanca, Salamanca, Spain
{aliciagh,luciagh,fgarcia}@usal.es
[3] Faculty of Informatics, Juraj Dobrila University of Pula, Pula, Croatia
tihomir.orehovacki@unipu.hr
[4] Faculty of Natural Sciences and Mathematics, University of Maribor, Maribor, Slovenia
{marjan.krasna,igor.pesek}@um.si
[5] University of Southern Denmark, Odense, Denmark
emanuela@sdu.dk, anva@mmmi.sdu.dk
[6] Oerestad Gymnasium, Copenhagen, Denmark
[7] I. Osnovna škola Čakovec, Čakovec, Croatia
ivana.ruzic@skole.hr
[8] Université Gustave Eiffel, Campus de Marne-La-Vallée, Val d'Europe, Serris, France
fraoua@u-pem.fr
[9] REMIT, IJP, Universidade Portucalense, Porto, Portugal
fmoreira@upt.pt
[10] IEETA, Universidade de Aveiro, Aveiro, Portugal
https://ror.org/02f40zc51

Abstract. The introduction of cloud technology in educational settings over the past ten years has enabled organizations to embrace a data-driven decision-making paradigm. Schools and colleges are undergoing rapid digital updating procedures due to the use of outside technological solutions in the cloud, affecting how students learn and are taught. Regarding data, teaching and learning processes are improved by technology that gathers and analyzes student data to present useful information. With this technological shift comes the pervasiveness of data thanks to cloud storage. This means that in many instances, outside the purview of schools and universities, certain actors may gather, manage, and treat educational data on private servers and data centers. This privatization allows data leaks, record manipulation, and unwanted access. To help primary and secondary schools understand what data-driven decision-making entails for an educational institution and what problems with data fragility are related to current educational technology and

P. Zaphiris and A. Ioannou (Eds.): HCII 2023, LNCS 14040, pp. 3–16, 2023.
https://doi.org/10.1007/978-3-031-34411-4_1

data academic management, the current paper outlines the main goals of the SPA-DATAS project, its organizational structure, and its key issues. It also offers tools and frameworks to safeguard the privacy, security, and confidentiality of students' data.

Keywords: Academic data · privacy · security · management · confidentially of student's data

1   Introduction

In the last 10 years, if we talk about educational environments, there has been an evolution that has made possible a decision-making paradigm based on data collected by themselves [8, 13, 25]. Regarding technology, and more specifically after the Covid-19 crisis, schools and universities are experiencing rapid processes of digitalization and ICT tools and services updating where the adoption of third-party technology solutions in the cloud results in changes in academic and learning processes (such as Big Data services, or Artificial Intelligence, Machine Learning, Learning Analytics, and Tutoring Systems) [2, 6, 7, 15, 19, 22, 23, 45]. Regarding data, technology that collects and analyzes students' data to present actionable information enhances teaching-learning processes [2, 3, 9, 20, 27, 48]. On the one hand, those organizations that understand the power of data can improve the educational context in very different manners [12, 44]. On the other hand, those who do not contemplate this change of data in the teaching-learning processes cannot benefit from the analytical results, and as can be seen from the results of previous work, adaptability to users through interactive, gamified platforms, with correctly designed management of user data and interactions, are options for guaranteed success implementations [16, 17, 26, 28, 29]. However, both perspectives have the same cloud-computed technology-associated problems regarding data fragility [1, 4, 5, 8, 9].

Cloud storage brings the ubiquity of data to this technological transition. However, in many cases, this suggests that certain actors, beyond the control of schools and colleges, collect, handle, and treat educational data on private servers and data centers [18]. This privatization enables the manipulation of stored records, data leaks, and unauthorized access. Hence, although the integration of cloud services in schools and universities has a positive shift, it also presents threats to all academic roles that need to be discussed regarding protection, privacy, and confidentiality.

Security denotes the extent to which an application protects users' data and information from unauthorized access and use [31]. It is composed from two relevant dimensions: integrity (the degree to which users' information and data are trustworthy and accurate) and confidentiality (the extent to which data and information can be accessed only by authorized users) [35]. Considering that security significantly contributes to the perceived usefulness and users' satisfaction [38], it is commonly used for quality evaluation of cloud computing applications employed in educational settings [32–34, 37, 40, 41] as well as other applications that have educational potential [36]. Apart from security, an important role in the adoption of cloud computing applications also have privacy and trust [39]. While privacy indicates the extent to which users' information and artefacts are protected from being shared with a third-party without their consent or knowledge, trust refers to the degree to which cloud computing application takes care about interests of its users [35].

Considering the context described above, in the SPADATAS project, a full awareness of data fragility comprehends the acquisition of those competencies exposed in DigiCompEdu regarding data literacy and responsible use in digital competence. Thus, the SPADATAS project aims to provide:

- Understanding and awareness to primary and secondary schools about what datadriven and decision-making imply for an educational institution,
- Which problems about data fragility are related to current educational technology and data academic management,
- Provide tools and frameworks to protect the privacy, security, and confidentiality of students' data.

Our approach focuses on the data fragility awareness acquisition by representatives, teachers, and students to promote data and self-data treatment good practices. In this sense, SPADATAS is aligned with the horizontal priority of: "Addressing digital transformation through the development of digital readiness, resilience, and capacity", and with the following two priorities according to the objectives of the project: Supporting teachers, school leaders, and other teaching professions; and development of key competences.

2 Project Description

The digital evolution of schools and universities means using third-party hardware and software, which mostly resides and executes in cloud computing forcing changes to educational institutions' culture and processes [24]. The growth of educational technology based on this approach has led to adopting educational decisions based on data in line with the big data analytics movement [8, 49]. On the one hand, institutions require permanent Internet connectivity, and therefore the data generated becomes ubiquitous and available at anytime and anywhere. On the other hand, changes in academic and educational processes raise new problems concerning generated data, because this type of hyperconnected educational environment has a strong ability to collect, store, process, and analyze large amounts of data through cloud computing.

Technological innovations and the cheapening of cloud computing have made Software as a Service (SaaS) [10, 11], which resides in the cloud, the most attractive option for the distribution of digital tools in the industrial field, and education [30]. Universities and schools are working to reduce costs by adopting SaaS solutions [14]. However, this results in many negative results, from data leaks to misuse. Consequently, digital educational technology tools (EdTech) raise new challenges and issues related to privacy, identity, confidentiality, and security of data and metadata for all educational roles. All these problems, issues, and threats to educational data are described as a data fragile context or data fragility problem.

When sending data to cloud it is mandatory to define and integrate processes and technologies that ensure ethical and legal data treatment. In this sense, there are a lot of questions without answers, among others:

- Do we need to send data to cloud, or we can use local-unplugged technologies?
- What data should be sent outside the institution that can be transferred without risking the students' identity?
- Do we need to send unsecured data, or can we send it anonymously?
- Can local technology be the only one to provide a trustworthy, private, and secure environment?

All the context and questions above are motives for the project. Answering the questions is not easy and needs different educational actors to be involved. Moreover, due to Europe having a General Data Privacy Regulation that frames the answers, funds are needed to help different actors from around Europe meet and work together to give answers.

Tree main actions have been defined for achieving our goals:

- Develop open and public web tools for data fragility awareness, auto-assessment, and data treatment processes mapping regarding data privacy and security treatment processes in primary and secondary schools (mixed method: quantitative research with qualitative evaluation).
- Conduct data fragility awareness workshops. The schoolteachers will be trained as data awareness agents to raise data fragility awareness among representatives, teachers, and students from their own and other schools who voluntarily apply to the project. The schoolteachers will conduct role-targeted workshops to spread data fragility awareness and extract good practices on students' data academic management.
- Develop a website and release a handbook of categorized good practices regarding data academic management to implement effective processes, or improve current, in primary and secondary schools to help protect the data privacy, security, and confidentiality of students, in collaboration with the communities and associations of a region and under the European Union's General Data Protection Regulation.

The results expected will be twofold: on the one hand, build a digital platform for auto-assessment of data treatment regarding data privacy and security of students; and on the other hand, publish resources focused on data privacy, security, and confidentiality of student's data to help any kind of educational institution the implementation of data treatment processes to reduce privacy and security issues. Both results aim to raise awareness of data fragility.

The Regulation (EU) 2016/679 sets the need for the protection of natural persons regarding the processing of personal data and the free movement of such data. It is an essential step to strengthen individual fundamental rights in the digital age. In this sense, the main priority of the European Union (EU) is to provide an inclusive data protection framework. The objectives of the SPADATAS project are in line with the EU data protection framework, where actions are set to reduce data fragility issues. This regulation also applies to data academic management in primary and secondary schools, being this one of the focuses of the project.

A systematic review of CORDIS and Erasmus + project results in databases was conducted to ensure the project is innovative and complementary to other projects already carried out. In this preliminary work, several projects found focused on digital security competencies, healthy digital life, internet safety, online security, cybersecurity, or data security. All the projects focus on student training, proposing actions, learning materials, and lesson plans to improve their digital skills to have an auto-regulated healthy digital life [21, 42, 43, 46–48]. However, there is a lack of projects, and there is not any official database, at least at a European level, that considers data academic management processes regarding data fragility issues and involves representatives and teachers. Namely, most of the projects are focused on digital skills for students instead of digital skills for reducing the digital fragility of students' data in teaching and academic processes, being one of the main innovations of the project.

The SPADATAS project is innovative because it is not focused only on student training, but also on providing resources and tools for representatives and teachers to fight data fragility issues on academic management in their primary and secondary schools.

3 The Consortium

We present a consortium with three levels of partners and associated partners (14 in total, with more than 25 teachers and researchers involved, to directly impact 100–200 school students during the project, and more than 1,000 schools in the dissemination processes of the project results, based on the capacity of connection between schools and institutions of the consortium.

Five universities and two schools form the partner consortium:

- La Salle, Ramon Llull University (URL), Spain.
- University of Salamanca (USAL), Spain.
- Juraj Dobrile University of Pula (UNIPUR), Croatia.
- University of Maribor (UM), Slovenia.
- University of Southern Denmark (SDU), Denmark.
- Oerestad Gymnasium School, Denmark.
- Elementary School "I. osnovna škola Čakovec", Croatia.

Also, the project has the support as associated partners of two universities from Portugal and France, two regional institutions from Spain that are managing a network of schools, and three more schools from Portugal, France and Croatia.

4 Methodology

The project duration is 30 months from October 2022 to March 2025 with a total budget approved of 250.000,00 €, and the activities are divided into different types:

- Project management and implementation activities:

  - A1 Overall project management.
  - A2 Quality Assurance.
  - A3 Dissemination and exploitation activity in the project.

- Intellectual outputs that represent the main actions developed in the project to achieve the objectives:

  – IO1: Open tool for data fragility auto-assessment and mapping in data academic management processes.
  – IO2: Digital handbook to reduce data fragility in data academic management.

- Transnational Project Meetings:

  – M1. Kick-off meeting in Salamanca, Spain.
  – M2. Setup the training in Barcelona, Spain.
  – M3. Follow-up meeting in Denmark.
  – M4. Laying the foundations in Pula, Croatia.
  – M5. Follow-up meeting in Slovenia.
  – M6. Follow-up and output completion in Barcelona, Spain.

- Joint staff training events:

  – C1. Teacher training in data awareness - Barcelona (Spain).
  – C2. Workshop awareness for teachers/coordinators – Schools.
  – C3. Workshop awareness for students – Schools.
  – C4. Workshop wrap-up for teachers/coordinators – Schools.

- Multiplier events, a set of events focused on spreading the results of the project and transferring the knowledge and practices developed in the Intellectual outputs. There will be four events to cover the different countries involved in the project:

  – E1. SPADATAS workshop Spain. Lead by USAL.
  – E2. SPADATAS workshop Croatia. Lead by UNIPUR.
  – E3. SPADATAS workshop Denmark. Lead by SDU.
  – E4. SPADATAS workshop Slovenia. Lead by UM.

The project is organized into five distinctive phases (as we can see in Fig. 1):

The first phase (M1 to M11) is data awareness assessment. It matches with the ongoing IO1. During the first six months, from M1 to M7, tasks will be executed to prepare and validate the data fragility questionnaire assessment, conduct a survey to schools' representatives, teachers and students, and report results. The results will serve as a baseline input for preparing the teacher training considered in the IO2. Also, it will serve as input for the development of the website tool, from M8 to M11, where any school could auto-assess their data academic management processes. The website will also serve as 1) a public observatory for data fragility awareness to foster connections between schools and the project that can help in the implementation or definition of the project activities, and 2) make available results of IO2. In resume the task (T#) defined are:

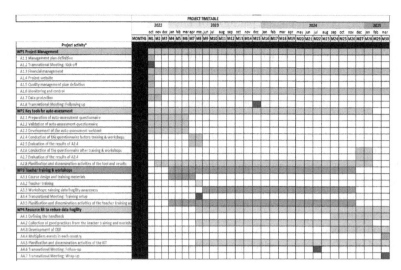

Fig. 1. Timeline of the project.

- T1.1 Preparation: Preparation of survey tools, system architecture, data collection processes, and questionnaires for data fragility assessment.
- T1.2 Validation: Validate resulting questionnaires from T1.1.
- T1.3 Conduct survey: Support schools in the survey execution using resulting survey tools from T1.1.
- T1.4 Reporting: Analyzing survey responses from T1.3 and sharing results with schools.
- T1.5 Website development: Development of a website to let any school auto-assess, map and report data fragility issues in their data academic management processes. Results will be anonymized and published as an observatory to raise data fragility awareness.

The second phase (M7-M27), training & Workshops will cover the first and second phases of the IO2. The first phase, from M7 to M11, considers tasks such as teacher training regarding data fragility awareness and co-creation of data awareness workshops. The teacher training design and execution will be led by URL-La Salle in conjunction with all the other partners considering their expertise and knowledge. The teacher training will have a double objective and will be divided into two main steps. As a first step, from M7 to M11 schools' partner teachers will receive training (C1) as data fragility awareness agents. As a second step, the co-design workshops sessions (C2, C3, and C4) will be conducted as part of the teacher training and must consider main objectives of the project: 1) raise data fragility awareness among representatives, teachers, and students, and 2) collect good practices regarding data academic management to reduce data fragility. The second phase, from M12 to M27, considers the execution of the workshops for representatives, teachers, and students. This phase covers the 2023–2024 school year and first part of 2024–2025, so each school can schedule its workshops depending on their academic program. The task identified are:

- T2.1 Training preparation: Preparation of knowledge pills for teacher considering materials, resources, activities, and learning platform.
- T2.2 Training execution: Teacher training in the equipment and applications necessary for the development of skills focused on data literacy and responsible use of digital competences.
- T2.3 Training evaluation: User profile assessment considering motivation, usability, and satisfaction.
- T2.4 Workshops co-design: Support schools in the design of the workshops that will be conducted in their schools considering their situation, context, and possibilities.
- T2.5 Workshops execution: Support schools in the execution of workshops in their schools.
- T2.6 Workshops evaluation: User profile assessment considering motivation, interest, and satisfaction.
- T2.7 Collect good practices: Support schools to collect good practices elements - described in IO2- during workshops execution.

The third phase (M8-M27), Follow up, will be developed in parallel to the 2nd phase because it will focus on the evaluation of the training and workshops (IO1). It will be centered on the user profile assessment, motivation, usability, and satisfaction (depending on the different variables associated with data academic management). This phase begins four months before the execution of workshops to prepare the evaluation protocol and the instruments used to collect the data and it will be finished two months after the end of the workshops to analyze the collected data. In resume the main task defined are:

- T3.1 Preparation: Prepare the evaluation protocol and the instruments used to collect the data centered on the user profile assessment, motivation, usability, and satisfaction.
- T3.2 Reporting: Analyze collected data from training and workshops.

The fourth phase (M13-M27), Mapping, matches with the execution of the IO2 and is divided into two stages. A first stage aims to collect good practices from communities, associations, companies, and non-profit organizations working on data fragility issues in the participant countries to identify all useful resources. A second stage aims to collect good practices resulting from workshops (IO1). The full mapping will serve as input for the handbook and its publication as web site also (IO2). The task will be:

- T4.1 Preparation: Preparation of the tools, documents and sharing points to fulfill with activities, initiatives, and methodologies by every participant.
- T4.2 Execution: Support on the search for activities, initiatives, and methodologies.

The last phase, (M24-M30) Integration, will consider the edition of the handbook and development of the website to share data academic management good practices (IO2). The data collected during the previous phase will be used to prepare the collection of resources that compose the handbook. Furthermore, the final task defined for this phase are:

- T5.1 Collection: Collect all resources resulting from PH2.T7 and PH4.
- T5.2 Handbook: Write and edit a handbook of good practices to raise data fragility awareness.
- T5.3 Website: Develop a website as a live resource to search for good practices regarding data fragility in data academic management.

5 Teacher Training

The project has defined a Teacher Training to help 1) understand and be aware about what data-driven and decision-making imply for an educational institution, 2) identify which problems about data fragility are related to current educational technology and data academic management, and 3) provide tools and frameworks to protect privacy, security, and confidentiality of student's data. Initially, a group of 3 teachers or staff from each partner institution will be involved in the short-term joint staff training event (C1), and the participants of the training will be the members of the project management teams and the partner institutions' teaching staff. Each partner's institution will be free to select the participants for the training event in the way as it suits them needs and possibilities to reduce data fragility in data academic management and raise data fragility issues awareness.

With workshops designed with a project-based learning approach we will focus the training on the following issues. This is a first proposal to be adapted in function of the school's needs and IO1 assessment results:

- How data in education enable data-based decision-making to improve context?
- How cloud technology supports data collection and analytics in education?
- How data fragility sets a sensitive context?
- How algorithms raise data fragility in education technology?
- How legality regulates data treatment in education and the needs of ethics?
- How data fragility examples let emerge solutions?
- How to regulate the use of digital technologies and new educational methods to reduce data fragility?

We expect that the teachers, considering the resources identified in the IO2 during the project, and with the training received in the seven topics identified, can be able to create awareness on data fragility and reduce privacy and security issues in their schools.

In the project, each training day is defined as an 8h/day schedule, with two workshops every day at morning (2 * 2h) and practice or visit time in the afternoon. In case of a morning visit the workshops will be scheduled in the same system but in the afternoon.

Our teacher training will basically focus on presenting key concepts, key problems, and key frameworks based on the seven previous points identified and considering the exchange of experiences with the teachers and other institutions. Teacher training is fundamental for the success of the Output 2 (IO2). A successful transmission of the contents for the teachers will empower them also to transmit knowledge acquired and raise data fragility awareness involving all the faculty. The proposed actions share a vision of data-based decision making where ethics is over legality, even though legality is a main aspect to consider as data academic management is subjected to the EU General Data Protection. The objectives of this training are addressed to:

- Training and empowering primary and secondary teachers (or equivalent level), in the responsible use of student's data during learning and teaching processes. It is validated by the studied study in continuous development in IO2.
- How to manage data in a data fragility context. The aim is to select those activities and best practices that fix better for the context of the school and the potential students involved. Although schools may have experience exploring and using educational data, they need some guidelines to define actions to empower students in the responsible use of data in a digital society.
- Promote team spirit among the group of teachers and members of the project, with the possibility of establishing new connections in the international network of schools that are addressing data fragility awareness projects.

6 Conclusions

The SPADATAS project focuses on improving educational data treatment processes in schools to reduce data privacy, security, and confidentiality issues. These issues are common in multiple fields, not unique for education. Maybe some data treatment processes could be unique to the educational context; however, data privacy and security issues can be organized into a few categories such as data leakage, data misuse, data unauthorized access, and data transfer to unauthorized third parties. Those are common issues in any field where data is treated.

Considering the above, problems of data privacy and security arises in other fields such as training, youth, and sports when initiating data treatment. Collecting, storing, and consulting data are sensitive processes that define a fragile context. This can be defined as the data fragility problem, where data privacy and security protection diminish and risks increments.

The results of the SPADATAS project will directly impact other fields different from education as the main objective is to raise data fragility awareness. The arguments supporting this data fragility awareness might fit in fields other than education. The objective of creating resources, frameworks, and tools specific for education to reduce data fragility might impact other fields, for instance enabling ideas and processes like those exposed.

Acknowledgements. With the support of the Erasmus+ Programme of the European Union in its Key Action 2 "Cooperation and Innovation for Good Practices. Strategic Partnerships for school education". Project SPADATAS (Security and Privacy in Academic Data management at Schools) (Reference number2022-1-ES01-KA220-SCH-000086363). The content of this publication does not reflect the official opinion of the European Union. Responsibility for the information and views expressed in the publication lies entirely with the authors.

References

1. Alier, M., Casany, M.J., Severance, C., Amo, D.: Learner privacy, a pending assignment. In: Proceedings of the Eighth International Conference on Technological Ecosystems for Enhancing Multiculturality, pp. 725–729. Association for Computing Machinery, New York (2020)

2. Amo, D., Alier, M., Casan, M.J., Casañ, M.J.: The student's progress snapshot a hybrid text and visual learning analytics dashboard. Int. J. Eng. Educ. **34**, 990–1000 (2018)

3. Amo, D., Alier, M., García-Peñalvo, F.J., Fonseca, D., Casañ, M.J.: Clickstream for learning analytics to assess students' behavior with Scratch. Future Gener. Comput. Syst. **93**, 673–686 (2019). https://doi.org/10.1016/j.future.2018.10.057

4. Amo, D., Cea, S., Jimenez, N.M., Gómez, P., Fonseca, D.: A privacy-oriented local web learning analytics javascript library with a configurable schema to analyze any edtech log: moodle's case study. Sustainability **13** (2021). https://doi.org/10.3390/su13095085

5. Amo, D., Fonseca, D., Alier, M., García-Peñalvo, F.J., Casañ, M.J., Alsina, M.: Personal data broker: a solution to assure data privacy in EdTech. In: Zaphiris, P., Loannou, A. (eds.) HCII: International Conference on Human-Computer Interaction. Learning and Collaboration Technologies. Designing Learning Experiences. Orlando, pp. 3–14 (2019)

6. Amo, D., Fox, P., Fonseca, D., Poyatos, C.: Systematic review on which analytics and learning methodologies are applied in primary and secondary education in the learning of robotics sensors. Sensors **21**, 1–21 (2021)

7. Amo, D., García-Peñalvo, F.J., Alier, M.: Social network analysis approaches for social learning support. In: García-Peñalvo, F.J. (ed.) Proceedings of the Second International Conference on Technological Ecosystems for Enhancing Multiculturality (TEEM 2014), pp. 269–274. ACM, New York (2014)

8. Amo, D., Gómez, P., Hernández-Ibáñez, L., Fonseca, D.: Educational warehouse: modular, private and secure cloudable architecture system for educational data storage, analysis and access. Appl. Sci. **11**, 806 (2021). https://doi.org/10.3390/app11020806

9. Amo, D., Torres, R., Canaleta, X., Herrero-Martín, J., Rodríguez-Merino, C., Fonseca, D.: Seven principles to foster privacy and security in educational tools: local educational data analytics. In: Eighth International Conference on Technological Ecosystems for Enhancing Multiculturality, pp. 730–737. Association for Computing Machinery, New York (2021)

10. Amo-Filvà, D., Fonseca, D., Alier, M., García-Peñalvo, F.J., Casañ, M.J.: Unplugged institutions: towards a localization of the cloud for learning analytics privacy enhancement. In: Proceedings of the Learning Analytics Summer Institute Spain 2022 (LASI Spain 2022). CEUR Workshop Proceedings, Salamanca, Spain, pp. 46–51 (2022)

11. Angel, N.A., Ravindran, D., Vincent, P.M.D.R., Srinivasan, K., Hu, Y.-C.: Recent advances in evolving computing paradigms: cloud, edge, and fog technologies. Sensors **22**(1), 196 (2022). https://doi.org/10.3390/s22010196

12. Baepler, P., Murdoch, C.: Academic analytics and data mining in higher education. Int. J. Scholarsh. Teach. Learn. (2010). https://doi.org/10.20429/ijsotl.2010.040217

13. Breiter, A., Light, D.: Decision support systems in schools-from data collection to decision making. AMCIS 2004 Proc. 248 (2004)

14. Bulla, C., Hunshal, B., Mehta, S.: Adoption of cloud computing in education system: a survey. Int. J. Eng. Sci. **6**, 6375–6380 (2016). https://doi.org/10.4010/2016.1532

15. Burgos, C., Campanario, M.L., de la Peña, D., Lara, J.A., Lizcano, D., Martínez, M.A.: Data mining for modeling students' performance: a tutoring action plan to prevent academic dropout. Comput. Electr. Eng. **66**, 541–556 (2018). https://doi.org/10.1016/j.compeleceng.2017.03.005

16. Cardona, J.S., Lopez, J.A., Vela, F.L.G., Moreira, F.: Older adults and games from a perspective of playability, game experience and pervasive environments: a systematics literature review. In: Rocha, A., Adeli, H., Dzemyda, G., Moreira, F. (eds.) Information Systems and Technologies, pp. 444–453. Springer, Cham (2022). https://doi.org/10.1007/978-3-031-04819-7_42

17. Constain Moreno, G.E., Collazos, C.A., Bautista, S., Moreira, F.: FRIDA, a framework for software design, applied in the treatment of children with autistic disorder. Sustainability 14, 14560 (2022). https://doi.org/10.3390/su142114560

18. Filvà, D.A., García-Peñalvo, F.J., Forment, M.A., Escudero, D.F., Casañ, M.J.: Privacy and identity management in learning analytics processes with blockchain. In: ACM International Conference Proceeding Series, pp. 997–1003. ACM Press, New York (2018)

19. Fonseca, D., García-Peñalvo, F.J.: Interactive and collaborative technological ecosystems for improving academic motivation and engagement. Univ. Access Inf. Soc. 18(3), 423–430 (2019). https://doi.org/10.1007/s10209-019-00669-8

20. Fonseca, D., García-Peñalvo, F.J., Camba, J.D.: New methods and technologies for enhancing usability and accessibility of educational data. Univ. Access Inf. Soc. 20(3), 421–427 (2020). https://doi.org/10.1007/s10209-020-00765-0

21. Fonseca Escudero, D., Redondo, E., Sánchez, A., Valls, F.: Educating urban designers using augmented reality and mobile learning technologies/Formación de Urbanistas usando Realidad Aumentada y Tecnologías de Aprendizaje Móvil. RIED Rev. Iberoam. Educ. Distancia 20, 141 (2017). https://doi.org/10.5944/ried.20.2.17675

22. García-Peñalvo, F.J., Corell, A., Abella-García, V., Grande, M.: Online assessment in higher education in the time of COVID-19. Educ. Knowl. Soc. 21 (2020). https://doi.org/10.14201/eks.23013

23. García-Peñalvo, F.J., Corell, A., Rivero-Ortega, R., Rodríguez-Conde, M.J., Rodríguez-García, N.: Impact of the COVID-19 on higher education: an experience-based approach. In: Information Technology Trends for a Global and Interdisciplinary Research Community (2021). https://www.igi-global.com/chapter/impact-of-the-covid-19-on-higher-education/www.igi-global.com/chapter/impact-of-the-covid-19-on-higher-education/269996. Accessed 10 Jan 2023

24. García-Peñalvo, F.J., et al.: Mirando hacia el futuro: Ecosistemas tecnológicos de aprendizaje basados en servicios Looking into the future: Learning services-based technological ecosystems. In: Fidalgo-Blanco, Á., Sein-Echaluce, M.L., García-Peñalvo, F.J. (eds.) La Sociedad del Aprendizaje. Actas del III Congreso Internacional sobre Aprendizaje, Innovación y Competitividad. CINAIC 2015 (14–16 de Octubre de 2015, Madrid, España). Fundación General de la Universidad Politécnica de Madrid, Madrid, Spain, pp. 553–558 (2015)

25. Lai, M.K., Hsiao, S.: Developing data collection and management systems for decision-making: What professional development is required? Stud. Educ. Eval. 42, 63–70 (2014)

26. Leal, F., Veloso, B., Pereira, C.S., Moreira, F., Durão, N., Silva, N.J.: Interpretable success prediction in higher education institutions using pedagogical surveys. Sustainability 14, 13446 (2022). https://doi.org/10.3390/su142013446

27. Llauró, A., Fonseca, D., Villegas, E., Aláez, M., Romero, S.: Educational data mining application for improving the academic tutorial sessions, and the reduction of early dropout in undergraduate students. In: Ninth International Conference on Technological Ecosystems for Enhancing Multiculturality (TEEM 2021), pp. 212–218. Association for Computing Machinery, New York (2021)

28. Mendoza, W., Ramírez, G.M., González, C., Moreira, F.: Assessment of curriculum design by learning outcomes (LO). Educ. Sci. 12, 541 (2022). https://doi.org/10.3390/educsci12080541

29. Moreira, F., et al.: TPS2 approach applied to requirements engineering curriculum course. In: Zaphiris, P., Ioannou, A. (eds.) Learning and Collaboration Technologies Designing the

Learner and Teacher Experience, pp. 461–477. Springer, Cham (2022). https://doi.org/10. 1007/978-3-031-05657-4_33

30. Navarro, J., Amo, D., Canaleta, X., Vidaña-Vila, E., Martínez, C.: Utilizando analítica del aprendizaje en una clase invertida: Experiencia de uso en la asignatura de Microprocesadores. Actas Las Jorn Sobre Enseñ Univ Informática **3**, 391–394 (2018)

31. Orehovacki, T.: Proposal for a set of quality attributes relevant for Web 2.0 application success. In: Proceedings of the ITI 2010, 32nd International Conference on Information Technology Interfaces, pp. 319–326 (2010)

32. Orehovački, T.: Perceived quality of cloud based applications for collaborative writing. In: Pokorny, J., et al. (eds.) Information Systems Development, pp. 575–586. Springer, New York (2011). https://doi.org/10.1007/978-1-4419-9790-6_46

33. Orehovački, T., Babić, S.: Qualitative approach to determining the relevant facets of mobile quality of educational social Web applications. In: 2016 39th International Convention on Information and Communication Technology, Electronics and Microelectronics (MIPRO), pp. 1060–1065 (2016)

34. Orehovački, T., Babić, S.: Identifying the relevance of quality dimensions contributing to universal access of social web applications for collaborative writing on mobile devices: an empirical study. Univ. Access Inf. Soc. **17**(3), 453–473 (2017). https://doi.org/10.1007/s10 209-017-0555-7

35. Orehovački, T., Babić, S., Etinger, D.: Identifying relevance of security, privacy, trust, and adoption dimensions concerning cloud computing applications employed in educational settings. In: Nicholson, D. (ed.) AHFE 2017. AISC, vol. 593, pp. 308–320. Springer, Cham (2018). https://doi.org/10.1007/978-3-319-60585-2_29

36. Orehovački, T., Babić, S., Etinger, D.: Modelling the perceived pragmatic and hedonic quality of intelligent personal assistants. In: Karwowski, W., Ahram, T. (eds.) IHSI 2018. AISC, vol. 722, pp. 589–594. Springer, Cham (2018). https://doi.org/10.1007/978-3-319-73888-8_91

37. Orehovački, T., Babić, S., Jadrić, M.: Exploring the validity of an instrument to measure the perceived quality in use of web 2.0 applications with educational potential. In: Zaphiris, P., Ioannou, A. (eds.) LCT 2014. LNCS, vol. 8523, pp. 192–203. Springer, Cham (2014). https:// doi.org/10.1007/978-3-319-07482-5_19

38. Orehovački, T., Blašković, L., Kurevija, M.: Evaluating the perceived quality of mobile banking applications in Croatia: an empirical study. Future Internet **15**, 8 (2023). https://doi.org/ 10.3390/fi15010008

39. Orehovački, T., Etinger, D., Babić, S.: Perceived security and privacy of cloud computing applications used in educational ecosystem. In: 2017 40th International Convention on Information and Communication Technology, Electronics and Microelectronics (MIPRO), pp. 717–722 (2017)

40. Orehovački, T., Granić, A., Kermek, D.: Exploring the quality in use of web 2.0 applications: the case of mind mapping services. In: Harth, A., Koch, N. (eds.) ICWE 2011. LNCS, vol. 7059, pp. 266–277. Springer, Heidelberg (2012). https://doi.org/10.1007/978-3-642-27997-3_26

41. Orehovački, T., Granić, A., Kermek, D.: Evaluating the perceived and estimated quality in use of web 2.0 applications. J. Syst. Softw. **86**, 3039–3059 (2013). https://doi.org/10.1016/j. jss.2013.05.071

42. Pereira, C.S., Durão, N., Fonseca, D., Ferreira, M.J., Moreira, F.: An educational approach for present and future of digital transformation in portuguese organizations. Appl. Sci. **10**, 757 (2020). https://doi.org/10.3390/app10030757

43. Redondo Domínguez, E., Fonseca Escudero, D., Sánchez Riera, A., Navarro Delgado, I.: Augmented reality in architecture degree: new approaches in scene illumination and user evaluation. J. Inf. Technol. Appl. Educ. JITAE **1**, 19–27 (2012)

44. Simon, D., Fonseca, D., Necchi, S., Vanesa-Sánchez, M., Campanyà, C.: Architecture and building enginnering educational data mining. Learning analytics for detecting academic dropout. In: Iberian Conference on Information Systems and Technologies, CISTI (2019)

45. Solé-Beteta, X., et al.: Automatic tutoring system to support cross-disciplinary training in big data. J. Supercomput. **77**(2), 1818–1852 (2020). https://doi.org/10.1007/s11227-020-033 30-x

46. Valls, F., Garcia-Almirall, P., Redondo, E., Fonseca, D.: From raw data to meaningful information: a representational approach to cadastral databases in relation to urban planning. Future Internet **6**, 612–639 (2014). https://doi.org/10.3390/fi6040612

47. Valls, F., Redondo, E., Fonseca, D., Garcia-Almirall, P., Subirós, J.: Videogame technology in architecture education. In: Kurosu, M. (ed.) HCI 2016. LNCS, vol. 9733, pp. 436–447. Springer, Cham (2016). https://doi.org/10.1007/978-3-319-39513-5_41

48. Vázquez-Ingelmo, A., García-Peñalvo, F.J., Therón, R., Amo Filvà, D., Fonseca Escudero, D.: Connecting domain-specific features to source code: towards the automatization of dashboard generation. Clust. Comput. **23**(3), 1803–1816 (2019). https://doi.org/10.1007/s10586-019-03012-1

49. Williamson, B.: Big Data in Education: The Digital Future of Learning, Policy and Practice. SAGE Publications Ltd., London (2017)

The Rallye Platform: Mobile Location-Based Serious Games for Digital Cultural Heritage

Jean Botev$^{(\boxtimes)}$, Sandra Camarda, and Claude Ohlhoff

University of Luxembourg, 4364 Esch-sur-Alzette, Luxembourg
{jean.botev,sandra.camarda,claude.ohlhoff}@uni.lu

Abstract. This paper presents the Rallye Platform, a software ecosystem that enables various mobile location-based serious games such as digital treasure hunts. Such games are an effective way to engage audiences in a cultural heritage context on-site, and beyond traditional museum spaces. We devised and employed the platform to develop two long-running deployments –the Légionnaires Rallye and the Minett Stories Rallye– in support of two major multimedia exhibitions in Luxembourg running between July 2021 and May 2022, which doubled as test cases for qualitative and quantitative analysis. The evaluation shows that the applications helped promote the physical exhibitions, engaged players, and sparked curiosity about the respective subject areas and historical contexts. Various changes implemented between the deployments further improved the user experience, and the mobile web applications were used even beyond the end of the exhibitions by students and other groups to explore the history and geography of the urban space.

Keywords: Serious Games and Gamification · Location-Based Learning · Mobile Learning · Cultural Heritage · Digital Storytelling

1 Introduction

For the past decades, museums have experienced a paradigmatic shift towards inclusiveness and participation, putting in place outreach strategies aimed at making exhibitions more experiential and interactive [2,19]. Expanding the museum beyond its walls helped reformulate the relationship between cultural heritage institutions and their audiences [16]. Additionally, the affordances of new digital technologies have increased the possibilities of providing enriching learning experiences. From an educational point of view, emotional involvement, enjoyment, and engagement are proven conditions to facilitate the acquisition of skills, the understanding and retention of information, and the improvement of knowledge [6–8,20]. Serious games, particularly those that provide task-based activities involving quizzes and puzzles, are particularly suited to be employed in cultural heritage settings [13]. Providing contextualized content, location-based

© The Author(s), under exclusive license to Springer Nature Switzerland AG 2023
P. Zaphiris and A. Ioannou (Eds.): HCII 2023, LNCS 14040, pp. 17–31, 2023.
https://doi.org/10.1007/978-3-031-34411-4_2

systems are seen as an effective solution to enhance cultural experiences both inside and outside the museums [1,5,9,12,15]. The urban space becomes the game board where players are invited to explore historical locations and cultural heritage sites while contextually solving cognitive tasks [18]. Mobile devices, employed as interfaces for gameplay, allow the interchange between the physical and virtual world, functioning as gateways to access various types of textual and audiovisual sources. Such kinds of pervasive games [11] can enrich and augment the visitors' experience representing both tangible and intangible heritage while transcending spatial and temporal barriers.

Storytelling represents another fundamental component in conveying information related to cultural heritage sites [14,17]. Location-based serious games can facilitate forms of both linear and non-linear storytelling, where the position and interaction of the player with the physical environment (for example, reaching a historical point of interest) triggers and advances the narrative and the game itself. Such forms of location-aware storytelling, where stories are generated interactively based on the user's location, can result in a more enjoyable and stimulating educational experience [10].

Starting from these assumptions, we built on the familiar concept of the treasure hunt game (Rallye, in Luxembourgish) to develop a solution to extend immersive multimedia exhibitions toward the urban space. With the Rallye platform, we created a tool that helped us realize and deploy games for two educational projects related to historical themes and national heritage.

Before discussing the details of the two concrete deployments in Sect. 3, we introduce the platform and its components in the following Sect. 2. We then discuss qualitative and quantitative results in the context of the evaluation of the test cases in Sect. 4 and conclude in Sect. 5 with a summary and outlook. The terms rallye, treasure hunt, and game are used interchangeably in this paper.

2   The Rallye Platform

The Rallye platform was built to develop, deploy, and manage location-based web applications that engage players in games, such as digital treasure hunts, around historical locations. The concept resulted from an interdisciplinary collaboration between the Luxembourg Centre for Contemporary and Digital History (C^{2}DH) and the VR/AR Lab of the University of Luxembourg. It was first developed during the early stages of preparing a temporary multimedia exhibition called Légionnaires on the history of the Luxembourgers in the French Foreign Legion at the Musée Dräi Eechelen in Luxembourg City (30 June 2021 to 27 February 2022) [4]. Players were given an interactive map and a series of riddles or hints that had to be solved in sequence to reach several secret locations. Each location, or point of interest (PoI), was related to a particular historical event, building, landmark, person, or group.

We designed the platform as a generic software ecosystem; the modular, container-based architecture is built with modern event-driven back-end technologies such as Node.js and allows for the easy addition of different activity types, multimedia content, or interaction modes. We chose the non-relational database MongoDB to process all data because of its flexibility and efficient query operations on geospatial information.

Aside from the server-side technologies, which constitute a back end for hosting treasure hunts in arbitrary locations and about different historical themes, the platform further consists of two front-end components providing interactive access to the different stakeholders: the game, i.e., the treasure hunt itself, in the form of a mobile web application, and a web-based staff tool providing various management functionalities, such as statistics and editing capabilities. One of the paramount design guidelines was to make the user interfaces simple, intuitive, and adaptable to provide a great user experience regardless of the level of digital literacy.

Fig. 1. Légionnaires Rallye web application, landing page on mobile device.

2.1 Mobile Web Application

Following a search-and-find game pattern, the user has to physically reach a string of fixed-point destinations in the game area. An anonymized cookie allows for saving the game progress and language preferences. From the landing page, the player chooses a preferred language from a set of options (see Fig. 4a and Fig. 1 offering three or four different options, respectively); this can also be changed at any point later through the game menu. Before starting the game, users must consent to store the anonymous cookie and allow the app to access their location (cf. Fig. 3a).

A tutorial containing the game instructions and some tips on how to follow such a trail of PoIs shows an interactive map marking the treasure hunt area and the user's current position. When starting the game, players are given a riddle/hint and an interactive map that displays their location as they move around, for instance, as shown in Fig. 3b or Fig. 4c. The player's current geographical position is tracked and displayed on the interactive map using the mobile device's GPS localization data throughout the game.

Assuming the player correctly guessed the solution and is heading towards the right location, within a larger radius from the destination, a pulsating circle will appear on the map, signalling that the target is close. The closer the PoI, the more frequent and vivid the rings of the pulsating circle will be. Finally, upon arriving at the destination, an animated pin drops on the map, followed by an image and a text explaining the historical significance of that specific site (cf., for example, Fig. 3c). Reaching the first location will unlock the second riddle, and so on.

The pulsating circle signaling that a location is nearby will only appear if the player is at that particular stage of the hunt; simply roaming around the area will not reveal the position of the other secret locations on the map. As the player solves the riddles and discovers the PoIs, a progress bar indicates the advancement. The discovered locations will now appear as greyed-out markers on the interactive map.

To allow players to finish the game within a reasonable time, the locations are all in walking distance from each other. From the moment they start the game, players have two weeks to finish the hunt; after this period, the game progress is deleted, and they will have to start anew.

The last hint takes the players to the museum or venue, where they can continue the experience by visiting the exhibition. As an incentive, upon successfully finding all secret historic locations, players receive a unique code that can be redeemed at the museum's reception for a small reward (cf. Fig. 3d) and share their achievement on social media. The completion codes are randomly generated and stored anonymously on the server. The players can now also revisit all discovered locations in the form of a gallery view (cf. Fig. 4b).

The rationale behind a realization as a web application is maximum diffusion and availability without the need to install a dedicated app. While connection issues might slow the game, free Wi-Fi is available in most urban areas nationwide, so users do not need to rely on their data plans for access. Furthermore, running the business logic server-side allows for better control and fast deployment of updates in case of any issues or bug fixes. The adaptive design adjusts locally and dynamically to different screen sizes, resolutions, and orientations, while the back end detects whether a qualifying mobile device is used; if not, a dedicated page indicates to switch the device.

No personal data is collected or stored, but generalized statistics are provided to monitor the status. These data are visualized and made available through the web-based interface discussed in Sect. 2.2.

2.2 Staff Tool

To facilitate the management and maintenance of a game instance, the Rallye Platform provides an online front end with different access types and feature sets (cf. Fig. 2). For instance, a visual editor allows for creating and editing trails and PoIs, while different statistics interfaces provide real-time status information or technical details about platforms and browsers.

In order to accommodate the different stakeholders, we have created three access levels that gradually provide additional functions, detailed in the following with respect to each role.

Front Desk. The front desk role only provides access to the completion certificates generated at the end of the game (cf. Fig. 2a). Since the idea is to offer on-site award prizes for the first few users successfully completing a rallye, local staff needs to be able to verify the code on the user's device. The certificate list provides various sorting options, temporal filters, or the direct search for specific certificate numbers. After the prize is handed out, staff can validate the code as used, updating the status to "redeemed". The validation can also be reversed.

Moderator. The moderator role provides two other essential functions. On the one hand, detailed real-time statistics, e.g., on how many people play the game, how long it takes them to complete it, and whether they stop at a specific point of the hunt. To a certain degree, this allows for addressing potential issues with the content (particularly if users tend to get stuck at a specific point of the hunt). On the other hand, moderators have access to a visual editor for creating and editing trails or individual PoIs, allowing them to build content easily.

Administrator. In addition to the front desk and moderator options, the administrator role provides an interface for accessing further device-related statistics (cf. Fig. 2b), such as browser types, platforms, or browser platform distribution, which are especially useful for prioritizing bug fixes or designing automated tests. The statistics can again be filtered to provide more detailed information about a specific period.

(a) Front desk interface, certificate validation.

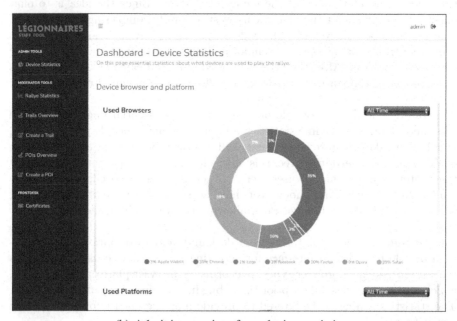

(b) Administrator interface, device statistics.

Fig. 2. Légionnaires Rallye staff tool, desktop screenshots (browser content only).

3   Deployments/Test Cases

Based on the Rallye platform introduced in Sect. 2, we developed and deployed two treasure hunts to accompany temporary multimedia exhibitions in Luxembourg.

The Légionnaires Rallye, in the context of the eponymous exhibition at the Musée Drāi Eechelen in Luxembourg City, running from July 2021 to February 2022, constituted the first test case. The second test case was the Minett Stories Rallye developed for the exhibition *Remixing Industrial Pasts: Constructing the Identity of the Minett* on the former ironworks of Belval in Esch-sur-Alzette, running from February to May 2022. As discussed in Sect. 1, both follow the same rationale to promote the events and transcend the exhibitions' physical space, giving them a transmedia dimension beyond the museum walls.

Application development began in 2020, and the chronological sequence allowed us to develop specific aspects between deployments further. We will discuss the individual implementations and their differences in the following sections.

3.1   Légionnaires Rallye

The exhibition *Légionnaires* was the outcome of a collaboration between the C^2DH and the Musée Drāi Eechelen, bringing together the results of a quinquennial investigation on the Luxembourgers in the French Foreign Legion conducted at the University of Luxembourg as well as the work of local specialists, public historians, and international experts. The exhibition also represented the last phase of *Éischte Weltkrich*, a digital public history project on WWI in Luxembourg. Highly visual and interactive, the project employed a multimedia and transmedia approach using multiple channels to delve into individual accounts and micro-histories. The Légionnaires Rallye treasure hunt constituted one of these channels, expanding the exhibition to the city and inviting tourists and local citizens to discover the history of the Luxembourgish legionnaires in the places that marked their passage.

The game area was restricted to the core of the city center where ten salient historic locations (PoIs) were identified. Players were given a fairly challenging single hint or riddle leading them to each secret location. The pulsating circle signalling the target's proximity on the interactive map was set at a radius of 50 m from the PoI (cf. Fig. 3b). To allow some leeway, the pin icon that drops on the map upon reaching the destination and the subsequent informative image and text (cf. Fig. 3c) were set to appear within a radius of 10 m. Given the length of the trail, users were allowed to stop and resume the game at any point. As an incentive for finishing the treasure hunt, however, we set a temporal constraint of two weeks, after which any progress would be deleted, and the game reset. Additionally, mystery boxes containing various prizes were promised to the first five players who would reach the final destination. Smaller rewards (a dedicated enamel badge) were also envisioned for the remaining players.

(a) Welcome screen, permissions.

(b) Map screen, hint extended.

(c) PoI screen, description.

(d) Completion screen, code.

Fig. 3. Légionnaires Rallye web application, screenshots (browser content only).

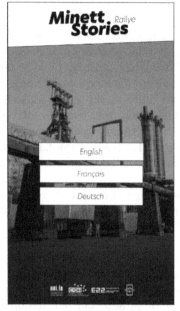

(a) Landing screen, languages.

(b) Final screen, gallery view.

(c) Map screen, hint extended.

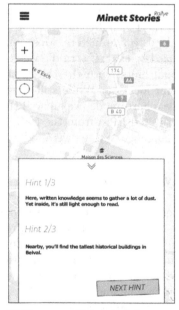

(d) Map screen, hints extended.

Fig. 4. Minett Stories Rallye web application, screenshots (browser content only).

3.2 Minett Stories Rallye

The Rallye platform was subsequently used in the frame of another project involving a different location and historical theme. The Minett Stories Rallye accompanied the opening of the temporary exhibition *Remixing Industrial Pasts: Constructing the identity of the Minett* (27 February 2022 to 15 May 2022), which was part of the European Capital of Culture Esch2022 programme. The exhibition explored the region's industrial past and was set in the Massenoire, a repurposed industrial hall within the former steelworks complex of Belval. The redevelopment project that over a period of twenty years converted the brownfield into a business and cultural center (today hosting the University of Luxembourg's main campus) radically transformed the landscape, erasing many old structures and buildings.

The game allowed to rediscover that past taking the players on a journey through the landmarks and relics of the former ironworks. The team of historians involved in the Remix project provided a new visual identity and a list of locations that mirrored the thematic structure of the exhibition for a total of nine PoIs (including the exhibition hall, where once a material known as *masse noire* or "black matter" was produced to close the tapholes of the blast furnaces). This new instance offered the opportunity to address a series of issues identified in the original Légionnaires Rallye, particularly concerning flow and balance between player challenge and frustration. This was achieved by significantly narrowing the distance between the PoIs, with a game area reduced to roughly one square kilometer. The reduction and compacting of the game area required an adjustment of the PoI radius down to 30 m instead of 50 m. The activation range was also halved to five meters. Most importantly, a three-tiered difficulty level was introduced so that, if a riddle was too obscure, every 30 s, players could unlock additional hints, with the third and last hint openly revealing the position of the secret location. While still providing a challenge for the players willing to embrace a hard mode, we allowed those experiencing difficulties to complete the game still and learn from the trail. Due to time constraints, the Minett Stories Rallye language options were reduced to three (English, French, and German).

4 Evaluation

The user tests conducted on a sample of players, as well as other metrics such as success rate and completion time, revealed an overall appreciation of this mode of asynchronous engagement. While the discussed test deployments were specifically aimed at promoting physical exhibitions, the platform enables the creation of stand-alone applications and games for exploring various contexts. This type of location-based game can thus offer a variety of possibilities for developing digital cultural heritage projects, strengthening the connection between the landscape and its stories while allowing players to discover history through an interactive experience that is both entertaining and educational. Although the games were not specifically intended to provide an alternative to the restricted museum visits during the COVID-19 pandemic, they offered the opportunity to access part of the exhibition content outdoors in safety.

4.1   Quantitative Results

While anonymous, the usage data provide a plethora of information and valuable insights into how the web applications were used.

User Growth Development. The plot in Fig. 5 shows the number of new users for the Légionnaires Rallye and the Minett Stories Rallye over time, for the duration of the exhibitions (shaded in the respective color) and beyond, until the cut-off date in November 2022. Around both exhibition openings (June/July 2021 and February/March 2022), the amount of new users peaks, and also the stabilization or increase following subsequent promotional initiatives is clearly discernible. Later spikes in January and March 2022 for the Légionnaires Rallye and October 2022 for the Minett Stories Rallye stem from groups using the web application well past the end of the exhibitions.

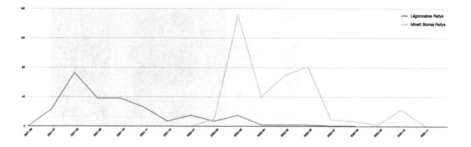

Fig. 5. User growth for both deployments; actual exhibition periods are shaded.

Completion Rates. The completion rate of the Légionnaires Rallye was alarmingly low, with high drop-out rates at the initial PoIs. This can only partly be attributed to unforeseen circumstances, such as the extreme flooding across Western Europe in the summer of 2021 that hit Luxembourg with devastating effects shortly after the web app's launch. While the torrential rain prevented people from playing for several weeks, the low completion rate is probably due to the relatively high difficulty of the riddles. Without the possibility to short-track and get further help within the application itself, few mustered the perseverance required to solve the puzzles. Another deterrent was represented by the length of the trail connecting the PoIs. While the gaming zone was confined to an urban area of circa five square kilometers, reachable on foot or by public transport, the game required crisscrossing the city center for several hours. Five of 223 players who started the Légionnaires Rallye game completed it. The Minett Stories Rallye, on the contrary, was more successful, with 393 players overall, of which

49 players succeeded, i.e., the completion rate was about 12%. The reasons for the positive reception are to be found in the influx of people visiting the area because of the Esch2022 events, in an effective promotional campaign, as well as in the game design improvements, namely a shorter duration of the session play, the delimitation of the game zone to a much smaller area, and the introduction of the three-tiered hint system that significantly lowered the game difficulty.

Device Statistics. The device statistics (cf. screenshot in Fig. 2b) provide interesting insights into the platform and browser distribution. Notably, around half of the players were using iOS devices, i.e., iPhones or iPads (45% for the Légionnaires Rallye, 52% for the Minett Stories Rallye). Fig. 6 furthermore shows the browser distribution for each platform, with the platform-native browsers (Chrome/Android and Safari/iOS) dominating and only Firefox or Facebook's app-internal browser as third-party browsers achieving more significant shares. The remaining 11% (Légionnaires Rallye) and 6% (Minett Stories Rallye) of the browser software could not be allocated.

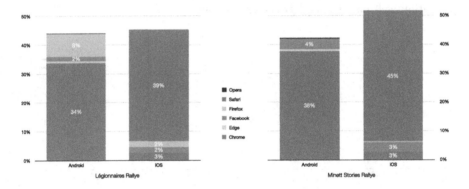

Fig. 6. Distribution of platforms and browsers for both deployments.

Language Selection. Both test deployments offered multiple languages to choose from. For the Légionnaires Rallye, most users played the game in English (33%) or French (30%), while 23% chose German and the remaining 14% Luxembourgish as a language. The Minett Stories Rallye did not include Luxembourgish as an option; the distribution of the remaining three languages among the players here was as follows: 37% French; 32% German; 31% English.

4.2   Qualitative Results

Complementing the quantitative data discussed in Sect. 4.1, we conducted a qualitative survey for the Minett Stories Rallye. Before the game went live, a group of 12 test users was asked to complete a questionnaire about their background and experience using the mobile web application. The survey was articulated in three main sections covering: 1) demographic segments; 2) game experience (focusing on the appeal and educational potential of the content); 3) usability and performance. For the most part, the test group was composed of female participants (75%) between the ages of 30 and 60. The majority (42%) were Luxembourgers, followed by German, French, Dutch, Spanish, and Bulgarian nationals. Contrarily to the general quantitative statistics, 58% of the test group chose German as their language option, 25% French, and the remaining 17% played the game in English. Six users were educational professionals with expertise in game-based learning belonging to the organizations IFEN (*Institute de Formation de l'Educaton Nationale*) and SCRIPT (*Service de Coordination de la Recherche et de l'Innovation Pédagogiques et Technologiques*), both entities of the Luxembourg Ministry of Education. The questionnaire included five-point Likert scale questions, as well as multiple-choice and open-ended questions. This combined survey method provided more granular and nuanced feedback and a reliable measure of the game experience. All users completed the game within an hour or two, with 83% playing in a single session without interruptions. Players were given the possibility of completing the game alone or in a group. 58% chose to play alone and the remaining 42% played with friends and family.

75% of the test users found the first hints very difficult and, on average, needed to unlock one additional hint before guessing the secret locations. 25% needed all three hints.

In regard to the storytelling, 92% of the users read the texts with full attention, enjoyed the content, and felt driven to complete the treasure hunt.

While 83% of the users declared to have already a moderate to very good knowledge of the geography and history of the site, all testers unanimously stated that playing the game taught them something new and made them more curious about Belval. Additionally, 42% of the users felt more motivated about visiting the exhibition. Their feedback helped to further address some minor geolocation issues, adjust the difficulty of some of the hints, and improve the quality of the content.

Overall, the quantitative results confirm the effectiveness of the additional features and improvements such as the adaptive hint system. Concerning aspects related to UI and UX design, more than 75% of the test users found that the app navigation was easy or very easy, while the majority approved of the general app design (83% like it or like it very much, the remaining 17% answered neutrally, i.e., there was no negative feedback in this regard).

5 Conclusion

This paper presented the Rallye Platform, a software ecosystem that enables various mobile location-based serious games like digital treasure hunts. Such games facilitate learning, helping to retain and understand information, and are effective ways to increase emotional involvement, enjoyment, and engagement, while task-based activities involving quizzes and puzzles are particularly appropriate for cultural heritage.

Therefore, we devised and employed the platform to develop two long-running deployments supporting two national, physical multimedia exhibitions running between July 2021 and May 2022, doubling as test cases for qualitative and quantitative analysis. The evaluation shows that the changes implemented from the Légionnaires Rallye to the Minett Stories Rallye deployments further improved the user experience.

The mobile web applications remained active well after the end of the exhibitions and continued to be used by students and other demographic groups as educational activities to explore the urban areas and their history. Shifting the focus towards discovery and away from the game challenge significantly increased the completion rates, helping to promote the physical exhibitions and sparking curiosity about the respective subject areas.

We intend to continue development and possibly integrate augmented reality techniques and other collaborative aspects and features as explored, for instance, in CollaTrEx [3] or similar projects.

References

1. Bellotti, F., Berta, R., De Gloria, A., D'Ursi, A., Fiore, V.: A serious game model for cultural heritage. ACM J. Comput. Cult. Herit. **5**(4), 1–27 (2013). https://doi.org/10.1145/2399180.2399185
2. Black, G.: Transforming Museums in the Twenty-First Century. Routledge, London and New York (2012)
3. Botev, J., Marschall, R., Rothkugel, S.: CollaTrEx – collaborative context-aware mobile training and exploration. In: Brooks, A.L., Brooks, E. (eds.) ArtsIT/DLI -2016. LNICST, vol. 196, pp. 113–120. Springer, Cham (2017). https://doi.org/10.1007/978-3-319-55834-9_13
4. Camarda, S., Sauer, A., Scuto, D., Reinert, F.: Légionnaires: Parcours de Guerre et de Migrations entre le Luxembourg et la France. Silvana Editoriale, Milano (2020)
5. Hjorth, L., Richardson, I.: Gaming in Social, Locative and Mobile Media. Palgrave Macmillan, London (2014). https://doi.org/10.1057/9781137301420
6. Hooper-Greenhill, E.: Museums and Education: Purpose, Pedagogy, Performance. Routledge, New York (2007). https://doi.org/10.4324/9780203937525
7. Kalmpourtzis, G.: Educational Game Design Fundamentals: A Journey to Creating Intrinsically Motivating Learning Experiences. CRC Press, Boca Raton (2018)
8. Kapp, K.M.: The Gamification of Learning and Instruction: Game-Based Methods and Strategies for Training and Education. Pfeiffer (2012)
9. Leorke, D.: Location-Based Gaming: Play in Public Space. Palgrave Macmillan, Singapore (2019). https://doi.org/10.1007/978-981-13-0683-9
10. Lombardo, V., Damiano, R.: Storytelling on mobile devices for cultural heritage. New Rev. Hypermedia Multimed. **18**(1–2), 11–35 (2012). https://doi.org/10.1080/13614568.2012.617846
11. Montola, M., Stenros, J., Waern, A.: Pervasive Games: Theory and Design. CRC Press, Boca Raton (2009). https://doi.org/10.1201/9780080889795
12. Mortara, M., Bellotti, F.: Introduction to special issue on serious games for cultural heritage. ACM J. Comput. Cult. Herit. **6**(2) (2013). https://doi.org/10.1145/2460376.2460377
13. Mortara, M., Catalano, C.E., Bellotti, F., Fiucci, G., Houry-Panchetti, M., Petridis, P.: Learning cultural heritage by serious games. J. Cult. Herit. **15**(3) (2014). https://doi.org/10.1016/j.culher.2013.04.004

14. Nack, F., Waern, A.: Mobile digital interactive storytelling-a winding path. New Rev. Hypermedia Multimed. **18**(1–2), 3–9 (2012). https://doi.org/10.1080/13614568.2011.641418

15. Rubino, I., Barberis, C., Xhembulla, J., Malnati, G.: Integrating a location-based mobile game in the museum visit: evaluating visitors' behaviour and learning. ACM J. Comput. Cult. Herit. **8**(3) (2015). https://doi.org/10.1145/2724723

16. Rudloff, M.: Extending museum walls. Reaching out with site-specific, digital, and participatory interventions. Nordsik Museologi (1), 35–55 (2012). https://doi.org/10.5617/nm.3117

17. Sharples, M., FitzGerald, E., Mulholland, P., Jones, R.: Weaving location and narrative for mobile guides. In: Drotner, K., Schrøder, K.C. (eds.) Museum Communication and Social Media: The Connected Museum, pp. 177–196. Routledge, New York (2013). https://doi.org/10.4324/9780203500965-13

18. de Souza e Silva, A., Sutko, D.M.: Digital Cityscapes: Merging Digital and Urban Playspaces. Peter Lang, New York (2009)

19. Simon, N.: The Participatory Museum. Museum 2.0 (2010)

20. Zirawaga, V.S., Olusanya, A.I., Maduku, T.: Gaming in education: using games as a support tool to teach history. J. Educ. Pract. **8**(15), 55–64 (2017)

An e-Learning Application for Children Suffering from Autism

Shubham Choudhary, Supriya Kaur(✉), Abhinav Sharma(✉), and Swati Chandna(✉)

SRH University Heidelberg, Heidelberg, Germany

{shubham.choudhary,supriya.kaur}@stud.hochschule-heidelberg.de,
ab88sharma@gmail.com, swati.chandna@srh.de

Abstract. Developmental impairment known as autism spectrum disorder (ASD) is brought on by variations in the brain. ASD sufferers have a recognized condition, like a genetic disorder. Other factors are still unknown. ASD begins before the age of 3 years and can last throughout a person's life, although symptoms may improve over time. ASD symptoms can appear in some kids within the first year of life. Others might not experience symptoms until they are 24 months old or older. Some ASD children develop new skills and reach developmental milestones up until the age of 18 to 24 months, at which point they cease doing so or lose the abilities they previously possessed.

As a result, several applications have been developed to improve symptoms from an early age. Because people with autism spectrum disorder usually lack knowledge and experience with many areas of modern technology, the accessibility of mobile applications designed for them is critical. As there is a need for an e-learning platform for ASD-affected children to make it more accessible and convenient for them to access educational material and learn at their own pace. Furthermore, because it is designed for ASD children, it will be more engaging and will provide a cost-effective alternative to traditional educational services for children with ASD. This study details the design and implementation of the "Autismic" mobile application's user interface (UI), as well as the standards for building an accessible user interface for people with autism spectrum disorders (ASD). The guidelines are based on current research on how to improve reading comprehension for both people with ASD and the user. Technology-based games are commonly utilized to teach students conceptual knowledge and skills. All the most important findings from this survey were considered to make this application as useful to the target users as feasible. Its primary purpose is to help children study better.

The paper primarily goes through the two version of the mobile application that was developed while considering all the procedures followed by the UI design, followed by the technologies that were used, usability testing, and interviews that were conducted to assess the efficacy and success rate among the target population. Furthermore, the paper discusses the second version of the program, which was produced following usability testing of the previous version, with changes in UI designs as with the feedback there were some improvements that were to be made as the user were having trouble with different ways to login, moreover the application was only in dark mode and there were trouble in navigating to next sections with this feedback there was a need of new functionality for implementation.

P. Zaphiris and A. Ioannou (Eds.): HCII 2023, LNCS 14040, pp. 32–41, 2023.
https://doi.org/10.1007/978-3-031-34411-4_3

Keywords: User experience · UI · Autism spectrum disorder · Mobile apps · UX · Competitor analysis · Prototype · LO-FI designs · Usability testing · HI-FI designs · Autismic · User Journey map

1 Introduction

Computer technology and the internet have already drastically altered the world. Meanwhile, technology has helped to make everyone's lives easier. The combination is also improving the lives of people suffering from various diseases and disorders. This research aims to provide an interface or application for students with ASD (autism spectrum disorder). This curriculum primarily helps students improve their learning ability and brain processes.

While autism was once a diagnosis, it is now known as autism spectrum disorder (ASD). This is since there are five separate illnesses that fall under the umbrella of ASD, each with varying symptoms and severity but are related enough to be classed together. To keep things straight, these five diseases were all classified as ASD under the Diagnostic and Statistical Manual of Mental Disorders, or DSM-5, in 2013 [1].

While Hans Asperger diagnosed the autism condition in four youngsters, he encountered in his clinic in 1944. Since the World Health Organization included this condition in 1992 [2]. Throughout the previous year, several parents and physicians gradually diagnosed this neurological condition. Children and teenagers with ASD experience neurological effects. They have the same intelligence as normal children, but the neurological difference affects how they perceive and respond to their surroundings. They struggle with generalizing their knowledge and skills, which is especially tough for children and teenagers with ASD. They frequently struggle to apply information and abilities in a variety of contexts and with others, as well as to absorb new knowledge and experience.

As, The Technology-Related Assistance for Individuals with Disabilities Act of 1988 describes assistive technology as any device that can assist those with disabilities. Assistive technology includes a variety of different Technologies. Children with autism often have an easier time processing visual data rather than listening to audio information. This means that the assistive technology and devices, which is usually visual, is targeting learning through many children's strongest learning centre [3].

As many autistic children attend traditional schools, though they frequently struggle with class participation. They also struggle with social interactions with other children. Many parents are unaware of these "early" signs of autism. Inadequate early-stage therapy and interventions. There is a growing need for e-learning platforms for children with autism spectrum disorder (ASD) since these platforms can give these children with a supportive and accessible environment to learn and develop critical abilities.

2 Related Work

In the past, such kind of application have been developed and gained popularity. Proloquo2go is one of the popular and widely used application, it works closely with the Augmentative and Alternative Communication (AAC) community. One of the most popular AAC apps is Proloquo2Go [4]. It combines symbol-based communication with typing and word prediction, making it adaptable and appropriate for both toddlers and adults whose demands may vary as they grow, or their health deteriorates. Proloquo2Go is the first AAC software with research-based vocabulary levels, (activity) templates to aid motor planning, ExpressivePowerTM to express oneself, and full bilingual support. And all with very little work on your part. Proloquo2Go is intended to improve communication skills and encourage language development. It is appropriate for all users, from beginners to advanced, and caters to a wide spectrum of fine-motor, visual, and cognitive abilities.

Mental Imagery Therapy for Autism (MITA). The MITA app was released in 2015 and quickly rose to the top of the "autism apps" charts [5]. MITA verbal activities start with simple vocabulary-building exercises and progress toward exercises aimed at higher forms of language, such as noun–adjective combinations, spatial prepositions, recursion, and syntax. For example, a child can be instructed to select the {small, large} {red|blue|green|orange} ball, or to put the cup {on|under|behind|in front of} the table. All exercises are deliberately limited to as few nouns as possible since the aim is not to expand a child's one-word vocabulary, but rather to teach him/her to integrate mental objects in novel ways by utilizing PFS. MITA activities outside of the verbal domain aim to provide the same PFS training visually through implicit instructions as has been described in Dunn et al. [7]. For example, a child can be presented with two separate images of a train and a window pattern, and a choice of complete trains. The task is to find the correct complete train and to place it into the empty square. This exercise requires not only attending to a variety of different features in both the train and its windows, but also combining two separate pieces into a single image (in other words, mentally integrating separate train parts into a single unified gestalt). As levels progress, the exercises increase in difficulty, requiring attention to more and more features and details. Upon attaining the most difficult levels, the child must attend to as many as eight features simultaneously. Previous results from our studies have demonstrated that children who cannot follow the explicit verbal instruction can often follow an equivalent command implicit in the visual set-up of the puzzle. Therefore, there is a need of an application which enables school children to learn from an early stage [6].

Autismic is solution for as an E-learning platform for autism spectrum disorder. It is a platform specifically catered to the needs of autistic children as target user. As ASD symptoms are usually known in the first five years of person's existence so this application targets the group of early children. As this app was designed for autistic children in early education. This contains different games and activities for the kids which can help them in leading a foundation in learning.

This application has a capability for parents to examine their children's progress, which was not available in other applications on the market. This application is specifically created for children with autism, and it will be available on mobile devices, as opposed to other applications that are ideal for large screens.

3 System Design and Implementation

To develop and design this application for autistic children we spoke with experts and families that support people with ASD. In order to get their feedback on the interactive prototype of the visual scheduling tool, we reached out to therapists, special education instructors, and parents. As they are the support provider or caretaker of the people with special needs their feedback was helpful.

Version 1.0:
See Fig. 1.

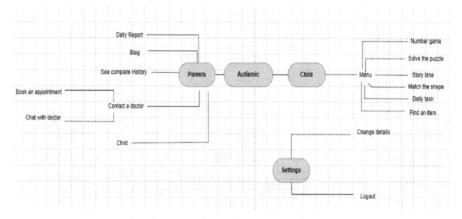

Fig. 1. Autismic's Information architecture

Application Flow: This application has different options for kids to choose their games or activities to play as:

1. Number game
2. Solve the puzzle.
3. Story time
4. Match the shape.
5. Daily task
6. Find an item.

As for parents they can check the daily report of there children progress and can book an appointment with doctor or can chat with them as well as they can change details in the account.

As in this application, there are features such as daily reports that parents can access, blogs that they can write, a complete history of the children's progress, and even the ability to connect with nearby doctors and schedule appointments, which was not seen in many other applications before, making it unique in comparison to others. In this service, parents can choose an age group ranging from 2 to 9 years old, and the system will adapt to the child's aptitude and comprehension level. Which make the application to be personalized.

Furthermore, this application requires changes because it was only available in dark mode, as well as modifications in the UI design because it was difficult to navigate to different pages.

In version 2, design enhancements were made to make navigation easier, and arrows were added to lead the user to pages. There are three modes in this version: day mode, dark mode, and one specifically developed for colourblind users. There are various options to choose from among activities and games, which were not present in the previous version and the addition of new activities and a music player feature to aid in the relaxation of children under stress.

Version 2.0:
See Fig. 2.

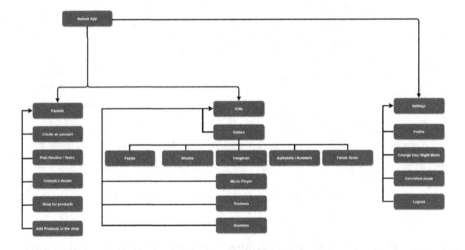

Fig. 2. Information Architecture version 2.0

As in version 2.0, the following enhancements were made as an extension of the prior version1.0 new categories have been added in the parents tasks now they can create account for their children as well as plan entire routine for them and sign them various tasks to perform with said that now the parents can add products to the online shop and can also shop products via application which will redirect them to the dedicated platforms.

As for kids' different games are introduced:

1. Wordle
2. Hangman
3. Learning alphabets
4. Music player

5. Routines

As in setting now there is dark mode and colourblind mode to choose from and now parents can update the profile also.

Implementation: To build the application MERN stack for front end was used and for backend Mongo express and Node JS. As mern stack is efficient for web or mobile applications. MERN Stack's React.js is best for UI layer abstraction. It executes code development quickly due to its collection of dynamic user interfaces readily available within the library. MERN acts the best in controlling and updating large dynamic JSON data that can smoothly navigate between the front end and the back end. The designing and prototypes were made through Figma.

As in the for the primary colours Blue, white and grey are chosen due to their soothing and calming effects. Figure 3 shows the first screen ASD children will notice as the design and colours chosen are muted so that they don not stress the autistic children and will visually appeal them. On this screen you have four options: Activities, Games, Doctors nearby and settings. The children can click on any of the options to choose from.

Fig. 3. Home screen

Figure 4 displays the activities and once the kid decide to choose the activities option this screen will be displayed. In the activities screen there are four options: Dotted alphabets, numbers, routine and expression. If you click on dotted alphabets another screen will open showcasing the aplhabets with dotted line where the kids had to join the dots.In this screen when you see the alphabet there is blue and red colored dots and lines drawn to connect the dots in the right direction.If you want to go to next alphabet it is below and just click on it to move further. If you wish to go back you can press the "arrow" button on the left side (Fig. 5).

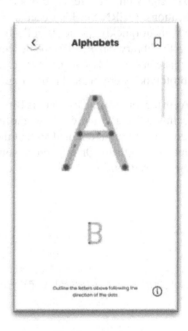

Fig. 4. Activities   **Fig. 5.** Alphabets

Figure 6 shows when you click on the routine option a display with the image of the task with explanation will be shown. So, as in figure below the task is to wake up and it will help kids to set a routine for themselves while visual images.

Once you click on expressions option Fig. 7. Expression screen will be displayed like below with the image of the kids being happy. And on the down left there is a sound icon while press the sound for the expression will be generated.

Figure 8 shows the games display of the application where there is puzzle, memory game, colouring and fit the shape. Once you click the puzzle option the display to puzzle will be open where you must select the right puzzle to make the picture and after completing the puzzle you can press "Finish" button and a success pop up will be displayed and you can move on to next image.

Fig. 6. Routine

Fig. 7. Expression

Fig. 8. Games

4 Usability Testing and Verification

Participants: The application is evaluated with the three people who are care takers of ASD children. Here, we conducted a study to understand the application from the user's perspective.

- Procedure: At first, we introduced the application and explained the concepts in detail. After that, we gave them approximately 15 min to get comfortable with the application. Some of the participants already started.

   We gave a few tasks to the participants to check the users' efficiency, effectiveness, and satisfaction. The tasks given to the participants are listed below:

1. You just got to know about this app and now you want to install and register on this application?
2. While creating the account you did a mistake in choosing wrong profile photo and now you want to change it?
3. Your kid creates an avatar for him/herself?
4. You want to schedule tasks for your kid to do while you are in your office, and he/she is at home?
5. While creating the account you did a mistake in choosing wrong profile photo and now you want to change it?
6. You want to review a doctor, and want to see the doctors nearby?
7. If you want to change your password which steps will you follow?

- Results

   1. due to the option being on the main menu it was easy to find.
   2. took some time to view all tasks but overall, the user experience was good.
   3. the user faced issue in locating the tasks options should have been more easily traceable.

5 Discussions

- **Target Audience:** Children with Autism spectrum disorder are the target audience for this application for learning.
- **Opportunities:** The application provides the features for the ASD kids which will help them in learning and developing skills. Thorough this application they get the basic learning foundation and a way they can express themselves.
- **Future Scope**: The current application helps the users to learn how to learn alphabets, numbers and they can even have a scheduled routine and different games to help them in communicating and practice social skills. The scope for the future of this project consists of the that with the help of AI the tactical games can be created which will be further helpful in learning process by using python.

6   Conclusion

To conclude, the developed application has provided a platform for autism spectrum disorder children who can learn alphabets, numbers and learn through playing games while at comfort and allows them to learn at their own pace. As discussed in the long term, the application will develop further and have more advanced features. It will stand out from other applications.

The application is built with MERN stack end React Native, an open-source framework that is entirely free to use and with mongo express react and.ode JS.As the application is built on react native it can be used both by android and IOS users.

References

1. https://www.psychiatry.org/psychiatrists/practice/dsm
2. Myles, B.S., Southwick, J.: Asperger Syndrome and Difficult Moments: Practical Solutions for Tantrums, Rage, and Meltdowns. AAPC Publishing (2005)
3. https://www.threadlearning.com/blog/autism-and-technology-how-digital-devices-help
4. https://www.assistiveware.com/support/proloquo2go/overview
5. .Vyshedskiy, A., Dunn, R.: Mental imagery therapy for autism (MITA)-an early intervention computerized brain training program for children with ASD. Autism Open Access **5**, 2 (2015)
6. Dunn, R., et al.: Comparison of performance on verbal and nonverbal multiple-cue responding tasks in children with ASD. Autism Open Access **7**, 218 (2017)
7. Dunn, R., et al.: Children with autism appear to benefit from parent-administered computerized cognitive and language exercises independent of the child's age or autism severity. Autism Open Access **7**, 1–12 (2017)

Two-Phases AI Model for a Smart Learning System

Javier García-Sigüenza⬤, Alberto Real-Fernández⬤,
Rafael Molina-Carmona⬤, and Faraón Llorens-Largo⁽✉⁾⬤

Grupo de investigación Smart Learning, University of Alicante, Alicante, Spain
{javierg.siguenza,alberto.real,rmolina,Faraon.Llorens}@ua.es

Abstract. Current Information Technologies are mature enough to favor the creation of adaptive learning systems that also encourages active, autonomous and persistent learning. A solution could be the creation of artificial intelligence algorithms capable of detecting the individual learning needs and features of the learners, what skills they are acquiring and how they do it, or how they behave, in order to offer them an adapted and personalized learning experience. This is what is defined a smart learning system.

Therefore, in this research we aim to propose an Artificial Intelligence (AI) model for a learning system to achieve this purpose. It is based on a learning model called CALM (Customized Adaptive Learning Model), that offers personalized learning through different learning paths and adapts to each learner by offering a specific activity at any time. The selection of this activity relies on an AI engine that detects the needs and characteristics of the learner and selects the most appropriate activity.

To implement an AI model for this purpose, applying CALM principles, we propose the use of both the information provided by activities and the learner's characteristics and progression. Combining these datasets with the use of deep learning techniques, we propose a two phases process. First, the model makes predictions that are personalized for each student, and then it applies a concrete instructional strategy to make the final decision, allowing the teacher to adapt and guide the student's learning.

Keywords: smart learning · artificial intelligence · deep learning

1 Introduction

Nowadays, due to the impact of Information Technology (IT) in society, education is involved in a digital transformation that aims to face a set of new needs

The development of the AI model that are part of the inference engine have been partially funded by CENID (Centro de Inteligencia Digital) in the framework of the Agreement between the Diputación Provincial de Alicante and the University of Alicante. The adaptive learning platform that supports this project is funded by the AdaptLearn project of the University of Alicante, within the UniDigital action of the Recovery, Transformation and Resilience Plan of the Government of Spain.

P. Zaphiris and A. Ioannou (Eds.): HCII 2023, LNCS 14040, pp. 42–53, 2023.
https://doi.org/10.1007/978-3-031-34411-4_4

and features that our current environment presents [1,2]. A changing process towards an environment with a dynamic, continuous and lifelong learning process, different to the traditional we knew, with completely different tools used by teachers and institutions [3,4]. But, if we want to fulfil an actual improvement in education environment, this transformation must embrace all the learning-teaching process and the learning model [5].

Moreover, if we focus in the learning process, we can see that each learner presents individual learning needs, styles and preferences, so we should aim this transformation to a personalized and adaptive learning [6]. The current evolution of IT, such as game-based learning environments [7] and learning analytics developments [8,9], makes it clear that they are evolved enough to allow the creation of adaptive learning systems that also encourages active, autonomous and persistent learning.

A solution could be the creation of Artificial Intelligence (AI) algorithms capable of detecting the individual learning needs and features of the learners, what skills they are acquiring and how they do it, or how they behave, in order to offer them an adapted and personalized learning experience. This is the definition of a smart learning system [10].

Therefore, we propose in this research an AI model for a learning system to achieve this purpose. Based on learning model called CALM (Customized Adaptive Learning Model) [11,12], we aim to design the AI model in charge of selecting the most suitable activity for a learner at a given time, adapting the learning process to them.

First we expose the background of the research, explaining CALM model, its selection engine and instructional strategies. Then we explain the AI model we propose, created in two phases, for the selection of activities.

2   Background

2.1   CALM

CALM is a theoretical model for a learning system that aims to meet the needs detected in the digital society, without neglecting the intentional objectives of teaching, making use of the potential of current technologies [11,12].

It is based on enhancing learner motivation, and other main concepts such as interaction, reward, and progression, providing learning results in real time and in a continuous learning cycle, giving the learner autonomy in their own learning process. It presents a wide range of activities, both in quantity and variety and serves as a complete teaching tool, offering different possibilities and options to view and manage the learning status of each learner.

CALM is composed by three main elements: competence map, activity bag and selection engine. Firstly, we define a competence as a set of skills and knowledge to be acquired by the learners. These competences will be connected between them in one direction, creating dependency relations, so that they are represented as a directed graph, what we call a competence map. These competences will be developed by a set of tasks that learners will perform, called activities, that compose the activity bag. And the selection engine will be in charge of assigning activities to be performed by the learners when they select a competence.

At the beginning, in the competence map all competences will be locked, except those considered as initial. Each competence has an associated score, called competence strength, which has an initial value of zero and will vary as the leaner performs activities. In this way, new competences will be unlocked, through thresholds assigned to the corresponding dependency connections, which mark the minimum strength value necessary to unlock that connection. Figure 1 shows an example of the competence map of a learner, which has some unlocked competences with a strength value, a competence already completed (C1) and some unlocked which strength value is zero.

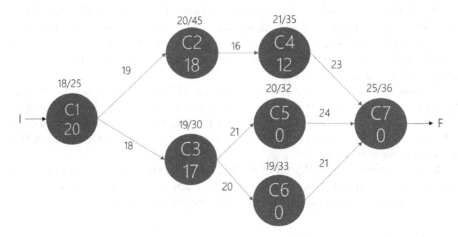

Fig. 1. Instance of a competence map for a learner in a concrete point, with a completed competence (C1 in green), some unlocked competences with a concrete strength value (C2, C3 and C4 in orange) and some that remain unlocked with zero strength value (C5, C6 and C7 in grey). (Color figure online)

Through the map the learner will interact with the system, where they will be able to select any of the available competences, choosing any of the possible available paths. At this point, the system will provide the learner with an activity to perform, developing the selected competence, which will change its strength value, thus unlocking and completing the competences on the map. All the activities with their respective characteristics will be stored in the aforementioned activity bag, of which there will be one instance for each learner. This will contain a subset of activities, those available and those completed, dynamically updated as the learner unlocks competences and completes activities. In Fig. 2 it can be seen an example of activity bag instance of a learner, with some available activities and others marked as done.

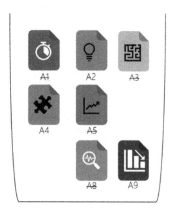

Fig. 2. Activity bag of a learner in a concrete point, with some available activities and others marked as done (A1, A3, A5 and A8).

The selection engine will be in charge of assigning an activity to a learner at a given time. This is where the logic of smart learning resides, managed by what we call the selection engine. It will be in charge of analyzing, for each individual learner, their state in the learning process, their learning needs and their characteristics, and provide him with the activity that best suits all this. This choice will be executed by an AI algorithm, which will receive as input data the mentioned information about the learner and the instructional strategy selected by the teacher, concept described further below. A general view of these concepts are shown in Fig. 3, where the selection engine manages and analyzes the information between competence map and activity bag, in addition to the learner features and the strategy selected.

2.2 Selection Engine

The entire logic of CALM's adaptive learning lies in the selection engine. Based on artificial intelligence, it is responsible for choosing the most appropriate activity for each learner at any given time.

When a learner selects a competence, the engine gives them the activity it considers most appropriate, which will depend, as mentioned above, on the individual characteristics of the learner, his state in the learning process and the available activities, as well as the selected instructional strategy, while maintaining his motivation and complying with the corresponding learning requirements. So that it will learn from each learner, knowing their characteristics, preferences and behavior, adapting to them as they progress in the learning process.

In order to do so, the system needs to store a set of readable and computable information to be obtained and analyzed, such as their progress, skills, knowledge, achievements, interaction and behavioral data, among others [13]. In CALM we do this in a data structure containing all the corresponding features, which we call feature vector [14,15]. And in order for the system to adapt to

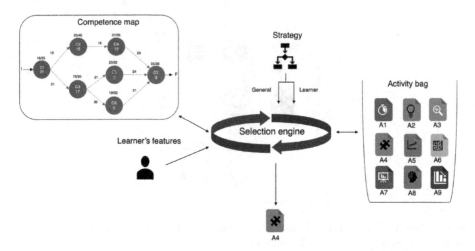

Fig. 3. General view of the selection engine, that manages and analyzes the information between competence map and activity bag of a learner, besides it features and the strategy selected.

each learner individually, it must also be able to characterize the activities, so their features, in this case static, are also stored individually in their own feature vector.

For example, one of the main characteristics of an activity will be its difficulty, which we can be defined in terms of the time and effort that learners will have to invest to successfully complete that activity [16]. Thus, there will be different levels of difficulty associated with each activity, to favor a progressive learning process. Thus, the system could provide activities with a progressively increasing difficulty, to maintain the learner's motivation, or maintaining the same if required. The difficulty will also influence the score obtained after completing an activity, adding more or less according to the corresponding level. In addition, there are other characteristics that can define an activity and so a leaner, such as the learning style, the cognitive level or knowledge type [17].

All this represents the core of the adaptation process of an adaptive learning system, in which both vectors are processed and interpreted by an algorithm (in our case, the one used by the selection engine) to choose the corresponding activity at all times and thus adapt individually to the learner in question.

2.3   Instructional Strategies

As we have mentioned, in CALM the selection of activities for a learner depends, among other factors already described, on the instructional strategy used. The teacher will be able to monitor the state of the overall course, and of each learner individually, being able to modify the strategy when they considers it appropriate, if they observe that the learning process is not progressing as expected, or if they detects certain needs to be covered.

The strategy establishes how the content will be shown, explained or assigned to the learners [18]. It is a set of techniques, approaches, models and methods that teachers use to optimize the learning process. Choosing the right strategy will help to foster learners' motivation and attention, understand and remember knowledge, and analyze their own learning [19].

It will be through the instructional strategy that the teacher will guide each learner to the learning objectives they intends him/her to achieve, and will mark how they does it. That is why these strategies are key in our system, since they will provide the guidelines that the selection engine will use, together with the rest of the learner's individual factors, to select the appropriate activity at each moment. Thus, the learning process of each learner will be aligned with the strategy, in order to achieve the objectives intended by the teacher, while achieving optimized learning for each learner according to their individual characteristics.

In this way, the selection engine will have the learner's vector and the vectors of the possible activities to be selected, which together with the patterns established by the instructional strategy, will allow the learner to choose the most appropriate activity at each moment.

Let us see how to define an instructional strategy. They are structured in what are known as dimensions, what represent a specific aspect of the strategy we want to consider, having a set of possible values to be assigned, called tactics. So a strategy will be defined by one or more dimensions, with at least one of their possible tactics selected. As is defined in CALM, a strategy can have multiple tactic values for each dimension, represented by weights, so each value will determine the weight a tactic represents in a strategy.

For example, let us suppose we want to set a strategy that manages the motivation of a learner, and we do this through their emotional state of a learner, following the Flow Theory of Csikszentmihalyi [20]. In this case, a dimension of the strategy will be called Emotional State and its tactics will be: Boredom, Apathy, Worry, Anxiety, Arousal, Flow, Control and Relaxation. So, although the aim is to keep the learner in a Flow state, there may be moments in which the teacher prefers to move them to an Emotional state, so the selected strategy will a have greater weight for Emotional tactic.

3 Activity Selection Phases

Deep learning [21] has been a revolution in the field of AI, allowing the development of new models with an accuracy never seen before. The capabilities of these new models allow accurate predictions to be made and AI to be applied to new fields, however, the development of deep learning brings with it the development of black boxes. This term refers to the fact that the developed models have a behavior that is too complex to be understood by people [22], so that the result obtained cannot be explained.

In the field of education, being able to explain the different decisions that guide student learning is especially relevant, since each student has unique characteristics that affect the development of learning. Therefore, it is necessary to understand the decision making of the model to understand if the learning is being adequate and adapted to the learner. There are different techniques to try to provide explainability to the predictions of deep learning models, which are included in the field of explainable artificial intelligence (XAI) [23]. However, these techniques are limited in that they allow understanding the behavior of the model, but do not allow influencing its behavior, preventing the teacher from adjusting the behavior of the model in case it is necessary.

Therefore, a two-phase model has been proposed: the first one, where an AI model obtains two metrics (score and time) that determine the performance of a student for each possible activity; and a second phase, which based on the two metrics obtained, allows to apply by algorithms one of the different instructional strategies available, allowing the teacher to guide and personalize the student's learning at any time.

3.1   Phase 1: Estimation of Student Performance

The data of the learning process is a combination of sequential data, in that the student presents an evolution in his knowledge based on the exercises performed previously, as well as structured and related to each other, since the activities are related to each other, having common knowledge and the result of some activities being more relevant than others depending on the context. That is why the information of the activities was interpreted and integrated as a sequence of graphs that is given as input to the model together with the student's characteristics.

In order to obtain a model that allows the use of both types of data, the Graph Convolutional Network (GCN) [24] architecture, which allows spatial information to be processed, and the Gated Recurrent Unit (GRU) [25], which allows temporal information to be processed, have been combined. In addition, a final convolutional layer has been used, which, after combining the data obtained from the graph sequence and the student's characteristics, allows obtaining the prediction of the score and the time for the different activities. The resulting architecture can be seen in Fig. 4, showing the input data in blue, the operations performed in yellow and the outputs of the AI model in green.

The model starts with an initial null state, which is given as input to the GCN layer of the model, together with the sequence of graphs, which represents the set of activities performed by the learner, as well as the evolution of the results obtained in each of the activities and the order in which they were performed. From this input, the GCN layer obtains information about the interdependencies between the different nodes, composed by the activities, through the use of convolutions, which through a series of filters learned during training, allows extracting information about the characteristics of each of the nodes and propagating the information through the graph. The output of the GCN layer, which encodes spatial information, is used as input for the GRU layer, which processes the temporal information and obtains a state, through a series of *gates* that process the input and decide how this data is processed and preserved. This new state obtained is used as the state for the next iteration of the sequence.

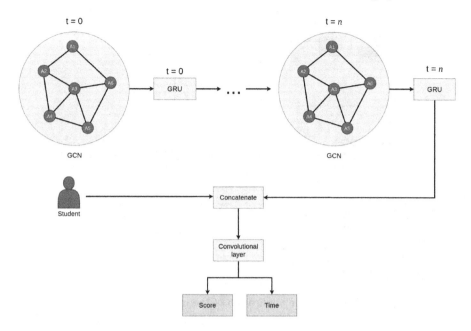

Fig. 4. Diagram of the deep learning model architecture.

Thus, by combining both layers, the spatial and temporal information of the student's progression and activities is combined. Finally, the information obtained from the graph is concatenated with the student's characteristics to obtain the input to the final convolutional layer. This last layer, through the use of another set of filters learned during training, allows to obtain the prediction of the score and time for the different activities given.

The model developed, once trained on the dataset, allows obtaining, for each of the possible activities, both an estimate of the score that the student will obtain and the time needed to perform the activity. Together, both metrics allow to have an estimate of the performance of each student for each of the possible options.

These metrics obtained are used as input for the second phase of the model, which allows the application of the chosen instructional strategy.

3.2   Phase 2: Application of Instructional Strategies

The application of instructional strategies adds a second phase to the model, allowing the introduction of the ability to guide the learner during learning based on the teacher's criteria. This structure changes the paradigm of the model compared to other AI models, whose use implies the use of a black box, where no intervention or explanation of the path chosen for the learner is possible. Instead, with this architecture, we get AI-assisted learning where the teacher can intervene in the learning.

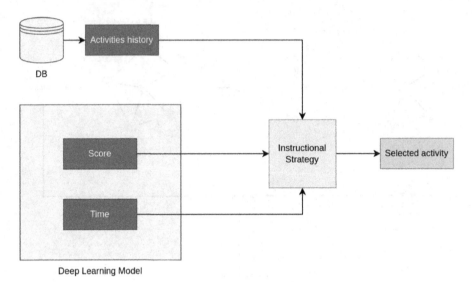

Fig. 5. Diagram of the application of the instructional strategy.

This second phase is applied through the use of different algorithms, implemented to represent each of the instructional strategies. These algorithms use the history of activities assigned to the user and the prediction of the outcome and time for each of the possible activities to select the activity that best fits the objective of the instructional strategy. This flow can be seen in Fig. 5.

Since the instructional strategies are the second part of the model, and since they are implemented using algorithms, the methodology used can be adjusted at any time. This implementation avoids the need to retrain the model if the learning objective is changed, and the training of the deep learning model can be focused on the accuracy of the metrics obtained, separating both components of the model.

For the implementation of instructional strategies, simple algorithms have been applied, based on a single goal, and other complex ones, which seek to maintain a specific flow in the learner's progress. Some of these simple algorithms, for example, seek to get the learner to obtain the best possible result, to maintain motivation, or seek to increase the difficulty, to make it challenging for the learner. One of the complex algorithms is *advance and reinstrength* , which aims to balance the difficulty iteratively, to keep the learner at an equilibrium point that helps to maintain the interest of the learner in the activities. To this end, the *advance and reinstrength* algorithm, at each iteration, seeks to maintain the difficulty between a maximum and minimum value, determining the target difficulty based on the results obtained by the student during the completion of the different activities. Another of these algorithms is *prick the bubble*, which, based on the history of activities and results obtained by the student, seeks to include among the selected exercises some of those that the student has done less

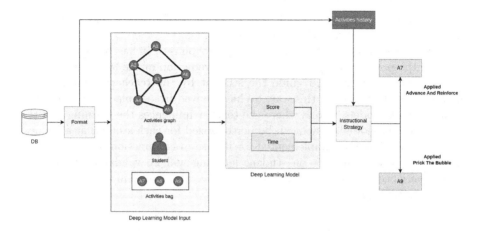

Fig. 6. Flow diagram of the model flow for three possible activities (A7, A8 and A9) and their output applying two different instructional strategies.

or that have different characteristics from the last ones the student has done, forcing the learner to adapt to these activities and leading to new skills.

For the development of the engine, a default strategy is established, which would be used for all students, but instructional strategies can be established at the course level or for a specific student, in order to be able to personalize the learning at any moment. For example, one could set *advance and reinstrength* as the default method for the engine, but for a learner who selects the same competences frequently, the teacher could set the use of *prick the bubble* to introduce the learner to other different activities and help them advance. Figure 6 shows an example of the engine flow, showing how from a bag of activities two different activities would be selected based on applying the *advance and reinstrength* or *prick the bubble* algorithm.

4 Conclusions

CALM proposes a theoretical model for a learning system that meets the needs of the digital society, for it aims to motivate the learner and follow other important principles such as interaction, reward and progression, providing learning results in real time and in a continuous learning cycle; adapting the learning process to each individual learner.

To achieve this, it provides each learner with the activity it considers most appropriate at each moment, based on the learner's characteristics, state and needs, and on the teaching strategy selected by the teacher. All this through a selection engine consisting of an artificial intelligence model.

Following CALM principles, we propose a two-phase design for such a model. The first phase, based on obtaining a predictor through the use of deep learning techniques, allows to obtain two metrics, score and time, to measure the performance of different students for each of the possible activities. The second phase uses an activity selector through the application of instructional techniques, implemented on the basis of a series of algorithms.

With the separation of the model into two phases, it has been possible to combine the power of deep learning, for the prediction of the two metrics, with the ability to influence and guide the student by the teacher, making use of instructional strategies. In this way, we have moved from a black box approach, as in other IA models, to one where the teacher influences the learning and the strategy to be followed, which can be personalized for each student at all times.

The model has been implemented for its use in conjunction with a learning platform, where its impact on student learning will be validated and tested. This experience will allow to adjust and evolve the model in a real execution environment.

References

1. Bedenlier, S., Bond, M., Buntins, K., Zawacki-Richter, O., Kerres, M.: Facilitating student engagement through educational technology in higher education: a systematic review in the field of arts and humanities. Australas. J. Educ. Technol. **36**(4), 126–150 (2020)
2. Manuel Area Moreira: La metamorfosis digital del material didáctico tras el paréntesis gutenberg. Revista Latinoamericana De Tecnología Educativa - RELATEC **16**(2), 13–28 (2017)
3. Area-Moreira, M., Adell-Segura, J.: Tecnologías digitales y cambio educativo. una aproximación crítica. REICE. Revista Iberoamericana Sobre Calidad, Eficacia Y Cambio En Educación (2021)
4. Goodwill, A., Chen, S.H.: Embracing a culture of lifelong learning: the science of lifelong learning. UNESCO Institute for Lifelong Learning (2021)
5. Daniela, L.: Smart pedagogy for technology-enhanced learning. In: Daniela, L. (ed.) Didactics of Smart Pedagogy, pp. 3–21. Springer, Cham (2019). https://doi.org/10.1007/978-3-030-01551-0_1
6. Robinson, K., Aronica, L.: Finding your element: how to discover your talents and passions and transform your life. Penguin (2014)
7. Min, W., et al.: Deepstealth: game-based learning stealth assessment with deep neural networks. IEEE Trans. Learn. Technol. **13**(2), 312–325 (2020)
8. Villagrá-Arnedo, C., Gallego-Durán, F., Llorens-Largo, F., Satorre-Cuerda, R., Compañ-Rosique, P., Molina-Carmona, R.: Time-dependent performance prediction system for early insight in learning trends. Int. J. Interact. Multimedia Artif. Intell. (2020)
9. Mangaroska, K., Vesin, B., Giannakos, M.: Cross-platform analytics: a step towards personalization and adaptation in education. In: Proceedings of the 9th International Conference on Learning Analytics & Knowledge, LAK 2019, pp. 71–75. Association for Computing Machinery, New York (2019)
10. Hwang, G.-J.: Definition, framework and research issues of smart learning environments-a context-aware ubiquitous learning perspective. Smart Learn. Environ. **1**(1), 1–14 (2014)
11. Real-Fernández, A.: CALM: un modelo de aprendizaje adaptativo y personalizado. Ph.D. thesis, Universidad de Alicante (2022)

12. Real-Fernandez, A., Llorens-Largo, F., Molina-Carmona, R.: Smart learning model based on competences and activities. In: Innovative Trends in Flipped Teaching and Adaptive Learning, pp. 228–251. IGI Global (2019)
13. Carberry, S., et al.: User Models in Dialog Systems. Springer, softcover reprint of the original, 1st edn. 1989 edition edition (2011)
14. Real-Fernández, A., Molina-Carmona, R., Pertegal-Felices, M.L., Llorens-Largo, F.: Definition of a feature vector to characterise learners in adaptive learning systems. In: Visvizi, A., Lytras, M.D. (eds.) RIIFORUM 2019. SPC, pp. 75–89. Springer, Cham (2019). https://doi.org/10.1007/978-3-030-30809-4_8
15. Real-Fernández, A., Molina-Carmona, R., Llorens-Largo, F.: Computational characterization of activities and learners in a learning system. Appl. Sci. 10(7), 2208 (2020)
16. Gallego-Durán, F.J., Molina-Carmona, R., Llorens-Largo, F.: Estimating the difficulty of a learning activity from the training cost for a machine learning algorithm. In: Proceedings of the Sixth International Conference on Technological Ecosystems for Enhancing Multiculturality - TEEM 2018, pp. 654–659. ACM Press (2018)
17. Real-Fernández, A., Molina-Carmona, R., Llorens Largo, F.: Characterization of learners from their learning activities on a smart learning platform. In: Zaphiris, P., Ioannou, A. (eds.) HCII 2020. LNCS, vol. 12205, pp. 279–291. Springer, Cham (2020). https://doi.org/10.1007/978-3-030-50513-4_21
18. Iglesias, A., Martínez, P., Aler, R., Fernández, F.: Learning teaching strategies in an adaptive and intelligent educational system through reinforcement learning. Appl. Intell. 31(1), 89–106 (2009)
19. Real-Fernández, A., Molina-Carmona, R., Llorens-Largo, F.: Instructional strategies for a smart learning system. In: Proceedings of the Seventh International Conference on Technological Ecosystems for Enhancing Multiculturality, TEEM 2019, pp. 671–679. Association for Computing Machinery, New York (2019)
20. Csikszentmihalyi, M.: Flow: The Psychology of Optimal Experience. Perennial Modern Classics. Harper & Row (1990)
21. LeCun, Y., Bengio, Y., Hinton, G.: Deep learning. Nature 521(7553), 436–444 (2015)
22. Rudin, C.: Stop explaining black box machine learning models for high stakes decisions and use interpretable models instead. Nat. Mach. Intell. 1(5), 206–215 (2019)
23. Arrieta, A.B., et al.: Explainable artificial intelligence (XAI): concepts, taxonomies, opportunities and challenges toward responsible AI (2019)
24. Kipf, T.N., Welling, M.: Semi-supervised classification with graph convolutional networks. CoRR, abs/1609.02907 (2016)
25. Cho, K., van Merrienboer, B., Bahdanau, D., Bengio, Y.: On the properties of neural machine translation: Encoder-decoder approaches. CoRR, abs/1409.1259 (2014)

Learning System for Relational Algebra

Erika Hernández-Rubio[1]([⊠]), Marco Antonio Rodríguez-Torres[2],
Humberto Vázquez-Santiago[2], and Amilcar Meneses-Viveros[3]

[1] Instituto Politécnico Nacional, SEPI-ESCOM, Ciudad de México, Mexico
ehernandezru@ipn.mx
[2] Instituto Politécnico Nacional, ESCOM, Ciudad de México, Mexico
[3] Departamento de Computación, CINVESTAV-IPN, Ciudad de México, Mexico
ameneses@cs.cinvestav.mx

Abstract. The interaction between the student and the pedagogical
material is essential in the learning process. eLearning tools allow this kind
of interaction. Also, learn about databases topics is important because the
handling of information has increased in recent decades. The relational
model allows the physical design of the data. To obtain operations on
the relational model, relational algebra is used. Relational algebra have
instruction set to obtain information about the data relationships. A web
system has been development to support the learning of Database courses,
allowing queries to be made to a database through a relational algebra language. The system has been tested in Databases courses at the Computing
School of National Institute Polytechnic in Mexico.

Keywords: Data bases · eLearning · relational algebra

1 Introduction

The interaction between the student and the pedagogical material is essential in
the learning process. It allows the student to learn and understand phenomena
through experimentation. In university-level courses associated with Internet
Communication Technologies, there are programming environments and platforms that allow students to learn concepts of curricular content such as programming paradigms and languages, image or data processing, among others [10,20].
Particularly in the Databases course, there are SQL query languages, or applications to make entity relationship diagrams and relational schemes, which allow
reinforcing the topics of data analysis, data model and queries.

This type of learning is important because the handling of information has
increased in recent decades. There are structured, semi-structured and unstructured data [1]. Structured data is stored in databases that allow the data model
to be maintained through a series of relationships between different tables. An
advantage of this type of database is that integrity constraints are satisfied and
different operations can be performed to perform queries.

The relational model allows the physical design of the data. To obtain operations on the relational model, relational algebra is used [26]. Relational algebra

P. Zaphiris and A. Ioannou (Eds.): HCII 2023, LNCS 14040, pp. 54–63, 2023.
https://doi.org/10.1007/978-3-031-34411-4_5

allows you to obtain information about the relationships of the data, that is, the relationships between the tables. Algebraic properties allow efficient and optimized queries. However, there are few Web applications where the student can practice this topic.

The fundamental operations that we can find within relational algebra are selection, projection, cross product, and the operations of set theory such as union, intersection, and difference, to name a few. There are also some operations that complement relational algebra such as joint, natural joint or external union.

Due to the importance of relational algebra, a school support Web system has been developed with a language to perform queries through relational algebra operators in a database. The system contains a relational algebra operator language in a database as well as an initial DB so that queries can be made through relational algebra. What allows to complete the tools that the student can have to complete his learning process in the matter of database. It also allows students to upload their own databases for queries. The system has been tested in Database courses at the Escuela Superior de Cómputo del IPN, Mexico.

2   Related Work

There are an increase of e-learning platforms such as course management systems [19], collaborative systems [25] or virtual and remote laboratories [3,22]. This availability of resources has allowed the establishment of new strategies in the learning process at the university level. Course management systems allow teachers to monitor the daily activities of students. In addition to having a concentration of tasks, tests and pedagogical resources, such as learning objects, to reinforce learning in the classroom.

With the increase in the use of data mining, artificial intelligence and big data to solve problems in different areas, the organization and management of data has generated that techniques for handling structured, semi-structured and unstructured data must be known [6,28]. For structured data, knowledge of relational database concepts is necessary, so teaching it is important. So, database is an important subject in the career of computer science and informatics. There are several efforts to improve the learning and teaching process [12,14].

Learning process take advantage by the use of e-Learning tools [10,17]. In the case of databases university courses, some works have been reported in the literature [11,17,21,27]. In [17] the impact of use of Learning Management Systems is presented for databases courses. In [11] authors present a study on the use of a Web application to teach the SQL languages in MySQL and SQLServer. Other works focus on game-based learning processes for the design of entity relationship diagrams [27]. Other tools automate the evaluation processes in activities for students, such as [21], where incorporating an Entity Relation Diagram evaluator into e-Learning environments.

There are some papers related to build a library or frameworks or systems to work with relational algebra [4,7,8,15,16,18,29,31,32]. There are works aimed at expressing an algebra with operators that allow expressing relational algebra and linear algebra [4,16]. Relax is a Web application developed by Innsbruck University [18], this application is based on manual data entry. Yang develop an interpreter for python to work with relational algebra [32]. Several work are oriented to translate sentences from relational algebra to SQL sentences, this translator are written in Java or Phyton [7,8,15]. In [31] authors make a system to process relational algebra through an iterative graphic interface that handles query trees.

The usability of e-Learning systems has been studied since the beginning of the 21st century [2,5,13,23,30]. Because there are various types of e-learning tools, several works have focused on studying the usability of a specific type of e-learning tool, for example, in [13] a usability review for Learning Management Systems is presented. Other authors have dedicated themselves to studying usability or developing tools and frameworks for usability applied to adaptive e-learning techniques [23].

3 Relational Model

Relational model was proposed by Codd in 1970. This model is based in the mathematical concept of relation. Cood and other authors extended this notion to apply it to design databases. Relational model is based in the relation concept that is represented as a table or two-dimensional array. In this physical representation rows are individual records and columns are attributes [24].

Attribute domain is a set with values allowed for every single attribute. Domains could be different or some attributes can have the same domain. Every row correspond to an individual record or entity instance. In the relational model, every row is a tuple. Most of characteristic specified of tables comes from properties from mathematical relations. A mathematical relationship is defined by a subset of cross product of sets. From databases point of view, a relation is any subset of cross product of the attributes domains. Usually, a relation is represented by a set of n-tuples, in which every element is selected from proper domain. Because a relation is a set, the order of the element does not matter. Therefore, the order of the elements in a table is irrelevant. In a set, no element is repeated. In the same way, in a table there are not repeating columns [24].

There are several languages used for relational database management systems. Relational algebra and relational are formal languages and could be not friendly to users. These languages are not natively implemented in database management systems. However, both languages has been used as a basis for another languages that manipulate upper level data for relational databases. So, these languages are interesting because show the basic operations for all data manipulation languages. Also, they are a comparative standard for another relational database languages [24].

Usability in relational algebra systems has focused on the use of operators in relational algebra grammar [9].

3.1   Relational Algebra

Relational algebra is a theoretical language with operators. This operators are applied to one or two relations to get another one. Then, the operands and results are tables. The basic operations of relational algebra are selection, projection, union, difference and cross product.

Projection and selection are unitary operations since they only operate on a relationship. Union, difference and cross product are binary operations since they operate on two relationships. Fundamental operations for relational algebra are explained in next.

Selection Operation. This operation select tuples that fulfill a given condition. σ symbol represent this operation. Condition is represented as σ subscript. The relation on which it operates is written in parentheses next to σ. The syntax for selection is:

$$\sigma(Conditon)(Relation) \tag{1}$$

This operation require comparative operators such as $=, \neq, \leq, <, >$ o $\geq$ and logic operators: conjuntion, disjuntion and negation.

Projection Operation. This operation only return selected arguments from a relation, in other words, projection act as a filter over the desired columns and eliminate duplicate attributes. Projection is represented by π greek letter. π subscript refer to the desired attributes to show in the result of the relation. The only argument is the relation on which it acts, so the attributes referred to in the subscripts would be in that relation. The syntax of a projection onto a relation is:

$$\pi(attribs)(Relation) \tag{2}$$

Union Operation. Union is a binary operation, its operands are relations. $\cup$ symbol is used to denote the union. The result is a relation with all tuples of initial relationships. Its syntax is:

$$Relation1 \cup Relation2 \tag{3}$$

It is necessary that the two relations that are operated in the union are compatible. If they are not, the union operation cannot be performed. Two relations are compatible if they meet these conditions:

1. Relations must have the same number of attributes.
2. Attribute domains must be the same.

Difference Operation. Difference is a binary operation. Two relations are its operands. Subtraction symbol $(-)$ is used to denote the difference. The result are all tuples contained in the first relation, but not in the second one. This operation is not symmetric. The syntax for difference is:

$$Relation1 - Relation2 \tag{4}$$

Like the projection operation, the relations would be compatible to execute the difference.

Cross Product Operator. Cross product allows to combine information of two relations and they do not need to be compatible. Symbol × is used to denote this operation. Cross product of two relation A and B is a new relation formed from the concatenation of tuples of A and B. The syntax for cross product is:

$$Relation1 \times Relation2 \tag{5}$$

4   Design

The objective of the system is to have a e-Learning tool to support the learning process in database courses at the *Escuela Superior de Cómputo del Instituto Politécnico Nacional* in Mexico. This tool allows to the students to solve queries using relational algebra. These queries are based on the design of a lexical and syntactic analyzer for relational algebra.

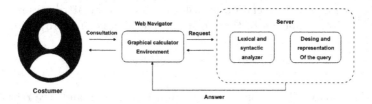

Fig. 1. System block diagram

The system design is based on client-server architecture. Figure 1 shows to the block diagram for the system. On the client side, user have a graphic user interface with a set of widgets such as buttons, field texts and menus. Users can perform relational algebra queries on pre-loaded databases, or they can load their own database files. On the server side, the lexical analyzer checks that the sentence written in real algebra is correct, that is, that the words and symbols are coherent together. In addition, it is verified that the semantics and syntax are adequate and that the names of the data exist within the available data set. After the statement is valid has been validated, the system sends the result of the query to the client to display the result.

The grammar for this relational algebra calculator includes the selection, projection, union, difference, and cross product operators. The grammar recognizes query statements such as those expressed in Eqs. 1, 2, 3, 4 and 5. The grammar include operator =, <, >, <=, >= y != for conditions. String values are enclosed in double quotes. Finally, the relation refers to the name of some table in the database.

4.1 The GUI Design

The main screen of the system allows the user to select a task among different options: review the theory of relational algebra, view system information, and perform a practice or query, Fig. 2.

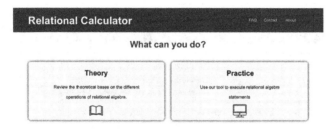

Fig. 2. Main Screen

The screen *Theory*, Fig. 3, contains various buttons associated with each relational operator. The action of each button presents the theoretical information of the selected operator. This screen allow to students have the theoretical framework for this type of query.

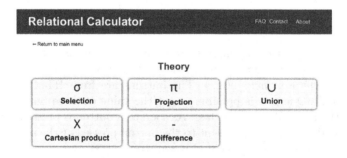

Fig. 3. Theory Screen

Practice screen describe to the user the way of use the system, Fig. 4. The user can choose the database to use, either one of the databases pre-loaded in the system, or a database loaded by the user. This view have a text field where the query is written en relational algebra. This query is written with the help of buttons that make it easy to insert conditional and relational operators. The system can detect when the user database field is not correct. After the user selects the database on which the query will be made, the result of the query will be displayed. If the query is wrong, an error notification will appear.

In order to make a query, *"Practica"* screen has several options. These options are: load file, select file, write a query (with relational algebra) and show results. *"Load file"* allows to the user store a file with a database structure and the system verify if this file is valid. Then the system create a temporal database and is added to the list of available data bases. With *"Select file"* option, the user can select a database from a lits of pre-loaded databases. Default database is *Schools*.

Fig. 4. Practice Screen

The main task of the system is to perform queries using relational algebra. Users can perform these queries by writing the expression through the buttons located above the text field, Fig. 4. The buttons are from HTML form. With JavaScript and JQuery it is possible to get the value of these buttons through their ID or their already defined class. As soon as a button is pressed, that value is obtained and the string equivalent to the button pressed at the position where the mouse cursor is currently located is sent to the text area.

Finally, there is a "Result Screen", where the result of query is showed. This screen display the database table and registers. There are another screens to displays another information such as *"FAQ"*, *"Contact"* or *"About.."*

5   Test and Results

The developed system was tested to verify its functionality and usability. The system was tested with the students of the Database of the *Escuela Superior de Cómputo del IPN*. Thirty-four students took the tests, twenty-eight men and seven women. The age range of the control group is between 20 and 22 years old. The tests were evaluated through questionnaires. Each subject performed three previously specified consultation operations, after carrying out the consultations they answered the questionnaire that was evaluated on a Likert scale. Each exercise increases the difficulty of the query. From simple selections to cross-product queries with selections. The students were able to obtain the expected results that were requested in each exercise. Although it was observed that the use of upper and lower case letters generated some problems when writing the queries.

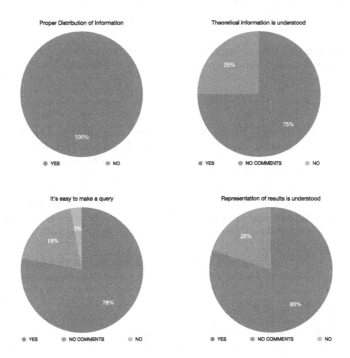

Fig. 5. Usability test results

Figure 5 shows the main usability test results. Of the questions that were asked to the control group, it was about the distribution of information on the system screens and 100% answered affirmatively. Another question that users were asked was whether the information presented is understandable. In this case, 75% answered affirmatively. For the question of whether it is easy to carry out the task of making a query in the system, 78% answered affirmatively, 19% did not answer and 3% answered no. Finally, the users were asked about the quality of the representation of the results, 80% answered that they agree with the way in which the results are presented, and 20% do not have a favorable or unfavorable opinion. In general the opinion. In general, the opinion of the users on the use of the system was favorable.

6   Conclusions

Based on the results of the tests carried out, it can be seen that the GUI design does not require major changes. The opinion of the users on the use of the system was favorable. However, improvements still need to be made in the handling of the query syntax, since the use of upper and lower case letters causes problems in the queries.

It is possible to have specific e-Learning tools that support the learning process. In particular, it is feasible to have systems that help to reaffirm relational algebra concepts in database courses at the university level.

Acknowledgements. The authors thank financial support given by the Instituto Politénico Nacional trough SIP program with the project number 20221447.

References

1. Acharjya, D.P., Ahmed, K.: A survey on big data analytics: challenges, open research issues and tools. Int. J. Adv. Comput. Sci. Appl. **7**(2), 511–518 (2016)
2. Ardito, C., et al.: Usability of e-learning tools. In: Proceedings of the Working Conference on Advanced Visual Interfaces, pp. 80–84 (2004)
3. Ballu, A., Yan, X., Blanchard, A., Clet, T., Mouton, S., Niandou, H.: Virtual metrology laboratory for e-learning. Procedia CIRP **43**, 148–153 (2016)
4. Barceló, P., Higuera, N., Pérez, J., Subercaseaux, B.: On the expressiveness of LARA: a unified language for linear and relational algebra. arXiv preprint arXiv:1909.11693 (2019)
5. Benson, L., et al.: Usability and instructional design heuristics for e-learning evaluation. In: Association for the Advancement of Computing in Education (AACE) (2002)
6. Boehm, M., Kumar, A., Yang, J.: Data Management in Machine Learning Systems. Springer, Cham (2022). https://doi.org/10.1007/978-3-031-01869-5
7. Carlyle, T.: Relational algebra translator (2011)
8. Cyganiak, R.: A relational algebra for SPARQL. Digital Media Systems Laboratory HP Laboratories Bristol. HPL-2005-170, vol. 35, no. 9 (2005)
9. Dadashzadeh, M.: Improving usability of the relational algebra interface. J. Syst. Manag. **40**(9), 9 (1989)
10. Dæhli, O., Kristoffersen, B., Lauvås, P., Jr., Sandnes, T.: Exploring feedback and gamification in a data modeling learning tool. Electron. J. e-Learn. **19**(6), 559–574 (2021)
11. Dela Rosa, A.P., Villanueva, L.M., San Miguel, J.M., Quinto, J.E.: Web-based database courses e-learning application. Int. J. Comput. Sci. Res. (2022)
12. Douglas, D.E., Van Der Vyver, G.: Effectiveness of e-learning course materials for learning database management systems: an experimental investigation. J. Comput. Inf. Syst. **44**(4), 41–48 (2004)

13. Freire, L.L., Arezes, P.M., Campos, J.C.: A literature review about usability evaluation methods for e-learning platforms. Work **41**(Suppl. 1), 1038–1044 (2012)
14. Hamzah, M.L., Rukun, K., Rizal, F., Purwati, A.A., et al.: A review of increasing teaching and learning database subjects in computer science. Revista ESPACIOS **40**(26) (2019)
15. Hirsch, R., Wagner, J.: Relational algebra translation application (2017)
16. Hutchison, D., Howe, B., Suciu, D.: LaraDB: a minimalist kernel for linear and relational algebra computation. In: Proceedings of the 4th ACM SIGMOD Workshop on Algorithms and Systems for MapReduce and Beyond, pp. 1–10 (2017)
17. Istambul, M.R.: E-learning design activity to improve student's knowledge and skills: a case study of database design courses. Int. J. Inf. Educ. Technol. **6**(6), 423 (2016)
18. Kessler, J., Tschuggnall, M., Specht, G.: Relax: a webbased execution and learning tool for relational algebra. In: BTW 2019 (2019)
19. Kim, K., Trimi, S., Park, H., Rhee, S.: The impact of CMS quality on the outcomes of e-learning systems in higher education: an empirical study. Decis. Sci. J. Innov. Educ. **10**(4), 575–587 (2012)
20. Landa-Durán, P., Silva-Rodríguez, A., Guarneros-Reyes, E.: Dispositional factors in psychology learning, a study supported by tics. Revista Electrónica de Psicología Iztacala **15**(4), 1476–1493 (2012)
21. Lino, A.D.P., Rocha, A.: Automatic evaluation of ERD in e-learning environments. In: 2018 13th Iberian Conference on Information Systems and Technologies (CISTI), pp. 1–5. IEEE (2018)
22. Martínez-Torres, M.D.R., Toral Marín, S., García, F.B., Vazquez, S.G., Oliva, M.A., Torres, T.: A technological acceptance of e-learning tools used in practical and laboratory teaching, according to the European higher education area. Behav. Inf. Technol. **27**(6), 495–505 (2008)
23. Mazon-Fierro, M., Mauricio, D.: Usability of e-learning and usability of adaptive e-learning: a literature review. Int. J. Hum. Factors Ergon. **9**(1), 1–31 (2022)
24. Ricardo, C.M.: Bases de datos. McGraw Hill Educación, New York (2009)
25. Salmons, J.E.: Taxonomy of collaborative e-learning. In: Encyclopedia of Information Technology Curriculum Integration, pp. 839–846. IGI Global (2008)
26. Santos, V., Belo, O.: Modeling ETL data quality enforcement tasks using relational algebra operators. Procedia Technol. **9**, 442–450 (2013)
27. Schildgen, J.: Monster park-the entity-relationship-diagram learning game. In: ER Forum/Posters/Demos, pp. 150–157 (2020)
28. To, Q.-C., Soto, J., Markl, V.: A survey of state management in big data processing systems. VLDB J. **27**(6), 847–872 (2018). https://doi.org/10.1007/s00778-018-0514-9
29. Villalobos-Murillo, J., Chavarría, S.B., Rivera, S.M.: Herramienta asistida por computadora para la enseñanza del álgebra relacional en bases de datos. Uniciencia **26**(1), 179–195 (2012)
30. Wong, S.K.B., Nguyen, T.T., Chang, E., Jayaratna, N.: Usability metrics for e-learning. In: Meersman, R., Tari, Z. (eds.) OTM 2003. LNCS, vol. 2889, pp. 235–252. Springer, Heidelberg (2003). https://doi.org/10.1007/978-3-540-39962-9_34
31. Xohua-Chacón, A., Benítez-Guerrero, E., Mezura-Godoy, C.: Tanquery: a tangible system for relational algebra learning. In: Proceedings of the XVIII International Conference on Human Computer Interaction, pp. 1–8 (2017)
32. Yang, J.: Ra (radb): a relational algebra interpreter over relational databases (2017)

Design and Simulation of an IoT Intelligent University Campus for Academic Aim

Mary Luz Mouronte-López[1](✉) ⓘ, Ángel Lambertt Lobaina[2],
Elizabeth Guevara-Martínez[2] ⓘ, and Jorge Alberto Rodríguez Rubio[3]

[1] Higher Polytechnic School, Universidad Francisco de Vitoria, Madrid, Spain
maryluz.mouronte@ufv.es
[2] Universidad Anáhuac México, Estado de México, Mexico
[3] Cisco Academy – Investigaciones y Estudios Superiores SC, Estado de México, Mexico

Abstract. Design, implementation, and experiments as well as the use of simulation technology are useful in learning telecommunication networks, allowing to put into practice real world alike scenarios. The fast development of IoT and its use in the most diverse context of human activity has motivated universities around the world to organize courses for their students in order to train and make them familiar with the use of this technology. The utilization of tools that simulate IoT networks functioning facilitates the teaching and training of future engineers in this area. This paper presents our experiences using tools that simulate IoT networks to facilitate teaching and training of future engineers.

Keywords: IoT · Cisco Packet Tracer · Network simulation · Smart buildings

1 Introduction

The term Internet of Things (IoT) was first coined by Kevin Ashton in 1999 [1].

IoT is consequence of Internet evolution. The IoT refers to the use of intelligently connected devices and systems to leverage data gathered by embedded sensors and actuators in machines and other physical objects. It makes the objects themselves identifiable, obtain intelligence, convey information about them and can access information gathered by other things. IoT lets us connect with people and things anytime and anywhere [2].

The use of IoT offers many advantages to create smart cities, buildings, and factories among many other applications. The 2020 Gartner Report [3] announced that investment in IoT would be critical to build smart cities. It anticipates that the use of data obtained through IoT devices would generate significant revenues. The report required the service providers to prioritize and to promote the utilization of the 5G mobile network technology. Later, in 2021, the Gartner Report [4] predicted that wireless communications will be of key importance for Industry 4.0 and smart factories. Researchers and companies have studied the issues connected to build of smart cities. Some analyses refer to the integration of 5G technology with IoT applications, and address aspects related to improving some communications functions [5]. Other investigations refer to security issues, suggesting solutions helping to preserve privacy of IoT environments

P. Zaphiris and A. Ioannou (Eds.): HCII 2023, LNCS 14040, pp. 64–78, 2023.
https://doi.org/10.1007/978-3-031-34411-4_6

[6, 7]. They also refer to the application of IoT in buildings, in order to save energy and increase the comfort of their residents [8]. Other researchers make a review of the state of the art of IoT technology, explaining the current situation in topics like architecture, infrastructure, communication systems and the most popular sensors [9].

The paper describes the use of a simulation tool in a seminar developed to introduce undergraduate students the principles of IoT. As part of the seminar, simulations of IoT based smart campus were carried out. An overview of the seminar, as well as the technical explanation of the devices and simulations created by students is described in the following sections.

The paper is structured as follows: Sect. 2 is a synopsis of the seminar; Sect. 3 briefly explains the tool used for the simulation, while Sect. 4 includes the initial requirements of the smart university campus and present the most creative solutions developed by students. Section 5 presents the evaluation and acceptance degree of the course. Finally, Sect. 6 contains conclusions.

2 Synopsis of the Seminar

The seminar had duration of 8 weeks. The students who attended the seminar belonged to the last two years of Computer Engineering and double degree in business analytics + computer engineering at Universidad Francisco de Vitoria in Madrid, and Information Technology and Telecommunications Engineering at Universidad Anáhuac México in México. Vocational training students, specifically those enrolled in the last years of higher education in administration of networked computer systems were also beneficiaries of this course.

However, the seminar could also be taught in courses at any other university with telecommunication network content in its curriculum.

Professors organized students in teams of no more than 4 students and presented the basic requirements of the smart university campus to be developed by students, which included standard networks services (implemented by using routers, servers, switches, access points, firewalls, etc.) and IoT based systems (with sensors, smart things, processing boards, etc.) to control access, climate and fire protection of the different areas.

The initial requirements of the IoT network were intentionally very simple to permit students a quickly understanding of the tool functionalities concerning the simulation of standard and IoT components to be used.

During the last sessions of the seminar, and under professors' supervision, the IoT networks were enriched and modified by the students themselves, creating more complex networks which meet requirements and performances of more realistic environments. By implementing new networks, students acquired deeper knowledge about IoT meanwhile developing skills using simulation tools.

Some network solutions created by students are presented to illustrate the knowledge and skills acquired during the seminar.

3   Briefly Explanation of the Tool Used for Simulation

The tool selected for the IoT network simulation was Cisco Packet Tracer version 8.0, a Cisco System Inc. proprietary multi-platform tool that enables students to create networking and IoT simulations without need of hardware and/or existing network. The tool can be downloaded freely and runs on the main operating systems. It allows users to execute simulations of networks of diverse complexity.

The development of an IoT network simulation based on a simple scenario permitted students a quickly understanding of the tool functionalities concerning the simulation of IoT systems. The IoT seminars were held in the second semester of 2021 at both Universidad Francisco de Vitoria in Madrid and Universidad Anáhuac México in México. The simulation allowed students to consolidate theoretical knowledge taught during the seminars.

Working with Cisco Packet Tracer is highly intuitive. Components to be used to build the network are selected among sets of different kind of components, which are then placed in the working area of the main window.

IoT components include smart devices (those that can connect directly to network's servers or gateways through their own network interfaces), non-intelligent components (sensors and actuators) and processing boards named MCU (microcontroller unit) and SBC (single board computer) which simulate popular Arduino and Raspberry Pi boards. Once the devices are selected, they must be connected and configured.

Depending on the devices to be interconnected, several types of cables will be used (from standard communications cables to special cables for IoT devices). There are two ways to configure the devices: by the user interface or by the Command Line Interface.

In addition to the logical simulation, Cisco Packet Tracer allows the simulation of networks at physical level creating different environments: cities, buildings, physical containers and wired cabins. From the main window it is possible to switch between logical and physical layers. In order to create several physical layers, the network is divided into different subnets, each one with different physical environments, permitting to create networks with more realistic characteristics during simulation such as physical length of cables, WAN coverage limitations, etc. During IoT network simulations, it is especially important to setup the values of environmental variables at different times of the day, because its influence on the behavior of many IoT devices which sense the environment.

Each physical layer (except wired cabins), allows to adjust the values of more than 50 environmental variables during 24 h, which permits to simulate real environments fluctuations.

4   Network Infrastructure

4.1   Campus Configuration Requirements

The network requirements of the university campus were simplified as much as possible: it consists of a single building with administrative offices, some classrooms and laboratories, and an open sports field adjacent to the building.

Campus Network Backbone. The backbone of the university campus network shall include standard network devices to connect it to an Internet Service Provider (ISP), to protect the network from access by intruders and penetration of viruses and malware that may affect its operation, and to provide IP telephony services.

Virtual LANs (VLANs) could be employed to connect the IoT sub-networks of classrooms and laboratories. Some Quality of Service (QoS) strategies that provide optimal use of network resources could also be implemented.

IoT Networks of Classrooms and Labs. All IoT classrooms and labs networks will have the same configuration: a router working as subnet gateway, a switch, and one IoT server to which all smart IoT devices are connected via the switch.

The IoT networks must have the following IoT based control systems:

1. Access control.
2. Climate control.
3. Fire protection.

Finally, IP phones, laptops and PCs will be included to the networks.

Sports Field IoT Network. The sports field irrigation system could or could not be directly connected to the university campus network. It has to perform the irrigation of the field during some hours of the day.

4.2   Best Solutions Created by Students

Campus Network Backbone. The most complete network backbone simulation developed during the seminar is shown in Fig. 1. The backbone consists of several connected conventional network devices which connects it to an Internet Service Provider (ISP), the 5G telephone network and the IoT sub-networks of classrooms and labs.

Most interesting issues of the solution were:

- The use of a firewall ASA 5505 from CISCO [10], enabling a secure interconnection of the university campus network to the ISP, and therefore the remote access to the network, including the access to the IoT devices and IoT backend servers of classroom and lab sub-networks.

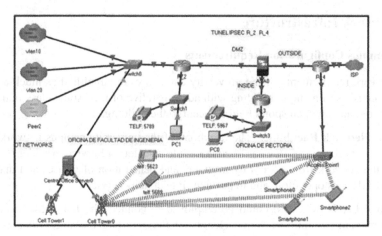

Fig. 1. Network backbone

The firewall was configured to ensure the following network security functions:

1. VLAN 1 INSIDE with security level 100.
2. VLAN 2 OUTSIDE with security level 0.
3. VLAN 3 DMZ with security level 50.
4. Operation policy configuration.
5. Configuration of network objects: (INSIDE, OUTSIDE), (DMZ, OUTSIDE).
6. Configuration of the OUTSIDE route
7. Configuration of the extended access control list (ACL) to manage the traffic allowing the firewall to control the voice traffic in all directions, to control the data traffic from INSIDE to lower security level interfaces, as well as from DMZ interface to OUTSIDE, from OUTSIDE to DMZ and prohibits the data traffic to INSIDE.
8. Configuration of tunnel IPsec [11, 12]. It permits to carry out the traffic from DZM to OUTSIDE, assuring the traffic encryption.

- The IP Telephony Network Configuration [12, 13] which provides the following functions:

1. Creating a DHCP to assign IPv4 addresses to IP phones.
2. Establishment phones and IPv4 router addresses to download the firmware to the phones.
3. Definition of telephone numbers.
4. Assigning the phone numbers to the Call Manager phones.
5. Configuration of the connection with the telephones.

- Other solutions that permits:

1. Communication between Subnets [14]. A dynamic routing protocol and static routes are used for communication between subnets.
2. Traffic Control between Subnets [15]. Extended access control lists (ACL) are used to control traffic between subnets.

3. Separation of Data and Voice Networks [16]. VLANs were created on routers to separate data and voice traffics.
4. Quality of Service (QoS) [17]. QoS policies are defined to adjust network performance to the service quality requirements. It is done by doing an appropriate use of the following technical parameters of network: bandwidth, latency, jitter and packet loss.
5. Access to the 5G Network. Permits the access to the campus network of 5G cellular phones by connecting it to cellular towers.

IoT Networks of Classrooms and Labs. An interesting solution of the IoT network of classrooms and laboratories was developed by another group which is shown in the Fig. 2. The IoT network has its own and simple backbone composed by a router, a switch and an IoT server. The connection of the IoT network to the campus network backbone was implemented via a VLAN. Standard network elements like PC and IP telephones are connected to the backbone via its switch.

Several smart IoT components were included to implement the access, fire protection and climate control systems.

- Access control. That includes a RFID reader, RFID cards and a door. The door is controlled (locked and unlocked) from the IoT network based on the output provided by the RFID card reader when a valid or invalid card is registered.
- Climate control. That includes an air conditioner, a furnace and a thermostat which controls them. Thermostat is remote controlled from the IoT server. The temperature is maintained within comfort limits between 20 and 28 °C. By alternating the operation of air conditioner and furnace (turning them on and off), the room temperature is adjusted.
- Fire protection. That includes a fire detector, a celling water sprinkler, a fan, a siren and a window. If fire is detected, the water jets located on the roof are put into operation, the window is opened, the fan is turned on and the alarm siren sounds.

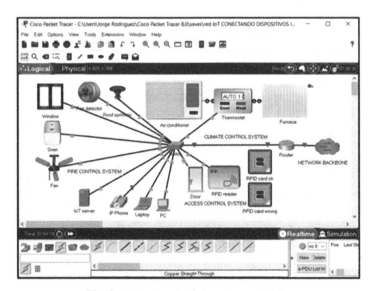

Fig. 2. IoT network of classrooms and labs

The IoT devices used in Cisco Packet Tracer simulations are grouped into four categories: smart devices, sensors, actuators and processing boards. Smart devices can be connected directly to the network (wired or wireless) and can be quickly configured using preloaded software. These devices include smart lights, home appliance, alarm sirens and a long list of smart sensors that can be connected directly to the IoT network. Smart devices are usually plug-and-play and only need to be connected to the local network. It is sometimes necessary to change their network interface from LAN to WLAN or vice versa, according to the required type of network used.

Once the IoT devices are physically connected to the network, they have to be connected by software to the IoT backend server, allowing users to check the operation of the IoT devices from a PC, laptop or smartphone connected to the network using a browser.

Figure 3 shows the IoT homepage created by students in the IoT server. Accessing the list of devices on the IoT server it is possible to view the status of each device, as well as to act with them remotely. By clicking Door device, more information about the device is shown: its status Open (green) or Close (red), and act with it to Lock or Unlock.

Furthermore, while connecting the IoT devices to the IoT homepage, it is also possible, by clicking on the Conditions tab, to setup basic IoT logic rules to create interactions between the IoT devices. Each rule has a set of conditions and a list of actions, which are executed if the conditions are satisfied.

Fig. 3. IoT homepage (Color figure online)

Figure 4 shows the interaction rules of IoT devices of the Fire (Fire detector), Access (Door unlock and Door locked) and Climate (Cooling and Heating) control systems.

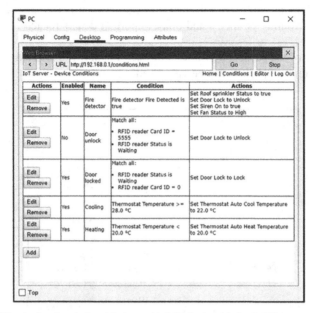

Fig. 4. Logic relationship between IoT devices at the IoT homepage

The rule named Fire detector related with IoT devices of the Fire Control System is shown in the Fig. 5.

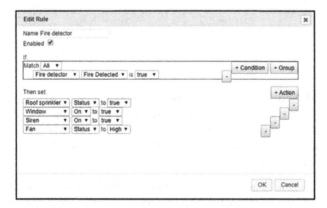

Fig. 5. Edited rule of the Fire Control System

One interesting feature of Cisco Packet Tracer is that it permits the user to switch simulations in real time from logic mode to simulation mode. Logic mode operation permits to create networks, connect devices and define the IoT logic on the backend servers.

However, only in simulation mode is it possible to validate that there are communication at the network layer between devices.

Student groups used this feature using Cisco Packet Tracer in simulation mode to see and analyze the traffic of different packets between nodes and devices to verify connectivity, routing protocols and other important details related to the networks functioning.

An example of the packets transmitted through the network is listed as is shown in Fig. 6. The contents of packets can be visualized.

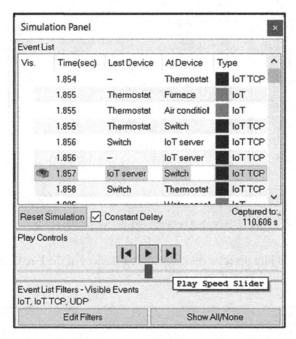

Fig. 6. Network packages captured in simulation mode

Sports Field IoT Network. There were two notable solutions of IoT system to irrigate the sport field, one connected to the network of the classrooms and labs and other working standalone. We will present the second one (see Fig. 7) which includes not only the interconnection of the devices, but also the programming of the processor board (SBC) to carry out the irrigation control.

Sport field irrigation control system includes a water level sensor, a SBC board and an outdoor sprinkler. The water level sensor indicates if the water level of the field is below a minimum. When it happens, the water irrigation starts, connecting the sprinkler until the target water level is reached.

Cisco Packet Tracer provides the use of non-intelligent devices such as sensors and actuators, something that frequently has to be done in real applications. Non-intelligent devices are not directly connectable to the network. If these devices are used (being

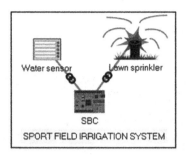

Fig. 7. Sports Field Irrigation System

connected to the IoT network or not), they must be connected to MCU or SBC processing boards by using a special IoT cable. Doing so, non-intelligent devices could be connected to the IoT network via the processing boards. However, non-intelligent devices sometimes are connected to processing boards to build local control systems not connected to the network, as the solution developed by students.

Connected or not to the IoT network, the processing boards always have to have a running program controlling non-intelligent devices. Generally, software reads input signals from sensors and executes an algorithm that produces output signals that operate on actuators. Cisco Packet Tracer provides Java, Phyton and Blockly programming languages to develop the programs which run on the processing boards. The first two languages allow full command and control of sensors and actuators.

Blockly is a visual programming language developed by Google [18]. It is an intuitive visual programming language based on graphical blocks that are visually edited. The user interface of the Blockly editor consists of a toolbox, which holds available blocks from where user can select blocks, and a workspace where user can drag and drop and rearrange blocks [18]. Finally, blocks are interpreted and executed [19]. Programs written using Blockly allow an easier visual development of program logic but sometimes don't permit a full control of sensors and actuators.

A Blockly program was developed to run in a SBC board to controls the irrigation of the sports field. It reads the water level status of the field; if the water level is less than or equal to 60, it starts the sprinkler irrigating the field (see Fig. 8). From the programming tab, it is possible to run or stop the program.

Sensors and actuators specifications can be found by clicking on the Specification tab of the selected device. The device specifications include all the necessary information to use the device: states, the type of input and output, etc. If more complex devices are used, programmer can use certain APIs previously developed to manipulate the devices.

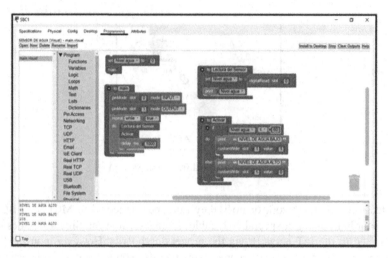

Fig. 8. Blockly program to control water supply to the sport field

5 Perception and Acceptance

5.1 What Professors Appreciated During the Seminar

The participative environment created during the seminar supported by Cisco Packet Tracer simulation tool allowed undergraduate students to acquire very quickly the basic knowledge which permit them to develop their owns IoT networks solutions of more complex scenarios with operating requirements closer to the real requirements of a university campus.

Students enjoyed sessions and learn very quickly during the seminar.

By discussing the different IoT network solution created by students, professors obtained information enough to evaluate the students' high degree of understanding and assimilation of theory and practice gathered during the seminar.

5.2 Seminar' Questionnaire

At the end of the seminar, a questionnaire was filled-out by students, which included questions about students' prior knowledge, the evaluation of the Cisco Packet Tracer as an IoT learning tool, and an open-ended question about recommendations for improving the course. The questionnaire applied is the following:

6. My prior knowledge related to computer networking before the seminar was:

    High level ___ Medium level ___ Low level ___ No knowledge ___

7. My prior knowledge related to IoT before the seminar was:

    High level ___ Medium level ___ Low level ___ No knowledge ___

8. Rating between 0 and 5 about Cisco Packet Tracer, assigning 5 if you strongly agree and 0 if you strongly disagree.
    a. Packet Tracer is an excellent tool for IoT learning.

   b. Using Packet Tracer I got a good understanding of basic IoT concepts.

   c. Packet Tracer is intuitive and easy to use

   d. The simulation exercises performed with Packet Tracer were adequate to achieve the learning goals.

9. On the content of the topics covered:

   a. I would like to have received a more basic pre-course related to computer networks. YES ____ NO ____

   b. I would like to have received a more basic previous course related to IoT. YES ____ NO ____

   c. The amount of received information was appropriate. YES ____ NO ____

   d. The course provided me with new knowledge. YES ____ NO ____

5.3 Survey Analysis

The answers to the questionnaires submitted by 42 students from both universities at the end of the courses yielded the following results.

As can be seen in Fig. 9, students have more prior knowledge of computer networks as only 17% said they did not know the subject, while 45% of the students had no prior knowledge of IoT.

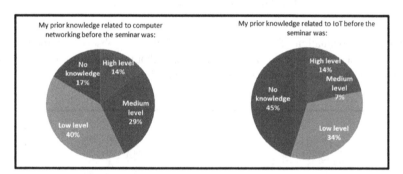

Fig. 9. Previous knowledge

Thus, the most requested previous course was IoT, as the results in Fig. 10 show.

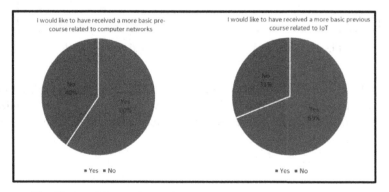

Fig. 10. Need for previous training about computer networks and IoT

Regarding the evaluation of Cisco Packet Tracer, it can be seen in Fig. 11 that most of the students of the course consider it a good tool to learn the basic concepts of IoT and that it is easy to use and intuitive. They also agreed that the proposed exercises were adequate to achieve the learning objectives.

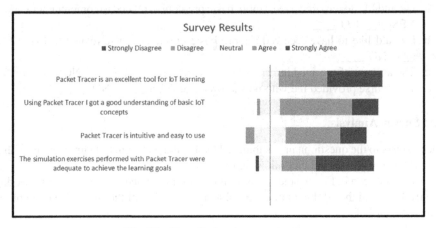

Fig. 11. Cisco Packet tracer evaluation

Finally, the evaluation of the course was satisfactory, as observed in the results of Fig. 12, the vast majority of the students considered that the content of the course was adequate since it allowed them to obtain new knowledge of IoT.

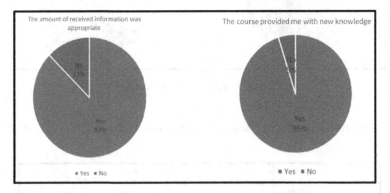

Fig. 12. Seminar evaluation: information and new knowledge

This is highly valuable information that allowed to evaluate Cisco Packet tracer as an IoT teaching tool and that will permit to improve the preparation and organization of IoT seminars in the future considering also the recommendations mentioned by the students.

6 Conclusions

Main conclusions are:

1. Simulation tool used in the seminars allowed undergraduate students of Computer Engineering at Universidad Francisco de Vitoria in Madrid and Information Technology and Telecommunications Engineering at Universidad Anáhuac México in México, to reinforce the knowledge and skills acquired during the IoT seminars.
2. By using Cisco Packet Tracer students simulated easily networks of a smart university campus by themselves because it is an environment very familiar to them. Students appreciated benefits provided by IoT systems.
3. During the seminars, students created, designed and simulated by themselves new IoT networks in more complex scenarios with functioning requirements closer to the real requirements of a university campus.
4. By using virtual private networks (VPN) combined with the multi-user working facilities provided by Cisco Packet Tracer will let students to link the networks created at different universities, working together, interchanging ideas and cooperating during the IoT design and simulation process.
5. The evaluation of the final questionnaire showed a good acceptance of seminar by the students.

The experience gained will allow professors to improve the quality and acceptance of IoT courses in the future.

Acknowledgements. This work was partially funded by Telefónica Chair at Universidad Francisco de Vitoria, Madrid, Spain.

References

1. Gabbai, A.: Kevin Ashton Describes "the Internet of Things". Interview. Smithsonian Magazine (2015)
2. GSM Association: Understanding the Internet of the Things (IoT). GSM Association (2014). https://www.gsma.com/iot/wp-content/uploads/2014/08/cl_iot_wp_07_14.pdf
3. Panetta, K.: Gartner top 10 strategic technology trends 2020 (2019)
4. Panetta, K.: Gartner top 10 strategic technology trends 2021 (2020)
5. Rong, B., Han, S., Kadoch, M., Chen, X., Jara, A.: Integration of 5G networks and internet of things for future smart city. Wirel. Commun. Mob. Comput. **2020**, Article ID 2903525 (2020)
6. Gheisari, M., Wang, G., Khan, W.Z., Fernández-Campusano, C.: A context-aware privacy-preserving method for IoT-based smart city using software defined networking. Comput. Secur. **87**, 101470 (2019)
7. Majeed, U., Khan, L.U., Yaqoob, I., Ahsan Kazmi, S.M., Salah, K., Hong, C.: Blockchain for IoT-based smart cities: recent advances, requirements, and future challenges. J. Netw. Comput. Appl. **181**(9) (2021)
8. Havard, N., McGrath, S., Flanagan, C., MacNamee, C.: Smart building based on internet of things technology (ICST). In: 12th International Conference on Sensing Technology, pp. 278–281 (2018)
9. Verma, A., Prakash, S., Srivastava, V., Kumar, A., Mukhopadhya, S.C.: Sensing, controlling, and IoT infrastructure in smart building: a review. IEEE Sens. J. **19**(20), 9036–9046 (2019)

10. Andrea, H.: Bonus tutorial Cisco ASA 5505 configuration (2020). http://www.cisco-tips.com
11. Bollapragada, V., Khalid, M., Wainner, S.: IPSec VPN design. CiscoPress (2005)
12. Voice and video enabled IPSec VPN (V3PN) solution reference network design, pp. 3.4–3.6 & 4.1–4.4. Corporate Headquarters Cisco Systems, Inc. (2020)
13. Implementing Cisco Unified Communications IP Telephony Part 1, Volume 2 Version 6.0. Student Guide. Editing production and web services (2008)
14. Chen, P.P.: Current issues of conceptual modeling: a summary of selective active research topics. In: Goos, G., et al. (eds.) Conceptual Modeling. LNCS, vol. 1565, p. IX–XXIV. Springer, Heidelberg (1999). https://doi.org/10.1007/3-540-48854-5_1
15. Stallings, W.: Data and Computer Communications, 10th edn. Pearson Education Ltd. (2014)
16. Tadimety, P.R.: OSPF: A Network Routing Protocol, 1st edn. Apress (2015). ISBN 1484214110, 9781484214114
17. Barreiros, M., Lundqvist, P.: QoS-enabled networks, 2nd edn. Wiley (2016). ISBN 978-1-119-10910-5
18. IONOS: ¿Qué es Blockly? (2020). https://www.ionos.es/digitalguide/paginas-web/desarrollo-web/blockly/. Accessed 20 June 2022
19. Google Developers: Introduction to Blockly, (Last updated 2022-12-06 UTC). https://developers.google.com/blockly/guides/overview. Accessed 21 Dec 2022

Behavioral Coding for Predicting Perceptions of Interactions in Dyads

Mohammadamin Sanaei[1]([✉]), Marielle Machacek[1], Stephen B. Gilbert[1], Coleman Eubanks[2], Peggy Wu[2], and James Oliver[1]

[1] Iowa State University, Ames, IA 50010, USA
asanaei@iastate.edu
[2] Raytheon Technology, Arlington, USA

Abstract. Verbal and non-verbal interpersonal interactions, if quantified, can be important factors for analyzing the performance of globalized team members. While using a survey is a common way to measure the interpersonal interactions, behavioral observation is a method that can effectively save time and avoid individual bias in interpretation. This between-subjects experiment collected data from 101 participants in a face-to-face (F2F), video conference (VC), and virtual reality (VR) training communication between the participant and a confederate trainer. The study explored whether the three conditions affected facial and interpersonal behavior differently. Secondly, the study examined whether future researchers could use the behavior markers to predict social and task variables. The dependent behavioral marker variables were Affirmation, Head Nod, Socializing, Question, Leaning Forward, Common Point of Reference, Mirroring, and Hand Gesture. Results showed that Affirmation and Question occurred significantly more often in F2F and VR than in VC. Participants also scored significantly higher in Head Nod in F2F than in VR and VC conditions, and VR socializing scores were also significantly higher than VC condition. Finally, correlation analysis showed that some self-report survey responses could possibly be replaced with behavioral observation methods. Future researchers who can automate the behavioral coding could thus use this approach rather than survey questions for those constructs.

Keywords: behavioral markers · interpersonal interactions · virtual reality · communication · videoconferencing · training

1 Introduction

Real-time remote collaboration spaces typically afford common visual references that could lead to richer remote teamwork. But their success may also be affected by multiple factors, like various levels of verbal and non-verbal interpersonal interactions [1, 2]. Quantifying perceptions about the quality of interpersonal interactions in remote collaboration can be difficult. The perceptions of participants are typically measured through surveys, but self-reports can be time-consuming and subject to individual interpretation and bias. Another potential method to predict collaborators' perception of an interaction is through behavioral observations. This study explores whether coded behavioral

© The Author(s), under exclusive license to Springer Nature Switzerland AG 2023
P. Zaphiris and A. Ioannou (Eds.): HCII 2023, LNCS 14040, pp. 79–90, 2023.
https://doi.org/10.1007/978-3-031-34411-4_7

observations predict participants' survey responses regarding social and task-oriented constructs.

Presence has been used to analyze interpersonal interactions [3]. It can be divided into three categories [4]: (1) physical presence, (2) social presence [5], and (3) emotional telepresence [5]. Analyzing emotional telepresence could be challenging since it manifests in complex ways [6]. Emotional aspect of co-presence in a learning context is measured in this paper by analyzing the users' gestures like facial expression, gaze, touch, etc. in face-to-face (F2F), videoconferencing (VC), and virtual reality (VR) environments.

Computer-mediated communication (CMC) has become popular after the COVID-19 pandemic in multiple domains containing learning contexts. Knowing more about the best affordances for CMC design could improve remote learning environments for students. Remote communication methods differ in emotional expression [7], and besides that, emotional facial expression can affect learning outcomes [8]. Considering the connection between CMCs, emotional expression, and learning outcomes, the sort of CMCs that is used by the subjects could affect users' learning.

Previous researchers have run studies to diagnose the differences in emotional expression between CMCs [9], exploring different chat conditions [7], text and video environment [6], and the differences between CMCs and F2F [10]. Some authors noted that expressing emotion in a CMC is more difficult than in the F2F condition [11, 12]. On the other hand, there are some papers that believe the difference between emotional expression between CMCs and the F2F condition is not notable and could even be disregarded over time [13, 14]. In the current study, first, the authors want to see if VC, VR, and F2F conditions affect facial and interpersonal behavior differently and then analyze the behavior marker results to see if future research can use the behavior markers to predict the social and task variables.

2 Approach

To understand the differences in emotional telepresence among three conditions (VC, VR, and F2F), after obtaining the Institutional Review Board (IRB) approval from Iowa State University, 106 participants were recruited from a Prolific research panel and social media. Participants were given training and then a test in a desktop non-immersive version of a 3D virtual environment called Circuit World [15]. To reduce variation due to cybersickness, participants had to report a low propensity for cybersickness during registration.

Circuit World is a training VR environment that was used as the working context for a participant and a trainer. Each participant was assigned to one communication condition for the training. In VC, the subject and the trainer saw each other via Zoom video while they viewed Circuit World on the trainer's shared screen. In F2F, the participant and trainer sat physically next to each other in front of a single desktop computer while the trainer used Circuit World on a screen in front of them. In VR, the participant used a head-mounted display (HMD) to experience the trainer as an avatar in an immersive version of the Circuit World environment.

In all the three training conditions, before the training phase, the participants first met the researcher, who explained the experimental procedure. Then, the trainer, a confederate, joined the session, and the interaction between the subject and the trainer started in either VC, VR, or F2F condition. The trainer explained a circuit board repair task for the subject. During the nine-minute training session, a camera on top of the monitor recorded the participant's body and facial gestures. These recordings were analyzed using Behavioral Observation Research Interactive Software (BORIS), an open-source software application for behavioral coding of videos [16].

Table 1. Behaviors, examples, and min-max ranges of the results

Behavior	Examples	Range
Affirmation	OK, yea, uh huh, nope, no Trainer: do you have any question; Participant: nope	0–76
Head Nod	[non-verbal]	0–72
Socializing	More about the study and not specifically about the task • Talking about internet connection/speed • "Is the trainer window supposed to be over here or there?" • Asking for help learning how to use the VR headset	0–18
Questions (Task)	"This part is called a what?"	0–29
Jargon	"So, after that, you put the ground wire in."	0–12
Leaning Forward	[non-verbal, e.g., participant has confused furrowed brow]	0–12
Common Point of Reference	Participant refers to an electrode: "So I move this thing over to the breadboard and plug it into this specific row"	0–4
Mirroring	[non-verbal, e.g., smile, frown, yawn, imitating body posture of trainer, such as returning to resting pose after trainer does; sitting up straight from resting pose after trainer does]	0–1
Hand Gesture	[non-verbal]	

Eight behavioral indicators of the subjects were coded and are described as follows. *Affirmation*: A phrase or word intended to inform the other that the person has understood; any type of response to what the trainer has asked. *Head Nod*: The participant nodded their head. *Socializing*: Verbal communication concerning something other than the task. *Questions (Task)*: The participant asked a question of the trainer concerning the task. *Jargon*: The participant used the proper name for a circuit item. *Leaning Forward*: The participant leaned in toward the trainer/screen. *Common Point of Reference*: The participant referenced circuit items but did not use the proper name. *Mirroring*: The participant displayed the same facial expressions as the trainer, or in the VR condition, held their avatar in the same posture as the trainer. A dual-coder protocol using interrater reliability was used to code behaviors, refine the behavior codebook, and ensure the reliability of coding. Cohen's kappa was calculated for interrater reliability estimates. Once coders reached a kappa score of 0.5, videos were then coded by only one coder. Examples for each of the variables are shown in Table 1.

This study compared the results of BORIS with the participant surveys of eight social and task-oriented variables gathered from the subjects via survey. The **social-oriented** variables surveyed were: engagement [17], co-presence [18], rapport [19], and trust [20]. The **task-oriented** variables were shared situational awareness [21], perceived ease of use [22], task experience (Rating scale: 5-point rating scale from very difficult to very easy rating 1 to 5 in terms of doing task), and mental workload [23].

2.1 Data Analysis Approach

Comparisons of the between-subjects VC, VR, and F2F conditions were made using the non-parametric Kruskal-Wallis test since the ANOVA assumption of normality was not met for any of the variables. Distribution was assessed by visual inspection of a boxplot. If there was a statistically significant different between groups, pairwise comparisons were performed using Dunn's (1964) procedure [24] with a Bonferroni correction for multiple comparisons.

To see if there was any similarity between the result of behavioral markers across all three condition and survey results, Pearson's correlations were conducted. Due to the dataset's low frequency of Common Point of Reference, Mirroring, and Hand Gesture, these behaviors were not considered.

3   Results

Data analysis first explored whether the communication condition (F2F, VC, VR) had an impact on the coded behaviors. Then a correlation analysis was completed to assess whether the behavioral codes could predict or be a proxy for the surveyed social-oriented and task-oriented constructs.

3.1   Difference by Communication Condition: Affirmation

A Kruskal-Wallis H test was conducted to determine if there were differences in median affirmation score between three different communication groups: the VC ($n = 40$), VR ($n = 29$), and F2F ($n = 32$) (see Fig. 1). Distributions of affirmation scores were similar for all groups, as assessed by visual inspection of a boxplot. Median affirmation scores were statistically significantly different between groups, $\chi 2(2) = 22.65, p < .001$. The post hoc analysis revealed statistically significant differences in median affirmation scores between the VC (8.5) and VR (22.0) ($p < .001$) conditions and between the VC (8.5) and F2F (23.0) ($p < .001$) conditions.

3.2   Difference by Communication Condition: Head Nods

A Kruskal-Wallis H test was conducted to determine if there were differences in median head nod score between three different groups (see Fig. 2). Distributions of head nod

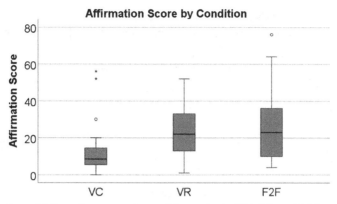

Fig. 1. Boxplots of Affirmation scores for participants in the VC, VR, and F2F conditions. VC was statistically significantly lower than in the other two conditions.

scores were similar for all groups, as assessed by visual inspection of a boxplot. Median head nod scores were statistically significantly different between groups, $\chi2(2) = 20.19$, $p < .001$. The post hoc analysis revealed statistically significant differences in median head nod scores between the VC (13.5) and F2F (22.5) $(p = .037)$, and VR (7.0) and F2F (22.5) $(p < .001)$ communication groups.

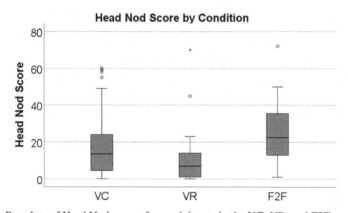

Fig. 2. Boxplots of Head Nod scores for participants in the VC, VR, and F2F conditions.

F2F was statistically significantly higher than the other conditions.

3.3 Difference by Communication Conditions: Socializing

A Kruskal-Wallis H test was conducted to determine if there were differences in median socializing score between three different groups (see Fig. 3). Distributions of socializing scores were similar for all groups, as assessed by visual inspection of a boxplot. Median socializing scores were statistically significantly different between groups, $\chi2(2) = 15.60$, $p < .001$. The post hoc analysis revealed statistically significant differences in median socializing scores between the VC (0.0) and VR (2.0) ($p < .001$) communication groups, but not between any other group combination. The median F2F score was 1.0.

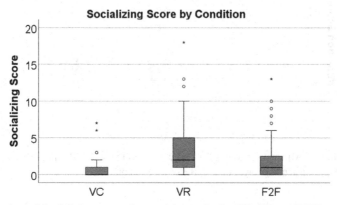

Fig. 3. Boxplots of Socializing scores for participants in the VC, VR, and F2F conditions. VR was statistically significantly less than VR.

3.4 Difference by Communication Conditions: Questions (Task)

A Kruskal-Wallis H test was conducted to determine if there were differences in median questions score between three different groups (see Fig. 4). Distributions of questions scores were similar for all groups, as assessed by visual inspection of a boxplot. Median question scores were statistically significantly different between groups, $\chi 2(2) = 9.98$, $p = .007$. This post hoc analysis revealed statistically significant differences in median question scores between the VC (0.0) and VR (2.0) ($p = .020$), and VC (0.0) and F2F (1.5) ($p = .025$) communication groups, but not between any other group combination.

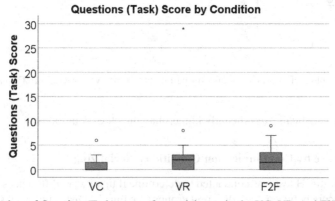

Fig. 4. Boxplots of Question (Task) scores for participants in the VC, VR, and F2F conditions. VC was statistically significantly lower than VR and F2F.

3.5 Difference by Communication Conditions: Jargon

A Kruskal-Wallis H test was conducted to determine if there were differences in median jargon score between three different groups (see Fig. 5). Distributions of jargon scores were similar for all groups, as assessed by visual inspection of a boxplot. Median jargon scores were not statistically significantly different between groups, $\chi 2(2) = 0.54, p = .763$. The median scores in each condition were VC (0.0), VR (0.0), and F2F (0.0).

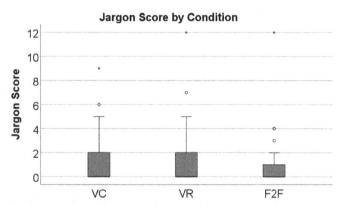

Fig. 5. Boxplots of Jargon scores for participants in the VC, VR, and F2F conditions. No significant differences by condition.

3.6 Difference by Communication Conditions: Leaning Forward

A Kruskal-Wallis H test was conducted to determine if there were differences in median leaning forward score between three different groups (see Fig. 6). Distributions of leaning forward scores were similar for all groups, as assessed by visual inspection of a boxplot. Median leaning forward scores were not statistically significantly different between groups, $\chi 2(2) = 1.46, p = .482$. The median scores in each condition were VC (0.0), VR (0.0), and F2F (0.0).

3.7 Relationship Between Behavioral Indicators and Constructs

There were several significant correlations between behavioral indicators and social-oriented constructs (see Table 2 and Table 3). For this analysis, "duration" variables represent the total duration of behaviors that lasted more than a moment in time. Engagement was significantly positively correlated with head nodding ($r = .21, p = .04$). Rapport was significantly positively correlated with asking task questions ($r = .26, p = .01$). Trust was significantly positively correlated with leaning forward duration ($r = .21, p = .04$). For all of three behaviors, a higher frequency of participants performing these behaviors was correlated with higher self-reports of these social-oriented constructs after the session.

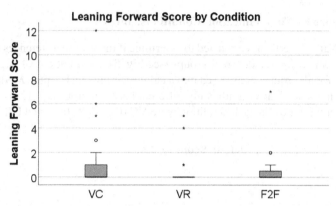

Fig. 6. Boxplots of Leaning Forward scores for participants in the VC, VR, and F2F conditions. No significant differences by condition.

Table 2. Behavioral codes correlated with social-oriented communication constructs: Co-Presence and Engagement. Gray highlighting indicates statistically significant correlations

	Co-Presence				Engagement			
	Overall	VC	VR	F2F	Overall	VC	VR	F2F
Affirmations	0.04	0.14	−0.02	−0.11	0.08	0.12	0.35	0.29
Head nods	0.11	0.16	0.25	0.02	0.21	0.31	0.18	0.21
Jargon	0.10	0.19	−0.04	0.09	0.03	0.10	0.08	0.02
Leaning Forward	0.07	0.27	−0.30	0.09	0.05	0.10	−0.04	0.03
Leaning Forward (Duration)	0.14	0.22	−0.05	0.09	0.03	−0.02	0.06	0.05
Questions about Task	−0.01	0.27	−0.05	−0.29	−0.09	0.04	0.04	−0.17
Questions (Duration)	0.04	0.27	−0.03	−0.14	−0.05	0.07	0.03	−0.04
Socializing	0.00	−0.06	−0.21	0.13	−0.06	−0.03	−0.04	0.15
Socializing (Duration)	0.00	−0.17	−0.10	0.14	−0.05	−0.06	0.00	0.17

Regarding task-oriented constructs (see Table 4 and Table 5), affirmation was significantly positively correlated with both Situational Awareness ($r = .27, p = .01$) and with Task Experience ($r = .20, p = .05$).

Table 3. Behavioral codes correlated with social-oriented communication constructs: Rapport and Trust. Gray highlighting indicates statistically significant correlations.

	Rapport				Trust			
	Overall	VC	VR	F2F	Overall	VC	VR	F2F
Affirmations	0.03	−0.13	0.38	−0.01	−0.05	0.01	−0.09	−0.17
Head nods	−0.06	-0.08	−0.08	−0.03	−0.11	−0.13	-0.1	-0.1
Jargon	0.04	−0.07	0.23	−0.03	−0.05	−0.01	-0.19	−0.04
Leaning Forward	0.01	−0.11	0.23	−0.07	0.08	0.23	−0.22	0.12
Leaning Forward (Duration)	0.00	0.002	0.38	−0.04	.21	0.32	−0.19	0.13
Questions about Task	.26	0.06	.52	0.27	0.002	0.04	0.19	−0.36
Questions (Duration)	0.17	−0.02	0.36	0.21	0.07	0.05	0.20	−0.12
Socializing	0.13	0.03	0.39	0.03	−0.08	0.15	−0.20	−0.23
Socializing (Duration)	0.11	0.08	0.3	−0.04	0.04	−0.14	0.10	−0.02

Table 4. Behavioral codes correlated with task-oriented communication constructs: Situational Awareness and Perceived Ease of Use. Gray highlighting indicates statistically significant correlations.

	Situational Awareness				Perceived Ease of Use			
	Overall	VC	VR	F2F	Overall	VC	VR	F2F
Affirmations	0.27	.32	−0.12	0.21	0.17	0.13	−0.28	0.07
Head nods	0.08	0.16	−0.15	0.15	0.02	0.10	−0.01	−0.15
Jargon	0.03	0.27	−0.09	−0.19	−0.001	0.24	−0.40	0.01
Leaning Forward	−0.01	0.09	−0.11	0.04	−0.11	−0.05	−0.43	0.23
Leaning Forward (Duration)	−0.05	−0.05	−0.20	0.03	−0.01	−0.07	−0.41	0.25
Questions about Task	0.03	0.20	−0.12	−0.19	−0.06	0.23	−0.41	−0.24
Questions (Duration)	0.03	0.21	−0.07	−0.27	−0.07	0.19	−0.43	−0.17
Socializing	0.10	0.09	0.003	−0.08	−0.13	−0.12	−0.68	−0.09
Socializing (Duration)	0.17	0.14	0.18	0.03	−0.07	−0.09	−0.40	−0.01

Table 5. Behavioral codes correlated with task-oriented communication constructs: Task Experience and Mental Workload. Gray highlighting indicates statistically significant correlations.

	Task Experience				Mental Workload			
	Overall	VC	VR	F2F	Overall	VC	VR	F2F
Affirmations	0.20	0.14	−0.33	0.2	−0.1	−0.1	0.19	0.1
Head nods	−0.04	0.01	0.01	−0.24	0.06	0.19	−0.14	0.09
Jargon	−0.04	0.18	−0.37	−0.11	0.05	−0.12	0.21	0.22
Leaning Forward	−0.09	-0.05	−0.29	0.22	0.07	0.09	0.06	0.02
Leaning Forward (Duration)	−0.01	−0.05	−0.25	0.19	0.08	0.13	−0.002	−0.02
Questions about Task	−0.13	0.11	−0.52	−0.32	0.08	0.004	0.38	0.23
Questions (Duration)	−0.13	0.11	−0.53	−0.26	0.12	−0.04	0.37	0.37
Socializing	−0.09	−0.002	−0.53	−0.21	0.11	0.03	0.28	0.42
Socializing (Duration)	−0.08	0.02	−0.42	−0.09	0.03	−0.1	0.20	0.08

4 Discussion and Conclusion

Affirmation and Question scores were significantly higher in F2F and VR in comparison to VC. Lack of social presence within video conferencing could be a prominent reason for these results. The VC condition may not provide the same level of social presence as VR and F2F conditions, which leads to less feeling of engagement within VC participants and possibly fewer affirmations and questions.

F2F participants nodded their heads more than participants in VR and VC conditions. This result may be explained in that Head Nod is a nonverbal communication method, and the F2F condition allowed for a greater nonverbal communication, such as facial expressions and body language, which could have led to more nods by the participant.

Participants in the VR condition had a higher score for unrelated task conversation (socializing) than in the VC condition. The reasons of this could be analogous with the analysis of the affirmation and question score (lack of social presence in VC), but it is interesting that there was no significant difference between the F2F and VC conditions. The median socializing score in F2F (1.0), like the VR (2.0), was higher than the VC (0.0), but it is possible that individual differences affecting participants' tendency to talk about unrelated topics led to too much variation in F2F to demonstrate a significant difference.

The significant correlations between behavioral markers and surveys showed that some self-reported survey responses could possibly be replaced with behavioral observation methods, especially if behavioral coding were performed automatically using machine learning. For example, head nods could replace an Engagement survey, leaning forward could be an indicator of Trust, questions could replace Rapport, and affirmations could replace Situational Awareness and Task Experience. However, these significant correlation values were all in the 0.20 – 0.27 range (weak), so perhaps these behaviors could be considered to be indicators of those constructs, but other behaviors would need to be included as well to more accurately predict the construct.

Acknowledgments. This research has been partially supported by an award from the Advanced Research Projects Agency-Energy (ARPA-E), U.S. Department of Energy associated with Award Number DE-AR0001097.

References

1. Sellen, A., Buxton, B., Arnott, J.: Using spatial cues to improve videoconferencing. In: Proceedings of the SIGCHI conference on Human factors in computing systems - CHI '92. pp. 651–652. ACM Press, Monterey, California, United States (1992). https://doi.org/10.1145/142750.143070
2. Ranjan, A., Birnholtz, J.P., Balakrishnan, R.: An exploratory analysis of partner action and camera control in a video-mediated collaborative task. In: Proceedings of the 2006 20th anniversary conference on Computer supported cooperative work, pp. 403–412 (2006)
3. Lee, K.M.: Presence, explicated. Commun. Theory. **14**, 27–50 (2004). https://doi.org/10.1111/j.1468-2885.2004.tb00302.x
4. Lombard, M., Ditton, T.: At the heart of it all: the concept of presence. J. Comput.-Mediat. Commun. **3** (1997). https://doi.org/10.1111/j.1083-6101.1997.tb00072.x
5. Tsetserukou, D., Neviarouskaya, A.: Emotion telepresence: emotion augmentation through affective haptics and visual stimuli. J. Phys. Conf. Ser. **352**, 012045 (2012). https://doi.org/10.1088/1742-6596/352/1/012045
6. Keynan, O., Brandel, N., Slakmon, B.: Students' knowledge on emotion expression and recognition in computer-mediated communication: a comparative case study. Comput. Educ. **189**, 104597 (2022). https://doi.org/10.1016/j.compedu.2022.104597
7. Kim, D., Frank, M.G., Kim, S.T.: Emotional display behavior in different forms of computer mediated communication. Comput. Hum. Behav. **30**, 222–229 (2014). https://doi.org/10.1016/j.chb.2013.09.001
8. Schneider, S., Krieglstein, F., Beege, M., Rey, G.D.: The impact of video lecturers' nonverbal communication on learning–an experiment on gestures and facial expressions of pedagogical agents. Comput. Educ. **176**, 104350 (2022)
9. Derks, D., Fischer, A.H., Bos, A.E.: The role of emotion in computer-mediated communication: a review. Comput. Hum. Behav. **24**, 766–785 (2008)
10. Kafetsios, K., Chatzakou, D., Tsigilis, N., Vakali, A.: Experience of emotion in face to face and computer-mediated social interactions: an event sampling study. Comput. Hum. Behav. **76**, 287–293 (2017). https://doi.org/10.1016/j.chb.2017.07.033
11. Culnan, M.J.: Information technologies. Handb. Organ. Commun.- Interdiscip. Perspect.-. (1987)
12. Rice, R.E., Love, G.: Electronic emotion: Socioemotional content in a computer-mediated communication network. Commun. Res. **14**, 85–108 (1987)
13. Walther, J.B., Burgoon, J.K.: Relational communication in computer-mediated interaction. Hum. Commun. Res. **19**, 50–88 (1992). https://doi.org/10.1111/j.1468-2958.1992.tb00295.x
14. Walther, J.B., Anderson, J.F., Park, D.W.: Interpersonal effects in computer-mediated interaction: a meta-analysis of social and antisocial communication. Commun. Res. **21**, 460–487 (1994). https://doi.org/10.1177/009365094021004002

15. Rozell, J., et al.: Circuit world: a multiplayer VE for researching engineering learning. In: 2021 IEEE Conference on Virtual Reality and 3D User Interfaces Abstracts and Workshops (VRW), p. 773. IEEE (2021)
16. Friard, O., Gamba, M.: BORIS: a free, versatile open-source event-logging software for video/audio coding and live observations. Methods Ecol. Evol. **7**, 1325–1330 (2016)
17. O'Brien, H.L., Toms, E.G.: The development and evaluation of a survey to measure user engagement. J. Am. Soc. Inf. Sci. Technol. **61**, 50–69 (2010)
18. Slater, M., Sadagic, A., Usoh, M., Schroeder, R.: Small-group behavior in a virtual and real environment: a comparative study. Presence. **9**, 37–51 (2000)
19. Bernieri, F.J., Davis, J.M., Rosenthal, R., Knee, C.R.: Interactional synchrony and rapport: Measuring synchrony in displays devoid of sound and facial affect. Pers. Soc. Psychol. Bull. **20**, 303–311 (1994)
20. McAllister, D.J.: Affect-and cognition-based trust as foundations for interpersonal cooperation in organizations. Acad. Manage. J. **38**, 24–59 (1995)
21. Taylor, R.M.: Situational awareness rating technique (SART): the development of a tool for aircrew systems design. In: Situational Awareness, pp. 111–128. Routledge (2017)
22. Davis, F.D.: Perceived usefulness, perceived ease of use, and user acceptance of information technology. MIS Q. **13**, 319–340 (1989)
23. Hart, S.G., Staveland, L.E.: Development of NASA-TLX (Task Load Index): results of empirical and theoretical research. In: Advances in Psychology, pp. 139–183. Elsevier (1988)
24. Dunn, O.J.: Multiple comparisons using rank sums. Technometrics **6**, 241–252 (1964)

Towards Accessible, Sustainable and Healthy Mobility: The City of Barcelona as Case Study

Mónica V. Sanchez-Sepulveda⬤, David Fonseca Escudero(✉)⬤, Joan Navarro⬤, and Daniel Amo-Filva⬤

La Salle, Ramon Llull University, Barcelona, Spain
{monica.sanchez,david.fonseca,joan.navarro,
daniel.amo}@salle.url.edu

Abstract. Sustainable mobility and circular economy are fundamental pillars in the fight against the climate crisis, covering all modes of transport with minimal or zero impact on the environment. The sustainable mobility of people and goods allows access to education, culture, housing, work, leisure, and food, it is part of millions of people every day and is one of the factors that most influence the path towards decarbonization, reduction of the greenhouse, gas emissions, improving the health of citizens and providing economic benefits. For this reason, it is essential to rethink mobility towards a more sustainable one by exploiting data and existing and in-the-field sensors. This project aims to build a platform capable of helping contemporary cities in the transformation towards sustainable, resilient, and healthy cities through the exploitation of data, both existing and sensors in the field. We propose to build a 2-layer platform committed to (1) quantitative data processing, which can be merged, processed, and visualized, using Big Data processing techniques to display relevant data and extract relevant information in the field of urban design, and (2) strategic system, which will assist in the definition of criteria to help citizens and regional governments to solve the problems derived from the design of contemporary cities. The efficient use of available technologies, aimed at improving the quality of life of the population, will lead to greater care for the environment and the reduction of social inequality. The proposed approach will integrate into existing decision support systems by providing quantitative and qualitative suggestions on sustainable policy architecture to drive healthy environmental and mobility management.

Keywords: Sustainable mobility · Big Data · urban design

1 Introduction

To preserve the value of resources and mitigate the acceleration of the set of environmental impacts derived from human activity and accelerated climate change, it is where circular economy and sustainable mobility are presented as valid solutions. The principles on which contemporary urbanism is based are not sufficiently aware of the dynamics of urban health and operate on macro-urban approaches that often ignore the daily life of the inhabitants, the local economy, and the environment [18]. In the European Union,

P. Zaphiris and A. Ioannou (Eds.): HCII 2023, LNCS 14040, pp. 91–104, 2023.
https://doi.org/10.1007/978-3-031-34411-4_8

transport generates more than 25% of CO2 emissions, and cars are the main pollutant, according to Eurostat [50]. More and more concern about global warming is generated and promoting sustainable mobility is necessary.

The circular economy brings great benefits to the climate and mobility sector, which can be classified into three large blocks: environmental, social, and economic. Among the environmental ones, we find the reduction of the negative impacts of transportation powered by fossil fuels, reducing the concentration of pollutants in the breathable air, while contributing to the slowdown of the greenhouse effect and particles and gases that are harmful to health.

Among the economic benefits, we find the increase in the income of public transport operators and operators of new sustainable mobility services; the reduction of costs related to transporting (fuel and maintenance) and energy consumption; the generation of new business opportunities and sources of income. Among the social benefits, we find the improvement of air quality and, therefore, reduction of health problems caused by pollution; reduction of congestion, stress, and noise generated by driving; healthier lifestyle, thanks to the use of bicycles and public transport; with a better quality of life for citizens by facilitating access to goods and services; improvement of the security in the displacements; better use of work time.

Pedestrian access and cyclability are essential to strengthen micro-urban fabrics, promote the occupation of space, encourage physical activity and contribute positively to community dynamics and the quality of life of citizens. According to a study presented by the Metropolitan Mobility Observatory (July 2021 Report (2019 Data-2020 Advance)), in Barcelona, they make an average of between 2.4 trips per person per day, and the modal distribution (work, study, and other reasons) 15.4% use a car or motorbike, 19.7% use public transport, 63.9% walk and bicycle and 1.0% others.

Cities like Barcelona, where most of the population and services are concentrated, with denser, public transport networks and with a greater number of exclusive areas for pedestrians or bicycles, present more sustainable modal splits. However, pollution in Barcelona due to suspended particles and nitrogen dioxide, largely caused by traffic, triples the new reference values for air quality set by the World Health Organization (WHO), according to the report 2021 of the "Contaminació.Barcelona" portal. From this situation arises the research question that motivates this project: How can we define quantitative and qualitative urban strategies to achieve accessible, sustainable, and healthy mobility of people and goods in contemporary cities?

To answer this question, we start from the following hypothesis: adjusting urban spaces to increase pedestrian traffic and cyclability would help to encourage physical activity among citizens and, therefore, improve their quality of life, as well as the health conditions of the population. In addition, this will also contribute to reducing the environmental impact of motorized transport.

Pedestrian prioritization and cyclability respond to a systemic social change and, according to this perspective, social innovation appears as a complementary mechanism to address social problems that go beyond the scope of traditional public policies based on efficient mobility and the reduction of traffic. Environmental impact. The overall health of a population is currently determined by multiple factors, including biology, genetics, lifestyle, and socioeconomic conditions. However, it has been found that the intrinsic environmental parameters related to the configuration of the access, the design of the facilities, and the design/use of the green areas are important factors that also contribute to the health conditions of the citizens.

Therefore, cities must seriously consider these factors to improve the health of their inhabitants and take advantage of new technologies to become smarter and healthier. Using new trends in Information and Communication Technologies (ICT), such as cloud computing (Cloud Computing), Big Data, and the Internet of Things to process, gamification [6, 17, 20, 47] or visualize and analyze data in real-time (for example using virtual or augmented reality [21, 22, 35, 37, 39, 43, 46]), it is now feasible to accurately monitor citizens, professionals, students, etc., and their interactions [15, 21, 30, 36, 42, 43, 46] with physical infrastructures and thus identify, learn and act to improve future public health conditions.

In recent years, Barcelona has become a world benchmark in the search for healthy intelligence and has organized various initiatives in this regard (for example, Smart City Expo World Congress, HEALTHIO, Open Data BCN). Following this initiative, this project proposes a technologically advanced pedagogy in a multidisciplinary way within the frameworks of Engineering, Architecture, and Urbanism to reduce negative impacts on the environment, influencing the improvement of the physical and psychological health of the public. Derived from the current design of cities.

Therefore, the general objective of this project is the creation of a data analysis and computation infrastructure that allows (1) to accurately assess the state, distribution, and dynamics of the use of the streets of Barcelona, (2) to extract automatically which architectural and urban design parameters have the most impact on the pedestrian traffic and cyclability of the streets, to (a) be able to automatically and objectively classify how healthy each street is for citizens, resources and the environment, and (b) provide a decision support tool for professionals and those responsible for designing urban spaces to make them healthier [49].

For this, a compliment will be created for decision support systems that use a prediction model to better understand and explain how each variable that architects and urban policies use to design our cities will affect the health of citizens and, consequently, how architects, local entities and the same citizens could improve their health by optimizing urban design [19, 40, 41, 48].

Specifically, this general objective leads to the following specific objectives:

SO1. Identify some strategic axes of the city of Barcelona of at least 500 m in length in which the proof of concept object of this project can be carried out.

o SO2. Prepare a data set (dataset) of at least 10 instances containing urban and architectural data related to the axis under study (OE1). Each instance will have at least 15 descriptors (ex. Width of sidewalks, location of fountains, types of trees, the density of pedestrian and motorized traffic, types of commerce, and crime rate...). Part of this data could be collected from ad-hoc sensors if necessary.

o SO3. Analyze the data obtained, develop a classification system, and from the descriptors used in OE2, assign a grade from 0 to 10 to the healthiness (referring to pedestrian traffic and cyclability) of an urban section.

o   SO4. Partition the axis of interest of SO1 into sections of 100 m and propose 3 urban measures per section that improve the health (referring to pedestrian traffic and cyclability) of the section by 30% by the system developed in SO3.
o   SO5. Use the SO3 tool in two other cities around the world to assess and quantify the degree of generalization of the results obtained.
o   SO6. Disseminate the results obtained in at least two international conferences and a first or second-quartile open-access JCR-indexed journal.

These objectives will make it possible to recognize the use that citizens make of these urban environments, and accurately measure the distribution of users in public spaces. From crossed readings on the routes, stays, frequencies, and the temporal chronology of the users, it will be possible to identify which areas and which spaces are the most used and which have less use. This information will be contrasted with the urban analysis of the relative position of the spaces, the urbanization, the textures of the pavement, the urban furniture, the vegetation, the road segregations, and the urban uses of the fragments of the free spaces, as well as the uses on the ground floor of the buildings. The contrast between the data information and the urban analysis will allow for recognizing intervention strategies that allow for substantially improving the quality of the urban space.

2   Methodology

The development of the project will focus on a strategic axis of the city of Barcelona. For the results to be extrapolated, a highly scalable system and methodology will be designed. Thus, the project is formulated to be worked on in different phases that work to achieve the objectives.

2.1   Methodologies to Achieve Objectives: SO1

Barcelona has an urban diversity that gives identity to each of its neighborhoods. They present different typologies and representative characteristics (as we can observe in Fig. 1). Axes will be identified in areas with a compact fabric such as the Gothic Quarter, one with a broad fabric such as in the Eixample, and another with a medium fabric such as in Gracia.

These axes must include common minimums such as a square or system of squares, and similar uses to carry out the proof of concept that is the object of this project.

Fig. 1. Data plotting [51].

2.2 Methodologies to Achieve Objectives: SO2

Using a systematic data collection process, we can obtain a massive amount of data in real-time to complement existing data repositories and feed applications related to health and the environment. Specifically, we propose three major analysis groups: network topology, commercial activity, and use analysis.

- About the first group, the built urban structure is a network topology derived from road geometry, which constitutes the fundamental base of the cities. Attempts to understand environments built through their geometric patterns have been carried out in the field of urban morphology studies. One of the most common approaches to extracting features of important urban structures is to consider them as a network and then realize analysis [3]. Centrality is an indicator of the importance of each element of the network and has several variants [31]. This proposal aims to analyze the urban structure of the city through different forms of centrality. For this, we have the urban structure data in vector format.
- The second large group of analyzes corresponds to commercial activity. The urban functions that satisfy the needs of the citizens are fundamental for the vitality of the cities since they allow the development of sustainable urban development [9, 10]. In this sense, urban planners have implemented two principles in cities: diversity and density. The diversity of functions, or mixed land use, has been recognized as a promoter of activities [5, 24, 38], and has shown effects positive on urban life [11, 12, 25], including the number of passengers in transport public [7, 16, 45]; public health [27]; and growth economic or dynamism [13, 23, 32] to your time, the density of functions has a positive impact in an area because produces different centralities within one city [26] and, from an economic perspective, stimulates an efficiency economy through externalities Marshallian [14]. This is precisely the basis on which the spatial economy works, defined as one that examines the mechanisms and rules behind the crowd's spaces at the city, region, country, or international level [44], considering the distribution of activities economic and its spatial clustering as a result of trade- between several forces (centripetal force and centrifugal force). For example, the physical proximity of entities economics facilitates communication and

mitigates the deterioration of information distance that generates externalities [29]. However, the density excessive in areas geographically limited decreases comfort and satisfaction, making the forces centrifuges be plus strong. Therefore, based on the processes of ascending and self-organizing typical of systems complex, these mutual interactions affect both the appearance and the form of cities [8, 28]. The supply of stores on each street is considered one of the most important factors that affect the behavior of pedestrians in cities [4]. Therefore, the present project is proposed to analyze the distribution of activities cheaply at the street level.

- Finally, the third large group of analyzes corresponds to the citizen's uses of the city. Model development behavioral math space is of special interest from the economic, social and environmental points of view of cities [33, 34]. Regarding interest economics, different actors are favored by this type of information due to the impacts potential in the billing of your stores and the values of their active real estate [34]. On another side, for the city authorities, said analysis can be used for the prediction of the consequences of urban planning and market shares (i.e., the effects of store substitution) or the management of crowd efficiency. We propose to apply the techniques of active data collection such as surveys or direct observation taking into account issues such as ethics and privacy [1, 2]. The collection of this data will allow us to understand better the behavior of citizens in different areas of the city.

2.3 Methodologies to Achieve Objectives: SO2 and SO3

IoT -based devices and sensors, which can be located in public spaces and facilities, and through the use of predictive analysis algorithms (machine learning and data mining) will allow us to build effective systems for inference and automatic recommendation of diagnosis and urban solutions (example, Fig. 2).

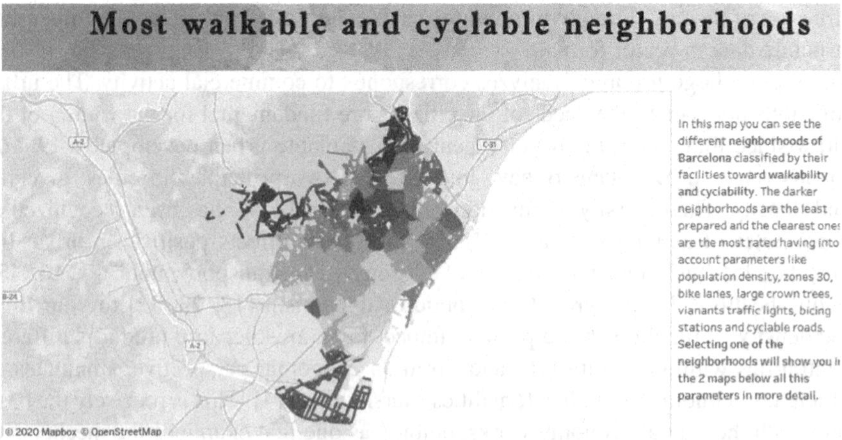

Fig.2. Most walkable and cyclable neighborhoods [52]

For this, it is proposed to build a 3-layer platform committed to:

(1) Acquisition and aggregation of data from multiple sources. For greater granularity, a highly scalable cloud computing infrastructure will be used to store and pre-process field data acquired through a distributed set of sensors and smart devices. On the other hand, the information layers related to network models to analyze the movement of people will also be hosted.

(2) Refinement and precise monitoring of associated data (for example, pollution, noise, natural or man-made risks, asthma epidemics) to complement existing data sets (for example, Open Data, Bicing, Transportes Metropolitanos de Barcelona, etc.) using Big Data processing and visualization techniques.

(3) Generation of scientific evidence to inform future political decisions, proposing new strategies, where the management of public spaces and facilities can be designed, developed, improved, and supported more flexibly. Therefore, the successful implementation of these ICT approaches will allow improving the political decision-making process in the field of urban design.

This infrastructure will allow:

- Capture and integrate data in real-time from the life of the city through the use of sensors and mobile devices (IoT technology).
- Integrate this data into an urban computer platform that allows the communication of said information between the various city services.
- Integrate complex analytics, modeling, optimization, and visualization of services to make better operational decisions for the city.

2.4 Methodologies to Achieve Objectives: SO4 and SO5

From the knowledge extracted from the data collected, we will study the particularities of the historic city, in comparison with the contrasts generated in more contemporary urban fabrics, considering the socio-urban dynamics that are reflected in the recent developments of popular urbanism. The decisive influence of new technologies is important for the generation of a new reality from economic, social, and urban points of view.

To collect this documentation, it will be necessary to prepare a methodological strategy on the priority questions that must be raised to properly focus the questionnaire and ensure that the documentation provided by the public is really useful for the research work. In this sense, the design of the questionnaire is essential to orient these questions so that they are well-directed toward the proposed objectives.

At the same time, it will be necessary to carry out an urban study of the selected areas. For this, cartographic material must be prepared on the position of said spaces about the urban fabric in which they are immersed and recognize their structural role, as well as it will also be necessary to analyze the road and pedestrian hierarchy and the accessibilities to said spaces. In turn, the arrangement of the commercial activities on the ground floor and the role of the facilities, either in the area of study or in its vicinity will be topics of discussion. For its part, and especially important is the fragmentation and uses of free space, considering the textures, the elements of urban furniture, the plant elements, and the urbanization of these spaces. Finally, the subdivision and its repercussion on the elevations, considering issues such as the aggregation of the plots and the new architectures and their languages should also be taken into consideration.

From the methodological point of view, the cross between the contributions of citizens and urban analysis, as well as the contribution of the technologies that will be applied in the detection of the use of these spaces by citizens should allow for establishing a rich scenario.

2.5   Methodologies to Achieve Objectives: SO6

Prepare semi-annual scientific-technical reports giving an account of the progress of the research issued at the end of each phase of the study. Process scheme (see Fig. 3):

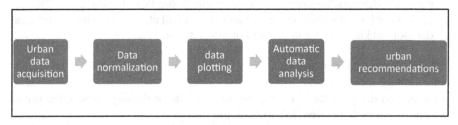

Fig. 3. Process outline.

3   Results

As a result of the achievement of these objectives, we expect:

- Conceive a Big Data infrastructure capable of processing mobility data from Barcelona and which can also apply to other contexts and topics. These models and their results will be especially useful to understand how the urban structure affects the movement of people and other derived effects, for example, the establishment of businesses. In addition, these techniques can be applied to other cities of interest, either in the surroundings of Barcelona or in any part of the world for which cartography is available in vector format. Additionally, the methodology for capturing data from commercial premises can be scaled to other cities in the world, and can even be supported by other services such as Google Street View.
- Design a protocol to distribute a predetermined set of Geographic Information System (GIS) points in the city of Barcelona, which will allow Architecture and Urban Planning experts to extract valuable information for intervention in specific and strategic areas.
- Define a methodology for the automatic and objective evaluation of the level of health (referring to pedestrian traffic and cyclability) of urban spaces.

- Define a set of quantitative and qualitative urban strategies to improve the general health of citizens in contemporary cities. These results may include different scales of intervention: some will involve inexpensive strategies and more typical of tactical urbanism, and which may involve soft and reversible interventions, while other strategies may be more structural according to the results obtained, and may specify more resources to carry them out.

3.1 Work Plan and Schedule

Next, we will identify each of the planned tasks, phases, or milestones about the objectives raised in the proposal for each of the phases. This schedule presented below is distributed over 18 months (M).

Planning Phase: M1.

- Development of the project plan:

- Description of project deliverables.
- The concretion of the content analytical of spaces urban
- Communication plan.
- Deadlines
- Risks and backup plans

  - Definition of the axes strategies to carry out the test object of this project

  Data Collection and Analysis Phase: M2 to M6

- Detailed map of the different streets of the city and their different degrees of centrality in the urban fabric.
- Data on the commercial activity of the city, classifying them into different categories of commercials and geolocating them.
- Elaboration of the analysis of urban areas of study.

  Diagnosis and Crossings Phase: M6 to M10

- Elaboration of the results analytical and diagnostic (deficits and opportunities) of the spaces urban.
- Preparation of the crossover method between studies in urban areas and the emptying of data from fieldwork.
- Preparation of intermediate scientific-technical reports giving an account of the progress of the investigation.

  Classification Phase and Degree of Generalization. M11 to M15:

- Development of an automatic classification system.
- Partition the axes and propose measures of urban planning by section.

- Use the tool in two other cities around the world to assess and quantify the degree of generalization of the results obtained.

  Results Phase M16 to M18:

- Process done cyclically for data processing _ obtained.

  Administrative Phases and Dissemination: M1 to M18

- Chores administrative – Follow-up, justification, or closure of the project.
- dissemination – Milestones related to presentations at congresses, conferences, talks, fairs, etc.

  Post-completion Dissemination Phase of the project: M18 to M21

- The results of the project will be disseminated through an article disseminating the results to be published and openly accessible through the municipal website (3 months after completion), together with a summary of the dissemination actions derived from the project.

La Salle -URL will be in charge of installing and admitting a set of tools that include folders shared storage for documents and work collaborative. The project platform for project management is based on Microsoft SharePoint where each collaborator may carry official documents. All project documents _ They will be available on the project platform. The documents public also will be available on a public website that will be created and will contain all public information about the project. Each team member will provide the coordinator with any information and documentation required for the preparation of progress reports, publications, and dissemination and to carry out the work sequential integration of the project into the social reality of the city and the social impact of the research:

- Knowing and measuring what is there, with the conjunction of digitization and Big Data, would promote sustainable mobility, improve the interconnected mobility system, unlocking even business opportunities that do not exist at the moment and helping to better manage mobility systems and maximize its complementarity with public transport. With this massive data, very useful tools can be created for companies that are engaged in logistics, distribution, tourism, among others.
- The mobility-processed data infrastructure can then be used for students and other interested parties.
- The design of a protocol to distribute a predetermined set of Geographic Information System points in a delimited metropolis of the Barcelona Metropolitan Area will allow architecture and pedagogy experts to extract valuable information from specific and strategic areas.
- Define a set of quantitative architectural policies and suggestions to improve the general health of citizens in contemporary metropolises by increasing their ability to walk and cycle.

- The urban strategies derived from the results will serve as scientific tools to inform future policy decisions.
- Synergy will be achieved between different research teams within the same university within La Salle-URL (GRETEL and GRITS) working with innovation as a priority objective that will contribute positively to the design, execution, application, and social impact of the project.
- The open-access dissemination of research results by all citizens has a positive impact on the city.

Acknowledgments. The project has been financed by the Barcelona City Council and the Ministry of Science and Innovation within the framework of Barcelona's Cultural and Scientific Capital. Acceptance grant code 22S09490-001.

References

1. Amo, D., Alier, M., García-Peñalvo, F., Fonseca, D., Casañ, M.J.: Privacidad, seguridad y legalidad en soluciones educativas basadas en Blockchain: Una Revisión Sistemática de la Literatura. RIED Revista Iberoamericana de Educación a Distancia **23**, 213 (2020). https://doi.org/10.5944/ried.23.2.26388
2. Amo, D., Alier, M., García-Peñalvo, F.J., Fonseca, D., Casañ, M.J.: Protected users: a moodle plugin to improve confidentiality and privacy support through user aliases. Sustainability **12**, 2548 (2020). https://doi.org/10.3390/su12062548
3. Barabási A-L Network Science the Scale-Free Property
4. Borgers, A.: Timmermans, H.J.P.: Modelling pedestrian behaviour in downtown shopping areas (2005)
5. Calthorpe, P.: The region. In: Ndubisi, F.O. (ed.) The Ecological Design and Planning Reader, pp. 506–514. Island Press/Center for Resource Economics, Washington (2014). https://doi.org/10.5822/978-1-61091-491-8_46
6. Calvo, X., Fonseca, D., Sánchez-Sepúlveda, M., Amo, D., Llorca, J., Redondo, E.: Programming virtual interactions for gamified educational proposes of urban spaces. In: (Eds.) PZ, Ioannou A (eds) LCT 2018, LNCS 10925. Springer International Publishing AG, part of Springer Nature 2018, pp. 1–13 (2018). https://doi.org/10.1007/978-3-319-91152-6_10
7. Cervero, R., Kockelman, K.: Travel demand and the 3ds: density, diversity, and design. Transp. Res. Part D: Transp. Environ. **2**, 199–219 (1997). https://doi.org/10.1016/S1361-9209(97)00009-6
8. Chiaradia, A., Hillier, B., Schwander, C., Barnes, Y.: Compositional and urban form effects on residential property value patterns in Greater London. Proc. Inst. Civil Eng. Urban Des. Plan. **166**, 176–199 (2013). https://doi.org/10.1680/udap.10.00030
9. Cohen, B.: Urbanization in developing countries: current trends, future projections, and key challenges for sustainability. Technol. Soc. **28**, 63–80 (2006). https://doi.org/10.1016/j.techsoc.2005.10.005
10. Cui, J., Dodson, J., Hall, P.V.: Planning for urban freight transport: an overview. Transp. Rev. **35**, 583–598 (2015). https://doi.org/10.1080/01441647.2015.1038666
11. Dovey, K., Pafka, E.: What is functional mix? An assemblage approach. Plan. Theory Pract. **18**, 249–267 (2017). https://doi.org/10.1080/14649357.2017.1281996
12. Dovey, K., Pafka, E., Ristic, M.: Mapping Urbanities: Morphologies, Flows, Possibilities. Routledge, New York (2017)

13. Duranton, G., Puga, D.: Diversity and Specialisation in cities: why, where and when does it matter? Urban Studies **37**, 533–555 (2000). https://doi.org/10.1080/0042098002104
14. Duranton, G., Puga, D.: Chapter 48 - Micro-foundations of urban agglomeration economies. In: Henderson, J.V., Thisse, J.-F. (eds.) Handbook of Regional and Urban Economics, pp. 2063–2117. Elsevier (2004)
15. Escudero, D.F., Domínguez, E.R., Valls, F.: Motivation and academic improvement using augmented reality for 3D architectural visualization. Educ. Knowl. Soc. **17**, 45–64 (2016). https://doi.org/10.1021/ja003055
16. Ewing, R., Cervero, R.: Travel and the built environment. J. Am. Plann. Assoc. **76**, 265–294 (2010). https://doi.org/10.1080/01944361003766766
17. Fonseca, D., Cavalcanti, J., Peña, E., Valls, V., Sanchez-Sepúlveda, M., Moreira, F., Navarro I., Redondo, E.: Mixed assessment of virtual serious games applied in architectural and urban design education. Sensors **21** (2021). https://doi.org/10.3390/s21093102
18. Fonseca, D., Sanchez-Sepulveda, M., Necchi, S., Peña, E.: Towards smart city governance. case study: improving the interpretation of quantitative traffic measurement data through citizen participation. Sensors **21**, 5321 (2021). https://doi.org/10.3390/s21165321
19. Fonseca, D., Valls, F., Redondo, E., Villagrasa, S.: Informal interactions in 3D education: citizenship participation and assessment of virtual urban proposals. Comput. Hum. Behav. **55**, 504–518 (2016). https://doi.org/10.1016/j.chb.2015.05.032
20. Fonseca, D., et al.: Student motivation assessment using and learning virtual and gamified urban environments. In: ACM International Conference Proceeding Series (2017)
21. Fonseca, D., Villagrasa, S., Navarro, I., Redondo, E., Valls, F., Sánchez, A.: Urban gamification in architecture education. In: Rocha, Á., Correia, A.M., Adeli, H., Reis, L.P., Costanzo, S. (eds.) Advances in Intelligent Systems and Computing. Springer International Publishing, Cham, pp. 335–341 (2017). https://doi.org/10.1007/978-3-319-56541-5_34
22. Fonseca Escudero, D., Redondo, E., Sánchez, A., Valls, F.: Educating urban designers using augmented reality and mobile learning technologies / Formación de Urbanistas usando Realidad Aumentada y Tecnologías de Aprendizaje Móvil. RIED Revista Iberoamericana de Educación a Distancia **20**, 141 (2017). https://doi.org/10.5944/ried.20.2.17675
23. Glaeser, E.L., Kallal, H.D., Scheinkman, J.A., Shleifer, A.: Growth in cities. J. Polit. Econ. **100**, 1126–1152 (1992). https://doi.org/10.1086/261856
24. Gómez-Varo, I., Delclòs-Alió, X., Miralles-Guasch, C.: Jane Jacobs reloaded: a contemporary operationalization of urban vitality in a district in Barcelona. Cities **123**, 103565 (2022). https://doi.org/10.1016/j.cities.2022.103565
25. Gurney, K.R., et al.: Comparison of global downscaled versus bottom-up fossil fuel CO_2 emissions at the urban scale in Four U.S. urban areas. J. Geophys. Res. Atmos. **124**, 2823–2840 (2019). https://doi.org/10.1029/2018JD028859
26. Hester Jr R.T.: Design for Ecological Democracy. MIT Press, Cambridge (2010)
27. Kostkova, P., et al.: Who owns the data? Open data for healthcare. Front. Public Health **4**, 7 (2016)
28. Krugman, P.: Confronting the mystery of urban hierarchy. J. Japan. Int. Econ. **10**, 399–418 (1996). https://doi.org/10.1006/jjie.1996.0023
29. Lucas, R.E.: On the mechanics of economic development. J. Monet. Econ. **22**, 3–42 (1988). https://doi.org/10.1016/0304-3932(88)90168-7
30. Navarro Delgado, I., Fonseca Escudero, D.: Nuevas tecnologías de visualización para mejorar la representación de arquitectura en la educación. Archit. City Environ. **12**, 219–238 (2017). https://doi.org/10.5821/ace.12.34.5290
31. Porta, S., et al.: Street centrality and densities of retail and services in Bologna, Italy. Environ Plann. B Plann. Des. **36**, 450–465 (2009). https://doi.org/10.1068/b34098
32. Quigley, J.M.: Urban diversity and economic growth. J. Econ. Perspect. **12**, 127–138 (1998). https://doi.org/10.1257/jep.12.2.127

33. Rasouli, S., Timmermans, H.: Assessment of model uncertainty in destinations and travel forecasts of models of complex spatial shopping behaviour. J. Retail. Consum. Serv. **20**, 139–146 (2013). https://doi.org/10.1016/j.jretconser.2012.05.001

34. Rasouli, S., Timmermans, H.: Incorporating mechanisms of social adoption in design and analysis of stated-choice experiments: illustration and application to choice of electric cars. Transp. Res. Rec. **2344**, 10–19 (2013). https://doi.org/10.3141/2344-02

35. Redondo Domínguez, E., Fonseca Escudero, D., Sánchez Riera, A., Navarro Delgado, I.: Augmented reality in architecture degree: new approaches in scene illumination and user evaluation. J. Inf. Technol. Appl. Educ. (JITAE) **1**, 19–27 (2012)

36. Redondo, E., Fonseca, D., Giménez, L., Santana, G., Navarro, I.: Alfabetización digital para la enseñanza de la arquitectura. Un estudio de caso. Arquiteturarevista **8**, 76–87 (2012). https://doi.org/10.4013/arq.2012.81.08

37. Redondo, E., Navarro, I., Sánchez, A., Fonseca, D.: Augmented Reality on architectural and building engineering learning processes. Two study cases. Ubiquit. Comput. Commun. J. **7**, 1269 (2012)

38. Register, R.: Ecocity Berkeley: Building Cities for a Healthy Future. North Atlantic Books (1987)

39. Riera, A.S., Dominguez, E.R., Escudero, D.F.: Developing an augmented reality application in the framework of architecture degree. In: UXeLATE 2012 - Proceedings of the 2012 ACM International Workshop on User Experience in e-Learning and Augmented Technologies in Education, Co-located with ACM Multimedia 2012 (2012)

40. Sánchez Riera, A., Redondo, E., Fonseca, D.: Geo-located teaching using handheld augmented reality: good practices to improve the motivation and qualifications of architecture students. Univ. Access Inf. Soc. **14**(3), 363–374 (2014). https://doi.org/10.1007/s10209-014-0362-3

41. Sanchez-Sepulveda, M., Fonseca, D., Franquesa, J., Redondo, E.: Virtual interactive innovations applied for digital urban transformations. Mixed approach. Future Gener. Comput. Syst. **91**, 371–381 (2019). https://doi.org/10.1016/j.future.2018.08.016

42. Sanchez-Sepulveda, M.V., et al.: Evaluation of an interactive educational system in urban knowledge acquisition and representation based on students' profiles. Expert Syst. **37** (2020). https://doi.org/10.1111/exsy.12570

43. Sanchez-Sepulveda, M.V., Torres-Kompen, R., Fonseca, D., Franquesa-Sanchez, J.: Methodologies of learning served by virtual reality: a case study in urban interventions. Appl. Sci. **9**, 5161 (2019)

44. Storper, M.: Keys to the City: How Economics, Institutions, Social Interaction, and Politics Shape Development. Princeton University Press, Princeton (2013)

45. Sung, H., Oh, J.-T.: Transit-oriented development in a high-density city: Identifying its association with transit ridership in Seoul, Korea. Cities **28**, 70–82 (2011). https://doi.org/10.1016/j.cities.2010.09.004

46. Valls, F., Garcia-Almirall, P., Redondo, E., Fonseca, D.: From raw data to meaningful information: a representational approach to cadastral databases in relation to urban planning. Future Internet **6**, 612–639 (2014). https://doi.org/10.3390/fi6040612

47. Valls, F., Redondo, E., Fonseca, D., Garcia-Almirall, P., Subirós, J.: Videogame technology in architecture education. In: Kurosu, M. (ed.) Lecture Notes in Computer Science (including subseries Lecture Notes in Artificial Intelligence and Lecture Notes in Bioinformatics). Springer, Toronto, pp. 436–447 (2016)

48. Valls, F., Redondo, E., Fonseca, D., Torres-Kompen, R., Villagrasa, S., Martí, N.: Urban data and urban design: a data mining approach to architecture education. Telematics Inform. **35**, 1039–1052 (2018). https://doi.org/10.1016/j.tele.2017.09.015

49. Vázquez-Ingelmo, A., García-Peñalvo, F.J., Therón, R., Amo Filvà, D., Fonseca Escudero, D.: Connecting domain-specific features to source code: towards the automatization of dashboard generation. Clust. Comput. **23**(3), 1803–1816 (2019). https://doi.org/10.1007/s10586-019-03012-1

50. European environment agency's home page — European environment agency. https://www.eea.europa.eu/. Accessed 14 Dec 2022

51. Towards Healthy smArt MetropOliS (THAMOS) I Blogs La Salle I Campus Barcelona. https://blogs.salleurl.edu/en/towards-healthy-smart-metropolis-thamos. Accessed 30 Jan 2023

52. BCNWalkability. In: Tableau Software. https://public.tableau.com/views/BCNWalkability/Dashboard1?%3Adisplay_static_image=y&%3AbootstrapWhenNotified=true&%3Aembed=true&%3Alanguage=es-ES&publish=yes&:embed=y&:showVizHome=n&:apiID=host0#navType=0&navSrc=Parse. Accessed 30 Jan 2023

53. THAMOS research project takes off! I LinkedIn. https://www.linkedin.com/pulse/thamos-research-project-takes-off-joan-navarro-phd/. Accessed 30 Jan 2023

Augmenting Online Classes with an Attention Tracking Tool May Improve Student Engagement

Arnab Sen Sharma[1] , Mohammad Ruhul Amin[2]([⊠]) , and Muztaba Fuad[3]

[1] Shahjalal University of Science and Technology, Sylhet, Bangladesh
arnab-cse@sust.edu
[2] Fordham University, Bronx, USA
mamin17@fordham.edu
[3] Winston-Salem State University, Winston-Salem, USA
fuadmo@wssu.edu

Abstract. Online remote learning has certain advantages, such as higher flexibility and greater inclusiveness. However, a caveat is the teachers' limited ability to monitor student interaction during an online class, especially while teachers are sharing their screens. We have taken feedback from 12 teachers experienced in teaching undergraduate level online classes on the necessity of an attention tracking tool to understand student engagement during an online class. This paper outlines the design of such a monitoring tool that automatically tracks the attentiveness of the whole class by tracking students' gazes on the screen and alerts the teacher when the attention score goes below a certain threshold. We assume the benefits are twofold; 1) teachers will be able to ascertain if the students are attentive or being engaged with the lecture contents and 2) the students will become more attentive in online classes because of this passive monitoring system. In this paper, we present the preliminary design and feasibility of using the proposed tool and discuss its applicability in augmenting online classes. Finally, we surveyed with 31 students asking their opinion on the usability as well as the ethical and privacy concerns of using such a monitoring tool.

Keywords: Gaze-Tracking · Augmenting Online Classes

1 Introduction

Most of the educational activities worldwide had shifted to online/remote learning during the COVID-19 pandemic outbreak to curtail its growth [1,2], and [3]. Teachers and students in every level of educational institutions (schools, colleges, and universities) have embraced and become adept at using online platforms and tools during this pandemic. Remote learning presents many unique opportunities including higher flexibility and greater inclusiveness [4]. For these reasons, this form of education is very likely to continue even in the post-COVID era.

P. Zaphiris and A. Ioannou (Eds.): HCII 2023, LNCS 14040, pp. 105–121, 2023.
https://doi.org/10.1007/978-3-031-34411-4_9

Many educational institutions have already introduced a hybrid system, a combination of online and offline classes [5]. Class engagement plays an important role in the learning process [6], but it is difficult for instructors to monitor student interaction during an online class [7].

To understand the problem with student engagement in online classes, we organized a round-table discussion on *"Ensuring Student Engagement in Online Classes"* with 12 university teachers who have taught online undergraduate courses during the lockdown period of COVID-19 pandemic. Among the participants, 8 were male and 4 were female. We requested them to share the challenges they have faced with student engagement while teaching online classes. We summarize the concerns raised in our discussion below.

– It is somewhat impossible to monitor all the students during an online class conducted through *Zoom*, *Google Meet*, or any other platforms they have tried. Especially, while the teacher is sharing the screen and presenting slides. On the other hand, many of the students feel reluctant to share their video feedback during an online class due to privacy issues or low internet bandwidth.
– Handful of the teachers informed their concerns that they have no way to understand whether students are listening to the lecture or not. The teachers mentioned they had to ask the class many times - *"Are you guys with me?"* or *"Does this make sense?"* - in order to get verbal feedback. However, usually the responses come from high-performing students while the majority remain silent. This is why all of the teachers we discussed with corroborate the importance of having some way of understanding the level of student engagement. In other words, they want to know how many of the students are listening to the lecture actively.
– Many of the teachers are also worried that their students might be taking online classes less seriously. They suspect that students might be engaging in other activities like; browsing social media or different websites while class is in progress. The teachers feel that since there is no way of making direct eye contact with the students of online classes, a monitoring tool might help make the students more attentive.

To address the above concerns, we present a tool that can help an instructor teaching an online class get better insights into how well the class is following the lecture. The main idea behind the tool is that at any particular moment during an online class, usually the instructor attracts students' attention to a particular region of the screen. If the students are indeed attentive to the class, their gaze patterns should align to some extent (Fig. 1). The tool has been designed to run in the background during an online class and collect gaze information of students via an webcam. To eschew ethical concerns, this tool does not collect video feedback from students, rather it collects students gaze on screen in the form of x,y coordinates. The tool will measure the density of the students' collective gaze in a particular screen area to rate the level of attention of the whole class. The instructor can utilize this score to gauge the engagement of students with the class.

In this study, we discuss the design and feasibility of this monitoring tool using existing gaze-tracking technology compatible with low-cost webcams.

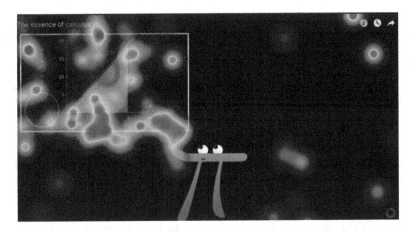

Fig. 1. A *YouTube* video named "The essence of calculus" by *3Blue1Brown* was shown to 3 students. The video was maximized to full-screen and students' gaze was recorded. The heatmap overlay on the figure represents students' gazes from 7:06 to 7:12 when the narrator focuses on the animation depicted in the top-left corner. The undergrad students were requested to try their best to maintain their full concentration while they watch the video clip. And, as expected, their gazes co-align (represented by the high concentration of gazes in the focused animation

We have collected gaze-stream data from 31 students using a prototype and discuss the performance of the gaze-tracking module. We hypothesize that certain patterns emerge in the aggregated gaze distribution while students are paying attention to a particular focus object (i.e., the item on screen the teacher is explaining) and verify our hypothesis using randomization test. Furthermore, we discuss the considerations and challenges to calculate an *attention* score for the whole class. Finally, we conduct individual interviews with students to get their perspective on the ethical and privacy concerns of using such a tool.

2   Related Works

Several studies have found positive correlations between visual attention and performance [8,9]. Finn [10] argued strong correlation between students' academic performance and class attention. Hutt et al. [11] and Wammes et al. [12] discussed the importance of monitoring students' attention state during a class. E Campbell [13] tried to establish a link between classroom engagement and the gaze pattern of primary-school aged students and found that students were more inclined to direct their gaze into their own work or the works of their classmates during the classroom discussion instead of fixating their gaze on teachers instructions. However, in our case, we are interested in measuring the attention of university-level students in online classes. University level theory classes primarily consist of lectures and students usually have less classroom activity apart from listening to and engaging with instructor's lecture.

Sharma et al. [14] introduced a gaze-based student-teacher co-attention score named `with-me-ness` which tries to answer a question from teachers' perspective - *"How much are the students with me?"*. They conducted a study by showing a MOOC video lecture to 40 participants and found positive correlation between the `with-me-ness` scores and scores achieved by students in a test conducted after showing the video lecture. They measure this `with-me-ness` value at two levels: *Perceptual* (if a student is looking at the items being referred by teacher's deictic acts – highlighting, annotating using digital pen, etc) and *Conceptual* (do students' look at the item the teacher is verbally referring to). Calculating this `with-me-ness` score requires extensive preprocessing steps that will be difficult or impossible to perform before every online class. In this study, we are interested in a system that works in real-time and does not require extensive preprocessing steps. Also the *Conceptual* part of the `with-me-ness` score can be infeasible to measure in real-time as the system will need to have extensive expertise in the topic being instructed as well as speech processing, natural language processing, and others. Our approach of calculating attention score rather depends on the density of collective gazing points on the screen. We argue that if the students are following the class their gaze patterns should follow regions of screens the teacher is attracting their attention and thus the gaze patterns should automatically align among themselves. An obvious limitation of our system is that it will fail to function when there is only one student in the class, which is rarely the case.

Srivastava et al. [15] extends Sharma et al's [14] work by introducing a matric `with-me-ness direction`, which tries to measure the video-watching attention patterns between a student's gaze and instructor's dialogue. They show that students gaze patterns can vary with their prior knowledge of the topic. And similar to `with-me-ness`, `with-me-ness direction` requires extensive preprocessing steps as well.

De Carolis et al. [16] has classified student engagement in a 4-point scale using Long Short-Term Memory (LSTMs) based on facial expressions, head movement, and gaze behavior. They have used the *OpenFace 2.0* toolkit to extract the eye-gaze estimation, head-pose, facial features from the video feed of a student. Yang et al. [17] and Rahul et al. [18] propose similar approaches for tracking attention during an online class using facial expressions, posture, and gaze pattern. Unlike our setting, all of the mentioned approaches expect video feed from students during an online class. Whereas, we only use a light-weight tool to track students gaze on the client-side.

According to the *eye-mind hypothesis* by Just et al. [19], we learn and process the information that we visually attend to. However, it is difficult to establish that visual attention transfers to learning activity or greater visual attention will result in better academic performance. But, in an online class setting, it is one of the very few information that can be exploited to *measure* student engagement in a class. In this study, we introduce a tool capable of following students gaze patterns during an online class, establish the usefulness of such tool by conducting interviews with university level teachers and students, and try to address possible ethical concerns raised by students while designing this system.

3   Design Considerations

A high-level overview of the tool is depicted in Fig. 2 below. An web application will interact with the webcam to collect gaze information during an online class (Fig. 2a). The gaze-stream in the form of 2D cartesian coordinates (x,y) will be sent to a server. At the server side, this gaze patterns will be aggregated to calculate an attention score for the whole class (Fig. 2b). The instructor will be alerted when the attention score goes below a predefined threshold. While designing this tool we took several considerations into account discussed below.

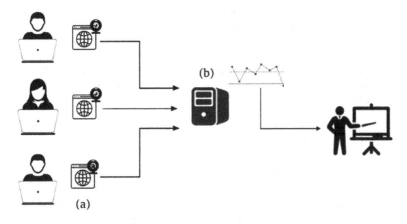

Fig. 2. Overview of the attention tracking tool.

– **Portability:** To ensure greater inclusiveness by not binding the students and teachers into specific operating systems or devices, we implemented this tool as a web application. This tool can be used with a modern browser on any device with a webcam running any operating system. The web application will run in the background while the online class is running on another platform (*zoom*, *meet*, or another tab of the browser). The application will download an eye-tracking module on clients' machines that runs in the browser sandbox.
– **Light-weight:** We cannot expect all the students to have high-end devices. So, we ensured that the tool is not too resource-hungry and does not require special processing units such as GPUs or TPUs to run. In practice, we adapt *WebGazer*[1], an open-source eye-tracking library by Papoutsaki et al. [20],

---

[1] https://webgazer.cs.brown.edu/.

which is implemented in JavaScript and it can be integrated into a web application. At the core, this library uses an eye-detection library to detect the pupils and then uses their location to linearly estimate the location on the screen where a user's current gaze is at. There is a brief calibration phase required before the tool can be used.

– **Ethical Concerns:** This tool does not expect video feedback from students. And, the attention score will be calculated for the whole class analysing the gaze-pattern of every student present in the class. This score will be used to alert the instructor only when the score goes below a certain threshold. So, the teacher will have no way of identifying the gaze pattern of an individual student. The main purpose of this tool is to make both students and the teacher self-conscious in order to ensure better class engagement. We expect that students will be more diligent during online classes because of this monitoring tool. Also, the students will be more accepting towards this monitoring tool as it has relatively less effect on their privacy. The teacher can use the attention score to understand when the class has become too difficult/tedious and upgrade their teaching styles and lecture contents.

In the following sections we discuss the feasibility of eye-tracking technologies with low-cost webcams to estimate gaze patterns which is an essential part of our tool. We set up a study with 31 undergraduate students to ascertain this tool's feasibility.

4   Data Collection

We arranged individual online meetings with each of the 31 students via *Zoom*, a popular platform of choice for online classes. Each of the participants was instructed beforehand to participate from a laptop or desktop with a webcam. We encouraged the participants to join in the sessions in the setting while they usually participate in online classes, which means: diverse backgrounds and different ambiance setups. Also, students were allowed to wear prescription glasses if they prefer to do so. Each session took around 20–25 min and each of the participants was paid 100 takas ($\sim$ 1.2 USD) in the form of mobile balance recharge for their contribution to this study (Table 1).

Table 1. Participants distribution in gender, their webcam resolution, and whether they wear prescription glasses or not. Total number of participants is **31**

Male	Female		Low (0.3MP)	High ($\geq$ 0.9)		With Glasses	Without Glasses
27	4		12	19		11	20

During the calibration phase, the participants were instructed to directly look at and click 3 times on some focus points. These focus points appear one by one,

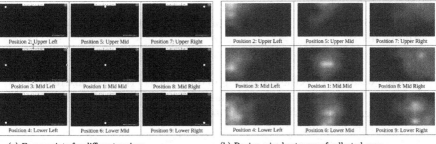

(a) Focus points for different regions

(b) Region-wise heatmaps of collected gaze patterns (for 31 students)

Fig. 3. Calibrating (a), heat-map of gazing (b)

a total of 20 times at predefined locations on the screen in a random sequence. The entire calibration phase takes about 35–40 s to complete. Although this calibration phase is required only once per device, we have found that performing calibration before each class results in improved gaze estimation performance.

We divided the screen into 9 regions. And we instructed the participants to focus their gaze on one of the regions for ~ 10 s while we record their gaze estimated by *WebGazer*'s eye-tracking module. To help the participants focus their gaze on a specific region of the screen, we show a focus point (Fig. 3a). All of the gaze points (x, y coordinates) received from students were divided by their screen dimensions (x/screen-width and y/screen-height) in order to normalize for different screen sizes and resolutions.

5   Gaze Estimation Result and Error Analysis

5.1   Emerged Gaze Patterns

The region-wise collected heatmaps of combined gaze-streams of 31 students are depicted on Fig. 3b. We can observe that almost in all cases the estimated gazes are concentrated in close proximity to respective focus points (Fig. 3a). This attests to this tool's reliability at predicting users' gaze on screen. We conduct randomization tests to verify that the aggregated gaze-stream for a specific region is different and separable from uniformly distributed 2D points. For this purpose, we coin a term *cohesiveness* which we define as the MSE loss for a gaze distribution with respect to its *centroid*.

$$cohesiveness = \frac{1}{N} \sum_{i=1}^{N} ((x_{centroid} - x_i)^2 + (y_{centroid} - y_i)^2) \qquad (1)$$

where N is the number of points in a gaze distribution (x_i, y_i), and $(x_{centroid}, y_{centroid})$ represents the *centroid* of the distribution.

To perform randomization test that gaze distribution is different from any random distribution of 2D points, we state the *null* hypothesis and *alternative* hypothesis below.

Let,

- `Random-Focus Diff` is the *cohesiveness* difference between a gaze distribution focused at a specific region and a random distribution of 2D points.
- `Random-Random Diff` is the *cohesiveness* difference between two random uniform 2D distributions.

Then,

- H_0: Focused gaze-distribution is *not* different from a random uniform 2D distribution. Meaning, the values `Random-Focus Diff` and `Random-Random Diff` are similar.
- H_1: Focused gaze-distribution is *significantly* different from a random uniform 2D distribution. That means, the values `Random-Focus Diff` and `Random-Random Diff` are separable with a clear margin.

Our randomization test consists of the following steps:

Step 1: For each of the nine regions (Fig. 3a), we take the gaze distribution (x_i, y_i). Then, we take a random sample of (x, y) co-ordinates from a uniformly distributed 2D points. To compare these two distributions, we calculate the difference between their *cohesiveness*. For example, for a specific region, we have the focused gaze pattern and the random uniform distribution depicted in Fig. 4. Using Eq. 1, we calculate the *cohesiveness* values for respective distributions shown below. To test the hypothesis, we will use the *cohesiveness* difference of the actual gaze and random uniform distribution (`Random-Focus Diff`).

    Random Cohesiveness: 0.17023544468407120
    Focus Cohesiveness : 0.07365995468797122
    Random-Focus Diff   : 0.09657548999609998

Step 2: To perform the randomization test, we compute the difference of *cohesiveness* between two random samples of size 5000. We measure the *cohesiveness* difference between these two new distributions (`Random-Random Diff`). And compare the `Random-Random Diff` with `Random-Focus Diff`.

Step 3: We run this simulation for 5000 times and plot the frequency of *cohesiveness* differences in Fig. 5 (the orange-colored line chart).

In Fig. 5, we can observe clear distinction between `Random-Random Diff` with `Random-Focus Diff`. In the plot, we can find the `Random-Random Diff` as the orange line-plot, where we observe that the smallest *cohesiveness* difference has the highest frequency of occurrence and it goes down as the *cohesiveness*

Fig. 4. Actual Gaze distribution vs Random uniform distribution

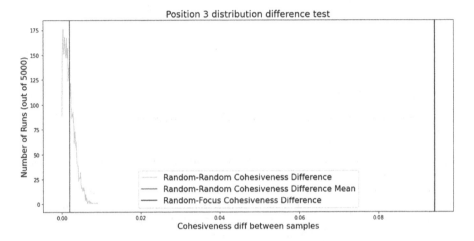

Fig. 5. Randomization Test Results. (Color figure online)

difference goes higher. The red vertical line represents the average of the `Random-Random Diff` values. The blue vertical line which is further apart on the rightmost side, represents the `Random-Focus Diff`. As we perform z-test to find if the blue vertical line is similar to the distribution in orange color, we find that it is rather significantly different at $p \ll 0.05$. Thus, we reject the *null* hypothesis and accept the *alternative* one. Similar trends were observed for all the 9 focus regions of Fig. 3a.

Thus, we can decisively conclude that gaze patterns emerge when multiple participants focused their gaze on a specific region and *Webgazer* is capable of capturing this pattern.

5.2 Error Analysis of the Gaze-Tracking Module

We calculated the mean square error of the gaze tracking module in different settings and find that the eye-tracking module yields satisfactory performance

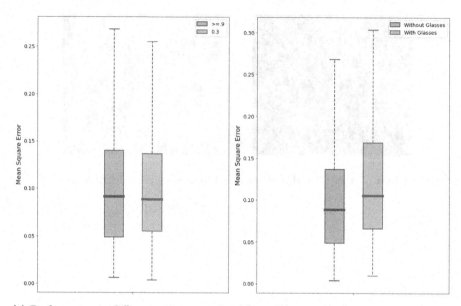

(a) Performance in different camera resolu- (b) Performance with vs without glasses
tions

Fig. 6. Mean square error of our presented tool in different camera resolutions (left) and whether the student was wearing prescription glasses or not (right). Our tool achieves a satisfactory performance with `MSE` ≤ 0.1 at predicting the gaze focus according to our collected data. Note that, all of the gaze points (`x, y` coordinates) were divided by the screen dimensions (`x/screen-width` and `y/screen-height`) in order to normalize for different screen sizes and resolutions.

on average (Fig. 6). Our gaze tracking tool archives a mean-square-error of less than 0.1 on average. Only when students are wearing prescription glasses the MSE slightly exceeds 0.1.

6 Considerations and Challenges to Measure Attention Score from Gaze Patterns

We have yet to finalize the procedure to calculate the attention score from a gaze distribution. However, we have been experimenting with a few ideas. Till now, we have found that **DBScan**, a clustering algorithm is showing some promising results. We have used the **DBScan** implementation of `scikit-learn` library by Pedregosa et al. [21] which expects two hyperparameters:

- *Epsilon*, in short `eps`: The maximum distance allowed between two points to be considered belonging to the same cluster. That means a point p will belong in a cluster $\mathbf{C}$ if and only if there is atleast one point q in $\mathbf{C}$ such that the distance between p and q is less than or equal `eps`.

– `min_samples`: The minimum number of samples in a cluster for a point to be considered as a core point. Effectively, there is atleast `min_sample` number of neighbouring points required to form a cluster.

During our experiments, we set the `min_samples` value to 100. This number has been established based on the observations during our experiments. We tune the `eps` value *dynamically* while analysing a collection of gaze patterns. The idea[2] is that, we can use nearest neighbours to reach a fair estimation of an *optimum* `eps` value. For each point, we find its distance from its $\lfloor min\_samples/3 \rfloor^{th}$ closest neighbour. Sorting these distance values give us an *exponential* like curve depicted at Fig. 7. The *optimum* `eps` value would be the y value at the **elbow** of the curve. There is a sharp rise after the **elbow**, which means some points are really sparse and they can be discarded as noise. We use the `kneedle` library by Ville Satopaa et al. [22] to find the **elbow** point.

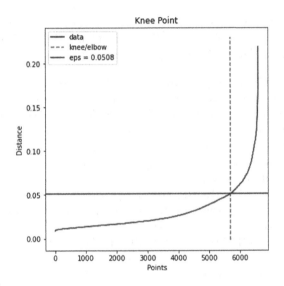

Fig. 7. Tuning the `eps` value for **Position 1**.

The performance of **DBScan** with tuning is depicted on Figs. 8 and 9. Figure 8 compares the performance of **DBScan** between a random distribution and the gaze distribution collected for focused regions. And Fig. 9 shows the results of **DBScan** when the gaze distributions of two different focused regions get mixed. We can observe clear distinction in the **DBScan** results and we are considering how this difference can be utilized to calculate an attention score.

---

[2] How to Use DBSCAN Effectively, link: https://towardsdatascience.com/how-to-use-dbscan-effectively-ed212c02e62.

There are some certain caveats, though. To reach a reliable attention score calculation method we need consistent results. But, in our collected data we observe some relatively bad clustering results of **DBScan**. In Fig. 10, we observe that for positions 4 and 6, **DBScan** identifies 3 and 4 clusters respectively. We have used the *WebGazer* library for gaze-tracking, which still has some room for improvements. During the calibration phase of our data collection the participants complained that the tracking module was not able to follow their gazes properly in the bottom regions of the screen, especially while the participants were wearing prescription glasses. There is a pupil-detection module at the core of the *WebGazer* library. We think that when a user is wearing glasses this pupil-detection module renders low performance. Further investigation is required in this regard.

7 Students Perspective of the Monitoring Tool

Following the data collection session, we conducted short interviews with the participants to ascertain the usability of this monitoring tool in a real-world online class setting. The findings from our discussions are summarized below.

- **Ease of use**: All of the participants found the tool to be easy to use. The students appreciated that it does not require them to install any new software as the tool works with a browser. Furthermore, the calibration phase takes only around 20–25 s. However, students who prefer to wear prescription glasses faced some issues during the calibration phase. They complained that the *Webgazer* tool could not track their gaze properly at the bottom layer of the screen (positions 4, 6 and 9).
- **Low resource and bandwidth consumption**: Students appreciated the fact that our tool consumes very low compute resource and internet bandwidth. Our tool was able to perform perfectly in relatively low-end devices (with core i3 processors and 2GB of RAM) without sacrificing the performance while the interview was in-progress via *Zoom*. The students were also content that this monitoring tool does not add much to the bandwidth payload.
- **Ethical and privacy concerns**: The participants were assured that only their gaze-stream data will be uploaded to a server where it will be aggregated into an attention measurement function. Thus, no one will have access to the video feed and the gaze data of an individual student. While 18 out of 31 participants were reluctant to share their video feed, only 2 participants raised concerns with sharing their gaze information during an online classes.
- **Efficacy of a passive monitoring tool**: We asked the students some additional questions regarding their attention span during an online classes: *why they lose their attention*, and *how likely this tool might help regarding this issue*. Some of the students blamed notification sounds of their smartphones

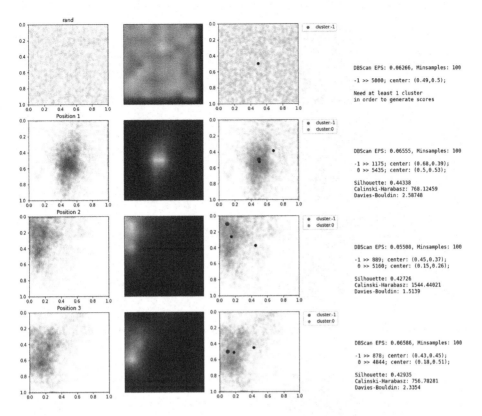

Fig. 8. DBScan performance on aggregated gaze-streams from a single focus region

from social media and messaging applications. In an online class with video feedback turned off, due to the lack of supervision some students (12 out of 31) said that they are often inclined to browse their social media sites when their attention gets interrupted by a notification or they find the lesson too difficult or tedious. They feel that as this tool might help the teacher understand when the lecture content is getting too difficult or monotonous for the students to follow, the teacher might be inclined to invest more time to explain the topic slowly, in a more understandable manner to reach most of the students.

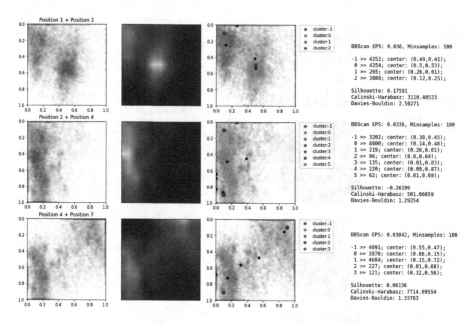

Fig. 9. DBScan performance on aggregated gaze-streams from two different focus regions

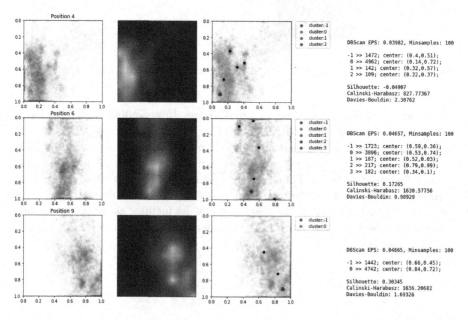

Fig. 10. DBScan *bad* performance on aggregated gaze-streams from a single focus region

– **Concerns raised by students**: Though the tool will not enable a teacher to monitor the *attentiveness* of an individual student some students raised concerns that the teacher might have a negative impression for the classes that have a low overall attention score. Some students raised concerns that this negative impression might have some impact on the overall grading for the course.

8   Conclusion

In this paper, we discuss the design and feasibility of a new monitoring tool that can augment online classes and make them more engaging. This tool will require only gaze-stream information in the form of x, y coordinates to function. We ascertain the necessity and feasibility of this tool in real-online classes consulting with both students and teachers. An obvious shortcoming of our tool is that it will fail to function properly if there is only one student attending the class. However, that is usually not the case. We discuss the considerations and challenges to finalize a method for calculating a reliable attention score by aggregating the continuous gaze-stream data from students during an online class. This work is very much in the preliminary phase. In this paper, we only present the results based on the data we have collected during our individual interview sessions with 31 students. As of now, we have not conducted any real online classes. To verify how our tool performs at deducing different levels of student engagement we will have to check how the attention scores correlate with student engagement of real classes. We have plans to take at least 10 online classes with 30+ students. The classes will be designed to allow a variable level of student engagement and each student will be directly monitored by a proctor to ascertain the level of his/her engagement during the course of each class. The data collected during these classes will serve as the gold standard for establishing the attention measurement methodology.

We pledge to make the tool open-source. Also, all our collected data and analysis code-base will be made publicly available. Our work-in-progress codebase can be accessed with the links below.

Student-Side (the gaze-tracking module)
Instructor-side (attention measurement module)

References

1. Lall, S., Singh, N.: COVID-19: unmasking the new face of education. Int. J. Res. Pharm. Sci. 48–53 (2020)
2. Jieun, Yu., Jee, Y.: Analysis of online classes in physical education during the COVID-19 pandemic. Educ. Sci. **11**(1), 3 (2020)

3. Pokhrel, S., Chhetri, R.: A literature review on impact of COVID-19 pandemic on teaching and learning. High. Educ. Future **8**(1), 133–141 (2021)
4. Ferri, F., Grifoni, P., Guzzo, T.: Online learning and emergency remote teaching: opportunities and challenges in emergency situations. Societies **10**(4), 86 (2020)
5. Adedoyin, O.B., Soykan, E.: COVID-19 pandemic and online learning: the challenges and opportunities. Interact. Learn. Environ. **31**, 1–13 (2020)
6. Webster, J., Trevino, L.K., Ryan, L.: The dimensionality and correlates of flow in human-computer interactions. Comput. Hum. Behav. **9**(4), 411–426 (1993)
7. Zhang, H., Miller, K.F., Sun, X., Cortina, K.S.: Wandering eyes: eye movements during mind wandering in video lectures. Appl. Cogn. Psychol. **34**(2), 449–464 (2020)
8. Yantis, S., Jonides, J.: Abrupt visual onsets and selective attention: voluntary versus automatic allocation. J. Exp. Psychol. Hum. Percept. Perform. **16**(1), 121 (1990)
9. Prinzmetal, W., Presti, D.E., Posner, M.I.: Does attention affect visual feature integration? J. Exp. Psychol. Hum. Percept. Perform. **12**(3), 361 (1986)
10. Finn, J.D.: Withdrawing from school. Review of educational research. Chem. Heterocycl. Compd. **25**(3), 319–325 (1989)
11. Hutt, S., Hardey, J., Bixler, R., Stewart, A., Risko, E., D'Mello, S.K.: Gaze-based detection of mind wandering during lecture viewing. Int. Educ. Data Mining Soc. (2017)
12. Wammes, J.D., Seli, P., Cheyne, J.A., Boucher, P.O., Smilek, D.: Mind wandering during lectures II: relation to academic performance. Scholarsh. Teach. Learn. Psychol. **2**(1), 33 (2016)
13. Campbell, E.R.: Can 'eye' tell if you are paying attention? the use of mobile eye-trackers to measure academic engagement in the primary-school classroom. In: White Rose eTheses Online. University of York (2014)
14. Sharma, K., Jermann, P., Dillenbourg, P.: "with-me-ness": a gaze-measure for students' attention in MOOCs. In: Proceedings of International Conference of the Learning Sciences 2014, number CONF, pp. 1017–1022. ISLS (2014)
15. Srivastava, N., et al.: Are you with me? Measurement of learners' video-watching attention with eye tracking. In: LAK 2021: 11th International Learning Analytics and Knowledge Conference, pp. 88–98 (2021)
16. De Carolis, B., D'Errico, F., Macchiarulo, N., Palestra, G.: "engaged faces": measuring and monitoring student engagement from face and gaze behavior. In: IEEE/WIC/ACM International Conference on Web Intelligence-Companion Volume, pp. 80–85 (2019)
17. Yang, F., Jiang, Z., Wang, C., Dai, Y., Jia, Z., Hirota, K.: Student eye gaze tracking during MOOC teaching. In: 2018 Joint 10th International Conference on Soft Computing and Intelligent Systems (SCIS) and 19th International Symposium on Advanced Intelligent Systems (ISIS), pp. 875–880. IEEE (2018)
18. Rahul, R.K., Shanthakumar, S., Vykunth, P., Sairamnath, K.: Real-time attention span tracking in online education. In: 2020 IEEE MIT Undergraduate Research Technology Conference (URTC), pp. 1–4. IEEE (2020)
19. Just, M.A., Carpenter, P.A.: A theory of reading: from eye fixations to comprehension. Psychol. Rev. **87**(4), 329 (1980)
20. Papoutsaki, A., Sangkloy, P., Laskey, J., Daskalova, N., Huang, J., Hays, J.: Webgazer: scalable webcam eye tracking using user interactions. In: Proceedings of the 25th International Joint Conference on Artificial Intelligence (IJCAI), pp. 3839–3845. AAAI (2016)

21. Pedregosa, F., et al.: Scikit-learn: machine learning in Python. J. Mach. Learn. Res. **12**, 2825–2830 (2011)
22. Satopaa, V., Albrecht, J., Irwin, D., Raghavan, B.: Finding a "kneedle" in a haystack: Detecting knee points in system behavior. In: 2011 31st International Conference on Distributed Computing Systems Workshops, pp. 166–171. IEEE (2011)

A Review on Modular Framework and Artificial Intelligence-Based Smart Education

Sarthak Sengupta[1] ⓘ, Anurika Vaish[1] ⓘ, David Fonseca Escudero[2] ⓘ,
Francisco José García-Peñalvo[3] ⓘ, Anindya Bose[4] ⓘ, and Fernando Moreira[5(✉)] ⓘ

[1] Indian Institute of Information Technology - Allahabad, Prayagraj, India
anurika@iiita.ac.in
[2] La Salle, Ramon Llull University, Barcelona, Spain
fonsi@salle.url.edu
[3] Department of Computer Science and Automation, Universidad de Salamanca, Salamanca, Spain
fgarcia@usal.es
[4] 6th Generation of Computing, London, UK
[5] REMIT, IJP, Universidade Portucalense, Porto & IEETA, Universidade de Aveiro, Aveiro, Portugal
fmoreira@upt.pt

Abstract. Smart educational systems have become an essential module for intelligent learning and teaching in educational institutions. A review of the literature was done on research studies around the globe to find the research aspects in the vibrant domain. The search keywords were extracted based on the secondary data collected along with Delphi method-based experts' survey analysis during the COVID-19 pandemic. The study helped in understanding the facets of research studies done on a modular framework, artificial intelligence, and smart education. Innovative strategies were also recommended to implement artificial intelligence-based smart education in institutions across the world.

Keywords: Artificial intelligence · Smart education · COVID-19 pandemic · Blended learning · Modular framework

1 Introduction

Interactive teaching and learning have become an integral part of education. The COVID-19 pandemic has transformed the education system drastically [1–3]. This study attempted to discuss smart education and artificial intelligence-based modular systems for the development of education. The online mode of teaching and learning had a huge potential which got implemented instantaneously due to the necessity created by the pandemic lockdown protocols. Artificial intelligence-based recommender systems for effective decision-making in the selection of the appropriate method to teach learners from different sections of society have become an important concern.

This study will help in achieving the growth in literacy rate for everyone irrespective of caste, religion, status, country, or background. Every human being on the earth has

P. Zaphiris and A. Ioannou (Eds.): HCII 2023, LNCS 14040, pp. 122–132, 2023.
https://doi.org/10.1007/978-3-031-34411-4_10

the right to become educated. An educated nation can pave the way for a prosperous economy. Online pedagogy can help in the enhancement of e-learning infrastructure as well as strategies for the implementation of e-governance. This study would help in the overall growth and development of society to support lifelong learning even during the COVID-19 pandemic.

Smart education-based pedagogy can perform an optimized amalgamation of technology with primitive teaching and interactive e-learning. New educational policies completely support massive up-gradation in technological usage [2]. The objective of most of the reliable studies is revolving around providing unbiased access to education for all sections of society. Many teachers want to teach knowledge but do not get the required mode to provide education. Solving these issues is the present requirement. Efficient resource management in providing effective education can be done by tactically managing the learners, course materials, capital investment, infrastructure, teaching methods, and the stakeholders' minds. The educational stakeholders include more or less everyone in the proximity of the learning process. For example, teaching a girl eventually educates her whole family.

This research paper is divided into various sub-sections. The next section discussed the review of literature and after that the methodology has been provided. The literature review discussed relevant research studies on the domain. The methodology comprised the research gap, problem, objective, statistical tools, and research methods needed to deploy the research endeavor. Later on, the analysis and findings were discussed followed by the conclusion. The analysis and findings provided the analytical techniques done to implement the research methodology along with the relevant findings. The conclusion discussed the conclusive insights along with the limitations and future scope of research.

2 Literature Review

Nowadays, all recommender systems are improving continuously because of AI. Thus, AI-based education systems can do wonders in learning retention and teaching pedagogy. The online e-learning mode is generating vast chunks of data that can be converted into meaningful information and valuable knowledge for massive enhancement in smart educational systems. Supervised machine learning (ML) algorithms can help in generating an optimized mix of course materials and unsupervised ML algorithms can automate the process eventually. Extensive AI-based educational data mining can help in forecasting appropriate methods for effective reach and efficient pedagogy.

The review of the literature provided a rich source of information to move ahead and pave the way for educational development [5–20]. The research study which motivated the researchers to move further discussed the importance of artificial intelligence and technology-based learning enhancement for educational development [21]. Artificial intelligence (AI) refers to a broader constellation of computing technologies [22] than machine learning (ML) approaches and should have active engagement with education [23]. Educational data mining (EDM) is primarily concerned with the development, research, and application of computerized methods for pattern detection in educational big data [24]. EDM and learning analytics (LA) have some commonalities along with distinctions with the common goal being educational improvement [25]. The EDM and

LAK (Learning Analytics and Knowledge) communities are somewhat closely related, and definitions are relatable [26]. Recommender systems and agents have an enormous contribution to the educational field in recommending the correct and appropriate methods. SARA [27] can be an example of a recommender agent that is even being studied for continuous analysis and importance [28]. Modular frameworks and systems have been significantly contributing to educational institutions. For example, the EMMeT MCQ Generator is trying to build a machine learning-based predictive model for better feasibility [29].

Various literature was reviewed meticulously on the areas of the study from the leading sources of research publications. It was found that less work had been done on the subject under study. It was also observed that most of the relevant studies were conducted during the COVID-19 pandemic. This justifies the proverb that "Necessity is the mother of invention".

3 Methodology

The study extensively searched and reviewed the top sources for leading research publications to explore the motivational studies done in the study's domain [30]. Various secondary sources and Delphi method-based experts' surveys were the primary sources of information for the research study. The year-wise analysis of publications in tabular form was done to have a panoramic view of the research publications which were based on the keyword-based search made till the year 2022. Firstly, the analysis based on the literature review is shown. Later on, the implications and conclusions were drawn accordingly. Last but not the least, the findings regarding essential tools and techniques to inculcate effective teaching and efficient learning has also been provided in the next section. These findings can help in implementing online pedagogy during the Coronavirus crisis for strategically achieving the new normal during such trying times. This study would help further researchers to move ahead in this domain and help learners and teachers to sustain themselves during the COVID-19 pandemic.

A major research gap found was lesser number of relevant research studies done on the domain. The problem of finding a tried and tested framework to deploy Artificial Intelligence for smart education with the help of modular sub-systems still persists. The objective of the study was to explore research studies around the global fraternity on artificial intelligence, smart education and modular framework.

4 Analysis and Findings

Research studies on the area were searched with the help of keywords namely "artificial intelligence", "smart education" and "modular framework". The keywords were extracted with the help of the review of the literature and the Delphi method-based experts' survey. The keywords helped in understanding these research concepts and motivational studies with deeper insights. After shortlisting the primary keywords based on priority and relevance to the study, feedback from subject matter experts was taken. The process started with an online poll with the help of the Mentimeter tool. The question asked was "Which Video-Conferencing platform is best?" to confirm the platform feasible for the subject matter experts. Figure 1 provides the result of the poll conducted on the Mentimeter tool which updated the responses dynamically, i.e., on a real-time basis. As per the survey-based poll, Google Meet was found to be the most suitable platform for conducting the experts' survey or the Delphi method. The discussion was mainly on validating the extracted keywords.

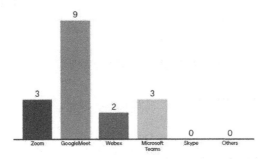

Fig. 1. Real-Time E-Polling results on finding the best video conferencing platform (Results generated by Mentimeter)

Moreover, after reviewing of literature, it was found that a few research studies have been done in this area. AND operator was used in finding the intersection set of research publications, i.e., the studies containing all the mentioned keywords. Although the process for advanced search varied for different publication sources, the objective was to check research studies containing all three main keywords were corroborated. Table 1 gives a summary of the research publications on basis of the keywords ("smart education" AND "artificial intelligence" AND "modular framework") to extract data from leading sources of research publication like Scopus, IGI Global, Emerald Insight, Google Scholar, ScienceDirect, IEEE Xplore, Web of Science (WebOfKnowledge), Springer Nature, ERIC, and JSTOR. The search was considered for all types of research publications like journals, conferences, workshops, seminars, books, book chapters, review papers, etc., encompassing all forms of research studies pursued so far. The date when the literature review-based search was done is till the month of the study undertaken, i.e., October 2022. So, all types of research studies have been taken till the date of the research study being done. Table 1 provided justifies this observation. It was also found that most of the research studies discussed strategic formulation, but the implementation and evaluation parts were still left to be studied. New problems are arising nowadays due to the Coronavirus crisis. Innovative technology adoption models are the need of the hour. The educational institutions witnessed the forced implementation of online pedagogy due to the COVID-19 pandemic. The pandemic had imposed travel restrictions and social distancing measures which resulted in a sudden halt in classroom teaching and in-campus learning pedagogy.

Table 1. Keywords-based extracted data of research publications from leading sources

Source of Research Publication	Number of Publication(s)	Time Range (in years)
Google Scholar	11	2012 to 2021
IGI Global	6	2008 to 2018
Springer Nature	4	2018 to 2022
Scopus	0	-
ScienceDirect (Elsevier)	0	-
Emerald Insight	0	-
IEEE Xplore	0	-
Web of Science (WebOfKnowledge)	0	-
ERIC	0	-
JSTOR	0	-

Note. Author's self-compilation from various sources

The research articles were explored. A total number of 21 distinct research publications between the years 2012 to 2022 were found from leading sources based on the keywords mentioned. The conference proceeding published in the year 2022 is a book chapter that has been published in a volume ahead of print. A literature review of research publications was done to find relevant inferences for the extraction and formulation of research gaps, problems, and objectives. The relevant inferences were drawn from highly revered and cited publications which are already provided in this section. The research study focused on developing a preliminary framework with the help of the keywords-based observational study along with the panoramic view of the year-wise data of the literature. But the main emphasis was given to the framework and new tools to help to achieve the new normal in online pedagogy during the COVID-19 pandemic. Figure 2 provides the year-wise analysis of research publications on the keywords based on this research study. The diagram is in the form of a well-depicted 3D column chart. The data was collected in Google Sheets and the chart was designed accordingly. In the figure, it can be observed that in the year 2018 the highest number of publications were witnessed, and the second highest was the year 2020. In the years 2010, 2012, 2019, and 2021 same number of research publications were found. No publications of relevant research studies were found in the year – 2009, 2011, 2013, 2014, 2016, and 2017.

No. of Publications v/s. Year

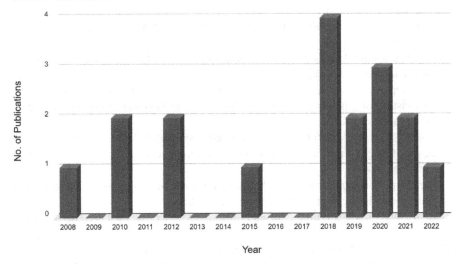

Fig. 2. Keywords based-Column Chart (Number of Research Publications V/S Year)

It was also found that services like MOOCs, Zoom, Microsoft teams, Webex, YouTube, Swayam, NPTEL, LinkedIn, ResearchGate, Facebook, Twitter, WhatsApp, Google Classroom/Meet, Coursera, Udemy, Moodle, Mentimeter, Flipgrid, Byju's, Edpuzzle, Canvas, etc., have an essential role in the growth of Information and Communication Technology (ICT) in education. The tools and platforms have been extensively used to justify their importance in this research study. These techniques can be a sustainable strategy to achieve the new normal-based online pedagogy during the COVID-19 pandemic. Based on the meta-analysis and exploration of these strategies, some of the tools and techniques were shortlisted but the list is not exhaustive. The various relevant services mentioned above are briefly described below:

- MOOC is Massive Open Online Courses (MOOCs) that provide online courses affordably and flexibly [3, 12].
- Zoom is used for video conferencing and teaching via online mode. It is a leading platform for video communications in educational institutions [32].
- Microsoft Teams is a communication platform used by teachers to teach their students [33].
- Cisco Webex is a famous platform for video communication and educational webinars [34].
- YouTube is a video-sharing platform comprising an enormous collection of educational videos [35].
- Swayam is a program to achieve educational policies namely access, quality, and equity [36].
- NPTEL provides e-learning courses for learners from all backgrounds [37].
- LinkedIn is a professional networking platform that provides effective learning solutions [38].

- ResearchGate is a social network for researchers who can connect, learn and collaborate accordingly [39].
- Facebook is a leading social networking platform that also provides educational services nowadays [40].
- Twitter is a microblogging social networking service that provides research and educational resources [41].
- WhatsApp is a messaging app-based service that has a major contribution to educational institutions mainly because of its interactive groups and instant messaging or sharing facilities [42].
- Google Classroom provides a student-teacher streamlined sharing platform [43] whereas Google meet is a video communication service used by educational institutions [44].
- Coursera provides online courses at reasonable prices but it was providing some free certifications during the COVID-19 pandemic [45].
- Udemy also provides online courses at affordable prices and for free occasionally [46].
- Moodle is an open-source learning management system [47].
- Mentimeter is a platform to create real-time feedback-based presentations and effective visualizations [48].
- Flipgrid provides a social learning environment along with interactive videos [49].
- Byju's is an online tutoring and learning platform that is growing at a fast pace [50].
- Edpuzzle helps in creating interactive videos for LMS integration [51].
- Canvas is a learning management system with an effective learning and efficient teaching platform [52].

Flipped classrooms and E-learning management systems acted as a boon for the education sector during this pandemic. The objective for overall growth and development in education is to plan for an integrated centralized system with all such services embedded into it.

The world's top educational institutions like Harvard University, Massachusetts Institute of Technology, Stanford University, etc., have one thing in common. They have a massive social media presence. Social networking-based platforms are the need of the hour. Services like LinkedIn, ResearchGate, Facebook, Twitter, WhatsApp, Google Classroom/Meet, Coursera, Udemy, etc., have a pivotal role. Providing education for all with special emphasis on poorer sections of society is essential. It has been observed that the literacy rate of many countries is still below the required level. The weaker sections of society are miles away from education. Moreover, the COVID-19 pandemic has drastically hit the education sector.

Some of the innovative methods and ways of learning are as follows: -

- Blended E-Learning– Innovative blended e-learning technology can be fused with social networking platforms. It can create a platform for an interactive e-learning pedagogy.
- Radio transmission- Nowadays, radio is easily accessible and it's inbuilt for free on most smartphones or mobiles. So, education can be provided with the help of radios on feasible schedules which can be notified through social networking platforms.

- Television-based educational channels– Some educational TV channels are providing courses along with social media-based discussion forums also. More publicity and growth of such channels can be done through social media marketing.
- Drones-based Internet access- UAVs (Unmanned Aerial Vehicles)/drone-based internet providers can help in internet services to remote areas for educational purposes.
- Crowdfunding/Crowdsourcing- With the help of crowdfunding, cheap educational laptops and smartphones can be designed that can have access to a social networking platform with educational courses. Crowdsourcing-based educational forums can also be done to share course content by cloud computing.

Electronic awareness (E-awareness) should be done among all sections of society because some educational institutions and organizations are already providing free education, but most people are not aware of it. Learners could access e-courses for free even during the COVID-19 pandemic. Therefore, all the stakeholders need to be motivated.

5 Conclusion

Artificial intelligence-based learning management systems (LMS) are the next big innovation in the educational sector. The strategies and innovative methods provided in the study will help in overall development and all-round growth of higher education institutions globally. The COVID-19 pandemic has deliberately increased the need to implement smart education virtually. The UNESCO 2030 agenda also discussed about the agenda regarding implementation of Artificial Intelligence (AI) in education but the ethical issues related to it should be observed continuously to address the challenges accordingly [53].

A limitation of this study was the roadmap to formulate the strategic model for effective implementation of the research plan. But further study is already being done by the team of authors to explore the future scope of research by developing a modular framework gradually.

An educated nation can pave the way for a prosperous economy. So, this novel study can provide the foundation to build a state-of-the-art infrastructure needed to implement AI in educational institutions.

Acknowledgements. This work was supported by the FCT – Fundação para a Ciência e a Tecnologia, I.P. [Project UIDB/05105/2020].

References

1. Sobral, S.R., Jesus-Silva, N., Cardoso, A., Moreira, F.: EU27 higher education institutions and COVID-19, Year 2020. Int. J. Environ. Res. Public Health **18**(11), 5963 (2021). https://doi.org/10.3390/ijerph18115963
2. GarcíaPeñalvo, F.J., Corell, A., AbellaGarcía, V., Grande, M.: La evaluación online en la educación superior en tiempos de la COVID-19. Educ. Knowl. Soc. (EKS) **21**(0), 26 (2020). https://doi.org/10.14201/eks.23013

3. GarcíaPeñalvo, F.J., Corell, A., AbellaGarcía, V., GrandedePrado, M.: Recommendations for mandatory online assessment in higher education during the COVID-19 pandemic. In: Burgos, D., Tlili, A., Tabacco, A. (eds.) Radical Solutions for Education in a Crisis Context: COVID-19 as an Opportunity for Global Learning, pp. 85–98. Springer, Singapore (2021). https://doi.org/10.1007/978-981-15-7869-4_6

4. Sengupta, S., Vaish, A.: Social networking mood recognition algorithm for conflict detection and management of Indian educational institutions. Soc. Netw. Anal. Min. **10**(1), 1–13 (2020). https://doi.org/10.1007/s13278-020-00701-3

5. Alier, M., Fonseca, D., Amo-Filvà, D., García-Peñalvo, F.J., Casañ, M.J.: Unplugged institutions: towards a localization of the cloud for Learning Analytics privacy enhancement (2022)

6. Llauró, A., Fonseca, D., Villegas, E., Aláez, M., Romero, S.: Educational data mining application for improving the academic tutorial sessions, and the reduction of early dropout in undergraduate students. In: Ninth International Conference on Technological Ecosystems for Enhancing Multiculturality (TEEM 2021), pp. 212–218

7. Amo, D., et al.: Learning Analytics Icons for analytics' transparency, information, and easy comprehension of data treatment of students. In Ninth International Conference on Technological Ecosystems for Enhancing Multiculturality (TEEM 2021), pp. 587–593, October 2021

8. Alier, M., CasañGuerrero, M.J., Amo, D., Severance, C., Fonseca, D.: Privacy and e-learning: a pending task. Sustainability **13**(16), 9206 (2021)

9. Fonseca, D., GarcíaPeñalvo, F.J., Camba, J.D.: New methods and technologies for enhancing usability and accessibility of educational data. Univ. Access Inf. Soc. **20**(3), 421–427 (2021). https://doi.org/10.1007/s10209-020-00765-0

10. Moreira, F., Ferreira, M.J., Pereira, C.S., Escudero, D.F., Collazos, C., Gomes, A.: Higher education teachers training (HET2) model: active learning in higher education environment. In: Rocha, Á., Adeli, H., Dzemyda, G., Moreira, F., Correia, A.M.R. (eds.) Trends and Applications in Information Systems and Technologies: Volume 3, pp. 103–112. Springer International Publishing, Cham (2021). https://doi.org/10.1007/978-3-030-72660-7_11

11. AmoFilvá, D., et al.: Local technology to enhance data privacy and security in educational technology. Int. J. Interact. Multimed. Artif. Intell. **7**(2), 262–273 (2021)

12. Petchamé, J., Iriondo, I., Villegas, E., Riu, D., Fonseca, D.: Comparing face-to-face, emergency remote teaching and smart classroom: a qualitative exploratory research based on students' experience during the COVID-19 pandemic. Sustainability **13**(12), 6625 (2021)

13. Campanyà, C., Fonseca, D., Amo, D., Martí, N., Peña, E.: Mixed analysis of the flipped classroom in the concrete and steel structures subject in the context of COVID-19 crisis outbreak. A pilot study. Sustainability **13**(11), 5826 (2021)

14. Moreira, F., Ferreira, M.J., Escudero, D.F., Pereira, C.S., Durão, N.: Teaching and learning Modelling and Specification based on gamification. In 2020 15th Iberian Conference on Information Systems and Technologies (CISTI), pp. 1–6. IEEE, June 2020

15. Fonseca, D., GarcíaPeñalvo, F.J.: Interactive and collaborative technological ecosystems for improving academic motivation and engagement. Univ. Access Inf. Soc. **18**(3), 423–430 (2019). https://doi.org/10.1007/s10209-019-00669-8

16. Moreira, F., Ferreira, M.J., Pereira, C.S., Gomes, A.S., Collazos, C., Escudero, D.F.: ECLECTIC as a learning ecosystem for higher education disruption. Univ. Access Inf. Soc. **18**(3), 615–631 (2019). https://doi.org/10.1007/s10209-019-00682-x

17. Cardona, J.S., Lopez, J.A., Vela, F.L.G., Moreira, F.: Older adults and games from a perspective of playability, game experience and pervasive environments: a systematics literature review. In: Rocha, A., Adeli, H., Dzemyda, G., Moreira, F. (eds.) Information Systems and Technologies: WorldCIST 2022, Volume 2, pp. 444–453. Springer International Publishing, Cham (2022). https://doi.org/10.1007/978-3-031-04819-7_42

18. Córdova, M., Díaz, J., ArangoLópez, J., Ahumada, D., Moreira, F.: Towards automatic gait analysis from an IT perspective: a kinesiology case. In: Rocha, A., Adeli, H., Dzemyda, G., Moreira, F. (eds.) Information Systems and Technologies: WorldCIST 2022, Volume 3, pp. 404–412. Springer International Publishing, Cham (2022). https://doi.org/10.1007/978-3-031-04829-6_36

19. Mendoza, W., Ramírez, G.M., González, C., Moreira, F.: Assessment of curriculum design by learning outcomes (LO). Educ. Sci. **12**, 541 (2022). https://doi.org/10.3390/educsci12080541

20. de Oliveira, C.F., Sobral, S.R., Ferreira, M.J., Moreira, F.: How does learning analytics contribute to prevent students' dropout in higher education: a systematic literature review. Big Data Cogn. Comput. **5**, 64 (2021). https://doi.org/10.3390/bdcc5040064

21. Loeckx, J.: Blurring boundaries in education: context and impact of MOOCs. Int. Rev. Res. Open Distrib. Learn. **17**(3), 92–121 (2016). https://doi.org/10.19173/irrodl.v17i3.2395

22. Fast, E., Horvitz, E.: Long-term trends in the public perception of artificial intelligence. In: Thirty-First AAAI Conference on Artificial Intelligence (2017). https://ojs.aaai.org/index.php/AAAI/article/view/10635

23. Cukurova, M., Luckin, R., Kent, C.: Impact of an artificial intelligence research frame on the perceived credibility of educational research evidence. Int. J. Artif. Intell. Educ. **30**(2), 205–235 (2019). https://doi.org/10.1007/s40593-019-00188-w

24. Romero, C., Ventura, S., Pechenizky, M., Baker, R.S.: Handbook of Educational Data Mining. Data Mining and Knowledge Discovery Series. Chapman and Hall/CRC Press, Boca Raton (2010)

25. Charitopoulos, A., Rangoussi, M., Koulouriotis, D.: On the use of soft computing methods in educational data mining and learning analytics research: a review of years 2010–2018. Int. J. Artif. Intell. Educ. **30**(3), 371–430 (2020). https://doi.org/10.1007/s40593-020-00200-8

26. Siemens, G., Baker, R.: Learning analytics and educational data mining: towards communication and collaboration. In: Proceedings of the 2nd International Conference on Learning Analytics and Knowledge (LAK 2012), pp. 252–254. Association for Computing Machinery, New York, NY, USA (2012). https://doi.org/10.1145/2330601.2330661

27. Greer, J., Frost, S., Banow, R., Thompson, C., Kuleza, S., Wilson, K., Koehn, G.: The student advice recommender agent: SARA. In: UMAP Workshops (2015). https://www.researchgate.net/publication/283323216_The_Student_Advice_Recommender_Agent_SARA

28. Mousavi, A., Schmidt, M., Squires, V., Wilson, K.: Assessing the effectiveness of student advice recommender agent (SARA): the case of automated personalized feedback. Int. J. Artif. Intell. Educ. **31**(3), 603–621 (2020). https://doi.org/10.1007/s40593-020-00210-6

29. Leo, J., et al.: Ontology-based generation of medical, multi-term MCQs. Int. J. Artif. Intell. Educ. **29**(2), 145–188 (2019). https://doi.org/10.1007/s40593-018-00172-w

30. García-Peñalvo, F.J.: Developing robust state-of-the-art reports: systematic literature reviews. Educ. Knowl. Soc. **23**, e28600 (2022). https://doi.org/10.14201/eks.28600

31. MOOCs. https://www.mooc.org/. Accessed 21 Nov 2022

32. Zoom. https://zoom.us/. Accessed 21 Nov 2022

33. Microsoft Teams. https://www.microsoft.com/en-in/microsoft-teams/group-chat-software. Accessed 21 Nov 2022

34. Cisco Webex. https://www.webex.com/. Accessed 21 Nov 2022

35. YouTube. https://www.youtube.com/. Accessed 21 Nov 2022

36. SWAYAM. https://swayam.gov.in/. Accessed 21 Nov 2022

37. NPTEL. https://nptel.ac.in/. Accessed 21 Nov 2022

38. LinkedIn. https://www.linkedin.com/. Accessed 21 Nov 2022

39. ResearchGate. https://www.researchgate.net/. Accessed 21 Nov 2022

40. Facebook. https://www.facebook.com/. Accessed 21 Nov 2022

41. Twitter. https://twitter.com/. Accessed 21 Nov 2022

42. WhatsApp. https://www.whatsapp.com. Accessed 21 Nov 2022
43. Google Classroom. https://classroom.google.com/. Accessed 21 Nov 2022
44. Google Meet. https://meet.google.com/. Accessed 21 Nov 2022
45. Coursera. https://www.coursera.org/. Accessed 21 Nov 2022
46. Udemy. http://www.udemy.com/. Accessed 21 Nov 2022
47. MOODLE. https://moodle.org/. Accessed 21 Nov 2022
48. Mentimeter. https://www.mentimeter.com/. Accessed 21 Nov 2022
49. Flipgrid. http://flipgrid.com/. Accessed 21 Nov 2022
50. Byju's. Home. BYJU'S. https://byjus.com/. Accessed 21 Nov 2022
51. Edpuzzle. http://edpuzzle.com/. Accessed 21 Nov 2022
52. Canvas. https://www.canvas.net/. Accessed 21 Nov 2022
53. FloresVivar, J.-M., GarcíaPeñalvo, F.-J.: Reflections on the ethics, potential, and challenges of artificial intelligence in the framework of quality education (SDG4). Comunicar **31**(74), 37–47 (2023). https://doi.org/10.3916/C74-2023-03

Technology and Education as Drivers of the Fourth Industrial Revolution Through the Lens of the New Science of Learning

Iulia Stefan[1]([✉])[iD], Nadia Barkoczi[2][iD], Todor Todorov[5][iD], Ivaylo Peev[5][iD], Lia Pop[2][iD], Claudia Marian[2], Cristina Campian[3][iD], Sonia-Carmen Munteanu[4][iD], Patrick Flynn[6][iD], and Lucía Morales[6][iD]

[1] Automation Department, Technical University of Cluj-Napoca, Cluj-Napoca, Romania
Iulia.Stefan@aut.utcluj.ro
[2] Department of Specialty with Psychopedagogical Profile, Technical University of Cluj-Napoca, Cluj-Napoca, Romania
{Nadia.Barkoczi,Lia.Pop,Claudia.Marian}@dspp.utcluj.ro
[3] Department of Structures, Technical University of Cluj-Napoca, Cluj-Napoca, Romania
Cristina.Campian@dst.utcluj.ro
[4] Department of Modern Languages, Technical University of Cluj-Napoca, Cluj-Napoca, Romania
Sonia.Munteanu@lang.utcluj.ro
[5] Department of Foreign Languages and Applied Linguistics, Technical University Sofia, Sofia, Bulgaria
{todobg,i_peev}@tu-sofia.bg
[6] Department of Accounting, Economics and Finance, Technological University Dublin, Dublin, Ireland
{patrick.flynn,lucia.morales}@tudublin.ie

Abstract. The economic needs imposed by our knowledge-based and digital economy require careful reflection and insights as we face new educational needs. This research paper explores the importance of a student-centred approach and the new science of learning paradigm to foster the development of new and innovative learning, teaching and research approaches. At EUt + we are working on a new concept coined as circular pedagogy. In our proposed innovative pedagogy, the roles of the learner, teacher and researcher are ever interchanging for a lifelong learning experience to navigate the challenges posed by the fourth industrial revolution and future new phases. The current work underlines the need for education and technology fusion to foster creativity and attractiveness towards sustainable learning processes for personal and cognitive skill development not limited to economic needs and demands. The context of European Universities' alliances through the lenses of EUt + is discussed as an internationally transformative strategy for enhancing educational opportunities for actors in the educational process, prioritising strong intercultural competencies development, underlining diversity, inclusion, and collaborative and open learning environments. The sustainable educational context is defined by the human being and well-being continuously engaged in adaptive tasks, learning processes, assessments, skill development and decision-making routines. The emphasis on stress-related reports underlines its negative impact on the learning process and the need for a learning environment designed to acknowledge specific personality profiles and vulnerabilities

© The Author(s), under exclusive license to Springer Nature Switzerland AG 2023
P. Zaphiris and A. Ioannou (Eds.): HCII 2023, LNCS 14040, pp. 133–148, 2023.
https://doi.org/10.1007/978-3-031-34411-4_11

to enhance a positive educational climate through technology that aligns with the needs of sustainable education.

Keywords: Technology · Fourth Industrial Revolution · New Science of Learning · STEM · Digital Economy · Knowledge-Economy · Inclusion · Cultural Clash · Sustainable Education

1 Introduction

The boundaries between the use of technology to support education are quite challenging to define. The discussions become more convoluted as we define the role of learners, teachers, and researchers through the intricacies of learning. Our develop-mental process is defined by cultural evolution and biological adaptation and by our ability to share and exchange knowledge. According to Meltzoff et al. [1], p. 1], human learning is characterised by its complexity as we engage with significant levels of abstraction and social interaction compounded by our ability to adjust and adapt. However, the speed of current transformations is impacting entire socio-economic and environmental systems that require a different response from our educational sector as we embrace the possibilities offered by new technologies and innovations [2]. We are facing rapid changes driven by the digital revolution that started in the middle of the last century as we witness the fusion between the physical, digital, and biological spheres coined as the Fourth Industrial Revolution [3]. Undoubtedly, we are immersed in dramatic changes that require a different response from our educational sector as we try to understand the interrelated dynamics of education and its impact on developing our economic systems and social relationships. Brynjolfsson and McAfee [4] have raised significant concerns, as technology supports progress and improves our living standards, but at the same time, our high-tech future is defined by uncertainty, inequality, a growing economic divide and rising levels of conflict [5]. Technological breakthroughs are critical to support our economic and sustainable development, but they can also contribute to the acceleration of inequalities, social marginalisation and health problems. In this context, the OECD [6, p. 1] underlines, for the year 2030, the importance of personal skills development to the same degree as the cognitive ones "in becoming a responsible and global citizen" Furthermore, technology and innovation are critical to helping us address ongoing and emerging challenges as we face severe environmental degradation derived from human economic activities that are well-known as the Anthropocene.

At Technological Universities, specifically at the European University of Technology (EUt+), we face significant challenges as we try to shape and define the university's future educational model focused on a student-centred approach. We aim to prepare and develop technologically savvy students capable of engaging with ever-changing socio-economic and environmental dynamics. Our reflections and discussions on the role that we will play as part of the educational system led us to examine by a systematic review of the literature in educational paradigms in relation to technology usage opportunities in educational process, the significance of bringing in new educational paradigms guided by innovative pedagogies that define and guide our teaching and learning processes. The new science of learning has significance as we try to understand and discern the implications and importance of having a student-centred approach that fosters learning for sustainable development [7]. Our ambition seeks to transform how we educate and engage with our students within a new learning paradigm where a circular role as learners, teachers and researchers emerges as outlined in our novel insights provided by Circular Pedagogy [8, 9]. To develop our discussions, the remainder of the paper explores the new science of learning in section two. The basic elements of the Fourth Industrial Revolution and the role of knowledge and the digital economy are detailed in section three. The discussion continues with the fourth section, where the analysis of the importance of internationalisation and implications for cultural clash are presented, followed by some reflections on the importance of inclusive learning environments for sustainable development in the sixth section. The paper concludes with a critical reflection on the significance of education in allowing a positive movement forward in our quest to trans-form education and how we engage with our students.

2   The New Science of Learning

Our European economic model is under severe pressure. The labour market requires the development of skills, capabilities and occupations that require digital knowledge that, in many cases, do not exist yet because we are looking at jobs that need to be created today for the needs of tomorrow. As part of the higher education community, we acknowledge the difficulties faced by teachers, students and researchers when trying to differentiate between the positive aspects that technological advances can bring to support and enhance educational models, the significance of a constructive learning experience and the needs of the labour market. In line with the guidelines of the European Commission to establish a common and standard European Learning Model (EML), as such a new ontology that provides a standardized vocabulary for the whole united model is needed [8]. The European Union's vision for a unified educational model is encouraged and supported by UNESCO to pursue a whole institutional approach that provides an educational framework to address the challenges associated with the United Nations' call aiming to develop an educational system for sustainable development [11–13].

The United Nations 2030 Agenda is overly ambitious, and it requires that we work together to enhance technological universities' educational offer attuned to our European and global reality. Technical education requires developing critical thinking, communication, collaboration, information skills, and problem-solving competencies, among others, that meet the demands of the future workplace and align with the needs of employment stakeholders in Europe [10, 14, 15].

The new science for learning needs to consider how technology is transforming education and learning by bringing new opportunities, but at the same time, we must be aware of its significant challenges. As part of the European Academic and research community, we have an important role to play as we try to identify an appropriate balance by defining curriculums that integrate different competencies that enable students to work and interact on dynamic and multi-diverse teams. Teams that can manage growing levels of information, fast-evolving technologies, as the need for communication, social and analytical skills are on the rise while being pushed by a growing socio-economic and digital divide [16–21].

To existing complexities, we must add pressures emerging from the needs of a fast-evolving labour market and growing situations of conflict that learners need to be able to navigate as part of their required working package skills without neglecting the need for social skills that are critical and the foundation of our societies. As we reflect and reconsider the significance of technical education, we bring forward the importance of thinking human first, and this means that our learning environments should not be detached from social, caring, and affective networks [9].

Our students are expected to develop digital skills in higher demand by the Information and Technology Sector combined with growing pressures to support STEM education while forgetting the significance of social sciences and the so-called "soft skills." The digital and knowledge economy is driving the educational agenda. Higher Education Institutions must adapt fast to the growing and evolving demands for a fast pace educational model that cherishes technical knowledge and the development of employability skills, but where are we leaving the social, caring, and affective relationships? Worrying questions and concerns are emerging as we reflect and reconsider the role to be played by Higher Education Institutions and their limited focus on the labour market and the interests of the business network. We argue that at technological universities, we are well-positioned to contribute significantly to developing needed skills within a learning framework that "Always Thinks Human First." However, we need to be aware of worrying trends emerging due to the overuse of technological advances within the learning, teaching and research context and their implications for students, researchers, and academics. Some of the most pressing issues are related to psychological and mental health problems, and social and cultural environments that can lead to discrimination, isolation and exclusion as we define the guiding paradigms of the "new science of learning." Within the European University of Technology (EUt+) context, we aim to provide critical insight into how transdisciplinary learning, teaching, and research environments can contribute to creating balanced spaces that enable collaboration and deep learning and that could lead to the development of A New Educational Model (ANEM). We are concerned about social issues and problems associated with inclusion, integration, diversity, cultural clashes, and isolation and how technology can enhance academia to facilitate and support collaborative learning spaces that nurture curiosity and the knowledge-sharing process through a student-centred approach. At the same time, we are interested in examining contemporary challenges in higher education derived from technology integration as part of learning processes and how technology can lead to a severe disruption of learning and affect students' ability to concentrate and focus. Academics and researchers must enable educational environments supported by technology, which means that we need to collaborate and engage with our students as we redesign learning models and processes supported by the co-creation of knowledge within different venues. Learning science environments offer academics and students an opportunity to work together to facilitate and develop flexible educational environments that integrate different elements that support personalised, flexible, and diverse learning environments that are supported by adequate assessment and feedback strategies.

3   The Fourth Industrial Revolution and the Knowledge and Digital Economy

The challenges introduced by the fourth industrial revolution, the digital economy and the knowledge-based economy are no longer about the need to innovate and digitise, but about the need for appropriate, high-quality education and training programmes designed to enable people to acquire new skills quickly. A definition of The Fourth Industrial Revolution, "Smart Factory" or Industry 4.0 is required to better understand its development context. As Klaus Schwab puts it, *"The Fourth Industrial Revolution builds on the digital revolution and combines multiple technologies that are leading to unprecedented paradigm shifts in the economy, business, society and individually."* [10].

The distinct phases associated with the Industrial Revolution started with the first phase, the First Industrial Revolution, dominated by steam, water, and mechanical production equipment. The division of labour defined the second phase, where the impact of electricity, mass production, and steam power usage to replace the intensive labour force and feverish economic model based on growth where the industrial era began. A Second Industry Revolution related to the extensive use of electricity and the development of automotive production emerged, followed by a Third Industry Revolution related to the interconnection between scientific research and their application in industry. Currently, we are witnessing how the unfolding of the Fourth Industrial Revolution – or Industry 4.0 that is surrounded by significant levels of uncertainty as we consider technology and scientific breakthroughs and their impact on sustainable development [11].

As we explore further the characteristics of the Industry 4.0, Rüttimann and Stöckl [12] identify core elements significant for our understanding of the learning process and how technological university learning models need to be reconsidered.

- Production: flexibility, dynamic manufacturing lines, smart product development for the three main actors related to the production outcome level of satisfaction: customer, employee, and the shareholders. The main shift resides in the flexibility of machinery interconnectivity and human mindsets. In the context of Industry 4.0, empowerment also moves the client in choosing and highly customising the product and the employee's empowerment is related to his recognition as a valuable element in the production process.
- Connectivity: Internet of Things (IoT) based manufacturing cell-based system, known under the paradigm of Cyber Physical Production System with an emphasis on "big data analytics, augmented reality, cyber security, cloud data management" [13].
- Empowering tools usage for rapid modernisation: mathematical models' usage in manufacturing and economic systems with human-based continuous improvement approach.

Fraga-Lamas, Varela-Barbeito, and Ferná [14] identify a new concept, Industry 5.0, that will follow Industry 4.0, as a revolution in the operation area of the industry. In this case, opposite to Industry 4.0, the focus is represented by research and innovation to increase sustainable production processes, with a strong emphasis on *"the well-being of the industrial workers that will be at the centre of the production process."* As such, Industry 5.0 seems to bring the human dimension of the economic process to the forefront by highlighting the importance of well-being. We question to which extent we might be able to connect the significance of thinking human first and how this can be reflected as part of our educational models that emerge as being a product that seeks to serve the needs of the labour market while forgetting *"the social, caring and affective networks."*

In this case of sustainable smart manufacturing systems, the Auto Identification technologies would play a vital role in providing automatic context data, a technology that still needs important developments in security assurance. Another critical component for Industry 5.0 would be guaranteed by Industrial Cyber-Physical Systems or the Industrial Internet of Things (IIoT) as a key for *"the digital transformation of manufacturing industries."* In the context of Industry 5.0, safety-critical cyber-physical systems (SC CPS), and industrial control systems. Ngo, DeAngelis, & Garcia [15] define human-based models to integrate into decision support systems of CPS implementation. Modelling human behaviour is based on digital big data collections using IoT and Auto-Identification technologies, artificial intelligence and human knowledge in modelling practices where the algorithms are improving, often based on the provided data related to *"the evaluation of physical and mental processes [that] guide the operator behaviour in system control"* [16]. An aspect that we might reflect upon is to which extent the human dimension is considered to enhance productivity levels and ensure that businesses can meet their economic and financial metrics. Undoubtedly, features of the human behaviour are becoming obviously important for the future, but fundamental questions and worries emerge regarding the purpose of human well-being to ensure economic goals. The knowledge and skills are stored to be translated into mathematical models to support a future smart factory with the focus on human well-being [14]. The model adaptation depends on the data collected from the human context. The better the skills, soft and hard, the better the chances to obtain a realistic model, depending again, for now, by the technical and personal skills of the human factor. From this point of view, the success of the next Industrial revolution depends on the knowledge and skills that will be developed and acquired through the educational process in a transdisciplinary approach where the interconnection of different fields is still to be discovered.

3.1 Knowledge and the Digital Economy

The combination of robots and human intelligence should be achieved under the magnifying glass of a human-centred approach to artificial intelligence with the introduction of digitisation in all economic sectors. The most important approaches are from the perspective of how education, training and lifelong learning can be reoriented towards the employers' needs and the labour market under the conditions of digitisation and how the content of education and training programmes should be adapted to form and upskill learners. Digital competences necessary in the framework of the fourth industrial revolution need to be complemented by the other seven European key competences. At the heart of the learning process, we identify the importance of literacy competences; multilingual competences; competences in science, technology, engineering, and mathematics; personal, social and learning to learn competences; citizenship competences; entrepreneurial competences; competences of cultural awareness and expression. Without the outlined competences we are imposing significant restrictions on our ability to work in environments where digitisation and robotics are emerging as critical players to support sustainable economic development [17]. The outlined competences complement the digital ones, emerging as essential as they stimulate the critical thinking needed to select information sources and understand new technologies. In Table 1 below, we offer some initial insights on relevant and updated research studies that highlight the challenges and opportunities associated with the fourth industrial revolution, the digital economy, and the knowledge economy. At EUt+ we are cognisant of the importance of examining the potential that technology offers, but we are also overly concerned about the challenges and problems that might emerge from its use.

Table 1. Challenges and opportunities of the Fourth Industrial Revolution, Knowledge, and Digital Economy

Authors	Challenges	Opportunities
Oke & Fernandes [18]	Teaching and learning retain its static character, despite the use of mobile (smart) devices and social media	Technology transforms learning and literacy only in combination with social and economic factors
	More than technology-driven change, disruptive innovation in higher education allows the boundaries between teaching and learning to blur through new modes of curriculum, new pedagogical models that bring new ways of teaching and new ways of learning	Artificial intelligence (AI) has a more active role
Xu et al. [19]	High-skilled jobs would be affected by machines and artificial intelligence, putting graduates at risk in the job market as they could lose out to machines capable of more sophisticated analysis and decisions	Knowledge management through the development of knowledge sharing strategies is imperative for the training of human resources
Scepanovič [21]	People can work from anywhere requiring new skills such as creative and critical interdisciplinary thinking while solving problems	Students can study in a project setting, rather than sitting in chairs for hours just listening and acquiring largely passive knowledge
Bonfield et al. [22]	Answers are needed on how institutions should design buildings, learning spaces, digital services and curriculum to best prepare the graduates of the future	Educational institutions apply subsets of artificial intelligence, such as machine learning, natural language processing, and computer vision, to improve student experience and teaching, learning, and assessment outcomes through personalised predictive analytics
Miranda et al. [23]	Rapid technological advancement and the need to develop essential skills in today's students encourages a development of technical, technological, analytical, and critical thinking skills	New knowledge is generated, and peer-to-peer information is transferred between colleagues, new innovative solutions are implemented and available technological resources are used

Technology and education are drivers of the digital transformation characteristic to the fourth industrial revolution through the lens of the new science of learning and Education 4.0 that holistically addresses:

"use of digital technologies, considering the specificities of students; adoption of organisational processes and practices in alignment with new social and work relationships; equip teachers with digital skills (do and be) to deal with native digital students; equip students with the technical, cognitive, social and emotional skills necessary for 21st century learning and work; and the adoption of innovative pedagogies focused on the transfer and acquisition of knowledge on demand to solve a problem or perform a task." [24, p. 288].

An option to enhance the learning experience could be provided through virtual and augmented realities. For better educational training programs, global companies such as Intel [25] and Adobe [26] are promoting VR as the future in STEAM education, underlining that these technologies are providing experiences that are not possible or can be difficult to understand in other circumstances. There are already on the shelf VR resources for entrepreneurial and innovation education [27], or for schools at undergraduate level [28].

The usage of AR and VR is extending dramatically towards new areas of critical usage, for example: e-health [29], automotive and maintenance [30], digital twin creation for object and system in cyber physical integration [31]. One can conclude that a drastic increase in technical skills for tool development in these specific areas is as needed as the augment in digital skills for usage.

Nevertheless, creativity is an essential human characteristic needed in Education 4.0. Powerful teaching tools such as visual learning, gamification, game-based learning, and project-based learning require teachers to become dynamic and more adaptive [32]. However, the growth of new knowledge and its increasing availability through digital media suggests that educational agents need to become more flexible and creative in their instruction to keep pace with future industrial innovation [33]. A big challenge that we face as educators and researchers as we consider the Fourth Industrial Revolution and our transition towards more sustainable economies and societies is the importance of knowledge and the digital economy. The connectivism approach and active learning through broad curriculum development, which should be engaged and student-centred, reminds us of the importance of individual student's needs and abilities, which should be appreciated socio-economically and academically.

4   Internationalisation and Cultural Clash

Along with the accelerated development of technologies, higher education institutions (HEIs) face a myriad of challenges resulting from the ever-increasing connectedness of our world. When economic, social, and cultural contexts are shaped by global trends as well as specific local ones, societies need to adapt and respond. For young populations, this often reflects dynamic expectations from education providers who are pressured to design strategies for a diverse and globally oriented student population. Internationalisation has thus become an integral component of the development strategies of most higher education institutions through which some of the most important goals are achieved: support for mobile students, providing professional global competences and global citizenship [34, 35]. Across Europe, universities have varying approaches to internationalisation, but recent initiatives try to further collaboration to engage students, cultivate and nurture research activities and shared learning practices that can help to accelerate the internationalisation of teaching, learning, research, and civic activities, to continue the Bologna Process and take the European Higher Education Area to a new level of integration and cooperation. The European Universities Initiative (EUI) is a policy instrument by which the European Commission fosters "excellence, innovation and inclusion in higher education across Europe." The higher education institutions created in the EUI, such as the European University of Technology (EUt+), prioritise mobility and exchange within the established European Alliances. However, as we grow and develop, we are engaging in a process where we share resources to innovate and reshape tertiary education, and we are in much need of resources to support our efforts. We are working at an educational framework that will offer joint qualifications, high-level research and educational models that respond to the societal needs of the Fourth Industrial Revolution, required digital skills, and the need to work towards education for sustainable development.

Integrating visions and approaches rooted in the local and national social, economic, and cultural models, the mission of European Universities is not without challenges. The EUI initiative has been criticised recently [36] for not being able to assist regional stakeholders in levelling the geographical imbalance between Western Europe universities participating in the initiative and the fewer Central and Eastern Universities participating, the latter also featuring fewer in coordination and steering of the alliances. The importance of working environments that integrate our rich European cultures presents a steep learning curve as we try to work together and find a way to communicate and value each individual and collective contribution to this ambitious project. In addition, governments and other national/regional authorities are not all equally committed to financially supporting the EUI. The outcome is that some universities are being privileged by having access to additional funding that contributes to the creation of a significant divide between involved universities as economic and power dynamics are at play. Rensimer and Brooks [36] show that the uneven funding reflects, in fact, conflicting approaches on the role and place of internationalisation initiatives versus efforts to support national higher education. Major concerns emerge as there is a huge risk of undermining the potential of the whole institutional approach as individual institutions' interests can take a central role in detriment to collaboration, cooperation, and the co-creation of knowledge. As an example, we can consider the case of the Netherlands, which chose not to additionally fund EUI, openly indicating that this internationalisation initiative can become elitist and, therefore, should not be supported at the expense of Dutch higher education (p.33). But to what extent does failing to fund educational projects and initiatives enhance and nurture the elitist dilemma that we are already facing? Education requires significant support and funding, and the idea of limited resources to support the development of our European universities is quite debatable and emerges as a potential failure to acknowledge the importance of developing our united and integrated European Educational Model.

Internationalisation of the curriculum is often a component of internationalisation strategy that involves the deepest and most widespread, systemic, transformation of universities [37]. Involvement in EUI triggers such changes at the level of curriculum development and creates co-curricular opportunities (i.e. joint degrees) for students. For teaching and research staff, the alliance networks underpin the growth of diverse disciplinary communities and communities of practice. The goals of an internationalised curriculum are closely interlocked with the development of intercultural competence. In fact, curriculum design with an internationalisation dimension must consider the integration of intercultural competence development as a specific learning outcome [38, 39]. In order to be able to deliver the wider promise of international education for Europe and our commitment to educate our students as global citizens that acknowledge their input as active actors for sustainability, we do need to consider our diversity, the richness of our cultures and how we can manage conflict as we find a way to work together. A more integrated curriculum for joint degrees, as envisaged by EUI requires harmonisation of viewpoints and approaches to all components: teaching, learning and assessment. Teaching staff involved in curricular design should therefore engage in the negotiation of disciplinary paradigms, re/consideration of emerging disciplinary paradigms and should be able to accept multiple and diverse perspectives on knowledge in and across disciplines [39]. Decisions on what should or should not be included in the curriculum are never neutral; wider local or national cultural bias often pervades the disciplinary culture, and, in particular, they tend to be dominated by Western approaches that hinder the contribution of non-Western countries. As Webb [40] observes, "content [...] does not arise out of a single cultural base but engages with global plurality in terms of sources of knowledge" (p.111). To avoid potential cultural clashes with adverse effects on cooperation in internationalisation of higher education initiatives, intercultural approaches must underpin all decision-making processes. Furthermore, intercultural competence development must feature as a priority of educational paradigms. In addition, diversity, inclusion, and collaborative and open learning environments are critical elements that we consider in the following section.

5 Learning Environments, Inclusion and Sustainable Education

Learning environments cannot be limited to academic walls; we are tempted to consider that the educational climate is enough to facilitate learning for our students because technology will support a proper transfer of information from the teacher to the student. However, education is not limited to the transfer of information; the role of the teacher and the student require to be reconceptualised, in a world of continuous evaluation and definition of multiple existential traits; the stringent need to reimagine the educational systems in order to survive on the earth, with the particularities of this volatile, complex and uncertain world, and against the damages of an economic model of education which generates violence and exclusion. The World Health Organization (WHO) reports depression as a mental disorder that affects more than 264 million people globally. Under these circumstances and in the context of the pressure of excelling the exams and assessments in order to face a competitive working and educational environment in which the pandemic period produced even more educational inequities [41], distressing trends have come to light as for example suicide is considered as second-highest leading form of death amongst 15–29 year olds [42]. Therefore, learning environments must cross beyond traditional university boundaries, technological equipment, and the development of digital skills; even if innovative learning environments are obviously significant and unprecedently required, we need to enhance and embrace more than ever "the social, caring and affective networks" [22, 56, 57]. Also, we cannot ignore the latest achievements in neuroscience and learning theories, which reveal that high-stress levels negatively affect the learning process and memory. More than that, learning is more effective when students have the ability to cope in an adaptative way with daily stress. Therefore, how we feel, and experience emotions correlate with the learn-ing process's quality and what and how much we learn. Even more, attention, memory and decision-making processes are framed within the emotion process and are aspects that we need to consider as part of the new science of learning [58, 59].

On the other hand, in the age of technology, we have to consider the new research on digital and virtual activities, which reveals that this kind of activity affects human behaviour. Individuals act differently when they are interacting with technology compared to face-to-face interaction. There are major problems associated with technology addiction as for example, "*smartphone addiction-type behaviours to being subjected to social technology, weapons of mass distraction*", which hijack attention, and then har-vest, profile, micro-target, monetise and subliminally manipulate" the user online [43]. Reflection on these elements points out not only the relevance of a human-centred app-roach in education, but the stringency of such an approach, education being essentially human. We argue on the need for a profound educational paradigm shift, a deep transfor-mation of mindsets and consideration of human well-being and security in the context of artificial intelligence, big-data and machine learning which raise ethical concerns. The focus on learning and the importance of innovative pedagogies to enable the creation of knowledge for living and considering philosophical and social thinking that emphasises potentials rejects determinism and expresses a flexible openness to new technologies and their value [5, 9]. *"The notion of "learning to become" also directs attention to the persistence of inequalities, continuing plagues of violence, and the increasing strains on a fragile planet – all of which demand that humanity become something it has not yet become"* [44].

In 2021, after three years of this UNESCO statement, a follow up report was published which presented the meaning of learning through beautiful words:" *learning means rais-ing the consciousness of multiple identities, needs and perspectives. We have to learn to become together*" [44]. In this regard and considering the importance of achieving a sustainable education that should be applicable to future generations, to children who are not born yet, we have to put the design of learning environments as a critical task for edu-cators. Learning environments should aim to integrate and support learners, they should communicate a space where everybody feels welcome, can contribute, and feels secure and valued. In HEIs such a learning environment has to address the gap between an ego-centric curriculum and more decolonised narratives and cultural diversity, highlighting our world's diverse nature. In order to put this in practice, academic staff is confronted with the need to learn how to succeed in diversity, how to act equitably, and how to be inclusive in an enlarged perspective, not only to include some students in learning activities, but to eliminate all barriers to accessing and participating in learning activities designed based on their different learning styles, backgrounds, personality profiles, straits, and vulnerabilities [45]. To accomplish constructive and welcoming learning environments, we need to think about the role played by educators and researchers and how they understand their relationship with students. The learning process has become a circular process of knowledge creation and co-creation. Therefore, we need support to develop a proper mindset in designing an adequate learning environment that acknowledges an active intervention from academic institutions that drive change, innovate, and actively contribute to transform our educational system.

At EUt+ we believe that the simple transfer of educational models from one country to another is unsuitable. We face different realities and have the privilege to enjoy different cultures and diverse working environments that can help us to develop a new vision for a new educational model. Therefore, the transposition of educational models from the west to our vision of the European Technological University will be unsuited to national contexts and the needs of the future global citizen [41]. We need to design and redesign our learning environments based on specific student learning outputs and guided by fostering Integration Inclusivity, Interconnectedness, Innovation, and Interculturalism [46].

We are looking to develop a disruptive educational model that embraces our differences so that we can create a positive educational environment that values every person and responds appropriately to different learning styles [54, 64, 65]. A learning environment in which a culture of trust, respect and belonging can be created, and cherished and where gratitude and equity emerge as valued guides to support innovative pedagogy with a focus on the best learning moments in which students perform and feel at their best. This is probably the best way to realise a lifelong learning attitude and a sustainable education that aligns with our vision to develop the foundations of our European Technological University.

6 Conclusions

The European University of Technology can benefit from the combination of learning sciences, digital skills, and an understanding of the needs driven by the digital and knowledge economy as we reflect and try to define our educational model. Our educational offer must reinforce learning skills that enable us to face the challenges of fast-growing services and products requiring significant digital skills to navigate modern life. Simultaneously, the academic community needs to find a balance between an educational offer that covers the labour market needs, and that does not forget that higher education should provide additional support to students, not limited to the needs and demands of the labour market. The fourth industrial revolution brings significant educational challenges as academics must identify how technological advances are integrated into the learning experience.

It is undeniable that the use of the Internet and web-based communication have come to occupy a central place in our contemporary society. The regular presence in the digital space has become an indispensable part of our daily lives, especially for the generation born after the year 2000, or, the so-called Generation Z, whose representatives, literally, before even being able to speak, demonstrate skilful use of a wide range of smart devices – iPhones, tablets, and computers. The ease with which children can barely walk, navigate the web to play electronic games, watch videos and listen to children's songs is truly amazing. Nonetheless, the ongoing research studies in the field continue to evaluate the effect of early mobile user devices on children's development and behaviour. As educators, our task is to ensure that we identify learning environments that nurture and foster our students' natural skills and support the development of additional ones.

Our research study explored some of the major challenges that we are facing as part of our global economy in need of an educational shift where we identify five different elements to be critical as we bring together the new science of learning within the demands of the fourth industrial revolution following a student-centre approach as follows:

a) The need for personalised learning environments. The learning experience should be constructed with the support of a scaffolding process where learners can benefit from technology and teachers' abilities according to their needs. Students' capabilities are considered as the learning material is provided to ensure a balanced approach that accommodates students' needs.
b) Our learning environments need to encourage diversity, flexibility, and adaptability. The learning experience should be supported by hybrid learning spaces where students benefit from in-person exchanges with their teachers/instructors. In parallel, learning environments must integrate online classes that are defined by interactive activities and blended classroom experiences that ensure that the human and technological elements offer multiple and diverse opportunities to students so that they can co-create, collaborate, and engage in problem-solving tasks.
c) Technology and innovation are critical players in developing hands-on learning activities to help students master their learning through active and cooperative learning environments as they acquire new knowledge and develop new skills.
d) The role of the student, teacher, and researcher is interchangeable and continuously evolving; feedback, communication and interaction emerge as vital to guide students through the learning process. A learning process that must integrate innovative assessment processes where technology can provide timely and constructive feedback to students helping to shape the learning experience and supporting students in the development of critical, analytical, and digital skills.
e) The development of social, caring, and affective networks cannot be neglected as part of our educational models. We are a social species that thrive by cooperating, collaborating, and working together. Our emotional, caring, and affective needs cannot be ignored as they are a critical element of our development and ability to grow.

The multicultural environment and the technology enhancements provide, through all the challenges and with all opportunities, the appropriate space to envision, design, co-create and develop the future of the next generations.

Acknowledgement. The current work was partially co-financed by the European Social Fund through the Human Capital Operational Program 2014–2020 through the project title: Entrepreneurial skills and excellent research in doctoral and postdoctoral study programs – ANTREDOC Project code: POCU/380/6/13/123927. Also, the current work is provided through the knowledge exchange and joint efforts within EUROPEAN UNIVERSITIES EPP-EUR-UNIV-2020 of ELaRA group members, mentioned as co-authors.

References

1. Meltzoff, A., Kuhl, P., Movellan, J., Sejnowski, T.: Foundations for a new science of learning. Science. **325**(5938), 2009 (2009)
2. World Bank: World Development Report 2018: Learning to Realize Education's Promise, Washington, DC (2018)
3. World Economic Forum: The Fourth Industrial Revoultion: What it means, how to respond 2(016)
4. Brynjolfsson, E., McAfee, A.: The Great Decoupling: An Interview with Eirk Brynjolfsson and Andrew McAfee (2015). https://hbr.org/2015/06/the-great-decoupling
5. Coetzer, J.-H., et al.: Enhancing human security by transforming education through science, technology, and innovations. Cadmus J. (2023)
6. OECD: Future of Education and Skills 2030. conceptual lerarning framework (2019). https://www.oecd.org/education/2030-project/teaching-and-learning/learning/skills/Skills_for_2030_concept_note.pdf
7. Schneegans, S., Straza, T., Lewis, J.: UNESCO Science Report: the Race Against Time for Smarter Development. UNESCO, Paris (2021)
8. European Union: Upcoming Lauch of the European Learning Model V3 (2022)
9. Licht, A., Tasiopoulou, E., Wastiau, P.: Open Book of Educational Innovation. European Schoolnet, Brussels (2017)
10. Schwab, K.: The Fourth Industrial Revoultion. What it Means and How to Respond (2015)
11. Bassi, L.: Industry 4.0: Hope, hype or revolution?. In: 2017 IEEE 3rd International Forum on Research and Technologies for Society and Industry (RTSI) (2017)
12. Rüttimann, B., Stöckl, M.: Lean and industry 4.0—twins, partners, or contenders? A due clarification regarding the supposed clash of two production systems. J. Serv. Sci. Manag. **9**, 485–500 (2016)
13. Islam, M.A.: Industry 4.0: skill set for employability. Soc. Sci. Human. Open. **6**(1), 100280 (2022)
14. FragaLamas, P., VarelaBarbeito, J., Ferná, T.M.: Next generation auto-identification and traceability technologies for industry 5.0: a methodology and practical use case for the shipbuilding industry. IEEE Access **9**, 140700–140730 (2021)
15. Ngo, S., DeAngelis, D., Garcia, L.: Modeling human-cyber interactions in safety-critical cyber-physical/industrial control systems. In: IEEE 19th International Conference on Mobile Ad Hoc and Smart Systems (MASS), Denver, CO, USA (2022)
16. Onyango, S.O.: Behaviour Modelling and System Control with Human in the Loop Stevine (2018). https://theses.hal.science/tel-01762668/document
17. European Commission: Directorate General for Education, Youth, Sport and Culture, Key competences for all: Policy design and implementation in European school education : final report. Publications Office (2022)
18. Oke, A., Fernandes, F.A.P.: Innovations in teaching and learning: exploring the perceptions of the education sector on the 4th industrial revolution (4IR). J. Open Innov. Technol. Market Complex. **6**(2), 31 (2020). https://doi.org/10.3390/joitmc6020031
19. Xu, M., David, J., Kim, S.: The fourth industrial revolution: opportunities and challenges. Int. J. Financ. Res. **9**(2), 90 (2018)
20. Anshari, M., Syafrudin, M., Fitriyani, N.L.: Fourth industrial revolution between knowledge management and digital humanities. Information **13**(6), 292 (2022). https://doi.org/10.3390/info13060292
21. Scepanovič, S.: The fourth industrial revolution and education. In: 8th Mediterranean Conference on Embedded Computing (MECO) (2019)

22. Bonfield, C.A., Salter, M., Longmuir, A., Benson, M., Adachi, C.: Transformation or evolution?: Education 4.0, teaching and learning in the digital age. Higher Educ. Pedagog. **5**(1), 223–246 (2020). https://doi.org/10.1080/23752696.2020.1816847
23. Miranda, J., et al.: The core components of education 4.0 in higher education: three case studies. Comput. Elect. Eng. **93**, 107278 (2021)
24. Oliveira, K.K.S., de Souza, R.A.C.: Digital Transformation towards Education 4.0. Informatics in Education (2021)
25. Intel: VR in Education: Advancing Learning through Immersive VR – Intel (2022). https://www.intel.com/content/www/us/en/education/transforming-education/vr-in-education.html
26. Babich, N.: How VR In Education Will Change How We Learn And Teach (2019). https://xd.adobe.com/ideas/principles/emerging-technology/virtual-reality-will-change-learn-teach/. Accessed 17 Feb 2023
27. Li, C.: The composition of VR system and the construction of VR teaching model in innovation and entrepreneurship education. In: 2nd International Conference on Information Science and Education (ICISE-IE), Chongqing, China (2021)
28. ClassVR: Virtual Reality for Schools (2023). www.classvr.com
29. Berciu, A.G., Dulf, E.H., Stefan, I.A.: PillCrop: the solution for the correct administration of medicine. IFAC-PapersOnLine **54**(15), 328–333 (2021)
30. Wundram, K.: Integrated AR-support for diagnoses and maintenance. In: AmE 2022 - Automotive meets Electronics GMM-Symposium, Dortmund, Germany, pp. 1–5 (2022)
31. Qi, Q., et al.: Enabling technologies and tools for digital twin. J. Manuf. Syst. **58**, 3–21 (2021). https://doi.org/10.1016/j.jmsy.2019.10.001
32. Puncreobutr, V.: Education 4.0: new challenge of learning. J. Human. Soc. Sci. (2016)
33. Costan, E., et al.: Education 4.0 in developing economies: a systematic literature review of implementation barriers and future research agenda. Sustainability **13**(22), 12763 (2021). https://doi.org/10.3390/su132212763
34. Wit, H.: Internationalisation of Higher Education in Europe and its assessment, trends and issues, 6 November 2022. https://www.eurashe.eu/
35. Wachter, B., Maiworm, F.: English-taught programmes in European Higher Education ACA. In: Papers on International Cooperation in Education (2015)
36. Rensimer, L., Brooks, R.: The European Universities Initiative: Championing Excellence and Inclusion? (2023)
37. Jones, E.: Internationalisation of the curriculum: challenges, misconceptions and the role of disciplines. In: Casper-Hehne, H., Reiffenrath, T., Bielefeld, W. (eds.), pp. 21–38 Bertelsmann Verlag (2017)
38. Byram, M.: Internationalisation in higher education –an internationalist perspective. On the Horizon **26**(2), 148–156 (2018)
39. Leask, B.: Internationalizing the Curriculum. Routledge, London (2015)
40. Webb, G.: Internationalisation of the curriculum: an institutional approach. In: Carroll, J., Ryan, J. (eds.) Teaching International Students: Improving Learning for All, pp. 109–118. Routledge, London (2005)
41. UNESCO: Global Education Monitoring Report 2021 – Central and Eastern Europe, the Caucasus and Central Asia – Inclusion and education: All means all, Paris (2021)
42. Chatterjee Singh, N., Duraiappah, A.K.: Rethinking learning: a review of social and emotional learning frameworks for education systems. UNESCO MGIEP, New Delhi (2020)
43. European Investment Bank: Life in cyberspace. Publications Office (2019)
44. UNESCO: Switzerland Contribution To Unesco's Futures Of Education Initiative. Futures of Education: Learning to Become How should what we learn, how we learn, and where we learn change in the future?, 12 April 2021. https://en.unesco.org/futuresof
45. OECD: Educational Opportunity for All: Overcoming Inequality throughout the Life Course (2017)

46. ICCGLOBAL: Future of education: learning to become initiative (2021). https://iccglobal. org/wp-content/uploads/World-Council-Futures-of-Education-Learning-to-Become-Initia tive_.pdf
47. OECD: The OECD Handbook for Innovative Learning Environments. OECD Publishing, Paris (2017)
48. Bucchianico, G., et al.: Inclusive higher education, Nakladatelství Gasset. In: Ceresnová, Z. (2018)
49. Banich, M.T., Compton, R.J.: Cognitive Neuroscience. Cambridge University Press (2018). https://doi.org/10.1017/9781316664018
50. OECD: Education at a Glance, 2022 OECD Indicators. OECD Publishing, Paris (2022)
51. ImmordinoYang, M.H., Damasio, A.: We feel, therefore we learn: the relevance of affective and social neuroscience to education. Mind Brain Educ. 1(1), 3–10 (2007). https://doi.org/ 10.1111/j.1751-228X.2007.00004.x
52. Paniagua, A., Istance, D.: Teachers as Designers of Learning Environments: The Importance of Innovative Pedagogis, Educational Research and Innovation. OECD Publishing, Paris (2018)
53. Harris, C., Straker, L., Pollock, C.: A socioeconomic related "digital divide" exists in how, not if, young people use computers. PLoS ONE 12(3), e0175011 (2017). https://doi.org/10. 1371/journal.pone.0175011
54. Johnson, A.M., Jacovina, M.E., Russell, D.E.: Challenges and solutions when using tech- nologies in the classroom. In: Crossley, I.S.A., McNamara, D.S. (eds.) Adaptive Educational Technologies for Literacy Instruction, pp. 13–29. Taylor & Francis, New York (2016)
55. OECD: Understanding the Digital Divide. OECD Digital Economy Papers, vol. 49m (2001)
56. Mubarak, F., Suomi, R., Kantola, S.-P.: Confirming the links between socio-economic vari- ables and digitalization worldwide: the unsettled debate on digital divide. J. Inf. Commun. Ethics Soc. 18(3), 415–430 (2020). https://doi.org/10.1108/JICES-02-2019-0021
57. Passaretta, G., Gil-Hernández, C.: The early roots of the digital divide: socioeconomic inequal- ity in children's ICT literacy from primary to secondary schooling. In: European Comission JRC Working Paper Series on Social Classes in the Digital Age, vol. 4 (2022)
58. UNESCO: Education for sustainable development. A Roadmap. UNESCO, Paris (2020a)
59. United Nations: United nations general assembly (2018). Decision 72/222. Education for sustainable development in the framework of the 2030 agenda for sustainable development (2017a)
60. United Nations: United nations general assembly (2018). Decision 74/223. Education for sustainable development in the framework of the 2030 agenda for sustainable development (2019)
61. World Economic Forum, "Bridging the digital divide between developing and developed Nations (2022)
62. Morales, L., Coetzer, J.-H., Barkoczi, N., Pop, L., Marian, C., Flynn, P.: A Circular Pedagogy for Higher Education (2022)
63. Pop, L., Barkoczi, N., Morales, L., Coetzer, J.-H., Marian, C., Flynn, P.: Circular Pedagogy for Smart, Inclusive and Sustainable Education. EUt+ ELaRA Working Paper Series (2022)
64. Kivunja, C.: do you want your students to be job-ready with 21st century skills? Change pedagogies: a paradigm shift from Vygotskyian social constructivism to critical thinking, problem solving and siemens' digital connectivism. Int. J. Higher Educ. 3, 81–91 (2014)
65. Voogt, J., Roblin, N.P.: A comparative analysis of international frameworks for 21st century competences: Implications for national curriculum policies. J. Curric. Stud. 44(3), 299–321 (2012). https://doi.org/10.1080/00220272.2012.668938

'How Do We Move Back?' – A Case Study of Joint Problem-Solving at an Interactive Tabletop Mediated Activity

Patrick Sunnen[1]([✉]), Béatrice Arend[1], Svenja Heuser[1], Hoorieh Afkari[2], and Valérie Maquil[2]

[1] University of Luxembourg, Porte Des Sciences 11, 4366 Esch-Sur-Alzette, Luxembourg
`{patrick.sunnen,beatrice.arend,svenja.heuser}@uni.lu`
[2] Luxembourg Institute of Science and Technology, Avenue Des Hauts-Fourneaux, 4362 Esch-Sur-Alzette, Luxembourg
`{hoorieh.afkari,valerie.maquil}@list.lu`

Abstract. The interactive tabletop activity 'Orbitia' aims at developing collaborative conduct among participants. We provide a detailed account of how a group of three participants jointly solve a problem in the Orbitia environment. In our conversation analytic case study, we analyze the situated processes at the group level of description to develop a better understanding of how problems are jointly solved in a group at an ITT-mediated activity and to gain design knowledge about inducing such episodes. More precisely, we identified six problem-solving moves: signaling a problem and accounting for it, formulating the problem and converging on a solution, seeking and identifying the competent first agent, co-instructing the first agent, assessing the solution(s), taking up a solution.

Keywords: interactive tabletop · collaboration · problem-solving · conversation analysis · case study

1 Introduction

Joint problem-solving can be a difficult matter and the mere joining of people's forces does not suffice unless people know how to collaborate. Hence, learning to learn and to work together must become an important goal in education and professional training. To support this enterprise, the design research project ORBIT [1] has developed the interactive tabletop (ITT) activity "Orbitia" that aims at developing collaborative conduct among participants [2–4]. Collaboration is understood here as "a coordinated, synchronous activity that is the result of a continued attempt to construct and maintain a shared conception of a problem" [5, p. 70].

In this paper we provide a detailed account of how a group of three participants jointly solve a problem in the Orbitia environment. In our case study we analyze "the situated processes that take place at the group level of description" [6, p. 542]. Thereby, we intend to develop a better understanding of the situated processes of problem-solving at a group level of description at an ITT-mediated activity and to gain design knowledge about inducing such episodes.

P. Zaphiris and A. Ioannou (Eds.): HCII 2023, LNCS 14040, pp. 149–162, 2023.
https://doi.org/10.1007/978-3-031-34411-4_12

2 Orbitia

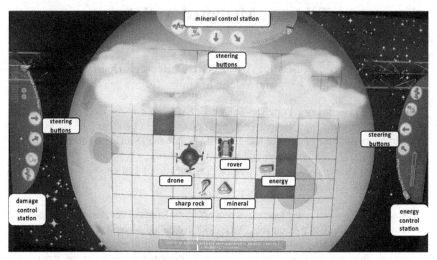

Fig. 1. Annotated screenshot of 'Orbitia'. Complementary responsibilities are distributed among the crew members: steering directions; damage control, mining & energy.

Orbitia is designed as a serious game where adult participants are acting as a space-mining crew on an imaginary planet (Fig. 1). The crew must collect minerals with a rover and rely on a camera drone for reconnaissance. Relying on pedagogical and design principles, several devices have been developed and implemented to induce collaborative conduct [3]. The relevant rover-steering-device (RSD) here consists of a rover with complementary control buttons distributed over three control stations (Fig. 2a). Two directions are missing and can only be taken through the composition of two other directions. Figure 2b shows the two ways to move north by one square, which becomes relevant in the analyzed extract.

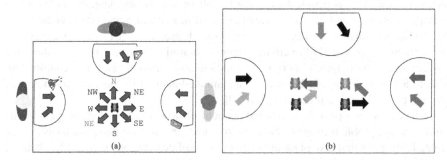

Fig. 2. RSD: (a) Distribution of directions (missing ones in red); for reasons of convenience the directions are represented by (inter)cardinal points (b) two ways of moving north by one square.

3 Joint Problem-Solving

In general, one speaks of a problem when there is a discrepancy between a current and a goal state, there is no ready-made solution [7], and the problem is considered worth solving [8]. Problem-solving then corresponds to finding the unknown [8] and can be undertaken as a joint endeavor. In the latter case, "to make sense of a problem together", participants must establish "common frames of reference", resolve "discrepancies in understanding", negotiate "issues of individual and collective action" and come to "joint understanding" [9, p. 404–5].

Unlike many other studies in this field, "we are not oriented toward theoretical hypotheses, statistical generalizations, individual mental representations, or sociocultural influences", rather we attempt to "understand the situated processes that take place at the group level of description in actual case studies" [6, p. 542]. To do this, we rely on an ethnomethodological conversation analytic (EMCA) inspired approach [10]. It has been shown that the latter approach has proven to be particularly suitable to address issues of design and collaboration [6, 11].

4 Setting and Study Design

The here analyzed excerpt is taken from the dataset of the first phase[1] of the project ORBIT. We considered the video recordings of the pilot study and three subsequent trials (14 group sessions lasting 30 to 40 min) and searched the data for moments where the participants explicitly discussed and reasoned among themselves on how to proceed. This frequently happened when they had identified a problem and were trying to solve it. In line with an emic approach (characteristic of EMCA), we interpret an incident as a problem when participants do so. Usually, one participant either verbally refers to an incident as a problem (for example, "we have a problem"), states the problem (for example, "so we don't know basically what is here"), or utters a response cry (for example, "oh shit" or "oh my God it's hard"), and at least one other participant then acknowledges the problem (for example, "ok"). So, the problem-solving episodes were not selected according to criteria "external to the interaction" but were "grounded in the discourse as structured by the participants" [6, p. 553]. We further found that 9 out of 20 episodes were related to the missing directions feature of the RSD (Fig. 2).

Since the RSD is one of our 'flagship' design features [3], we focused on the identified instances to investigate how it induces collaborative conduct by reconstructing how participants interactionally accomplish doing joint problem-solving. This means tracking "in detail the various conversational strategies and devices which inform and drive its production" [12, p. 114]. According to conversational analysis (CA), communication is sequentially organized. Sequences are ordered series of turns through which participants accomplish and coordinate an interactional activity. The most common type are dyadic adjacency pairs uttered by two different speakers producing one turn each; for example, a question creates a conditional relevance for an answer [13]. The "understanding of

---

[1] The Orbitia version of the first phase is designed to induce 'smooth' collaboration among the participants. In the second one, the underlying foundational rules are unexpectedly modified to put to the test participants' previously established collaboration procedures.

the preceding turn displayed by the current speaker" then constitutes "the basis for any other type of intersubjective understanding" [14, p. 156].

To investigate participants' problem structuring, Stahl [6] relies on EMCA and introduces, among others, the concept of 'discourse move'. Each move includes a base adjacency pair, which drives the interaction (several utterances of secondary structural importance may, however, introduce, interrupt, or extend the base pair) and is part of a longer chain of moves to accomplish discussing the conversational topic. In the here analyzed case, the topic corresponds to finding a way to reach a destination not directly accessible through the operation of one single steering command.

5   Analysis

The analyzed episode takes place about 3 min after the beginning. During this time, the three participants (Ava, Viv and Joe[2]) have explored Orbitia. In particular, they have discovered some of their competencies regarding the different control stations [2]. They now jointly designate a destination for the rover and decide to go there. More precisely, Ada suggests a potential destination for them ("on[3]") by pointing towards the visible mineral icon. Both Joe and Viv agree. Furthermore, Viv identifies and declares herself as the competent participant ("I", li 03), which is validated by Ada. In other words, they formulate and agree on a common project (reaching the square with the mineral). However, things will not proceed accordingly, as we are about to see.

Transcript 1.

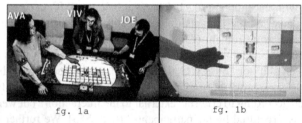

fg. 1a   fg. 1b

```
01   ADA: peut-être on doit être dans le: dans le (inaud.)
          maybe we have to be in the: in the (inaud.)
02   JOE: oui
          yes
03   VIV: O.K. je vais essayer
          O.K. I will try
04   ADA: oui
          yes
```

---

[2] French is a common language for these participants, although none of them is a native speaker.
[3] Grammatically speaking, "on" is a personal pronoun that is not attributed in a definite way; in social interaction, however, it is frequently used as a personal pronoun attributed to the collective ("we").

5.1 Problem-Solving Move 1: Signaling a Problem and Accounting for It

Viv pushes her straight arrow (S) twice. The rover moves accordingly and overshoots the targeted square with the mineral (fg. 2). This event is witnessed by all parties and triggers three overlapping reactions. First, Viv produces a response cry ("oh shit", li 07), followed by an account of her exclamation resp. Action ("I was too fast", li 07) [15, p. 693]. By uttering this imprecation, she produces a trouble alert signaling that there is some sort of problem. Through this elaboration, she links the trouble to something she previously did and went wrong (self-blame). Second, Joe acknowledges that something occurred ("o.k.", li 09); he reports what happened on the screen ("it was two times", li 09) and points to a consequence regarding his competency as the one overseeing energy ("it has taken way too much energy", li 10). So, he reads Viv's response cry as signaling trouble. However, by relying on an impersonal formulation ("that", li 09) and by referring to the rover ("it", li 10), he does not sanction Viv[4]. Rather, he produces a factual description ("<u>that</u> was two times", li 09), and an interpretation of what could be problematic here: the rover's excessive energy loss (li 10). Third, Ada starts smiling after Viv's self-declared mishap, thus acknowledging that something noticeable occurred.

Transcript 2.

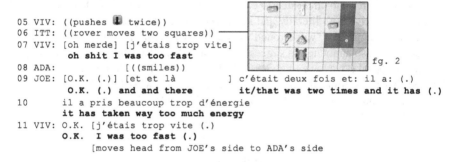

```
05 VIV: ((pushes ⬇ twice))
06 ITT: ((rover moves two squares))
07 VIV: [oh merde] [j'étais trop vite]
        oh shit I was too fast
08 ADA:          [((smiles))
09 JOE: [O.K. (.)] [et et là      ] c'était deux fois et: il a: (.)
        O.K. (.) and and there     it/that was two times and it has (.)
10      il a pris beaucoup trop d'énergie
        it has taken way too much energy
11 VIV: O.K. [j'étais trop vite (.)
        O.K. I was too fast (.)
        [moves head from JOE's side to ADA's side
```

fg. 2

So, they all concur that there is some kind of trouble. However, there is no shared understanding of the 'nature' of the problem yet. Viv causally links the trouble to her 'clumsiness' in the past, Joe highlights a consequence, and Ada does not utter an interpretation. Viv then chooses not to expand Joe's topic of excessive energy loss but restates her position (oversteering). So, the driving move here consists of calling out a problem and – beyond acknowledging – accounting for it. Next, we shall see how they start grasping the problem.

5.2 Problem-Solving Move 2: Formulating the Problem and Converging on a Solution

Here, Viv provides a formulation of the problem: "how do we move back" (li 12). Moreover, beyond specifying the problem ("how" to do it?), her phrasing also contains a solution ("move back") and points to its distributive character ("we"), meaning they

---

[4] He does not say, for example, "you pushed twice, and you made us lose too much energy.".

must all participate in solving the problem. In light of this statement, her wandering gaze (transcript 2, li 11) can be read as a lookout for the competent participant (who is the one who is able to move back). Both Ada and Joe acknowledge Viv's problem formulation by repeating it simultaneously, and their laughter further displays a shared interpretation of the problem situation.

Transcript 3.

```
12 VIV: O.K. [comment on recule
        O.K.  how do we move back
             [moves head from JOE's side to ADA's side
13 ADA:      [eh:
14 JOE: et [comment est-ce qu'on recule
        and how do we move back
15 ADA:    [comment est-ce qu'on recule
           how do we move back
16 VIV: [((laughs))
17 JOE: [((laughs))
```

Viv announces the proposal of a joint solution (li 18) and lays it out by performing circling movements with her right hand, first in the vertical (li 18) and then in the horizontal plane (li 21, fg. 3a-3c). So, she accounts for her understanding of the designed constraint that there is no direct steering option to directly move towards her (i.e., "back" from her perspective both literally and in the sense of undoing her previous 'mishap') and gesturally suggests a 'workaround' solution (by roughly pointing out a route for the rover). Ada also announces a suggestion ("maybe", li 19) and then verbalizes Viv's embodied proposal ("we have to go around", li 19). After displaying insight ("oh yes", li 20) Joe also aligns himself with the proposal. Finally, Ada confirms her endorsement of the workaround solution ("we have to go around", li 22) and verbally emphasizes the location ("there", li 22).

Transcript 4.

```
18 VIV: maintenant[on doit
        now       we have to
                  [((making turning gesture with hand in the vertical plane →))

19 ADA: peut-être [on doit faire le tour
        maybe     we have to go around
20 JOE:           [ah jo on doit faire le tour
                  oh yes we have to go around
21 VIV:           [(peut-être [on doit)
                  maybe we have to
                            [(((→moves hand around mineral in horizontal plane))
```

```
        fg. 3a  fg. 3b  fg. 3c
```

```
22 ADA: on doit y faire le tour
        we have to go around there
```

So, the participants jointly announce and ratify a solution. Ada's formulation carries the insight that the solution cannot be implemented by one participant alone and consists in a workaround. Indeed, the option of moving back directly is (by design) not available. The emerging solution of "moving back" (li 11–15) is multimodally transformed here into "going around." Thus, the problem-solving move we witness here is composed of posing the problem ('how to move back') and proposing a first approach to the solution ('going around'). Now, we will see how they begin to implement and specify the solution.

5.3   Problem-Solving Move 3: Seeking and Identifying the First Agent

While Joe starts objecting (li 23), Viv requests the information on who can move forward (li 24). While turning her head towards Ada resp. her station and pointing toward the target location for the rover (fg. 4a – fg. 4b), she refers to Ada and so provides herself with the requested information in the same turn. Ada overlappingly moves her left hand towards her steering controls and points to the NE-arrow (li 25), which moves the rover to the designated square (fg. 4b). Joe confirms ("yes", li 26) and points with his finger to ADA (fg. 5). Simultaneously with Joe's hand movement, Ada moves her finger between her control arrows (li 28, fg. 5).

Transcript 5.

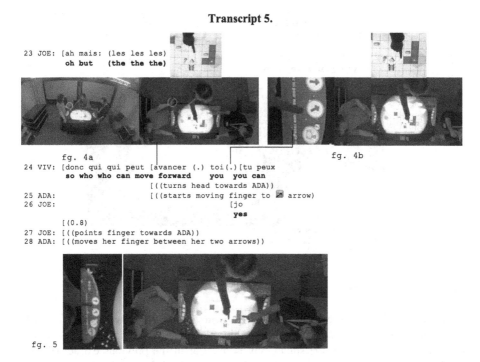

Viv's multimodal utterance (li 24) does the following work: the first step of the solution is formulated ("move forward" & *pointing to a target location*); the competent participant is sought and identified ("who" - "you" & *gaze/head movement*). Through Ada's overlapping action, she self-identifies as competent and accepts the attribution of being the competent first agent regarding movement. The just described action of seeking and identifying the first agent drives the interaction here. Despite this rather straightforward discourse move, Ada is facing somewhat ambivalent displays of direction giving. Viv points to the square that can directly be reached by Ada's diagonal arrow (NE), and Joe's straight pointing finger matches her straight-forward steering arrow (E). Ada reacts to this display of conflicting directions by positioning her finger between the two moving options (E & NE), thus expressing some hesitancy while remaining ready for both options.

5.4   Problem-Solving Move 4: Co-instructing the First Agent

In response to Ada's hesitant conduct, Viv prompts Ada to move forward (li 29). The latter shows no apparent reaction, so Joe multimodally instructs her to proceed (li 30), which is endorsed by Viv (li 32). Ada then asks for confirmation (li 33) and displays her understanding of 'move forward' by positioning her finger over the E-arrow (fg. 6). Both Joe and Viv validate (li 34 & 35), at least temporarily.

Transcript 6.

```
29 VIV: [tu peux avancer
30       you can move forward
         [((moves finger to home position))

31 JOE: [toi tu avances
          you you move forward
         [((whipping finger movement))

32 VIV: oui
         yes
```

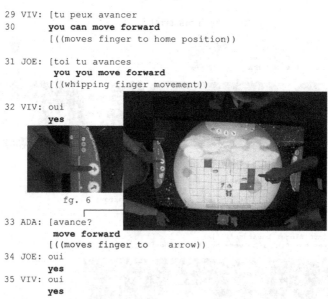

```
         fg. 6

33 ADA: [avance?
         move forward
         [((moves finger to    arrow))
34 JOE: oui
         yes
35 VIV: oui
         yes
```

So, we can observe here that the meaning of "move forward" is not straight forward. There appears to be some ambiguity here, which slows down the process. Does "move forward" mean moving to the square Viv pointed at in the previous extract (fb. 4), entailing pressing the NE-button, or literally moving forward from Ada's perspective, entailing pressing the E-button. Thus, the central move here is an instructed action that is not fully completed. A directive ("move forward") is issued to Ada, and by requesting a clarification, the addressee acknowledges that she is willing to operate the appropriate direction button. However, she does not carry out her part (yet), so the instructed action remains open and pending, which will trigger an evaluation of the procedure.

5.5 Problem-Solving Move 5: Assessing the Solution(s)

Transcript 7.

```
36 JOE: ou:
        or
37 VIV: ah non
        ah no
38 JOE: [une fois une (.) une fois
        one time one      one time
```

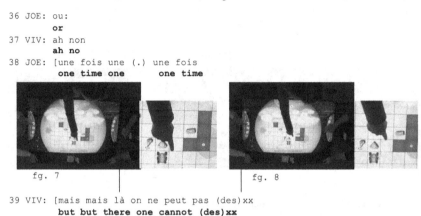

```
        fg. 7                          fg. 8
```

```
39 VIV: [mais mais là on ne peut pas (des)xx
        but but there one cannot (des)xx
```

The carrying out of the instruction to move forward remains pending. Ada is not moving "forward." So, Joe announces an alternative (li 36), but then – regarding Ada's finger position on the E-button – specifies his previous instruction by indicating the number of moves ("one time", li 38) twice. Viv initiates a repair (li37) and challenges Joe's directing by multimodally pointing (li 39, fg. 7 & fg. 8) to the constraint that they cannot move towards her from the position Joe is directing the rover to.

Transcript 8.

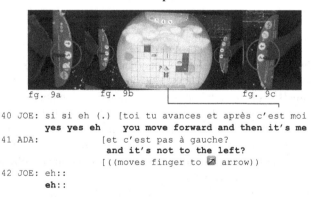

```
        fg. 9a        fg. 9b                      fg. 9c
```

```
40 JOE: si si eh (.) [toi tu avances et après c'est moi
        yes yes eh    you move forward and then it's me
41 ADA:              [et c'est pas à gauche?
                     and it's not to the left?
                     [((moves finger to ⬈ arrow))
42 JOE: eh::
        eh::
```

Joe reaffirms his suggestion ("yes yes"), repeats his previous instruction ("you move forward"), and adds the next prospective step ("and then it's me", li 40) to lay out the complete path and address Viv's concern. Ada reacts to the raised doubt by placing an alternative first move on the table. She moves her 'trigger'-finger to her second steering button (NE) and inquires whether they do not have to turn left (from her perspective, the NE-arrow can reasonably be described this way). Her option challenge Joe's instructing and the carrying out of her alternative would take the rover to the square Viv was previously pointing to (fg. 8). Joe shows some puzzlement and attempts to hold the floor ("eh:").

Transcript 9.

```
fg. 10                                          fg. 11
43 VIV: ah peut-être [si [on [peut aller comme
        ah maybe        if we can go like
                        [((makes diagonal hand movement))
44 JOE:                 [((looks at Viv's hand))
45 JOE:                     [un des deux (.) un des deux
                            one of the two (.) one of the two
        peu eh peu importe
        no eh no matter
46 ADA: j'essaie
        I try
47 VIV: [oui essaie
        yes try
        [((points to    ))
48 JOE: peu importe
        no matter
49 VIV: essaie
        try
50 ADA: ((pushes    ))
```

Viv now displays insight into Joe's variant and multimodally takes up his second move suggestion (li 43, fg.10–11). Upon noticing Viv's beginning hand movement (fg. 10), which parallels his NW-button, and Ada's hesitation, Joe points out that Ada can operate any of her two steering buttons. So, he validates both options as equally valid (li 45). Nevertheless, Ada still asks for confirmation (li 46), which is granted both by Viv, who expresses a preference by pointing to the NE-arrow (li 47), and by Joe (li 48). When Ada continues to hesitate, Viv prompts her one more time (li 49), and Ada takes up Viv's previously suggested option.

The outside observer can easily spot the two equivalent bi-step ways to "move-back" (see Fig. 2b) and that the controls to carry out both ways are equally distributed among Ada and Joe. However, the participants must first figure this out and jointly agree on how to proceed. Ada's display of hesitation leads to an exchange where the two options are multimodally displayed and recognized as being alike. So, both alternatives are on the table, and the designed first operator (Ada) is verbally given the choice, although Viv embodiedly endorses the NE-direction.

In other words, Joe's announcement of an alternative and Viv's objection indicate that the first step of the projected solution is put to the test. Viv then negatively assesses a potential second step by pointing out its non-feasibility (the unavailable N-direction). Joe then disagrees with her evaluation and explains why the challenged first step (E) is a valid option. Then follows a series of questioning, disagreeing, suggesting an alternative, and finally, two trajectories (E-NW, NE-E) are validated as equivalent. Now that both solutions are positively assessed, one must be taken up.

5.6   Problem-Solving Move 6: Taking up a Solution

After Ada has moved the rover, Viv validates the option chosen by Ada and induced by herself. She then points to the result ("but that's it", li 52) which also does the work of closing the first step (NE) and orienting to the next action [16]. Joe then goes on to identify himself as the competent participant and simultaneously announces and carries out the second move to reach the mineral (li 53). Viv overlappingly confirms this (li 54). After the rover has moved (li 55), she introduces herself as the next competent participant and highlights the next step by pointing to the means (the crane button) to perform it (li 56, fg. 12). Joe validates both Viv's competency and the next step (li 57). So, Viv picks up the mineral (li 58), Joe and Ada close the whole procedure (li 61 & 62).

Transcript 10.

They have now solved the problem of how to move back and concluded their initial project of collecting a previously designated mineral. Note that they do not just carry out the steps to move back in a coordinated and smooth way, but they also announce and substantiate the projected or carried out actions (instructing themselves and one another). By vocalizing their actions, they render the physical actions mutually accountable and establish a shared awareness of 'moving back'. So, what drives the interaction here, is the actual joint uptake of a previously outlaid solution. This steering maneuver(s) now become(s) a stable resource for their ongoing task accomplishment. Furthermore, the procedure will subsequently be adapted to move back by two squares by combining the NE and the NW steering buttons, enabling faster and more efficient progress if necessary (not shown here due to space limitations).

6   Conclusion

We thoroughly analyzed the multimodally embodied conduct of the three participants engaged in the ITT-mediated game activity Orbitia. So, we reconstructed how they interactionally accomplished jointly solving a problem in situ, or, in other words, we told the 'story' of their collaborative endeavor to do so. One participant signaled the problem ("oh shit I was too fast"), and they acknowledged resp. Accounted for it. So, they all became aware that there is a problem, and they could start developing a shared conception of it [5]. They did this by formulating it, and this formulation ("how do we move back") was also the first approach to an upcoming solution. The competent first agent was sought and identified, and her two co-players started instructing her. However, her hesitation in front of two 'floating' options lead to a positive assessment of both of them and an uptake of one.

By means of these six identified discourse moves, they coordinated themselves and constructed and maintained a shared conception [5] of their problem at hand, thus collaborated. That this particular sequential organization took place is "evidence that the machinery for its production is culturally available, involves members' competencies, and is therefore possibly (and probably) reproducible" [13, p. 50]. The additional instances of problem-solving, we have identified in our video corpus, are currently analyzed, and will contribute to the establishment of a collection of similar patterns of joint problem solving. Since nine instances are related to the RSD, we can reasonably assume that this design feature, especially designed for Orbitia [3], has a solid potential to induce collaborative problem-solving.

Note on Transcription Conventions.
ADA/JOE/VIV: participant speaking or doing the embodied action
ITT: action of interface
((pushing the button)) non-verbal conduct
? question
[overlapping talk
(0.6) timed pause
(.) micro pause
fg. frame grab

Acknowledgements. We thank the Luxembourg National Research Fund (FNR) for funding the ORBIT project under the CORE scheme.

References

1. Sunnen, P., Arend, B., Maquil, V.: ORBIT-Overcoming Breakdowns in Teams with Interactive Tabletops. In: Kay, J., Luckin, R. (eds.) Rethinking Learning in the Digital Age: Making the Learning Sciences Count, pp. 1459–1460. ISLS, London (2018)
2. Arend, B., Sunnen, P., Heuser, S., Maquil, V., Afkari, H.: Being a space mining crew: how participants jointly discover their complementary resources while engaging into a serious game at an interactive tabletop. In: Gomez Chova, L., Lopez Martinez, A., Candel Torres, I. (eds.) EDULEARN20 Proceedings, pp. 1769–1779. IATED, Valencia (2020)
3. Sunnen, P., Arend, B., Heuser, S., Afkari, H., Maquil, V.: Developing an interactive tabletop mediated activity to induce collaboration by implementing design considerations based on cooperative learning principles. In: Stephanidis, C., Antona, M. (eds.) HCI International 2020 - Posters, pp. 316–324. Springer International Publishing, Cham (2020). https://doi.org/10.1007/978-3-030-50729-9_45
4. Maquil, V., Afkari, H., Arend, B., Heuser, S., Sunnen, P.: Balancing shareability and positive interdependence to support collaborative problem-solving on interactive tabletops. Adv. Human-Comput. Interact. **2021**, 1–17 (2021). https://doi.org/10.1155/2021/6632420
5. Roschelle, J., Teasley, S.: The construction of shared knowledge in collaborative problem solving. In: O'Malley, C. (ed.) Computer Supported Collaborative Learning, pp. 69–97. Springer, Berlin (1995)
6. Stahl, G.: Investigation 25. structuring problem-solving. In: Stahl, G. (ed.) Theoretical Investigations Philosophical Foundations of Group Cognition. CCLS, vol. 18, pp. 541–567. Springer, Cham (2021). https://doi.org/10.1007/978-3-030-49157-4_25
7. Bransford, J.D., Steon, B.S.: The Ideal Problem Solver, 2nd edn. W. H. Freeman and Company, New York (1993)
8. Albanese, M.A., Dast, L.C.: Problem-based learning. In: Huggett, K.N., Jeffries, W.B. (eds.) An Introduction to Medical Teaching, pp. 57–68. Springer, Dordrecht (2014). https://doi.org/10.1007/978-94-017-9066-6_5
9. Barron, B.: Achieving coordination in collaborative problem-solving groups. J. Learn. Sci. **9**(4), 403–436 (2000)
10. Moore, J.: Ethnomethodology and conversation analysis: empirical approaches to the study of digital technology in action. In: Price, S., Jewitt, C., Brown, B. (eds.) The SAGE Handbook of Digital Technology Research, pp. 217–235. Sage, London (2013)
11. Koschmann, T.: Conversation analysis and collaborative learning. In: HmeloSilver, C.E., Chinn, C.A., Chan, C.K.K., O'Donnell, A. (eds.) The International Handbook of Collaborative Learning, pp. 149–167. Routledge, New York (2013)
12. Hutchby, I., Wooffitt, R.: Conversation Analysis. Polity Press, Cambridge (2008)
13. Psathas, G.: Conversation Analysis. Sage, London (1995)
14. Peräkylä, A.: Conversation analysis. In: Seale, C., Gobo, G., Gubrium, J.F., Silverman, D. (eds.) Qualitative Research Practice, pp. 153–167. Sage, London (2007)

15. Bert, M., Bruxelles, C., Etienne, C., Mondada, L., Tesston, S., Traverso, V.: Oh: oh là là, oh ben...', les usages du marqueur 'oh' en français parlé en interaction. In: Durand, J., Habert, B., Laks, B. (eds.) Congrès mondial de linguistique française, 17 pages. Institut de Linguistique Française, Paris (2008)
16. Haileselassie, A.: Voilà, an orientation shift marker in modern French discourse: a conversation analytic perspective. Dissertation. University of Illinois, Urbana (2015)

Designing a Pedagogical Strategy for the Implementation of Educational Technology in Collaborative Learning Environments

Tord Talmo[1]([⊠])[iD], Robin Støckert[1], Begona Gonzalez Ricart[2], Maria Sapountzi[3], George Dafoulas[4], George Bekiaridis[3], Alessia Valenti[5], Jelena Mazaj[5], and Ariadni Tsiakara[4]

[1] Norwegian University of Science and Technology, Trondheim, Norway
{tord.m.talmo,robin.stockert}@ntnu.no,
europrojects3@fygconsultores.com
[2] FyG Consultores, Valencia, Spain
[3] Active Citizens Partnership, Athens, Greece
[4] Middlesex University, London, UK
{G.dafoulas,a.tsiakara}@mdx.ac.uk
[5] CESIE, Palermo, Italy
{alessia.valenti,jelena.mazaj}@cesie.org

Abstract. Educational Technology (Ed. Tech) can provide different approaches to our learning designs and engage and motivate students to achieve their academic aims. However, few efforts have been made to use response tools in collaborative settings systematically. It has been argued that removing the social factor in a collaboration, i.e., the ability to micro-communicate and socially interact, makes it challenging to enhance the learning experience. This article investigates a possible pedagogical strategy to mitigate the potential adverse effects of moving the collaboration into an online or hybrid environment. The article aims at determining which pedagogical strategies are necessary to implement to heighten the learning outcome from collaborative work when using Ed. Tech. The results are extracted from previous research in the project iLikeIT2 and quantitative and qualitative data obtained through instructor training in four different countries with 46 participants. The data is analyzed according to codes and interpreted in the research group. The results provide recommendations on what to consider when using Ed. Tech in collaborative settings. For instance, how to design groups, how to do assessments, the type of facilitation needed, the amount of individual work within the group, and more.

Keywords: Education Technology · pedagogical strategy · collaboration

P. Zaphiris and A. Ioannou (Eds.): HCII 2023, LNCS 14040, pp. 163–181, 2023.
https://doi.org/10.1007/978-3-031-34411-4_13

1 Introduction

The 21st Century will include digital tools in learning environments at all levels of the educational system, also within higher education institutions in Europe. In addition, digital strategies on governmental and international levels are shaping and transforming our digital future within education.

Digital tools with innovative functionalities, ICT expertise, and various infrastructures and platforms enable students and instructors to explore and investigate new ways of interaction. At the same time, one can distribute and manage learning and teaching differently than earlier. However, these new possibilities require a higher focus on learning design and pedagogical approaches to maximize the potential of the tools.

New digital tools also demand that instructors and experts worldwide acquire new skills and competencies to take full advantage of the innovations to adapt, improve and sometimes change their existing methodological approach. When introducing Educational Technology (Ed. Tech) in modern learning environments, in-class or online, one always needs to keep both these aspects in mind. Technology can enhance the learning experience in various ways, heightening motivation, improving communication, creating engagement, and more. However, one is still most interested in ensuring a better student learning outcome in a learning environment. Technology does not work without pedagogy; therefore, it is necessary to work with both technology and pedagogy simultaneously. Including expertise from different areas of the educational system, like students, instructors, AudioVisual (AV) personnel, and IT, should be the standard when working with Ed. Tech.

The study presented in this article aims to determine which pedagogical strategies are necessary to implement to heighten the learning outcome from collaborative work when using Ed. Tech.

2 Background

Digitizing has often been used to move from one medium to another without changing or adapting the content: Same content, new wrapping/mode of delivery. In other words, technology is a direct substitute/digitized version of traditional activities and materials with no functional change. This statement coincides with the first level in the SAMR – model [1]. Furthermore, the higher levels in the SAMR- model describe enhancement, modification, and redefinition of educational practices and the creation of new tasks due to digital tools/technology. There are also other models for connecting pedagogy and technology, showing that the challenge is real. Still, a literature review shows that the area is still not sufficiently explored [2].

Hence, one needs to investigate further which functionalities in the new technologies can improve existing pedagogical practices and how pedagogical practices can improve the development of new functionalities in technologies. Traditional methods are in use for a reason; they work, and therefore innovative technology needs to be different and bring something new to the table to have an effect. Ordinarily, traditional exercises and activities have mainly been copied and pasted into the digital form, with obvious advantages of distance learning and faster distribution of materials and tasks to the students, allowing students to be more effective. However, there has been too little focus on applied pedagogy when using technology in learning environments. As the 21st-century technological revolution has changed our lives, the view on digitalization has changed accordingly. Digital tools and skills can change the concept of time, place, and format, enabling "on-the-fly" learning and ownership of the learning process and improving motivation and interest [3]. Utilizing these effects can create new and exciting learning environments that can improve traditional and conservative pedagogical approaches, for instance, considering how one conducts group work.

Modern technology provides new opportunities, like active collaborative learning approaches, fast access to learning materials, and possibilities to investigate materials in a new way. And instant access to an increasing amount of external sources. Consequently, the students can be active in setting the terms for communication and interaction in the classroom. Obtain a clearer view of their knowledge and perception, and maybe even better their self-regulation of learning processes. These new opportunities do not mean that digital tools solve all problems or even make it easier to be a teacher; on the contrary. The need for a pedagogically and digitally competent instructor is even higher today than ten years ago. Therefore, one must find ways to integrate the technology with existing knowledge and expertise. Otherwise, it will only cost lots of time and effort without much gain.

We know it is often difficult in a classroom to get students involved in discussions with peers and the teacher. Some students are seldom able to raise their voices, discuss, or enhance their analytical and social skills in an academic environment. There have been and are many initiatives in order to overcome this challenge. Educational technology is "the combined use of computer hardware, software, and educational theory and practice to facilitate learning" [4]. It has the advantages of involving students, raising engagement and motivation, enhancing peer learning, and ensuring easy diagnosis for the student groups when used correctly [5]. It also provides the lecturer with possibilities of facilitating the usage of EdTech, giving immediate feedback to the group, and it should be easy to integrate into existing lectures.

Collaborative work has the advantages of enhancing social skills, redirecting educational and social strategic goals for the students, and enhancing the learning environment [6, 7]. Collaborative learning is nothing new, neither in work life nor higher education, and it has gained interest in recent years, often connected to concepts of active learning [8]. Allowing students to learn from peers, refine their arguments in a "safe" environment, and take active control of their learning process is something that all lecturers seek. There are several ways to perform collaborative learning in class and online, but they should all caretake the student's various needs to achieve the highest possible learning outcome from these activities. In order to have a successful implementation of online learning environments, it is necessary to encourage students to actively participate and create a sense of belonging to a community of learning. "In the new culture of learning, people learn through their interaction and participation with one another in fluid relationships that result from shared interests and opportunity" [9]—implying that the pedagogy behind the activities is even more crucial than before. This paper's essence is how to combine new and innovative Ed. Tech with pedagogical strategies.

2.1 iLikeIT2

The results presented in this paper are part of the Erasmus + co-funded project "Learning Through Innovative Collaboration Enhanced by Educational Technology (iLikeIT2)", running from 2020 to 2023 [10]. This paper elaborates on one of the four significant outcomes of the project: The pedagogical strategy for implementing Educational Technology in a collaborative learning environment.

The project iLikeIT2 focuses on sharing innovative practices in the field of education and, in particular, creating a collaborative learning platform that enables computer-supported cooperative learning functionalities, including communication, coordination, and collaboration tasks [11]. The platform functions mainly as a response tool that builds on research done throughout the three years the project has been running. To build a functioning prototype, it is necessary to (i) identify different aspects of collaborative learning that can support students in their learning, (ii) determine those functionalities that are necessary for enhancing collaborative learning processes, and (iii) design a platform that can support instructor-student-group collaboration, communication, and coordination. These elements are the essential parts of a system that might enhance the learning effects of introducing Ed. Tech in a learning environment.

2.2 Previous Research

In a previous study in the project iLikeIT2, the focus was on functionalities inherent in digital tools and their ability to facilitate better collaborative work [12]. The study based its theoretical framework on ideas of Computer Supported Collaborative Learning (CSCL). CSCL has been proven in previous studies to improve "student motivation and critical thinking" [13]. During the early years of shaping CSCL, Lehtinen et al. (1999) argued that "there are not too many well-controlled experiments which could answer the questions concerning the wider applicability of CSCL in normal classrooms and the added value of computers and networks in comparison to collaborative learning environments without technology" [14]. Of course, there has been a radical improvement in the CSCL framework since the beginning of this millennium. The refinements have shown six categories essential for developing functional tools for collaborative work.

- Delivery – we believe it is necessary to enable instructors and learners to collaborate and communicate without interrupting learning delivery, such as: A teaching presentation, demonstration of an application, use of a browser to show a website, display of visual content or video, and sharing files.
- Interaction – we determined that the leading exchanges between instructors and learners during a teaching session would be assessment, questioning, and polling.
- Learner support – we anticipated that learner support during scheduled sessions is affected by the emphasis on covering certain content. Therefore small interventions should be driven by the instructor's ability to access statistics about the entire class's progress, the performance of certain groups, and the achievement of individual learners.
- Communication – we expected that instructors and learners would use either audio or chat functions to exchange information during a session.

- Collaboration – we determined that collaboration would require team formation and allocating roles.
- Coordination – we established that instructors would need to coordinate the learning activity by (i) reflecting on whether specific tasks need improvements, (ii) appraising which topics are challenging for the learners, (iii) testing which questions are appropriate for the session, (iv) evaluating whether groups perform according to certain thresholds and (v) assessing individuals' knowledge and understanding [12].

Table 1. Areas identified as essential for improving collaboration when using Ed.Tech

CSCL categories	Areas of interest	CSCL categories	Areas of interest
Delivery	Time efficiency & control Split screen Visuals Dynamics Misuse Cost & fees Connection	**Communication**	Sharing Communi-cation Regularity Messaging system
Interaction	Recording Learning effect Responsibility Teacher view Statistics/results	**Collaboration**	Peer learning Collaboration Indicating uncertainty Roles
Learner support	Initiation Preparation Control system for the moderator Learning design	**Coordination**	Collaboration/ Assignments Coordination Grouping Teachers' preparation

In order to figure out what instructors and students found useful when using Ed. Tech as a collaborative tool, the study first performed pilots on different functionalities using different tools and distributed a questionnaire to all involved informants. Secondly, the study conducted a reflectional conversation with 31 participants (11 students and 20 instructors). Finally, the study identified 28 areas of interest within the six defined CSCL categories based on the results.

These areas provide insight into technological features necessary for developing a tool that aids collaboration and academic achievements in such a work. Nevertheless, technology is nothing without pedagogy, and when incorporating Ed. Tech in a collaborative setting, one needs to analyze and design the work pedagogically. Thus, there is a need for a pedagogical strategy when implementing Ed. Tech in collaborative learning environments.

2.3 Theoretical Framework Pedagogical Strategy[1]

The pedagogical strategy includes a theoretical framework. In order to design the framework, the consortium has identified key factors and categories necessary to consider when working with Ed. Tech and collaborative work. The following elements have been identified as necessary. However, in this paper, they are only mentioned in order to frame the included data, interpreted and analyzed to expand results underlining the research aim:

1. Educational technology as a part of Higher Education
2. Learning environments in a modern age
3. Mobile learning
4. Response technology
5. Active learning
6. Collaborative learning
7. Digital competencies
8. Formative assessment
9. Moods of delivery, mainly focusing on face-to-face, hybrid and online moods

These nine areas frame the idealization of a collaborative tool with functionalities that might enhance the learning outcome of collaborative work. Within the frame, a teacher/instructor needs to build learning designs, cases, aims, and more to utilize the effects digital tools might provide in a modern learning environment. The question remains in which areas are essential to consider and how to redefine strategy when implementing Ed. Tech in collaborative work?

In the following, we will focus on pedagogical aspects that traditionally are discussed when doing collaborative work, and the study also shows what both theory and real-life instructors claim to be more or less critical in this case.

3 Methodology

In order to ensure data that reduced the bias, it was decided to use a three-stage methodology in the study. First, the consortium wanted quantitative and qualitative data from the research, and the methodology should enhance results from previous phases in the project. It was also crucial that the data collected should aid the building of a prototype of a response tool under construction, which would be piloted according to the methodology at a later stage in the project.

3.1 Literature Review

The consortium started with an integrative literature review [15]. Previous research in the project had focused on how Educational Technology can best enhance collaborative work and which functionalities need to be present to make the tool work positively for the collaborative work (see chapter 2.2 Previous research). The main results from this research showed 28 areas of importance when using Ed. Tech in collaborative learning

---

[1] The full strategy can be retrieved from the homepage of iLikeIT2 [10].

environments. These areas were thus the basis for developing a pedagogical strategy for implementing Ed. Tech in collaborative settings. In order to investigate which pedagogical aspects were most valid for the best integration possible, the consortium decided that an integrative approach was most suitable when conducting the literature review.

The searches was based on the keywords "collaboration", "communication", "coordination", "Educational Technology," and "pedagogy". However, the search was revised to "collaboration + Educational Technology" due to many potential hits. The findings were then related to the data collected previously in the project.

The data collected from the integrative literature review was interpreted using qualitative content analysis [16]. As described previously, five experts from different countries collected articles from different databases. In the abstracts from the articles, the researchers looked for combinations of "collaborative work", "Educational Technology" and "pedagogy/didactics". However, only a few articles matched all requirements, and some were included for the theoretical framework in the pedagogical strategy.

3.2 Expert Discussion

Results from the integrative literature review were discussed in the consortium, moderated by the authors of this paper. The consortium includes researchers, teachers, programmers, AV experts, and stakeholders involved in and working with Ed. Tech for several years. Hence, the consortium is considered an expert group on the subject. Therefore, the discussions obtained a multifaceted view and shared experiences to caretake all stakeholder opinions. The discussions were structured as small group discussions [17]. The discussions were based on principles developed by Vennebo and Aas (2019), called Leading professional group discussions (LPGD).

The process for finding elements from the literature that were influential for the pedagogical approaches to be implemented consisted of four stages; 1) setting the stage, 2) Examining, 3) Interpreting and 4) considering results [18]. The discussions identified fifteen elements as most important when achieving increased learning outcomes from collaborative work. The elements were also considered vital when designing collaborative work in different learning environments; face-to-face, hybrid mode, and online environments.

3.3 Instructor Training

To ensure the results were adequate, they needed to be validated. This result will be a strategy and pedagogical approach for the instructor in the project. Therefore it was necessary to include more voices from these types of end-users. The consortium designed and held five instructor training activities in four countries (Norway, Italy, Greece, and Spain), focusing on using Ed. Tech in collaborative settings. In total, 46 instructors were involved.

The training consisted of a project presentation and an introduction to both Ed. Tech and collaborative work, and the practical use of a tool of the trainer's choice. The last part consisted of a questionnaire and discussions on how to use Ed.Tech in collaborative learning environments.

Data collected from the instructor training were gathered and included in the work with the pedagogical strategy. During the training, teachers (and some other participants, consultants, and IT employees) were presented with a case-based survey in three parts.

- Part A was designed to get the participants in the right mood, asking for individual perceptions of the importance of 12 elements when doing collaborative work. The participants were asked to rate the importance on a Likert-scale from 1–5, 5 being very important.
- Part B was directed toward the individual usage of Ed. Tech when lecturing. The participants were asked 12 questions to be answered with yes or no.
- Part C consisted of three allegations concerning the central elements of collaborating with Ed. Tech. that the participants needed to discuss. One of the involved participants collected notes from the discussion, and all the collected data was submitted to the consortium for processing

4   Results

In the following, we will present the instructor training's results and discuss them according to the background materials presented in parts 1 and 2 of this article.[2]

4.1   Quantitative Results from Instructor Training

As mentioned earlier, part A of the questionnaire was individual and designed to get instructors into the mindset of collaborative work in a learning group.

Table 2. Results from answers to the questionnaires part A

Part A	Identify, on a scale 1 (low) – 5 (high) Your perception of the importance of the following elements when doing collaborative work	Average score	Score category
Coordination	The roles allocated to group members	4,04	**4,35**
	The division of tasks within the group	4,37	
	The possibility of interaction between the group members	4,76	
	The possibility of storing and sharing information between members	4,22	
Cooperation	The infrastructure (i.e. classroom set-up, breaks, comfort, number of members, and more) of the group context	4,09	**4,29**
	The ability to gain insight into other members' ideas and thoughts	4,26	
	The ability to comment on other members' ideas and thoughts	4,33	
	The possibility to think together, visually or orally	4,46	
Communication	The possibility of discussing content	4,54	**4,24**

(*continued*)

[2] The quantitative results from this article has also been discussed in a smaller format in an article presented at INTED2023, to be held in Valencia, Spain 6th – 8th March 2023.

Table 2. (*continued*)

Part A	Identify, on a scale 1 (low) – 5 (high) Your perception of the importance of the following elements when doing collaborative work	Average score	Score category
	The ability to micro-communicate (i.e., mimic, sighs, smile, and more)	3,78	
	The possibility of indicating that you are uncertain of something	4,28	
	The possibility of indicating that you want to say something	4,35	

Part B of the questionnaire was designed to get participants to reflect on their use of Educational Technology in general, both the software and the functionality inherent in the software.

Table 3 Results from answers to the questionnaires part B

Part B	Indicate your usage of educational tools for collaboration by answering yes or no to the following questions	Numbers Y/N	Score category
Coordination	Do you use an LMS or similar to upload curricular elements?	36/10	**145/39**
	Do you send texts/e-mails/notifications to students via an LMS or similar?	34/12	
	Do you collect answers/opinions using an educational tool during lectures?	36/10	
	Do you allow students to organize group-work digitally?	39/7	
Cooperation	Do you use any type of shared screen to cooperate with students and/or colleagues?	35/11	**129/55**
	Do you use chat functions to cooperate/talk with students or colleagues?	41/5	
	Do you allow students to use social media to cooperate in lectures?	25/21	
	Do you use animations/GIFs or similar to illustrate your talking points in a lecture or with student assignments?	28/18	
Communication	Do you have the ability to discuss content digitally with your students?	42/4	**141/43**
	Do you use an educational tool that allows you to monitor the student's progress during a lecture?	26/20	
	Do you allow students to digitally post anonymous/private questions during a lecture?	32/14	
	Do you allow students to raise their hands digitally during a lecture?	41/5	

4.2 Qualitative Results from Instructor Training

Qualitative results are collected through a discussion monitored by an expert in the consortium. The participants were divided into groups of approximately five participants at each training and asked to discuss and comment on the following three statements:

1. It is essential to have a collaborative setting where group members are physically present and close to one another.

2. Educational technology can enhance any type of collaborative work, both in class and in an online/hybrid environment.
3. Videoconferencing is the online environment that best resembles physical presence. Thus, it is the only way to solve a problem when collaborating online.

The participants discussed one and one statements and tried not to progress until all topics were fully debated. During the discussion, the expert was supposed to monitor passively, only providing insight or questions if the discussion was at a dead end or on the wrong track. One of the involved participants was asked to take notes of the discussion, refine them, and send them to the consortium [19] to reduce the possible sources of error in collecting data. It negatively impacts the data if the survey designers interfere too much; this could lead the participants in a specific direction in their discussion. The same is the case if the facilitators themselves take notes. It could lead to only favorable notes being registered. The facilitator naturally took their own notes, and after the training, the data has been interpreted and aligned with the notes from the facilitator. There has been no need to remove any data. The authors have not corrected spelling mistakes in the delivered materials (Fig. 1).

Fig. 1. Wordcloud illustrating the data provided from instructor training

The qualitative data was later processed through the NVivo programme [20]. All comments and keywords have been collected by participants in the five trainings throughout Europe. The document has been included in NVIVO three times to reduce bias. One researcher has been doing the interpretations of the materials, and the results presented in 2–5 are based on the codes created by the research group.

Previous research indicates that the three C's (Communication, Collaboration, Coordination) frames collaborative work, including Ed. Tech in a sensible way and functions well for designing a new collaborative software [21, 22]. In the project iLikeIT2 this has been the fundament for all the work being done. Therefore, it was natural that real-life instructors' comments were also interpreted and analyzed according to these three keywords.

In Fig. 2, we can see the distribution of results coded according to the three C's: Collaboration, communication, and coordination.

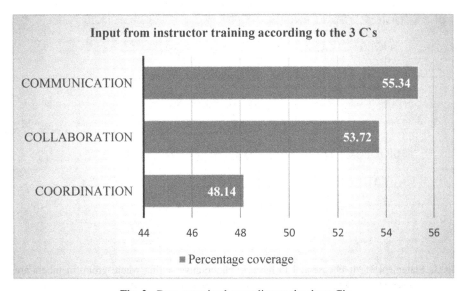

Fig. 2. Data organized according to the three C's

These codes do not give us much and show no significant differences considering the three C's. However, it says that instructors consider collaboration, communication, and coordination critical when discussing Ed. Tech in collaborative learning environments.

Analyzing the word-cloud and connecting the data to the theoretical framework and literature review, it seemed that some categories were more interesting than others. We, therefore, processed the data two more times in NVIVO. As a result, seven categories were identified; 1) Digital competencies, 2) Efficiency, 3) Modes of delivery, 4) Pedagogical advantages, 5) Pedagogical challenges, 6) Tools – advantages, and 7) Tools – challenges.

Figures 3, 4 and 5 shows the distribution of references coded to each category, and Table 4 summarizes the findings throughout the statements.

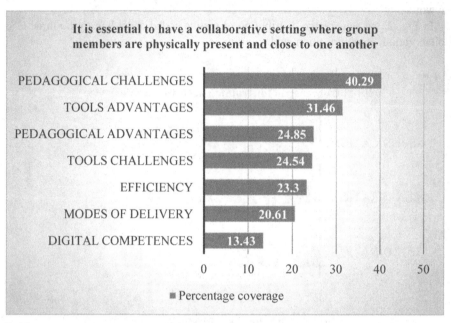

Fig. 3. Statement 1: "It is essential to have a collaborative setting where group members are physically present and close to one another" coded according to categories

To verify the results, the data was analyzed a third time to see if there was any significant difference between the categories, and how often they were mentioned in the materials. As seen in Table 4, the instructors has been led to think about digital tools, and their inherent advantages (27%) and challenges (12%), but there are also a lot of discussions about pedagogical advantages (16%) and challenges (15,5%) in the discussions (Tables 1, 2 and 3).

It was expected that instructors would be concerned about different modes of delivery, i.e., F2F, hybrid, and online modes. Considering we have experienced two years of pandemic conditions and learned a lot about both online and hybrid learning delivery, it was anticipated that instructors would also be aware of this duality in collaborative settings. However, 7,5% of the comments mentioned "modes of delivery", which is lower than expected. It indicates that collaborative learning environments revolve more around pedagogics and structures than physical rooms and environments. Still, instructors are very aware of the pitfalls in different modes. Some of these will be commented on later in this section.

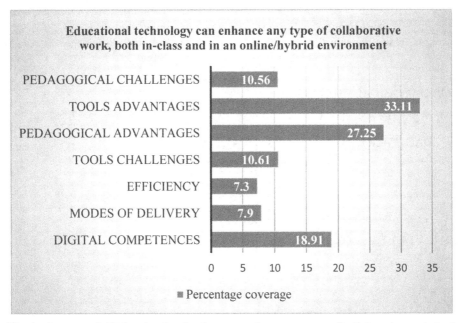

Fig. 4. Statement 2: "Educational technology can enhance any type of collaborative work, both in-class and in an online/hybrid environment" coded according to categories

4.3 Discussion

Several exciting findings need to be commented on in this study's materials. First, looking at the quantitative data, it is evident that instructors, to a large degree, recognize and acknowledge the literature identified as important by the consortium (see 3.1: Literature review). The average scores are high throughout the whole sample of elements included. With a variation from an average score of 3,78 to 4,76 of 5,0, we find that instructors agree that these are all important areas.

Secondly, from the quantitative data, we see that instructors are more concerned about the challenges and possibilities introduced via Ed. Tech than what might be called more traditional elements. For example, we see that challenges concerning learner roles and communication score pretty low, while interacting and thinking with others are rated very high.

Considering the low(er) scores on communicative elements in the quantitative data, it is a paradox that communication is discussed the most during part C of the training (see Fig. 2). This might be due to instructors' focus more on communication WHEN using Ed. Tech. The qualitative data gives us more insight into the materials later in the discussion.

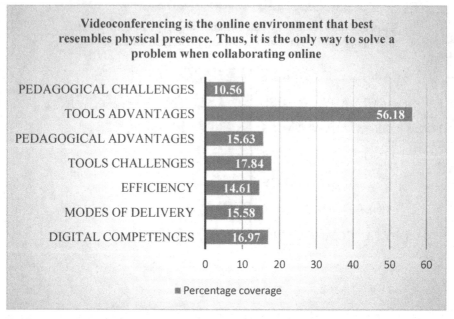

Fig. 5. Statement 3 "Videoconferencing is the online environment that best resembles physical presence. Thus, it is the only way to solve a problem when collaborating online" coded according to categories

Table 4. Summary codes in all three statements instructor trainings iLikeIT2

Code	References	Percentage
Digital competencies	23	12,5
Efficiency	17	9,5
Modes of delivery	14	7,5
Pedagogical advantages	29	16
Pedagogical challenges	28	15,5
Tools - advantages	49	27
Tools - challenges	22	12

When instructors were asked if they use an LMS or similar to upload curricular elements, 36 of 46 attendees answered yes. At the same time, the average score on the question about the possibility of storing and sharing information between members was as high as 4,22. Even if this is no surprise, the finding is emphasized during the discussions. Several instructors mention coordination as a positive effect of Ed. Tech in various ways. Still, there are discussions that even if there is an abundance of different tools available, the tools need to be adapted or used in a good way to function positively. If not, the technical difficulties and the sheer inclusion of an extra element might reduce the learning outcome. When implementing technology to distribute better and gain access to statistics and theory, the instructor should consider the effectiveness and coordinative function of the tool.

In the theoretical framework, the need for heightened digital competency is high-lighted, and the instructors often mention the need to train both themselves and the students in using the tools before applying them in the learning environment. The instructors are concerned with both the effectiveness of new tools, specific languages (like mathematics), ethics, and general behavior when using digital tools in the classes. Consequently, this might also be why the lowest average score in our materials is on whether instructors allow students to use social media to communicate during lectures (average score 3,78). When instructors introduce and use Ed. Tech in Higher Education classrooms, the fear of tools disturbing or causing reduced attention spans is still high.

Another interesting finding concerns the room structure when doing collaborative work. This was especially connected to online environments, and it seems as if the instructors, to some degree, seek to represent ordinary classroom structures also in online environments. Looking at the Communication category in part B of the questionnaire, we see that instructors want students to raise their hands during online lectures (41 YES/5 NO), while they are not too interested in anonymous questions during the lecture (32 YES/14 NO). At the same time, we see that the instructors cannot monitor the student's progress during the lecture (26 YES/ 20 NO). It is evident that even if the instructors have the tools, they do not use them to differentiate the lectures from ordinary lectures. During the training, one instructor had an interesting observation concerning how to work in an online environment. When discussing if online teaching can function without video-conferencing, a lecturer at the university level claims that video-conferencing is just a worse replica of physical presence. It includes the argument that video conferences can never achieve the same aims as a physical collaboration, thus, one should never seek to replace something with something else that is not as good. Instead, one needs to find the inherent advantages in the learning environment available for the work.

Pedagogy engaged in the discussions with every aspect of the collaborative work. There are comments on elements of coordination, peer learning, and heightened digital and cooperative skills. There are especially two things that are mentioned often, which can also help improve the pedagogical approach for a new teacher. First, it seems as if one is to introduce Ed. Tech in a collaborative setting, one needs to have a clear pedagogical purpose. The primary pedagogical approach that Ed. Tech aids, according to the discussions, is interactivity. This includes simple functionality like emojis, raise hand, shared screen, digital post-its and more, but it also makes the plenary parts or lectures more engaging. One could, for example, introduce GIFs or animations to a PP to enliven it. When answering individually on the question if instructors use these elements, it is almost 50–50, showing that this is something that is considered attractive, but not introduced and used to its fullest yet.

We all know that one of the most essential learning aspects of collaborative work is communication between the participants, which increases engagement [23]. This is also something that the instructors regard as important. When discussing the statements, the instructors are aware of the lack of micro-communication and body language when doing digital lectures. At the same time, they claim that often the discussions are better, freer in terms of exchanging ideas and experiences when the camera is turned off. Some claim that digital tools themselves improve the student's ability to communicate and collaborate and that students are more willing to defend their arguments via a more anonymous setting in a digital framework. It is essential to consider this when designing rules and guidelines for internal discussions and when starting collaborative work. At the same time, it is mentioned that the implemented tools must be adapted for the purpose and that participants must be trained in digital etiquette and manners to make the communication work.

The qualitative data also shows some concern about students staying inactive and passive in discussions, especially when doing an online collaboration. It indicates that there is a need for smaller groups when introducing Ed. Tech in collaborative work. It can also shed some light on the results from the individual parts. For example, in part A, they are asked about the importance of micro-communication (i.e., use mimic, sighs, smiles and more), and the average score is the lowest we find (3,78). Accordingly, the scores indicating uncertainty (4,28) and turn-taking (4,35) are not impressively high. These are elements that come more naturally when doing more traditional collaborative work.

Since more or less the introduction of Ed. Tech in learning environments, the aim of efficiency has been central to the development of new tools and strategies [24]. It is undoubtedly one of the advantages of introducing and using Ed. Tech in a classroom is evident that the teachers are aware of it in data presented in this survey. 9,5% of the mentions all together in the materials is about the efficiency of digital tools, mostly in a positive manner (see Table 4). Some comments claim that the tools may make learning less efficient than physical presence, but this effect is often reduced by training or the number of digital competencies in the student and instructor group. Digital competencies are naturally mentioned a lot (12,5%), and very often in connection with how to make the tools work in a collaborative setting (see Table 4). It is also noteworthy that instructors repeatedly mention infrastructural elements considering digital competencies, like GDPR, ethics, and how to use the tools themselves.

Learning design is always the most important when considering pedagogy in any situation. In a collaborative work, the students should learn from each other; therefore, the learning designs need to aim for this. When introducing Ed. Tech, the learning design needs to utilize strengths and benefits that cannot be found in a traditional F2F-situation. It is interesting to look at the answers from the individual questionnaires in the instructor training to see how the learning design reflects this view.

When answering individual questions in the instructor training, the three first questions might give insight into what a good learning design should provide in a collaborative setting. The instructors agree that the division of tasks within the group (average score 4,37 of 5,0) and the possibility of interaction between the group members (4,76) is the most important when collaborating. Less critical, it seems, is the roles allocated to group members (4,04, with a standard deviation of 0,83). Interestingly, as many as 21 out of 46 instructors do not allow their students to use social media to interact during the lecture. It means that one either has to facilitate physical or online interaction or create a chat channel or shared screen opportunity to utilize the benefits of communication in the learning situation.

5 Conclusion

Several factors need to be considered when designing a pedagogical strategy for integrating educational technology in a collaborative learning environment. In order to answer the research question on which pedagogical strategies are necessary to implement to heighten the learning outcome from collaborative work when using Ed. Tech, we will try and summarize some of the most significant findings in our materials.

The basis for every collaborative work, including Ed. Tech needs to be the three C's: Collaboration, coordination, and communication.

When implementing Ed. Tech in digital learning environments task/cases should allow for a monitoring role more than a facilitating/participative role for the instructor.

All tasks must be designed to enable all participants to be seen and heard. Thus, all will experience the same quality/effects of the learning experience. It can be done via asynchronous lectures (available online resources) when the curriculum/theory is the lecture's main element.

All cases and tasks provided need to be designed to allow both cooperation and individual work. It is one of the inherent advantages that Ed. Tech provides and needs to be utilized to its fullest.

One of the most important recommendations is to provide small training tasks before the participants start their work. The training should be directed towards turn-taking, attention to the speaker and coordinating the work, especially considering sharing of materials.

Digital competency is an obvious factor, both for students and instructors. If there is a discrepancy between the experience in a group, one should cater to this and ensure that all involved participants have an adequate level for participating actively in the work-related tasks.

There are already many digital tools being used by both instructors and students. Instructors should not be afraid to use existing tools and train students to use them for coordination, communication, and collaboration. In addition, it will raise awareness of the tools and their pedagogical effects.

Maybe the most crucial recommendation is that the learning design needs to facilitate using opportunities found in the introduced Ed. Tech. One needs to find new ways of using ED. Tech to reach a higher learning aim than possible in traditional lectures.

The both qualitative and quantitative data point to the coordinative functions in Ed. Tech-tools are the single most important innovations for collaborative work. Thus, the coordinative role in the group is more important. Make sure always to include one strong coordinator in each group. It is essential to consider the coordinative role in the group when dividing members—introducing Ed. Tech makes this role more complex and vital than in more conservative collaborative environments.

These are primarily recommendations based on the research presented in this article and not a complete list of pedagogical approaches. Still, the data shows the significance of these recommendations, and considering these will improve the quality of a collaborative learning environment when introducing Ed. Tech to it.

Acknowledgements. Parts of the research has been co-funded with support from the European Commission through the project Learning Through Innovative Collaboration Enhanced by Educational Technology (iLikeIT2) (Nr. 2020-1-NO01-KA203-076434). This publication reflects the author's views only, and the Commission cannot be held responsible for any use which may be made of the information contained therein.

References

1. Puentedura, R.R.: SAMR: A contextualized introduction. Lecture at Pine Cobble School (2014). Accessed 13 Mar 2014
2. Blundell, C.N., Mukherjee, M., Nykvist, S.: A scoping review of the application of the SAMR model in research. Computers and Education Open, vol. 3. ISSN 2666-5573 (2022). https://doi.org/10.1016/j.caeo.2022.100093.
3. DeGani, A., Geoff Martin, G., Stead, G., Wade, F.: Mobile Learning Shareable Content Object Reference Model (m-SCORM) Limitations and Challenges, Tribal Education, UK (2010)
4. Wikipedia: Educational Technology (2022). https://en.wikipedia.org/wiki/Educational_tec hnology
5. Kukulska-Hulme, A., Jones, C.: The next generation: design and the infrastructure for learning in a mobile and networked world. In: Olofsson, A.D., Lindberg, J. O. (Eds.) Informed Design of Educational Technologies in Higher Education: Enhanced Learning and Teaching, pp. 57–78. Information Science Reference (an Imprint of IGI Global). Hershey, PA (2011a)
6. Goodfell, A., Smith, B.L., MacGregor, J.: Collaborative Learning: A Sourcebook for Higher Education. Natl Center on Postsecondary (1994)
7. César, M., Santos, N.: From exclusion to inclusion: collaborative work contributions to more inclusive learning settings. Eur. J. Psychol. Educ. **21**(3), 333–346 (2006). https://doi.org/10.1007/bf03173420
8. Prince, M.: Does active learning work? A review of the research. Res. J. Eng. Educ. **93**(3), 223–231 (2013). https://doi.org/10.1002/j.2168-9830.2004.tb00809.x
9. Thomas, D., Seely Brown, J.: A new culture of learning: cultivating the imagination for a world of constant change. CreateSpace Independent Publishing Platform, p. 50 (2011)
10. ilikeIT2.eu (2022). https://ilikeit2.eu
11. Talmo, T., Dafoulas, G., Martinez, P.C., Bekiaridis, G., Valenti, A.: Learning through innovative collaboration enhanced by educational technology (ILIKEIT2), EDULEARN21 Proceedings, pp. 10602–10611 (2021)
12. Talmo, T., Sapountzi, M., Dafoulas, G., Valenti, A.: Collaborative learning using technological tools - a framework for the future. In: Zaphiris, P., Ioannou, A. (eds.) Learning and Collaboration Technologies. Designing the Learner and Teacher Experience, pp. 478–496. Springer International Publishing, Cham (2022). https://doi.org/10.1007/978-3-031-05657-4_34
13. Knutas, A., Ikonen, J., Porras, J.: Computer-supported collaborative learning in software engineering education: a systematic mapping study. Int. J. Inf. Technol. Secur. **7**(4), 1-28 (2019)
14. Lehtinen, E., Hakkarainen, K., Lipponen, L., Veermans, M., Muukkonen, H.: Computer Supported Collaborative Learning: A Review (1999)
15. Snyder, H.: Literature review as a research methodology: an overview and guidelines. J. Bus. Res. **104**, 333–339 (2019). https://doi.org/10.1016/j.jbusres.2019.07.039
16. Mayring, P.: Qualitative content analysis. Forum Qual. Sozialforschung/Forum: Qual. Soc. Res. **1**(2), 20 (2000). http://nbnresolving.de/urn:nbn:de:0114-fqs0002204

17. Hafezimoghadam, P., Farahmand, S., Farsi, D., Zare, M., Abbasi, S.: A comparative study of lecture and discussion methods in the education of basic life support and advanced cardiovascular life support for medical students. Turkish J. Emergency Med. **13**(2), 59–63 (2013)

18. Vennebo, K.F., Aas, M.: A supportive tool for principals in guiding professional group discussions. Educ. Res. **62**(3), 266–283 (2020). https://doi.org/10.1080/00131881.2020.179 6518

19. Ezzy, D.: Qualitative Analysis. EBook August 2013. ImprintRoutledge (2002). https://doi.org/10.4324/9781315015484

20. NVIVO (2023). Homepage. https://www.qsrinternational.com/nvivo-qualitative-data-analysis-software/home

21. Stahl, G.: Group practices: a new way of viewing CSCL. Int. J. Comput. Support. Collab. Learn. **12**, 113–126 (2017). https://doi.org/10.1007/s11412-017-9251-0

22. Ze, S., Ruihua, K., Xiongkai, S.: CSCW-based virtual team cooperation platform analysis and design. In: Conference proceedings Informatics in Control, Automation and Robotics (CAR), 2010 2nd International Asia, vol. 3. (2010)

23. Blasco-Arcas, L., Buil, I., Hernández-Ortega, B., Sese, F.J.: Using clickers in class. The role of interactivity, active collaborative learning and engagement in learning performance. Comput. Educ. **62**, 102–110 (2013). ISSN 0360–1315. https://doi.org/10.1016/j.compedu.2012.10.019.

24. Keough, S.M.: Clickers in the classroom: a review and a replication. J. Manage. Educ. **36**(6), 822–847 (2012). https://doi.org/10.1177/1052562912454808

Discovering Best Practices for Educational Video Conferencing Systems

Tord Talmo$^{(\boxtimes)}$ and Mikhail Fominykh

Norwegian University of Science and Technology, Trondheim, Norway
{tord.m.talmo,mikhail.fominykh}@ntnu.no

Abstract. Digitalization of higher education is amongst the most important and most researched areas in recent years. The COVID19 pandemic ensured rapid movement into less known environments of the digitization process, online environments and synchronous teaching, otherwise known as Video Conferencing (VC). New areas of interest concerning hardware, software, pedagogical approaches, support services and regulations and rules emerged. In this paper, we present results of a study aiming at investigating how VC is being implemented and used in a Norwegian context. The study aims at identifying the challenges experienced when using online conferencing systems and specify best practices from different contexts to be used for later ideation and models for developing a new system for VC. These aims are being achieved in the study through focus group collaborative work considering different problems occurring when doing VC, and through seven in-depth interviews with different personnel employed at the Norwegian University of Science and Technology. The data collected are analyzed using content analysis and used to design a best practice according to the PACT framework. The results show that even if the resources are available, we still have a way to go working with the culture of being digital and providing good VC experiences for lecturers and students. We also derived best case scenarios for using the inherent advantages found in technology. This in turn can provide better academic learning outcomes from VC if used in a proper way.

Keywords: Video Conference · online environment · PACT-framework · pedagogy · software features

1 Background

Higher education educators, students, education leaders, and support staff are facing a situation caused by COVID-19 pandemic that no one was prepared for. Online teaching that can give the same interaction and engagement of a large classroom of mathematics students, designers in a design studio, or freshmen in a physics laboratory requires fundamental rethinking in making the activities possible.

The study presented in this paper aims to contribute empirical data to the design of video conferencing toolkits and best practices for supporting the teachers in higher

The original version of this chapter was revised: a minor error in the author's name has been corrected. The correction to this chapter is available at
https://doi.org/10.1007/978-3-031-34411-4_46

education, educational leaders, support staff, and students. We identify and document the diverse scenarios that the video conferencing systems mediated classes representing the physical resources, the teaching styles and learning preferences in play, and the behavioral and social interaction factors that are beyond the technological solution scope.

During COVID-19 restrictions, video conferencing became a de facto environment for higher education classrooms attended by students both face-to-face and online. The use of hardware accessories, video conferencing software, recorded video sharing, and use of hardware and software functionalities for various types of teaching-learning activities are continuously experimented by teachers, tech support, e-learning consultants, and pedagogical designers. The suitable solutions are highly context-dependent, but the use-case scenarios in terms of purpose and pedagogical design are similar. The activities involving lectures, student presentations, group-formation and group work, live quizzes, peer-group assessment, and collaborative design and facilitation are some of the activities that require integration of video-conferencing functionalities and various web-based software. The digital capabilities in the online teaching context involve even the use of camera setup, light settings, body language, eye-contact, and other digital and non-digital tools - depending on the field of study. The new roles and competencies required from teachers and students for engaging in video-conferencing systems that bring the learning experience closest to face-to-face classroom requires strategic "diffusion of innovations" [1]. The diversity of available digital systems (hardware accessories and software) and the pedagogical designs with technology setup for engaging classes are context sensitive. The integrated video conferencing systems are insufficient and the software systems with portable devices (for example, laptops) require an additional camera, microphone and loudspeaker, live streaming, and recorded video sharing facilities. Engaging and facilitating students' activities and discussion require additional online applications (for example, breakout rooms, quizzes, collaborative writing/presentation/design tools). Therefore, the innovation process includes two broad scopes. First, the hardware accessories and software functionalities that enable conducting some of activities. Second, the pedagogical designs that enable the designs for ensuring valuable learning experience for students and teachers.

The definition of portable video conferencing in this study includes but not limited to 'mobile video conferencing' [2], additional hardware including wireless speakers and microphones, separate webcam, pen tablets to substitute whiteboard, or streaming separate camera views for the teacher and whiteboard/blackboard, etc.

1.1 Context of the Organization and Culture at NTNU

Norwegian University of Science and Technology (NTNU) is the largest university in Norway today in 2023 and has a history dating back to 1910. NTNU's vision is to create knowledge for a better world aiming to provide solutions that can change and improve everyday life. This solicitates for a solid base financing, innovative experience and intentions of providing updated and high-tech solutions for many possible learning scenarios.

At NTNU, students can choose between 400 study programs. The university offers Norway's widest range of programs in technology, health, teacher education, the arts and music disciplines. The three-campus situation creates some specialized needs and challenges for the university, something that also includes research and innovation considering video conferencing between cities, both synchronous and asynchronous.

NTNU aims to provide education distinguished by quality at a high international level and has two Centers of Excellence in Higher Education designated by the Norwegian Agency for Quality Assurance in Education. The university is committed to innovative education, especially increased use of learning methods with active student participation and digitalization. This is also emphasized in the strategy of the university. Concerning education and learning environments it is stated: "Students are involved in developing content and learning processes in a tailored learning environment. New technology enables stimulating and varied approaches to learning and assessment, and facilitates access to lifelong education." [3]. New technologies are also explicitly mentioned concerning campus development: "Develop sustainable technological solutions" [3]. Other than these two quotations, the strategy focuses on other developments than specific ICT competence, and there are no places where the strategy talks solely about video conferencing.

One would still claim that NTNU is aware of the new demands in the 21st Century. To achieve the visions for the future, NTNU points at digitalization as the most important point concerning the development of the whole institution:

NTNU'S capacity for development

NTNU sets priorities for resources to ensure high quality in our core activities, and develops a leading position in our disciplines so that we can meet society's changes, needs and expectations. NTNU has user-friendly and effective support systems. Future-oriented digital services focused on user needs are available to students and staff. NTNU has robust systems to meet the need for information security, emergency response capacity and protection of privacy.

Development goals

NTNU will: Have resource management that contributes to increased productivity and creates room for manoeuvre in terms of strategic priorities and renewal at all levels Launch digitalization initiatives and improvements that support integrated, standardized procedures and work processes [3].

This sets a context for the possibilities for NTNU to set a standard also when it concerns video conferencing. During the pandemic, students and instructors were mainly satisfied with the way the lectures were performed. This is also consistent with the demands from the Norwegian government, which is the owner of the University.

1.2 Norwegian Governmental Strategies and Demands

The Norwegian government issued in 2017 a new strategy for digitalization of Higher Education in Norway [4]. As Talmo et.al. show, the Norwegian digitalization strategy has been connected to single persons initiatives and anchored mainly in the management [5]. In addition, it is interesting that new teachers have not been provided sufficient training in developing their digital skills. This meant that the pandemic provided several challenges in Norway as well as the rest of the world considering the shift to an online and/or hybrid mood of Education. In the Norwegian context, this led to a governmental action plan for digital transition in Higher Education ("Handlingsplan for digital omstilling i høyere utdanning og forskning") for the period 2021-2025 [6]. The action plan came as a consequence of the COVID19 pandemic, and follows up on many of the ongoing actions already started in the previous plan [4]. There is still a higher focus on shared digital learning resources and flexible education. The institutions are urged to make more courses available for more people and in different life situations. At the same time, there should be infrastructure designed for more usage of digital tools. It is obvious in the action plan that the usage of online videoconferencing is highly appreciated, and that Norway wants more of this in the future.

As it was also shown in a recent report from The Norwegian Directorate for Higher Education and Skills (HKDIR, previously DIKU) [7], promoting the use of digital skills in workplace is one of the priorities that has been successfully introduced in Norway's tertiary education and this is a positive step towards its digitalization. The action plan until 2025 develops this idea also for higher educational institutions and claims in 3.2 Digital innovation in lecturing and learning (authors translation) that it is necessary with educational digital competence if we are to realize this digitalization in lecturing and education. Especially important is the connection between digital, professional and pedagogical competence in order to reach this [6].

The government, as the institutions themselves, is concerned about the academic performance of the students, and emphasizes the fact that students also need to have the opportunities of developing their digital skills, and have access to modern and personalized learning environments that enhance amongst others flexible and digitized learning experiences [4]. Accordingly, the teacher should also implement applications, digital tools and services to support both the learning process but also the professional development of the teacher. The governmental strategies thus emphasize and facilitate highly innovative and modern video conferencing, if and when needed. For this study it is also interesting to see that the strategies are aiming at improving the infrastructure at the institutions, in order to create more flexible learning environments, especially designed for personal learning environments and mobile and dynamic studies. Still, even in the new action plan, the responsibility for the development is mainly placed on an institutional level. NTNU is therefore both responsible for implementation, and in charge of solutions chosen to a high degree. It is therefore even more interesting to see how VC has been implemented and used at an institutional level at NTNU.

The Norwegian strategy for digitalization corresponds well with other overarching policies, like the ones from the European Union [8]. There are still few means and resources for implementing the strategy provided by the government, thus the institutions need to implement the new demands in their plans for the future, allocate resources and create incentives for actual development in the scientific staff, for example considering the idea of a recognition system for pedagogical development in all institutions.

NTNU needs to be aware of both international and national strategies and demands for better and more digital solutions and provide necessary incentives for innovation and development, both concerning infrastructure updated hardware and applicable software. NTNU is therefore in front when it comes to new solutions for delivering video conferencing systems, and better off than many other institutions throughout Europe and the world. On the other side, a university of this size has an inherent culture that might be challenging to change considering lectures. This in turn leads us to the aim of this study.

1.3 Research Aim

The aim for the study presented in this paper is twofold. First, we aim to identify challenges experienced when using online conferencing systems. Second, we aim to specify best practices from different contexts to be used for later ideation and models for developing a new system.

In the wider scope of the research project, the data on video conferencing-mediated teaching is collected using surveys, interviews, observations, and other methods. The innovation is the explored diversity of contexts and the contexts of use, particularly the portable video conferencing systems integrated with the various online tools for engaging students. The study conducted at NTNU in Norway, contributed by conducting seven interviews and two focus-group workshops.

The underlying objective is to identify the scenarios that work in the local settings and the challenges faced in the process of adopting video conferencing systems and engaging students during online classes. The results of the study at NTNU will be combined with the results of similar studies conducted in six universities in other countries to define the problems and ideate possible solutions for engaging students in the different scenarios of teaching at a later stage in the project.

2 Methodology

In this study two different approaches were chosen to achieve the results needed to answer the research aim. First, we performed focus groups, collecting data through the problem tree methodology [9, 10]. In these groups we included three students, and a total of four employees; One IT-expert, one AV-expert, one leader and one teacher. Second, we did focused interviews with personnel employed at NTNU in different functions (see description later)

2.1 Activity 1 – Focus Groups

A problem tree methodology is a form of focus group interview, where the participants should work together in small groups and identify different connections between variables around a problem [9].

The first focus group consisted of three students at university level. They had some previous experience from lectures in both hybrid and online formats from High School, and mostly meetings and individual guidance at university level.

The second group consisted of four people employed at NTNU and included one leader, one lecturer, one IT expert, and one Audio-Video (AV) expert. They have between 10 and 25 years of experience working in Higher Education and have all been involved in video conferencing. This group performed the focus group twice, with two different problem statements.

Both groups were asked the same questions. They were asked to initially explain their experience with video conferencing and identify a problem statement they found interesting when working within this field of education. The problem statement was written in the middle of a paper to be visualized. Then all participants were asked to identify (a) multiple causes of the problem and (b) multiple effects of the problem. These causes and effects were written on post-its andhung on the paper. After a discussion, the researcher involved took a photo of the problem tree (pictures are available through the authors) and processed the data in an Excel-file. No personal information was collected.

2.2 Activity 2 Individual Interviews

The interviews were conducted by two researchers [11]. One researcher asked the questions, whilst the other took detailed notes and clarified answers provided by the interviewee.

We used the PACT framework – People, Activities, Contexts, Technologies to structure the interviews, and specifically the scenario descriptions in the interviews [12]. We also used the same framework to analyze the data collected from the interviews afterwards. These, together with findings from the focus groups, collectively gives an overview of best scenarios for video conferencing in a Norwegian context.

To get the best overview and mitigate eventual sources of errors an interview guide was decided on before the interviews. Two researchers would be conducting the interview, while one participant would be responding. One researcher would be asking the questions, whilst the other one would take notes, and follow up on the answers if anything was unclear.

Participants in this study consisted of two lecturers, two AV/IT- experts, one lecturer/pedagogical support and finally two people working as pedagogical/technological support. All involved informants have experience with video conferencing solutions. All interviews lasted for approximately 45 min. Notes were taken, transcribed and approved by the informant afterwards (all interview notes are available by contacting the authors of this paper) (Table 1).

Table 1. Interview questions

PACT aspect	Question
Introduction	1. Describe the best scenario of using video conferencing. 1a. To represent the best possible scenario, please, describe the video conferencing activities that work best, and students like them. 2. Describe how you use video conferencing in your teaching/e-learning support/tech. support activities.
People	3. Describe the roles of the people who you work with. 3a. For a teacher, this would be students and other teachers and teaching assistants. 3b. For an e-learning consultant, this would be teachers and IT support, perhaps.
Activities	4. Name the activities that you do in the "contact hours". 5. What works well and what does not? 5a. Examples: lecture, monitoring, meetings, guidance. 6. What didactics and methods do you use? 6a. Example: group work in Zoom

(continued)

Table 1. (*continued*)

PACT aspect	Question
Context	7. Define the context of your video conferencing experience. 8. What are the core tasks of the unit you work at (e.g., for academic departments, these are usually teaching and research; for IT-support units, these can be supporting personal computers or other infrastructure)? 9. What are the organizational guidelines that you follow? 9a. Example, for teachers, this would be course name, study program, if the students are at home or in the class, what kind of class/lab/studio etc.
Technologies	10 What technologies, both hardware and software, are you dealing with? 11. How various technological features and tools are used during a videoconference-mediated contact session? 12. What tools do you use for engagement and how? 13. What works well that you would recommend to others? 14. What are some of the main concerns that you would ask other roles/colleagues to address?

2.3 Data Analysis

The data analysis was done using the content analysis method [13]. Two researchers worked synchronously together to code the interview transcripts. NVivo software was used for the coding. The unit of analysis was defined as a statement or an idea, ranging in length from a single phrase to a paragraph. The researchers defined few codes beforehand and derived most other codes from the data responsively [14]. Each interview was coded two times, with both researchers involved both times. In the first coding cycle, the researchers were discovering new codes, while the second cycle was used to control that all statements were included in all codes.

In this study, we aimed to see which elements in the PACT-framework were most frequent in the sample of informants involved. Analyzing statements using content analysis means that each statement needs to be interpreted and coded according to several criteria. There are different approaches to a content analysis, some claim that codes should be mutually exclusive, whilst others find more complexity in the codes, like parent-child [15]. In this study the second approach is applied; even if the codes are analyzed and interpreted one by one, the results are then merged into the four categories of the PACT framework.

3 Results

3.1 Focus Groups

In the focus groups, two different set of groups participated: a) Students, and b) employees. The second group included both teachers, leaders, AV and IT-personnel. The groups were gathered for app. One hour for each problem statement, and decided on the group division and work themselves after the initial introduction from the researcher.

In total, three problem statements were identified, one amongst the students (n. 3) and two amongst the employees (n. 4). The problem statements were:

1. Quality in all included digital solutions - hardware and software
2. How can VC provide added value compared to physical lectures?
3. Pedagogical challenges: Just mirroring what you do in physical class into digital domain do not work.

In the first group, the students, the scenarios described were lectures, meetings and one-to-one-interaction. In the second group, several scenarios were described, including f2f-lecturing, online lecturing supervision, hybrid teaching and multicampus-teaching. The second group had a special focus on hybrid education, especially due to the multi-campus situation at NTNU (campuses in three different cities).

In Figure 1, the data are processed by the researchers at NTNU. All three problem statements are listed, and the causes and effects correspond to these through interpretation. All causes are mentioned by one or two of the groups. The causes and effects are also mentioned according to one or more of the statements.

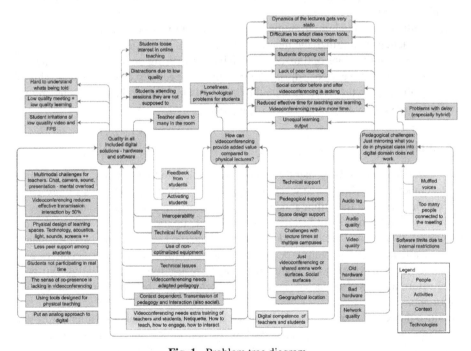

Fig. 1. Problem tree diagram

There are many more causes than effects presented in the materials, even if many of the causes also can be interpreted as effects themselves. There are also more insights gained from the employee group, which is anticipated seeing that this group has discussed and elaborated more on the lectures during the pandemic than students. The most interesting interpretation is the fact that most allegations can be connected to problem statement number 3: Pedagogical challenges: Just mirroring what you do in physical class into digital domain do not work. This is also the problem statement that attracts the most different categories considering PACT. This clearly shows the need for adjusted pedagogy when doing VC. Other than this statement, most causes and effects are connected to context, mainly because all informants were influenced by the recent pandemic situation.

It is noteworthy that the students have a different view, or at least it seems like it in this group, concerning technology than the employees. In problem statement 1: Quality in all included digital solutions – hardware and software, there are several causes and effects not mentioned or discussed in the second group when working on problem statement. This indicates that lecturers and support personnel trust that the technological solutions should be sufficient, whilst the students have more difficult conditions on their own hardware and software. At the same time, all agree that usage of non-optimized equipment is bad for the learning experience.

We also observe that the second group, the employees, are more concerned about pedagogical challenges when using VC than the students. They focus on how to deliver a good experience for a larger group, more than the individual focus on each student in a video conference.

It is difficult to conclude from the focus groups, but it is obvious that one needs to look for practices that utilize the inherent advantages in digital technology, ensure that all technical solutions are optimized, especially considering audio and video quality, and consider support services adjusted to the context specific scenario (Fig. 1). This is further elaborated in the discussion on the interviews in Chapter 3.2. The focus groups can be seen as a base for the interviews being done.

3.2 Interviews

Two researchers worked together throughout the whole interview process, from October to December 2022. There were seven interviews performed, six with physical presence and one interview in the online mode. All seven informants hold different positions at NTNU. Two informants are lecturers, two work as support personnel within AV and IT, one works both as a lecturer and provides pedagogical support, and two informants work at a department providing pedagogical and technical support for lecturers and students. The interviews were done according to restrictions set by GDPR. No personal information was collected, notes were taken, transcribed, and approved by the informants.

Since the researchers were both doing the interviews and analyzing afterwards, the data were already processed once, and the PACT-framework defined some general codes to look for in the analysis. In processing the data, the researchers categorized the codes according to PACT, but kept the single codes for interpretation. Thus, some codes have few references, but they are still interesting and provide insights not found in other codes (see Tables 2, 3, 4 and 5).

Table 2. Codes and quantitative analysis of the interviews (PACT: People)

Code(s)	Number of interviews it appears	Number of references
Digital competencies	5	19
Involved departments	7	18
Organizational rules/guidelines	7	19
Personnel roles	7	58
Total		114

Table 3. Codes and quantitative analysis of the interviews (PACT: Activities)

Code(s)	Number of interviews it appears	Number of references
Asynchronous teaching	4	6
Group work	3	9
Hybrid	5	14
Meetings	3	5
Research and development	2	4
Synchronous teaching	7	16
Total		54

Table 4. Codes and quantitative analysis of the interviews (PACT: Context)

Code(s)	Number of interviews it appears	Number of references
Hardware and room design	6	12
Pedagogical challenges	5	13
Pedagogy	7	42
Physical room design	4	8
Sound and rooms	2	3
Technological challenges	6	11
Time issues	3	8
Total		97

Table 5. Codes and quantitative analysis of the interviews (PACT: Technologies)

Code(s)	Number of interviews it appears	Number of references
Camera and image	5	8
Hardware and networks	5	7
Ped-Tech-Room interaction	3	13
Software	7	41
Software features	5	30
Video and sound recordings	6	15
Total		114

In total, 23 codes were created, and 379 references were found for these codes in the interview notes. The distribution of the references is presented in Tables 2, 3, 4 and 5. All seven informants talked about *involved departments, organizational guidelines, pedagogy, different personnel roles,* and *synchronous teaching. Personnel roles* is the code most frequently used in the interviews (58 references), followed by an overarching code *pedagogy* (48 references). This is natural, as all the time informants are employed in a role at a university and were asked about it during the interview. It is also worth mentioning that all interviews started with a general question about the interview, which means that all talked about themselves and their role in the organization.

There was no need to discard any of the codes. All codes will therefore be interpreted below, and the connection between the codes will be exemplified in the summary section that presents best practices according to the PACT framework.

Codes Classified to PACT: People. We classified four codes into the People category of the PACT framework (Table 2).

Digital Competencies. The informants are aware of the heightened competence obtained through the pandemic. All use more advanced tools, and especially tools making collaboration easier. The most frequent point is that best practice does not necessarily need the best equipment but knowing the tools and having the competence to use that specific tool.

Involved Departments. The most common reference about involved departments is the division between different departments. IT is mentioned as the most frequent support service, but also technical, AV and learning support is mentioned. The informants mainly mention these services to illustrate the division between different tasks that need to be supported. The main issue seems to be whether the support services should be operational support or development included in the department.

Organizational Rules/Guidelines. The organization set guidelines mainly through strategies and work plans for the involved personnel. Rules are mainly connected to standardized software solutions and sharing of information (GDPR-regulated). Some governmental demands affect the choices. Mainly it appears that there are more recommendations than rules, and both support and help lines/drop-in-meetings are available. Some basic training was offered, but not sufficient.

Personnel roles. The informants show a well-designed structure for support services, which is very specialized. As long as one knows what is needed, you are directed to the correct department. The aid is provided on a wide range, from pedagogical support, via IT-help to design of new rooms and buildings to aid the educational needs. The different support services are not known enough amongst staff. Working in collaboration with others, both students, staff and learning assistants, is common. Normally people ask for tech-help first, and then advances to ped.-tech.-related problems. Mostly about hardware during the pandemic, more on software today.

Codes classified to PACT: Activities. We classified six codes into the Activities category of the PACT framework (Table 3).

Asynchronous Teaching. Asynchronous teaching was mainly connected to recordings, evaluation on LMS and questions and answers. Provides opportunity of flipped classroom approaches, using small, pre-made videos. Also allowing time for contact hours online is mentioned.

Group Work. Group work is a way to facilitate more learning in video conferencing. Small groups of 4-5 students preferred, and always summarize in plenary. This facilitates peer learning processes. The plenary could be facilitated through digital tools, like response tools or whiteboards to write on.

Hybrid. There are many different aspects mentioned when it comes to hybrid solutions. The social dimension seems important, to create a sense of belonging no matter where you are located. Thus, the camera should be on, and one needs to work mentally with the shift from one environment to another. Hybrid solutions require different set-ups, and are costly, for example, considering technology needed and room designs. Most lecturers used streaming but were aware of the shortened attention span online.

Meetings. Important to have short, efficient meetings when attendees are in different locations. Being able to focus on content more than technology is vital. Using a platform that is suited for the format aids abovementioned problems. Meetings online are used mainly for discussions about pedagogy and logistics.

Research and Development. Video conferencing is still considered innovative, and a lot of both formal and informal, local and international projects are being done. Common is the fact that students are closely involved in the process.

Synchronous Teaching. The informants state that it is difficult to resemble a physical lecture in a digital environment. To enliven the interaction lots of digital tools are implemented, and there might be a demand to keep camera on and be present. Technology provides an opportunity for meeting when physical presence is not possible. Still there are few solutions that work for synchronous teaching. It is difficulties with real time sound and audio, and frame rate might be an issue. It is easy to miss questions in chat, but also difficult to get students to speak orally. Thus, one uses break-out rooms to meet a smaller group. When doing VC, it is important to explain and present the plan for the lecture.

Codes Classified to PACT: Context. We classified seven codes into the Activities category of the PACT framework (Table 4).

Hardware and Room Design. New physical rooms are often designed for collaboration and interaction, thus facilitating student-active learning. This requires a good set-up with quality technologies like headset, microphones, cameras, video systems and microphones. When attending a VC, one needs to ensure the same on the receiver side, especially good screens, and headset.

Pedagogical Challenges. There are several different pedagogical challenges addressed, but the most frequent is connected to the usage of cameras and microphones. The students are unwilling to turn the cameras on, and rarely answer questions orally. This, combined with stress and home environment problems, makes the online environment colder and reduces the sense of interactivity. More and more lecturers are gaining interest in using hybrid spaces/rooms, thus more questions connected to tech-ped-challenges appear. One problem is that the technology does not always cater for the type of lecture intended.

Pedagogy. Considering pedagogical approaches in VC it is obvious that two things are the main concern; 1) achieving more student active learning and 2) making sure the students feel a sense of belonging to the group. This is done through resembling f2f-classes, for example by introducing icebreakers, smiling, enhancing transparency and structure and giving regular pauses. The most common structure seems to be group discussions followed by plenary discussions, and then questions one on one. To enhance interaction and engagement lots of digital tools are applied, especially response tools like Mentimeter, and MiroBoard to visualize thoughts and ideas.

Physical Room Design. The informants emphasize sound and image as the most important when designing rooms for VC. This involves a lot of people from different positions (teachers, learning support, designers, architects, IT, AV) in order to make sure the quality of both sound systems, acoustics in room, colors, flexibility for the lecture is sufficient. Enough space for movement and moving equipment around is important.

Sound and Rooms. Two informants talked about this, and all three statements coded states that sound is more important than image.

Technological Challenges. The technological challenges are connected to three dimensions. We see the challenges of the tools themselves, like connection issues, quality of equipment and the design of the room that does not fit the lecture format. Secondly, it is obvious that informants have needs from the technology that might aid the pedagogical approach, like sharing screen to multiple rooms, pinning of windows in some software and getting different feedback (individual vs. community). Lastly, there are also statements concerning how to make technology aid pedagogy.

Time Issues. There are concerns that time is a resource when it comes to technology. The less time you have, the more reluctant you are to invest time in learning and developing methodology considering technology. With time to learn the tools, students and lecturer get familiar with them, and spend less time on the processes. It is also stated that everything takes more time in an online environment, and you need to adapt time spent with this in mind.

Codes Classified to PACT: Technologies. We classified six codes into the Technologies category of the PACT framework (Table 5).

Camera and Image. All statements except one is about having camera on or off during a VC. One teacher does not like to have a camera on himself, but all agree that "camera on" is necessary to achieve the wanted learning outcome. It is also important to focus on sound over image in the beginning.

Hardware and Networks. It is stated that best practice does not necessarily need the best equipment, the most important is that it works for the user. It is still mostly help with hardware asked for, but after the pandemic it is more constant due to the fact that the hardware is purchased. The informants are concerned about variation in the tools, mostly to ensure that all can use a tool. High quality is emphasized also here.

Ped-Tech-Room Interaction. When considering the connection between pedagogy, technology and rooms, it is dependent on the format of the lecture. Monologue based lectures are easy in VC, whilst collaboration is more difficult. When you are to collaborate in VC, one needs to deliver the same sense of presence and to all participants. This also means that new rooms and environment at NTNU are built specifically for interaction and collaboration, and not necessarily suited for monologue-based lectures. All hardware, furniture and infrastructure must be specifically designed for the activity. New rooms also foster new pedagogy. It is also important to remember that rooms are more expensive to build when designed for hybrid lectures.

Software. Obvious that rules and recommendations set by the institution affect which software is being used. The informants mainly use some sort of video-platform, Panopto for recordings and videos and a response tool to engage the students. There are some rules connected to security that limit the possibilities. The informants are concerned about finding software that fosters engagement and student-active learning. This includes, as well as response tools, streaming solutions, anonymity in responses, questions and evaluations via LMS and software that allows for movement and dynamics in the screen. There are less discussions about VC in itself now, more on functionalities and inherent pros and cons. Support services do not want to recommend single tools but allow for variation.

Software Features. Lecturers mainly choose their software based on the inherent features. In order to engage the students, features that enhance interactivity, sense of belonging and social effects are important. It is also important to include features that activate the students, like break-out rooms for collaboration, whiteboard or annotation tools for collaborative writing and share screen functionality that works sufficiently. Many of the features are used to structure a lecture and communicate to the whole group at once.

Video and Sound Recordings. One emerging technological feature is podcasts, used both for repetition, lecturing and training. The same is the case with short videos, either recorded beforehand or during the lecture. Informants like the opportunity of recording their streamed lectures, no matter if the recordings are used for anything after the session.

Best Practices of Videoconferencing. The summary of the findings is based on interpretations of the references in each code. Every reference is read and categorized according to keywords and key sentences. The keywords most frequently found are emphasized more in the summary then single or few keywords, even if these have been used to further underline the content in the summary.

All summaries have been merged to describe possible best practices for VC based on the interviews and according to the PACT framework. There are some tools and technologies mentioned, this is due to the fact that these were mentioned many times, thus functions as a best practice tool at NTNU.

People.

- Easy to access tools. The less spent on learning the tool itself, the better it is.
- In order to succeed one needs to have specialized support services, which is well-known by staff and students.
- All tools must be GDPR-safe. Training must be available and constant, also considering these issues.
- Support services should be concerned mainly on problems concerning pedagogy and technology combined.
- Drop-in-meeting room available, to ask questions and receive help when needed.

Activities.

- When doing an activity in VC one should use the advantages provided in technology. Response tools, annotations, interactive boards to facilitate plenary discussions and tools like Miroboard to think together, create interaction.
- A VC needs a coherent structure, even more than a traditional lecture.
- It is important to involve students in the whole process when designing learning in a VC.
- Apply break out rooms to create collaboration and interaction (smaller groups)
- Mitigate the lack of social presence, for example by using extensive group work combined with plenary explanations and discussions. Camera should be on at both sides, and anonymous answers via a response tool is a good idea.

Context.

- Ensure time to test all technical equipment.
- Make the camera and microphone less frightening, for example by introducing all students in the group to an introductory round with the camera on.
- Important with high quality in all solutions, especially everything connected to sound. Physical rooms for education need to facilitate good sound.
- Student active learning and interactivity should be the aim, both between students and student to teacher.
- Response tools like Mentimeter and other software need to be easy to use or integrate in VC.
- Easy set-up ensures that technological solutions work. This in turn saves time for the involved parts, that can be spent on deciding ped.-tech.-challenges and solutions.

Technologies.

- It is obvious that technology, environments, and pedagogy influence each other. Thus, one needs to consider all three elements as equal and how they mutually benefit each other. Monologue-based activities can be implemented in small videos made in Panopto or podcasts, whilst collaborative activities need different features in the chosen hard- and software.
- It is necessary to start with the pedagogical approach. Simple solutions might be sufficient, as long as the technology works, and the lecturer knows how to handle the equipment.

– To enhance the learning experience, one should include possibilities for collaboration, interaction and student-active learning. Shared screen options like you find in Zoom and Blackboard Collaborate, collaborative writing areas, chat functionality and a possibility to raise one's voice, preferably anonymous, needs to be included.

Some of the results and practices presented above are interesting to investigate and comment on further. It is also interesting to compare results from the interviews with findings from the focus groups (Fig. 1).

When considering the delivery of VC, it is clear that the relationship between pedagogy, technology and space (or environment) is vital to consider to achieve the aims. This is mentioned several times in all the interviews. The Pedagogy-Space-Technology framework is quite simple [16]. Still, it is a good framework to work within, and it can be scaled and applied to many various scenarios, both physical, hybrid, and online. Considering our data, the logical starting point for this cyclical process should always be pedagogy. Depending on what one wants to deliver, the technology and space designs need to be adjusted accordingly, which again will influence the pedagogy in a cyclical process.

The informants obviously talked a lot about different software implemented in their VC, and how they used these. It is especially interesting to see that different response tools, mainly Mentimeter and Padlet, were mentioned and discussed often. A response tools has the advantage that it involves, engages, and allows all students to answer, often anonymously [17]. This is fully aligned with the emphasis our informants put on student-active learning. Even if this is nothing special for VC, it might be even more difficult to activate the students in an online environment.

The idea of active learning is further elaborated in the focus on interaction and dynamics, both in the delivery of the lecture and on the screen itself. One informant states that *e dozed off when being student if the screen was filled purely with a slides, and thus sought tools and activities that enlivened the screen. This makes it important to include such tools, and actively use them.

At NTNU we see that there are some regulations when it comes to software allowed to use. NTNU uses BlackBoard as a learning management system, which includes the platform Blackboard Collaborate, but still we see that Zoom is preferred amongst our informants. Mainly this is because Zoom works more fluently than BlackBoard, and that some of the features are better in this platform. The same goes for Panopto, which is the preferred and recommended tool for recordings and videos.

One of the innovations shown in the materials is podcasting. Several of the informants explain both how they use podcasts, and how rooms are set up for this usage. Interestingly podcasts are mentioned as often as something for training colleagues and/or assistants as for being used directly in lectures. This shows potential for further innovation, and at NTNU there are several rooms built solely for this purpose.

It is also worth mentioning that both the focus groups and the interviews mentioned the same problem areas when discussing the hardware needed in a room set up for VC. It needs to work, and any difficulties with hardware, especially considering sound, will greatly affect the delivery of the lecture or meeting.

There are only 11 references to the code technological challenges (see Table 4). This is surprising all the time we were discussing VC. Probably this is due to two factors.

First, NTNU is, as shown earlier a modern and well-equipped university, meaning that both physical rooms, home equipment and network connections are of good quality. Second, our informants were more concerned about the pedagogical approaches than the technology itself. This meant that the discussions were more directed towards this dimension.

4   Conclusions

As shown in section 1.1, NTNU is a highly modern and large university, with good access to modern equipment and support services. This means that discussions at NTNU often move from debating tools on to the connection between pedagogy and technology. As one of the informants states when asked if they get questions about hardware: "It was during the pandemic. We now have the hardware, and people no longer need to purchase and test new things. It is more constant now". Thus, one moves on to asking how technology can aid pedagogy. This is worse, seeing that support personnel often have a lot of respect for the lecturer and their competence: "The challenging part is that the teachers are often pedagogues themselves, and have the right competence." This indicates that it is more the culture of lecturing, and the interest and time to understand the technological approach that might hold the digitalization of education back at NTNU. Considering for example time issues it is stated that most employees want to spend time on their profession and the topic, not the technology itself. This also means that there are not too many initiatives towards improving the approaches used in VC. This is underlined by the fact that several of the informants state that there are few good solutions for rooms designed for hybrid delivery of lectures today.

The same results can be found in problem statement three from the focus groups. Often it seems as if we are just mirroring what happens in a physical lecture hall into an online environment. This means that we lose "the power of being digital", as one of the informants states it. Thus, we need to utilize the advantages found in digital tools to enhance the VC experience for both teacher and student. It is difficult to state exactly what this "digital power" is, but from the materials it clearly includes involvement, engagement, active learning and anonymity.

Even if it seems like the culture can be hard to change, we see the high ambitions especially from the government towards using new and innovative technology (see Sect. 1.2). This is also reflected in our materials. We see that all the support personnel are concerned about development, both in the dimension pedagogy-technology, but also pedagogy-technology-rooms, for physical or hybrid lectures. This shows a willingness to fulfill aims decided on a national, and also institutional, level.

When considering the usage of VC today, one still must consider it a new way of interacting. This also means that there are a lot of technologies and software features left to explore, in order to maximize the potential. Something is already obvious, like one of the informants states: "Technology can give the possibility to be together, when meeting in person is not an option". When including technology that enhances the effects one is looking for, the interaction can be better and even enhance the learning experience.

There are clear limitations to this research. The data has been collected at one institution in Norway, and the informants providing insight has been limited to 12 in total.

We also see from the materials that the informants involved are all people already at a quite high level of digital competency, meaning that they will have different issues and problems than other possible objects. The research has been performed by a small group of involved researchers. Also, the results depend upon valid interpretation, which can always be debated. Even if all these limitations have been mitigated through methodological approaches and ethical standards, it would still be interesting to enlarge the study. Including a higher number of lecturers with limited experience in VC to the focus groups would be highly interesting, and something that is pursued by the research group already. It would also be interesting to interview stakeholders, i.e. leaders at the institution, to get more insight into policies and economy especially. Still some recommendations stand after the study.

As shown in our summary of best practices, it is possible to identify elements to be included in best practice scenarios in a Norwegian context for VC. Mainly a best practice VC needs to include high quality hardware, that the lecturer and students can access easily and know how to use. One should always look for solutions that utilize the advantages inherent in digital tools, for example by creating more interaction and engagement in the student group. This can be done via the use of response tools, break-out rooms or shared screens with annotation possibilities. It is necessary to include enough time to train and learn the tools, the support services need to be available and known to the user, and it is an advantage if they are specialized. Pedagogy needs to define the tools chosen, but one always needs to consider all three dimensions, pedagogy, space, technology, in order to have full effect of the VC. Even more in online environments than in physical lectures, it is important to aim for student-active learning. This reduces the effects of lowered attention span, enhances the social dimension of the lecture and makes the learning effects better. Thus, a good VC set-up needs to include possibilities of changing environments and group sizes instantly.

Acknowledgement. Parts of the research presented in this paper has been supported by the Portable Video Conferencing Toolkits and Online Applications for Engaging Learning Experience Design in Higher Education Classroom project (EdViCon https://edvicon.compute.dtu.dk/). The project was funded by the European Union's Erasmus Plus program, grant agreement 2021-1-DK01-KA220-HED-000023313. This publication reflects the authors' views only, and the Commission cannot be held responsible for any use which may be made of the information contained therein.

The methodology applied in this paper has been designed in collaboration with other partners in the EdViCon project.

References

1. Rogers, E.M.: Diffusion of Innovations. The Free Press, New York (2003)
2. Neustaedter, C., Procyk, J., Chua, A., Forghani, A., Pang, C.: Mobile video conferencing for sharing outdoor leisure activities over distance. Human-Comput. Inter. **35**(2), 103–142 (2020)
3. Communication Division, Norwegian University of Science and Technology: Strategy 2018-2025. Knowledge for a better world. Trondheim, Norway (2018). https://www.ntnu.edu/strategy-2018-2025

4. Kunnskapsdepartementet: Digitaliseringsstrategi for universitets- og høyskolesektoren 2017–2021 (2017). https://www.regjeringen.no/contentassets/779c0783ffee461b88451b9a b71d5f51/no/pdfs/digitaliseringsstrategi-for-universitets--og-hoysk.pdf
5. Talmo, T., et al.: Digital competences for language teachers: do employers seek the skills needed from language teachers today? In: Zaphiris, P., Ioannou, A. (eds.) HCII 2020. LNCS, vol. 12205, pp. 399–412. Springer, Cham (2020). https://doi.org/10.1007/978-3-030-50513-4_30
6. Kunnskapsdepartementet: Strategi for digital omstilling i universitets- og høyskolesektoren 2021–2025. (2021). https://hkdir.no/vaare-tenester/handlingsplan-for-digital-omstilling-i-hoeyere-utdanning-og-forskning
7. DIKU: Digital tilstand 2018: Perspektiver på digitalisering for læring i høyere utdanning. 6/2019 (2019). https://diku.no/rapporter/digital-tilstand-2018-perspektiver-paa-digitalisering-for-laering-i-hoeyere-utdanning
8. European_Commission: Shaping the digital transformation in Europe. EU Publications (2020). https://doi.org/10.2759/294260
9. Dillon L.B.: Problem tree analysis. https://sswm.info/taxonomy/term/2647/problem-tree-analysis
10. Narayanasamy, N.: Participatory rural appraisal: principles. Methods Appl. (2009). https://doi.org/10.4135/9788132108382
11. DeCarlo M.: Qualitative interview techniques, scientific inquiry in social work (2019). https://scientificinquiryinsocialwork.pressbooks.com/chapter/13-2-qualitative-interview-techniques/
12. Benyon, D.: Designing User Experience: A guide to HCI, UX and interaction design, 4th edn. Pearson Education Limited, London (2019)
13. Stemler S.: An overview of content analysis. Pract. Assess. Res. Eval. 7, 17 (2019)
14. Haney, W., Russell, M., Gulek, C., Fierros, E.G.: Drawing on education: using student drawings to promote middle school improvement. Schools Middle 7, 38–43 (1998)
15. Weber R.P.: Basic Content Analysis. Quantitative Applications in the Social Sciences, 2 edn. SAGE Publications, Inc., Newbury Park, California (1990)
16. Radcliffe, D.: A pedagogy-space-technology (PST) framework for designing and evaluating learning places. Paper presented at the Learning spaces in higher education: Positive outcomes by design: Proceedings of the Next Generation Learning Spaces Colloquium (2008).
17. Einum, E.: Response Technology and Student-centring of Language Education. Norwegian University of Science and Technology, Trondheim (2019)

Experimental Design and Validation of i-Comments for Online Learning Support

Jiaqi Wang[1] , Jian Chen[2] , and Qun Jin[3]([envelope])

[1] Graduate School of Human Sciences, Waseda University, Tokorozawa, Japan
jiaqi.wang.x@toki.waseda.jp
[2] Faculty of Information Technology and Business, Cyber University, Fukuoka, Japan
jian_chen@cyber-u.ac.jp
[3] Faculty of Human Sciences, Waseda University, Tokorozawa, Japan
jin@waseda.jp

Abstract. Online learning provides flexibility and accessibility, however, lack of interaction and support leads to decreased satisfaction and brings feelings of loneliness. Studies explored ways to promote social interaction and collaboration among learners, but there remain challenges in addressing the issues of relying on asynchronous communication in online learning. In this study, we explored which pattern of scrolling comments is beneficial and effective for online learning support. Based on the i-Comments model, we design an experiment, in which three groups of subjects are randomly assigned to view the video only, the video with i-Comments pattern I and video with i-Comments patternII. During the learning process, the subjects' concentration is detected by an eye-tracking device, while their peaceful level is monitored through the emWave system. After viewing the videos, the subjects are requested to take a quiz to test their comprehension, and a questionnaire is used to investigate cognitive load, fatigue, loneliness, and satisfaction. The results showed that i-Comments with more relevant knowledge, larger quantity, and appearance when viewing the third and last video were found to significantly improve learning comprehension, enhance learning satisfaction, keep a peaceful state, and alleviate the sense of loneliness in online learning.

Keywords: Individualized comments · Online learning support · Online learning interaction · Eye tracking · emWave system

1 Introduction

Online learning is a field that has seen significant growth and development in recent years, particularly after the COVID-19 pandemic. Online learning uses technologies to deliver learning content and support learning outside of traditional classroom settings. The main advantage of online learning is that it allows

P. Zaphiris and A. Ioannou (Eds.): HCII 2023, LNCS 14040, pp. 201–213, 2023.
https://doi.org/10.1007/978-3-031-34411-4_15

for more flexible and accessible learning opportunities for learners, regardless of their location.

While online learning provides many advantages, it has its own set of disadvantages. Online learning often lacks interaction and support that can be easily found in a traditional classroom setting. What's more, the feeling of loneliness and disconnecting from others while learning online often result in decreased satisfaction and motivation. And these also have a negative impact on learning performance [12].

There are a few research works focused on addressing the issues above. For example, creating opportunities for learners to connect with each other, such as online forums, chat rooms, and virtual learning communities. These can be used to facilitate social interaction and counteract feelings of loneliness [5]. Additionally, using technologies and tools to support collaboration, such as collaborative documents or virtual whiteboards encourages learners to work together on projects or assignments [12]. However, these methods still do not effectively address the online learning platforms that rely on asynchronous communication, which makes it difficult for learners to engage in online learning and generate a sense of companionship.

Facing these challenges, we propose a new interaction model of on-screen individualized comments, namely the i-Comments model [17]. One feature of i-Comments is the comments that accompany videos are projected over the video image in a scrolling column of text. This means the movement of comments across the screen and the 'pseudo-synchronicity' created by the way they are projected produces a feeling of companionship for learners, it can effectively solve the problems of loneliness. [21].

Therefore, in this paper, we focus on three elements of i-Comments, i.e., content, quantity, and timing. We aim to find an optimal pattern by analyzing the variation in biological indicators so that can make the appropriate content with the appropriate quantity to appear at the appropriate time. The optimal i-Comments pattern could be expected to facilitate positive learning states of learners. It also contributes to further improving learning comprehension and experience.

The rest of this paper is organized as follows. Section 2 introduces the related work, Sect. 3 describes our experiment design, and our experiment results and discussion are given in Sect. 4, finally, Sect. 5 makes a conclusion.

2   Related Work

The impact of social interaction on online learning has been extensively studied, and the results indicate that it plays a crucial role in determining the success of online learning. It has been found that the lack of social interaction is the main cause of high dropout rates among online learners [20]. Furthermore, numerous studies have shown that learners who have opportunities for social interaction experience improved learning performance and satisfaction, which leads to increased motivation and a higher possibility of successfully completing the course [14]. These findings highlight the importance of incorporating social interaction in online learning to enhance learning performances and improve overall student satisfaction.

One emerging technology of user-generated content is called *danmaku* or bullet screen, which is a real-time commentary system that enables users to view and add commentary on videos. The unique feature of this method is the integration of the comment section into the video display screen. User-generated comments are displayed over the video image in a scrolling column of text, creating a sense of "live" viewing through the illusion of a virtual time shared between users. The movement of comments across the screen and their pseudo-synchronization with the video enhances the viewing experience [10].

This kind of commentary presentation has a lot of potential advantages in facilitating learning performance. Studies have shown that it can provide a synchronous experience in asynchronous learning situations [6] and foster a sense of companionship among learners and instructors [21].

However, little attention has been paid to what type of scrolling comments are suitable for online learning. While viewing the video lectures with comments, learners are required not only to process the current learning content but also to deal with the information transmitted by the comments. According to Mayer's multimedia learning cognitive theory, the learner's working memory capacity is limited, and their attention can only be allocated to a small part of the incoming information at once [4].

Therefore, in our previous study, we proposed a new interaction model of on-screen individualized comments, namely the i-Comments model [17] to explore this issue.

Based on the related work, it is significant to explore the types of individualized comments that are suitable for online learning. In this paper, experiments are designed and analyzed based on the i-Comments model. Furthermore, we validate the effectiveness of the model and find out the appropriate patterns of i-Comments.

3   Experiment Design

3.1   Definition of the Three Elements of i-Comments

In our previous study, we defined three elements of i-Comments as follows.

(1) Content of i-Comments: According to Yerkes-Dodson law [16], it is known that the learning state of a learner changes with stress, and either too low or too high stress is not a good learning state, keep a peaceful state is beneficial for the learner. Therefore, by adjusting the content of i-Comments, we can regulate the peaceful level of the learner to promote learning under an optimal peaceful state.

(2) Quantity of i-Comments: We determine the quantity of i-Comments based on the cognitive load theory. When the cognitive load is too high, learning performance is usually not very satisfactory. We need to adjust the quantity of i-Comments within a reasonable range.

(3) Timing of i-Comments: Learners' concentration is generally declining after 10–15 min, The change in the concentration of learners with the passage of time is called the concentration curve [19]. In addition, fatigue also increases with the time spent learning. Therefore, the i-Comments would appear on the video when the course proceeds to the stage where the learner is losing concentration and feeling fatigued.

3.2 Group Control and Subjects

In order to validate the effectiveness of our model, this study employs a control experimental design. The control group view video only, while the two experiment groups view video with i-Comments in different two patterns.

In the control group, the learning content was provided to learners by a common, non-commentary video. For Experiment Group I, firstly, we collected the comments from the video website, which came from all video viewers on the web, and the comment contents were freely generated by video viewers. Secondly, we screened and refined the collected comments, excluding some irrelevant and duplicated comments, leaving only those comments that were related to the learning content. Experiment Group II was a further augmentation of Experiment Group I, in which an appropriate amount of additional knowledge related to the learning content was added to the comments.

The purpose of using three different types of videos is to validate which pattern is more beneficial to learners for online learning by comparing learners' comprehension and learning states.

Subjects are undergraduate and graduate students recruited from a university. Participation was voluntary and with informed consent from all subjects. A total of 12 students participated, and each subject was instructed to view three learning videos, one from the control group, one from Experiment Group I, and the other from Experiment Group II.

3.3 Learning Contents

During the experiment, three video clips of learning content (A, B, C) were used, each video had an average duration of approximately 6.5 min, with a total duration of approximately 19.5 min. These video clips were taken from NHK's learning video "High School Lecture Japanese History" website[1]. Video content is independent and do not interfere with each other.

---

[1] https://www.nhk.or.jp/kokokoza/tv/nihonshi/index.html.

For validation purposes, each clip's video was prepared with a version for the control group, and a version for Experiment Group I (in this version, video clip A has 20 i-Comments, B has 40 i-Comments, and C has 20 i-Comments), and a version for Experiment Group II (in this version, video clip A has 40 i-Comments, B has 60 i-Comments, and C has 60 i-Comments), as shown in Table 1. And the combination of videos viewed by all subjects is shown in Table 2. For example, Subject 1 will watch the video clips in the order of A, B-40 and C-60, which means there will not appear i-Comment from beginning to 6.5 min, and 40 i-Comment will appear from 6.5 min to 13 min, and 60 i-Comment will appear from 13 min to 19.5 min.

Table 1. Three Groups of Video Clips.

Control Group	Experiment Group I	Experiment Group II
A	A-20	A-40
B	B-40	B-60
C	C-20	C-60

Table 2. The Combination of Video Clips.

Subject Number	First (1-6.5min)	Second (6.5–13 min)	Third (13–19.5 min)
1	A	B-40	C-60
2	A	B-60	C-20
3	A-20	B	C-60
4	A-40	B-40	C
5	C	A-20	B-60
6	C-20	A	B-60
7	C-20	A-40	B
8	C-60	A-20	B
9	B	C-20	A-40
10	B-40	C-60	A
11	B-40	C	A-40
12	B-60	C	A-20

3.4 Measures

(1) Learning Comprehension Test. The pre-questionnaire aims to gather information about the subject's background and experiences related to online learning, and Japanese history education. It contains some basic information, such as gender, age, experience of online learning, experience of watching videos with scrolling comments, knowledge level of Japanese history, experience of taking classes about Japanese history, and interest in learning more about Japanese history. The data collected from this pre-questionnaire will provide insights into the subject's backgrounds and help in understanding their performance.

(2) Comprehension Quiz. This quiz test is designed with reference to NHK High School Lecture Japanese History comprehension test [2], to check a subject's comprehension and understanding of video content. Three single-choice questions are prepared for each video. Each correct answer is given 1 point, and wrong or no answer is given 0 points. Finally, the point scores are converted into a percentage scale. The score range is between 0 and 100.

(3) Cognitive Load Questionnaire. We adopt the NASA task load index (NASA TLX), which is a tool for measuring and conducting a subjective mental workload (MWL) assessment. This questionnaire contains six dimensions: mental demand, physical demand, temporal demand, performance, effort, and frustration. It is commonly used to determine the MWL of a subject while they are performing a task [8]. Then we convert the scores into a percentage scale, the range is between 20 to 100.

(4) Fatigue Questionnaire. We use the Maslach Burnout Inventory student survey (MBI-SS), which is a self-report questionnaire used to assess fatigue of students [9]. The response is scored on a 5-point Likert scale ranging from 1 (strongly disagree) to 5 (strongly agree). The converted percentage scores range from 20 to 100.

(5) Loneliness Questionnaire. We adopt the UCLA Loneliness Scale to measure a subject's loneliness in online learning [13]. Eight items are used to assess the level of loneliness and social loneliness experience. Subjects are asked to rate their agreement with each item on a scale ranging from "never" to "often". The items on the scale measure various aspects of loneliness such as emotional loneliness, social loneliness, and perceived social loneliness. The converted percentage scores range from 25 to 100.

(6) Satisfaction Questionnaire. Satisfaction is measured by adopting five items [11]. For the purpose of this study, we have made modifications to the original scale. Each item is answered on a 5-point Likert scale ranging from one (strongly disagree) to five (strongly agree). After conversion to a percentage scale, the scores will range from 20 to 100.

(7) Peaceful Monitoring. An emWave system is used to assess the peaceful states of subjects. The hardware device of the system includes an ear pulse sensor, and a USB module. By measuring the rate of blood flow to the ear lobe, the sensor calculates both the Heart Rate (HR) and Heart Rate Variability (HRV) values.

In the context of the emWave technology, coherence refers to a physiological state in which the heart, brain, and autonomic nervous system are functioning in synchrony and harmony. When a person is in a state of coherence, the state has been associated with improved emotional regulation, reduced stress and anxiety, and overall better physical and mental well-being [3, 15]. We call this kind of state as peaceful state. The scoring algorithm updates the coherence score every 5 s during an active session and adds them together and sums them as achievement on the app displays [1]. The interface screen of the emWave software program is shown in Fig. 1.

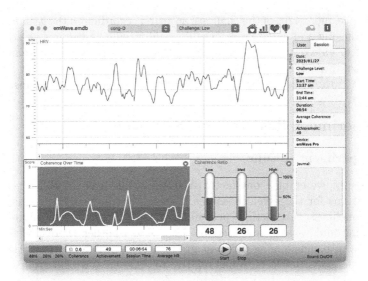

Fig. 1. The interface screen of the emWave software program

Fig. 2. Tobii Pro Glasses device (https://www.eyetracking.com/glasses/)

(8) Eye-tracking Data. Tobii Pro Glasses is a wearable device for eye-tracking research as shown in Fig. 2. We use the number of saccades as an indicator of concentration. The number of saccades and eye movements, during reading or visual tasks, has been found to be related to the level of concentration and focus. In general, a higher number of saccades is often associated with decreased concentration and increased mind wandering. Conversely, fewer saccades are often seen as a sign of increased focus and attention [7,18].

3.5   Procedure

Subjects viewed video clips individually in the experiment room. There are three steps in the experiment as follows.

(1) A subject is asked to fill out a pre-questionnaire.

(2) The subject is guided to sit in a chair in front of a computer, and the experiment procedure and precautions are explained. Then the subject is equipped with a mobile eye-tracking device, an emWave sensor, and headphones. The distance and height of the chair are adjusted according to the situation. After the eye-tracking and emWave devices are calibrated, the video is presented.

(3) After videos viewing is completed, the subject is requested to answer the learning comprehension quiz and questionnaire.

Steps (2) to (3) are repeated to complete the other two video clips.

4   Experiment Results and Discussion

4.1   Experiment Results

In this study, we employ one-factor ANOVA to analyze the difference among three patterns for the seven measures: learning comprehension, cognitive load, fatigue, loneliness, satisfaction, peacefulness, and the number of saccades. Both the F-value and p-value are used to determine whether there are significant differences in means among different groups. The F-value measures the magnitude of differences between groups relative to differences within groups, where a larger F-value suggests that the factor under study may have a greater impact on the outcome. The p-value indicates the probability of observing an F-value as extreme as, or more extreme than the one observed. If the p-value is less than the significance level (usually 0.05 or 0.01), indicating that there are significant differences in means among different groups.

It can be seen from Table 3, the three measures of comprehension ($F = 3.652$, $p = 0.037 < 0.05$), loneliness ($F = 20.273$, $p = 0.000 < 0.01$), and satisfaction ($F = 5.363$, $p = 0.010 < 0.01$), peacefulness ($F = 6.606$, $p = 0.004 < 0.01$) showed significant differences. The other three measures of cognitive load ($F = 0.390$, $p = 0.680$), fatigue ($F = 1.161$, $p = 0.326$), the number of saccades ($F = 0.399$,

$p = 0.674$) do not show significance ($p > 0.05$) across the different patterns, which means that the different patterns demonstrated consistency and no difference in these three measures.

Table 3. ANOVA Results of Three Groups.

Group(M ± SD)	Comprehension	Cognitive Load	Fatigue	Loneliness	Satisfaction	Peacefulness	Number of Saccades
CG($n = 12$)	66.67 ± 40.25	51.00 ± 10.23	42.08 ± 7.69	73.50 ± 9.85	62.67 ± 19.09	79.92 ± 21.13	546.42 ± 130.58
EP I ($n = 12$)	66.92 ± 14.29	52.92 ± 13.21	43.58 ± 9.39	58.08 ± 5.93	71.33 ± 9.77	59.25 ± 10.34	530.50 ± 140.77
EP II ($n = 12$)	91.75 ± 14.92	48.42 ± 13.94	38.58 ± 7.51	52.92 ± 8.41	80.67 ± 9.16	91.67 ± 30.24	501.83 ± 95.61
F	3.652	0.390	1.161	20.273	5.363	6.606	0.399
p	0.037*	0.680	0.326	0.000**	0.010**	0.004**	0.674

*$p < 0.05$ **$p < 0.01$

From the box plots in Fig. 3, it can be inferred that in terms of comprehension, the comparison results of group mean scores with significant differences are EPII > EPI ($t = -4.164$, $p = 0.000 < 0.01$); in terms of loneliness, the comparison results are EPII < CG ($t = 5.460$, $p = 0.000 < 0.01$), EPI < CG ($t = 4.645$, $p = 0.000 < 0.01$); as for satisfaction, the comparison results of the mean scores of the groups with more obvious differences are EPII > CG ($t = -2.944$, $p = 0.010$), EPII > EPI ($t = -2.414$, $p = 0.025 < 0.05$); and for peacefulness, the comparison results are EPII > EPI ($t = -3.514$, $p = 0.004 < 0.01$), CG > EPI ($t = 3.043$, $p = 0.006 < 0.01$).

Table 4. Summary of Comparison Results.

Group	Comprehension	Loneliness	Satisfaction	Peacefulness
CG				√
EP I		√		
EP II	√	√	√√	√

As summarized in Table 4, the results demonstrate that the experimental group II has significant advantages in comprehension, loneliness, satisfaction, and peacefulness.

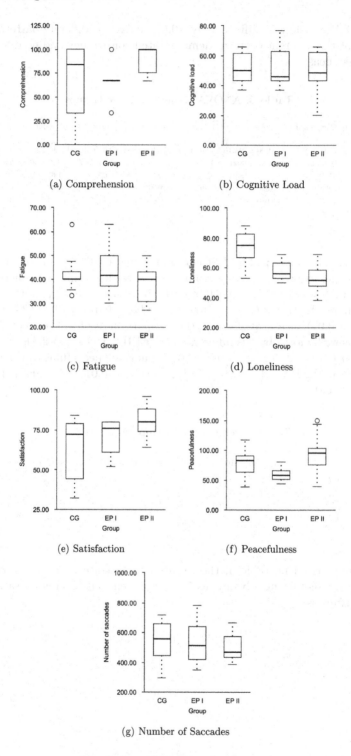

(a) Comprehension

(b) Cognitive Load

(c) Fatigue

(d) Loneliness

(e) Satisfaction

(f) Peacefulness

(g) Number of Saccades

Fig. 3. Box plots of seven measures.

4.2 Discussion

The results of our analysis showed that the pattern of i-Comments in Experiment Group II could improve comprehension, enhancing satisfaction, keep a peaceful state, and relieve the sense of loneliness. Although the potential increase in the amount of information to be processed by subjects, our findings suggested that it did not result in an increase in cognitive load or lead to feelings of fatigue and attentional distraction.

Next, we analyzed why i-Comments in Experiment Group II have demonstrated a positive impact in the following four aspects.

(1) Content of i-Comments. The i-Comments of Experiment Group I mainly came from the viewers' own submissions. Upon extraction of comments related to the video content, it was found that the viewers' comments mostly consisted of personal expressions of emotion during the viewing process (e.g., interesting, thanks), and questions about the unclear knowledge points. These constituted the i-Comments of Group I. As for Experiment Group II, on the basis of the above comments, additional knowledge related to the current content was added. According to the feedback from the subjects, this part of the content was what they needed most and could improve their comprehension.

(2) Quantity of i-Comments. Regarding the quantity, as mentioned in the experiment design, the quantity of i-Comments in Experiment Group I was 20, 40, and 20 respectively. The quantity of i-Comments in Experiment Group II was 40, 60, and 60. Based on the results of this experiment, it can be seen that the quantity of i-Comments around 40 to 60, means approximately 6 to 9 i-Comments per minute has a better-supporting effect.

(3) Timing of i-Comments. In the video combination viewed by the subjects, as shown in Table 2, we can observe that the majority of videos in Experiment Group II appeared in the third stage, which was from 13 to 19.5 min. This result suggests that i-Comments appearing at this timing have a greater impact on promoting learning. It also fits the concentration curve.

(4) Limitation. In this study, survey questionnaires were used to measure subjects' cognitive load, fatigue, loneliness, and satisfaction. However, these four indicators are not completely independent, as fatigue and cognitive load can influence each other, and all indicators can affect satisfaction. Therefore, the questionnaire items need to be further adjusted.

And only two physiological indicators were analyzed in this experiment, which is not very comprehensive. In future work, more physiological data should be measured and analyzed to make the results more objective.

Additionally, due to the factors of the pandemic, the number of subjects in the experiment is limited. Therefore, more time should be devoted to collecting data from more subjects.

5   Conclusion

In this paper, we designed and conducted an experiment to validate the i-Comments model. The two patterns of i-Comments were designed for our proposal. The results showed that i-Comments in Experiment Group II had a positive impact on online learning. The optimal i-Comments pattern consisted of a combination of personal expressions and questions from learners, as well as additional knowledge related to the current learning content, which was found to be highly beneficial for learners. The optimal quantity of i-Comments was found to be between 40 to 60. Additionally, the timing of i-Comments appeared to have a greater impact on learning when they were placed during the third stage, from 13 min to the end. These findings suggest that the optimal i-Comments pattern can effectively improve comprehension, enhance satisfaction, keep a peaceful state, and alleviate the sense of loneliness associated with online learning.

For our future work, we will consider additional elements to compose more patterns and validate them in experiments with more subjects and continue to optimize the i-Comments model and validate its effectiveness in the online learning environment.

Acknowledgements. This work was in part supported by JST SPRING (Grant No. JPMJSP2128).

References

1. Institute of heartmath. https://www.heartmathbenelux.com/doc/HeartCloud
2. NHK high school lecture Japanese history website. https://www.nhk.or.jp/kokokoza/tv/nihonshi/index.html
3. Aranberri-Ruiz, A., Aritzeta, A., Olarza, A., Soroa, G., Mindeguia, R.: Reducing anxiety and social stress in primary education: a breath-focused heart rate variability biofeedback intervention. Int. J. Environ. Res. Public Health **19**(16), 10181 (2022)
4. Baddeley, A.: Working memory. Science **255**(5044), 556–559 (1992)
5. Chang, S.H.H., Smith, R.A.: Effectiveness of personal interaction in a learner-centered paradigm distance education class based on student satisfaction. J. Res. Technol. Educ. **40**(4), 407–426 (2008)
6. Chen, Y., Gao, Q., Rau, P.-L.P.: Understanding gratifications of watching danmaku videos – videos with overlaid comments. In: Rau, P.L.P. (ed.) CCD 2015. LNCS, vol. 9180, pp. 153–163. Springer, Cham (2015). https://doi.org/10.1007/978-3-319-20907-4_14
7. Godijn, R., Theeuwes, J.: The relationship between exogenous and endogenous saccades and attention. Mind's Eye 3–26 (2003)
8. Haga, S., Mizukami, N.: Japanese version of NASA task load index sensitivity of its workload score to difficulty of three different laboratory tasks. Jpn. J. Ergon. **32**(2), 71–79 (1996)
9. Hu, Q., Schaufeli, W.B.: The factorial validity of the maslach burnout inventory-student survey in china. Psychol. Rep. **105**(2), 394–408 (2009)
10. Johnson, D.: Polyphonic/pseudo-synchronic: animated writing in the comment feed of nicovideo. Jpn. Stud. **33**(3), 297–313 (2013)

11. Keržič, D., et al.: Academic student satisfaction and perceived performance in the e-learning environment during the COVID-19 pandemic: evidence across ten countries. PLoS ONE **16**(10), e0258807 (2021)
12. Kurucay, M., Inan, F.A.: Examining the effects of learner-learner interactions on satisfaction and learning in an online undergraduate course. Comput. Educ. **115**, 20–37 (2017)
13. Masuda, Y., Tadaka, E., Dai, Y.: Reliability and validity of the Japanese version of the UCLA loneliness scale version 3 among the older population. J. Japan Acad. Commun. Health Nurs. **15**(1), 25–32 (2012)
14. Razami, H.H., Ibrahim, R.: Distance education during COVID-19 pandemic: the perceptions and preference of university students in Malaysia towards online learning. Int. J. Adv. Comput. Sci. Appl. **12**(4) (2021)
15. Sha'ari, N.S., Amin, M.: Resilience building among university students: a heart rate variability biofeedback study. In: IOP Conference Series: Materials Science and Engineering, vol. 1051, p. 012015. IOP Publishing (2021)
16. Teigen, K.H.: Yerkes-dodson: a law for all seasons. Theory Psychol. **4**(4), 525–547 (1994)
17. Wang, J., Chen, J., Jin, Q.: i-comments: on-screen individualized comments for online learning support. In: 2022 IEEE International Conference on Dependable, Autonomic and Secure Computing, International Conference on Pervasive Intelligence and Computing, International Conference on Cloud and Big Data Computing, International Conference on Cyber Science and Technology Congress (DASC/PiCom/CBDCom/CyberSciTech), pp. 1–5. IEEE (2022)
18. Wang, J.Z., Kowler, E.: Micropursuit and the control of attention and eye movements in dynamic environments. J. Vis. **21**(8), 6–6 (2021)
19. Wang, J.: Research on the emergency education model of liberal arts in universities and its quality assurance. In: International Conference on Education Studies: Experience and Innovation (ICESEI 2020), pp. 462–467. Atlantis Press (2020)
20. Xavier, M., Meneses, J.: Persistence and time challenges in an open online university: a case study of the experiences of first-year learners. Int. J. Educ. Technol. High. Educ. **19**(1), 1–17 (2022)
21. Zhang, Y., Qian, A., Pi, Z., Yang, J.: Danmaku related to video content facilitates learning. J. Educ. Technol. Syst. **47**(3), 359–372 (2019)

Tailoring Persuasive, Personalised Mobile Learning Apps for University Students

Xiaoran Zhao, Yongyan Guo[✉], and Qin Yang

East China University of Sience and Technology, No 130 Meilong Road, Xuhui District, Shanghai, China
{zhaoxiaoran,y81210094}@mail.ecust.edu.cn, g_gale@163.com

Abstract. The widespread use of English has stimulated a strong demand for learning in all countries. However, there has been little research on persuasive techniques for behavioural change in the field of MELL (Mobile English Language Learning). This paper therefore examines persuasive techniques-based MELL application in order to help students learning well. Research aims: Firstly, to explore the relationship between personality and different persuasive techniques in MELL behaviour; Secondly, to propose guidelines for the design of persuasive techniques in developing MELL application for students with different personalities. Research methods: In order to advance research in the area of personality and MELL, this paper firstly conducted a literature review to establish the background of persuasive technology for this paper; Secondly,the study serves as exploratory work by focusing on 5 commonly studied FFM personality traits illustrated on storyboards, 241 samples were collected using Likert scale questionnaires and semi-structured interviews; Finally, a structural equation model showing the relationship between personality traits and the persuasive power of different persuasive techniques was developed through the Amos, and the attitudes of different personality groups towards the 16 persuasive techniques were analysed. The results show that there are significant differences in the evaluation of persuasive skills by different personalities in the field of English language learning. These results provide valuable suggestions for the design of mobile applications in the field of MELL.

Keywords: Persuasive technology · English language learning · FFM · Persuasiveness measurement

1 Background

English has become the lingua franca of the modern world and is used as the primary language for communication with people in many fields (business, academia). With the widespread use of English, many countries whose first language is not English have integrated English language learning into their basic education, so the development of modern assistive learning tools to support effective English language learning is a key issue in the field of English language education [1].

P. Zaphiris and A. Ioannou (Eds.): HCII 2023, LNCS 14040, pp. 214–234, 2023.
https://doi.org/10.1007/978-3-031-34411-4_16

With the advent of mobile applications, the learning population can use their mobile devices to complete the act of learning anywhere, anytime. The concept of mobile learning (m-learning) is introduced [2] and research has shown that the most concentrated area of m-learning research is English vocabulary learning. English learning involves a large amount of vocabulary memorization, so vocabulary learning is a major part of English learning. The learning of English vocabulary can be done anytime and anywhere by the learning population through mobile applications, and accordingly many studies combining mobile learning with language learning have emerged, and the concepts of Mobile-assisted Language Learning (MALL) [3] and Mobile English Language Learning (MELL) [4] have been proposed.

Persuasive technology (PT) aim to change users' attitudes or behaviour through various strategies [5] and have been used by various research scholars in different fields. The use of persuasive technology in mobile learning (m-learning) can increase the effectiveness of mobile applications. Eliasn, M et al. present guidelines for the development of mobile game applications for English language vocabulary learning, which contain 16 principles based on persuasive technology [6]. Although there has been research into the application of persuasive technology to vocabulary learning for mobile learning, most existing apps take a non-tailored approach to their design; what works for one person may not work for another, and the use of the same persuasive technology may have diametrically opposed persuasive effects on users with different personalities [7]. Studies have also shown that customized persuasive apps can increase their effectiveness in promoting target behaviours compared to generic apps [8]. Considering the general nature of English language learning and the lack of research on customized persuasive apps for English language learning, there is a need for research on different personality types of persuasive techniques for English vocabulary learning behaviour.

2 Literature Review

2.1 Mobile Learning (m-learning)

Mobile learning is a specific type of learning model using mobile technology [2]. Crompton et al. define mobile learning (m-learning) as the social and content-based interaction through the use of personal electronic devices to accomplish educational acts in a variety of environments [9]. Mobile learning (m-learning) improves learning and academic performance by allowing students to learn remotely through mobile devices at their own comfort level [10]. Its aim is to put the education sector and associations at the center of academic progress in order to meet the needs of users for universality and flexibility [11]. Based on the flexibility of mobile learning, the act of learning gradually becomes learner-centered, with flexible access in the sense of time, place or interaction [12], And by allowing flexible access to rich examples of digital resources, mobile learning is rapidly expanding the realm of learning in areas outside of formal education (i.e. informal learning) [13]. And in the context of the new crown epidemic, where the probability of online classes (formal education) has increased significantly, research on m-learning is even more important. In addition to flexibility, mobile learning (m-learning) can improve the accessibility and quality of education and training as well as reduce costs and increase the cost-effectiveness of education [14]. The US government has tried to reduce costs by encouraging schools to transition from paper to digital textbooks over the next five years [15].

Based on these advantages, the field of application of mobile learning (m-learning) has gradually expanded in recent years: Some researchers have suggested that mobile learning (m-learning) can be used to improve the accessibility and quality of medical education [16]. For example, in clinical medicine teaching for assessment, inspection, collecting monitoring reports and student feedback and downloading specific course materials [17]; Survey shows 80% of US doctors use smartphones or medical apps in their practices [18]. In addition, mobile learning (m-learning) is becoming increasingly popular among those learning English and this web-based language learning gradually developed into Mobile Assisted Language Learning (MALL) [12] and Mobile English Language Learning (MELL) [4].

The learning behaviour of mobile learning is mainly done through mobile devices, which are described as tools for accessing resources [19] and can facilitate learning activities including searching and accessing documents, researching, summarizing, reading books, recording videos, taking photos, sharing information and taking notes [20]. And based on the hardware requirements of the mobile devices needed for mobile learning, higher education students are likely to engage in mobile learning more than students in high school and below, as mobile devices are very common on college campuses [21] and many universities in the United States have been pioneering mobile learning. Therefore, when studying mobile learning, the population sample and site selection should be best for college students on campus.

2.2 Persuasive Techniques

The Persuasion Technology (PT) was first introduced by Professor Fogg, who defined it as "an interactive computing system designed to change people's attitudes and behaviours [22], contains seven rules. Subsequently, Oinas Kukkonen et al. define persuasion systems as "computerized software or information systems designed to reinforce, change or shape attitudes or behaviour or both without the use of coercion or deception" and propose the Persuasion Systems Design Model (PSD) [23] The PSD model then divides the 28 principles of persuasion systems into four main categories: primary task support, dialogue support, system credibility support and social support. With widespread interest from scholars both nationally and internationally, PSD has been applied to a number of fields including healthcare, fitness and education. Relevant research in the field of education is as follows:

Llagostera et al. studied the persuasive power of a set of strategies and proposed a Persuasion Inventory (PI) questionnaire for this set of strategies: reward, competition, social comparison, credibility and social learning. Subsequently, a number of scholars have adapted the PI to examine students' sensitivity to persuasive strategies [24]. Abdullahi et al. examined students' cognitive ability scores in relation to their sensitivity to persuasive strategies (social learning, credibility, rewards) [25]. Orji et al. instead adapted the PI to investigate the use of social influence strategies (social comparison, competition, social learning) to design personalised learning components to enhance learning engagement, and the researchers will personalise the system according to the susceptibility of different students to different strategies [26].

Elaish, M et al. et al. combine persuasive technology with educational components to present a guide for the development of a mobile game application for English language learning. 16 principles from the guide provide the context for this paper's research in persuasive technology and are summarized in Table 1 [6]. With this, Elasish, M et al. developed a mobile game to increase students' motivation to learn vocabulary. The concept of Persuasive Education Systems (PES) was first introduced in 2021 and is defined as "interactive systems designed for educational settings that allow students to develop, change or reinforce optimal attitudes or behaviours for learning through persuasive strategies" [27].

Table 1. Description of the persuasion techniques

Factors	Description of the persuasion techniques
Reduction	Makes the system simpler
Tunneling	A method to guide the user through a set of predetermined sequence actions to encourage or dampen behavior
Self-monitoring	Allows users to monitor their progress and performance
Tailoring	The experimental design depends on requirements, personality, interests, and the usage of context or any aspect which belongs to the users' group
Convenience	Easy to access
Mobile simplicity	This relates to applications on mobile phones that are uncomplicated to utilize and which have a greater chance of persuasion
Mobile loyalty	Serves its own user needs and wishes
Information quality	Delivers current, pertinent, and well-arranged information
JiTT (Just In Time Teaching)	Gives suggestion at the right moment
Social facilitation	Shows to the user other people performing the same behaviour
Social comparison	Allows comparison
Social learning	Allows users to observe the performance of others
Competition	Technology motivates users to adopt a target behaviour or attitude to leverage the natural drive of human beings to compete with each other
Cooperation	Technology motivates the user to adopt a target behaviour or attitude to leverage the natural drive of human beings to cooperate
Recognition	By making the public aware of whether an individual on a group computing technology can raise the chance that an individual or a group will accept a particular behaviour or attitude
Conditional rewards	Rewards depend on target behaviour

2.3 FFM

The Big Five Factor Model of Personality (FFM) [28] is the most accepted personality model among others,it classifies people according to five different personality dimensions (Ramstedt, 2007): *Agreeableness, Conscientiousness, Neuroticism, Extraversion* and *Openness,* which are summarized in Table 2 Johnson, D. M et al. showed that personalised persuasive apps are more effective in promoting individual target behaviour, and the findings of this study further explain why FFM is widely used to customize personalised persuasive apps [29]. As the use of FFM by scholars has increased, so too has the need for the efficiency of FFM measurement, with Cosling, S. D et al. noting the need for short FFM questionnaires [30]. Scholars have gradually developed a number of short, time-saving FFM questionnaires, such as the 44-item Big Five Inventory (BFI-44) [31], the 10-item Big Five Inventory (BFI-10) [28], the 20-item Mini-IPIP [32], and 10-item TIPI [30]. The context of this paper is instead based on the Chinese version of the 10-item Big Five Personality Inventory (TIPI-C) [33].

Table 2. Description of the FFM.

Factors	The five traits represent the tendency to…
Agreeableness	…be considerate, cooperative, tolerant, friendly, caring, and helpful
Extraversion	… be outgoing, expressiveness, seek out new opportunities, and ambitious
Conscientiousness	…be self-discipline, actively plan, goal-oriented, dependable, and organized
Neuroticism	…be nervous, fearful, sensitive, distrustful, and emotionally unstable
Openness	…be curious, imaginative, hold unconventional values, and creative

Several HCI researchers have investigated how persuasive applications can be tailored to users' personalities through FFM. In the health field, Garnett, C et al. investigated how persuasive messages could be tailored to promote individual physical activity through different personality types [34]. Orji, R et al. studied the effectiveness of 10 persuasive strategies in promoting healthy eating among users with different personality types [35]. Felwah, A et al. explored FFM personality and 16 persuasive strategies [self-monitoring, reminders, verifiability (trusted information), credibility (privacy policy), personalization, distraction, suggestions, rewards, praise, encouragement, social support, customization, relaxation exercises, relaxation audios, security lock features, and contact for help] to promote mental and emotional [8]. In the field of education, however, despite the importance of mobile learning (m-learning), there is still no relevant research on the impact of FFM personality factors. Therefore, there is a need to examine the relationship between a persuasive mobile learning application (English language vocabulary learning) and different personality types.

3   Study Design and Methods

The main aim of this study was to investigate the relationship between the FFM personality [*Agreeableness, Conscientiousness, Neuroticism, Extraversion and Openness*] and the 16 principles of persuasive techniques in the mobile game app development guidelines developed by Elaish, et al. [*Reduction, Tunneling, Self-Monitoring, Tailoring, Convenience, Mobile Simplicity, Mobile loyalty, Information Quality, JiTT, Social Facilitation, Social comparison, Social learning, competition, cooperation, Recognition, Conditional Rewards*],between them to develop a guide for using persuasion strategies tailored to personalise English vocabulary learning mobile apps for different personality groups in order to achieve the effect of increasing the motivation of English language learners (ELL) to learn English.

3.1   Study Instrument

We have created interview story cards for the 16 persuasive techniques in the Mobile Application Development Guide. The content on each story card includes the name of the Persuasive technology, an explanation of the term, an example of an existing mobile app in use and a picture of the example. To ensure that the story cards conveyed the meaning of the persuasion strategy clearly and accurately, five experts were invited to discuss the design of the story cards, and based on their feedback, the interview story cards were revised and finalized. Figure 1 shows an example of a 'self-monitoring' strategy card. Prior to the main study, a pilot study was conducted with university students at East China University of Science and Technology to ensure the validity of our interview story cards. Each interview story card had a corresponding Perceived Persuasion Scale, adapted from [35], which consisted of the following questions:

"This persuasive technology will influence me to undertake English vocabulary learning"

"This persuasive technology will convince me to do English vocabulary learning"

"This persuasive technology is not relevant to me"

"This persuasive technology will make me reconsider my English vocabulary learning"

These scales were measured using a five-point Likert scale ranging from "1 = Strongly disagree" to "5 = Strongly agree".

We also collected data using the Chinese version of the 10-item Big Five Personality Inventory (TIPI-C) to assess the personality traits of each participant. Personality traits were measured using a 7-point Likert scale (ranging from '1 - Absolutely Disagree' to '7 - Absolutely Agree'). We also collected demographic information from the participants: gender, age and asked if they had ever used a mobile app to memorize words for learning purposes.

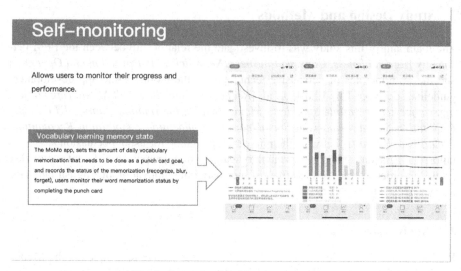

Fig. 1. Example of an interview story card

3.2 Data Collection

We have collected data through an online and offline approach.

The data for the online survey was obtained from online interviews and online questionnaires. The online interviews were conducted through online social networking tools such as WeChat and Tencent Meetings, and involved university students and postgraduate students from various universities in China, including East China University of Technology, South China University of Technology, Xihua University, Southwest Jiaotong University and Communication University of China. The 16 storyboards of persuasive strategies were explained in detail and respondents were invited to fill in the corresponding online scale questionnaires, and were further asked about their personal feelings and perceptions.

In the offline study, the participants were university and postgraduate students at East China University of Science and Technology. After the participants had been interviewed, they were given a short introduction to the study objectives, asked for their personal information, invited to look at the persuasive techniques interview story card and add to them, and invited to fill in the evaluation scales for the respective persuasive techniques, and finally conducted semi-structured interviews.

3.3 Participant Demographic Information

After screening the questionnaires with short response times and incomplete returns, we collected a total of 241 valid samples. We then used frequency statistics to summarize the demographic information of the 241 valid samples in Table 3.

Table 3. Description of the distribution of sample characteristics

		Frequency	Percentage
Age	15–20	13	5.40%
	20–25	174	72.20%
	25–30	54	22.40%
Gender	Male	86	35.70%
	Female	155	64.30%
Is there memorization of words	YES	221	91.70%
	NO	20	8.30%
Educational level	University students	104	43.20%
	Postgraduate	137	56.80%

4 Data Analysis

The main purpose of this study was to explore the relationship between the FFM personality and the 16 principles of persuasive techniques in the mobile game app development guidelines developed by Elaish, M. The aim was to examine whether there were differences in the perception of various persuasive techniques by users of different personality types and to develop guidelines for tailoring persuasive app features to the individual's personality type. To achieve this, we have employed a variety of tools and procedures to analyse our data. In this section, we summarize the various steps taken to analyse the data.

1. We calculated descriptive statistics (frequencies) for demographic variables.
2. To determine the suitability of our data for analysis, we calculated the Kaiser–Meyer–Olkin (KMO) sampling adequacies and the Bartlett Test of Sphericity (Kaiser 1970) using SPSS.

3. Next, we examined and compared the persuasiveness of the features by computing the average score for each feature and conducting a repeated-measure ANOVA (RM-ANOVA) followed by pairwise comparison, after validating for the ANOVA assumptions using SPSS.
4. Finally, we used Amos for structural equation modelling to develop models showing the relationship between personality traits and the persuasiveness of various characteristics in order to analyse the attitudes of different personality groups towards the 16 persuasion techniques.

4.1 Assessing the Suitability of Data

We determined the suitability of our data for further analysis using the KMO sampling adequacies and the Bartlett Test of Sphericity. Our results show that the KMO was 0.915, well above the recommended value of 0.6; that the Bartlett Test of Sphericity was statistically significant (χ^2 (3003) $= 14675.093\ p < 0.0001$). These results show that our data was suitable for further analysis [36].

4.2 Confidence and Validity Analysis

1. Indicator reliability: We examined the indicators loadings of the models and they were all above the recommended value which is 0.708 [37].
2. Internal consistency: We assessed the internal consistency and reliability using composite reliability (CR) and Cronbach's alpha and all were higher than their threshold value of 0.7 [37].
3. Convergent reliability: We also checked the data for convergent reliability by assessing average variance extracted (AVE) and all constructs have an AVE above the recommended threshold of 0.5 [37].
4. Discriminant validity: We assessed discriminant validity using the Heterotrait-Monotrait (HTMT) ratio of correlations and found that HTMT was all below the recommended limit of 0.9 [37].

4.3 Structural Equation Modelling

We developed models showing the relationship between personality traits and the persuasiveness of various characteristics using amos, and all five core fit indicators of this structural equation model were excellent, as shown in the following figure (See Fig. 2).

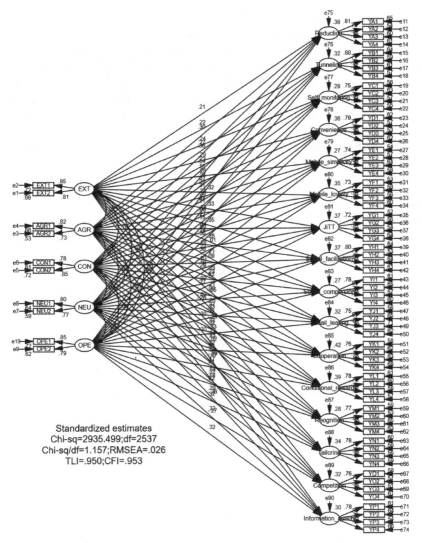

Fig. 2. The relationship between personality traits and the persuasiveness of various characteristics

5 Results

In this section, we first present the results of comparing the overall persuasiveness of the features. Then, we present the results of the relationship between the FFM personality traits and the features of a persuasive app.

5.1 Comparing the Persuasiveness of the Features Overall

The results of the repeated measures ANOVA in Table 4 indicate that (, the type of persuasive technique employed by the application had an effect on overall persuasiveness

(F $= 1.986$, p < 0.05). For the overall evaluation of persuasive technology susceptibility, means were calculated for the participants' rating data. As shown in Table 6, the means for each persuasive technology for the study sample represent the sample group's ratings of susceptibility to the use of persuasive techniques in MELL application. The means for all 16 persuasive techniques are above the median, indicating that the sample group did perceive these persuasive techniques as having an impact on the use of MELL application. The mean scores of the five strategies, *Tunneling, Mobile-simplicity, Social-facilitation, Social-learning, and Cooperation,* were high, indicating that the sample group believed that these three strategies played a greater role in improving the ease of use of MELL application.

Table 4. Means and standard deviations of the overall persuasiveness of the 16 features of a persuasive app

	Mean	SD
Reduction	2.9855	0.85714
Tunneling	3.0498	0.83361
Self-monitoring	2.9523	0.87815
Convenience	2.9907	0.80923
Mobile-simplicity	3.0322	0.81698
Mobile-loyalty	3.0508	0.87367
JiTT	2.8485	0.80064
Social-facilitation	3.0114	0.87804
Social-comparison	2.972	0.88829
Social-learning	3.0737	0.8886
Cooperation	3.0456	0.90369
Conditional-rewards	2.9699	0.81737
Recognition	2.9471	0.85881
Tailoring	2.8838	0.85512
Competition	2.9481	0.84219
Information-quality	2.9066	0.9189

5.2 The Structural Model

The structure of the model suggests that the personality of the participants affects the persuasive power of the persuasive techniques. In this section, we discuss and compare the persuasive power of different persuasion techniques for different personality types according to Table 7, and we find that some of the data is supported by the participants' comments (see Table 5).

Table 5. Description of the distribution of sample characteristics

Factors	EXT	AGR	CON	NEU	OPE
Reduction	0.211	**0.302**	**0.356**	0.157	**0.315**
Tunneling	0.217	**0.271**	−**0.339**	0.196	0.207
Self-monitoring	**0.241**	0.224	**0.309**	0.240	0.148
Convenience	**0.289**	**0.238**	0.203	0.214	**0.357**
Mobile-simplicity	**0.257**	0.240	–	0.238	**0.295**
Mobile-loyalty	**0.322**	**0.330**	–	0.218	**0.291**
JiTT	**0.331**	**0.345**	−0.182	0.157	**0.270**
Social-facilitation	**0.354**	–	–	**0.393**	−**0.255**
Social-comparison	**0.260**	–	**0.332**	–	−**0.296**
Social-learning	0.210	0.230	–	**0.363**	**0.298**
Cooperation	**0.334**	–	**0.328**	−**0.335**	**0.347**
Conditional-rewards	0.214	**0.370**	**0.319**	0.224	0.208
Recognition	**0.246**	**0.374**	–	0.173	0.221
Tailoring	−**0.245**	**0.415**	–	0.178	**0.320**
Competition	–	−0.195	**0.318**	−**0.362**	−**0.270**
Information-quality	–	–	**0.286**	**0.319**	**0.322**

Not bolded means p < 0.05, bolded means p < 0.001, "-" means no significant correlation.

5.3 The Relationship Between Personality Traits and the Persuasive Power of Different Persuasion Techniques

Reduction. The *Reduction* strategy makes the software simple to use, converting complex behaviours into simple task steps to help users achieve their goals. The results of the study showed that people who are high in extraversion, agreeableness, conscientiousness, neuroticism, openness are more easily persuaded by the *reduction* in completing English language learning behaviours using the ELA application ($\beta = 0.211$, $p < 0.05$), ($\beta = 0.302$, $p < 0.001$), ($\beta = 0.356$, $p < 0.001$), ($\beta = 0.157$, $p < 0.05$), and ($\beta = 0.315$, $p < 0.001$). The above results were supported by comments from participants as follows.

> "I really need the help of this strategy as it looks like it will optimize the operational process of my multi-software"

> "Simpler software steps would certainly be better"

Tunneling. *Tunneling* in MELL application is manifested in a predetermined set of sequential actions to guide the user through the English language learning behavior and prevent user error.

Our results show that *self-monitoring* is a significant motivator for people who are high in extraversion, agreeableness, neuroticism and openness ($\beta = 0.217$, $p < 0.05$), (β

= 0.271, p < 0.001), (β = 0.196, p < 0.05), (β = 0.207, p < 0.05). The above results were supported by comment from participants as follows.

"The software feels like it would be difficult to use the software without this technology."

However, for people who are high in conscientiousness, *tunneling* is not a significant motivating factor and even had a negative impact (β = −0.339, p < 0.001).

Self-monitoring. *Self-monitoring* refers to allowing users to track their performance status, which in the case of the MELL application is shown to users as a demonstration of their past and current learning. Our results show that *self-monitoring* is a significant motivator for people who are high in extraversion, agreeableness, conscientiousness, neuroticism and openness (β = 0.241 p < 0.001), (β = 0.224, p < 0.05), (β = 0.309, p < 0.001), (β = 0.240, p < 0.001), (β = 0.148, p < 0.05). The above results were supported by comments from participants as follows.

"I like this kind of app that can detect my learning status, especially since some apps use forgetting curves"

Convenience. *Convenience* means that the application is designed to be easy to access, with no unnecessary steps, and in the case of MELL application, this is reflected in the act of opening the software and going straight to the core functions to complete the learning. Our results show that *Convenience* is a significant motivator for people who are high in extraversion, agreeableness, conscientiousness, neuroticism and openness (β = 0.289, p < 0.001), (β = 0.238, p < 0.001), (β = 0.203, p < 0.05), (β = 0.214, p < 0.05), (β = 0.357, p < 0.001). The above results were supported by comments from participants as follows.

"Some of the software is really cumbersome, a whole lot of features I haven't used"

Mobile-simplicity. *Mobile-simplicity* means that apps that are simple to use will be more compelling. Our results show that *Mobile-simplicity* is a significant motivator for people who are high in extraversion, agreeableness, neuroticism and openness (β = 0.257, p < 0.001), (β = 0.24, p < 0.05), (β = 0.238, p < 0.05), (β = 0.295, p < 0.001).
However *mobile simplicity* has no significant effect on the conscientiousness.

Mobile-loyalty. *Mobile loyalty* refers to the need and desire of the application-side system to serve its users. Our results show that *Mobile loyalty* is a significant motivator for people who are high in extraversion, agreeableness, neuroticism and openness (β = 0.322, p < 0.001), (β = 0.330, p < 0.001), (β = 0.218, p < 0.05), (β = 0.291, p < 0.001). The above results were supported by comments from participants as follows.

"I definitely want the software provider to listen to one of my requests"

However, *Mobile loyalty* did not have a significant impact on the conscientiousness.

JiTT. *JiTT* refers to giving advice at the right time. In the case of MELL application, this can be in the form of reminders for users to complete learning behaviours. Our results show that *JiTT* is a significant motivator for people who are high in extraversion, agreeableness, neuroticism and openness ($\beta = 0.331, p < 0.001$), ($\beta = 0.345, p < 0.001$), ($\beta = 0.157, p < 0.05$), ($\beta = 0.27, p < 0.001$). The above results were supported by comments from participants as follows.

"I sometimes forget and some software reminds me on time and can help me to stick to it"

However, *JiTT* had a significant negative effect on the conscientiousness ($\beta = -0.812, p < 0.001$), which was also supported by the following comment.

"I don't like that the software keeps sending me notifications, I remember myself"

Social-facilitation. *Social facilitation* shows users who are performing the same behaviour. In the case of MELL application this could be in the form of seeing an online learning status alert for a particular person, etc. Our results show that *Social facilitation* is a significant motivator for people who are high in extraversion and neuroticism($\beta = 0.354, p < 0.001$),($\beta = 0.393, p < 0.001$). The above results were supported by comments from participants as follows.

"This has a facilitating effect on me I see others learning and I want to learn too, I Don't want to be left behind"

However *Social facilitation* had no significant effect for the agreeableness and conscientiousness but a significant negative effect for the openness ($\beta = -0.255, p < 0.001$), which was also supported by the following comments.

"This won't motivate me, I don't want to roll it"

"I can't roll it, it's too tiring, how much others learn won't affect me"

Social-comparison. *Social comparison* points to an individual using his or her children as a comparison for self-evaluation in the absence of objectivity. In the case of MELL application this can be expressed in terms of showing the user the learning process of other users, etc. Our results show that *Social-comparison* is a significant motivator for people who are high in extraversion, conscientiousness ($\beta = 0.260, p < 0.001$), ($\beta = 0.332, p < 0.001$).

However, *social comparison* had no significant effect for the agreeableness but a negative effect for the openness ($\beta = -0.296, p < 0.001$)

Social-learning. *Social learning* points to allowing users to observe what others are doing. This can manifest itself in MELL application by seeing what everyone else is using, recommendations from acquaintances, etc. Our results show that *Social learning* is a significant motivator for people who are high in extraversion, agreeableness, neuroticism and openness ($\beta = 0.210, p < 0.05$), ($\beta = 0.230, p < 0.05$), ($\beta = 0.363, p < 0.001$), ($\beta = 0.298, p < 0.001$).

However, *social comparison* had no significant effect for the agreeableness and conscientiousness.

Cooperation. *Competition* refers to the natural drive to motivate users to adopt a target attitude or behaviour through human competition. In the case of MELL application this can be expressed as PK lists.

Our results show that *Competition* is a significant motivator for people who are high in extraversion, agreeableness and openness ($\beta = 0.334$, p < 0.001), ($\beta = 0.328$, p < 0.001), ($\beta = 0.347$, p < 0.001), which was also supported by the following comments.

> "Collaboration is a great stimulus and the reward of achievement from a win-win situation is much more enjoyable"

> "I like the stimulating effect of cooperation"

However, *Competition* did not have a significant effect on the extraversion but had a significant negative effect on the neuroticism ($\beta = -0.347$, p < 0.001).

Conditional-rewards. *Conditional rewards* refer to rewarding the user for completing a goal. This could be expressed on an ELA application as a reward of points or other rewards for completing learning behaviours.

Our results show that *Conditional rewards* is a significant motivator for people who are high in extraversion, agreeableness, conscientiousness, neuroticism and openness ($\beta = 0.214$, p < 0.05), ($\beta = 0.37$, p < 0.001), ($\beta = 0.319$, p < 0.001), ($\beta = 0.224$, p < 0.05), ($\beta = 0.208$, p < 0.05), which was also supported by the following comments.

> "I'm more likely to stick around if there's a reward."

Recognition. *Recognition* refers to the process of assigning a behaviour to a public consciousness in order to change the user's attitude towards it and make them more likely to complete the behaviour. In the case of English learning apps, this can be seen in the way in which the act of learning is given a communal awareness of the environment to encourage the user to persist in their studies and complete the clock. Our results show that *Recognition* is a significant motivator for people who are high in extraversion, agreeableness, neuroticism and openness ($\beta = 0.246$, p < 0.001), ($\beta = 0.374$, p < 0.001), ($\beta = 0.173$, p < 0.05), ($\beta = 0.221$, p < 0.05), which was also supported by the following comments.

> "I like it, it makes me feel like I'm doing something worthwhile."

However, *Recognition* did not have a significant effect on the conscientiousness.

Tailoring. *Tailoring* means that the design of the application depends on the individual needs of the user. Our results show that *Tailoring* is a significant motivator for people who are high in agreeableness, neuroticism and openness ($\beta = 0.415$, p < 0.001), ($\beta = 0.178$, p < 0.05), ($\beta = 0.320$, p < 0.001).

However, *Tailoring* did not have a significant effect on the conscientiousness but had a significant negative effect on the extraversion ($\beta = -0.245$, p < 0.001)

Competition. *Competition* refers to the natural drive to motivate users to adopt a target attitude or behaviour through human competition. This can be manifested in English learning apps as PK lists. Our results show that *Competition* is a significant motivator for people who are high in conscientiousness ($\beta = 0.318$, $p < 0.001$).

However, *Competition* did not have a significant effect on the extraversion but had a significant negative effect on the agreeableness, neuroticism and openness ($\beta = -0.195$, $p < 0.05$), ($\beta = -0.362$, $p < 0.001$), ($\beta = -0.27$, $p < 0.001$), which was also supported by the following comments.

"I prefer a win-win partnership to competing with others"

"Competition doesn't motivate me very much"

Information-quality. *Information quality* refers to the provision of up-to-date, relevant and well-organized information. This can be seen in English learning applications by providing relevant meanings and phrases when learning English vocabulary, etc. Our results show that *Information quality* is a significant motivator for people who are high in conscientiousness, neuroticism and openness ($\beta = 0.286$, $p < 0.001$), ($\beta = 0.319$, $p < 0.001$), ($\beta = 0.322$, $p < 0.001$), which was also supported by the following comment.

"I would love to be given relevant information when I am studying, such as the explanation of a word in various dictionaries and such"

However, *Information quality* did not have a significant effect on the extraversion and agreeableness.

6 Discussion

6.1 Designing for Users with a Specific Personality Type

Our research has shown that it is essential to tailor the functionality of MELL application to the user's personality.

For people high in extraversion, our results show that they have a strong preference *Reduction, Tunneling, Self-monitoring, Convenience, Mobile-simplicity, Mobile-loyalty, JiTT, Social-facilitation, Social-comparison, Social-learning, Cooperation, Conditional-rewards, Recognition.*

However, *Tailoring, Competition and Information quality* are features that is perceived as negative by people with a high level of conscientiousness. Therefore, when designing a MELL application to specifically appeal to people high in extraversion, designers should employ *Reduction, Tunneling, Self-monitoring, Convenience, Mobile-simplicity, Mobile-loyalty, JiTT, Social-facilitation, Social-comparison, Social-learning, Cooperation, Conditional-rewards, Recognition* but should avoid *Tailoring, Competition and Information-quality.*

For people high in agreeableness, our results show that they have a strong preference *Reduction, Tunneling, Self-monitoring, Convenience, Mobile-simplicity, Mobile-loyalty, JiTT, Social-learning, Conditional-rewards, Recognition and Tailoring,* they are more likely to be motivated by systems employing these features. However, *Competition* is the only feature that is perceived as negative by people with a high level of conscientiousness.

Therefore, when designing a MELL application to specifically appeal to people high in agreeableness, designers should employ *Reduction, Tunneling, Self-monitoring, Convenience, Mobile-simplicity, Mobile-loyalty, JiTT, Social-learning, Conditional-rewards, Recognition and Tailoring* but should avoid *Competition*.

For people high in conscientiousness, our results show that they have a strong preference *Reduction, Self-monitoring, Convenience, Social-comparison, Cooperation, Conditional-rewards, Competition, Information-quality*. However, *Tunneling and JiTT* are features that is perceived as negative by people with a high level of conscientiousness. Therefore, when designing a ELL mobile app to specifically appeal to people high in extraversion, designers should employ *Reduction, Self-monitoring, Convenience, Social-comparison, Cooperation, Conditional-rewards, Competition and Information-quality* but should avoid *Tunneling and JiTT*.

For people high in neuroticism, our results show that they have a strong preference *Reduction, Tunneling, Self-monitoring, Convenience, Mobile-simplicity, Mobile-loyalty, JiTT, Social-facilitation, Social-learning, Conditional-rewards, Recognition, Tailoring, Information-quality*. However, *Cooperation and Competition* are features that is perceived as negative by people with a high level of conscientiousness. Therefore, when designing a MELL application to specifically appeal to people high in extraversion, designers should employ *Reduction, Self-monitoring, Convenience, Social-comparison, Cooperation, Conditional-rewards, Competition and Information-quality* but should avoid *Cooperation and Competition*.

For people high in openness, our results show that they have a strong preference *Reduction, Tunneling, Self-monitoring, Convenience, Mobile-simplicity, Mobile-loyalty, JiTT, Social-learning, Cooperation, Conditional-rewards, Recognition, Tailoring, Information-quality*. However, *Social-facilitation, Social-comparison, and Competition* are features that is perceived as negative by people with a high level of conscientiousness. Therefore, when designing a MELL application to specifically appeal to people high in extraversion, designers should employ *Reduction, Tunneling, Self-monitoring, Convenience, Mobile-simplicity, Mobile-loyalty, JiTT, Social-learning, Cooperation, Conditional-rewards, Recognition, Tailoring and Information quality* but should avoid *Social-facilitation, Social-comparison, and Competition*.

6.2 Design Guidelines

By comparing the findings of the five personality types, we established differences in the effectiveness of persuasive traits across personality types, and we summarize these findings as design guidelines in Table 6.

Table 6. Description of the distribution of sample characteristics

Persuasive technology	FFM				
	EXT	AGR	CON	NEU	OPE
Reduction	+	+	+	+	+
Tunneling	+	+	+	+	+
Self-monitoring	+	+	+	+	+
Convenience	+	+	+	+	+
Mobile-simplicity	+	+		+	+
Mobile-loyalty	+	+		+	+
JiTT	+	+	−	+	+
Social-facilitation	+			+	−
Social-comparison	+		+		−
Social-learning	+	+		+	+
Cooperation	+		+	−	+
Conditional-rewards	+	+	+	+	+
Recognition	+	+		+	+
Tailoring	−	+		+	+
Competition		−	+	−	−
Information-quality			+	+	+

7 Limitation

The study has a number of limitations. First, our study is based on self-reported data obtained from questionnaires and interviews. These persuasive techniques have not been validated over time in MELL application and the actual persuasive power of these persuasive techniques may differ from the findings of the study. Secondly, our sample group was not evenly split in terms of gender and gender was not included in the research variables at the time of the study. Finally, English language learning behaviour exists not only on university campuses but also on secondary school campuses, but our sample group for the study was mainly concentrated on university campuses. In terms of groups, there are differences in the learning states and learning mindsets of university students and secondary school students, i.e. our findings cannot be generalized to all learning groups.

8 Conclusion and Future Work

Firstly, we explored the relationship between personality types and features of MELL application, providing insight into how individuals' personality traits determine their preferences for different persuasive technique features. Our results suggest that people's personality types play an important role in their preferences for different persuasive techniques, providing valuable suggestions for the design and development of mobile apps in the English language learning domain. Secondly, we found that the sample group was more averse to persuasive techniques such as competition, social facilitation and social comparison, which use the representation of others' learning status to motivate users themselves, and this was confirmed by user comments we received during the interviews. In addition, we assessed the overall persuasive power of these persuasive techniques and the results showed that they have some persuasive power in the area of English language learning.

Future research will focus on the characteristics of persuasive techniques preferred by different groups of learners at different stages of learning, and should also examine the persuasive power of MELL application in practice based on participants' long-term use and evaluation of MELL application.

References

1. Chen, C.-M., Chung, C.-J.: Personalized mobile english vocabulary learning system based on item response theory and learning memory cycle. Comput. Educ. **51**(2), 624–645 (2008)
2. Yuen, S.C.-Y., Yuen, P.K.: Mobile Learning. IGI Global (2008)
3. Kukulska-Hulme, A.: Language learning defined by time and place: a framework for next generation designs innovation Qian Kan the use of ICT in supporting distance Chinese language learning. J. Technol. Chin. Lang. Teach. **4**(1), 1–13 (2012)
4. Elaish, M.M., Shuib, L., Ghani, N.A., Yadegaridehkordi, E.: Mobile english language learning (MELL): a literature review. Educ. Rev. **71**(2), 257–276 (2019)
5. Fogg, B.J.: Persuasive technology: using computers to change what we think and do. Ubiquity 2002 (December) (2002)
6. Elaish, M., Ghani, N., Shuib, L.: Mobile game applications (MGAs) for english language learning: a guideline for development (2017). Author, F., Author, S.: Title of a proceedings paper. In: Editor, F., Editor, S. (eds.) Conference 2016, LNCS, vol. 9999, pp. 1–13. Springer, Heidelberg (2016)
7. Kaptein, M., De Ruyter, B., Markopoulos, P., Aarts, E.: Adaptive persuasive systems: a study of tailored persuasive text messages to reduce snacking. ACM Trans. Interact. Intell. Syst. (TiiS) **2**(2), 1–25 (2012)
8. Alqahtani, F., Meier, S., Orji, R.: Personality-based approach for tailoring persuasive mental health applications. User Model. User-Adap. Inter. **32**(3), 253–295 (2021)
9. Crompton, H.: A historical overview of mobile learning: toward learner-centered education. Handb. Mob. Learn. **3**, 3–14 (2013)
10. Ishaq, K., Mat Zin, N.A., Rosdi, F., Jehanghir, M., Ishaq, S., Abid, A.: Mobile-assisted and gamification-based language learning: a systematic literature review. PeerJ Comput. Sci. **7**, e496 (2021)
11. Ishaq, K., Rosdi, F., Zin, N.A.M., Abid, A.: Usability and design issues of mobile assisted language learning application. Int. J. Adv. Comput. Sci. Appl. **11**(6), 86–94 (2020)
12. Klimova, B., Poulova, P.: Learning technologies and their impact on an educational process in the Czech Republic. In: Proceedings of the International Conference on Computer Science and Information Engineering 2015, pp. 429–434 (2015)
13. Cheon, J., Lee, S., Crooks, S.M., Song, J.: An investigation of mobile learning readiness in higher education based on the theory of planned behavior. Comput. Educ. **59**(3), 1054–1064 (2012)

14. Bates, T.: Restructuring the University for Technological Change. Murdoch University (1997)
15. Hefling, K.: Obama administration's challenge to schools: embrace digital textbooks within 5 years. Huffington Post (2012)
16. Masika, M.M., Omondi, G.B., Natembeya, D.S., Mugane, E.M., Bosire, K.O., Kibwage, I.O.: Use of mobile learning technology among final year medical students in Kenya. Pan Afr. Med. J. **21**(1), 127 (2015)
17. Lumsden, C.J., Byrne-Davis, L.M.T., Mooney, J.S., Sandars, J.: Using mobile devices for teaching and learning in clinical medicine. Arch. Dis. Child.-Educ. Pract. **100**(5), 244–251 (2015)
18. Klímová, B.: Mobile learning in medical education. J. Med. Syst. **42**(10), 194 (2018)
19. Kukulska-Hulme, A., Traxler, J.: Mobile Learning: A Handbook for Educator and Trainers (2005)
20. Mcquiggan, S., Mcquiggan, J., Sabourin, J., Kosturko, L.: Mobile Learning: A Handbook for Developers, Educators, and Learners. John Wiley & Sons (2015)
21. Traxler, J.: Current state of mobile learning. Mob. Learn.: Transforming Delivery Educ. Training **1**, 9–24 (2009)
22. Fogg, B.J.: Persuasive technology: using computers to change what we think and do. Ubiquity 2002 (2002)
23. Oinas-Kukkonen, H., Harjumaa, M.: Towards deeper understanding of persuasion in software and information systems. In: First International Conference on Advances in Computer-Human Interaction 2008, pp. 200–205. IEEE (2008)
24. Llagostera, E.: On gamification and persuasion. In: Proceedings of the SBGames, pp. 2–4. Rio de Janeiro, Brazil (2012)
25. Abdullahi, A.M., Orji, R., Nwokeji, J.C.: Personalizing persuasive educational technologies to learners' cognitive ability. In: 2018 IEEE Frontiers in Education Conference (FIE) 2018, pp. 1–9. IEEE (2018)
26. Orji, F.A., Greer, J., Vassileva, J.: Exploring the effectiveness of socially-oriented persuasive strategies in education. In: Persuasive Technology: Development of Persuasive and Behavior Change Support Systems: 14th International Conference, PERSUASIVE 2019, pp. 297-309. Springer (2019)
27. Murillo-Muñoz, F., et al.: Characteristics of a persuasive educational system: a systematic literature review. Appl. Sci. **11**(21), 10089 (2021)
28. Rammstedt, B., John, O.P.: Measuring personality in one minute or less: a 10-item short version of the big five inventory in english and german. J. Res. Pers. **41**(1), 203–212 (2007)
29. Johnson, D.M., Gardner, J.A.: Personality, motivation and video games. In: Australasian Computer-Human Interaction Conference 2010 (2010)
30. Gosling, S.D., Rentfrow, P.J., Swann, W.B., Jr.: A very brief measure of the big-five personality domains. J. Res. Pers. **37**(6), 504–528 (2003)
31. John, O.P., Donahue, E.M., Kentle, R.L.: The big five inventory—versions 4a and 54. In: Berkeley, C.A. (ed.) University of California, Berkeley, Institute of Personality (1991)
32. Donnellan, M.B., Oswald, F.L., Baird, B.M., Lucas, R.E.: The mini-IPIP scales: tiny-yet-effective measures of the big five factors of personality. Psychol. Assess. **18**(2), 192 (2006)
33. Li, J.: Psychometric properties of ten-item personality inventory in China. Chin. J. Health Psychol. **21**(11), 1688–1692 (2013)
34. Garnett, C., Crane, D., Michie, S., West, R., Brown, J.: Evaluating the effectiveness of a smartphone app to reduce excessive alcohol consumption: protocol for a factorial randomised control trial. BMC Public Health **16**(1), 1–10 (2016)
35. Orji, R., Vassileva, J., Mandryk, R.L.: Modeling the efficacy of persuasive strategies for different gamer types in serious games for health. User Model. User-Adap. Inter. **24**(5), 453–498 (2014)

36. Kupek, E.: Beyond logistic regression: structural equations modelling for binary variables and its application to investigating unobserved confounders. BMC Med. Res. Methodol. **6**(1), 1–10 (2006)
37. Chin, W.W.: The partial least squares approach to structural equation modeling. Mod. Methods Bus. Res. **295**(2), 295–336 (1998)

Understanding the Learning Experience

Investigating the Critical Nature of HE Emergency Remote Learning Networks During the COVID-19 Pandemic

Allaa Barefah[1]([✉]), Elspeth McKay[2], and Walaa Barefah[1]

[1] Taif University, P.O. Box 11099, Taif 21944, Saudi Arabia
{aobarefah,Walaa.o}@tu.edu.sa
[2] Cogniware.com.au, Unit-3,, 109 Whitehorse Road, Vic. 3010 Blackburn, Australia
e.mckay@cogniware.com.au

Abstract. In 2020, the world experienced a historical community lockdown caused by the COVID-19 pandemic. The unprecedented spread of this highly infectious disease imposed the closure of educational institutions to contain transmission of the virus. In response, universities transitioned immediately into emergency (online) remote learning (ERL) pedagogies to ensure continued education [1, 2]. This rapid shift into ERL created a new educational ecosystem [3] different from the widely published eLearning pedagogies experienced by higher education (HE) before the pandemic. This article describes a research study in the Saudi Arabia HE sector to uncover students' learning networks formed in such a chaotic environment by examining how interactions between the different instructional strategies contributed to student learning. The research design employed a mixed-methods approach; a qualitative study explored the formation of learning networks through the actor-network theory (ANT), providing the ERL feedback as content for an online questionnaire; a five-level Likert agreement scale was used to prepare the data for the quantitative study. A Rasch measurement theory (RMT) model [4] was used to analyse the questionnaire. Overall results identified influencing learning actors, while conclusions from the Rasch analysis identified gender performance differences.

Keywords: Emergency remote learning (ERL) · COVID-19 pandemic · Higher Education (HE) · Actor-Network Theory (ANT) · Continuity of learning · Synchronous learning pedagogies · Asynchronous learning pedagogies · Instructional systems design (ISD) · Rasch measurement theory (RMT) · Learning analytics

1 Introduction

The world experienced historical global lockdowns resulting from the widespread COVID-19 pandemic. The unprecedented spread of this highly infectious virus disrupted the globe, profoundly prompting governments to impose educational institutions to contain the transmission of the virus. In response, universities decided upon the pedagogical

---

The original version of this chapter was revised: the word "Title" at the beginning of the title has been deleted. The correction to this chapter is available at
https://doi.org/10.1007/978-3-031-34411-4_45

P. Zaphiris and A. Ioannou (Eds.): HCII 2023, LNCS 14040, pp. 237–255, 2023
https://doi.org/10.1007/978-3-031-34411-4_17

transition into an emergency remote learning (ERL) approach to enable continued student learning. Moreover, the arrival of the pandemic coincided with the middle of a teaching semester in most universities. This rapid shift into ERL created a new educational ecosystem different from the widely studied eLearning pedagogy experienced in higher education (HE) learning environments.

Universities responded in various ways to the challenges and opportunities caused by the pandemic to keep their students' learning processes flowing smoothly within this emerging educational ecosystem. However, the new 'normality' formation implied a change in the pedagogical structure underpinning the learning process, key actors, and influential roles supporting the learning [5]. Furthermore, this rapid shift into ERL means that learning now occurs outside university classrooms and beyond the scheduled lecture halls. This disruption is suggested here as appearing in a complex and digitally networked environment. Thus, it is necessary to uncover these technological networks formed in such a chaotic environment and examine how interactions between different entities may have contributed to learning continuity.

During the COVID-19 pandemic, the ERL occurred in a networked social environment of innumerable objects, actors, complex associations, and assemblies. For this purpose, it was essential to adopt an appropriate analytical lens that considered all the actors' contributions. The ANT originated from social research as a socio-technical approach assuming that everything in the social world is a constantly changing network of relationships. These relationships occur between hybrid entities (actors) of both human beings and socio-technical elements. ANT treats actors equally in the same way in terms of their contributions to constructing a network. Therefore, ANT is relevant in analysing the continuity of learning at HE institutions, which are considered complex social entities that depend heavily on technology (socio-technical) to achieve their goals. In ANT, the ERL is a product of networked interactions between different parts: universities; instructors; learners; computers; plans; and leadership; whose actions are taken collectively and examined as a combined work [6].

ANT assumes that meaningful activities, such as the continuity of learning, were formed through the interactions between actors, which produced the network [7]. On this premise, ANT is concerned with the mechanism of power that results from the formation of networks made up of actors (human-being and socio-technical elements). In other words, the underlying meanings of a phenomenon reside in the dynamic and complicated relationships between the actors [8]. This article explores how ERL networks formed during the forced transition into fully online learning. Also, to identify the influencing actors (human-being and socio-technical elements) and follow their interactions which played a crucial role in supporting the continuity of learning within the uncertain realities of the COVID-19 pandemic. Therefore, ANT fits well with this study accounting for the contributions from both human-being actors and socio-technical elements. However, understanding how students learn in this pandemic is beyond this article's focus, and it would be more appropriate to apply a learning theory serving that purpose.

This examination is through the lens of ANT for adopting ERL to help identify and quantify novel and potentially useful ERL pedagogy designs for Saudi Arabia. This article is organised as follows:

Starting with the extant literature on emergency remote learning discusses continued learning under such emergencies. Following on is the qualitative research design and methods used. Then there are key findings and a summary to follow the analysis of the interaction within the ERL network. Then there is the quantitative empirical research design and methodology employed, describing the data triangulation and a rationale for the researchers to increase the credibility and reliability of their findings confidently. Finally, the article ends with a Discussion and Conclusions section with future research work directions.

2 Related Work

Since the outbreak of the COVID-19 pandemic, the ERL literature is still growing to understand how the pandemic impacted the learning continuity in higher education institutions (HEI) [9, 10]. This increased interest prompted improving HE institutions' preparedness in dealing with future emergencies. Many studies have documented the responses of HEI in adapting to the new ERL requirements. On an administration level, [11] explored HE policy responses to the pandemic in Canada. The study recommended collaborative efforts between HEI and federal and provincial governments for their critical roles towards recovery. Other studies, like [12], examined HEI communication responses in China, Canada, and the USA using a framework ased on situation crisis communications theory (SCCT). During the initial response to the crisis, they explored HEI policy and management, relying on three elements: crisis stages, leadership response, and stakeholder responsibility. Their findings supported leadership and communication as central to managing the continuity of learning during emergencies. Some studies have highlighted HEI technological readiness as a critical element in mitigating the transition [13].

Other studies investigated the adaptation of instructors as crucial to maintaining continued learning during emergencies. Some research focused on instructors' perceptions of ERL as being influential in facilitating the transition [14]. Other research attempts tended to focus on their needs for training [15, 16]; and professional development [17, 18] to adapt and design instructional strategies for ERL. Other factors, such as: instructors' prior online experience; their gender [19]; and the level of their IT-skills [20]; were also investigated in the ERL literature. Several studies took a learner-centred approach and focused their investigations on: learners' perceptions [21]; accessibility to technology [22]; motivation [23]; and engagement [1]; drawing on their lived experiences of ERL. Much literature has been published on learners' and instructors' challenges during ERL. These challenges can be grouped into three categories; (a) the psychological, physical and mental health concerns resulting from COVID-19, (b) academic relating to courses, instructional techniques, evaluation of assessment methods and (c) personal adaptation to the new situation, in terms of privacy and distraction during the learning process [24, 25, 46].

While previous studies give much attention to instructors, learners, and institutions, less attention was given to instructional designers and the practice of designing instructional strategies for ERL [26, 27]. Some research proposed educational frameworks for

COVID-19 ERL to be used in future emergencies. For example, [28] adopted a participatory design methodology to provide practitioners with a future emergency remote teaching environment framework. When designing responsive ERL, their framework considered shifting variables like learners' age and socio-economic status, subject areas, and school district. Another approach for sustaining learning during emergencies proposed the integration of social media to foster active understanding/learning [29]. [30], introduced the academic communities of engagement (ACE) framework to design instruction in light of (a) the course community (instructors, peers, administrators) and (b) the learners' personal community (parents, siblings, friends). Despite the extensive pedagogies and frameworks in the ERL literature, little is known about the cultural adaptations to ERL pedagogical designs and tools [31]. This issue is particularly important for future practical implications.

In the context of Saudi Arabia, the ERL literature reveals a healthy variety of investigations focused on technology and its use during the transition to maintain continued learning [32]. Also, studies explored learners' perceptions [33], preferences [34], and engagement [35]. In addition, there have been some calls in the literature, such as the work of [36], for the Saudi HE administration to formulate a contingency strategy for ERL and provide training for learners and instructors to improve their preparedness for future emergencies. Other research trends draw on instructors' experience to investigate students' engagement during COVID-19 ERL [37], in which the findings supported the effects of local culture on students' engagement. Accordingly, such differences and considerations were necessary when undergoing the instructional systems design (ISD) process [38].

In these scenarios, it is important to understand that ERL occurred in a digitally networked environment that includes different entities (actors) of both human beings and socio-technical elements. In this sense, the interactions between these entities influence the learning continuity during the COVID-19 pandemic. However, although extensive research has been conducted on the continuity of learning under the COVID-19 pandemic, more investigation is needed to fully understand how the nature of ERL forms through the interaction between influencing actors. There would seem to be a definite need for a holistic approach that accounts for all actors contributing to continued learning within their social and cultural environments. In this light, it would be possible for HEI to improve their future responses to emergencies and develop customised and culturally responsive ERL.

3   Qualitative Research Study

Taking the ANT analytical approach meant it was necessary to uncover the ERL network and its underlying structure before any data measurement or evaluation occurred. Furthermore, during this pandemic, relying on educational technology to deliver instruction meant that the changing educative roles of institutions, learners, and instructors may give rise to a complexity affecting the continuity of learning. It was then essential to explore the ERL network components concerning the actors, their relationships, and the network learning continuity outcomes during the COVID-19 pandemic.

3.1   Materials and Method – Qualitative Study

A four-staged qualitative research design represented: the literature review to formulate the interview questionnaire items; two pilot studies to locate the instrument's reliability; and the main study. Three separate processes were necessary to conduct the research: participants to provide the qualitative data; devising the instrumentation for the data collection; and the data analysis. The following parts describe these processes in turn.

Participants. There were 13-participants involved in semi-structured interviews, and the researchers collected the data for the qualitative analysis at the early stage of the pandemic in 2020. Formation of the ERL network from an instructor's perspective revealed they were immersed in designing, teaching, communicating, and delivering distant instruction to the learners. Although the targeted sample involved mainly instructors, other ANT actors were interviewed as influential for the continuity of learning to uncover the ERL network's underlying structure. The sample included: nine male and female instructors; one academic administrator; two learners; and one IT support team member who were teaching, studying, or working at universities in Saudi Arabia, representing different colleges that included: Business Administration; Applied Science; Design; Medical Science; and Engineering.

Instruments and Procedure. Interviews conducted involved an iterative validation process of revision and analysis. The first stage reviewed the existing literature: (1) identified the initial actors influencing the continuity of learning under emergencies; and (2) designed the interview questions based on the themes that emerged from the literature review. Then, two participants were interviewed during the second stage (pilot-1) to test the interview questions' validity. A set of additional actors arose from the pilot-1 analysis, which showed the need to revise some interview questions. During the third stage (pilot-2), three participants were interviewed to validate the revised interview questions and reconfirm the actors' set to influence continuous learning under emergencies. The final research stage was the main study, which involved eight participants who were interviewed based on the previously validated interview questions.

Due to restrictions imposed to control the spread of COVID-19, participants were contacted by phone calls that lasted between 30 and 40 min. The interview questions were designed using the themes from the literature review devised consecutively during the data collection stages. Interview protocol uncovered participants' lived ERL pandemic experience; first-person, entity, or tools of contact that helped them continue the learning experience during the early days of the pandemic; and their approach to facing critical challenges during the transition into ERL. The questions were left open-ended to allow participants to expand their responses from a personal perspective [39]. All interviews were recorded and transcribed. Interviews were conducted in Arabic, and answers were translated into English to comply with the NVIVO software requirements. The translation into English was done after analysing the data to elicit meaning and concepts. The forward translation was performed immediately after the quotes selection, and two expert editors transferred informal Arabic into Standard Arabic. This step ensured translation was equivalent to the original scripts conceptually, semantically, and culturally [40]. Back-translation was then conducted by two professional translators.

Data Analysis. A standard qualitative analysis followed a three-coding model. First, the transcripts were read thoroughly and coded independently by two researchers to extract initial coding. Descriptive codebooks included the definition and description of each code developed to ensure similar interpretation of data. Both researchers read the exact text, conducted the coding independently, and discussed areas of discrepancies with emerging themes compared to the researchers' content review. A second coding round was performed using Microsoft Word to group initial codes into meaningful themes to conform with manual coding. The interviews' data were imported into the NVIVO tool to confirm data coding and thematic analyses.

3.2 Results – Qualitative Study

The qualitative study results follow in the next two sections. The first section outlines the actors' list as the most influencing actors to the learning continuity from an instructors' perspective. The second section provides an analysis of the nature of the ERL network during the COVID-19 pandemic. The final section presents a brief description of emergent themes.

List of Actors. The results revealed that the ERL network comprised five sets of black boxes, including actors identified by instructors as having the most significant influence on the ERL continuity. The actors were listed based on instructors' recording of their importance and perceived impact coinciding with their first appearance in the network. Although not a complete list, it only included the most influential actors according to participants' views on the strength of their interaction that formed the ERL network actors: COVID-19; university leadership; technology; college; and IT support team.

Complex Nature of the ERL Network. The ERL network changed over time, with the learning continuity progressing in four main phases: a stay-at-a-home decision; the transition into ERL; adaption to the ERL; and the optimal application of ERL.

Each phase had: a distinctive nature of learning continuity; key influencing actors who affect the development of the learning process; and inhibitors identified as hampering the flow of learning. Participants experienced the continuity of learning, going through these phases at a different pace depending on their interaction with key actors and their differences, and communication skills. The section below presents an analysis of each phase based on three network premises: commencement, maintenance, and the network's disintegration. In all phases, it appeared that the changing nature of the learning continuity corresponded with the time instructors spent during the COVID-19 pandemic. For instance, the more time instructors utilised technology to interact with other actors, innovate effective teaching methods and learning strategies, the more they could support learning continuity.

Phase-1: Stay at Home Decision – Commencement: The COVID-19 virus was the phase initiator described by many instructors, learners, and academic admins waiting for university leadership instructions. The flow of learning continuity was vague and several attempts to initiate the network by instructors failed. *Development:* Despite interruptions, instructors could form facilitating relationships with academic admins, which allowed the network to become established (technology functioned here as a mediator). *Disintegration:* Instructors' unanswered inquiries and wait for guidance directed their interaction with actors outside the educational system, such as unofficial social media personal accounts.

Phase-2: Transition into ERL – Commencement: The university's official announcement of the transition into ERL was the second phase's initiator. *Development:* the learning process flowed in two emergent patterns (positive and passive). The positive path of continued learning was noticed with instructors who took adaptive steps towards the transition by initiating virtual lectures using the university's LMS relying on their personal knowledge and digital skills. On the other hand, the passive path of learning flow appeared with instructors who could not adapt to the transition as they resisted the change. However, the interviews revealed that the lack of technical skills and instructors' perception of eLearning effectiveness were the dominant inhibitors that prevented the learning continuity from flowing. *Disintegration:* The IT support team members who prepared reports on virtual lectures for the university leadership were alarmed about the absence of some instructors. To revive the learning process, the university leadership imposed strict procedures that involved regular reports and follow-ups on instructors' attendance.

Phase-3: Adaptation to ERL – Commencement: Instructors activated the adaptation of ERL as they were leading the process of learning continuity. The instructors' practices to improve learners' ERL experience distinguished the instructors' role. Instructors exerted efforts in supporting the continuity of learning by ensuring the delivery of smooth lectures and enhancing communication with the learners. *Development:* the learning flow changed when instructors interacted with the course. The learning flow slowed when instructors dealt with the nature of some courses' instructional content. As ERL complexities increased, the learning flow diverted consistently from its path due to interruptions' inhibiting effects (huge number of learners per lecture). As Participant-8 explained:

> *"every lecture, I deactivate the chat function, I know that I'm lessening the chance of interaction with my students. But I have to do this because many students send irrelevant issues in the chat box that would distract their peers, or cause a technical problem."* P8.

Disintegration: The end of this phase aligned with the start of final exams and announcing the first semester's results in the pandemic. Some instructors faced a significant challenge in conducting electronic exams as it was their first time setting up an exam electronically. The technical support team exerted great effort in supporting this process virtually through training workshops.

Phase-4: Optimal ERL Application By this phase, most of the instructors reached optimal ERL literacy, which enabled continued learning. *Commencement:* The continuity of remote learning during the lockdown in the second semester was the start of this phase. The more time spent in lockdown, the more the reliance on technology improved instructors' IT skills and signaled a transition into a more disciplined approach to remote learning. Instructors showed advanced management and technical skills and enhanced communication with other actors. *Development:* Due to the availability of informative resources and continuous IT support, manifested in the training workshops and instant response. The learning remained vivid, and instructors overcame the effects of minimal interruptions of some procedural activities. *Disintegration:* The learning discontinued at the end of the second semester of lockdown. Instructors were waiting for a changing event, such as the approval of vaccination or further instructions from the university leadership regarding the ongoing approach, indicating a pause in the learning cycle.

Emergent Themes and Categories.   Our analysis revealed two emergent themes related to the ERL (continuity of learning and instructors); five categories (managerial issues, technology, cultural barriers, personal characteristics and work-related challenges); and 12 sub-categories.

3.3   Summary – Qualitative Study

The study confirmed the complex changing nature of the ERL network through the phases that characterised the learning continuity during the COVID-19 pandemic. Although it was a difficult transition, robust opportunities for learning occurred throughout these phases. As recommended by [41], HE can target these opportunities to improve ERL design to enhance continued learning. For example, university leadership would benefit from the set of the identified inhibitors and facilitators from each phase used as a guide in formalising risk-management and recovery plans, which can empower the HE sector with sustainability resilience [41]. Alternatively, instructors can benefit from the results in facilitating continued learning during any transitional situation under emergencies. As the complicated nature of ERL was revealed and the actors influencing the continuity of learning identified, it was now possible to measure the ERL effectiveness within this context.

4   Quantitative Empirical Research Study

A key focus of an educational researcher is to design reliable test instruments for measuring performance or agreement outcomes in particular settings. In this sense, the reliability characteristics (or behaviour) of the effectiveness of ERL agreement points describe how consistent or error-free the measurements were [41]. Such test-measurement results show whether agreement levels achieved represent whether or not these agreements occurred and whether or not instructional technologies, strategies, and assessment methods were helpful for that particular set of stakeholders. In addition, it was beneficial to understand initial reactions to the questionnaire items. For instance: consistently low agreement levels across the measured stakeholder cohort may indicate a need for remedial ERL strategies (for particular stakeholders). Or where questionnaire items were not showing much agreement among others, requiring additional ERL strategy-solving activities to stretch those stakeholders cognitively.

4.1 Materials and Method – Quantitative Study

The main aim of the quantitative data analysis was to examine the questionnaire results in terms of the individual participant or person Likert agreement-scores, relative to other participant's agreement-scores, and behaviour of online questionnaire-items, relative to each questionnaire-item, on a common unidimensional scale [42]; whether there was variation in responses between males and females; and whether individual item responses had expected outcomes, or had anomalous distributions.

The parameterisation used was the Andrich rating scale model, otherwise known as the polytomous Rasch model (PRM) [43]; whereby observed distance between response categories on the Likert rating scale were identical across items, and the data fit the rating scale parameterisation [44]; [45], including the conditional estimation of item parameters independently of person parameters [4] p: 131, providing the sufficient statistics for all parameters [46].

In the past decade, a vast body of expertise in Rasch model theory (RMT) has expanded from the educational sector [45] into the medical/healthcare and business sectors. The contributions, for example, include: an exploratory factor analysis conducted on an active support measure using a dataset of 884 participants living with intellectual disabilities in Australian group homes, collected between 2010 and 2018 [47]; measuring the perceived quality of student services at the reception office of an Italian university [48]; and a customer satisfaction survey [49]. However, the current digital transformation [50] within the education sector is forging innovative digital pedagogy solutions such as carefully customised online learning questionnaires [51], brought about by COVID community lockdowns, and increasing interest in psychometric testing of online skill development. In recognition of this demand, the Australian Council for Educational Research (ACER) supports the importance of management and human raters measurement [52].

The application of the RMT in this study was to overcome the limitations of the Classical Test Theory (CTT), such as testing sample dependency [53, 54]. The Rasch model allows a rigorous validation of the measuring instruments by evaluating item-difficulty against participant-ability on the same logit scale. Additionally, an RMT analysis can detect potential measurement issues, such as local item dependency, allowing for improved measurement quality [55]. Another essential feature of an RMT analysis is ensuring that the data fit the model, thus contributing to reliable inferences by showing any misfit items that may require modifications. Therefore, this study applied the RMT analysis to evaluate the effectiveness of ERL collectively reflected in three constructs by employing a context-developed survey instrument.

Participants. The participant sample consisted of 334 graduate students receiving ERL during the COVID-19 pandemic at different universities in the Kingdom of Saudi Arabia. The questionnaire was disseminated electronically to participants enrolled in one of the following colleges (Medical, Applied Science, Pharmacy, Business Administration, Humanities, Islamic Jurisprudence and Law, Computer and Information Technology, Science and Engineering, Science, Design and Arts, Education), in the academic year 2020–2021. More females (60.2%) responded to the questionnaire than males (39.8%). Therefore, the study sample was assumed to represent the universities' population [56].

Participants were aware of the aim of the study and informed that their personal information and responses would be handled securely. All respondents participated voluntarily. The questionnaire remained open for four weeks.

Instruments and Procedure. The design of the measuring instrument involved the following steps; (1) establishing the research constructs, (2) developing items, and (3) assessing instrument validity. Relying on the results from phase-1 (Stay at home decision – Qualitative Study), three main constructs were used to measure the effectiveness of technology in supporting continued learning during ERL; (Educational Technologies, Educational Strategies, and Assessment Methods). These constructs commonly appear in ERL literature [57, 58]. The questionnaire included 19-items in which each item was believed to contribute to a single construct: Educational Technologies (10-items); Educational Strategies (5-items); and Assessment Methods (4-items). Items were carefully worded and structured to avoid ambiguity and then scored on an ordinal scale using a five-level Likert agreement scale (1:never been used, 2:not effective, 3:effective to some extent, 4:effective, 5:very effective) (see Appendix for a full list of items).

Statistical Data Analysis. The Qualitative Study (phase-1) results revealed a sudden shift into the ERL during the COVID-19 pandemic. It was seen as forging various digital pedagogical strategies, indicating the need for an inclusive evaluation through a reliable measurement approach.

Survey items were analysed using the Rasch PRM [59] software. It was important to validate the questionnaire item design and ensure the reliability of the testing instrumentation.

The RMT analysis focused on the following aspects:

1. the overall agreement level of participants relative to the questionnaire COVID strategy agreement levels);
2. whether there was a variation in responses between the different colleges/schools;
3. whether there was a variation in responses between males and females; and
4. whether individual item responses had expected outcomes or had anomalous distributions).

4.2 Results – Quantitative Study

The results support the questionnaire items as having excellent psychometric properties. The summary statistics include the unidimensional Rasch logit-scale location and fit residual statistics (Fig. 1). Although the Summary Statistics revealed a Power of Analysis of Fit as excellent, it was used in conjunction with other analysis indicators [43].

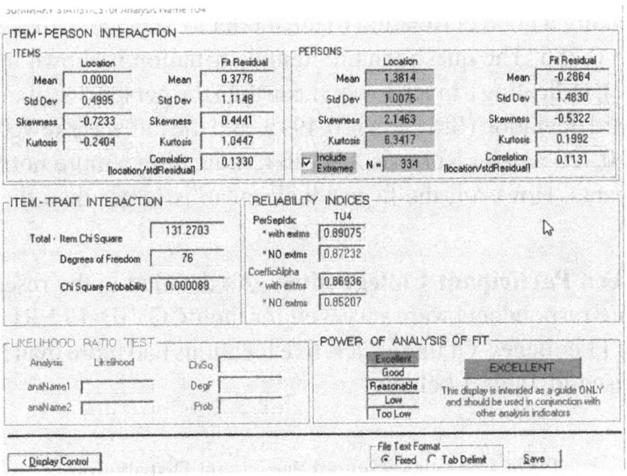

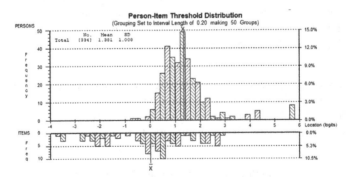

Fig. 1. RUMM 2030 Summary Statistics

Person-Item Interaction. The proverb that a picture speaks a thousand words is used here to communicate the initial research results. The starting point was to examine the questionnaire results in terms of the individual participant/person Likert agreement-scores relative to each participant's agreement-score and the behaviour of each questionnaire-item relative to each questionnaire-item on a common unidimensional scale. This scaling concept is shown in the Person-Item Threshold Distribution below (Fig. 2). There were 334-participants involved in the questionnaire. The Summary Statistics included the unidimensional Rasch logit-scale location and fit residual statistics. There were 19-items in the questionnaire, each with five levels of Likert agreement).

Fig. 2. Person-Item Threshold Distribution

The threshold distribution for participants (red boxes above the Logit scale, Fig. 2) showed a bimodal distribution with a mean value of 1.381 and a standard deviation of 1.008. The distribution is relatively tight on the left side of the mean. However, a long tail of values to the right gave a positive skewness of 2.146 and a large Kurtosis of 6.3417. Cronbach's Alpha Coefficient was 0.869, and the Rasch model Person Separation Index was 0.891, indicating a good correlation to the model's expected values. The fit residual mean was only −0.286. The questionnaire item distribution is shown in blue under the logit scale (Fig. 2), indicating a much lower mean than the person distribution on the same scale. The standard deviation (Std Dev) is 0.4995, and the tail was skewed to the left with a skewness of −0.7233 and a Kurtosis −0.2404, indicating a more normal distribution than the participants. However, the fit residual: mean is larger than the participants at 0.3776.

Variation Between Participant College Sites. As detailed in the research methodology, questionnaire respondents were surveyed for their COVID-19 ERL strategy agreement levels from 11 colleges. Of these sites, five locations had more than five participants and are summarised in Table 1 below:

Table 1. College/School Participant Distribution

Group	# Partic	Mean	SD	Skew
4	12	0.939	0.551	−0.112
5	8	0.849	0.724	−1.095
9	289	1.438	1.011	2.112
10	9	0.875	0.636	0.514
11	6	0.899	0.385	2.363
Total Sample	**334**	**1.381**	**1.0075**	**2.146**

This analysis shows that the smaller college samples had a lower COVID-19 strategy agreement with the mean for the four small sample groups, approximately 0.9 on the logit scale. The main survey site of 289 participants had a mean logit score of 1.438, which significantly affected the overall analysis outcome. This college clearly had a well-applied COVID-19 strategy, with a large portion of the cohort in agreement that the strategies were effective.

Variation Between Genders. The gender split of participants was 134 males and 200 females. Seven of the eight extreme high scores (Fig. 2) were males, which skewed their mean value by 0.22 logits. These extreme scores were therefore removed in this analysis to better illustrate the variation between genders. Table 2 summarises the analysis:

Table 2. Gender Participant Distribution

Group	# Partic	Mean	SD	Skew
Males	127	1.426	0.921	1.074
Females	199	1.184	0.633	1.096
Total Sample	**326**	**1.381**	**1.0075**	**2.146**

The male participants had a mean logit score of 1.426 (1.644 including extremes) compared to a mean value for females of 1.184 logits. This variation is significant and may indicate that the male cohort was more involved in developing the college COVID-19 strategy and was engaged in implementing that strategy.

Individual Item Analysis. As mentioned in the methodology, the questionnaire had 19-questions grouped into three categories:

1. Educational Technologies (items 1 to 10);
2. Educational Strategies (items 11 to 15); and
3. Assessment Methods (items 16 to 19).

The Rasch model theory (RMT) item characteristic curve (ICC) identifies class intervals that show the relative ability of a question/item to discriminate among adjoining knowledge constructs (traits) along a linear scale (Fig. 3). Rather than compare individual participant scores against the expected model curve, the Rasch Model divides the sample into either quartiles or, in this case, quintiles. So, it determines the mean logit score of each 20% of the participant sample (0.402, 0.835, 1.175, 1.518 and 2.344). As evident in the expected value plots for individual questions, these red marks on the person logit scale do not change. However, the observed value of the group (the black dot within the plot) does change for each question. For example, Fig. 3 for question 11 (the strategy of allowing direct questions during virtual lectures) illustrates that the observed score for each quintile closely matches the expected value from the model distribution (i.e. all black dots are very close to the expected value curve). In addition, the fit residual is very low at only -0.036, indicating a strong correlation between the observed scores and the model's expected values.

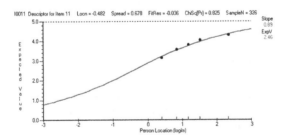

Fig. 3. Item characteristic curve (ICC) – question/item-11

The analysis strength of the ICC is that the variation in responses to each item between participant groupings, such as genders and between the different college sites in the study can be visualised and measured. For example, Fig. 4, using item-11 as a typical question, where observed responses correlated well with the model's expected value curve, illustrates that both males and females conform reasonably well to the expected curve. However, the females generally performed better than the males on this question, which was opposite to the overall study results.

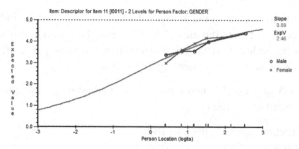

Fig. 4. Item characteristic curve (ICC) with Gender distribution – question/item-11

However, some items have irregular distributions and poor correlation to the model's expected curve. For example, item-5 (questioning the use of cameras in online communications) showed a relatively poor correlation with a fit residual of 3.366, with the lowest quintile scoring above the model curve and the highest quintile scoring well below the expected curve (Fig. 5).

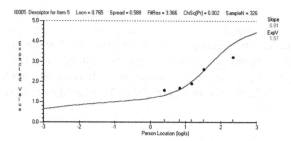

Fig. 5. Item characteristic curve (ICC) – question/item-5

The Items-5 gender distribution ICC (Fig. 6) shows the female result distribution roughly following the expected value curve, and as with the overall study result, the females were slightly below the overall study expected value. However, the male observed value on this question was irregular and clearly did not correlate well with the model's expected value curve.

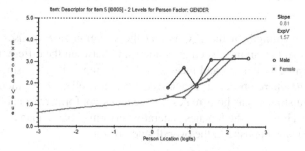

Fig. 6. Item characteristic curve (ICC) with Gender distribution – question/item-5

Although the college variance was more difficult to identify due to the significant differences in participant numbers at different college sites, it was still useful to review this data. For Item-11 the main participant site (Group 9) correlated well with the expected curve. This result was predictable as the expected curve is largely built around the 289 participants at this college. Group-4 was the second largest college site, and they performed better than expected on both items-11 and item-5. However, Group-5, with only eight participants, showed anomalous distribution on both items, indicating that the sample size at this site was insufficient within the overall study to yield a consistent expected outcome.

4.3 Summary – Quantitative Study

The RMT analysis successfully identified the participants' overall agreement levels of COVID ERL strategies relative to the online questionnaire items with an excellent fit and small fit residual mean of -0.2864. The data analysis indicated that the larger colleges had better-developed ERL strategies than the smaller cohorts and that male participants had a higher agreement level than the females. Individual item responses showed anomalous distributions relative to the expected outcomes, with the item category often reflected in the response variations.

5 Discussion and Conclusions

In this work, we investigated the formation of the complex changing nature of ERL to support learning continuity during the COVID-19 pandemic. We also identified influencing actors and their interaction which uncovered the connected structure of the network. We then measured how effective the ERL was in supporting continued learning. It is clearly visible from the presented findings that the transition into ERL was not smooth and took collective efforts, drastic changes, and lengthy waits. As the network changed over time, the learning continuity progressed in four main phases. These findings are particularly important to universities' leadership in their institutional response to emergencies. Instead, what is required from universities is an inclusive response that considers all the influencing actors and gives equal importance to their changing roles in supporting the continuity of learning. This mixed methods research project endeavoured to identify the critical nature and elements of the ERL network that formed the continuity of learning during *an* initial period of the COVID-19 pandemic *by* measur*ing* how effective the ERL was in supporting continued learning.

The qualitative study investigated the formation of (socialised learning) networks in the early days of transitioning from traditional online learning pedagogies to an ERL environment in Saudi Arabia's HE. This examination was through the lens of ANT for adopting ERL to help identify and quantify novel and potentially useful ERL pedagogy instructional designs for Saudi Arabia. The main influencing actors were identified, and their interactions were woven into an ERL imposed without consideration for what was happening in places external to Saudi Arabia. In the light of three broad change requirements for continued learning, like levels of interaction among the ANT actors involved, different educational technology tools to support learning pedagogies, and effective leadership to overcome challenges. The interrelated nature of the ERL network of all the actors is complicated and dependent on actor skill levels, timely communications and clear University directives. Considering all actors (human and socio-technical) that contribute to learning continuity during emergencies and their interactions, this holistic view expands the understanding of ERL strategies for future implementations. However, the qualitative sample size was small and confined to a limited number of colleges within Saudi Arabia. Therefore, future studies need to increase the sample and expand to other countries and contextual settings.

The quantitative study examined three latent trait categories (educational technologies, educational strategies, and assessment methods) in a 19-item online questionnaire. The main aim of the data analysis was to examine individual participants' online questionnaire results using a person's Likert agreement scores, whether individual item responses had expected outcomes or anomalous distributions, and whether there was a variation in responses between males and females. The parameterisation used a polytomous Rasch model to provide sufficient statistics for all parameters.

The Rasch PRM analysis outcome indicated an excellent fit with only eight extremes in the online cohort of 334 participants. In addition, the fit residual mean of -0.2864 and reliability indices between 0.85 and 0.89 also indicated a reasonable data fit to the Rasch model estimate. However, further analysis of participant groupings identified variations across the full questionnaire analysis and on individual questionnaire items. Male participants had a mean logit value of 1.426, whereas females had a lower mean score of 1.184 Rasch logits. Larger college samples had a higher agreement level to the ERL strategies than the smaller college sites. This result may be related to the small sample size at some of these colleges and therefore require expanded participant numbers in future studies.

Cultural norms in Saudi Arabia may have influenced male and female responses, especially on specific items such as the use of personal images in online forums (Item-5). Although females scored below the expected value curve, they followed the form of the curve, whereas the male cohort had an inconsistent outcome compared to the expected value curve (Fig. 6). Future studies should evaluate whether overall male-to-female response (mean values) and variations on specific items (cameras in online communication strategies) are peculiar to the current sample, Saudi Arabia in general, Islamic countries or a global consistency across the online environment.

References

1. Khlaif, Z.N., Salha, S., Kouraichi, B.: Emergency remote learning during COVID-19 crisis: students' engagement. Educ. Inf. Technol. **26**, 7033–7055 (2021)
2. Toquero, C.M.: Emergency remote education experiment amid COVID-19 pandemic in learning institutions in the Philippines. Int. J. Educ. Res. Innov. (IJERI) **15**, 162–176 (2020)
3. Mustafa, A.-J., Kurshan, B.: Educational ecosystems: a trend in urban educational innovation. Penn GSE Perspect. Urban Educ. **12**(Spring), 7 (2015)
4. Andrich, D.: Rasch models. In: Peterson, P., Baker, E., McGaw, B. (eds.) International Encyclopedia of Education (Third Edition), pp. 111–122. Elsevier, Oxford (2010)

5. Tesar, M.: Towards a post-Covid-19 'new normality?': physical and social distancing, the move to online and higher education. Policy Futures Educ. **18**(5), 556–559 (2020)
6. Elder-Vass, D.: Disassembling actor-network theory. Philos. Soc. Sci. **45**(1), 100–121 (2015)
7. Fenwick, T., Edwards, R.: Actor-Network Theory in Education. Routledge (2010)
8. Belsey, C.: Poststructuralism: A Very Short Introduction. OUP Oxford, USA (2002)
9. Ferdig, R.E., et al.: Teaching, Technology, and Teacher Education During the COVID-19 Pandemic: Stories from the Field. Association for the Advancement of Computing in Education Waynesville, NC (2020)
10. Manca, S., Delfino, M.: Adapting educational practices in emergency remote education: continuity and change from a student perspective. Br. J. Edu. Technol. **52**(4), 1394–1413 (2021)
11. El Masri, A., Sabzalieva, E.: Dealing with disruption, rethinking recovery: policy responses to the COVID-19 pandemic in higher education. Policy Des. Pract. **3**(3), 312–333 (2020)
12. O'Shea, M., et al.: Communicating COVID-19: analyzing higher education institutional responses in Canada, China, and the USA. High Educ. Pol. **35**(3), 629–650 (2022)
13. Cutri, R.M., Mena, J., Whiting, E.F.: Faculty readiness for online crisis teaching: transitioning to online teaching during the COVID-19 pandemic. Eur. J. Teach. Educ. **43**(4), 523–541 (2020)
14. Rahayu, R.P., Wirza, Y.: Teachers' perception of online learning during pandemic covid-19. Jurnal Penelitian Pendidikan **20**(3), 392–406 (2020)
15. Oliveira, G., et al.: An exploratory study on the emergency remote education experience of higher education students and teachers during the COVID-19 pandemic. Br. J. Edu. Technol. **52**(4), 1357–1376 (2021)
16. Gacs, A., Goertler, S., Spasova, S.: Planned online language education versus crisis-prompted online language teaching: lessons for the future. Foreign Lang. Ann. **53**(2), 380–392 (2020)
17. Sadler, T.D., et al.: Technology-supported professional development for collaborative design of COVID-19 instructional materials. J. Technol. Teach. Educ. **28**(2), 171–177 (2020)
18. Clausen, J.M., Bunte, B., Robertson, E.T.: Professional development to improve communication and reduce the homework gap in grades 7–12 during COVID-19 transition to remote learning. J. Technol. Teach. Educ. **28**(2), 443–451 (2020)
19. Scherer, R., et al.: Profiling teachers' readiness for online teaching and learning in higher education: Who's ready? Comput. Hum. Behav. **118**, 106675 (2021)
20. Cicha, K., et al.: Distance learning support measures for teachers in Poland during the COVID-19 pandemic. Int. J. Environ. Res. Public Health **19**(13), 8031 (2022)
21. Sharma, A., Alvi, I.: Evaluating pre and post COVID 19 learning: an empirical study of learners' perception in higher education. Educ. Inf. Technol. **26**(6), 7015–7032 (2021)
22. Basch, S., Covarrubias, R., Wang, S.: Expanding access: Minoritized students' lived experiences with pandemic-era remote learning. Collaborative Research for Equity in Action (2021). https://cpb-us-e1.wpmucdn.com
23. Kılınç, H.: Opinions of field experts on practices that will increase the motivation levels of learners during the COVID-19 pandemic process. In: Bozkurt, A. (ed.) Handbook of Research on Emerging Pedagogies for the Future of Education: Trauma-Informed, Care, and Pandemic Pedagogy, pp. 191–208. IGI Global (2021). https://doi.org/10.4018/978-1-7998-7275-7.ch010
24. Adedoyin, O.B., Soykan, E.: Covid-19 pandemic and online learning: the challenges and opportunities. Interact. Learn. Environ. **31**(2), 863–875 (2020). https://doi.org/10.1080/10494820.2020.1813180
25. Dhawan, S.: Online learning: a panacea in the time of COVID-19 crisis. J. Educ. Technol. Syst. **49**(1), 5–22 (2020)
26. Xie, J., Gulinna, A., Rice, M.F.: Instructional designers' roles in emergency remote teaching during COVID-19. Distance Educ. **42**(1), 70–87 (2021). https://doi.org/10.1080/01587919.2020.1869526

27. Bellaby, A., Sankey, M., Albert, L.: Rising to the occasion: Exploring the changing emphasis on educational design during COVID-19. In: Conference: ASCILITE 2020: ASCILITE's First Virtual Conference (2020)

28. Whittle, C., et al.: Emergency remote teaching environment: a conceptual framework for responsive online teaching in crises. Inform. Learn. Sci. 121(5/6), 311–319 (2020)

29. Greenhow, C., Chapman, A.: Social distancing meet social media: digital tools for connecting students, teachers, and citizens in an emergency. Inform. Learn. Sci. 121(5/6), 341–352 (2020)

30. Borup, J., et al.: Supporting students during COVID-19: Developing and leveraging academic communities of engagement in a time of crisis. J. Technol. Teach. Educ. 28(2), 161–169 (2020)

31. Bhatnagar, R., Many, J.: Striving to use culturally responsive pedagogy online: perceptions of novice teachers in high-needs schools during COVID-19. J. Online Learn. Res. 8(2), 181–202 (2022)

32. Al Shammari, M.H.: Devices and platforms used in emergency remote learning and teaching during Covid19: a case of English major students in Saudi Arabia. Arab World English J. (AWEJ) Special Issue on Covid 19, 80–94 (2021)

33. Alzain, E.: Examining saudi students' perceptions on the use of the blackboard platform during the COVID-19 pandemic. Int. J. Learn., Teach. Educ. Res. 20(6), 109–125 (2021)

34. Al Shammari, M.H.: Digital platforms in the emergency remote education: the students' preferences. Arab World English J. (AWEJ) 12, 19–36 (2022)

35. Oraif, I., Elyas, T.: The impact of COVID-19 on learning: investigating EFL learners' engagement in online courses in Saudi Arabia. Educ. Sci. 11(3), 99 (2021)

36. Alqurshi, A.: Investigating the impact of COVID-19 lockdown on pharmaceutical education in Saudi Arabia–A call for a remote teaching contingency strategy. Saudi Pharm. J. 28(9), 1075–1083 (2020)

37. Aladsani, H.K.: A narrative approach to university instructors' stories about promoting student engagement during COVID-19 emergency remote teaching in Saudi Arabia. J. Res. Technol. Educ. 54(sup1), S165–S181 (2022)

38. McKay, E.: Prescriptive training courseware: IS-design methodology. Australasian J. Inform. Syst. 22, 8 (2018)

39. Frankfort-Nachmias, C., Nachmias, D.: Research Methods in the Social Scences, vol. 4, Fifth edn. Open Journal of Business and Management, Arnold, London (1996)

40. Giusti, E., Befi-Lopes, D.M.: Translation and cross-cultural adaptation of instruments to the Brazilian Portuguese language. Pró-Fono Revista de Atualização Científica 20, 207–210 (2008)

41. Frisbie, D.A.: Reliability of Scores from Teacher-Made Tests. Educ. Meas.: Issues Pract. 7(1), 25–35 (1988)

42. Briggs, D.C., Wilson, M.: An introduction to multidimensional measurement using Rasch models. J. Appl. Meas. 4(1), 87–100 (2003)

43. Andrich, D.: Understanding the response structure and process in the polytomous Rasch model. In: Nering, M., Ostini, R. (eds.), Handbook of Polytomous Item Response Theory Models: Developments and Applications. Lawrence Erlbaum Associates, Inc. (2009)

44. Guttersrud, Ø., Petterson, K.S.: Young adolescents' engagement in dietary behaviour – the impact of gender, socio-economic status, self-efficacy and scientific literacy. Methodological aspects of constructing measures in nutrition literacy research using the Rasch model. Public Health Nutr. 18(14), 2565–2574 (2015)

45. Andrich, D.: A rating formulation for ordered response categories. Psychometrika 43(4), 561–573 (1978)

46. Rasch, G.: Probabilistic Models for Some Intelligence and Attainment Tests. Nielsen & Lydiche, Copenhagen (1960)

47. De_Losa, L.: Living with Disability Research Centre Research – July Seminar Series. Obser-rving the Quality of Staff Practice. https://www.latrobe.edu.au/events/all/living-with-disabi lity-research-centre-research-seminar-series17 (2021)
48. Aiello, F., Capursi, V.: Using the Rasch model to assess a university service on the basis of student options. Appl. Stoch. Model. Bus. Ind. **24**, 459–470 (2008)
49. De-Battisti, F., Nicolini, G., Salini, S.: The Rasch model. In: Kennett, R., Salini, S. (eds.) Modern Analysis of Customer Surveys: with applications using R. Wiley & Sons Ltd, Chichester, UK (2012)
50. Weill, P., Woerner, S.L.: What's Your Digital Business Model? Six Questions to Help you Build the Next-Generation Enterprise, vol. 239. Harvard Business Review Press, USA (2018)
51. Razali, S.N., Shahbodin, F., Hafiez Ahmad, M., Nor, H.A.M.: Measuring validity and reliability of perception of online collaborative learning questionnaire using Rasch model. Int J Adv Sci, Eng. Inform. Technol. **6**(6), 966 (2016). https://doi.org/10.18517/ijaseit.6.6.1343
52. Lee, D.: Understanding Rasch Measurement Theory for Language. ACER Discover (2020)
53. Sondergeld, T.A., Johnson, C.C.: Using Rasch measurement for the development and use of affective assessments in science education research. Sci. Educ. **98**(4), 581–613 (2014)
54. Dunya, B.A., McKown, C., Smith, E.: Psychometric properties and differential item functioning of a web-based assessment of children's emotion recognition skill. J. Psychoeduc. Assess. **38**(5), 627–641 (2019)
55. Müller, M.: Item fit statistics for rasch analysis: can we trust them? J. Stat. Distrib. Appl. **7**, 5 (2020)
56. Scoulas, J.M., De Groote, S.L.: The library's impact on university students' academic success and learning. Evid. Based Libr. Inform. Pract. **14**(3), 2–27 (2019)
57. Whittle, C., Tiwari, S., Yan, S., Williams, J.: Emergency remote teaching environment: a conceptual framework for responsive online teaching in crises. Inform. Learn. Sci. **121**(5/6), 311–319 (2020)
58. Ferri, F., Grifoni, P., Guzzo, T.: Online learning and emergency remote teaching: opportunities and challenges in emergency situations. Societies **10**(4), 86 (2020)
59. RUMM-2030: RUMM2030 Getting Started Manual. RUMM_Laboratory_Pty_Ltd., WA (2015)

Decoding Student Error in Programming: An Iterative Approach to Understanding Mental Models

Francisco J. Gallego-Durán⬡, Patricia Compañ-Rosique⬡,
Carlos J. Villagrá-Arnedo⬡, Gala M. García-Sánchez⬡,
Rosana Satorre-Cuerda⬡, Rafael Molina-Carmona$^{(\boxtimes)}$⬡,
Faraón Llorens-Largo⬡, Sergio J. Viudes-Carbonell⬡,
Alberto Real-Fernández⬡, and Jorge Valor-Lucena⬡

Smart Learning Research Group, University of Alicante, Alicante, Spain
{fjgallego,patricia.company,villagra,galamariagarcia,rosana.satorre,
rmolina,faraon.llorens,sergio.viudes,alberto.real,jorge.valor}@ua.es
https://web.ua.es/en/smart-learning/

Abstract. In computer programming education, despite yearly changes in teaching methodologies, students still struggle to grasp the concepts. When they advance to more complex projects, gaps in their basic knowledge become evident. It seems that the knowledge they learn in the first course is forgotten or not well understood. This proposal aims to explore students' mental models of computer programming concepts to better understand and identify any misconceptions. An iterative methodology is proposed to identify, test, analyse and evidence students' erroneous mental models in programming. Characterising these mental models is a first step to deepen our understanding and designing strategies to help students improve them. The proposed methodology is exemplified in detail through an undergoing use case at the University of Alicante, and some early results are discussed.

Keywords: Programming · Learning · Mental Models

1 Introduction

Learning to program is fundamental for Computer Engineers and Scientists. However, it has proven challenging over time. Most students show frustration and lack of understanding while learning. Teachers try many strategies to ease this frustration and foster learning: metaphors, sketches, different languages, Gamification, programming challenges... [3]. All combined, along with a lot of effort, students learn to program, pass their exams and obtain their grades.

However, are exams and assignments enough to detect flaws in their learning? This question arises from our experience at the University of Alicante. During fourth year, students at the Multimedia Engineering Degree develop a Computer

P. Zaphiris and A. Ioannou (Eds.): HCII 2023, LNCS 14040, pp. 256–273, 2023.
https://doi.org/10.1007/978-3-031-34411-4_18

Game as a project for seven subjects. In groups of five or six, they invest around 3500–4200 h (~700 hours per student) in seven months. This project is three to four orders of magnitude greater than their usual assignments and exams.

This scale challenges our students, making their developments fail in many different ways. However, contrary to expected, failures do not arise from intermediate or advanced programming concepts; they arise from very basic knowledge. The knowledge our students learn in first year, and use in second and third years, seems to be misunderstood or even forgotten.

What do students actually learn? How can we test it? Can we help ensure the basic knowledge is properly acquired? To answer these questions, we consider conceptual and mental models. Students form their own mental models of different concepts. Like in the process of science, their models evolve to fit the observations and challenges (exams and assignments). The ideal situation would be their models becoming asymptotically similar to the conceptual models. However, based on our experience, seems possible that mental models close to their initial form are enough to pass exams and/or assignments. Even more, seems possible that these models persist over time, arriving without much evolution from first to fourth year.

This work proposes a way to explore students' mental models. The focus is on analysing, understanding and detecting erroneous mental models. The aim is to characterise students' models to help design strategies to improve them. We propose a methodology to achieve this goal and the design of the first step in this methodology.

Section 2 presents definitions of conceptual and mental models, along with the bibliography on the subject, with particular emphasis on programming. Afterwards, Sect. 3 defines the research questions that motivate this work and which one is selected for this first research step. Then, the proposed methodology is presented in Sect. 4. To help understand the methodology in practice, a complete example of application is presented step by step in Sect. 5. This example shows the exact process we have been following at the University of Alicante and the preliminary results for our early analyses. Finally, Sect. 6 summarizes the conclusions of this work.

2 Conceptual and Mental Models

The topic has been of interest in this field for a long time. In [11] two experiments are reported that indicate providing subjects with insightful representations of example programs and guiding them through an "ideal" problem-solving strategy facilitates learning.

In [10], it is highlighted that novice programmers have inconsistent and faulty mental models of basic programming concepts. The development of a multiple-choice questionnaire is presented to obtain and measure the consistency of a novice programmer's mental model of arrays.

In [8], it is highlighted that a beginner builds a mental model of program execution while learning to program. Any erroneous concepts during this phase lead to the development of a discrepant mental model. One way to prevent this situation is to carefully and explicitly uncover the details of program execution. This is achieved through the use of the Little Man Computer (LMC), which has an interactive visual interface that helps the programmer internalize how software interacts with hardware to achieve the programmer's goal. The experience received positive feedback from students and other teachers who taught classes in subsequent semesters.

In [1], a study is presented on the accuracy of beginners' mental models in computer science about linked lists. Learning fundamental abstract concepts that require students to understand memory management can be very difficult and result in misunderstandings that are transferred to advanced topics. Therefore, two-hour semi-structured interviews are conducted with 11 university students to understand the accuracy of their mental models. The results suggest that none of the participants have an accurate mental model of simple linked lists after having learned about them and applied them in their data structures course.

In [7], an evaluation is developed that uses a concept inventory to profile students based on their understanding of certain programming concepts. The goal is to identify incorrect mental models that obstruct their progress. The research allowed defining nine profiles.

The analysis of students' mental models in the realm of recursion has been studied several times. In [9], the focus is on the difficulty that novice programmers have in building an adequate mental model of the concept of recursion, specifically of the program stack and control flow back from the last invocation of the recursive method. To overcome this difficulty, a visual interface is employed that does not require the novice programmer to apply the solution steps through a programming language. By offering a language-independent approach, the novice programmer can come to understand the concept of recursion such that they are capable of developing an algorithm that can be programmed using any programming language. [2] is based on the Pieces of Knowledge (KiP) framework which offers a view of the dynamic nature of knowledge. The authors classify the results based on a proposed classification of recursive mental models. These approaches are not new: decades ago, there have been other similar approaches with different implementation schemes but similar aims and results [5,6,15].

Another way to detect if students have a correct mental model is through the spontaneous gestures or movements they make with their hands when explaining code [12]. During communication, gestures can be an external representation of the students' understanding of the code. In addition to gestures, some studies have shown the importance of verbal feedback in students' understanding of code. Verbal feedback allows students to correct their incorrect mental models and refine their understandings. For example, [13] found that effective verbal feedback increases students' problem-solving and code understanding.

In general, students' formation of mental models to understand code is a complex process that involves multiple factors. Educators and software development professionals should take these factors into account to help students develop a correct mental model and fully understand the code. This study will only focus on detecting and characterising the incorrect mental models already formed as a first step to trace their origin and devise methods for correcting them and preventing their formation.

3   Research Questions

Following general research questions have motivated this study:

- How are students' mental models formed?
- How similar are these models to their respective conceptual models?
- How flexible are these models? Do they change over time? How much?
- Can students pass their exams and assignments with weak mental models?
- How much can erroneous mental models persist over time?
- Do mental models become less flexible over time?
- Can an erroneous mental model solidify and difficult learning progress?
- Can we help students refine their mental models? How?

These are really complex questions that require long term research. Therefore, this study proposes an starting point: analysing erroneous mental models. The initial research question then becomes:

- Can we design a method to characterise students' erroneous mental models?

For this question we propose an iterative methodology and a initial method to analyse students' erroneous mental models and refine the analysis over time.

4   Characterising Students' Mental Models

The method we propose to characterise students' mental models is akin to standard scientific method. The initial references or a priory are the models of the concepts being tested (the conceptual models). One or more teachers should have deep understanding of these conceptual models and experience teaching them. These two inputs enable teachers to hypothesise about students' erroneous mental models.

Starting with the teachers' hypotheses, the method comprises the next five steps:

1. **List of models.** The teachers create a list of the erroneous mental models projected from their own hypotheses. Models are described in such a way that they could be falsifiable/testable.

2. **Question design.** Questions are derived from each model from the list. Each question should be specifically conceived to test on or several models. The questions should be open-ended: they should ask students for explanations, code development or similar types of answers. It is important not to resort to closed-answer sets or directed questions. Testing models require insight into students' minds; it is highly relevant to encourage them to give information from their own thoughts.
3. **Questionnaire.** Conduct a questionnaire with the students. It is preferably to conduct it in person and limit their ability to use devices to search for answers. Tools such as Moodle's Safe Browser could be utilised. An atmosphere of concentration could also help. Raising awareness on students about the importance of their explanations for improving and learning is also recommended.
4. **Analysis of Results.** There are several dimensions to consider here. First, every answer should be tested against the list of models to decide if it fits one or more of them. That should result in a true/false mapping, that could be used to count the number of students who fit into each model for any given question. This gives information in both the prevalence of each model as well as the relevance of each question. But apart from this, the open-ended nature of the questions will probably yield new patterns to explore. Finding patterns of erroneous answers will help devise other mental models not previously foreseen.
5. **Iterate over models and questions.** In response to the results, eliminate models that are not clearly present on students' minds. For those models with enough evidence, discard or redesign questions that have given less evidence. Maintain most prolific questions and generate variations of them with two purposes: reinforce the evidence on the model and ensure that the evidence is clear. Take into account that questions could yield results due to biases on how it is formulated or even the conditions in which it was answered. Therefore, even best performing questions should be complemented and tested with variants. Take erroneous patterns devised on analyses and add new hypothetical mental models to the list, along with questions for testing them.

Figure 1 summarises this method visually. The general idea behind this method is to continuously improve the knowledge about the erroneous mental models the students develop. The teachers start by formulating their hypotheses based on their experience, and the evidence collected guides the iterative process. Evidence from students confirms or refutes hypothetical models and helps formulating new hypotheses. This last part is key, and requires the students to give explanations, not just simple answers. This is why the questions have to be open-ended.

5   Design Example

To exemplify the use of the method proposed, let us follow its steps at the University of Alicante. In the Multimedia Engineering Degree, students have

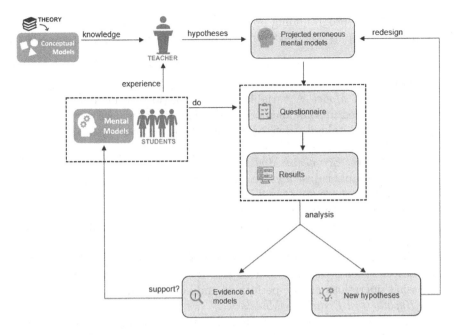

Fig. 1. Iterative methodology to gather evidence on students' mental models

two introductory programming subjects in their first year. This two subjects have these syllabus (summarised):

1. **Programming 1**
   - Introduction to programming
   - Elementary Datatypes (constants, variables, operators, basic types)
   - Control Structures (conditionals, loops, iterations, expressions)
   - Modular programming (functions, parameters, value and reference)
   - Basic recursivity (recursivity concept and characteristics)
   - Data structures (static and dynamic arrays, structs)
2. **Programming 2**
   - Dynamic memory management
   - Object oriented programming: classes, objects and methods
   - Inheritance and Polymorphism
   - Error handling. Input/Output

5.1 Step 1: Listing Hypothetical Mental Models

When students reach their fourth year, they have to program a complete computer game in C++ language from scratch. During the seven months they take to program their games, they exhibit many programming problems related to the concepts involved in the subjects Programming 1 and 2 from their first year. As proposed in the method, the teachers start with two inputs: the experience with students and their programming problems, and the conceptual models involved. With these two inputs, the next list of hypothetical erroneous mental models is elaborated:

- **Variables**
  - *Conceptual Model.* A variable is a symbol (identifier) that refers to an object stored in some memory space. The object is data with a concrete codification, taking a defined amount of consecutive bytes and with a set of valid operations.
  - *Hypothetical Erroneous Models*
    * A variable is just a value, not an object.
    * Variables are not stored in memory.
    * Some variables are not stored in memory.
    * Parameters are not variables (or are variables of a different nature)
- **Data Types**
  - *Conceptual Model.* The type of a variable is meta-information about the object it refers to: how much space it requires, how it is encoded, and what operations can be performed and how they are done.
  - *Hypothetical Erroneous Models*
    * "Type" only refers to basic types (struct or array are not types)
    * The type only indicates values and range for a variable.
    * A field of a struct is an independent variable.
    * Being a pointer is not part of the type.
    * Operations are not part of the type.
- **Char Data Type**
  - *Conceptual Model.* A 1-byte-sized integer object, encoded in standard binary (positional) in two's complement. Supports integer mathematical operations. It is often used to represent symbols, by number-symbol correspondence (ASCII standard).
  - *Hypothetical Erroneous Models*
    * Can only store characters.
    * A char is a letter/character, not an integer number.
    * Thinking memory stores letters directly, apart from binary numbers.
    * Believing that letters and binary numbers are different objects.
    * Not understanding that memory is made only of binary numbers.
- **Pointers**
  - *Conceptual Model.* A pointer is a variable that stores a memory address. Its type describes the object at the memory address stored (the object pointed to). Arithmetic operations on the pointer are scaled by the size of the object pointed to. The operator* (in-direction) refers the object pointed to (l-value).
  - *Hypothetical Erroneous Models*
    * Thinking the pointer IS the object it points to.
    * Thinking operators direction (&) and/or in-direction (*) produce a value and not an object (&: a pointer, *: the pointed-to object).
    * Thinking a pointer and a reference are the same.

* Thinking the type refers to the pointer, not to the object pointed-to.
- **Parameters**
  - *Conceptual Model.* A parameter is a new local variable created in the stack when the scope of its function begins, and dropped when the scope ends. It is initialised with an argument: a value given by the caller. The parameter is the variable, the argument is its initial value.
  - *Hypothetical Erroneous Models*
    * Consider parameters something different than local variables (kind of special items).
    * Believe that arguments are objects (l-values), not values (r-values).
    * Confounding parameters and arguments (local variables with their initial values).
    * Thinking that a pointer parameter is equal to a C++ reference (and failing to understand that is a normal pointer variable).
- **Memory Management**
  - *Conceptual Model.* When allocating, an object is created. A pointer is used to refer to it. The object will life until being explicitly deallocated.
  - *Hypothetical Erroneous Models*
    * Thinking 'new' returns the object allocated and not a pointer to it.
    * Thinking of the pointer being the allocated object, and not a variable holding its address (do not separate both objects).
    * Thinking the pointer must be released, and not the allocated object (through any pointer to its address).
    * Thinking that releasing the allocated object affects the pointer variable.
    * Thinking that the pointer must be set to NULL/0.

5.2   Step 2: Designing Questions to Test the Models

The next step, based on our hypothesis regarding the mental models that the students may have developed, is to design open-ended questions to assess their understanding. An effective question should have the potential to reveal one or more mental models. The clarity and directness of the question in relation to the specific concept being tested will determine the clarity of the answer categories. Students exhibiting one or more of the mental models being evaluated will consistently fall into a specific category. However, this may require multiple iterations and tests to achieve the desired quality level. The usefulness of each question will ultimately be determined by the evidence gathered from the students' answers.

Taking everything into account, the following questions where designed to test the models. Note that spaces used for clarity have been removed from code segments to reduce the space they take on paper.

Q1 What is a variable?
Q2 List all the variables you can find in this code

```
float c[5] = {0.0f};
char const* p;
int main(int argc, char**argv) {
  char b = 'a';
  int a;
  p = argv[0];
  return 0;
}
```

Q3 In the latest code, list the differences between variables p and b, if there are any.

Q4 In the latest code, where is each variable stored?

Q5 In the latest code, Would you be able to get the address of none/some/all the variables? How?

Q6 Explain in detail what the type of a variable is

Q7 List all the variables along with their types

```
typedef struct { float num; char name[10]; } S;
float f[5] = {0.0f};
S const* p;
int main(int argc, char**argv) {
  int  a = argv[0][0];
  char b = 'a';
  S ss;
  p = &ss;
  ss.num = argc;
  ss.name[0] = b;
  ss.name[1] = a;
  ss.name[2] = 0;
  return p->num;
}
```

Q8 Let T be a type. Could this function be problematic? Justify your answer.

```
T sum(T a, T b) { return a + b; }
```

Q9 List differences between variables a and b in this code

```
void doStuff() {
  int  a;
  char b;
  //... do things
}
```

Q10 If this function contains errors, list them and explain. If it is correct, what will it return?

```
char letstry() {
    char a = 'A';
    char b = 65;
    return a - b;
}
```

Q11 Complete the code for this function

```
int moveIfAorD(char const key) {
    // If key is A, return -1 (move left)
    // If key is D, return 1 (move right)
    // return 0 otherwise
}
```

Q12 What is a pointer?

Q13 Explain using words what you understand these pointers are

```
char * p1;
int const * p2;
float * const p3;
long ** p4;
void(*p5)(int);
```

Q14 What type will the p parameter be

```
void doSomething(int n, --TYPE?-- p) {
    // do something....
}
int main(int argc, char**argv) {
    char* program = argv[0];
    doSomething(argc, program);
}
```

Q15 For each function, state if it is correct or contains errors. For those with errors, explain them. For those correct, state what they return.

```
int f1(int a, int b) { int* p =  a; return &p; }
int f2(int a, int b) { int* q = &b; return  q; }
int f3(int a, int b) { int* r = *a; return  r; }
int f4(int a, int b) { int* s = &a; return *s; }
int f5(int a, int b) { int* t = *b; return &t; }
```

Q16 Complete the code to accumulate bonuses in the score. You should modify only the commented line.

```
int timeBonus();
int lifeBonus();
void accumulateBonuses(int* score) {
    int tb = timeBonus();
    int lb = lifeBonus();
    //.....................
}
```

Q17 Explain in detail what a function parameter is.

Q18 Explain lines 4 and 5 in detail, how sum is called and how parameters are passed.

```
1 int sum(int const s1, int const s2) { return s1 + s2; }
2 int main() {
3     int a = 5;
4     int b = sum(a, 10);
5     return sum(a, b);
6 }
```

Q19 What value does update function return? Explain your answer

```
void move(float x, float const vx) { x += vx; }
float update() {
    float px = 2.5;
    float pv = 0.75;
    move(px, pv);
    return px;
}
```

Q20 What do the functions update1, update2, and update3 return? Explain your answer.

```
void increment_by_1(unsigned* val) {  val += 1; }
int update1() {
    unsigned points = 10;
    increment_by_1(&points);
    return points;
}
int update2() {
    unsigned points = 10;
    unsigned* p = &points;
    increment_by_1(p);
    return points;
}
int update3() {
    unsigned points = 10;
    unsigned* p = &points;
    increment_by_1(p);
    return *p;
}
```

Q21 Give a detailed explanation on what do operators new and delete do.

Q22 Explain what happens on lines 5 and 6. Can we modify the Point in line 7? Why?

```
1 typedef struct {
```

```
2    int x, y;
3 } Point;
4 int main() {
5     Point* p = new Point{1, 2};
6     p = nullptr;
7     //...........
8 }
```

Q23 Indicate if there are errors in this code and explain them. Can we modify Point1, 2 in line 8? Why?

```
1    typedef struct { int x, y; } Point;
2    int main() {
3        Point* p1 = new Point{1, 2};
4        Point* p2 = new Point{2, 3};
5        Point* a = p1;
6        delete a;
7        a = p2; delete a;
8        //.............
9    }
```

Q24 You receive this code and you need to review it (code review). Would you propose to make any changes? Why?

```
struct Node { int val; Node* next; };
int main() {
    Node* n = new Node{1, nullptr};
    n->next = new Node{2, nullptr};
    //... Do many things....
    Node* temp = n;
    delete n;
    delete temp->next;
}
```

Each question was designed with one or several mental models in mind to test. The correspondence between models and questions designed to test them is summarised in Table 1.

5.3 Step 3: Questionnaire

All the questions were compiled into a questionnaire, which was then administered to the students. The questionnaire included additional questions to assess correlations with other influential factors identified in previous studies [4,14]. These questions related to:

– The students' level of enjoyment for programming
– Characterising their sleeping habits and patterns

Table 1. Correspondence between hypothetical mental models and detection questions.

Mental models	Questions
- A variable is just a value, not an object - Variables are not stored in memory - Some variables are not stored in memory - Parameters are not variables (or are variables of a different nature)	Q1, Q2, Q3, Q4, Q5
- "Type" only refers to basic types (struct or array are not types) - The type only indicates values and range for a variable - A field of a struct is an independent variable - Being a pointer is not part of the type - Operations are not part of the type	Q6, Q7, Q8
- Can only store characters - A char is a letter/character, not an integer number - Thinking memory stores letters directly, apart from binary numbers - Believing that letters and binary numbers are different objects - Not understanding that memory is made only of binary numbers	Q9, Q10, Q11
- Thinking the pointer IS the object it points to - Thinking operators direction (&) and/or in-direction (*) produce a value and not an object (&: a pointer, *: the pointed-to object) - Thinking a pointer and a reference are the same - Thinking the type refers to the pointer, not to the object pointed-to	Q12, Q13, Q14, Q15, Q16
- Consider parameters something different than local variables (kind of special items) - Believe that arguments are objects (l-values), not values (r-values) - Confounding parameters and arguments (local variables with their initial values) - Thinking that a pointer parameter is equal to a C++ reference (and failing to understand that is a normal pointer variable)	Q17, Q18, Q19, Q20
- Thinking 'new' returns the object allocated and not a pointer to it - Thinking of the pointer being the allocated object, and not a variable holding its address (do not separate both objects) - Thinking the pointer must be released, and not the allocated object (through any pointer to its address) - Thinking that releasing the allocated object affects the pointer variable - Thinking that the pointer must be set to NULL/0	Q21, Q22, Q23, Q24

- Reflection on the programming questions and the doubts and certainties they elicited

The purpose of these questions was to serve as performance indicators and to identify potential causes. For example, students who have less interest in programming are likely to have invested less time in learning and have a greater likelihood of having erroneous mental models. Similarly, poor sleeping habits could negatively impact a student's ability to generalise and improve their mental models. Finally, student reflection on the questions provides insight into their beliefs and can reveal the strength of patterns ingrained in their thinking.

The questionnaire was administered to fifty students from the Multimedia Engineering Degree at the University of Alicante during a regular lesson, and took one and a half hours to complete. The students were informed ahead of time that the questionnaire was not an exam and were informed on the importance of their answers in identifying and resolving programming problems. The teachers emphasised the importance of providing detailed explanations, even if they were correct, and encouraged the students not to feel bad about mistakes. This pre-intervention helped students try their best on each question and provide more detailed explanations.

5.4   Step 4: Analysis of Results

The analysis of results is currently being undertaken following this approach:

1. Construct a table relating student answers and hypothetical mental models
2. Analyse answers one by one with respect to each of the possible mental models, then categorise as 0 or 1. A classification of 1 means that there is enough evidence in the student answer to deduce that he/she thinks as the hypothetical mental model states. A 0 means that the student might or might not think like the model, but there is not enough evidence in the answer to make the connection.
3. Each answer is also evaluated from 1 to 5 points depending on its correctness and completeness. A score of 0 is assigned to questions that are left unanswered by the students.
4. While analysing answers, observations are also annotated in order to devise patterns in the explanations of the students. The detected patterns will later be used to form new hypotheses regarding their mental models.
5. With all the answers analysed, evaluations are averaged and classifications are added. This gives scores of 0–5 points to each question depending on how well students performed, and also scores of 0–50 points for each mental model and each question, depending on how many students were having classified as thinking like the model.

At the time of writing, the analysis of results is ongoing, but some initial observations can be made:

- There seems to be enough evidence of students that think that parameters are not variables. Also, most of them have difficulty determining where variables are stored, and think that might not be stored in memory.
- We have found clear evidence that most students do not think that the type of a variable restricts the operations that can be performed on it. Also, most students think that the type only affects to the size and range of valid values of the variable.
- There is strong evidence in favour of students thinking that the char type can only used to stores characters. Also, almost all students seem to think that characters can be directly stored in memory, failing to understand that memory only stores bits/bytes and characters are only a number-symbol correspondence through the ASCII table.
- There also seems to be strong evidence for the students confusing the type of a pointer with the type of the object it points to. Similarly, most seem to confound the pointer itself with the object being pointed-to, and think that operators & and * result in values instead of objects.

5.5   Step 5: Iterate over Models and Questions

The summaries of scores for both questions and models allow us to assess their validity, discard those who without enough evidence and select and continue analysing the promising ones. The score for a mental model indicate the number of students that shown evidence of thinking like the model. With respect to questions, their score shows the number of students that were classified into a mental model since their answers to the question. In both cases, the higher the score, the most relevant the item (model or question). Alternatively, questions can also be considered in terms of their evaluation: a question in which many students fail will have a low evaluation, even if answers do not fit into models.

To classify scores for both models and questions (S_m, S_q), we propose a simple Gaussian analysis as a first step. Let us start by calculating the mean (μ) and the standard deviation (σ) score of all questions and all mental models, and then classify each question and model in the distribution. Then let us consider low (L), average (A) and high (H) scoring models and questions as defined by Eq. 1.

$$
\begin{aligned}
L_i &= \{i/S_i < \mu - \sigma\} \\
A_i = \{i/\mu - \sigma &\ <= S_i <= \mu + \sigma\} \\
H_i &= \{i/S_i > \mu + \sigma\} \\
&\quad i \in \{m, q\}
\end{aligned}
\tag{1}
$$

Then, with questions and models classified, a default way to start a new iteration would be as follows:

- Discard all L_i
- Select all H_i and reuse them in next iteration to continue gathering evidence. New evidence will continue confirming models and questions or can discard them later (early evidence could have been a statistical artifact)

– Rethink and redesign all A_i. Consider the models and questions and reflect on what they reveal about the students. An interesting idea would be to generate two or three new versions of each item, by varying the test idea to analyse the reasons of not being supported by evidence.

After this procedure, the output should be an updated list of models and questions. Then, the list of models should be taken to the first step and completed with new hypotheses. Ideally, these new hypotheses should come from the patterns observed during the analysis in step 4. However, it could also be interesting to add new hypotheses coming from teachers' experience that may arise at any moment.

This will restart the process, as new questions should be generated from the freshly added models. These questions would then join the ones from reiteration, and a new questionnaire would then be ready to continue the refining process.

6   Conclusions

This work started by considering the question on why do our students exhibit programming problems in final years of their degree, related to what they learn in first years. The approach taken was to considering conceptual models (the theory to be learnt) and mental models students have developed (how they think). The problem with this approach is that mental models are inside students' head and all evidence teachers have is indirect through teaching experience.

To gather evidence on the students' erroneous mental models, this study proposed an iterative methodology composed of five steps: defining a list of hypothetical mental models, designing a questionnaire with open-ended questions, analysing results, selecting and redesigning questions and models, and repeating the process. This methodology can help to study students' mental models over time in a more scientific manner and may lead to the development of strategies to make students aware of their models and improve them.

An example of the application of the proposed methodology was demonstrated at the University of Alicante with fourth-year students in the Multimedia Engineering Degree. The students were tested on twenty-six erroneous mental models related to first-year programming concepts using twenty-four questions. The initial results indicated that the students may be confusing and misunderstanding some concepts, supporting some of the hypothetical mental models.

This is only the first step in gathering evidence on the topic, and larger samples and multiple iterations will be necessary to draw definitive conclusions. Nevertheless, this study highlights the need for further research in this field to better understand and help students to become better professionals. The authors encourage the scientific community to take on this challenge.

References

1. Almadhoun, E., Parham-Mocello, J.: Exploratory study on accuracy of students' mental models of a singly linked list. In: 2021 IEEE Frontiers in Education Conference (FIE), pp. 1–9 (2021). https://doi.org/10.1109/FIE49875.2021.9637318. ISSN 2377-634X
2. Chao, J., Feldon, D.F., Cohoon, J.P.: Dynamic mental model construction: a knowledge in pieces-based explanation for computing students' erratic performance on recursion. J. Learn. Sci. **27**(3), 431–473 (2018). https://doi.org/10.1080/10508406.2017.1392309
3. Figueiredo, J., García-Peñalvo, F.J.: Design science research applied to difficulties of teaching and learning initial programming. Universal Access in the Information Society (2022). https://doi.org/10.1007/s10209-022-00941-4
4. Gallego-Durán, F.J., Villagra-Arnedo, C.J., Compañ Rosique, P., Real-Fernández, A.: Memoria de trabajo o hábitos de sueño, qué influye más en las habilidades de programación? In: Actas de las XXVIII Jornadas sobre Enseñanza Universitaria de la Informática, vol. 7, pp. 271–278. Asociación de Enseñantes Universitarios de la Informática (AENUI), Valencia (2022). https://aenui.org/actas/pdf/JENUI_2022_035.pdf
5. Ginat, D., Shifroni, E.: Teaching recursion in a procedural environment-how much should we emphasize the computing model? In: The Proceedings of the Thirtieth SIGCSE Technical Symposium on Computer Science Education, New Orleans, Louisiana, USA, pp. 127–131. ACM (1999). https://doi.org/10.1145/299649.299718. https://dl.acm.org/doi/10.1145/299649.299718
6. Gunion, K., Milford, T., Stege, U.: Curing recursion aversion. ACM SIGCSE Bull. **41**(3), 124–128 (2009). https://doi.org/10.1145/1595496.1562919. https://dl.acm.org/doi/10.1145/1595496.1562919
7. Henry, J., Dumas, B.: Developing an assessment to profile students based on their understanding of the variable programming concept. In: Proceedings of the 2020 ACM Conference on Innovation and Technology in Computer Science Education, ITiCSE 2020, pp. 33–39. Association for Computing Machinery, New York (2020). https://doi.org/10.1145/3341525.3387400
8. Javed, N., Zeeshan, F.: LMC + scratch: a recipe to construct a mental model of program execution. In: English, R., Stewart, C. (eds.) 6th Conference on Computing Education Practice, CEP 2022, pp. 33–36. Association for Computing Machinery, New York (2022). https://dl.acm.org/doi/proceedings/10.1145/3498343
9. Law, R.: Introducing novice programmers to functions and recursion using computer games. In: European Conference on Games Based Learning, pp. 325–334. Academic Conferences International Limited, Reading (2018)
10. Mazumder, S.F., Pérez-Quiñones, M.A.: Eliciting a novice programmer's mental model of arrays. In: Proceedings of the 52nd ACM Technical Symposium on Computer Science Education, SIGCSE 2021, p. 1302. Association for Computing Machinery, New York (2021). https://doi.org/10.1145/3408877.3439647
11. Pirolli, P.L., Anderson, J.R.: The role of mental models in learning to program. Technical report, N/A (1984). https://eric.ed.gov/?id=ED265177. eRIC Number: ED265177
12. Solomon, A., Pradeep, V., Li, S., Guzdial, M.: The role of gestures in learning computer sciences: (abstract only). In: Proceedings of the 49th ACM Technical Symposium on Computer Science Education, SIGCSE 2018, p. 1100. Association for Computing Machinery, New York (2018). https://doi.org/10.1145/3159450.3162316

13. Tiam-Lee, T.J., Sumi, K.: Analyzing facial expressions and hand gestures in filipino students' programming sessions. In: 2017 International Conference on Culture and Computing (Culture and Computing), Kyoto, pp. 75–81. IEEE (2017). https://doi.org/10.1109/Culture.and.Computing.2017.12. http://ieeexplore.ieee.org/document/8227348/

14. Walker, M.P.: Sleep, memory and emotion. In: Progress in Brain Research, vol. 185, pp. 49–68. Elsevier (2010). https://doi.org/10.1016/B978-0-444-53702-7.00004-X. https://linkinghub.elsevier.com/retrieve/pii/B978044453702700004X

15. Wu, C.C., Dale, N.B., Bethel, L.J.: Conceptual models and cognitive learning styles in teaching recursion. In: Proceedings of the Twenty-Ninth SIGCSE Technical Symposium on Computer Science Education - SIGCSE 1998, Atlanta, Georgia, United States, pp. 292–296. ACM Press (1998). https://doi.org/10.1145/273133.274315. http://portal.acm.org/citation.cfm?doid=273133.274315

What Do Students Think About Learning Supported by *e-Schools* Digital Educational Resources?

Goran Hajdin[✉] (ID), Dijana Plantak Vukovac (ID), and Dijana Oreški (ID)

University of Zagreb Faculty of Organization and Informatics, Varaždin, Croatia
{goran.hajdin,dijana.plantak,dijana.oreski}@foi.unizg.hr

Abstract. Today's students use digital educational resources (DER) to a significant extent, especially after the COVID-19 pandemic made classical teaching in the classroom impossible for several months. It is therefore important that digital educational resources are of high quality and enables meaningful learning even in cases when the teacher is not present. Research which is presented in the paper focuses on DER for primary and secondary level students and their opinions about DER which were created in the *e-Schools* project. Those DER are primarily focused on providing support for students' process of learning and must follow requirements and guidelines that were prescribed by the tender documentation. In this paper we describe eight pedagogical requirements, then overall technical requirements, along with the guidelines for the development of multimedia and interactive elements within DER that are aligned with the principles of multimedia learning. The research study was focused on three research questions related to the relation of variables among students' opinions about DER (RQ1), relations among profiles of primary and secondary school students' opinions and different aspects of DER (RQ2), and correlation between clusters related to a school class of primary or secondary school students (RQ3). Research results are based on the 11827 students' answers. Results show three factors consisting of variables which are related. Further, we identified four profiles of students, and lastly, there is no linear relationship between students' school and obtained cluster. The overall conclusion is that DER which were created within the *e-Schools* project have consistent quality for all levels of education.

Keywords: Digital educational resources (DER) · e-Schools · Pedagogical requirements · Multimedia learning · Survey

1 Introduction

Digital educational resources (DER) are present over two decades [1] under different terms such as digital educational materials [2], digital educational content [3] and digital educational resources [4], while in some cases the term *education* is replaced with learning [5]. DER are often intervened in contemporary teaching with modern pedagogical approaches such as flipped classroom, project-based learning, inquiry-based learning, problem-based learning, and others [6]. In addition to the pedagogical aspects of DER, an important part of DER is the integration of rich media into it. Multimedia and interactivity within DER play an important role since media can facilitate meaningful learning when designed according to the principles of multimedia learning [7–10], while interactive media stimulate learning engagement of the students [11] and enhance the achievement of learning outcomes [12–14]. DER are often connected to the concept of open educational resources. Many authors discuss the importance and role of open educational resources, as well as what is the concept of openness. Some DER are open, while others are closed, and certain aspects of the open concept could be implemented in part of the DER [15–17].

DER can be used primarily by teachers or students or created as a universal resource for both subjects to be used during the learning and/or teaching process. Thus, its quality can be perceived from teachers' and from students' perspectives [18, 19]. Researchers focus on different levels of education when exploring DER and they focus on different subjects and fields. According to research findings, DER was more often used during the COVID-19 pandemic where it helped to maintain accessible education, while providing additional value and diverse pedagogical approaches in the online teaching environment [20–22].

The use of digital educational resources was also encouraged during the pandemic in Croatia. There were two sources of DER for students based on primary and secondary school curricula: a) those developed within the project *e-Schools Programme* that started in 2015 and is still led by the Croatian Academic Research Network (CARNET); DER are accessible at the repository https://edutorij.e-skole.hr/, and b) DER that were developed as an aid for students and teachers during emergency remote teaching and was led by the Croatian Ministry of Science and Education; DER are available at https://i-nastava.gov.hr/.

In this paper, we provide results of a broad investigation of students' experience and perceptions of *e-Schools* digital educational resources (*e-Schools* DER), that were used by students in primary and secondary schools in Croatia during the first half of the year 2020. *e-Schools* digital educational resources (*e-Schools DER*) is a part of *e-School e-contents*, one of the main pillars of the *e-Schools Programme,* that are further described in the next section. Our research is focused on the differences among primary and secondary school students' opinions related to various aspects of *e-Schools* digital educational resources.

The structure of the paper is as follows: in the *Introduction* the context of the study is explained, while the second section contains a broader description of the *e-Schools* project and *e-Schools* digital educational resources developed within the project, with prescribed criteria and guidelines. In addition, aspects of *e-Schools DER* are put in the context of another related research. In the third section research methodology is explained. The fourth section provides a description of research results. Finally, the fifth section concludes the paper.

2 Research Background

2.1 About *e-Schools*

The *e-Schools Programme*, with its full title "e-Schools: a comprehensive informatization of school operation processes and teaching processes aimed at the creation of digitally mature schools for the 21st century", is the biggest educational project currently carried out in Croatia. The program is coordinated by the Croatian Academic Research Network (CARNET) and mostly financed (85%) by the Structural Funds of the European Union. The main goal of the *e-Schools Programme* is to strengthen the capacity of the primary and secondary education system with the aim of training students for the labor market, further education, and lifelong learning [23]. The program consists of two phases: a pilot project "e-Schools: Establishing a System for Developing Digitally Mature Schools (pilot project)" implemented in the period from 2015 until 2018 and the major project "e-Schools: Development of a System of Digitally Mature Schools (second phase)" which is carried out from September 2018 until October 2023. The pilot project included a selection of 151 public primary and secondary schools which participated in piloting organizational, technological, and educational concepts of introducing ICT in the educational and operational processes. The major project includes all the schools founded by the Republic of Croatia, a unit of local (regional) self-government or a religious community: 907 elementary schools, 364 secondary schools, and 50 art schools and centers for upbringing and education [24].

e-Schools Programme is organized into 4 main pillars: a) *Infrastructure*, which enables the establishment of adequate data centers, the establishment of school infrastructure by equipping classrooms and staff, and the establishment of regional training centers, b) *e-contents*, which includes the creation of digital educational resources and teaching scenarios, c) *e-services*, which enables the upgrade of existing services for teaching and business processes, and creation of new e-services and d) *Education and support*, which enables education for the development of staff digital competence, then the establishment of the community of practice, and provision of support (helpdesk and mobile experts teams) [24].

e-contents within e-Schools Programme are divided into two main categories [24]: digital educational resources (*e-Schools DER*) which accompany the subject curriculum for various school subjects from 5th-grade primary schools to 4th-grade secondary school, and teaching scenarios (*e-Schools TS*) for all school subjects developed for teachers to integrate contemporary pedagogical methods and appropriate digital tools into their teaching, including interdisciplinary curricular topics such as health, entrepreneurship, personal growth and development etc. This paper focuses on *e-Schools DER* developed during the e-School pilot project and the first part of the *e-Schools* major project.

2.2 About *e-Schools* Digital Educational Resources

Development of DER was carried out after a carefully planned public procurement process [25] to which main book publishers, multimedia developers and other stakeholders for primary and secondary school levels in Croatia have responded. Requirements and guidelines for the development of DER were set up in the *e-Schools* pilot project, then upgraded for the first phase of the *e-Schools* major project and refined for the second phase of the project which currently takes place. Those requirements had to ensure that all developed DER have the same structure and conform to high standards of technical and pedagogical quality.

The tender documentation prescribed the structure and elements of DER. Each DER should be structured into modules and units, while units should have an introduction with motivation, then an elaboration of learning content, and be finalized with a conclusion. Documentation also prescribed a minimum number of various multimedia elements, interactive elements, elements of assessment of the adoption of educational outcomes, and learning activities within DER. In the first phase of the project, teams created 16 DER for school subjects of biology, chemistry, mathematics and physics for 7th and 8th grade of primary level of education and 1st and 2nd grade of secondary level of education. In the second phase of the project, teams are developing over 190 DER for all mandatory subjects in primary level of education from 5th to 8th grade and all four grades of general education (gymnasiums) in secondary level of education.

One DER should cover at least 60% of a subject curriculum. Since *e-Schools DER* are focused on students and their learning process, they must comply to the pedagogical requirements which are defined through eight criteria:

1. compliance with the national curriculum – all learning outcomes must be based on the national curriculum for specific subject, which is relevant for each DER, including interdisciplinary topics which help connect subjects with generic skills,
2. motivation and appropriateness to student's developmental level – as all learning which is placing the student in the center of the process, students should be motivated by DER content and the content must be fully appropriate for students age and learning needs,
3. content clarity – content must be easy for students to understand and they should be able to use it on their own, without much help and assistance from the teacher's side,
4. systematicity, scaffolding and applicability of the content – content should be organized in a meaningful way, respecting didactic principles which focus on accelerated learning and knowledge, skills and attitudes which are relevant for different real-life situations,
5. student's activity and contemporary teaching methods – DER must support contemporary pedagogical approaches and enable student's engagement both, within and outside (because of technical limitations) of DER; DER should promote inquiry-based learning, problem solving, project activities and other contemporary learning approaches which facilitate learning process and enable students' active participation,
6. content differentiation and integration – DER should be organized into meaningful sections – modules and units which should further be organized into chapters and paragraphs that help students perceive content structure,
7. feedback and self-evaluation of student's achievements – DER should provide interactive (self)evaluation activities, alongside more complex ones which will be carried out outside of DER and evaluated by peers or teacher; when possible, DER should provide timely feedback to students and help them in the learning process,

8. individualized approach – DER content must be created in such a way to respect
   different needs of students, especially those with special learning needs; DER enables
   students to learn at their own pace, choose topics order and preferred learning strategy.

All sections of DER must incorporate all 8 pedagogical criteria which was a
challenging task for the authoring teams.

In each DER various multimedia elements and interactive elements should prevail
over the text in the approximate ratio of 60% versus 40%. Multimedia elements included
images (photos, illustrations, graphs), sound, video, and 2D and 3D animation. Interactive elements were divided into those of medium level of interactivity, such as moving
or grouping parts of the content by drag & drop action, filling out the form, marking
answers, entering text or formulas, enlarging the images etc., and high level of interactivity, such as didactic games, simulations with the ability to enter input parameters
and display results depending on the entered parameters, interactive video, elements that
enable input and verification of the programming code through an interactive simulation of the programming language (so-called REPL elements). An example of a DER
is presented in Fig. 1, showing two segments of the webpage for one unit in the DER
Informatics 6 (Informatics for the 6th grade of primary schools), module 2, Computer
thinking and programming.

Technical requirements included parameters related to the quality of audio and video,
then description of metadata, compliance with HTML, CSS and WAI W3C standards,
responsiveness, and implementation of all DER to *e-Schools* central repository *Edutorij*
[26].

Guidelines for the development of multimedia and interactive elements within DER
were based on principles of multimedia learning proposed by Mayer [8, 27] and other
relevant studies (e.g. [9, 28]). Since one of the main requirements of the DER structure
is the dominance of multimedia, authoring teams should prepare educational content
that combines text and various forms of media, such as static and dynamic pictures,
to adhere to the multimedia principle. In order to reduce the cognitive load for students learning through DER, the content should be designed in accordance with several
principles. In creating videos and animations, authoring teams were advised to develop
them in accordance with the modality principle (narration is used to explain a process
or a procedure in a video or animation), the temporal contiguity principle (narration is
presented simultaneously with the corresponding scene in the video or animation), the
signaling principle (important elements in the video or animation should be enhanced)
and the spatial contiguity principle (important elements in the video or animation should
be described with the keywords). Both the signaling and spatial contiguity principles
should be used with images (explanation of graphs or photographs). To conform to
the redundancy principle (avoidance of on-screen text when narration is present), text
in the video or animation should be integrated in the form of subtitles that could be
switched on-off. To comply with the coherence principle (exclusion of extraneous material), background music should not be used when the narrator is explaining the content,
while interesting content was suggested to be created only sparsely and at the beginning
of the DER unit to motivate the students to further explore DER content.

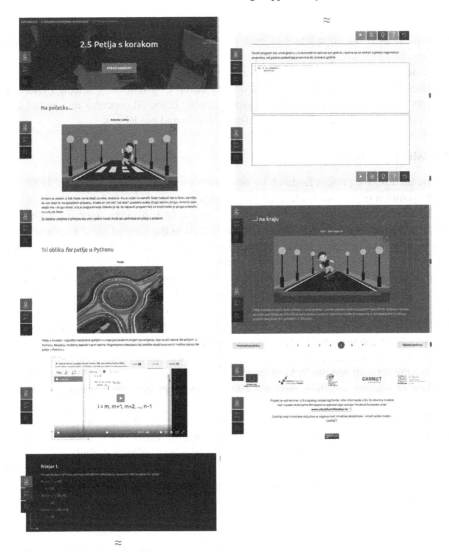

Fig. 1. A unit "Loop with the step" of *e-School DER* Informatics 6

Principles of multimedia learning were explained and demonstrated with examples to the authoring teams in several workshops, to secure consistency in DER design and quality.

The quality of content is ensured by the review process. DER are reviewed individually by independent reviews. The review process was performed in stages: during stage one in which 20% of DER content was created and during stage two or three in which 80% of DER content was created. The review process consisted of two parts, collaborative and final. The collaborative part of the review included the continuous monitoring of the creation of the DER including authors and reviewers, and serves to harmonize the views on the content of the DER and/or its individual parts. The final part of the review takes place after the completion of each stage of delivery of a certain part of the DER content. Both reviewers and authors participated in workshops that prepared them for the review process. Between the collaborative and the final part of the review, CARNET collaborative team performed internal quality control on randomly selected DER, to monitor the work of authors and reviewers, resolve potential concerns and assure that DER are developed according to the defined criteria and guidelines.

2.3 Similar Studies

In this section, we present research by other authors about various aspects of DER and the disposition of *e-Schools DER* about a particular aspect.

DER are a broad concept discussed and researched in many scientific papers. It has been researched for over 20 years, as presented in the state-of-the-art review paper where authors conducted a mixed methods review and focused on the repositories which store DER. Their findings indicate that there are few studies focused on the potential of DER and its use in education institutions. Further findings indicate relevant cultural and institutional differences between users who use DER, especially when focused on perceptions, attitudes and practices of use [1]. In the context of *e-Schools DER*, one of the goals of the *e-Schools Programme* was to promote DER and teaching scenarios among teachers and their students, and to explore who are the actual users of those e-contents.

DER are often connected to the concept of open educational resources. Many authors discuss the importance and role of open educational resources, as well as what is the concept of openness. While certain aspects of the open concept are implemented in some DER, others are either completely open or entirely closed. Findings point out that DER as an open concept is an attempt to answer challenges that are emerging from the everchanging education field, especially the shift from textbooks to online resources, use of information and communication technologies and individually tailored learning process [15–17]. In the context of *e-Schools DER*, all e-contents are open educational resources. With each DER a technical documentation is available that describes the technical characteristics of DER, its authors and reviewers, and the terms of use with a license CC BY-NC-SA [26].

DER are often intervened in contemporary teaching with modern pedagogical approaches such as flipped classroom, project-based learning, inquiry-based learning, problem-based learning, and others. Based on the findings, learning supported by DER enables students' active participation and flexible learning, while teachers have "more freedom in the presentation of teaching materials" [6]. As described in the previous section, *e-Schools DER* were developed in accordance with eight pedagogical criteria that promote contemporary teaching and learning practices.

DER can be used primarily by teachers or students or created as a universal resource for both subjects to be used during the learning and/or teaching process. Thus, its quality can be perceived from teachers' and from students' perspectives [18, 19]. Research results conclude that teachers have positive attitudes about DER and that it can help their students in learning. Further, they think that DER are motivational to students. On, the other hand, teachers point out importance of appropriate infrastructure to use DER [18]. In the context of *e-Schools DER*, teachers' perception on intention to re-use DER/DEC was investigated in [3]. The perceptions were analyzed from the responses of 1623 teachers from primary and secondary schools by applying CRISP-DM methodology. The most important predictors of intention to re-use DEC were *Content that students find harder to understand, is well explained in DEC by using pictures, videos or animations* (females teachers' intention), *Students navigate easily through the content of the DEC* (males teachers' intention) and *DEC encourages students to learn* (primary and secondary school teachers' intention to re-use DEC predictive models).

Researchers focus on different levels of education when exploring DER and they focus on different subjects and fields. According to research findings, DER was more often used during the COVID-19 pandemic where it helped to maintain accessible education, while providing additional value and diverse pedagogical approaches in the online teaching environment. Further, DER enables countries to support their education even through exceptional situations, such as COVID-19, but such shocking events also facilitate digital transformation of education [20–22]. According to the analytics from *Edutorij*, the use of *e-Schools DER* rapidly arose in the beginning of COVID-19 pandemic. This paper presents the results of *e-Schools DER* usage during the first pandemic wave of COVID-19.

Concept of DER, or as it was called in the research "Digital Educational Materials" is presented through two main aspects of quality – educational and technological, which consist of three sectors of application for the standard – academic, governmental/institutional and business. Presented results promote use of quantifiable and rubric elements to evaluate DER [2]. Another approach to evaluation of DER is described through the theoretical framework based on the TPACK + S model where PK represents pedagogical knowledge domain, CK content knowledge, TK technological knowledge and S standards knowledge domain. Presented model is evaluated through rubric which has four to seven criteria for each of the four domains [4]. Possible approach to evaluation of DER quality was also presented through a similar approach – four sections: academic, pedagogical, didactic and technical which was each subdivided into two to four criteria for evaluation [5]. In the context of *e-Schools DER* and its quality, the effects of DER was investigated within a broad research on the effects of the e-Schools pilot project. Only limited results and conclusions on using one DER were provided: that specific DER was a negative predictor of the emotion of anger and orientation towards work avoidance and did not yield an impact on specific cognitive learning outcomes [29]. Thus, additional research on various aspects of *e-Schools DER* was needed.

3   Research Methodology

3.1   Research Approach

In collaboration with the CARNET, a team from the University of Zagreb Faculty of Organization and Informatics compiled an online questionnaire that was shared with school teachers and students who used *e-Schools DER* during the first half of the year 2020. A broad goal of the questionnaire was to determine the experience and to investigate the satisfaction of students and teachers in using *e-Schools DER* in order to improve DER quality in the next development phase. To identify relevant aspects for improvement, the questionnaire focused on 8 closed-type statements which were followed by four open-type questions which helped us better understand and interpret quantitative results (see Appendix). *e-Schools DER* was designed by teams of authors consisting of educational experts and was further reviewed before its application in schools. Schools that participated in the project had a contract signed with CARNET related to their participation and activities relevant to the follow-up research and monitoring. As a part of the research for the development of *e-Schools DER* all schools distributed the questionnaires while participation for students was on a voluntary basis. Since the team of expert reviewers already reviewed *e-Schools DER* and the questionnaire did not incorporate any sensitive personal information, questions, or ethical dilemmas, there was no further need to review the questionnaire by the ethical committee. The questionnaire was verified by an expert from the field of school psychology as well as three university professors. Finally, schools asked parents of the students to sign informed consent about voluntary and anonymous participation of the student in the study.

This paper presents results of the students' perceptions about DER, with a focus on the following research questions:

- RQ1: Which variables among students' opinions about digital educational resources are related?
- RQ2: Which profiles of primary and secondary school students' opinions related to different aspects of digital educational resources can be identified?
- RQ3: Is there a correlation between clusters related to a school class of primary or secondary school students?

In order to answer those questions, the following research methods/analysis techniques were used:

1. *Factor analysis* – In factor analysis, a set of measured variables is divided into a small number of independent linear combinations (factors), each of which captures as much variability in the original variables as possible. In addition to being a tool for exploratory data analysis, factor analysis is a dimension-reduction technique. By using as few variables as possible, factor analysis is used to represent the data's structure as completely as possible.
2. *Cluster analysis* – Latent Class Cluster Analysis (LCCA) clustering algorithm is applied in order to group students into meaningful groups. The use of categorical and continuous variables is allowed in LCCA for clustering. Numerous cluster analyses were conducted separately. The optimal number of clusters was determined using Log-Likelihood, Bayesian Information Criterion (BIC), and Akaike's Information Criterion (AIC). Model fit is evaluated using information-based metrics AIC and BIC.
2. *Correlation analysis* – Correlation analysis seeks for the linear relationship between obtained clusters and students' level of education. Relationship is measured through correlation coefficient and evaluated by value of statistical significance of the relationship (*p-value*).

4 Research Results

4.1 Students' Demographics and Factor Analysis

The following results present student demographic information. Our convenient sample consisted of 15152 students from primary and secondary schools all over Croatia. Data preparation phase indicated various inconsistencies in data (e.g., student indicated age 12 and identified himself as secondary school student). Accordingly, the initial dataset was cleaned and such and similar cases were excluded from further data analysis. Final number of 11827 students was included in data analysis with demographic characteristics as presented in Table 1.

Table 1. Distribution of students by gender and school type

Gender	School type	N
female	Primary	4507
	Secondary	2289
male	Primary	3752
	secondary	1279

Those students learned from 59 unique *e-Schools DER*, of which 35 DER were related to primary schools' subjects from the 5th to 8th grade (Croatian language, English language, German language, Mathematics, Informatics, Technical Education, Nature, History, and Geography), while 24 DER were related to secondary schools' subjects from 1st to 4th grade (Croatian language, English language, German language, Mathematics, Informatics, Physics, Biology, Chemistry, History, and Geography).

Students answered to the following statements, i.e. variables used in the factor analysis: T1 *e-Schools DER encourages me to learn*, T2 *e-Schools DER explains the material well to me*, T3 *Contents that are difficult for me to understand are well explained in e-Schools DER using pictures, videos or animations*, T4 *Moving through the contents of the e-Schools DER is simple and easy*, T5 *I like the way e-Schools DER looks*, T6 *e-Schools DER look modern*, T7 *e-Schools DER makes learning easier for me*, and T8 *Some parts of the material in e-Schools DER are not presented in an interesting way*.

As indicated in Table 2, results from the factor analysis reveal three factors which consist of: *Factor 1* – T2, T3 and T7; *Factor 2* - T4, T5 and T6; and *Factor 3* – T1. T8 was not included in any of the factors even when we changed the values from negative to positive, since T8 is the only statement that was formulated with a negative stance (for further details consult *Appendix* – Extracted Parts from Questionnaire for Students Satisfaction with *e-Schools DER*). Factors are logically grouped where *Factor 1* is focused on statements that reflect that *e-Schools DER* makes learning easier. *Factor 2* is focused on statements which are relevant for DER good appearance. *Factor 3* is related to the single statement which is targeting motivation.

Table 2. Factor analysis based on 8 variables

Factor Loadings

	Factor			Uniqueness
	1	2	3	
T1			0.998	0.00498
T2	0.853			0.32539
T3	0.769			0.40648
T4		0.408		0.57433
T5		0.910		0.20109
T6		0.613		0.54481
T7	0.595			0.40408
T8				0.96585

Note. 'Minimum residual' extraction method was used in combination with an 'oblimin' rotation

4.2 Clusters and Correlations

By using eight categorical variables, cluster analysis LCCA was performed. First step is to determine the optimal number of clusters. In order to do so, five independent cluster models with solutions involving two, three, four, five, and six clusters were carried out. The two-step cluster technique was used to calculate the number of clusters. An optimal number of clusters was determined using Log-Likelihood, Bayesian Information Criterion (BIC), and Akaike's Information Criterion (AIC). Model fit is evaluated using information-based metrics AIC and BIC. Both are based on the LogLikelihood method, which aims to estimate a model's parameters [30]. The model with the lesser BIC and AIC values is regarded as superior when comparing the BIC and AIC values for two models.

Table 3. Cluster evaluation

Number of clusters	BIC	AIC	Best
2	204879	204517	
3	194900	194354	
4	189502	188403	Smallest BIC, smallest AIC
5	189993	189078	
6	191659	190929	

Table 3 presents the results of cluster analysis, which led to the selection of 4 clusters (smallest BIC and smallest AIC). The four-cluster approach was also chosen as the optimal after considering sample sizes in each cluster and interpretability. The four identified cluster distributions are listed in Table 4.

The largest cluster, Cluster 1, consists of almost half of the students (42%) who are satisfied with all aspects of DER. Cluster 2, the second largest cluster, consists of students who are very satisfied with DER. Those two clusters contain two-thirds of the students from our sample. Clusters 3 and 4 refer to the students who are slightly unsatisfied with DER (cluster 3) and completely unsatisfied (cluster 4 consisting of only 7%).

Table 4. Distributions of students in clusters

Cluster	Percentage of students	Cluster name
Cluster 1	42%	Satisfied students
Cluster 2	26%	Completely satisfied students
Cluster 3	25%	Slightly unsatisfied students
Cluster 4	7%	Completely unsatisfied students

Figures 2 and 3 visualize identified clusters by each variable. Each variable is presented with four bars that represent distribution of students' (dis)agreement for each statement. The abbreviation meanings are as follows: CD – completely disagree, D – disagree, A – agree, CA – completely agree.

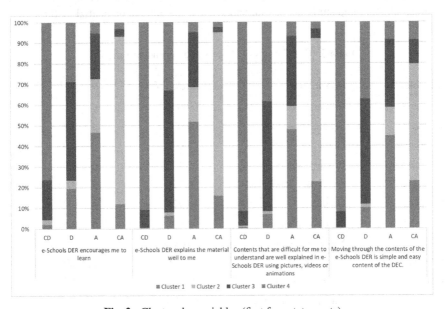

Fig. 2. Clusters by variables (first four statements)

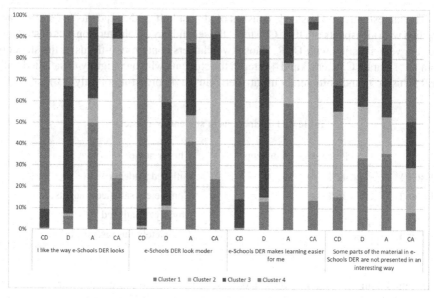

Fig. 3. Clusters by variables (second four statements)

Correlation analysis is performed to identify if there is linear relationship between obtained clusters and students' school and grades. Results are presented in Table 5.

Table 5. Correlations of clusters and dependent variables

Variable	by Variable	Correlation	p
Cluster 1	Primary school	0.0037	p > 0.05
Cluster 1	Secondary school	−0.0037	p > 0.05
Cluster 1	Grade	0.0076	p > 0.05
Cluster 2	Primary school	0.1126	p < 0.05
Cluster 2	Secondary school	−0.1126	p < 0.05
Cluster 2	Grade	0.0720	p < 0.05
Cluster 3	Primary school	−0.0902	p < 0.05
Cluster 3	Secondary school	0.0902	p < 0.05
Cluster 3	Grade	−0.0616	p < 0.05
Cluster 4	Primary school	−0.0474	p < 0.05
Cluster 4	Secondary school	0.0474	p < 0.057
Cluster 4	Grade	−0.0340	p < 0.05

According to the results, there is no correlation coefficient higher than 0.2. This leads us to the conclusion that there is no correlation between clusters related to a school class of primary or secondary school students.

The whole analysis answered three research questions. Analysis results indicate three factors which consist of: Factor 1 – eSchools DER makes learning easier, Factor 2 – eSchools DER has good appearance and Factor 3 – students' motivation. Variables in each factor are related (RQ1). Regarding the profiles of primary and secondary school students' opinions which are related to different aspects of digital educational resources (RQ2), we identified four profiles of students. Profiles are identified according to different aspects of digital educational resources: two larger groups of satisfied students (68%) and two smaller groups of slightly unsatisfied and unsatisfied students (32%). We expected to have a distribution among positive and negative opinions, with a larger group of positive one, since students were mostly satisfied with DER. Views of the students about DER are aligned with the previously explored views of the teachers which are presented in the previous paper [31]. This provides further confirmation of DER quality which were developed within the e-Schools project, since students' and teachers' views are similar.

Regarding the third research question (RQ3) focusing on correlation between clusters related to a school class of primary or secondary school students we can conclude that there is no linear relationship between students' school and obtained clusters. Such results imply there are no differences in students' opinions between students in primary and secondary school, nor among students with different grades. Based on the results we can conclude that DER which were developed within the *e-Schools* project have rather consistent quality for all levels of education. This is further confirmation of *e-Schools* concept of DER.

5 Conclusions

This paper presents survey results about the quality of *e-Schools* digital educational resources (*e-Schools DER*) which were developed within the currently biggest educational project in Croatia, aimed at raising digital maturity of primary and secondary schools. We explained the complex process of creating and reviewing of more than 200 *e-Schools DER* which share the same design and development approach. All *e-Schools DER* had to be developed in accordance with the eight pedagogical criteria and guidelines of multimedia learning, as well as to conform to minimal technical requirements. Given that those *e-Schools DER* were developed by various authoring teams, it was crucial to identify if the quality of DER is consistent across various schools subjects for various schools classes at various educational levels (primary and secondary school).

In this paper we explored overall quality of *e-Schools DER* from the perspective of students in primary and secondary schools. Altogether, 15152 students participated in the study and provided opinions about the *e-Schools DER* of 59 schools subjects of various school classes. After data cleaning, answers from 11827 participants were used for the analyses.

We sought for variables among students' opinions about DER that are related (RQ1) and used exploratory factor analysis, which uncovered three factors: *Factor 1* related to easier learning with *e-School DER*, *Factor 2* related to *e-School DER* good appearance and *Factor 3* related to motivational aspect of *e-School DER*. To identify profiles of primary and secondary school students' opinions related to different aspects of DER (RQ2), cluster analysis LCCA was performed. Four profiles of students' opinions were discovered, that were further grouped into two larger groups of satisfied students (68%) and two smaller groups of unsatisfied students (32%) with different aspects of e-School DER. Finally, we sought for correlation between clusters related to a school class of primary or secondary school students (RQ3) and found no linear relationship between students' school and obtained clusters.

All those analyses support our opinion that DER developed within *e-School Programme* are of good quality from the pedagogical and technical aspects: they are motivational, visually attractive and enable easier learning. Furthermore, those quality aspects are consistent throughout *e-School DER*, regardless of the school level. This implies that various teams who designed and developed various DER considered requirements and guidelines prescribed by the tender documentation, in addition to the review process which was well-performed. Finally, majority of students are satisfied with learning supported by *e-School DER*, which further indicates the quality of the created DER. We can speculate that the good quality of DER is also due to the well-planned process of managing the *e-School* project, as well as the development of DER based on guidelines from established research. The lessons learned from this process can serve as a solid foundation for future projects of a similar nature and facilitate the sharing of best practices with other educational systems.

However, there are several limitations of this research. First, sample size is convenient consisting of students which used DER and which responded to the survey. Second limitation refers to statistical analyses. Optimization of parameters is data biased, so generalization of the results should be performed cautiously.

Future research could focus on identifying variations in students' satisfaction levels among different subjects' DER or on exploring the relationship between authoring team performance and students' satisfaction. One potential avenue for future research could involve replicating this study while incorporating DER that were developed in the later stages of the *e-Schools* project. These DER feature advanced multimedia materials, such as interactive video content and virtual reality learning materials.

Acknowledgment. This work is supported by the project "e-Schools: a comprehensive informatization of school operation processes and teaching processes aimed at the creation of digitally mature schools for the 21st century" funded by the European Union.

Appendix – Extracted Parts from Questionnaire for Students Satisfaction with *e-Schools DER*

The following statements refer to the characteristics of digital educational resources (DER). For each feature, mark the answer that best corresponds to your perception of how visible that feature was when using digital educational resources. The degrees on the scale mean:

1 – I do not agree at all.

2 – I mostly disagree.

3 – I neither agree nor disagree.

4 – I mostly agree.

5 – I completely agree.

NA – I cannot estimate.

T1. *e-Schools DER* encourages me to learn.

T2. *e-Schools DER* explains the material well to me.

T3. Contents that are difficult for me to understand are well explained in *e-Schools DER* using pictures, videos or animations.

T4. Moving through the contents of the *e-Schools DER* is simple and easy.

T5. I like the way *e-Schools DER* looks.

T6. *e-Schools DER* look modern.

T7. *e-Schools DER* makes learning easier for me.

T8. Some parts of the material in *e-Schools DER* are not presented in an interesting way.

Open-type questions:

1. List the features of digital educational resources that you like the most.
2. List the features of digital educational resources that you like the least.
3. What problems have you encountered in the application of digital educational resources?
4. What would be your message and advice to authors who create digital educational resources?

Demographic questions:

1. Year of birth
2. Sex
3. Name of the school
4. Class year
5. List of subjects where you used DER
6. The grade which you got in those subjects in the past school year

References

1. Rodes-Paragarino, V., Gewerc-Barujel, A., Llamas-Nistal, M.: Use of repositories of digital educational resources: state-of-the-art review. IEEE Rev. Iberoam. Tecnol. Aprendiz. **11**, 73–78 (2016). https://doi.org/10.1109/RITA.2016.2554000
2. Fernández-Pampillón, A.M.: A new AENOR project for measuring the quality of digital educational materials. In: Proceedings of the First International Conference on Technological Ecosystem for Enhancing Multiculturality, pp. 133–139. ACM, Salamanca Spain (2013). https://doi.org/10.1145/2536536.2536557
3. Oreski, D., Hajdin, G., Plantak Vukovac, D.: Modelling teachers' intention to re-use digital educational content. Presented at the 14th International Conference on Education and New Learning Technologies, Palma, Spain July (2022). https://doi.org/10.21125/edulearn.2022.1306

4. Xie, K., Di Tosto, G., Chen, S.-B., Vongkulluksn, V.W.: A systematic review of design and technology components of educational digital resources. Comput. Educ. **127**, 90–106 (2018). https://doi.org/10.1016/j.compedu.2018.08.011

5. El Mhouti, A.E., Nasseh, A., Erradi, M.: How to evaluate the quality of digital learning resources? Int. J. Comput. Sci. Res. Appl. **3**, 27–36 (2013)

6. Drozdikova-Zaripova, A.R., Sabirova, E.G.: Usage of digital educational resources in teaching students with application of "flipped classroom" technology. Contemp. Educ. Technol. **12**(2), ep278 (2020). https://doi.org/10.30935/cedtech/8582

7. Guo, P.J., Kim, J., Rubin, R.: How video production affects student engagement: an empirical study of MOOC videos. In: Proceedings of the first ACM conference on Learning @ scale conference. pp. 41–50. ACM, Atlanta Georgia USA (2014). https://doi.org/10.1145/2556325.2566239

8. Mayer, R.E.: Cognitive theory of multimedia learning. In: Mayer, R.E. (ed.) The Cambridge Handbook of Multimedia Learning, pp. 43–71. Cambridge University Press (2014). https://doi.org/10.1017/CBO9781139547369.005

9. Mayer, R.E., Moreno, R.: Nine ways to reduce cognitive load in multimedia learning. Educ. Psychol. **38**, 43–52 (2003)

10. Tani, M., Manuguerra, M., Khan, S.: Can videos affect learning outcomes? Evidence from an actual learning environment. Educ. Technol. Res. Dev. **70**, 1675–1693 (2022). https://doi.org/10.1007/s11423-022-10147-3

11. Barut Tugtekin, E., Dursun, O.O.: Effect of animated and interactive video variations on learners' motivation in distance education. Educ. Inf. Technol. **27**(3), 3247–3276 (2021). https://doi.org/10.1007/s10639-021-10735-5

12. Roemintoyo, Efendi, A., Budiarto, M., Wibawanto, H.: The effect of interactive multimedia to improve the cognitive learning outcome in senior high school's student. Int. J. Educ. Knowl. Manag. **4**, 1–9 (2021). https://doi.org/10.37227/IJEKM-2021-01-34

13. Sahronih, S., Purwanto, A., Sumantri, M.S.: The effect of interactive learning media on students' science learning outcomes. In: Proceedings of the 2019 7th International Conference on Information and Education Technology. pp. 20–24. Association for Computing Machinery, New York, NY, USA (2019). https://doi.org/10.1145/3323771.3323797

14. Zhang, D.: Interactive multimedia-based e-learning: a study of effectiveness. Am. J. Distance Educ. **19**, 149–162 (2005). https://doi.org/10.1207/s15389286ajde1903_3

15. Stracke, C.M., Downes, S., Conole, G., Burgos, D., Nascimbeni, F.: Are MOOCs open educational resources? A literature review on history, definitions and typologies of OER and MOOCs. Open Prax. **11**, 331 (2019). https://doi.org/10.5944/openpraxis.11.4.1010

16. Tuomi, I.: Open educational resources and the transformation of education. Eur. J. Educ. **48**, 58–78 (2013). https://doi.org/10.1111/ejed.12019

17. Wiley, D., Bliss, T.J., McEwen, M.: Open educational resources: a review of the literature. In: Spector, J.M., Merrill, M.D., Elen, J., Bishop, M.J. (eds.) Handbook of Research on Educational Communications and Technology, pp. 781–789. Springer, New York (2014). https://doi.org/10.1007/978-1-4614-3185-5_63

18. Alberola-Mulet, I., Iglesias-Martínez, M.J., Lozano-Cabezas, I.: Teachers' beliefs about the role of digital educational resources in educational practice: a qualitative study. Educ. Sci. **11**, 239 (2021). https://doi.org/10.3390/educsci11050239

19. Saliyeva, A.Z., Zhumabekova, F.N., Saurbekova, G., Tauasarova, D., Sakenov, J.: On the students' ability to use digital educational resources. Int. J. Environ. Sci. Educ. **11**, 4669–4679 (2016)

20. Pocinho, R., Carrana, P., Margarido, C., Santos, R., Milhano, S., Trindade, B., Santos, G.: The use of Digital Educational Resources in the Process of Teaching and Learning in Pandemic by COVID-19. In: Eighth International Conference on Technological Ecosystems for Enhancing

Multiculturality, pp. 810–816. ACM, Salamanca Spain (2020). https://doi.org/10.1145/343 4780.3436589

21. Rodríguez, M.L., Pulido-Montes, C.: Use of digital resources in higher education during COVID-19: a literature review. Educ. Sci. **12**, 612 (2022). https://doi.org/10.3390/educsci12 090612

22. Sanz-Labrador, I., Cuerdo-Mir, M., Doncel-Pedrera, L.M.: The use of digital educational resources in times of COVID-19. Soc. Media Soc. **7**, 205630512110492 (2021). https://doi. org/10.1177/20563051211049246

23. CARNET: e-Schools Programme. http://www.e-skole.hr/program-e-skole/. Last accessed 3 Jan 2023

24. CARNET: e-Schools: Development of the System of Digitally Mature Schools (second phase), https://www.e-skole.hr/wp-content/uploads/2022/02/e-Skole-brosura.pdf (2019)

25. CARNET: Public procurement: https://pilot.e-skole.hr/en/public-procurement/. Last accessed 3 Dec 2022

26. Edutorij » Digitalni obrazovni sadržaji - e-Škole, https://edutorij.e-skole.hr/share/page/dos-eskole. Last accessed 22 Feb 2021

27. Mayer, R.E.: Multimedia Learning. Cambridge University Press, Cambridge, New York (2009)

28. Bouki, V., Economou, D., Angelopoulou, A.: Cognitive theory of multimedia learning and learning videos design: the redundancy principle. In: SIGDOC'11, pp. 271–277. ACM, Pisa, Italy (2011)

29. Center for Applied Psychology, Faculty of Humanities and Social Sciences, University of Rijeka: Scientific Research on the Effects of the Project "e-Schools: Establishing a System for the Development of Digitally Mature Schools (Pilot Project)": Conclusions and recommendations. https://pilot.e-skole.hr/wp-content/uploads/2019/11/Conclusions_and_recomm endations.pdf (2018)

30. Burnham, K.P., Anderson, D.R.: Multimodel inference: understanding AIC and BIC in model selection. Sociol. Methods Res. **33**, 261–304 (2004). https://doi.org/10.1177/004912410426 8644

31. Oreski, D., Hajdin, G., Vukovac, D.P.: Identifying clusters of primary and secondary school teachers according to their educational digital content perceptions. In: 2021 IEEE Technology & Engineering Management Conference – Europe (TEMSCON-EUR). pp. 1–6. IEEE, Dubrovnik, Croatia (2021). https://doi.org/10.1109/TEMSCON-EUR52034.2021.9488651

A Human or a Computer Agent: The Social and Cognitive Effects of an e-Learning Instructor's Identity and Voice Cues

Tze Wei Liew[1]([⊠]) [iD], Su-Mae Tan[1] [iD], Chin Lay Gan[1] [iD], and Si Na Kew[2] [iD]

[1] Multimedia University, Jalan Ayer Keroh Lama, 75450 Melaka, Malaysia
twliew@mmu.edu.my
[2] Universiti Teknologi Malaysia, Jalan Iman, Johor Bahru, 81310 Johor, Malaysia

Abstract. An instructor in an e-learning video can identify as a human or a computer agent. Relatedly, they can project a human-recorded voice or a machine-voice generated from a classical text-to-speech engine. This study examines the effects of an e-learning instructor's identity and voice cues on an instructor's social ratings, learners' cognitive load, and learning performance. A between-subjects laboratory experiment was conducted where university undergraduates (n = 108) interacted with either one of the four e-learning videos featuring different pairings of an instructor's identity (human versus agent) and voice (human-voice versus machine-voice) cues that delivered a lesson on programming algorithms. The findings affirmed the voice effects in multimedia learning in that the human-voice enhanced social and learning outcomes more than the machine-voice, irrespective of the identity cues. Credibility ratings were diminished when an instructor identified as a computer agent projected a human-voice than a machine-voice—additionally, endowing a human-identified instructor with a machine-voice prompted learners to assign lower intrinsic cognitive load. These observations imply the congruence/incongruence effects of identity-voice cue pairings on social and cognitive load outcomes. Theoretical and practical implications are discussed in this paper.

Keywords: E-learning · Multimedia learning · Social agency · Voice effect · Identity cue · Cognitive load

1 Introduction

E-learning videos are pervasive today. They are cost-effective, highly accessible anytime, anywhere, and can convey rich instructional content through visual and verbal information. Converging visual and verbal information in an e-learning video promotes meaningful learning through the multimedia effect that accords with human's dual-channel (visual and verbal) cognitive architecture [1]. In addition, an e-learning design must conform to the principles grounded on the Cognitive Load Theory, which denotes the three types of cognitive load that can impact e-learning performance—intrinsic, extraneous, and germane load [1, 2].

P. Zaphiris and A. Ioannou (Eds.): HCII 2023, LNCS 14040, pp. 292–304, 2023.
https://doi.org/10.1007/978-3-031-34411-4_20

Another design imperative is based on the Social Agency Theory, which avers that e-learning videos should be designed around priming learners to regard e-learning engagement as a social communication rather than an information delivery process [2, 3]. An e-learning video devoid of social cues may compel the learners to assume that e-learning is purely a one-way impersonal information delivery mechanism, which offers little incentive for them to process the information deeply. On the other hand, when learners adopt a social communication mindset during e-learning, they apply the human-to-human social rule of cooperation. Following this social rule, learners commit more effort to comprehend the message as a reciprocate response to acknowledging that the speaker is attempting to convey a clear and meaningful message.

Many e-learning videos feature an instructor as a computer agent [4]. Also known as pedagogical agents, they exhibit human-like traits and cues, albeit not intentionally portraying themselves as real or actual people but as software-generated simulacra of human beings. The popularity of computer agents embodying e-learning instructors is attributed to cheaper, faster, and more scalable productions compared to video recordings of humans. Further, AI agents such as Apple's Siri, Amazon's Alexa, and Google Assistant increasingly permeates people's lifestyle, including education, where they assume instructional roles [5]. Moreover, nascent technology avails computer agents to express realistic social and emotional cues, including artificial voices that sound human-like to support teaching and learning activities [6–10]. Given the emerging role of computer agents as instructors, examining how the identity (human versus agent) and voice cues affect the learners' social ratings of the instructor, cognitive load, and learning performance is vital.

1.1   Voice Cue

Derived from the Social Agency Theory, the Voice Principle asserts that the e-learning instructor's voice conveying the verbal information should be human-than machine-voice [3, 11–14]. Text-to-speech voice, especially generated through classical vocalizers, is characteristically machine-like. The machine-like tone runs counter to the familiar human-to-human communication schema and, therefore, cannot prime learners to forge an ideal social connection with the e-learning speaker. On the other hand, when a human voice is used, learners are easily primed to engage socially with the e-learning instructor, thus driving increased efforts to understand the learning materials. Noteworthy, some modern text-to-speech vocalizers can convey artificial voices that sound sufficiently human-like and natural. These are equally effective in causing learners to feel a social connection toward the e-learning instructor, leading to optimal cognitive effort and learning outcomes [5, 15, 16].

1.2 Identity Cue

Per the Social Agency Theory, human-like traits and cues from a social model embedded in an e-learning environment, irrespective of their identity as a real-life human or an artificial agent, can prompt learners to equate the e-learning activity to a social communication that merits their active attention to and cognitive engagement with the conveyed learning material. This hinges fundamentally on the media equation theory [17], which assumes that people will treat technological artifacts as fellow humans, especially when the entities showcase human-like traits. The process is considered automatic and mindless, even when people recognize that artificial agents are not real humans. Termed the Ethopoeia Concept, it has been inferred that irrespective of whether a human or a computer agent depicts a social model, they will induce similar social responses in learners as long as they exhibit sufficient and appropriate social cues [18].

However, this research highlights a potential caveat: while users apply human-to-human social rules to engage with digital entities, the elicited social responses are not equal between the model's identity framed as a computer agent versus a human [19–23]. People may assign less trustworthiness and credibility to the information they perceive as derived from a "computer algorithm" than a human [21], believing that computer agents are less sophisticated and less capable than human partners, which, in turn, influence social responses [19]. From the Social Agency Theory perspective, Schroeder and Adesope's review [24] suggests that while both a human and a pedagogical agent can prime learners to sense a social presence and arouse social responses, this effect is relatively more pronounced with a human than an agent as a social model. For instance, Burgoon et al. [23] revealed that interacting with a computer agent produced smaller effects on social ratings, including trust, expertise, sociality, and competence, than interacting with a human partner in a digital task environment. The different social responses can implicate computer-based learning tasks, with studies indicating that the perception of engaging with a computer agent instead of a human negatively impacts performance [19–21].

Relatedly, the Threshold Model of Social Influence [25] posits that users' feelings of social presence and subsequent social responses toward the social model differ depending on the identity cue: a human or a computer agent [26]. People will fundamentally only engage in social behavior with the social model in a virtual environment if they perceive them as another human being (e.g., an avatar controlled by a human) but significantly less so when they know that the social model is a mere computer agent. Under the condition where users identified the social model as a computer agent, the agent must exhibit adequate human-like qualities that exceed a specific behavioral realism threshold to elicit comparable social responses from users. Contrariwise, a social model that users identify as a human partner will always induce social presence and reactions in users, irrespective of the entity's degree of behaviouralism realism cues.

While the Threshold Model of Social Influence primarily addresses the agency effects (an avatar controlled by a human versus a computer agent) within an interactive virtual environment, we adopt this paradigm in exploring the identity cue and voice effects of an e-learning instructor. In line with this model, an e-learning instructor's human-voice emits high behaviouralism cues while a machine-voice radiates low behaviouralism cues. At the same time, learners' perception of the e-learning instructor as a human or an agent may influence their sense of social presence and agency, affecting cognitive and learning outcomes. Moreover, the e-learning instructor's identity cue as an agent or a human may influence the Voice Principle effects. It can be conjectured that when learners regard the e-learning instructor as a human, they will always sense a sufficient social presence that elevates cognitive effort and learning performance, regardless of whether the instructor's voice is human-like (high behaviorism realism cue) or machine-like (low high behaviorism realism cue). Whereas, if the e-learning instructor is perceived as an agent, only a human-voice (high behaviorism realism cue) compared to a machine-voice (low high behaviorism realism cue) can effectively evoke learners' sense of social presence and social responses that drive cognitive effort and learning performance.

1.3 Congruence/Incongruence Effect

In addition to the above, this paper addresses the congruence between the identity (human versus agent) and voice (human-voice versus machine-voice) cues. Drawing on the cognitive consistency principle, a contradiction between identity and voice cues imposes additional cognitive processing to categorize the social model and induces unfavorable social perceptions [27, 28]. Gong and Nass [28] discovered that participants engaging with social models exhibiting mismatched face-voice attributes (a human picture with a computer-generated voice and a computer-agent face with a human-recorded voice) negatively impact judgment and social ratings compared to those engaging with social models exhibiting congruous face-voice attributes.

Relatedly, mismatching identity cues and their corresponding social traits can violate users' expectations [29–31]. Generally, users tend to have lower onset expectations toward a social model framed as a computer agent than a human—this promotes positive appraisals if the agent's social cues' qualities exceed users' already-restrained expectations and simultaneously dispels disappointment if the social cues are deemed inferior [29, 30]. However, expectation violations can also occur if a social model framed as a computer agent exhibits more human-centric traits, which contravenes users' machine heuristics that the computer agent would manifest machine-like instead of human-like cues [31]. Go and Sundar [31] found that the chatbot identified as program-operated but had a human picture led to lower social ratings, less favorable attitudes, and lower behavioral intentions than the chatbot identified as human-operated and had a human picture. Moreover, users attributed the chatbot identified as human-operated but had a non-human image with lower social ratings, less favorable attitudes, and lower behavioral intentions than the chatbot identified as program-operated and had a non-human picture.

1.4 The Present Study

Overall, this paper proposes two competing perspectives. On the one hand, it can be inferred that a computer agent and a human social model will evoke equivalent social responses, provided they adequately manifest favorable social cues. Adopting this stance implies that a human-voice will lead to more positive social, cognitive, and learning outcomes than a machine-voice, regardless of the e-learning instructor's identity cue (human or agent). On the other hand, the countervailing perspective suggests that the social model's identity as a computer agent versus a human will elicit unequal social responses, thereby influencing social, cognitive, and learning outcomes. Further, there are plausible joint effects across varied identity-voice cue pairings, as implied through the lens of the Threshold Model of Social Influence [25], cognitive consistency principle [28], and violation expectancy theory [29–31]. To shed light on this research stream, this work examines the confluence between the effects of an e-learning instructor's identity and voice cues on learners' social, cognitive, and learning outcomes. Formally, we ask:

RQ: To what extent do an e-learning instructor's identity (human versus agent) and voice (human-voice versus machine-voice) cues affect the instructor's social ratings, learners' cognitive load, and learning performance?

2 Method

2.1 Research Design

This study employed a 2 (identity cue: human versus agent) X 2 (voice cue: human-voice versus machine-voice) between-subjects experiment in which learners interacted with the respective multimedia learning presentation in a computer laboratory.

2.2 Multimedia Learning Material

We utilized Adobe Animate and PowerPoint to develop a 12 min-long multimedia learning presentation that conveyed step-by-step demonstrations on interpreting the outputs of programming algorithms, i.e., IF statement, IF-ELSE statement, and NESTED IF statement. The presentation format followed the principle of worked example effect, where learners were shown fully worked examples rather than attempting to seek solution steps to a novel problem [32]. The presentation converged sample program codes, flowcharts, and animated markers to inform learners on basic concepts of programming algorithms, including initial value, condition, and statement. Figure 1 illustrates the e-learning environment.

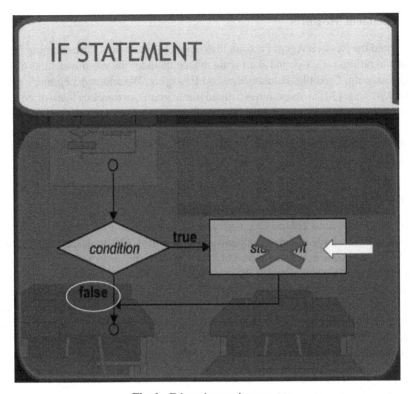

Fig. 1. E-learning environment.

2.3 Identity and Voice Cues

We designed four variants of the multimedia learning material per the e-learning instructor's identity (human versus agent) and voice (human-voice versus machine-voice) cues. To distinguish between the identity cues, the experimenters told the participants that they would engage with the e-learning presented by a human or a computer agent instructor. Moreover, at the beginning and two more intervals within the multimedia learning program, the e-learning instructor verbally introduced himself as either "Michael, a human person recording this lecture for you!" (human-identified) or "Michael, not a real human, but a computer agent programmed to deliver this lecture to you!" (agent-identified). The e-learning video did not visibly feature the instructor to avoid confounding factors. Concerning voice cues, the multimedia learning material was narrated using a male human-recorded speech (human-like) or Microsoft TTS David (machine-like). Ultimately, the experimental stimuli featured:

1. Human-identified instructor with a human-voice,
2. Human-identified instructor with machine-voice,
3. Agent-identified instructor with a human-voice,
4. Agent-identified instructor with machine-voice.

2.4 Dependent Measures

We adopted the Revised Agent Persona Instrument [33] to assess the e-learning instructor's social ratings on a 5-point Likert scale, which includes the sub-dimensions of Facilitating Learning, Credible, Human-like, and Engaging. We adopted Leppink's eleven-
point Likert scale [34] to assess intrinsic load (three items), extraneous load (three items),
and germane load (four items). Learning performance was measured via a pencil-and-
paper posttest comprising recall and application questions concerning the flowchart
diagram, program statements, and program outcomes, with a maximum score of 10
marks.

2.5 Participants and the Experimental Procedure

We obtained a sample comprising first-year, first-semester undergraduates pursuing
Diploma in IT at a large private Asian university (n = 108, 87% males, all aged between
18 and 22). They were novice learners who had yet to take any programming courses. The
learners voluntarily participated in the experiment and were informed they could quit it
anytime. They were randomly divided and ushered into the computer labs with individual PCs and headsets featuring one of the four multimedia learning program variants,
resulting in an equal 27 participants in each experimental condition. The experimenters
steered the participants to complete the approximately one-hour experimental process
comprising the following:

1. Listen to the briefing,
2. Sign the informed consent,
3. Interact with the multimedia learning program,
4. Complete the surveys and learning posttest,
5. Listen to the debriefing, thanked, and dismissed.

3 Data Analyses and Results

3.1 Social Ratings

A series of 2 (identity cue: human versus agent) $\times$ 2 (voice cue: human-voice versus
machine-voice) analysis of variance (ANOVA) was computed with the learner's scores
for Facilitating Learning, Credible, Human-like, and Engaging as dependent variables.
Figure 2 illustrates the means for the social ratings. The results detected significant main
effects of voice cues on Human-like $[F(1,104) = 5.13, p < .05]$ and Engaging ratings
$[F(1,104) = 7.56, p < .01]$, with the human-voice led to higher ratings than the machine-
voice. A significant interaction effect was found for Credibility ratings $[F(1,104) = 6.01,$
$p < .05]$. The simple main effect analyses demonstrated that the e-learning instructor
identified as an agent with a machine-voice led to higher Credibility ratings than the
e-learning instructor identified as an agent with a human-voice $[F(1,52) = 7.01, p < .5]$.
The other main or interaction effects were non-significant.

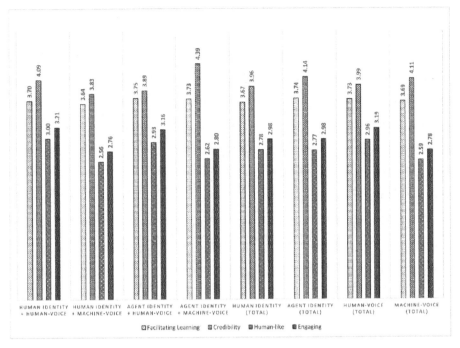

Fig. 2. Means for social ratings.

3.2 Cognitive Load Ratings

A series of 2 (identity cue: human versus agent) × 2 (voice cue: human-voice versus machine-voice) analysis of variance (ANOVA) was computed with the learner's ratings for the intrinsic, extraneous, and germane load as dependent variables. Figure 3 illustrates the means for the cognitive load ratings. The results indicated an interaction effect for intrinsic load [$F(1,104) = 4.98, p < .05$]. The simple main effect analyses showed that the e-learning instructor identified as a human with a machine-voice resulted in the lowest intrinsic load ratings and was significantly lower compared to the e-learning instructor identified as a human with a human-voice [$F(1,52) = 4.05, p < .5$] and the e-learning instructor identified as an agent with a machine-voice [$F(1,52) = 6.50, p < .5$]. The main and interaction effects for extraneous and germane load were non-significant.

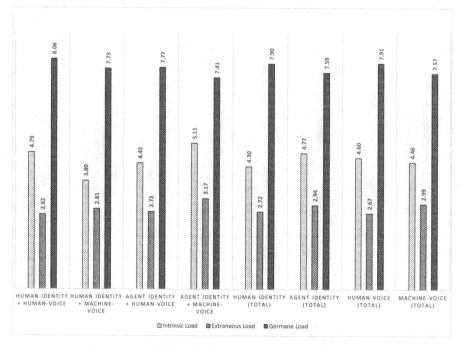

Fig. 3. Means for cognitive load ratings.

3.3 Posttest Scores

A 2 (identity cue: human versus agent) × 2 (voice cue: human-voice versus machine-voice) analysis of variance (ANOVA) was computed with the learner's posttest scores as a dependent variable. Figure 4 presents the means for the posttest scores. The outcome showed a significant main effect of voice cue on posttest scores [$F(1,104) = 6.01$, p < .5]. Irrespective of whether the e-learning instructor was identified as a human or an agent, the human-voice led to better posttest scores than the machine-voice. No other effects were significant.

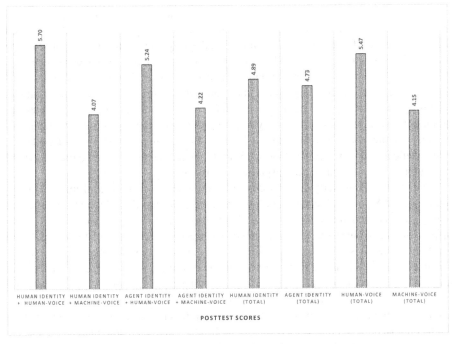

Fig. 4. Means for posttest scores.

4 Discussion

Overall, this study revealed that an e-learning instructor's voice has a robust effect on the instructor's social ratings and learning outcome, in that the learners attributed higher social traits concerning "human-like" and "engaging" to the instructor and also performed better in the posttest when they engaged with the e-learning instructors with a human-voice than a machine-voice. These effects were observed regardless of whether the e-learning instructor was identified as a human or a computer agent, affirming the Voice Principle in e-learning [3, 12, 13].

The framing of the e-learning instructor's identity cue as a human or an agent alone did not directly influence learners' social, cognitive, and learning outcomes. However, when considered with the voice cue, certain nuances were revealed concerning social and cognitive load outcomes. Specifically, endowing an agent-identified instructor with a human-voice than a machine-voice reduced credibility. This discovery could be attributed to the identity-voice cues incongruity effects [27, 28, 31], which negatively impacts social perception toward the instructor as a trustworthy information source. When the e-learning instructor frames himself as a computer agent, the identity cue will trigger the machine heuristics in the learners' minds [31]; hence, learners anticipate the instructor to project a machine-voice. The expectation violation due to using the human-voice than the machine-voice caused the learners to assign less credibility to the agent-identified e-learning instructor.

Another interesting observation is that the e-learning instructor, who was identified as a human but was endowed with a machine-voice (incongruent pairing), prompted learners to assign lower intrinsic cognitive load ratings, particularly compared to the human-identified instructor with a human-voice (congruent pairing) and agent-identified instructor with a machine-voice (congruent pairing). This finding implies that the congruence effects of identity and voice cues can affect learners' cognitive load ratings regarding the difficulty and complexity of the learning contents. A plausible interpretation is that the mismatched identity-voice traits caused the learners not to regard or engage with the learning content seriously; thus, the learning content was assumed to be easier (reflected as low intrinsic load) than when the learners encountered the e-learning instructors with harmonious identity-voice attributes.

The results of this study do not accord with the supposition adopted from the Threshold Model of Social Influence model, which suggested that the e-learning instructor's identity cue as a human rather than a computer agent will robustly prime stronger social responses and facilitate better performance for learners regardless of the human- and machine-voice cues. This outcome implies that it is inconsequential whether an e-learning material features a human or a computer agent as an instructor. Instead, what matters for enhancing social, cognitive, and learning outcomes are the appropriate and sufficient social cues, including human-voice cues associated with the social model [3, 11–13]. From a practical viewpoint, rendering computer agents for e-learning environments offers a cheaper, faster, and more scalable alternative than humans, as long as they are endowed with human-recorded speech or contemporary human-sounding artificial voice. [5, 15, 16]. However, we recommend more research to clarify further to what extent identity-voice cues pairings shape social and cognitive outcomes.

5   Limitations and Recommendations for Future Work

This study adopted an experimental design that supplies valuable insights into cause-and-effect relationships, albeit with certain drawbacks that limit validity and generalization. The artificial laboratory settings in the experiment may not apply to real-world scenarios containing the complexity and nuance of e-learning engagements. In addition, our sample was limited to Asian learners who were novices in the subject matter; thus, the results are not generalizable to the broader population. The short duration of the e-learning material might have influenced the findings; this study cannot ascertain the identity and voice cue effects for a long-duration e-learning video. Future research can extend this research stream through field experiments that enable researchers to assess the identity and voice cues in a real-world setting. Such an endeavor increases generalizability via stronger external and ecological validity in that the findings better reflect the effects naturally and authentically. Moreover, future work can be conducted with more diverse sample learners and with longer-duration e-learning materials.

Acknowledgment. This research was supported by the Malaysia Ministry of Higher Education (FRGS/1/2021/SS0/MMU/02/8), which was awarded to Su-Mae Tan.

References

1. Mayer, R.E.: Thirty years of research on online learning. Appl. Cogn. Psychol. **33**, 152–159 (2018). https://doi.org/10.1002/acp.3482
2. Mayer, R.E., Fiorella, L., Stull, A.: Five ways to increase the effectiveness of instructional video. Educ. Tech. Research Dev. **68**(3), 837–852 (2020). https://doi.org/10.1007/s11423-020-09749-6
3. Pelletier, C.: The cambridge handbook of multimedia learning. Inform. Design J. **16**, 81–83 (2008). https://doi.org/10.1075/idj.16.1.12pel
4. Li, J., Kizilcec, R., Bailenson, J., Ju, W.: Social robots and virtual agents as lecturers for video instruction. Comput. Hum. Behav. **55**, 1222–1230 (2016). https://doi.org/10.1016/j.chb.2015.04.005
5. Liew, T.W., Tan, S.-M., Pang, W.M., Khan, M.T.I., Kew, S.N.: I am Alexa, your virtual tutor!: the effects of Amazon Alexa's text-to-speech voice enthusiasm in a multimedia learning environment. Educ. Inf. Technol. **28**, 1455–1489 (2022). https://doi.org/10.1007/s10639-022-11255-6
6. Liew, T.W., Tan, S.-M., Kew, S.N.: Can an angry pedagogical agent enhance mental effort and learning performance in a multimedia learning environment? Inform. Learn. Sci. **123**, 555–576 (2022). https://doi.org/10.1108/ils-09-2021-0079
7. Liew, T.W., Mat Zin, N.A., Sahari, N.: Exploring the affective, motivational and cognitive effects of pedagogical agent enthusiasm in a multimedia learning environment. HCIS **7**(1), 1–21 (2017). https://doi.org/10.1186/s13673-017-0089-2
8. Kim, Y., Baylor, A.L.: Research-based design of pedagogical agent roles: a review, progress, and recommendations. Int. J. Artif. Intell. Educ. **26**(1), 160–169 (2015). https://doi.org/10.1007/s40593-015-0055-y
9. Wang, Y., Gong, S., Cao, Y., Lang, Y., Xu, X.: The effects of affective pedagogical agent in multimedia learning environments: a meta-analysis. Educ. Res. Rev. **38**, 100506 (2023). https://doi.org/10.1016/j.edurev.2022.100506
10. Sikström, P., Valentini, C., Sivunen, A., Kärkkäinen, T.: How pedagogical agents communicate with students: a two-phase systematic review. Comput. Educ. **188**, 104564 (2022). https://doi.org/10.1016/j.compedu.2022.104564
11. Mayer, R.E., DaPra, C.S.: An embodiment effect in computer-based learning with animated pedagogical agents. J. Exp. Psychol. Appl. **18**, 239–252 (2012). https://doi.org/10.1037/a0028616
12. Atkinson, R.K., Mayer, R.E., Merrill, M.M.: Fostering social agency in multimedia learning: examining the impact of an animated agent's voice. Contemp. Educ. Psychol. **30**, 117–139 (2005). https://doi.org/10.1016/j.cedpsych.2004.07.001
13. Mayer, R.E., Sobko, K., Mautone, P.D.: Social cues in multimedia learning: role of speaker's voice. J. Educ. Psychol. **95**, 419 (2003). https://doi.org/10.1037/0022-0663.95.2.419
14. Liew, T.W., Tan, S.-M., Tan, T.M., Kew, S.N.: Does speaker's voice enthusiasm affect social cue, cognitive load and transfer in multimedia learning? Inform. Learn. Sci. **121**, 117–135 (2020). https://doi.org/10.1108/ils-11-2019-0124
15. Craig, S.D., Schroeder, N.L.: Reconsidering the voice effect when learning from a virtual human. Comput. Educ. **114**, 193–205 (2017). https://doi.org/10.1016/j.compedu.2017.07.003
16. Davis, R.O., Vincent, J., Park, T.: Reconsidering the voice principle with non-native language speakers. Comput. Educ. **140**, 103605 (2019). https://doi.org/10.1016/j.compedu.2019.103605
17. Reeves, B., Nass, C.: The media equation: how people treat computers, television, & new media like real people & places. Comput. Math. Appl. **33**, 128 (1997). https://doi.org/10.1016/s0898-1221(97)82929-x

18. von der Pütten, A.M., Krämer, N.C., Gratch, J., Kang, S.-H.: "It doesn't matter what you are!" Explaining social effects of agents and avatars. Comput. Hum. Behav. **26**, 1641–1650 (2010). https://doi.org/10.1016/j.chb.2010.06.012
19. Crompton, C.J., MacPherson, S.E.: Human agency beliefs affect older adults' interaction behaviours and task performance when learning with computerised partners. Comput. Hum. Behav. **101**, 60–67 (2019). https://doi.org/10.1016/j.chb.2019.07.006
20. Caruana, N., Spirou, D., Brock, J.: Human agency beliefs influence behaviour during virtual social interactions. PeerJ **5**, e3819 (2017). https://doi.org/10.7717/peerj.3819
21. Spatola, N., Chevalère, J., Lazarides, R.: Human vs computer: What effect does the source of information have on cognitive performance and achievement goal orientation? Paladyn, J. Behav. Robot. **12**, 175–186 (2021). https://doi.org/10.1515/pjbr-2021-0012
22. Aharoni, E., Fridlund, A.J.: Social reactions toward people vs. computers: how mere lables shape interactions. Comput. Human Behav. **23**(5), 2175–2189 (2007). https://doi.org/10.1016/j.chb.2006.02.019
23. Burgoon, J.K., Bonito, J.A., Bengtsson, B., Cederberg, C., Lundeberg, M., Allspach, L.: Interactivity in human–computer interaction: a study of credibility, understanding, and influence. Comput. Hum. Behav. **16**, 553–574 (2000). https://doi.org/10.1016/s0747-5632(00)00029-7
24. Schroeder, N.L., Adesope, O.O.: A systematic review of pedagogical agents' persona, motivation, and cognitive load implications for learners. J. Res. Technol. Educ. **46**, 229–251 (2014). https://doi.org/10.1080/15391523.2014.888265
25. Blascovich, J.: A theoretical model of social influence for increasing the utility of collaborative virtual environments. In: Proceedings of the 4th international conference on Collaborative virtual environments, pp. 25–30 (2002). https://doi.org/10.1145/571878.571883
26. Fox, J., Ahn, S.J., Janssen, J.H., Yeykelis, L., Segovia, K.Y., Bailenson, J.N.: Avatars versus agents: a meta-analysis quantifying the effect of agency on social influence. Human-Comput. Interact. **30**, 401–432 (2015). https://doi.org/10.1080/07370024.2014.921494
27. Hu, P., Wang, K., Liu, J.: Speaking and listening: Mismatched human-like conversation qualities undermine social Perception and Trust in AI-based voice assistants. In: Proceedings of the 23rd Pacific Asia Conference on Information Systems: Secure ICT Platform for the 4th Industrial Revolution (2019)
28. Gong, L., Nass, C.: When a talking-face computer agent is half-human and half-humanoid: human identity and consistency preference. Hum. Commun. Res. **33**, 163–193 (2007). https://doi.org/10.1111/j.1468-2958.2007.00295.x
29. Mark Grimes, G., Schuetzler, R.M., Giboney, J Scott: Mental models and expectation violations in conversational AI interactions. Decis. Support Syst. **144**, 113515 (2021). https://doi.org/10.1016/j.dss.2021.113515
30. Burgoon, J.K., et al.: Application of expectancy violations theory to communication with and judgments about embodied agents during a decision-making task. Int. J. Hum Comput Stud. **91**, 24–36 (2016). https://doi.org/10.1016/j.ijhcs.2016.02.002
31. Go, E., Sundar, S.S.: Humanizing chatbots: the effects of visual, identity and conversational cues on humanness perceptions. Comput. Hum. Behav. **97**, 304–316 (2019). https://doi.org/10.1016/j.chb.2019.01.020
32. Chen, O., Kalyuga, S., Sweller, J.: The worked example effect, the generation effect, and element interactivity. J. Educ. Psychol. **107**, 689–704 (2015). https://doi.org/10.1037/edu0000018
33. Schroeder, N.L., Romine, W.L., Craig, S.D.: Measuring pedagogical agent persona and the influence of agent persona on learning. Comput. Educ. **109**, 176–186 (2017). https://doi.org/10.1016/j.compedu.2017.02.015
34. Leppink, J., Paas, F., Van der Vleuten, C.P.M., Van Gog, T., Van Merriënboer, J.J.G.: Development of an instrument for measuring different types of cognitive load. Behav. Res. Methods **45**(4), 1058–1072 (2013). https://doi.org/10.3758/s13428-013-0334-1

The Study on Usability and User Experience of Reading Assessment Systems: A Preliminary Research

Peiying Lin and Guanze Liao[✉]

National Tsing Hua University, Hsinchu City, Taiwan
peiying22120@gapp.nthu.edu.tw, gzliao@mx.nthu.edu.tw

Abstract. In modern society, digital reading has become an essential ability in daily life. Reading assessment systems provide teachers with various digital texts and instant assistance to observe students' reading performance and learning progress to make informed decisions on curriculum design or remedial instruction. In addition, students can have personalized learning experiences and practice self-regulated learning with systems at any time and place. Although there are already several reading platforms and assessment instruments on the market, research on these educational technology tools is relatively rare. The usability and user experience greatly influence learning effectiveness and continual usage willingness; therefore, this study aims to investigate user needs, improve the usability of reading assessment systems, and provide design strategies for developers. The presented study consists of three research stages: requirement analysis, proposing design strategies and prototypes, and user testing. This preliminary research focuses on middle school educators and learners, and our system environment is in Mandarin Chinese.

Keywords: Usability · Digital reading · Reading assessment system

1 Introduction

Nowadays, emerging digital resources that significantly change reading habits and bring people new challenges gain the attention of researchers and governments. In 2009, Program for International Student Assessment (PISA), an authoritative international test measuring 15-year-old students' performance in reading, mathematics, and science literacy, updated their assessment to evaluate their reading abilities in digital contexts [1]. In the meantime, an increasing number of students are choosing digital textbooks and online resources as learning tools [2, 3], and teachers of all grades tend to use e-books or online articles rather than print [4, 5].

As people gradually tend to read on screens, research has confirmed that competencies required for reading and understanding in digital spaces are entirely different from reading conventional linear texts [6–8]. Furthermore, some researchers indicated that youth cannot read profoundly and stay engaged while reading in a digital environment [9, 10]. In response to the booming trend of digital reading and all the problems that come with it, many platforms and tools have been launched to train learners' reading skills and assist educators in various teaching approaches, including electronic textbooks, digital libraries, and online reading platforms.

Concerning different reading platforms and assessment systems launched in recent years, the usability of these tools and how learners and other stakeholders perceive these tools are essential [11]. Several studies have revealed that the perceived usability of systems greatly influences students' learning experience [12]. Moreover, learners will use the system more frequently if the user interface is easy to use. Conversely, if the system is considered hard to use, it takes learners more time to learn to operate it than to use it [13].

Additionally, the interaction design for educational technology tools may need to be revised to ensure their adoption [14]. Although many researchers have noticed the importance of usability, as shown in accessible research data, discussions of usability issues in educational technologies are relatively lacking [11, 12]. Therefore, to ensure educators and learners a practical and comfortable experience in digital reading environments, this study investigates user needs of reading assessment systems (RAS), proposing and validating design strategies to improve the usability and user experience. This preliminary research focuses on middle school educators and learners, and our system environment is in Mandarin Chinese.

2   Case Studies

This study focuses on reading assessment systems (RAS) that provide many digital texts and quiz questions to help students train digital reading skills and strategies. With the assistance of RAS, students can have personalized reading experiences and practice self-regulated learning at their own pace. Moreover, RAS not only supplies teachers with various digital texts to prepare their courses but also provides instant data analysis, such as students' reading performance, answering records, and learning progress, to assist them in making informed decisions on curriculum design or remedial instruction. The following section will discuss various reading assessment platforms and systems in the Mandarin Chinese market.

2.1   Science Students

Science Students currently provides subscription-based services that send science articles and reading test questions for middle school students to assist them in practicing digital reading. By subscribing, users can get two science articles and literacy-oriented test questions in line with the teaching progress in schools every week. In addition, users also receive two articles related to the latest scientific research news per month to supplement new knowledge outside of the school. When users complete the reading test online, they can instantly see their reading time, answering time, correct answer rate, and other learners' performance (see Fig. 1). Furthermore, parents can have an account to receive articles their children read and check the reading performance of their children.

Fig. 1. The results of answering Science Students

2.2 PinXueTang Reading Comprehension System (PRCS)

PRCS currently provides services on a subscription basis. This platform offers a variety of digital texts and quizzes to help users understand their performance in reading comprehension. After subscribing to the service, users can browse articles of different topics, types, or formats and answer quiz questions. Educators who subscribe to PRCS for their students can create their classes and distribute articles and test questions to learners on the platform. After the due date, educators can view each student's learning status and reading performance through data analysis. Students can also conduct self-directed learning on PRCS if they have a device connecting to the Internet. Furthermore, PRCS provides text analysis, extended thinking, and extended reading to assist students in higher-level thinking and broader reading (see Fig. 2).

Fig. 2. The article page of PRCS

2.3 PaGamO Literacy School (PLS)

PLS currently offers a subscription-based service, including personal and school subscriptions, with a gamification learning environment (see Fig. 3), digital texts, and test questions that meet the needs of students at different stages. After subscribing, four articles and topics are distributed automatically to learners every week, and special assessments are also delivered every month. Each question group in PLS has detailed audio and video explanations recorded by teachers to help understand the article more comprehensively. Moreover, students and their parents can understand their learning status and reading performances through data analysis such as radar charts.

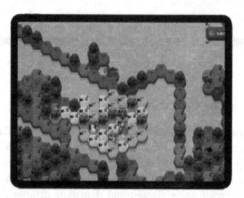

Fig. 3. The gamification environment of PLS

3   Research Design

This study uses qualitative and quantitative methods to gain insights into user needs and validate the usability of proposed design strategies and prototypes. The research stages are as follows.

3.1 Requirement Analysis

We invited 24 middle school teachers and students who had used RAS for at least one semester to attend our semi-structured interviews. In doing so, educators' and learners' ideas and needs can be considered. The interview questions (see Table 1) include usage motivation, daily operation modes, functional requirements, frequently encountered difficulties, and so forth. During the interview, participants can use the tablet to recall and explain their thoughts.

After user interviews, verbatim transcripts were organized and summarized into eight design concepts for future systems by the affinity diagram, known as the KJ method. Firstly, all the key sentences were extracted from transcripts and written on sticky notes. Then, according to the meaning of each sentence, we sorted these notes into several related groups and labeled each of them. Based on their relationships, these small groups were combined into larger groups and named into categories. After that, we combined these categories into larger related clusters and wrote summaries of each set. Lastly, the results of the affinity diagram were transformed into design concepts.

Table 1. The outline and questions of the semi-structured interview

Focus area	Questions	
	Teacher	Student
Motivation and purpose of use	What is your motivation for using RAS in class? What do you expect students to learn from RAS?	What is your motivation for using RAS? What do you expect to learn from RAS?
Functional requirements and operation modes	How do you prepare before using RAS in class? What teaching contexts do you use RAS? How do you use RAS after class?	How do you usually use RAS in the classroom? How do you use RAS after class? Do you need other tools to use RAS for learning?
Frequently used functions and difficulties encountered	What functions do you commonly use RAS? What difficulties have you had when using RAS?	What functions do you commonly use on RAS? What difficulties have you had when using RAS?

3.2 Prototype Design

After concluding our design strategies for RAS, this study gradually transformed this result into a tablet version of RAS. First, the information architecture was developed according to our design concepts from the previous stage. Next, based on information architecture, the author sketched a low-fidelity prototype to present the basic appearance of RAS and arranged necessary elements on the interface, including functions, titles, text content, and so on (see Fig. 4). Finally, a high-fidelity functional prototype was built so that we could evaluate and improve these design concepts (see Fig. 5).

Fig. 4. The low-fidelity prototype of RAS

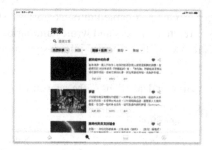

Fig. 5. The high-fidelity prototype of RAS

3.3 Evaluation

To validate our design concepts and prototype, we conducted user testing based on features most frequently used by teachers and students. During the test, participants were instructed to conduct tasks with the thinking-aloud method on an iPad. After completing each task, the moderator asked several questions to understand participants' views and feelings toward the current system environment. In the end, participants filled out post-test questionnaires.

Participants

This study collected data from six middle school Chinese teachers and six students. All participants had not used any reading assessment system before, but eleven of them had experience using technology tools to teach or learn, such as digital books, online videos, and Google Classroom, to name but a few.

Task Scenarios

Task goals and scenarios (Table 2) were set based on usage contexts and design concepts to guide participants in operating and testing RAS. Most tasks are identical, but some are adjusted to user needs of different identities.

Table 2. Task goals and scenarios of user testing

	Teacher	Student
Task1	Searching articles: Please find an article that is related to Ukraine and suitable for novices	
Task2	Adding articles to reading lists: Please find three natural science articles with graphs and save them in a new reading list named "scientific reading"	
Task3	Assigning tasks: Please distribute a reading task to class 201, including an expository article on social science and two natural science articles that have just been added to your reading list	Receiving tasks: Please check the article topic and type of the reading task your Chinese teacher just assigned on RAS

(continued)

Table 2. (*continued*)

	Teacher	Student
Task4	Checking class performance: Supposing you've been using RAS for a while and want to know students' performance. Please check the submission status of Reading Task 1, finding the average grade of class 201 and the average time spent on each article	Checking personal performance: Supposing you've been using RAS for a while and want to know your reading performance so far. Please check which topics you most frequently read and your reading performance of different topics
Task5	Finding extended materials to teach: Students' reading score of *Swedish Dessert Cinnamon Rolls* is relatively low, so you want to check the answering records find extended materials to teach. Please find answering records, Extending Reading and Article Analysis on this page	Finding extended materials to learn: Supposing you find that the reading score of *Swedish Dessert Cinnamon Rolls* is relatively low, so you want to review it again and find further information to learn. Please find Extending Reading and Article Analysis on this page
Task6	Finding similar articles with tags: *Swedish Dessert Cinnamon Rolls* is an article related to diet. Please use this article (page) to find more new articles on the topic of diet	
Task7	Marking highlights: After reading *Swedish Dessert Cinnamon Rolls*, you find that the first line of the second paragraph ("In the 18th century, the Swedes brought back precious spices such as cinnamon and cardamom from overseas") was the key point. Please mark this sentence in pink	

Evaluation Methods

This study uses the ISO 9241–11 definition of usability and evaluates three metrics: effectiveness, efficiency, and satisfaction. The completion rate of each task measures effectiveness. Efficiency is the required time and steps to complete a task. The questionnaire determines satisfaction for user interaction satisfaction (QUIS). Moreover, this study also uses the system usability scale (SUS) as the post-test questionnaire to measure the overall usability level.

The questionnaire for user interaction satisfaction (QUIS). In this study, QUIS version 7.0 is used to measure user satisfaction with the proposed design concepts and prototype. QUIS was developed by researchers from the human-computer Interaction Laboratory at the University of Maryland to Assess Subjective Satisfaction, Especially For The Human-Computer Interface. The questionnaire can be rearranged and choose only some sections to follow various research needs. This study selects five facets of QUIS, including overall system satisfaction, screen, terminology and system information, learning, and system capabilities, totaling 21 questions. To facilitate the subjects' responses, we change them to a five-point scale.

The system usability scale (SUS). This study utilizes the SUS questionnaire to evaluate the overall usability of RAS. SUS is a 5-point Likert scale proposed by John Brooke in 1986 to measure the usability of computer systems. The questionnaire contains positive and negative-oriented items, which are presented in an alternate order. For positively worded questions, researchers subtract one from the user responses. For negatively worded questions, researchers subtract the score from five. The total score of 10 items is added and multiplied by 2.5 to get a final score.

4 Results

4.1 Design Strategies

Based on the result of requirement research, we transformed user expectation and needs into the following design concepts. These design concepts come from the voices of middle school Chinese teachers and students, providing an important foundation for subsequent design prototype (Table 3).

Table 3. Design strategies of RAS

User needs	Design strategies
Searching for articles is the most common action, so users hope related functions can be placed in an easy-to-find location and make the search process more efficient	Integrating search and filter functions into the same page: Integrate search and filtering on the same tab, allowing users to find articles in different ways and conditions at the same time
Users want to have a folder where they can collect articles. Because when they find an article they like, they don't always have time to read it right away, and some articles they want to read over and over again	Providing Reading Lists as sorting tools: The function of Reading List allows users to quickly create their own folders for collection or classification and enter short notes to record personal thoughts
Users want to have all course-related information or content on one page. This way, teachers can keep track of the status of each class, and students will not miss course announcements or messages	Integrating all course information into one space: Teachers can find the class they are looking for to assign assignments or check students' reading performance more quickly. Students can complete reading tasks and browse rankings by entering the learning environment of their class
Students mention that real-time analysis of reading skills is helpful for personal learning. Teachers indicate that analysis of long-term data could help them track the reading performance of individual students	Automatically analyzing reading performance: Teachers can instantly see the submission status and reading performance of students' assignments in the classroom environment. In addition, long-term changes in students can be tracked through graph analysis. Students can see their own reading records and performance analysis in the personal account area

(continued)

Table 3. (*continued*)

User needs	Design strategies
Teachers want to use digital tools that allow students to extend their reading from a single article to a related article. In particular, when students are learning independently, teachers hope platforms to provide some guidance for students	Assisting users with extended information on Article Page: At the end of the article, Extended Thinking and Further Reading, including link to other articles and videos, provide teachers and students with more diverse learning approaches besides answering questions. Additionally, the teacher edition's Article Page can also see the list of students for each option to see how students responded
Students and teachers often mark highlights or take notes when reading paper-based materials, so there is a need for related functions in the digital reading environment	Providing convenient highlighter function: After the function of the highlighter is activated by long-pressing, the screen displays a toolbar with different color highlighters immediately. By clicking on the color, users can add a mark
Users sometimes just browse RAS casually, such as looking for inspiration or learning something new, so they want RAS to be like a social platform that recommends articles according to different topics or user interests	Providing personalized recommendation and article exhibition: Personalized recommendation is carried out on the homepage, and articles of different theme series are displayed to provide users with more diverse and rich content
Users think that if some games or peer interaction, such as leaderboards or points, can be added, it should enhance students' motivation to learn	Integrating gamification design into RAS: Leader boards can provide opportunities for students to observe each other in class. In addition, competition and stimulation can motivate students to read and practice on the platform

4.2 The Prototype of RAS

This study uses black, white, and green as primary visual colors to provide a simple and calming interface. The environment of RAS mainly consists of four parts: Home, Exploration, My Class, Member Area, and Article Page. The details are as follows.

Home
The Home page (see Fig. 6) includes Personalized Recommendations and Topic Exhibitions. Personalized recommendations are presented as article tags, and the recommended content is based on articles that users have read on RAS. Topic exhibitions are shown as sliding banners and organized similar articles into the same series for users to explore new topics.

Fig. 6. The Home page of RAS

Exploration

The Exploration page (see Fig. 7) includes Search Bar, Filter, and Top Ranking. The search bar and filter are put together to make searching specific articles easier for users. Also, when users are out of ideas or want to browse around, they can see the ranking of articles. After seeing the search result, users can add articles to their reading lists. This study uses black, white, and green as primary visual colors to provide a simple and calming interface. The environment of RAS mainly consists of four parts: Home, Exploration, My Class, Member Area, and Article Page. The details are as follows.

Fig. 7. The Exploration page of RAS

My Class

All course announcements and information are presented in My Class (see Fig. 8), which contains Reading Tasks and Leader Board. Students and teachers can view all reading tasks, including ongoing or expired ones, and see the rank of students' reading performance after joining their class. Additionally, assigning articles is added to the educator version, so teachers can directly assign articles to students in the environment of their classes.

Fig. 8. The My Class page of RAS

Member Area

The Member Area page (see Fig. 9) consists of three parts: Basic Setting, Reading Performance, and Reading List. Generally, personal data and records are organized on this page. Reading Performance provides personal reading records and analysis, including Overview, Article Ratio, and Topic Proficiency. For students who prepare for exams, reading performance information can help them better understand their learning situation and make adjustments.

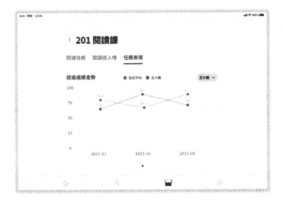

Fig. 9. The Member Area page of RAS

Article Page

The section of the Article Page (see Fig. 10), which includes Article Content, Extended Thinking, Further Reading, Text Analysis, and Test question, is mainly for teachers and students to read, answer and review. Users can long-press the sentence to mark it in different colors as they read the article. When finishing reading, users can answer test questions on the right side of the Article Page. After the test, users can find detailed explanations and article analysis on the same page to understand their blind spots.

Fig. 10. The Article Page of RAS

4.3 User Testing

The result of user testing includes effectiveness, efficiency, and satisfaction. Also, the SUS score shows the overall usability of RAS, and post-test interviews provide further information for reference.

Effectiveness
The completion rate of each task measured effectiveness in this study. If participants finish the task without prompting or assistance, it will be considered completed; otherwise, it will be considered a failure. Figure 11 presents completion rates of teacher and student subjects.

Efficiency
Efficiency in the present study was measured by how much time participants took to complete a task correctly and how many steps were required. If users fail the task, the time spent on the particular task will not be counted in the calculation. Table 4 presents the time used by teacher and student users to complete each task.

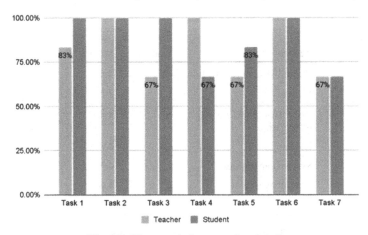

Fig. 11. The completion rate of each task

Table 4. Time used by participants to complete each task

	Teacher		Student	
	Time	Steps	Time	Steps
Task 1	1 min. 1 s	4	30 s	4
Task 2	1 min	16	57 s	16
Task 3	2 min. 36 s	21	17 s	3
Task 4	41 s	4	26 s	3
Task 5	64 s	4	43 s	3
Task 6	22 s	2	21 s	2
Task 7	16 s	3	12 s	3

Satisfaction

The scores for overall satisfaction were collected from QUIS. As shown in Table 5, the average QUIS scores of teachers and students are 4.7 and 4.6. The aspect of Learning receives the highest marks, respectively 4.8 and 4.8. Notably, "Learning to operate the system (difficult - easy)" gets full marks from both respondents. It shows that DRAP has a certain learnability and is friendly to novice users.

The SUS Score

The results of the SUS questionnaire are presented in Table 6. The average score is 80, which is higher than the figure in [15]. In addition, compared to the grading scale and the acceptability ranges proposed in [16], all scores range from Good to Excellent. Therefore, for middle school teachers and students, the usability of RAS is acceptable.

Table 5. The result of QUIS

Items of QUIS	Teacher	Student
Overall system satisfaction	4.5	4.6
Screen	4.3	4.6
Terminology and system information	4.5	4.7
Learning	4.8	4.8
System capabilities	4.7	4.5
Overall average	4.7	4.6

Table 6. The result of SUS questionnaire

Code	ET1	ET2	ET3	ET4	ET5	ET6	ES1	ES2	ES3	ES4	ES5	ES6
Score	85	72.5	72.5	87.5	75	75	70	80	87.5	92.5	82.5	80
Average	80											

5   Discussion

In terms of the results of effectiveness, both teachers and students had more difficulties in task 7 (Marking highlights). Although many people reported that the interaction design of long-press is similar to how they usually use electronic products, some participants mentioned that it would be better if there were a visual reminder. For teacher participants, task 3 (Assigning tasks) and 5 (Finding extended materials to learn) exhibit lower completion rates. In task 3, ET3 and ET4 replied that combining the function of assigning reading tasks in My Class was very convenient; however, the process and interaction design needed to be more intuitive and simpler. And some teachers suggested adding operating instructions during the process of assigning tasks. In task 5, two teacher participants did not find that clicking on the article's title in the answering records would link directly to the article; thus, the font design needs to be more differentiated. For student participants, only the completion rate of task 4 (Checking personal performance) is lower, but the effectiveness is quite well.

Concerning the result of efficiency, as indicated in Table 4, task 6 (Finding similar articles with tags) and 7 (Marking highlights) are relatively easy for both participants on RAS. Many participants said the topic tags are very similar to the functions and operation methods on social platforms, which align with their usual usage habits. About task 1, although the two types of participants performed the same task content, teacher participants kept thinking about choosing appropriate texts for their students and spent more time completing the task.

Comparing effectiveness and efficiency, the most challenging task for teachers is task 3 (Assigning tasks). This may be caused by the complexity and steps of the task, and the process of assigning reading materials to the class should be simple or offer operational guidance. As for student participants, task 5 (Finding extended materials to learn) cost them more time to complete. Some users mentioned that it took them longer to browse the entire page to find supplementary materials at different spots, so we suggest that learning or teaching resources should be placed as close as possible.

Regarding the result of QUIS, the less satisfactory aspect for teachers is the Screen, and the score is deficient in "Highlighting on the screen simplifies task (not at all – very much)." Compared with effectiveness and efficiency, the functional prompts of distribution and highlighter need to be improved. Student participants give the lowest score to "I think PRCS is (dull - stimulating)." We assume that because the style of user interface and simple gamification do not fully meet the expectations of students, RAS appears to be rigid to student users.

6 Conclusion

Regarding digital reading assessment tools, developers and designers should gain a comprehensive and deep understanding of the frequently used products or services by teachers and students. In user testing, many teachers and students mentioned that My Class on RAS is similar to Google Classroom, which they are familiar with, so it is intuitive and easy for them to operate. Also, Article Tags and Personalized Recommendations, which students like, are similar to functions of social media platforms, such as hashtags on Instagram and Facebook. Moreover, in user interviews, some teachers indicated that educational technology tools with different interfaces and operating modes cost them a lot of time and energy to learn and teach students how to operate. Therefore, this study suggests that the design of educational technology products must match with software or websites which educators and learners often use in their daily lives so that they can get started more quickly.

This study aims to improve the usability and user experience of reading assessment systems by exploring the usage scenarios, usage motivations, needs, and pain points of teachers and students. However, the present study is limited to only utilizing semi-structured interviews to understand users' requirements because the time points when teachers use digital tools in class are difficult to be determined in advance. Also, it is inconvenient for some teachers to allow outsiders to observe their courses directly, so we did not have much chance to enter the classrooms.

As for our design strategies and prototype, although this study has constructed various interactive functions and the prototype of a digital reading assessment system, due to considerations of time and technical, some special user requirements have yet to be included in this design. Moreover, teaching modes and learning methods are highly diverse. If future research can conduct more detailed research based on different teaching years, curriculum design, or learning methods, it will vastly improve the user experience of digital reading assessment tools.

References

1. OECD: PISA 2009 Results: What Students Know and Can Do (2010)

2. Aharony, N.: The effect of personal and situational factors on LIS students' and professionals' intentions to use e-books. Libr. Inf. Sci. Res. **36**(2), 106–113 (2014)
3. Potnis, D., Deosthali, K., Zhu, X., McCusker, R.: Factors influencing undergraduate use of e-books: A mixed methods study. Libr. Inf. Sci. Res. **40**(2), 106–117 (2018)
4. Baron, N.S.: Reading in a digital age. Phi Delta Kappan **99**(2), 15–20 (2017)
5. Park, H.R., Kim, D.: English language learners' strategies for reading online texts: Influential factors and patterns of use at home and in school. Int. J. Educ. Res. **82**, 63–74 (2017)
6. Afflerbach, P., Cho, B.-Y.: Identifying and describing constructively responsive comprehension strategies in new and traditional forms of reading. Handbook of research on reading comprehension, 69–90 (2009)
7. Coiro, J.: Predicting reading comprehension on the internet: contributions of offline reading skills, online reading skills, and prior knowledge. J. Lit. Res. **43**(4), 352–392 (2011)
8. OECD: PISA 2018 Reading Framework (2019)
9. Lenhart, A., Purcell, K., Smith, A., Zickuhr, K.: Social Media & Mobile Internet Use among Teens and Young Adults. Millennials. Pew Internet & American Life Project (2010)
10. Ortlieb, E., Sargent, S., Moreland, M.: Evaluating the efficacy of using a digital reading environment to improve reading comprehension within a reading clinic. Read. Psychol. **35**(5), 397–421 (2014)
11. Orfanou, K., Tselios, N., Katsanos, C.: Perceived usability evaluation of learning management systems: Empirical evaluation of the System Usability Scale. The International Review of Research in Open and Distributed Learning **16**(2), 227–246 (2015)
12. Vlachogianni, P., Tselios, N.: Perceived usability evaluation of educational technology using the System Usability Scale (SUS): A systematic review. Journal of Research on Technology in Education, 1–18 (2021)
13. Ardito, C., et al.: An approach to usability evaluation of e-learning applications. Univ. Access Inf. Soc. **4**(3), 270–283 (2006)
14. Tselios, N., Avouris, N., Komis, V.: The effective combination of hybrid usability methods in evaluating educational applications of ICT: Issues and challenges. Educ. Inf. Technol. **13**(1), 55–76 (2008)
15. Sauro, J.: Measuring usability with the System Usability Scale (SUS) (2011). https://measuringu.com/sus/
16. Bangor, A., Kortum, P., Miller, J.: They are determining what individual SUS scores mean: Adding an adjective rating scale. J. Usability Stud. **4**(3), 114–123 (2009)

Learning with Videos and Quiz Attempts: Explorative Insights into Behavior and Patterns of MOOC Participants

Bettina Mair⬤, Sandra Schön(✉)⬤, Martin Ebner(✉)⬤, Sarah Edelsbrunner⬤, and Philipp Leitner⬤

Graz University of Technology (TU Graz), Graz, Austria
{sandra.schoen,martin.ebner}@tugraz.at

Abstract. Many MOOCs use units with videos and quizzes, where a successful attempt after several tries is the basis for a MOOC certificate. A first in-depth analysis of quiz behavior within a MOOC at the Austrian MOOC platform iMooX.at had shown several quiz attempts patterns (Mair et al. 2022). As a next step, the researchers now collected details on video watching within a new edition of the same MOOC and therefore could combine data on quiz and video behavior. This analysis shows similar distribution of the quiz attempt patterns as in our first analysis. Additionally, the analysis indicates that learners who completed more quiz attempts than needed for full point results or passing have a higher average video watching time than learners who only made attempts until reaching a full score or passing.

Keywords: MOOC; quiz behavior · Video behavior · Learning · Learning analytics

1 Introduction

MOOCs are often structured in units with videos, a discussion forum for learners and quizzes to test learners' progress. At the Austrian national MOOC platform iMooX.at the quizzes can therefore be attempted up to five times; the best result is counted. Participants with at least 75% of the maximum points for each quiz (and therefore, unit) obtain the MOOC certificate. Within our learning analytics research, the data on quiz activities has always been attractive, but analyzing the data is not trivial. In our first approach, we looked at the first quiz attempt and if it correlates to later MOOC success. Somewhat surprisingly, the analysis showed no statistically significant correlation within the analyzed MOOC data [1]. In another MOOC, we analyzed and visualized the quiz attempts, which gave us the opportunity to explore a potential set of quiz attempt patterns: We have identified four quiz attempt patterns as shown in Fig. 1: pattern I "full points are enough" (attempts until 10 points are reached in each quiz), pattern II "training with a quiz is more important than full points" (further attempts even after a full points result), pattern III "minimal success" (attempts until passing each quiz) and pattern IV "passing is okay,

P. Zaphiris and A. Ioannou (Eds.): HCII 2023, LNCS 14040, pp. 321–332, 2023.
https://doi.org/10.1007/978-3-031-34411-4_22

but a better result would be nicer" (further attempts even after passing each quiz). We can also identify superordinate groups of learners who have full points in each quiz at the end (group A: full score) or a second group that made attempts until all quizzes were at least passed (group B: passed; at least 75% of the points in each quiz). Additionally, there is a third group who failed at least one quiz or did not participate in at least one quiz. In this group, no special patterns could be found (group C: failed). Figure 1 also shows the distribution of learners from the MOOC the data was taken from [2].

DIFFERENT QUIZ RESULT GROUPS AND QUIZ ATTEMPT BEHAVIOR PATTERNS

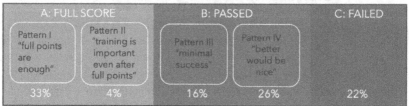

Analyzed MOOC: LULIIWS20 at iMooX.at (Mair et al. 2022, n=605, all who did a quiz)

Fig. 1. Patterns of quiz attempts and their distribution among learners in a MOOC who attempted at least one quiz (n = 605). Analyzed MOOC: LULIIWS20 at iMooX.at. Source: Own illustration of Mair et al., Table 2 [2]. Please note: pattern names were slightly adapted.

Although we already have been conducting learning analytics at iMooX.at for several years and have published on the topic, e.g. [3–6], we have not regularly filed data on details of video watching. Only one of our papers analyzed video data and compared how learners in a MOOC deal with H5P-based interactive videos versus videos without such interactions [6]. Of course, other researchers have already dealt with video data of MOOCs. For example, the 'popularity' of a video was defined as the average viewing duration divided by video length [7]; in another instance, video data was analyzed with the help of SPARK [8]. Nevertheless, to our knowledge and research, quiz attempts and video watching behavior in a MOOC have not been analyzed in combination often before. So, when conducting the same MOOC, a year later, the relevant video data was tracked as well. This paper analyses whether the previously identified quiz attempt patterns can be found again and how video watching behavior interferes with quiz behavior.

2 Material and Method

The basis for the analysis is user data of the MOOC "Lehren und Lernen mit digitalen Medien II". This MOOC was delivered in winter term 2021/2022, addressing the topic "Teaching and learning with digital media" (available at https://imoox.at/course/LUL IIWS21). The MOOC started on 4 October 2021 and ended on 31 July 2022. It is designed for the target group of future teachers but was available for free and open to everyone who wanted to participate. In total, six quizzes as well as 19 videos were provided. The MOOC was co-designed by lecturers from six Austrian universities and integrated into their regular lecture system in the first year of master studies. The MOOC served as the "lecture" part in a combined "lecture with practical" setting at all partner universities.

In other words, the universities asked their students to join the MOOC and additionally take part in a face-to-face practical course. The final grading is based on a final exam with partly the same multiple-choice questions as in the MOOC and a piece of project work.

All participants of iMooX.at agreed to the analysis of their learners' data for the further development and adaptations of the platform, MOOCs and services. User behavior data concerning quiz attempts and video watching was collected during the time frame of the MOOC and analyzed in an exploratory manner using object-oriented programming in Python. In the analysis, we further developed and used visualization approaches already used in our former publication [2].

3 Results

The analysis of quiz and video behavior is presented in the following paragraphs. As mentioned above, the analyzed MOOC started in October 2021 and was available online for self-study until the end of July 2022. In this timeframe, 791 registered participants and 412 successful participations were counted.

3.1 Quiz Attempts, Durations, and Patterns

At the end of July 2022, 501 of the 791 registered course participants had taken at least one quiz (63.3%) and 290, that is 36.7% of the registered course participants, did not complete single quiz. As described, there are up to 5 attempts possible for each quiz, which is a maximum of 30 possible attempts throughout the entire course. In sum, we count 4,483 quiz attempts, so considering only those who attempted at least one quiz, on average about 9 quiz attempts were made throughout the whole course.

Quiz Attempts. As can be seen in Fig. 2, the overall number of attempts made decreases slightly from quiz to quiz (exception quiz 5). Overall, the dropout rates are similar across all quizzes. About half of those who made the first attempt made a second attempt (dropout between 43 and 56%). The same can be observed regarding the third attempt. From the fourth attempt on, the dropout becomes a bit higher - between 50 and 80% do not make a further attempt (see Fig. 2).

Quiz Duration. If we look at the duration of the attempts of quiz 1 (see Fig. 3), we see that the attempt duration tends to become shorter and shorter, especially the first attempt usually takes significantly longer. In quiz 1, about 50% of the learners took more than 4 min for the first attempt, while concerning attempt 5, for example, almost no one took longer than 2 min. In this respect, it must be noted that there are only a few people who made 5 attempts in quiz 1 (about 3.5% of the participants of quiz 1).

This is contrasted with the attempt durations of the 6th quiz (Fig. 4). You can already see on the x-axis that the attempts in quiz 6 were completed much faster than in quiz 1. Here, apart from a few outliers, most people needed less than 2.5 min even on the first attempt. Attempts 4 and 5 were consistently under one minute. Again, quiz 6 shows a similar dropout from attempt to attempt as quiz 1. Only about 2% of the participants of quiz 6 made 5 attempts.

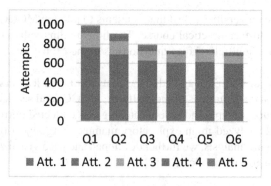

Fig. 2. Number of attempts by quiz.

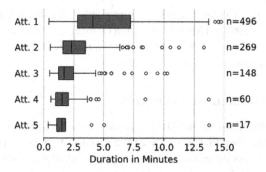

Fig. 3. Duration of quiz attempts of quiz number 1.

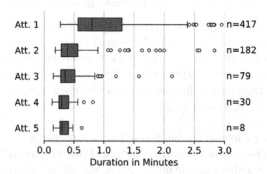

Fig. 4. Duration of quiz attempts of quiz number 6.

Finally, in the following plot the mean duration of all attempts per quiz is presented (Fig. 5). We see that not only are the attempts within a quiz completed faster and faster (as described above), but also that the mean duration of all attempts of a quiz tends to shorten over the course of the MOOC (especially from quiz 2 to quiz 3 and from quiz 3 to quiz 4. Without further analysis, we do not know whether this is based on a learning effect regarding the whole procedure of quiz attempts, or whether certain quizzes are simply easier than others.

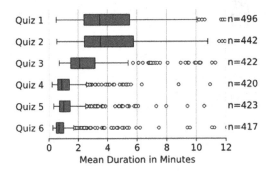

Fig. 5. Average duration of all quiz attempts of the 6 quizzes.

Quiz Attempts Route According to Full Points, Passing and Failure. Figure 6 for quiz 1 and Fig. 7 for quiz 6 show to what extent, depending on the result of the previous quiz attempt, the participants make further attempts. One can see for both quizzes that people almost always stop when they have reached 10 points for the first time. Additionally, it is evident that in quiz 6, 10 points are reached much more often in the first and following attempts than in quiz 1, where the minority of participants achieves 10 points on their first attempt.

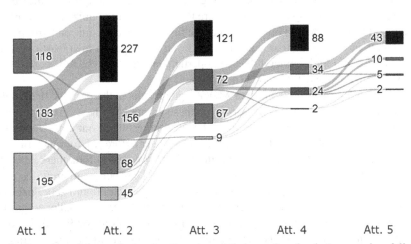

Fig. 6. Overview of (up to five) quiz attempts and their results of quiz 1: green is a full-point result, blue is a passed result (at least 75%) and yellow is a failed result (less than 75%).

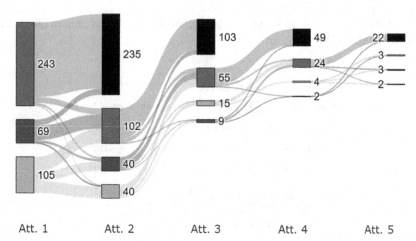

Att. 1   Att. 2   Att. 3   Att. 4   Att. 5

Fig. 7. Overview of (up to five) quiz attempts and their results of quiz 6: green is a full-point result, blue is a passed result (at least 75%) and yellow is a failed result (less than 75%).

3.2 Frequency of Learners Who Failed and Succeeded and Quiz Attempt Pattern Distribution

This section describes the general performance of the participants of the MOOC "Teaching and learning with digital media II" and the distribution of patterns of quiz attempt behavior. As a first step in identifying possible pattern trajectories of completing each quiz attempt in the MOOC, we first differentiated all course participants who made at least one quiz attempt (n = 501) into three groups as in our description of the general quiz behavior above: group A has a full score (10 points) in each quiz, group B passed each quiz (at least 7.5 points) but did not get the full score in each quiz and group C has failed (less than 7.5 points in at least one quiz or no participation in at least one quiz). As can be seen in Fig. 8, about 40% of the participants reached the full score in all 6 quizzes, 42% passed and 18% failed (n = 501).

Based on our observations of other MOOC quiz results in the past, we then looked for a presumed pattern of quiz behavior within these groups. Are there certain groups of people that always work consistently toward a specific result? In our beforementioned analysis of the same MOOC with different leaners a year before [2], four patterns were identified. As shown in Fig. 8, as in the same MOOC one year before, there is again a big group of learners who belong to pattern I (33.7%). They belong to group A (green in Fig. 8) and – in each quiz – make attempts until they reach the full score once and then stop making attempts. The other people in Group A form a smaller group that makes additional (training) attempts even after a full point result (6.6%). 18.8% of all participants who made at least one quiz attempt made attempts until passing all 6 quizzes (pattern III). The second biggest group of people with 23.2% percent also belongs to group B and shows pattern IV "passing is okay, better would be nice". They often make further attempts after passing a specific quiz, but they do not get the full score in each quiz.

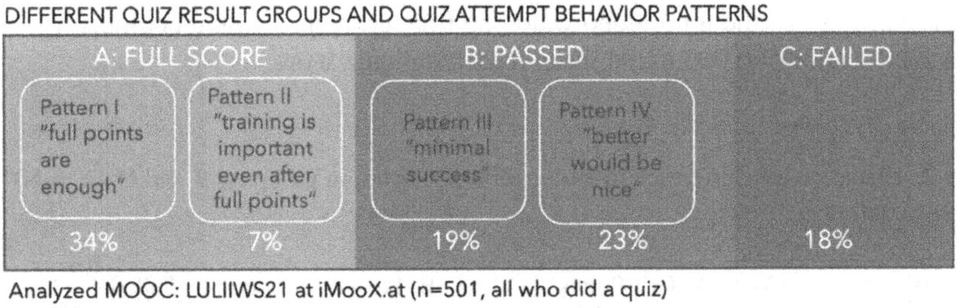

DIFFERENT QUIZ RESULT GROUPS AND QUIZ ATTEMPT BEHAVIOR PATTERNS

Analyzed MOOC: LULIIWS21 at iMooX.at (n=501, all who did a quiz)

Fig. 8. Overview of four quiz attempt patterns: pattern I "full points are enough", pattern II "training is important even after full points", pattern III "minimal success" (no more attempts after passing) and pattern IV "better would be nice" (n = 501, all who made at least one attempt in one quiz; the total is 101% to due a rounding error). Analyzed MOOC: LULLIIWS21 at iMooX.at

3.3 Quiz Activities and Video Watching

Video Watching. There was a total of 19 videos in the 6 units, ranging in length from 3.8 to 15.3 min. In total, 428 of all registered people watched 554.8 h of video. This is an average of 1.3 h per learner who shows video activity.

Using Videos and/or Quizzes as Resources. An additional analysis concerning the video watching behavior shows on the one hand that not all participants who made quiz attempts watched videos within the course, and on the other hand that not all participants who watched videos made quiz attempts.

Table 1. Used resources in the MOOC. n = 557 (all who did a quiz and/or watched a video)

Used resources	Number of Learners	Percentage of learners
Video only	56	10.1%
Quiz only	129	23.2%
Video and quiz	372	66.8%
Sum	557	100.0%

A total of 557 people was recorded as having taken a quiz and/or watched a video. Approximately 10% of these only watched videos, 23.2% only took quizzes and the remaining 66.8% show both quiz and video activities. In other words, about a tenth of the learners with any recorded activity only watched videos, although the MOOC cannot be successfully completed without quiz success.

Video Watching by Overall Quiz Results. Table 2 shows how long learners watched videos, categorized by their overall quiz results. While group A and B show similar amounts of video watching, with about 40% of these participants watching more than an hour of video, in Group C over 40% did not watch any video at all. On average, the most successful group by quiz results (group A) also has the highest video watching time. There is a weak positive correlation between the extent of video watching and the overall quiz results: the total video watching time correlates with a coefficient of 0.24 and a significance of 0.000 to the mean maximum quiz score.

Table 2. Extent of watching time of participants separated in group A, B and C. (n = 501, all who did a quiz)

Duration	Group A: Full Points	Group B: Passed	Group C: Failed	All
none	23.8%	21.0%	41.6%	25.7%
< 10 min	16.3%	25.2%	32.6%	23.0%
10 to 60 min	19.3%	13.8%	19.1%	17.0%
> 60 min	40.6%	40.0%	6.7%	34.3%
Average in min	81	70	14	64
n	202	210	89	501

When Do Learners Watch Videos?   Another question that arose during the process of analyzing the data was related to the aspect of when participants watch videos throughout the course. Do they do so before their quiz attempts as envisaged by the structure of the MOOC? Fig. 9 shows an example of the course of activities of a MOOC participant. The participant's activities all happened within 3 h on Day 288 of the MOOC. First, the participant watched video footage (marked by the black arrows in the graph), then he completed all quizzes without watching videos again. The different colors of the lines symbolize different quizzes. As can be seen, the participant completed all 6 quizzes and belongs to quiz behavior pattern III. He has tried to score more than 7.5 points in all quizzes, but not has not worked towards full score in each quiz.

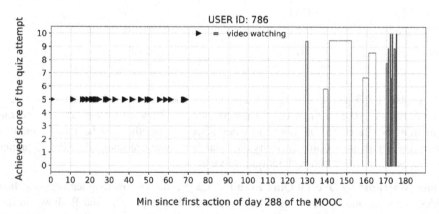

Fig. 9. Course of activities of user 786. Note: The colored lines show quiz attempts with their duration (x-axis) and the achieved score (y-axis). The different colors resemble different quizzes.

Another example of course activities is shown in Fig. 10. This participant has scored 10 points in each quiz and then stopped making further attempts. So, this person belongs to quiz attempt pattern I. While user 786 first watched videos and then made all quiz attempts, user 23204 watched videos before the attempts of each quiz.

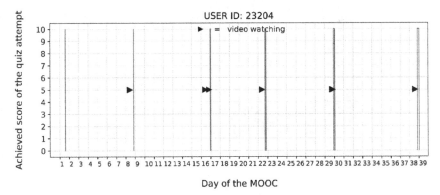

Fig. 10. Course of activities of user 23204. Note: The colored lines show quiz attempts with their duration (x-axis) and the achieved score (y-axis). The different colors resemble different quizzes.

Both exemplary users never watched videos between their attempts of a specific quiz. Therefore, we looked at all other users to see if this is the common strategy. In Fig. 11 the videos were first assigned to the respective quiz units. Then it was analyzed if video activities occurred between the start time of the first quiz attempt and the end time of the last attempt of the same quiz, or if it occurred exclusively before or after the attempts. More than half of the learners watched videos in each unit exclusively before quiz attempts (57.3%). About 24% of the learners show video activity before the start of the first quiz attempt and after the end of the last attempt, and just under 9% show video activity before the first attempt and between attempts. The remaining combinations occur very rarely, most notably watching only after, only in between, or after and in between. Overall, of the 372 people with quiz and video activities, nearly 95% watched videos in at least one unit before the first quiz attempt was made, nearly 32% show video activity after the quiz attempts, and about 15% watched videos in any unit between attempts.

Differences of Users by Quiz Patterns Concerning Their Video Watching Behavior. Finally, Fig. 12 shows how the quiz attempt patterns correlate with average video watching in a cross table. Above we have shown that on average, Group A shows the highest amount of video watching. However, not all the people with full points in all quizzes (namely pattern I and II) have such a high video consumption. It is the small group with quiz attempt pattern II that watched by far the most video sequences. The second highest average duration belongs to pattern IV in group B; in other words, the patterns where additional attempts are made even after full points (pattern II) or passing (pattern IV) are those with a long average video watching duration.

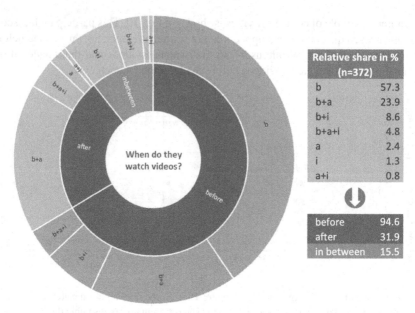

Fig. 11. How often are videos watched before, in between or after quiz attempts? (n = 372, all who show quiz and video activities). Note: b = between, a = after, i = in between.

DIFFERENT QUIZ RESULT GROUPS AND QUIZ ATTEMPT BEHAVIOR PATTERNS
AND THEIR AVERAGE TIME USED FOR VIDEO WATCHING

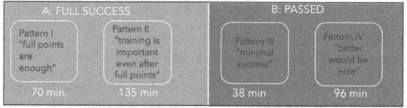

Analyzed MOOC: LULIIWS21 at iMooX.at (n=412 who suceeded)

Fig. 12. Mean video watching time in minutes of learners with different quiz patterns (n = 412, all who succeeded the MOOC)

4 Discussion

One important result of this paper is that learners of the MOOC one year later show similar quiz attempt patterns as in the year before (see Fig. 1 and Fig. 8, [2]). Additionally, we could show that the average duration of video watching is longest amongst learners with full points, shorter among learners who just passed the quizzes and shortest among learners who failed one or more quizzes. The analysis of video consumption by quiz attempt patterns gives surprising insights: Learners with the pattern to make more attempts than needed, as they have already passed or reached 10 points, show a quite higher average time of video consumption. It might be interpreted that these learners use the quizzes and videos for more intense learning activities than the others. The shorter average video watching time of pattern I (full points is enough) might be related to existing prior knowledge and less need to really learn with the resources. A detailed analysis of when a video was watched in relation to the respective quiz in a unit showed, as in Fig. 9, that only about 57% of the learners exclusively watch videos before their quiz attempts. Obviously, it is common as well to start a quiz or make a first attempt and then watch the respective video after an (unsuccessful) attempt. Additionally, we have seen in a learners' survey for another MOOC from our platform [6] that many learners, in this MOOC also students, use the video transcripts for learning. Future research must therefore also investigate how often and by whom video transcripts were downloaded and potentially used for learning. We guess that a relevant number of people (n = 129, see Table 1), especially with pattern I might use transcripts as well and not just the videos for learning.

In the analysis presented in this paper we used the same MOOC with new learners to be able to directly refer to the first analysis of the same MOOC. Nevertheless, the special MOOC setting with the main target group of future teachers does not allow us to infer that the quiz attempt patterns that have emerged again in this analysis are possible patterns for learners in other MOOCs as well. For this, future research with different MOOCs is needed.

Acknowledgement. This research was co-funded by the Austrian Federal Ministry of Education, Science and Research within the project "Learning Analytics" (2020–2023). We kindly thank Mario Reinwald and Christoph Bodlos; their ideas inspired us to compare quiz attempt patterns with video usage.

References

1. Schön, S., Leitner, P., Ebner, M., Edelsbrunner, S., Hohla, K.: Quiz feedback in massive open online courses from the perspective of learning analytics: role of first quiz attempts. In: Auer, M.E., Hortsch H., Michler O., Köhler T. (eds.) Mobility for Smart Cities and Regional Development - Challenges for Higher Education. ICL 2021. LNNS, vol. 389. Springer, Cham (2021). https://doi.org/10.1007/978-3-030-93904-5_94
2. Mair, B., et al.: Patterns of quiz attempts in a MOOC. The full-points-pattern and other patterns on the way to a successful MOOC in a lecture setting (Preprint). In: EdMedia Proceedings 2022 (2022), https://doi.org/10.3217/xkc5m-g1555. https://repository.tugraz.at/records/xkc5m-g1555
3. Khalil, H.; Ebner, M.; Leitner, P.: Using learning analytics to improve the educational design of MOOCs. Int. J. Educ. Learn. 4(2), 100–108 (2022). https://doi.org/10.31763/ijele.v4i2.641
4. Leitner, P., Ebner, M., Geisswinkler, H., Schön S.: Visualization of learning for students: a dashboard for study progress - development, design details, implementation, and user feedback. In: Sahin, M., Ifenthaler, D. (eds.) Visualizations and Dashboards for Learning Analytics. Advances in Analytics for Learning and Teaching. Springer, Cham (2021). https://doi.org/10.1007/978-3-030-81222-5_19
5. Leitner, P., Maier, K., Ebner, M.: Web analytics as extension for a learning analytics dashboard of a massive open online platform. In: Ifenthaler, D., Gibson, D. (eds.) Adoption of Data Analytics in Higher Education Learning and Teaching. AALT, pp. 375–390. Springer, Cham (2020). https://doi.org/10.1007/978-3-030-47392-1_19

6. Thurner, S., et al.: An exploratory mixed method study on H5P videos and video-related activities in a MOOC environment. Int. J. Technol. Enhance. Educ. **1**(1), 1–18 (2022). https://doi.org/10.4018/IJTEE.304388
7. Luo, Y; Zhou, G.; Li, J.; Xiao, X.: A MOOC video viewing behavior analysis algorithm. Math. Probl. Eng. **2018**, 7560805, 7p (2018). https://doi.org/10.1155/2018/7560805
8. Hu, H., Zhang, G., Gao, W., Wang, M.: Big data analytics for MOOC video watching behavior based on Spark. Neural Comput. Appl. **32**(11), 6481–6489 (2019). https://doi.org/10.1007/s00521-018-03983-z

Doctoral Education in Technology-Enhanced Learning: The Perspective of PhD Candidates and Researchers

Anna Nicolaou[1]([⊠]) [iD], Maria Victoria Soule[1] [iD], Androulla Athanasiou[1] [iD],
Elis Kakoulli Constantinou[1] [iD], Antigoni Parmaxi[1] [iD], Mikhail Fominykh[2] [iD],
Maria Perifanou[3] [iD], Anastasios Economides[3] [iD], Luís Pedro[4] [iD], Laia Albó[5] [iD],
Davinia Hernández-Leo[5] [iD], and Fridolin Wild[6] [iD]

[1] Cyprus University of Technology, Limassol, Cyprus
{anna.nicolaou,mariavictoria.soule,androulla.athanasiou,
elis.constantinou,antigoni.parmaxi}@cut.ac.cy
[2] Norwegian University of Science and Technology, Trondheim, Norway
mikhail.fominykh@ntnu.no
[3] University of Macedonia, Thessaloniki, Greece
maria.perifanou@uom.edu.gr, economid@uom.gr
[4] University of Aveiro, Aveiro, Portugal
lpedro@ua.pt
[5] Pompeu Fabra University, Barcelona, Spain
{laia.albo,davinia.hernandez-leo}@upf.edu
[6] Open University, Milton Keynes, UK
f.wild@open.ac.uk

Abstract. The field of Technology Enhanced Learning (TEL) in recent years has drawn much attention and has been widely researched. Research has mainly focused on the theory, implementation in various disciplines and modes, and the role of TEL, especially in Higher Education. Researchers, however, are called upon to focus on the interdisciplinarity of TEL as well as on its potential in supporting doctoral students, one level above the usual research carried out on undergraduate courses. This paper aims at presenting part of the quantitative results yielded from an online survey which collected information on doctoral education in TEL from PhD candidates and researchers involved in doctoral education or carrying out research in TEL. The findings have shown that despite the increase in the availability of resources and materials as doctoral students move to more advanced stages of their studies, they need adequate support and training in academic writing and research methodologies. This has prompted the design and implementation of a training program for doctoral students by the Doctoral Education for Technology-Enhanced Learning project (DE-TEL), which aimed to improve and innovate the European doctoral education in TEL, by developing a new program and Open Education Resources in this field.

Keywords: Technology-enhanced learning · Doctoral education

P. Zaphiris and A. Ioannou (Eds.): HCII 2023, LNCS 14040, pp. 333–348, 2023.
https://doi.org/10.1007/978-3-031-34411-4_23

1 Introduction

1.1 Background

The increased use of technology in various aspects of our lives has been experienced for quite a few years now, offering an abundance of opportunities in facilitating achievement in various fields. The field of education has not remained immune to these developments and their implementation. In fact, the use of technology in education is gaining much ground and is widely implemented, aiming to achieve learning outcomes and to equip students with necessary skills in order to develop lifelong learning. The role of Technology Enhanced Learning (TEL) in education, therefore, is of vital importance since it "harnesses the power of interactivity and has the potential to enhance what is learned, how we learn and how we teach" [1]. TEL is being widely researched [1–3], in various disciplines [4], while some researchers [5] emphasize its interdisciplinary nature.

With growing knowledge, data, and published works in every field, requirements on researching TEL become more challenging. Research conducted on the use of technologies to support doctoral students' learning suggests that the affordances of technologies can be beneficial for doctoral students [6]. This applies especially where co-construction of knowledge is a course expectation and in cases where transnational doctoral students wish to share experiences. The appropriate choice of technologies can lead to a richer learning environment, inclusivity, intercultural communication and more engagement. Thus, training and guidance in conducting research and using technologies for learning at the doctoral level may be a key activity in dealing with the ever-growing requirements in research. In particular, Chen has identified that "due to a lack of formal research training and experience, students can find completing research projects a daunting task. This, coupled with a fear of statistics, can culminate in quite an overwhelming experience for many students" [7]. Dermo [8] stated that the key aspect would be to improve the quality of students' learning experience in higher education. Similarly, Pammer-Schindler et al. [5], based on the results of the Doctoral Education for Technology-Enhanced Learning (DE-TEL) project, have also identified the need for providing doctoral training in TEL related areas. In particular, the DE-TEL project aimed to improve and innovate the European doctoral education in TEL, by identifying good practices in doctoral education in TEL and developing a new program for doctoral education in TEL and OERs (Open Education Resources).

1.2 Aim of Study

This paper presents part of the quantitative results yielded from an online survey which was conducted in the context of the DE-TEL project. The survey aimed at collecting information on doctoral education in TEL from PhD candidates and researchers involved in doctoral education or carrying out research in TEL.

2 Literature Review

2.1 Technology-Enhanced Learning

In an attempt to define the term Technology Enhanced Learning (TEL), O'Donnell and O'Donnell [9] state that it supports teaching and learning through the use of technology and can carry a similar meaning to 'e-learning'. The term was coined in the context of working groups initiated by the European Commission in 2000. Bourdeau and Balacheff [10] gave a researcher-perspective definition of TEL describing it as "a field of research aiming at improving learning by integrating current technologies and designing innovative ones". Kirkwood and Price [4] also give a similar meaning to the term, although they also say that there are very few explicit statements as to what meaning it may carry and that, frequently, it is related to equipment and infrastructure. Wild [11], however, provides a definition of TEL that moves away from the mere use of technology, focussing on the use of tools "that afford isolated or collaborative endeavours in formal and informal situations" and that are aimed at developing human competence both in educational and professional contexts.

Fominykh and Prasolova-Førland [12] indicate that TEL is not limited to the use of technologies for teaching purposes, but it being "a research field that explores new ways of learning enabled by technology and designing new technologies that can support learning in new ways". The term TEL has also been used together with multiple overlapping concepts and synonyms 'Educational Technology', 'Digital Education', 'Learning Engineering', or 'Learning Informatics', with the latter two implying that this area requires technical competence in order to become involved in learning and development initiatives especially in areas that methodologically depend on data science, Computer Science, and the Learning Sciences [5]. According to the authors, all terms "recognize the need of epistemic fluency to facilitate interdisciplinary dynamics", highlighting how the specific field overlaps with a variety of disciplines. This interdisciplinary aspect can become an indicator of the vast amount of research that has been conducted and will be carried out in the future.

Although this fluency is highlighted as a very important component of TEL interdisciplinarity [13], when we approach this discussion from a research methods standpoint, the discussion is more varied. Fominykh et al. [14] highlight the interdisciplinarity of TEL, connecting it to the master-level education in the field, which is dominated by interdisciplinary TEL and educational subjects in their curricula and lack of computer science subjects. Scanlon and Conole [15] report the existence of tensions between the methodological approaches that are put forward and that mirror existing siloed ideas and ways of making research. According to these authors, the mixed methods approaches that are valued in TEL often collide with visions that "[s]ingle discipline research is generally more highly regarded in terms of research excellence initiatives, and much interdisciplinary research is often accused of being methodologically muddled or less rigorous than work done within disciplinary norms".

Passey [16] echoes this idea and introduces an interesting perspective where he claims that "[as] research study contexts move more towards ecologies of technologies, the selection of research focus, what theoretical principles underpin that focus (or focuses), and implications for methodological approaches, all need to be carefully considered".

At its core, these discussions seem to reflect an old "paradigm war" [17], and may be harmful as they "generate a polarization of positions, and are unlikely to lead to methodological progress". At the same time, there is a general call to analyse critically existing perspectives on doctoral education [18].

Previous studies on students' doctoral journeys identified the importance of efficient supervisors [19], courses [20], networking such as academic conferences [21] and writing groups [22, 23], libraries and subscribed databases [24, 25] among others. However, many PhD programs do not include intersectoral or interdisciplinary courses that can broaden graduates' career outside and inside academia [26]. So, there is a need to enrich PhD programs with intersectoral and interdisciplinary courses.

Effective PhD supervision is also essential for successfully developing a PhD dissertation [19]. PhD candidates receiving sporadic supervision had more chances to interrupt their studies [27]. PhD candidates would also like to have knowledgeable supervisors who will be involved in the writing process too [28]. In addition, a PhD supportive network is a measure of success [19]. PhD students participating in a community for academic writing can enhance their writing skills for preparing their dissertation proposals and final dissertations [22, 23].

2.2 Research Questions

This study investigates the perceptions of TEL PhD candidates and TEL PhD holders on doctoral education in TEL. The study attempts to answer the following research questions (RQs):

RQ1: What courses and educational materials do TEL PhD candidates need?
RQ2: What research methods do TEL PhD candidates use?
RQ3: What learning sources do TEL PhD candidates use?

3 Method

This study collected quantitative and qualitative data from an online survey which gathered information on doctoral education in TEL from PhD candidates and researchers involved in doctoral education or carrying out research in TEL.

3.1 Participants

The study involved 229 participants: 103 (45%) were PhD students at the time of the data collection, 92 (40.2%) of whom were holding a PhD, 26 (11.4%) were holding a Master's degree or equivalent, and 8 (3.5%) held a degree that was lower than a Master's or equivalent. This study reports on the first two groups of participants, PhD candidates and PhD holders. As for the PhD candidates, it is worth mentioning that they were in different stages of their doctoral studies: 54 (52.4%) were in their late stage, this is, less than one year before their PhD thesis submission and defense; 27 (26.2%) were in their middle stage; and 22 (21.4%) were in their early stage, this is first year students.

The participants' ages were distributed as follows: 28 (12.2%) were 29 years old, 92 (40.2%) were 30–39 years old, 62 (27.1%) were 40–49 years old, and 43 (18.8%)

were 50 and above (1.7%, preferred not to specify their age), with 118 (51.5%) female and 103 (45%) participants, (3.4% preferred not to specify gender). As per their origin, participants were from 40 different countries around the globe, being Spain, Germany, and Portugal the three countries with a bigger representation (34.1% all three) followed by Greece, Norway, and Estonia (17.4% all three).

With regard to the participants' PhD topics, these are presented in Table 1:

Table 1. Participants' PhD Topics.

PhD topic	Number	Percentage
Computing / IT applied to learning (e.g., designing new apps or digital content for learning)	41	17.9
Education using technologies (e.g., applying technology for learning in practice)	75	32.8
Approximately equal efforts in development of educational technologies and applying them for learning	36	15.7
Management of TEL (e.g., managing digitalization and integration of technologies in education in organizations)	9	3.9
Computing / IT	9	3.9
Education	12	5.2
None of the above	47	20.5

3.2 Instrument

The instrumentation consisted of a survey that was implemented as an online question-naire using Lime Survey. It included 31 (close and open) questions and was composed of seven sections designed to obtain information on the participants' (1) professional background, (2) thematic content related to the need of courses and educational mate-rials on TEL topics, (3) general PhD training topics, (4) research methods, (5) learning sources, (6) challenges, and (7) supervision and mentoring. The report published by the DE-TEL consortium includes further information about the questions included in the survey[1]. This paper reports on the results of Sects. (3), (4) and (5).

3.3 Data Collection and Analysis

Participants' responses were gathered from September 2020 to February 2021. The survey was distributed via multiple channels, including the European Association for

---

[1] Laia Albó, Mikhail Fominykh, María Victoria Soulé, Luis P. Prieto, Davinia Hernández-Leo, Anna Nicolaou, Androulla Athanasiou, Luis Pedro, Viktoria Pammer-Schindler, Carlos Santos, Lorena Azevedo de Sousa, Anastasios Economides, Maria Perifanou, Aurelio Ruiz García, Maren Scheffel, Christian Glahn, and Fridolin Wild (2022) Doctoral Education for Technology-Enhanced Learning in Europe: report. DETEL Consortium. https://ea-tel.eu/de-tel/detel-report https://doi.org/ 10.13140/RG.2.2.32762.98243.

Technology-Enhanced Learning (EATEL) website (https://ea-tel.eu/de-tel/survey) and social media accounts of EATEL, institutional and individual professional accounts of the DE-TEL project partners, and the mailing lists of EATEL and of the national professional communities of the countries represented in the DE-TEL consortium.

Computerized data analysis was performed with SPSS 25 to analyze close-ended questions. Descriptive statistics included the calculation of frequencies and percentages for the specific sections mentioned above. Inferential statistics were performed to identify whether any differences between the participants' groups were statistically significant.

4 Results

In the following sections, we provide the results obtained on the participants' opinions related to the need of courses and educational materials on general PhD training topics, research methods, and learning sources.

4.1 General PhD Training Topics

The analysis of the participants' responses in terms of their needs for courses and educational materials on the general PhD training topics revealed that PhD candidates and PhD holders coincide in their need for 'academic writing' courses as the most relevant course (21.5% PhD candidates and 25.3% PhD holders). It is well accepted that PhD candidates need to publish in order to gain a PhD degree and later an academic position [29–33]. In order to enhance their academic writing skills, they can participate in academic writing groups [22], writing retreats [34–37], etc. Both groups of participants discern in their rank order of preferences for other courses. For instance, PhD candidates selected 'dissemination of research results' as the second most relevant course in which they would like to be trained in (20.7%), while for PhD holders, the second most relevant course pertains to the 'project management' category (14.7%). These differences are also observed in the third most selected course for both groups. While PhD candidates identified 'project management' as the third course in which they would like to receive training (16.4%), PhD holders are more interested in 'dissemination of research results' (14%) and 'research ethics' (14%). Interestingly, this course was the least selected by PhD candidates (5.5%). 'Communication about research' is the fourth course in the rank order of preferences for both groups (15.2% for PhD candidates, and 13.2% for PhD holders). Results are displayed in Fig. 1.

Regarding the availability of courses and materials, we were interested in investigating at what stage of their PhD studies PhD candidates have access to useful courses or educational materials on each of the following thematic areas: 'academic writing', 'research ethics', 'communication about research', 'dissemination of research results', 'well-being', 'project management', and 'entrepreneurship'. Three stages were indicated on the survey questionnaire: early stage (first year of PhD), middle stage, and late stage (less than one year before PhD thesis submission and defense). The descriptive statistics run in SPSS indicated that the more students progress in their PhD studies, the more available are the courses and materials in the aforementioned thematic areas. Therefore, PhD students seem to gradually gain access to relevant resources. Figure 2

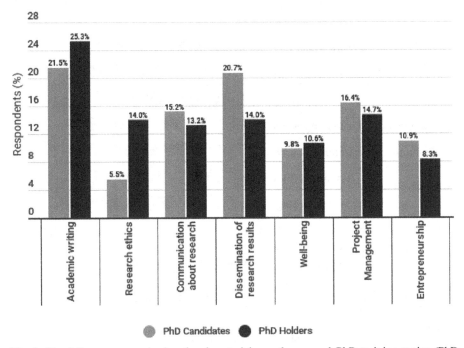

Fig. 1. Need for courses and educational materials on the general PhD training topics (PhD candidates vs. PhD holders).

demonstrates the descriptive statistics indicating the availability of courses and materials for PhD candidates by the stage of their PhD studies.

Subsequently, a one-way analysis of variance (ANOVA) was computed in SPSS to evaluate the significance of mean differences. The analysis of variance showed that the effect of the PhD stage on the availability of courses and educational materials was significant in the variable 'academic writing' (i.e. academic languages style, supporting arguments with references, formats of academic journals and conferences), $F(2,91) = 6.23$, $p = .003$ at a 0.05 significance level. In addition, an analysis of variance showed that the effect of the PhD stage on the availability of courses and educational materials was significant in the variable 'communication about research' (i.e. presenting research, pitching, addressing different target audiences, dealing with the defence), $F(2,86) = 3.95$, $p = 0.23\ 0.05$ at a 0.05 significance level. A Tukey post hoc test revealed that the availability of courses and materials was statistically significantly higher after the PhD candidates have progressed to the middle and late stage of their PhD studies. Table 2 demonstrates the analysis of variance.

4.2 Research Methods

Participants were asked about the research methods they used, building on the methods survey inventory developed in Meyer et al. [38], but dropping the items determined as non-significant there, as well as dropping 'ethnographic methods' and adding 'secondary

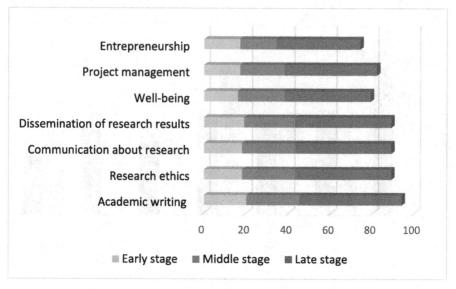

Fig. 2. Availability of courses and materials for PhD Candidates by Stage

Table 2. Analysis of variance

Availability of courses and materials for PhD Candidates by Stage	df	F	Sig
Academic writing			
Between Groups	2	6.237	.003
Within Groups	91		
Total	93		
Communication about research			
Between Groups	2		
Within Groups	86		
Total	88	3.951	0.23

research' (i.e., desk research). Additionally, their training needs for research methods were investigated. Results are displayed in Figs. 3 and 4.

Compared to the survey conducted in Meyer et al. [38], the drop in percentages can be explained by the reformulation from an agreement Likert scale to binary yes/no, as well as in the more precise formulation of 'primary' methodological approach investigated here, whereas Meyer et al. [38] had asked for methods use in general, complementing rather than contradicting the general trend identified.

A comparison of the data presented in Figs. 3 and 4 indicates that both groups would like to receive more training in the research methods that they are already using. This might point out at the different levels of expertise in the research methods listed

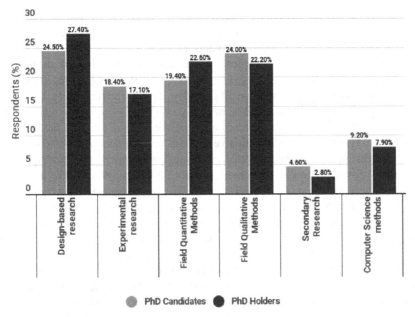

Fig. 3. Research methods used by PhD candidates and by PhD holders

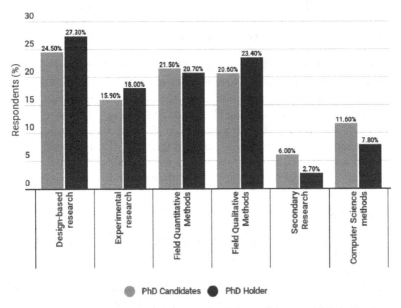

Fig. 4. Research methods training needs (PhD candidates vs. PhD holders)

in the survey, indicating particularly the need for more advanced training rather than introductory. For instance, 'design-based research' was selected as the method most used by both PhD candidates and PhD holders, and it was also selected as the research method most needed for training by both groups of participants. Indeed, design-based research has been successfully adopted by doctoral dissertations [39–42]. 'Qualitative methods' are reported to be the method most used by PhD candidates, while 'quantitative methods' are reported to be the method most used by PhD holders. The reverse image can be observed in their needs of training, since the second research methods most needed by PhD candidates are 'quantitative methods', and 'qualitative methods' by PhD holders. Interestingly, our data does not seem to suggest a temporal shift from qualitative to quantitative, neither in use (quantitative: early 36.4%, middle 37.0%, late 37.0%; qualitative: early 59.1%, middle 33.3%, late 46.3%), nor in training need (quantitative: early 50%, middle 55.6%, late 44.4%; qualitative: early 45.5%, middle 59.3%, late 40.7%), painting a more differentiated picture in that exploratory stages would be more qualitative, and summative validation oriented final stages would be more quantitative.

Other methods used include 'experimental research', which was the fourth option selected by both groups, and 'computer science methods', which were selected only by 9.7% of the PhD candidates, and 7.8% by PhD holders. The least method used was 'secondary research' (i.e., desk research). Similar results were obtained for training needs in research methods: the fourth research method selected by both groups was 'experimental research', and the two least methods selected were 'computer science' and 'secondary research'. However, while for the PhD holders the percentage for these categories remained the same as in their responses to the use of research methods, there was a slight increase of percentage in the PhD candidates' interest in receiving training in the same categories.

The relationship between PhD topics and the research methods used in each one of those topics was also investigated. There is a visible variation of the research methods that are most used according to the different PhD topics. 'Design-based research' is the most used method in 'Computing/IT applied to learning' PhDs whereas 'experimental research' and 'field qualitative methods' are the methods that respondents in the field of 'Education using technologies' reported the most. 'Design-based research' is again the most used method in PhDs where there are approximately equal efforts in the development of educational technologies and applying them for learning (see Fig. 5).

4.3 Learning Sources

Moreover, we further investigated the learning sources used in terms of TEL topics, general PhD-level training topics and research methods. Figure 6 displays the results for PhD candidates.

According to the selection made by PhD candidates, two sources emerge as the most relevant across the three categories: (1) 'Academic publications' (20.6% TEL topics, 15% PhD training, 17.7% Research methods), and (2) 'Supervisor help' (15.3% TEL topics, 16% PhD training, 17.7% Research methods). 'Courses in PhD programs' seem to be relevant for general PhD training (14.7%) and 'Research methods' (14.2%), but less for TEL topics (9.5%). Another important learning source for the participants is 'Academic conferences' (15.30% TEL topics, 10.60% PhD training, 9.10% Research

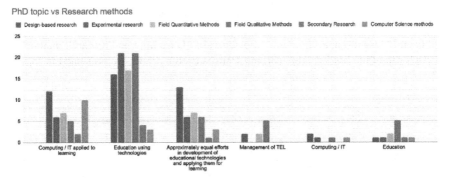

Fig. 5. Research methods used by PhD topic

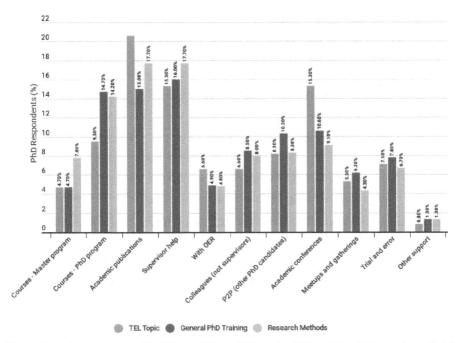

Fig. 6. Learning sources used by PhD candidates (TEL topics, PhD training & Research methods)

methods). Doctoral students develop their knowledge, research, and learning by using libraries [25], participating in academic conferences [21] and consulting their advisors [43–47], among other methods. The doctoral supervisors may deliver transformative learning experiences for doctoral students [45]. However, previous studies argue that doctorate students hold a mix of fantasies and unrealistic or contradictory expectations regarding their supervisors' roles [48].

We can also see differences of learning sources between the learning domains of TEL topics, general PhD training, and Research methods. Learning sources for TEL topics stand out by the 'academic publications', 'academic conferences' and 'OER' being significantly more popular than for the general PhD training and research methods. At the same time, 'courses in PhD programs' become learning sources for TEL topics significantly less often, compared to the general PhD training and research methods.

As for the PhD holders, the learning sources used by them are presented in Fig. 7.

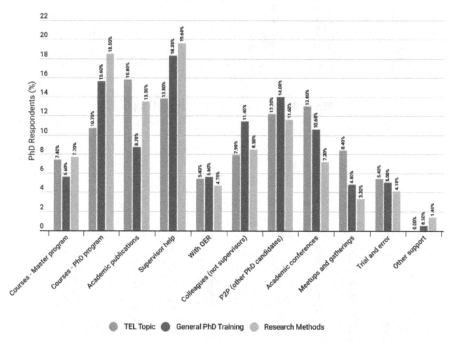

Fig. 7. Learning sources used by PhD holders (TEL topics, PHD training & Research methods)

The results displayed in Fig. 7 indicate that there are some similarities in the selection made by PhD students (see Fig. 5) but also some important differences. For instance, both groups consider 'Supervisor help' as one the most relevant sources across the three categories (13.8% TEL topics, 18,3% PhD training, 19.6% Research methods). Another similarity between the two groups resides in the participants' perception towards 'Courses in PhD programs' which, according to the PhD holders, are one of the learning sources most used in terms of general PhD training (15.6%) and Research methods (18.5%). 'Academic publications' also appear as one of the most relevant learning sources, but in the PhD holders' case, this learning source only seems to be relevant for the TEL topic (15.8%) and Research methods (13.5%) categories. 'Academic conferences' also constitute relevant learning sources for this group, but only for TEL topics (13%). A distinctive characteristic of this group is found in the 'From colleagues (other than supervisors)' and 'Peer-to-peer (from other PhD candidates)' sources, which are perceived fairly relevant, the former for the general PhD training category, and the latter across all three categories.

5 Discussion

Findings on the need of courses and educational materials on the general PhD training topics show that both PhD candidates and PhD holders agree on the need for 'academic writing' courses as the most relevant course. However, both groups discern in their rank order of preferences for other courses. With regard to the availability of courses and materials for PhD candidates, the inferential results of the study showed statistically significant differences when it comes to the stage of PhD of students. Specifically, as PhD students progress to the middle and late stages of their studies, they seem to have access to a wider range of resources and materials in topics related to 'academic writing' (e.g. academic language style, supporting arguments with references, formats of academic journals and conferences) and 'dissemination of research results' (e.g. submitting manuscripts to academic journals, research databases, open data, open science, social media, and reproducibility consideration). This may suggest that as the students advance in their doctoral studies, they either receive greater support in terms of courses and materials or they establish ways to access them due to their experience. All in all, regardless of the stage in their studies, both PhD candidates and PhD holders indicated the need for training in 'academic writing' and other courses.

With regards to research methods, responses indicated that 'design-based research' is the most common method for both PhD students and PhD holders. An exception are researchers working in the field of 'Education using technologies', where 'experimental research' and 'field qualitative methods' are the most reported methods. Regardless of the level of training, the participants reported a need for more training in the research methods they work with.

The changing emphasis between method focus and its reversed training need between PhD candidates and holders is surprising, but especially the switch in emphasis from candidates to holders regarding training needs clearly speaks against a natural order of advancement in methodology. The explanation that this may reflect the temporal order in which methods quite often are applied seems more convincing: Qualitative methods are generally used more widely in exploratory phases of research, while summative validation-oriented phases rely more generally on quantitative methods. This, of course, is only a general tendency, with notable exceptions presented in particular in more advanced use of these methodological fields (e.g., validation case studies, or the exploratory use of affect polar scales in surveys). In any case, the shift in emphasis and our interpretation regarding levels indicates the need for advanced methods training, both qualitative and quantitative methods as well as experimental design.

In terms of the learning sources used by the participants, the latter indicated that these were influenced by their educational background, although all tended to choose the 'academic publications' as their primary learning source for TEL topics. For the general PhD-level training topics both PhD candidates and PhD holders selected the 'supervisor help' as their primary learning source. Additionally, the data has also shown that three learning sources seem to be the most used by PhD candidates and PhD holders with regards to research methods: 'supervisor help', 'academic publications', and 'courses in the PhD program'.

6 Conclusion

Technology-enhanced learning has become an essential part of higher education, and as a result, there is a growing need for well-trained professionals who can design, implement, and evaluate technology-enhanced learning environments. This study has shown that the need for training for PhD candidates varies in terms of academic writing, research ethics, communication about research, dissemination of research results, well-being, project management, and entrepreneurship, whilst both PhD candidates and PhD holders voice the need to receive more training in the research methods that they are already using. The rapid pace of technological change and the complexity of technology-enhanced learning require ongoing training and professional development to stay current and effective. Therefore, it is essential that institutions and organizations continue to invest in training programs that support the development of skilled and knowledgeable professionals who can meet the needs of the ever-evolving landscape of technology-enhanced learning.

Acknowledgement. This work was partially supported by the European Commission under the Erasmus Program, as part of the DE-TEL project (Grant Agreement No. 2019-1-NO01-KA203-060280). This publication reflects the views of the authors only. The European Commission support for the production of this publication does not constitute an endorsement of the contents which reflects the views only of the authors, and the Commission cannot be held responsible for any use which may be made of the information contained therein.

References

1. Duval, E., Sharples, M., Sutherland, R.: Research themes in technology enhanced learning. In: Technology Enhanced Learning: Research Themes, pp. 1–10. Sprimger, Cham (2017). https://doi.org/10.1007/978-3-319-02600-8
2. Bower, M.: Design of Technology-Enhanced Learning: Integrating Research and Practice. Emerald Group Publishing, Bingley (2017)
3. Flavin, M.: Technology-enhanced learning and higher education. Oxf. Rev. Econ. Policy **32**(4), 632–645 (2016)
4. Kirkwood, A.: Price, L: Technology-enhanced learning and teaching in higher education: what is 'enhanced' and how do we know? A critical literature review. Learn. Media Technol. **39**(1), 6–36 (2014)
5. Pammer-Schindler, V., et al.: Interdisciplinary doctoral training in technology-enhanced learning in Europe. Front. Educ **5**, 150, Frontiers Media SA (2020)
6. Boulton, H.: Crossing boundaries: the affordances of new technologies in supporting a collaborative learning environment for doctoral students learning transnationally. Technol. Pedagog. Educ. **28**(3), 255–267 (2019). https://doi.org/10.1080/1475939X.2018.1559761
7. Chen, H.X.: Approaches to Quantitative Research: A Guide for Dissertation Students. Oak Tree Press, Cork (2012)
8. Dermo, J.: e-Assessment and the student learning experience: a survey of student perceptions of e-assessment. Br. J. Edu. Technol. **40**(2), 203–214 (2009)
9. O'Donnell, E., O'Donnell, L.: Challenges in developing adaptive educational hypermedia systems. In: Khosrow-Pour, M. (ed.) Encyclopedia of Information Science and Technology, 4th edn. pp. 2380–2391. IGI Global, Hershey (2018)

10. Bourdeau, J., Balacheff, N.: Technology-enhanced learning: from thesaurus and dictionary to ontology. Dans Jovanovic, Jelena et Chiong, Raymond (dir.), Technological and Social Environments for Interactive Learning, pp. 1–33. Informing Science Press (2014)
11. Wild, F.: Learning Analytics in R. Springer, Berlin (2016)
12. Fominykh, M., Prasolova-Førland, E.: DE-TEL-A European Initiative for Doctoral Education in Technology-Enhanced Learning. ERCIM News e-ISSN: 1564-0094, vol. 120, Special theme: Educational Technology (2019)
13. Kalz, M., Specht, M.: Assessing the cross-disciplinarity of technology-enhanced learning with science overlay maps and diversity measures. Br. J. Educ. Technol. **45**, 415–427 (2014). https://doi.org/10.1111/bjet.12092
14. Fominykh, M., Weidlich, J., Kalz, M., Hybertsen, I.D.: What do they TEL(L)? A systematic analysis of master programs in technology-enhanced learning. Int. J. Educ. Technol. High. Educ. **19**(1), 1–25 (2022). https://doi.org/10.1186/s41239-021-00305-7
15. Scanlon, E., Conole, G.: Interdisciplinarity in technology enhanced learning: an interview study. J. Interact. Media Educ. **2018**(1), 1–8 (2018). https://doi.org/10.5334/jime.476
16. Passey, D.: Technology-enhanced learning: rethinking the term, the concept and its theoretical background. Br. J. Educ. Technol. **50**(3), 972–986 (2019). https://doi.org/10.1111/bjet.12783
17. Hammersley, M.: Paradigm war revived? On the diagnosis of resistance to randomized controlled trials and systematic review in education. Int. J. Res. Method Educ. **31**(1), 3 (2008). https://doi.org/10.1080/17437270801919826
18. Carter, S., Smith, K., Harrison, N.: Working in the borderlands: critical perspectives on doctoral education. Teach. High. Educ. **26**(3), 283–292 (2021)
19. Fisher, M.C., et al.: Strategies for success in a nursing PhD program and beyond. J. Prof. Nursing **39**, 187–193 (2022). https://doi.org/10.1016/j.profnurs.2022.01.004
20. Franklin, C., Lightfoot, E., Nachbaur, M., Sucher, K.: A study of PhD courses and curricula across schools of social work. Res. Soc. Work. Pract. **32**(1), 116–126 (2022). https://doi.org/10.1177/10497315211039187
21. Fakunle, O., Dollinger, M., Alla-Mensah, J., Izard, B.: Academic conferences as learning sites: a multinational comparison of doctoral students' perspectives and institutional policy. Int. J. Doc. Stud. **14**, 479–497 (2019). https://doi.org/10.28945/4383
22. Déri, C.E., Tremblay-Wragg, E., Mathieu-C, S: Academic writing groups: history and state of play. The Int. J. Higher Educ. Res. **11**(1), 85–99 (2022). https://doi.org/10.5430/ijhe.v11n1p85
23. Grady, M.L.: Online doctoral education: strategies and resources for faculty advisors. J. Learn. Higher Educ. **14**(1), 17–20 (2018)
24. Grigas, V., Juzeniene, S., Velickaite, J.: "Just Google It"–the scope of freely available information sources for doctoral thesis writing. Inf. Res. Int. Electr. J. **22**(1), n1 (2017)
25. Ince, S., Hoadley, C., Kirschner, P.A.: The role of libraries in teaching doctoral students to become information-literate researchers: a review of existing practices and recommendations for the future. Inf. Learn. Sci. **120**(3/4), 158–172 (2019)
26. Kosvyra, A., Filos, D., Mountford, N., Cusack, T., Isomursu, M., Chouvarda, I.: PhD courses and the intersectoral experience: a comprehensive survey. In: Proceedings of the 7th International Conference on Higher Education Advances (HEAd'21) pp. 1131–1139 (2021)
27. Pyhältö, K., Vekkaila, J., Keskinen, J.: Fit matters in the supervisory relationship: doctoral students and supervisors perceptions about the supervisory activities. Innov. Educ. Teach. Int. **52**(1), 4–16 (2015). https://doi.org/10.1080/14703297.2014.981836Previous
28. Helfer, F., Drew, S.: Students' perceptions of doctoral supervision: a study in an engineering program in Australia. Int. J. Doct. Stud. **14**, 499–524 (2019). https://doi.org/10.28945/4368
29. Hatch, T., Skipper, A.: How much are PhD students publishing before graduation? An examination of four social science disciplines. J. Sch. Publ. **47**(2), 171–179 (2016). https://doi.org/10.3138/jsp.47.2.171

30. Li, Y.: "Publish SCI papers or no degree": practices of Chinese doctoral supervisors in response to the publication pressure on science students. Asia Pacif. J. Educ. **36**(4), 545–558 (2016). https://doi.org/10.1080/02188791.2015.1005050
31. Lindqvist, M.H.: Reconstructing the doctoral publishing process. Exploring the liminal space. High. Educ. Res. Dev. **37**(7), 1395–1408 (2018). https://doi.org/10.1080/07294360.2018.148 3323
32. Xu, L., Grant, B.: Doctoral publishing and academic identity work: two cases. High. Educ. Res. Dev. **39**(7), 1502–1515 (2020). https://doi.org/10.1080/07294360.2020.1728522
33. Xu, L.: Chinese international doctoral students' perceptions of publishing: a time–space perspective. Teach. High. Educ. (2022). https://doi.org/10.1080/13562517.2022.2067473
34. Kornhaber, R., Cross, M., Betihavas, V., Bridgman, H.: The benefits and challenges of academic writing retreats: an integrative review. High. Educ. Res. Dev. **35**(6), 1210–1227 (2016). https://doi.org/10.1080/07294360.2016.1144572
35. Quynn, K., Stewart, C.: Sustainable writing for graduate students: writing retreats offer vital support. J. Furth. High. Educ. **45**(10), 1385–1397 (2021). https://doi.org/10.1080/0309877X. 2021.1875200
36. Stevenson, N.: Developing academic wellbeing through writing retreats. J. Furth. High. Educ. **45**(6), 717–729 (2020). https://doi.org/10.1080/0309877X.2020.1812549
37. Tremblay-Wragg, E., Vincent, C., Mathieu-C., S., Lison, C., Ponsin, A., Déri, C.: Writing retreats responding to the needs of doctoral candidates through engagement with academic writing. Qual. Res. Educ. **11**(1), 29–57 (2022). https://doi.org/10.17583/qre.9195
38. Meyer, P., Kelle, S., Ullmann, T.D., Scott, P., Wild, F.: Interdisciplinary cohesion of TEL – an account of multiple perspectives. In: Hernández-Leo, D., Ley, T., Klamma, R., Harrer, A. (eds.) EC-TEL 2013. LNCS, vol. 8095, pp. 219–232. Springer, Heidelberg (2013). https:// doi.org/10.1007/978-3-642-40814-4_18
39. Anderson, T., Shattuck, J.: Design-based research: a decade of progress in education research? Educ. Res. **41**(1), 16–25 (2012). https://doi.org/10.3102/0013189x11428813
40. Kennedy-Clark, S.: Research by design: design-based research and the higher degree research student. J. Learn. Des. **6**(2), 26–32 (2013). https://doi.org/10.5204/jld.v6i2.128
41. Goff, W., Getenet, S.: Design-based research in doctoral studies: adding a new dimension to doctoral research. Int. J. Dr. Stud. **12**, 107–121 (2017)
42. Mandran, N., Vermeulen, M., Prior, E.: THEDRE's framework: empowering PhD candidates to efficiently implement design-based research. Educ. Inf. Technol. **27**(7), 9563–9586 (2022). https://doi.org/10.1007/s10639-022-10993-x
43. González-Ocampo, G., Castelló, M.: How do doctoral students experience supervision? Stud. Contin. Educ. **41**(3), 293–307 (2019). https://doi.org/10.1080/0158037X.2018.1520208
44. Gube, J.C.C., Getenet, S.T., Satariyan, A., Muhammad, Y.: Towards "operating within" the field: Doctoral students' views of supervisors' discipline expertise. Int. J. Dr. Stud. **12**, 1–16 (2017). https://www.informingscience.org/Publications/3641
45. Lee, A.: How can we develop supervisors for the modern doctorate? Stud. High. Educ. **43**(5), 878–890 (2018). https://doi.org/10.1080/03075079.2018.1438116
46. Overall, N.C., Deane, K.L., Peterson, E.R.: Promoting doctoral students' research self-efficacy: Combining academic guidance with autonomy support. High. Educ. Res. Dev. **30**(6), 791–805 (2011)
47. Sverdlik, A., Hall, N.C., McAlpine, L., Hubbard, K.: The PhD experience: a review of the factors influencing doctoral students' completion, achievement, and well-being. Int. J. Dr. Stud. **13**, 361–388 (2018). https://doi.org/10.28945/4113
48. Xu, L.: Moving between fantasies, fallacies and realities: students' perceptions of supervisors' roles in doctoral publishing. In: Teaching in Higher Education, pp. 1–15 (2020). https://doi. org/10.1080/13562517.2020.1832065

Analyzing Students' Perspective for Using Computer-Mediated Communication Tools for Group Collaboration in Higher Education

Eric Owusu[1]([✉]), Adita Kulkarni[1], and Brittani S. Washington[2]

[1] Department of Computing Sciences, State University of New York, Brockport, 350 New Campus Drive, Brockport, NY 14420, USA
{eowusu,akulkarni}@brockport.edu
[2] Department of Business Information Systems and Operations Management, University of North Carolina at Charlotte, 9201 University City Blvd, Charlotte, NC 28223, USA
bwashington@uncc.edu

Abstract. Advancement in technology has changed the way humans communicate with one another significantly. Post the COVID-19 pandemic, computer-mediated communication (CMC) has become an essential part of an instructor's course deliverable process in technology-oriented courses in higher education. It has affected the way instructors communicate with their students, and the way students communicate among themselves. Throughout their higher education curriculum, students work on at least one group project. Collaboration skills obtained while working on such group projects are important as they help the students in their post-graduation career. This work analyzes the use of CMC tools for group collaboration in higher education from the students' perspective. There are five measures of performance (MOP) indicators – payload, time, range, features and speed, used in this analysis. The observation is that student responses in all the indicators are skewed towards agreement, satisfaction, and effectiveness of the use of CMC tools.

Keywords: Computer-mediated Communication · Collaborative · Measure of performance

1 Introduction

Accreditation boards such as Accrediting Board for Engineering and Technology (ABET) provides assurance that a college or university program meets the quality standards of the profession for which that program prepares graduates in higher education [1]. Group collaboration forms part of the educational learning outcomes for all students. By this standard, students can perform better in teams at their workplace. Computer-mediated communication (CMC) tools such as Blackboard, Canvas, and Brightspace, integrate effectively with Zoom, Microsoft teams, Cisco Webex, Goggle meet, GoToMeeting, GroupMe etc., for effective communication. CMC tools use different forms of communication over a network in a synchronous or asynchronous

© The Author(s), under exclusive license to Springer Nature Switzerland AG 2023
P. Zaphiris and A. Ioannou (Eds.): HCII 2023, LNCS 14040, pp. 349–365, 2023.
https://doi.org/10.1007/978-3-031-34411-4_24

way [2–4]. In a research study conducted by Owusu and Washington, it was revealed that although higher education and institutions provide recommended CMC tools to be used, students preferred using open-source applications for group collaboration [5].

This study examines student perspectives on performance and use of computer mediated communication tools in group collaboration in higher education. Having an effective collaborative tools students can communicate and produce high-quality project delivery which could result in higher rate of knowledge exchange and sharing, increase the speed to turn around projects deliverables, group performance, higher engagement, and the ability to receive real-time feedback from groupmates through features such as chat and live video.

2 Background of the Study

Group collaboration projects are one of the main forms of interaction students encounter throughout their higher education career. It allows for students of all levels and backgrounds to be exposed to a collaborative learning and working style that prepares them for team projects post their college career [6]. Students can apply the objectives, perform the methods learned throughout the course, and display them to their audience in the way the instructor deems necessary. Displaying their work affords the opportunity for them to receive feedback from their peers, instructors, or both [7]. With any setting for interacting with your peers there are advantages and disadvantages. These advantages and disadvantages can have an impact on the performance of the individual as well as the overall group; however, variables such as perspective, classification year (class year), and experience play a role in determining which side of the spectrum the group project falls on.

2.1 Advantages and Disadvantages of Group Collaboration Projects

What might be an advantage to one person may be a disadvantage to another person. This perspective allows individuals from various backgrounds to bring in a unique way of thinking. The benefit of alleviating the one-sided mentality, exploring different avenues of creativity, and allowing the group to have different perspectives presents an expanded opportunity. However, it can also cause a clash where an individual thinks their direction is correct and the other is not. The objective of exploring different perspectives brings a balance to decision-making to alleviate as many biases as possible.

A component that impacts group projects is the class year which focuses on experience based on status. Students enrolled in the course may be of different classifications (i.e., Freshman, Sophomore, Junior, Senior), depending on the individual's academic standing and credits earned or transferred at the time of semester enrollment. If a Sophomore and a Freshman were enrolled in the course and they had to work on the same project, the Sophomore may have more experience due to their previous exposure of group projects during their freshman year. A first-year student is new to the higher education experience. Upper class students such as sophomores, juniors, and seniors with time have had the opportunity to learn from their mistakes as well as the mistakes of their peers.

Another component that impacts the experience is the difference between traditional and non-traditional students. The rate of non-traditional students is growing at a substantial rate, but there still is a clear difference between these two types of students. A traditional student is a student who enters their post-secondary experience without a lapse in prior education [8]. A non-traditional student is a student whose race and ethnicity, gender, age, whether they are full-time or part-time, married, or has dependents may impact when and how they are enrolled in school [9]. They are most impacted by external factors and are more goal oriented [10]. Gender is now playing a role in defining a non-traditional student. The American Psychological Association defines gender as a male, female, or an alternative gender that may not have anything to do with the sex that they were assigned [11].

The following research questions were examined:

- Does the measure of performance of CMC tools affect group collaboration in higher education?
- Does system functionality affect students' collaborative effort in group work?
- Does optimizing CMC tools, and analyzing open-source CMC tools for higher education institutions impacts student's outcome in group work?
- Does personal preference of CMC tools affect students' outcome of group collaborative work?

2.2   Measure of Performance and CMC Tools

Measure of Performance (MOP) measures that characterize physical or functional attributes relating to the operations, and it focuses on what is right and what is wrong [12]. The variables that are defined under the measure are described in Table 1.

Table 1. Measure of performance attributes

Payload	The accuracy of tracking material movement totals against performance targets
Time	The specific time allowed to execute
Speed	The speed at which the user operates a feature within the tool
Features	The service components available per tool
Range	The range of the availability of the tools

CMC is how humans communicate with one another through software that was designed for collaborative use [3]. In higher education, the use and the development of CMC tools has evolved. As per survey [5], CMC tools such as Zoom, Microsoft Teams, and Group Me are some of the tools that are primarily used today as a means of communication in higher education. These tools have common components as well as features that are unique to them. Also, some components vary based on the plans the end-user selects for use.

Software such as Zoom, and Microsoft Teams utilizes features like the waiting room to provide an additional security measure to control who can enter a Zoom meeting. This feature is disabled by default which means the meeting host must have the knowledge to enable this feature [13]. This feature keeps the meeting participants in a virtual room before entering the meeting space. This way the meeting host can verify that those who entered the meeting are actual participants. Depending on the length of your participants list, time and payload may play a significant role. It will be easier to add to the meeting a list of 10 participants than a list of 60 participants.

For time performance measurement, the more participants that you have with the enabled waiting room feature may require the following:

- The host with assistance from those established as co-hosts to let participants into the meeting, or
- Starting the meeting early and informing the participants, so that you as the host have more time to enter participants into the meeting.

For payload performance measurement, the more participants that you have may require assistance in managing features, such as:

- Questions and Answers,
- Polling,
- Monitoring and managing the Chat,
- Monitoring and acknowledging the raise hand feature, or
- Breakout rooms.

The purpose of breakout rooms during a video conference is to engage in discussions with a group size smaller than those participating in the meeting. The range of features that are enabled during the meeting in the main room are also available within each breakout room, that is only available for the view of those in that breakout room [14, 15].

2.3 Blackboard and Canvas Integration with CMC Tools

Applications such as Zoom and Microsoft Teams integrate in the Canvas and Blackboard learning management systems (LMS) in the same manner. The differences between the platforms are how the external CMC tool is accessed within the system configuration for initial setup. The difference between the instructor's point of view and the student's experience is how the instructor configures the CMC tool inside of the platform. Other variables that may impact the integration of the LMS with CMC tools are the different instructors and the differences in the course. Additional CMC tools such as GroupMe are identified as stand-alone applications and do not integrate with the LMS platforms.

2.4 Accrediting Board for Engineering and Technology (ABET) Accreditation

ABET accreditation is used to ensure higher education institution's programs meet a certain standard to prepare student in the fields of applied and natural science, computing, engineering, and engineering technology to be ready with the knowledge they need to enter the workforce [16]. The Computing Accreditation Commission (CAC) of ABET focus on the institutions who have programs within the following areas [17]:

- Associate Cybersecurity and Similarly Named Programs - associate computing programs using cybersecurity, cyber operations, computer security, information assurance, information security, computer forensics, or similar titles.
- Computer Science and Similarly Named Computing Programs - computer science theory and software development fundamentals similar titles.
- Cybersecurity and Similarly Named Computing Programs - cybersecurity, cyber operations, computer security, information assurance, information security, computer forensics, or similar titles.
- Information Systems and Similarly Named Computing Programs - management of information systems within an information systems environment, or similar titles.
- Information Technology and Similarly Named Computing Programs – computing technologies, or similar titles.

Students enrolled in a CAC classified program must have the availability to [17]:

- Analyze the complexity of computing problems, and apply principles taught to identify solutions.
- Design, implement, and evaluate computing-based solutions using a set of specific computing requirements.
- Communicate effectively.
- Recognize professional responsibilities and make informed judgments based on legal and ethical principles.
- Serve as a member or leader of team engaged activities such as group projects.

The more exposure students get to understanding their personal style of work and that of their peers, it sets them up for success in group collaboration environments. Their quality of work puts them in a better position for employments opportunities, having access to loans, grants, and scholarships, and allows them to be marketable globally [18].

3 Methodology

This study used mixed methods, quantitative and qualitative descriptive approach in analyzing data and generalizing the results collected from 200 undergraduate students in the United States. The study focused on the human computer factors that assist in MOP of CMC tools for group collaboration in higher education. The connotation is that, if a student was aware or knew how to use the tools that are applicable for collaborative use, they will produce a high-quality project deliverable that will increase their degree of success. The goal of measuring performance reveals the ability of a system to meet a specified need from a particular viewpoint [5].

A questionnaire was developed using Qualtrics to capture the data needed, so that higher education professionals are aware of the current state of team collaboration and productivity of group projects. The study was based on a recommendation from the previous study on measuring the impact of accessing mechanisms for group collaboration for students during the COVID-19 pandemic. It proposed more research to be conducted in the aspect of performance measure for CMC tools. A Likert scale questionnaire was distributed to active enrolled undergraduate students at a higher education institution to participate in this study. Participants were recruited through Department Chairs who chair departments who house students that 18 years of age or older and are enrolled in technology-related majors. All participants enrolled in the study must have completed at least one semester at the institution as an undergraduate, be enrolled in the minimum amount course credit requirements to be considered at least part-time working toward a bachelor's degree, and be classified as a Freshman, Sophomore, Junior, or Senior. The estimated time of completion for each participant was 15 min from start to finish.

3.1 Design Approach

Twenty survey questions associated with the MOP indicators were collected and reviewed from the previous study. Supportive factors were identified in the questionnaire that validated the results. The data gathered were consolidated from a 5-point Likert scale to a 3-point Likert scale. The following were combined into one grouping - Agree and Strongly Agree, Strongly Disagree and Disagree, Very Effective and Effective, Very Satisfied and Satisfied, Unsatisfied and Very Unsatisfied. This was because, as stated earlier, this study is an extension of our previous work [5]. The 5-point Likert scale was used for the quantitative analysis in the previous study [5]. The qualitative analysis in this work aimed to measure the agreement, effectiveness, and satisfaction of students. Questions reviewed with similar performance indicators such as Payload, Time, Speed, Features and Range were grouped. Students age, gender, majors, and class year were captured in the category for demographics.

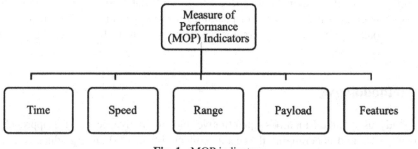

Fig. 1. MOP indicators

3.2 Research Limitations

Basing the study on a larger sample size for quantitative purposes could have generated more accurate results. A larger sample will show a true representation of the group collaboration performance within higher education. The lack of previous studies in the study area was a challenge. The IRB does not mandate all participants to answer all the questions on the survey.

4 Results

4.1 Time

Table 2. Time Indicator Responses

Questions	Disagree	Neutral	Agree
Enough time was allocated that allowed students to work on their group projects inside of the classroom	17.69%	20.73%	61.58%
Enough time was allocated that allowed students to work on their group projects outside of the classroom	5.45%	16.97%	77.57%
My team interacted with one another at least one time per week	12.27%	13.50%	74.23%
The team spent very little time complaining about things we cannot control	10.91%	26.06%	63.03%

In this section, we study the student responses to the questions related to the time indicator. We observe that most participants agreed with the questions related to this indicator. Around 62% and 78% of participants agree that they had sufficient time inside and outside of the classroom, respectively, to work on group projects. Around 74% of participants agreed that their team interacted at least once per week, which ensured that they completed their project on time. 63% of participants agreed that they spent little time complaining about things that they cannot control.

4.2 Features

Table 3. CMC Tool Features Comparison [13–15]

Components	Zoom	Teams	GroupMe
Price	$0 to $20.00 per month per user	$0 to $12.50 per month per user	$0
Capacity	Up to 1,000	Up to 300	Up to 5,000
Time	Up to 40 min on free plan; 30 h on paid plans	Up to 60 min on free plan; 24 h on paid plans	Up to 24 h, with Skype integration
Common			
Voice and Video Calling	Yes	Yes	Yes, with Skype integration
Chat	Yes	Yes	Yes
Screen Share	Yes	Yes	No
Mobility	Yes	Yes	Yes

(*continued*)

Table 3. (*continued*)

Components	Zoom	Teams	GroupMe
Breakout Rooms	Yes	Yes	No
Additions			
Whiteboard	Yes	Yes	No
Filters	Yes	Yes	No
Meeting Recordings	Yes	Yes	No
Meeting Transcripts	Yes	Yes	No
Host Webinars	Yes	Yes	No
Cloud File Storage	Yes	Yes	No
Integrates with Blackboard and Canvas	Yes	Yes	No
User reporting and analytics	Yes	Yes	No

Table 4. Features Indicator Responses

Questions	Unsatisfied	Neutral	Satisfied
Are you satisfied using collaboration tools in your school projects activities?	9.25%	24.28%	66.48%
How is the look and feel (design) of the collaboration tool you use for group work?	6.35%	28.90%	64.74%
Are you comfortable with the collaboration's tools?	5.21%	23.12%	71.68%
How reliable is completing tasks inside the collaboration's tool i.e. (completing an action)?	4.63%	24.86%	70.52%
	Not Effective	Neutral	Effective
How effective is virtual group collaboration versus in-person group collaboration?	33.52%	21.39%	45.09%
	Disagree	Neutral	Agree
The collaboration tools features enhance my social capabilities (Break rooms) with my team?	11.56%	27.17%	61.27%
Majority of the various functions in the collaborative tools were used?	19.08%	32.95%	47.98%

In this section, we present the student responses to the questions related to the features indicator. Table 2 shows the comparison of all the features that are useful in team projects for the three most popular tools amongst our participants – Zoom, Teams and GroupMe. Table 3 shows all the questions asked about the features indicator and the participants' responses to them. We see that most participants are satisfied with the collaboration tools they used and found them reliable for group projects. Most of the participants agreed that they made use of maximum functionality of the tools, and it enhanced their experience with teamwork. Although most of the participants (45%)

agreed that virtual group collaboration was effective, there is a considerable number of participants (33.52%) who still prefer working on group projects in-person.

4.3 Range

Table 5. Range Indicator Responses – Determining Factor in picking a Tool for collaboration.

What was the determining factor of using each tool?	Response
Group collaboratively determined the tool of use	43.66%
Instructor determined the tool of use	32.84%
Team Member determined the tool of use	13.06%
Project Leader determined the tool of use	10.45%

Table 6. Range Indicator Responses – Other questions

Questions	Disagree	Neutral	Agree
I would feel uneasy if I was given a school project where I had to use only CMC tool school had?	14.45%	41.04%	44.5%
I feel that I might not be able to collaborate effectively if I don't use other open sources of CMC tools?	13.3%	43.93%	42.77%
If you had a list of recommended tools to use for group collaboration, would that positively impact their collaborative efforts with your peers?	4.63%	27.17%	68.21%
If a student was aware of, or knew how to use the tools that are applicable for collaborative use, they will produce a high-quality project deliverable that will increase their degree of success	2.89%	21.39%	75.72%
The institution provides collaborative tools that increases my level of confidence in the success of my group project?	13.87%	27.17%	58.95%

Table 4 and Table 5 show responses to the questions related to the range indicator. We observe in Table 4 that most of the students (~44%) selected a CMC tool to use collectively as a group, followed by (~33%) selection of a tool by the course instructor. Table 6 shows that many students agreed that they would prefer a range of tools to choose from to be effective in teamwork, but there are significant students who do not care if they are given an option or not (Table 7).

4.4 Speed

Table 7. Speed Indicator Responses

Question	Unsatisfied	Neutral	Satisfied
How easy and satisfying is it learning to use your collaboration's tools?	6.39%	24.42%	69.18%

In this section, we present the student responses related to the speed indicator. The question asked to the survey participants was how easy and satisfying they found the CMC tools they used with respect to the speed at which they operate a feature within the tool. About 69% of participants were satisfied with the CMC tools they used (Table 8 and 9).

4.5 Payload

Table 8. Payload Indicator Responses – Number of courses per year

How many courses in the past year required the completion of a group project?	Response
4	14.88%
3	35.71%
2	46.43%
1	2.98%

Table 9. Payload Indicator Responses – Number of courses per year

Question	Disagree	Neutral	Agree
The use of collaborative tools has a positive effect on project outcome?	3.51%	32.75%	63.74%

We next present the responses to the payload indicator which analyzes efficiency of students with respect to the amount of workload they have. Students in our survey work on group projects for a duration between 5 and 16 weeks (about 3 and a half months) depending on the course. As per our survey, only about 3% of the participants worked on a group project in the given academic year. All other participants worked on 2 or more courses with a maximum of 4 courses in the academic year. We observe that around 64% of participants agreed that the use of CMC tools had a positive effect on the outcome of all the projects they worked on.

4.6   Demographics

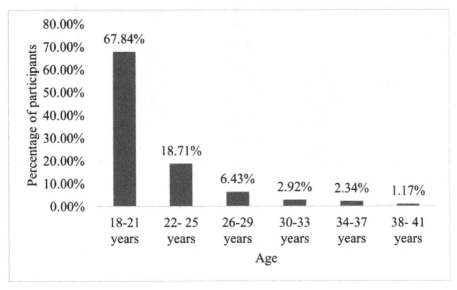

Fig. 2. Age

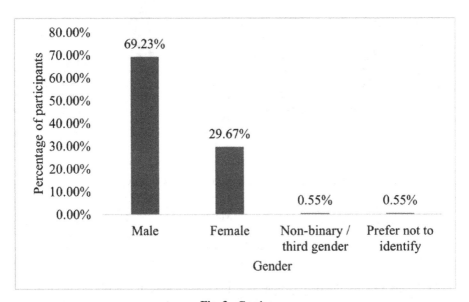

Fig. 3. Gender

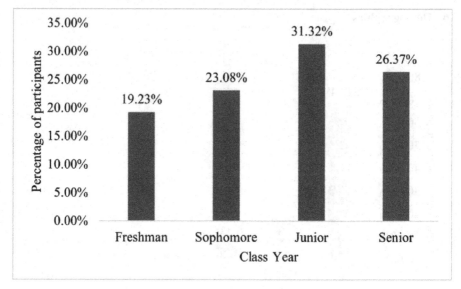

Fig. 4. Class Year

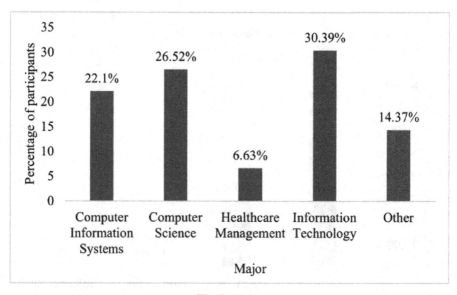

Fig. 5. Major

We finally present the demographics of the participants. From Fig. 1, we observe that most participants who took the survey are between 18 and 25 years. Only 13% of the participants are over 25 years. Figure 2 shows that the survey participants have more male students compared to female or non-binary. Around 58% of the participants are upper division students, i.e., juniors or seniors (Fig. 3). We observe from Fig. 4. That the highest number of participants are majoring in Information Technology, followed by Computer Science, Computer Information Systems, and Healthcare management, respectively. Finally, in our survey, we have 96.15% full-time students whereas only 3.85% students are enrolled in a program part-time (Fig. 5).

5 Discussion

Measuring the performance of all indicators based on student response, most of the results presented above were skewed towards agreement, satisfaction, and effectiveness of the use of CMC tools. This could be due to social influences or behavioral intension. To better understand the results, the unified theory of acceptance and use of technology (UTAUT2) conception of behavioral intension is a significant predictor from the finding of the results [20]. UTAUT2 focuses on individual perceptions in the adoption of technology and explains user variances in technology adoption. Factors such as performance expectancy - the degree to which using a technology will provide benefits to consumers in performing certain activities, effort expectancy - the degree of ease associated with the consumers' use of technology, social influence - the degree to which individuals perceive that other important to them believe they should use a technology, and habit - conceptualized as self-reported perception of automatically engaging in a certain behavior, are all significant factors that explain why students' responses were heavily skewed to agreeance, satisfaction and effectiveness [20]. The UTAUT2 framework implies that if a student has a positive or enjoyable experience while using any CMC tool, they are more likely to repeat using the CMC tools. Repeated use of the technology results in routine behavior or habit which reduces the enjoyability of using the technology and reduces behavioral intention. To sustain the use of CMC tools and improve behavioral intention, it will be necessary to introduce features that will motivate or drive the interest of group collaboration, such as chats and video calls for user feedback. Table 3 explains the ease of use of CMC tools for better group collaboration (Table 10).

In this study, most of the participants (43.93%) were neutral when it came to how they felt using CMC tools that were not recommended by the instructors. If the student wasn't required to use the CMC tools in a prior course, it may be difficult to use. For example, GroupMe is not a recommended tool for communication set forth by universities. However, since many students are familiar with the CMC tool, it's easier for them to communicate with their peers. A study conducted by Hao-Chang, revealed that after a student has received training in the use of CMC tool in the first two weeks of this course, they showed significant growth in confidence and familiarity with using the tool. This indicates that the training in CMC tools is beneficial for students to ensure that they can participate in learning activities via these communication tools [4].

Table 10. MOP Usability Comparison Overview

Level of Ease	Zoom	Microsoft Teams	GroupMe
Payload	High – Payload isn't impacted due to each user having their own license and running multiple meetings at a time, but only when a shared account is being used	High – Due to each user having their own license and running multiple meetings at a time	Low – Due to needing to utilize a third-party application for conference calls with no ability to. No ability to track movement of performance with common features
Time	High – Common Features Medium – Additional Features require more learning based on the CMC tool Low – Dependent on the end users experience	High – Common Features Medium – Additional Features require more learning based on the CMC tool Low – Dependent on the end users experience	High – Due to the limited common features
Speed	Medium – Speed is dependent on multiple factors such as internet connection, knowledge of application, the knowledge of the features, capacity of the device running the application	Medium – Speed is dependent on multiple factors such as internet connection, knowledge of application, the knowledge of the features, capacity of the device running the application	Medium – Due to the low range of features the tool is fairly accessible. The Skype integration component is more so impacted by the speed due to needing a fair internet connection
Features	High – Serves a high volume of needs	High – Serves a high volume of needs	Low – Limited features
Range	High - Variety of features	High - Variety of features	Low - Limited features

Group projects can reduce the grading time needed for instructors who find themselves with many more students. However, factoring in that all students' contribution isn't equal presents complexity to this scenario. Just like working in the field post-graduation, working in groups is one of the most disliked avenues of teaching structures from the student's perspective due to communication and time [10]. In multiple studies where a questionnaire was conducted as it relates to the stance of group collaboration effort in higher education, the responses skewed more towards the time allotted inside of the classroom is more productive and valuable than time allotted outside of the classroom due to many external factors. ABET requires IT graduates to attain soft skills, or the ability to communicate well, work in teams, and manage conflict [1]. During the lifespan of a course, working in groups trains students how to be better prepared for group decision making and cross-functional interaction amongst teams within the workplace

[21]. To ensure that the instructor obtains quality work where the contribution levels are equal, and for the student's level of satisfaction to remain high, the amount of time allotted inside and outside of the classroom plays an important role [5].

This study has approximately 32% non-traditional students. A non-traditional student is classified as typically older and working, with a growing percentage within the United States [21]. For many employees, when they join a company and a series of years have passed, many are looking for growth opportunities. Growth in an organization traditionally comes with training and other career development opportunities sponsored or reimbursed by the employer. Over time, research has shown that companies could more than likely retain their employees if they have career development opportunities [22]. This narrative, when implemented, has changed the way in how and when education is consumed. Non-traditional students' lives differ from those between the ages of 18 to 19 enrolling in college directly after receiving their high school diploma. Their external lives play a huge role in the decision-making process for enrollment, course structure and capabilities, and continuing enrollment. Also, their academic skill set, and technology use may not be as strong due to the length of time they have been out of a school setting as a student [23]. Due to the full-time workload of a non-traditional student, it may be difficult for them to take three or more classes per semester which classifies them as part time students.

The data revealed that the majority of the students were taking three or more project-based classes per semester. Students' course load indicated that the chances for them to succeed in project collaboration depended on the effectiveness of CMC tools which are user friendly and had more features. Also, the student's behavior and preferences of this type of tool is triggered by the emerging class of Gen Z and the way the tool embraces prompt communication among classmates. Higher education institutes use popular CMC tools such as Zoom and Teams because it has the flexibility of integrating external components like whiteboard, filters, meeting recordings, meeting transcript, host webinars, cloud file storage and user reporting and analytics on platform of Blackboard, Canvas and Brightspace. This comparison is outlined in Table 2. Significantly, although participants (45%) in the study agreed that virtual group collaboration was effective, there was a considerable number of participants (32.52%) who still prefer working on group projects in-person.

6 Conclusion

Findings from this study on performance indicators reveal that participants were more likely to use CMC tool based on the level of ease of use. Garrett (2010) revealed in his study that "every product that is used by someone has a user experience [24]" Using open-source CMC tools allows students to pick tools that makes them comfortable. How people feel about a tool and their satisfaction when using it can impact student outcome. Specifically, the overall impact of how good CMC tool is to use is centered on MOP indicators. This study has the potential to contribute to learning in higher education by developing usable CMC tools with the human centered approach. It also has the potential to benefit students and instructors. The familiarity of the tools being used increases the chances of a high-quality group project deliverable. The more exposure a student gets to understanding their personal style of work as well as the style of work of their peers, it sets them up for success in group collaboration environments. Their quality of work puts them in a better position for employment opportunities and allows them to be marketable globally. This study assists instructors to be effective in offering project-based courses which ensure student success.

References

1. ABET. Criteria for accrediting computing programs, 2023–2024. ABET. https://www.abet. org/accreditation/accreditation-criteria/criteria-for-accrediting-computing-programs-2023-2024/
2. Lee, E., Oh, S.Y.: Computer-mediated communication. Communication. https://doi.org/10. 1093/obo/9780199756841-0160
3. Treem, J.W., Leonardi, P.M., van den Hooff, B.: Computer-mediated communication in the age of communication visibility. J. Comput.-Mediat. Commun. 25(1), 44–59 (2020)
4. Lo, H.C.: Utilizing computer-mediated communication tools for problem-based learning. J. Educ. Technol. Soc. 12(1), 205–213 (2009)
5. Owusu, E., Washington, B.: The impact of accessing mechanisms for group collaboration for students in higher education. In: Antona, M., Stephanidis, C. (eds.) Universal Access in Human-Computer Interaction. User and Context Diversity, pp. 78–93. Springer, Cham (2022). https://doi.org/10.1007/978-3-031-05039-8_6
6. Hammar Chiriac, E. (2014). Group work as an incentive for learning - students' experiences of group work. Front. Psychol. 5. https://doi.org/10.3389/fpsyg.2014.00558
7. Lozoya-Santos, J.d.J., et al.: Transdisciplinary Learning community: a model to enhance collaboration between higher education institutions and society. In: 2019 IEEE Global Engineering Education Conference (EDUCON), 2019, pp. 622–627 (2019). https://doi.org/10. 1109/EDUCON.2019.8725108
8. Johnson, M.L., Nussbaum, E.M.: Achievement Goals and coping strategies: identifying the traditional/nontraditional students who use them. J. Coll. Stud. Dev. 53, 41–54 (2012)
9. Grabowski, C., Rush, M., Ragen, K., Fayard, V., & Watkins-Lewis, K. (2016). Today's nontraditional student: Challenges to academic success and degree completion. Inquiries Journal, 8(03). http://www.inquiriesjournal.com/a?id=1377
10. Eppler, M.A., Carsen-Plentl, C., Harju, B.L.: Achievement goals, failure attributions, and academic performance in nontraditional and traditional college students. J. Soc. Behav. Pers. 15, 353–372 (2000)
11. Oxford University Press. (n.d.). Oxford languages and google - english. Oxford Languages. Retrieved from https://languages.oup.com/google-dictionary-en/
12. Smith, N., Clark, T.: An exploration of C2 effectiveness–A holistic approach. In: 2004 Command and Control Research and Technology Symposium (2004, September)
13. Zoom US. (n.d.). Video conferencing, web conferencing, webinars, screen sharing. Zoom Video Communications. https://zoom.us/pricing
14. Microsoft. (n.d.). Compare microsoft teams options: Microsoft teams. Compare Microsoft Teams Options | Microsoft Teams. https://www.microsoft.com/en-us/microsoft-teams/com pare-microsoft-teams-options?activetab=pivot%3Aprimaryr1&pricing-tab=1
15. GroupMe. (n.d.). The best way to chat with everyone you know. GroupMe. https://groupme. com/en-US/
16. Accrediting Board for Engineering and Technology. (n.d.). Accreditation: Setting the Standard Worldwide. ABET. https://www.abet.org/accreditation/

17. Accrediting Board for Engineering and Technology. (n.d.). Why ABET Accreditation Matters. ABET. https://www.abet.org/accreditation/what-is-accreditation/why-abet-accred itation-matters/

18. Accrediting Board for Engineering and Technology. (2021, December 3). Criteria for Accrediting Computing Programs, 2022–2023. ABET. https://www.abet.org/accreditation/accredita tion-criteria/criteria-for-accrediting-computing-programs-2022-2023/

19. Petersen, D.: Setting goals measuring performance. Prof. Saf. **50**(12), 43–48 (2005)

20. Venkatesh, V., Thong, J.Y., Xu, X.: Consumer acceptance and use of information technology: extending the unified theory of acceptance and use of technology. MIS Q. **36**(1), 157–178 (2012)

21. ABET.: Criteria for accrediting computing programs, 2023–2024. ABET. https://www.abet. org/accreditation/accreditation-criteria/criteria-for-accrediting-computing-programs-2023-2024/

22. Leverence, M.E.: A study of nontraditional students' perceptions of their library research skills. Ref. Libr. **27**(58), 143–161 (1997). https://doi.org/10.1300/j120v27n58_14

23. Bai, J., Liu, J.: A study on the influence of career growth on work engagement among new generation employees. Open J. Bus. Manag. **6**(2), 300–317. https://doi.org/10.4236/ojbm. 2018.62022

24. Chapman, K.J., Van Auken, S.: Creating positive group project experiences: an examination of the role of the instructor on students' perceptions of group projects. J. Mark. Educ. **23**(2), 117–127 (2001). https://doi.org/10.1177/0273475301232005

25. Garrett, J.J.: The Elements of User Experience: User-Centered Design for the Web and Beyond, 2nd edn, New Riders Press (2010)

Exploring Factors Affecting User Perception of Trustworthiness in Advanced Technology: Preliminary Results

Iuliia Paramonova[(✉)], Sonia Sousa, and David Lamas

School of Digital Technologies, Tallinn University, Tallinn, Estonia
{juparam,scs,drl}@tlu.ee

Abstract. People perceive advanced technologies to be nondeterministic as they become increasingly complex and opaque. Therefore, the issue of trust in technology is becoming crucial, particularly in risky domains where the consequences of misuse can cause significant harm or loss. There is a lack of design heuristics that consider the users' perspective on the trustworthiness of technologies to support practitioners in promoting trust in technologies. In this exploratory study, we aimed to understand how users perceive the trustworthiness of advanced financial technologies. A survey was conducted to assess users' risk propensity and trust in technology, followed by semi-structured interviews with 12 participants to examine their behaviours and perceptions when using cryptocurrency platforms. We use the observation method to triangulate the data, asking participants to show us how they use the application. The grounded theory analysis identified the following factors that affect users' perceptions of trustworthiness in advanced financial technologies: Usability, Credibility, Risk Mitigation, Reliability, and Level of Expertise.

Keywords: Value-sensitive design · Human-centered design, Human-computer trust · Trustworthy technology

1 Introduction

People perceive advanced technologies to be nondeterministic as they become increasingly complex and opaque. In this context, "complex" refers to a system or software with many components whose functions and design elements are challenging to accept and justify [1]. The concept of complexity also considers a series of non-linear interactions [2]. The characteristics of complex systems include robustness and lack of central control with autonomous and independent behaviour [3].

Although advanced systems continue improving in sophistication, their inner processes remain mostly opaque, earning them the label "black boxes" in the literature [4] due to the difficulty in comprehending how they function to verify the results and trust in technology. According to Lewis and Weigert [5] and Moellering [6], trust can serve as a functional alternative to rational prediction to reduce complexity. Moreover, nondeterminism leads to uncertainty when people do not know all the information, they

P. Zaphiris and A. Ioannou (Eds.): HCII 2023, LNCS 14040, pp. 366–383, 2023.
https://doi.org/10.1007/978-3-031-34411-4_25

need to set accurate odds to assess outcome probability [7]. Uncertainty could lead to risk and loss aversion [8]. According to Kahneman's prospect theory, people are likelier to avoid actions that could lead to losses, even if gains are probable [8]. Perceived risk is interconnected with trust [9, 10]. Therefore, in order to increase trust in advanced technologies, it is necessary to reduce risk and uncertainty [11].

Trust is impacted by contextual factors, for example, by the perceived level of risk [12]; therefore, trust in technology is becoming crucial, particularly in risky domains such as healthcare [13, 14], robotics and automation [15] and finance [16]. It is worth mentioning that advanced systems such as decision support tools, recommendation systems, and autonomous vehicles are often viewed as promising to eliminate human error and augment individual abilities, they can also be misused and cause harm. For instance, personal data and privacy issues with Facebook [17], Amazon purchasing manipulations [18], or social disinformation with deep fake news during US presidential elections [19]. The lack of comprehensive explanations of system performance and outcomes affects users' trust in everyday applications such as film recommendations, social networks, and navigation systems because users need to assess the system's trustworthiness [20].

Scholars also approach the concept of trustworthiness from a technical perspective, focusing on developing explainable agnostic agents or algorithms that can provide some level of self-explanation. For example, Diprose et al. [21] conducted an experimental study on machine learning decision support systems and found a significant correlation between explainability, understanding, and trust. However, more research is needed to understand the role of users' perceptual tendencies in evaluating different explainability methods.

Nevertheless, the results of the study conducted by Ribes et al. [22] indicate that user trust is not affected by provided stimuli in a low-risk context tested on a news aggregator interface prototype because trust is crucial in a scenario where there is more to lose than gain.

It has been observed that average users may perceive advanced technologies and existing software systems that do not utilise machine learning as nondeterministic, as they may appear complex to understand from the user's perspective [23]. Given this, we focus our investigation on cryptocurrency exchange platforms (CEPs) for the current study. CEPs are defined as centralised platforms for exchanging digital assets. Trust is a critical aspect of the adoption of cryptocurrency [24]. Users should trust the exchange's ability to hold their funds securely to complete transactions to store and trade assets [25]. Moreover, cryptocurrency and blockchain concepts are complex and incomprehensible from the users' perspective, particularly for novices and users with a non-technological background [26, 27].

Currently, research on trustworthy technologies tends to focus on AI-infused systems. While the HCI community and the EU have proposed principles, guidelines, and legal regulations for designing trustworthy AI systems [28–31], there needs to be more heuristics for designing advanced technologies that are trustworthy.

By understanding the user's perspective on what makes a technology trustworthy, we can reduce risk by providing users with a desirable user experience and the information they need to assess risks. In this exploratory study, we aimed to understand how users perceive advanced financial technology's trustworthiness and provide preliminary findings on trustworthy factors influencing users' trust.

2   Related Works

2.1   Trust

Trust is a multidimensional phenomenon, and it is difficult to define it [12, 32, 33]. In the context of human relationships, trust was defined by Mayer et al. [12] as "the willingness to be vulnerable to the actions of another party based on the expectation that they will perform an action that is important to the trustor". According to Luhmann [34] and Giddens [35], trust has a circular relationship with risk. Risk represents the difference between controllable and uncontrollable factors, and that trust is directly related to the subjective ability to make risk-taking decisions Luhmann [34]. Furthermore, it has been found that interpersonal trust is impacted by contextual elements, including the stakes at hand, the balance of power, the perceived level of risk, and the alternatives available to the trustor [12].

Additionally, the context of the relationship affects both the necessity of trust and the assessment of trustworthiness [12]. However, trust helps people cope with risk and uncertainty in human relationships; this study focused on trust in technology, which reflects beliefs that a specific technology has the necessary attributes to perform as expected in a given situation where negative consequences are possible [12]. Trust in advanced technology is a factor that facilitates increasing users' confidence in a system by making them comfortable while controlling and using it [36].

Some scholars associate trust in technology with privacy and security [37, 38], some with transparency and accountability [39], and others focused on ethics and reliability [40], which leads to approaching trust from a half-side perspective. Trust is a multi-dimensional phenomenon and should be considered a complex of aspects and come from an interdisciplinary perspective. For instance, Human-Computer Trust Model (HCTM) which is following a socio-technical approach and measures trust in technology considering both system and human-like characteristics [10, 41]. It is an empirically tested model based on prior trust-measuring instruments [42, 43], which uses a psychometric Human-Computer Trust Scale (HCTS) to measure trust in technology. The HCTM assess trust based on users' perceptions of three indicators: Perceived Risk, Competence, and Benevolence [10]. Perceived risk is the user's subjective evaluation of the potential threats and consequences posed by the system. Competence refers to the perceived ease with which a user can use the system to complete a task successfully. Benevolence is the user's belief that the system will act in their best interests and that most other users of the system share similar social behaviours and values. Additionally, the HCTM account for the mean of results for reporting the general level of trust to justify result acceptability [10, 41].

The dynamic nature of trust should be considered when measuring trust. Initial trust refers to the trust that is established at the beginning of the relationship with technology [44]. This can be achieved through various means, such as demonstrating the technology's functionality and reliability or providing user-friendly support and documentation [21]. Maintaining trust refers to the ongoing effort to sustain the trust established in the relationship with the technology [45]. This can involve consistently updating and maintaining the technology to ensure its continued functionality and reliability and providing timely and effective user support [46]. Calibrating trust refers to the process of adjusting the level of trust based on new information or experiences with the technology [47]. This can involve reassessing the technology's trustworthiness and adjusting one's level of trust accordingly [48]. It is important to recognise that trust in technology is a fluid and dynamic process that requires ongoing effort and attention to maintain and calibrate.

2.2 Trustworthiness

Trust and trustworthiness are related concepts, but they are not the same. Trust refers to the belief that someone or something is reliable and likely to act in a trustworthy manner. Trustworthiness, on the other hand, refers to the actual qualities or characteristics that make someone or something trustworthy [33]. In the context of technology, trustworthiness refers to the set of properties that can be attributed to a system or an entity to increase trust [49].

Caldwell and Clapham [33] identified a model of organizational-level trustworthiness that consists of seven duties: competence (the level of knowledge and ability to achieve results), quality assurance (adherence to standards of quality), interactional courtesy (respect and courtesy shown to others), procedural fairness (opportunities for stakeholders to participate in fair processes), responsibility to inform (communication to stakeholders about organisational objectives and outcomes), legal compliance (understanding and following applicable laws), and financial balance (maintaining financial stability). These duties, which were originally identified in the context of the human resource profession, are directly comparable to the Mayer et al. [12] model of interpersonal trustworthiness, which consists of three factors: ability (the trustor's perception of the trustee's competence, expertise, and ability to complete the task or fulfil their responsibilities), benevolence (the trustor's perception of the trustee's intentions and willingness to act in the trustor's best interests), and integrity (the trustor's perception of the trustee's honesty, reliability, and consistency in their actions and words). Together, these three factors make up the trustor's overall assessment of the trustworthiness of the trustee in an interpersonal relationship.

According to McKnight et al. [32], trust in technology can be based on system characteristics such as functionality (the belief that the technology has the necessary capabilities or features), helpfulness (the belief that the technology provides adequate and responsive help to users), and reliability/predictability (the belief that the technology will consistently operate properly, and its behaviour can be forecast). Hasselbring and Reussner [50] propose the following trustworthy system qualities. Correctness refers to the absence of improper system states, while safety refers to the absence of catastrophic environmental consequences. Moreover, quality of service includes availability, the probability of readiness for correct service; reliability, the probability of correct service for a given duration of time; and performance, response time and throughput. Security refers to the absence of unauthorised access to a system, and privacy indicates the absence of unauthorised disclosure of information. These attributes are important to consider in order to ensure the trustworthiness of software systems [50].

The trustworthiness of automation technology and autonomous systems is often influenced by characteristics such as performance, purpose, and process [51]. Performance refers to the competency or expertise of the automation as demonstrated by its ability to achieve the operator's goals. Purpose refers to the extent to which the automation is being used in accordance with the designer's intent. Process refers to the appropriateness and effectiveness of the automation's algorithms in achieving the operator's goals [51].

There is widespread agreement that advanced technologies should be trustworthy, incorporating criteria for trustworthy systems such as technical robustness and safety, transparency, non-discrimination, and fairness [31]. Developers also aim to design and develop trustworthy applications by increasing their technical robustness and explainability [52], fairness [53], and transparency [39]. In addition to the trustworthy design of systems, it is important for users to be able to accurately assess the trustworthiness of systems [54]. This is especially relevant for professionals in high-risk domains, such as physicians or loan officers, who rely on systems in their decision-making processes. If users overestimate or underestimate the trustworthiness of a system, it can lead to negative consequences such as undertrust or overtrust and disuse.

2.3 Designing Trustworthy Technologies

There are two main approaches to designing trustworthy technologies: normative and pragmatic [55]. The normative approach involves considering ethical and legal considerations at the governmental level. Some examples of this include the UK House of Lords' [56] UK AI Ethical Code, the Organisation for Economic Co-operation and Development's [57] OECD Recommendation of the Council on Artificial Intelligence welcomed by G20 leaders, and the White House's Office of Science and Technology Policy's Trustworthy AI Principles [58]. The European High-Level Expert Group on AI (AI-HLEG) [31] also released the Ethics Guidelines for Trustworthy AI.

The pragmatic perspective shows how researchers are exploring trustworthy design in practice. There are various guidelines that have been developed to help communicate trustworthiness in technology. Nielsen's [59] ten usability heuristics are a well-known set of principles that, although not specifically focused on trust, can ensure a system's usability, which refers to trustworthiness [60]. Nielsen [61] identified four ways to communicate trustworthiness with interface design: 1) design quality (such as presenting organised content and navigation, following current trends in visual design, and avoiding typos and mistakes), 2) upfront disclosure of customer relationships (specifying details of responsibilities, costs, and overall information in a clear and accessible way), 3) comprehensive, correct, and current content (presenting the full range of services or products and keeping them up to date), and 4) connection to the rest of the web (including links to external sources such as customer reviews, social media, or news outlets).

Shneiderman [62] proposes a different set of guidelines based on two principles: 1) inviting participation by ensuring trust, which involves offering assurance before the relationship through four guidelines (disclosing patterns of past performance, providing references from past and current users, getting certifications from third parties, and making it easy to locate, read, and enforce policies involving privacy and security), and 2) accelerating action by clarifying responsibility and obligations, which is translated into three guidelines (clarifying each participant's responsibilities, providing clear guarantees with compensation, and supporting dispute resolution and mediation services).

Borg et al. [63] used Assessment List for Trustworthy AI (ALTAI) to assess advanced driver-assistance systems (ADAS) under development. The study shows that ALTAI applies to some extent to evaluating ADAS, but some parts regarding human agents and transparency can be discarded in ADAS. Also, researchers proposed additional suggestions for the further revision of ALTAI, such as life cycle variants, domain-specific adaptations, and removing redundancy.

Siau and Wang [64] analysed the trust concept from various perspectives and proposed a list of factors to establish initial trust and support continuous trust in AI-based technology.

Schlicker and Langer [65] explored the relationship between user perceptions of trustworthiness and actual system trustworthiness using Brunswik's Lens Model and the Realistic Accuracy Model. They identified cues, which are observable pieces of information, as a means for users to assess the trustworthiness of a system. These cues can include the appearance of a user interface, information about the system's inputs and outputs, the classifier's displayed accuracy, information about uncertainty in classification outputs, a rationale for the system's recommendations, or the company logo [65].

While there was research conducted in recent years to propose trustworthy characteristics, principles, and guidelines, there is a lack of design heuristics that consider the perspective of users in order to help designers effectively communicate the trustworthy characteristics of technologies in a way that allows users to accurately assess the actual trustworthiness of the system and build trust.

3   Study Design

In this exploratory study, we aimed to improve our understanding of how users perceive the trustworthiness of advanced financial technology, specifically centralised cryptocurrency platforms, and to provide preliminary findings on factors that affect users' perception of trustworthiness. The survey study was followed by semi-structured interviews with the same sample. During the semi-structured interviews, the observation method was used to triangulate the data, with participants being asked to show how they use applications to assess trustworthiness. The collected data were analysed using descriptive statistics and a grounded theory approach. The mixed-method approach allowed us to understand the extent to which users trust cryptocurrency platforms and then explain why they trust them, identifying the factors that affect user perceptions of system trustworthiness. Our study follows a user-centred perspective, with a pragmatic influence and a focus on problem-solving [66]. However, the study has been paused to avoid biases due to a major cryptocurrency platform collapse in November 2022 [67].

3.1   Piloting

The pilot study had a similar structure to the main study, but some changes were made. Firstly, the object of the investigation was changed from real estate crowdfunding platforms to cryptocurrency platforms due to the broader spread of the latter. As a result of the low response rate to the planned interview among the 37 (N = 37) participants recruited through Amazon Mechanical Turk who completed the survey, it was decided to conduct in-person interviews and add a survey study as an additional preliminary step. For further study, we decided to use alternative channels for recruitment instead of Amazon Mechanical Turk. Finally, the survey stimuli of the trust assessment scale was modified during the second iteration of the pilot study. The stimuli was changed from a short video describing the risks of scams and fraud when using technology to a real-world scenario of money loss shared by one of the interview participants. This change was made in order to align the stimuli with the research objectives and to ensure that the survey was more relevant and engaging for the participants.

3.2 Survey

We conducted an unmoderated survey study in order to understand participants' propensity to risk, level of trust in technology, collect general data and data about participants' investment behaviour. During the screening process, participants provided consent to participate in the study and confirmed that they met the requirements of being over 18 years old and having experience using cryptocurrency platforms. The sample includes 12 (N = 12) users of cryptocurrency platforms living in Estonia, Tallinn. The sample consists of 3 females and 9 males ranging from 18 to 47. Participants were recruited through advertisements on Facebook and at Tallinn University. They were scheduled for in-person interviews and provided a link to an online platform to complete the unmoderated survey before the interview.

The survey consisted of several sections, including an introduction, screening, general information and investment experience, risk propensity and trust in cryptocurrency assessment, and open-ended questions about participants' assessment behaviour. The introduction provided information about the study's requirements, goals, and procedures. The general information section included demographic questions and questions about participants' experience using cryptocurrency platforms, the platforms they used, the frequency of their use, and the overall amount of cryptocurrency investment. This information was used to understand participants' investment profiles and inform user modelling to follow a user-centred approach.

The General Risk Propensity Scale (GRPS) was used to assess participants' tendency to take risks. Developed by Zhang et al. [68], this tool consists of a series of 8 questions that measure an individual's risk propensity. The Human-Computer Trust Scale [10] was also employed as a survey instrument to assess users' trust in technology based on Perceptions of risk, Benevolence, and Competence. The trust assessment section of the survey included a scenario that provided respondents with information about the nature of the technology and its risks and ensured a common understanding of the context among respondents [69]. This scenario was created using data from the pilot study and was based on a real user experience of loss.

In addition to these structured questions, the survey included several open-ended questions to understand participants' assessment behaviours. These questions were also used to sensitise participants for the upcoming interviews.

3.3   Interview with an Element of Observation

Semi-structured interviews were conducted with the same sample as the survey.

We used notes taking template for each participant to organise qualitative data during and after the interviews. The TEDW method, which promotes conversations over interviews by using open-ended questions such as "Tell me about...?", "Explain what you mean by...?", "Describe...", and "Walk me through..." was employed in this research study. By asking questions this way, we could elicit more detailed and comprehensive responses from participants rather than limiting them to simple yes or no answers. Additionally, the TEDW method was combined with a focus on asking about past experiences, which allowed for a deeper understanding of the participants' perspectives and experiences. This method helped to provide insights into the motivations and reasoning behind participants' actions and behaviours. During the interviews, we asked participants to show how they use platforms to assess trustworthiness, particularly platform features, visual cues, data visualisation and valuable information. We made photos of participants' screens to collect the data. The observation method was used to triangulate the data.

4   Data Analysis

The qualitative data was analysed using the ground theory method, a technique commonly used in human-computer interaction for data analysis (Muller and Kogan 2012). The open coding process was performed iteratively, forming categories with codes serving as subcategories (Alfarraj et al. 2015). The core category was identified, and the relationships between categories were established based on the research goal of identifying the factors affecting user perception of trustworthiness (Fig. 1). The main categories identified were Usability, Risk Mitigation, Level of Expertise, Credibility and Reliability. The analysis showed that the core category is Usability, which was mentioned by all 12 participants. It refers to how easy it is to use the platform, how easy it is to understand content and functionality, how easy it is to learn how to use the platform and how users are satisfied after having the experience of using it. In Sects. 5.1 and 5.2, the identified factors are discussed in more detail.

Due to the small sample size ($N = 12$) in the current study stage, there is low statistical validity and reliability of the overall scores obtained from the scales used. Therefore, the quantitative data can only provide a tendency of scores for each participant and serves to support the qualitative analysis.

To assess the reliability of the General Risk Propensity Scale (GRPS), we calculated Cronbach's alpha reliability coefficient, which should be above 0.7, according to Tavakol and Dennick [70]. The GRPS satisfied this condition with a Cronbach's alpha of 0.7 and an overall score of 3.3 (SD = 1.1). The Human-Computer Trust Scale (HCTS) data were analysed by constructs (Risk Perception, Benevolence, Competency and Overall Trust) and specific scale questions. The Risk Perception (RP) construct received the lowest score, 2.2 (SD = 1.05), with a Cronbach's alpha of 0.7, indicating that users perceive the object of investigation as risky. The question "I believe that there could be negative consequences when using the Cryptocurrency platform" received the lowest score in the Risk Perception (RP) construct, with a score of 1.8, indicating that users believed that there could be negative consequences when using the platform.

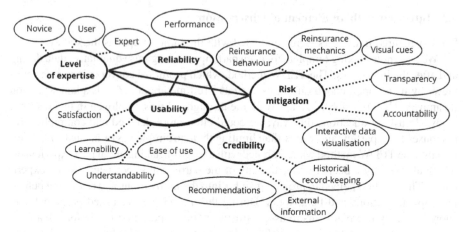

Fig. 1. Core category, main categories, and subcategories relationships

5 Results

The results identify the following factors affecting users' perceptions of trustworthiness in advanced financial technologies: Usability, Credibility, Risk Mitigation, Reliability, and Level of Expertise. These factors, namely Usability, Credibility, Risk Mitigation, and Reliability, can be considered advanced technology trustworthy characteristics, whereas the Level of Expertise is a user characteristic.

In this research, we have adopted a user-centred perspective and have presented the preliminary results referring to the factor of user characteristics in the form of user persona defined as hypothetical archetypes of actual users [71]. However, it is important to note that the persona presented here is a draft based on preliminary findings that will need further verification with additional data. User persona provides a detailed understanding of the users' archetype motivations, goals, behaviour, needs and frustrations.

Section 5.2 describes identified factors that affect users' perceptions of trustworthiness and can be considered as trustworthy characteristics of advanced financial technologies.

5.1 Level of Expertise in Technology: The User Characteristic Affecting Perceptions of Trustworthiness in Advanced Financial Technologies

During the analysis, we identified three levels of expertise in technology adopting Lui et al. [72] classification that influences participants' trustworthiness and risk assessment behaviour: Expert, User, and Novice. An "Expert" is someone who has a strong understanding of the core knowledge in a domain and can answer most questions about it, having detailed knowledge of specific subtopics within the domain and being proficient in using any related tools. A "User" has some advanced knowledge and can provide relatively good answers but lacks a thorough understanding of basic concepts and is not proficient in advanced knowledge within a domain. They can use one or a few tools with a graphical interface related to their domain of expertise. A "Novice" is someone who is just starting to learn about a domain and is asking questions about basic concepts. They are also learning how to use a tool with a graphical interface related to their domain of expertise. In this context, a "Tool" refers to advanced technology with either a hard interface or a graphical interface.

Sensitising research data, we created a draft of Expert persona referring to their motivations, goals, behaviour, needs and frustrations when interacting with cryptocurrency platforms.

An Expert User Persona (Draft). About: Mark is a 37-year-old man from Tallinn, Es-tonia, who is an expert in blockchain technology and cryptocurrency. He is an active investor in cryptocurrency, with a significant portfolio worth over 10,000 euros, which is 50-70% of his overall investments. Mark is highly skilled in trading. His goal is to maximise returns on his investments while minimising his risks. He believes it is generally safe to use established platforms with a long history and are well-trusted. Alt-hough Mark perceives cryptocurrency as risky, he is enjoying the trading process.

[P7] "… I trusted the legacy. A platform that has been about for many years. You should never add funds to a new platform unless you know and understand you can trust it. The biggest exchanges are already established."

Behaviour: Mark assesses risks using real-time data visualisation tools and carefully evaluates the liquidity and credibility of platforms before making trades. He also takes into account the insurance strategies of the platforms he uses. Mark uses different platforms to trade specific coins to diversify his portfolio and optimise his trades. He makes trading decisions according to his own assumptions and analysis. After completing a trade, he promptly transfers the coins to a cold wallet, which is not connected to the internet, to reduce the risk of security breaches. Mark is familiar with advanced features, such as the API functionality for Binance Staking, and has knowledge of DeFi protocols, which he uses in conjunction with his ledger:

[P7] "I use the platforms for leveraged investment only. The rest, I prefer DeFi".

[P6] "… They are just about to release a transparency feature for owners of the funds, and we can actually assess the stake by API and perform a full audit of everything they are holding now."

He is comfortable with high-risk investments such as futures but uses the stop-loss function to constrain potential losses. Despite knowing that decentralised exchanges and hard wallets are generally safer, Mark prefers centralised platforms for trading due to their convenience and efficiency. He keeps up-to-date on the latest news about cryptocurrency by following Twitter and other channels.

Needs: He requires flexibility in the setting of data visualisation to meet his individual needs, as well as a clear and user-friendly interface. He also places importance on platform transparency, including the API access on the core technology provided by the platform and the ability to compare prices and track transaction information. Mark is waiting when DeFi protocol applications became more efficient and convenient.

[P7] "And I would say, like UX wise, it's still a way to go to be more simplified because take your Metamask that is the biggest wallet of all. And it's still buggy as hell, and you have to do so many steps to pay for your lunch. "

He believes that it is necessary to have more legal regulations for blockchain and cryptocurrency technology.

[P6] "… no, so like, stop technology advancing, but just be regulated enough that it can't collapse like FTX did."

Frustrations: Centralized platforms can collapse, even older ones. Mark knows that hard wallets are more trustworthy, but he uses exchange platforms due to their convenience and efficiency. However, he does not recommend storing money or coins on exchange platforms due to the risk of security breaches. He also has concerns about losing or damaging his ledger.

[P7] "…., if I look back, I know all the risks. I know that using a decentralised exchange, and my ledger is a lot safer. But I still use a centralised exchange, and the reason is convenience."

5.2   Factors Affecting User Perception of Trustworthiness in Advanced Technology

The following factors affected users' perceptions of trustworthiness in advanced financial technologies: Usability, Credibility, Risk Mitigation, and Reliability. Mentioned factors can be considered advanced technology trustworthy characteristics.

Provided trustworthy characteristics contribute to further developing design heuristics to support practitioners in promoting trust when developing advanced technologies.

Usability.   In this context, usability is a system quality factor that assesses the plat-form's ease of use in achieving user goals and completing tasks, the comprehensibility of the platform's content and functionality, and the degree to which the platform facilitates user learning [74]. Usability also encompasses user satisfaction, which is the user's response to interaction with the platform and includes attitudes towards its use [74]. Furthermore, it refers to the degree to which user needs are satisfied when a plat-form is used. The usability issues and complex user interface of cryptocurrency plat-forms are obstacles to technology acceptance and adoption. In other words, there is a tendency to use less trustworthy but easier and more convenient systems [75]. For instance, Novice users noticed that it is difficult to understand how starting to use the platform and highlighted a need for support in their first steps in comprehending what to do and how it works.

[P10] "In bank trading app, I have got training on how to use the app to invest; it helps me a lot."

[P4] "So, Binance is really difficult and complex. The learning curve can be high, especially if you do not understand what you are doing and all these cryptocurrency terms."

[P10] "If I do not understand, I do not use."

[P11] "As a beginner, I was looking for something easy to use and clear. Like: exchange rate - buy/sell the click. That is why I preferred OKX over Binance."

There are well-established ways to assess the system's usability [59] and user satisfaction [75]. From the perspective of the Human-Computer Trust Model, we can assume that Usability links to the Competency construct, which refers to the perceived ease with which a user can use the system to complete a task successfully. A system with high levels of satisfaction is likely to be recommended by its users to others, as people are more likely to recommend products or services they are satisfied with. Therefore, usability relates to other identified trustworthy factor, namely, Credibility.

Credibility. Credibility is a measure of the confidence that others have in the accuracy and validity of the information or results produced by a system [77]. It is often considered a key predictor of trust in technologies [78], as it reflects the perceived competence and expertise of the system. Our study's results showed that the platform's credibility was one of the main factors in the participants' perceptions of trustworthiness. Some participants cited recommendations from friends and social media, community choice, and the platform's reputation, contributing to its credibility.

[P3] "I trust it because a lot of people are using it".

[P4] "I followed some advice from my friend, whom I trust."

[P6] "I know they've got lots of Twitter followers."

[P7] "So, you trust those who survive, so time is an element that you cannot cheat; in a sense, they have been around for a very long time."

In other words, a technology that is perceived as credible is more likely to be trusted because it is seen as knowledgeable and capable. It can help to mitigate risk by reducing uncertainty and increasing the likelihood that a desired outcome will be achieved. According to the Human-Computer Trust Model, credibility can support users' subjective evaluations of the potential threats and consequences a system poses, which relates to the construct of Risk Perception. Therefore, Credibility is an essential factor which is interconnected in our study with the Risk Mitigation factor.

Risk Mitigation. It is worth noting that, according to the results of the Human-Computer Trust Scale in our study, the participants perceived cryptocurrency platforms as risky but still used the technology to achieve their goals. In addition, Risk Mitigation was a frequent topic of discussion during the interviews. We defined Risk Mitigation as the strategies or techniques used to reduce the risks associated with a system or to mitigate the consequences of potential failures or disruptions. Interactive real-time data visualisation was found to be a helpful tool for participants in mitigating risk by allowing them to analyse financial trends and compare digital asset prices. Most participants used external applications for this purpose because they were more flexible in terms of customisation. This is a context-specific factor that is commonly used in investing and trading. In addition to analysing trends, the visualisation also displayed users' activity in buying and selling assets, which supported participants' decision-making.

Furthermore, the participants mentioned that platforms use visual cues, such as badges and risk indicators, to communicate trustworthiness. For example, in peer-to-peer transactions, some users display a verification badge, which was perceived as trustworthy by the participants. However, they were unsure what the badge signifies or how to obtain it. When opening a margin account, which allows a user to borrow funds, the platform may provide a risk indicator in graphical and numeric form. The users perceived this indicator as a risk management mechanism and a trustworthy cue that helped them to assess risk.

Additionally, the participants in our study noted that certain platforms had implemented reinsurance policies to enhance user trust. One such platform is Binance, which was highly popular among the participants. Binance has established the Secure Asset

Fund for Users (SAFU), valued at 1 billion dollars [78]. According to Binance, the company has dedicated a portion of its trading fees towards growing the fund in an effort to protect its users. In addition, Binance offers an API for Staking technology to promote transparency for asset owners. Coinbase, another popular platform, has made its financial reports publicly available in order to promote accountability. These measures were perceived as trustworthy by the participants. Moreover, it was noticed that participants have behavioural patterns when using the system, periodically assessing risk and how the system meets their expectations. They prefer to control their losses by using the platform's constraint features, for instance, the stop-loss feature on Binance. Additionally, participants compare their options regarding different attributes, for example, peer attributes for peer-to-peer transactions (verification badge, number of successful operations, etc.) or compare gains and losses in futures trading. However, Binance provides the amount of profit when placing a bet for futures; it does not show losses if the user's bet is wrong. It was mentioned as a disadvantage of Binance because the user must manually calculate losses.

According to the ISO/IEC 25010:2010 System and Software Quality Requirements and Evaluation standard, the quality in use characteristic of Freedom of Risk refers to the extent to which a product or system mitigates potential risks to economic status, human life, health, or the environment [79]. Additionally, the ISO 9241-11 Ergonomics of human-system interaction states that a system should provide appropriate outcomes to avoid negative consequences and risks [73]. There is potential for future research in the field of Human-Computer Interaction (HCI) to explore how risk management can be incorporated into the design for trust and how it impacts users' perceptions of trustworthiness. This could include identifying risky moments that appeared during the user experience when reassurance is needed, examining the various strategies and techniques that can be used to mitigate risks, and evaluating the role that these play in building trust with users.

Reliability. During the analysis, we established a category called Reliability, which refers to the ability of an advanced system to maintain a specific level of performance under specified conditions [80]. The participants in our study identified system performance under high demand as a trustworthy factor. However, for some participants, low-performance levels did not significantly impact their choice of platform. Instead, they placed more emphasis on the credibility of the platform. In addition, according to the participants' perceptions, system failures were seen as scams. It is noticed that plat-forms did not track harmful failures or report them.

[P4] "... last trades were like scammed by Binance. My trades were not closed when they reached the level of my Take. And I did not see any comments provided by Binance about it. So yeah. It's really bad. And I am thinking about moving to Bybit. "

[P5] "I was trying to withdraw some money. And it didn't work for some reason. I find it hard to actually reach customer service. So I had to google online and follow the other people having the same problems."

In the context of technology, Reliability is often considered a key aspect of trustworthiness, as it reflects the ability of the system to perform as expected and to deliver on its promises [40, 50, 79]. However, further research may find it less significant to investigate due to its technical nature.

5.3   Future Works

This paper presents preliminary results from research that is currently in progress. We plan to collect data from an additional 18 participants to enrich the current results. It is also planned to generalise the findings using another subject of investigation, and it will be other advanced technologies perceived by users as nondeterministic. These preliminary results guide future literature review on risk mitigation behaviour and design in advanced technologies. Additionally, future research should consider user characteristics, defined as the Level of Expertise in technology that impacts user perception of trustworthiness in a way that Novice users who are less proficient in a field and platform application are more vulnerable to losses [81] and require more support to assess the system's trustworthiness [26, 27]. Furthermore, trust is a dynamic concept that changes over time. Therefore, future investigations need to examine separately how trustworthy factors influence initial trust and how trust can be maintained or adjusted over time. In order to narrow the scope of the research, the further study will focus its attention on Novice users who are in the process of forming initial trust with technology.

5.4   Limitations

This research investigates cryptocurrency exchange platforms, which are a specific type of financial technology application. Users of these platforms require experience in investment and trading due to the presence of various terms and processes related to traditional financial investment. Incorporating data from other relevant subjects of investigation may provide more comprehensive results and enhance preliminary findings.

The sample size in this study is not large enough for quantitative analysis, but it was used to inform the outcomes of qualitative analysis.

Overall, there is insufficient data to generalise trustworthy design heuristics, and further empirical research is required.

6   Conclusion

This research towards the design of trustworthy heuristics explores how users perceive trustworthiness in advanced financial technology. The preliminary results justify the notion that design for the trust should refer to a socio-technical approach. We identify the following factors to support the design of trustworthy technologies: Usability, Credibility, Risk mitigation, and Reliability. Besides, the Level of Expertise was found as a user characteristic that affects the perception of technology trustworthiness.

The identified factors relate to prior research that explores trustworthiness and trust. Usability, Credibility, and Reliability are widely recognised attributes contributing to users' perceptions of trustworthiness [32, 61, 73, 79]. Some studies [12, 33] suggest that the Level of Expertise is also a key factor in building trust. Risk Mitigation can be linked to software engineering and ergonomic standards, aiming to ensure the quality of use and minimise negative consequences and risks [73, 79]. To a certain extent, Risk Mitigation can be connected to the HCTM Risk Perception construct. Likewise, Usability and Reliability are related to the HCTM constructs of Competence and Benevolence. The

380   I. Paramonova et al.

Level of Expertise aligns with the Ability component in the Mayer et al. [12] model of interpersonal trustworthiness. Furthermore, Mayer et al. highlight that Perceived Risk plays a critical role in shaping interpersonal relationships [12]. Thus, it is vital to understand how to reassure users and reduce risk during the trust formation process. Further research is needed to justify identified trustworthy factors with other advanced technology targeting a precise population according to the level of expertise in technology. Justified trustworthy factors conceptualised with theoretical literature will form the set of heuristics to support practitioners in designing trustworthy advanced technologies.

Funding. This research was funded by the Trust and Influence Programme [FA8655–22-1-7051], the European Office of Aerospace Research and Development, and the US Air Force Office of Scientific Research.

References

1. Magee, C. L., de Weck, O. L.: 3.1. 3 complex system classification. In: INCOSE International Symposium, vol. 14, No. 1, pp. 471–488 (2004, June)
2. Spongberg, M., Curthoys, A., Caine, B.: K. In: Spongberg, M., Curthoys, A., Caine, B. (eds.) Companion to Women's Historical Writing, pp. 300–303. Palgrave Macmillan UK, London (2005). https://doi.org/10.1007/978-1-349-72468-0_11
3. Cilliers, P.: Complexity and Postmodernism: Understanding Complex Systems. Routledge, London (2002)
4. Adadi, A., Berrada, M.: Peeking inside the black-box: a survey on explainable artificial intelligence (XAI). IEEE Access **6**, 52138–52160 (2018)
5. Lewis, J.D., Weigert, A.: Trust as a social reality. Soc. Forces **63**(4), 967–985 (1985)
6. Möllering, G.: The nature of trust: from Georg Simmel to a theory of expectation, interpretation and suspension. Sociology **35**(2), 403–420 (2001)
7. LeRoy, S.F., Singell, L.D., Jr.: Knight on risk and uncertainty. J. Polit. Econ. **95**(2), 394–406 (1987)
8. Levy, J.S.: An introduction to prospect theory. Polit. Psychol. **13**, 171–186 (1992)
9. Hudson, B.: Trust: towards conceptual clarification. Aust. J. Polit. Sci. **39**(1), 75–87 (2004)
10. Gulati, S., Sousa, S., Lamas, D.: Design, development and evaluation of a human-computer trust scale. Behav. Inf. Technol. **38**(10), 1004–1015 (2019)
11. Lankton, N.K., McKnight, D.H., Tripp, J.: Technology, humanness, and trust: rethinking trust in technology. J. Assoc. Inf. Syst. **16**(10), 1 (2015)
12. Mayer, R.C., Davis, J.H., Schoorman, F.D.: An integrative model of organizational trust. Acad. Manag. Rev. **20**(3), 709–734 (1995)
13. Markus, A.F., Kors, J.A., Rijnbeek, P.R.: The role of explainability in creating trustworthy artificial intelligence for health care: a comprehensive survey of the terminology, design choices, and evaluation strategies. J. Biomed. Inform. **113**, 103655 (2021)
14. Larasati, R., De Liddo, A., Motta, E.: AI healthcare system interface: explanation design for non-expert user trust. In: ACMIUI-WS 2021: Joint Proceedings of the ACM IUI 2021 Workshops (2903). http://ceur-ws.org/Vol-2903/IUI21WS-TExSS-11.pdf
15. Papagni, G., Koeszegi, S.: Understandable and trustworthy explainable robots: a sensemaking perspective Paladyn. J. Behav. Robot. **12**(1), 13–30 (2021)
16. Murawski, J.: Mortgage providers look to ai to process home loans faster. Wall Str. J. **18**(2019)
17. Graham-Harrison, E., Cadwalladr, C.: Revealed: 50 million Facebook profiles harvested for Cambridge Analytica in major data breach (2018, March 17). The Guardian. https://amp.the guardian.com/news/2018/mar/17/cambridge-analytica-facebook-influence-us-election

18. Matsakis, L.: The subtle tricks shopping sites use to make you spend more (2020, August 6). Wired. https://www.wired.com/story/amazon-online-retail-dark-patterns/
19. Ahmed, S.: Who inadvertently shares deepfakes? Analyzing the role of political interest, cognitive ability, and social network size. Telematics Inform. **57**, 101508 (2021)
20. Eiband, M., Schneider, H., Buschek, D.: Normative vs. pragmatic: two perspectives on the design of explanations in intelligent systems. In: IUI Workshops (2018)
21. Diprose, W.K., Buist, N., Hua, N., Thurier, Q., Shand, G., Robinson, R.: Physician understanding, explainability, and trust in a hypothetical machine learning risk calculator. J. Am. Med. Inform. Assoc. **27**(4), 592–600 (2020)
22. Ribes, D. et al.: Trust indicators and explainable ai: a study on user perceptions. In: Human-Computer Interaction – INTERACT 2021. INTERACT 2021 LNCS, vol. 12933. Springer, Cham (2021). https://doi.org/10.1007/978-3-030-85616-8_39
23. Weber, T., Hußmann, H., Eiband, M.: Quantifying the demand for explainability. Hum. Comput. Interact. **2021**, 652–661 (2021)
24. Fröhlich, M., Waltenberger, F., Trotter, L., Alt, F., Schmidt, A.: Blockchain and cryptocurrency in human computer interaction: a systematic literature review and research agenda. arXiv preprint arXiv:2204.10857(2022)
25. Adamik, F., Kosta, S.: SmartExchange: Decentralised trustless cryptocurrency exchange. In: Business Information Systems Workshops, pp. 356–367 (2019)
26. Fröhlich, M., Kobiella, C., Schmidt, A., Alt, F.: Is it better with onboarding? Improving first-time cryptocurrency app experiences. In: Designing Interactive Systems Conference 2021, pp. 78–89, 2021, June
27. Glomann, L., Schmid, M., Kitajewa, N.: Improving the blockchain user experience - an approach to address blockchain mass adoption issues from a human-centred perspective. In: Ahram, T. (ed.) AHFE 2019. AISC, vol. 965, pp. 608–616. Springer, Cham (2020). https://doi.org/10.1007/978-3-030-20454-9_60
28. Amershi, S., et al.: Guidelines for human-AI interaction. In: Proceedings of the 2019 CHI Conference on Human Factors in Computing Systems, pp. 1–13 (2019, May)
29. Jacovi, A., Marasović, A., Miller, T., Goldberg, Y. Formalizing trust in artificial intelligence: prerequisites, causes and goals of human trust in AI. In: Proceedings of the 2021 ACM Conference on Fairness, Accountability, and Transparency, pp. 624–635 (2021, March
30. Chatila, R., et al.: Trustworthy AI. In: Braunschweig, B., Ghallab, M. (eds.) Reflections on Artificial Intelligence for Humanity. LNCS (LNAI), vol. 12600, pp. 13–39. Springer, Cham (2021). https://doi.org/10.1007/978-3-030-69128-8_2
31. High-Level Expert Group on AI, Ethics guidelines for trustworthy AI, 2019, European Commission. https://www.aepd.es/sites/default/files/2019-12/ai-ethics-guidelines.pdf
32. Mcknight, D.H., Carter, M., Thatcher, J.B., Clay, P.F.: Trust in a specific technology: an investigation of its components and measures. ACM Trans. Manag. Inform. Syst. **2**(2), 1–25 (2011)
33. Caldwell, C., Clapham, S.E.: Organizational trustworthiness: an international perspective. J. Bus. Ethics **47**(4), 349–364 (2003)
34. Luhmann, N.: Trust and Power. p. 103, Wiley (2018)
35. Giddens, A.: The Consequences of Modernity, p. 27. Polity Press, Cambridge (1990)
36. Vilone, G., Longo, L.: Explainable artificial intelligence: a systematic review. arXiv preprint arXiv:2006.00093 (2020)
37. Pearson, S., Benameur, A.: Privacy, security and trust issues arising from cloud computing. In: 2010 IEEE Second International Conference on Cloud Computing Technology and Science, pp. 693–702. IEEE (2010, November)
38. Hoekstra, M., Lal, R., Pappachan, P., Phegade, V., Del Cuvillo, J.: Using innovative instructions to create trustworthy software solutions. HASP@ ISCA, **11**(10.1145), 2487726–2488370 (20130)

39. Rizal Batubara, F., Ubacht, J., Janssen, M.: Unraveling transparency and accountability in blockchain. In: Proceedings of the 20th Annual International Conference on Digital Government Research, pp. 204–213 (2019, June)
40. Ryan, M.: In AI we trust: ethics, artificial intelligence, and reliability. Sci. Eng. Ethics 26(5), 2749–2767 (2020)
41. Sousa, S., Lamas, D., Dias, P.: A model for Human-computer Trust. In: Zaphiris, P., Ioannou, A. (eds.) LCT 2014. LNCS, vol. 8523, pp. 128–137. Springer, Cham (2014). https://doi.org/ 10.1007/978-3-319-07482-5_13
42. Compeau, D. R., Higgins, C.A.: Computer self-efficacy: development of a measure and initial test. MIS Q.18, 189–211 (1995)
43. McKnight, D.H., Choudhury, V., Kacmar, C.: Developing and validating trust measures for e-Commerce: an integrative typology. J. Inf. Syst. Res. 13(3), 334–359 (2002)
44. McKnight, D.H., Cummings, L.L., Chervany, N.L.: Initial trust formation in new organizational relationships. Acad. Manag. Rev. 23(3), 473–490 (1998)
45. Kim, P.H., Dirks, K.T., Cooper, C.D.: The repair of trust: a dynamic bilateral perspective and multilevel conceptualization. Acad. Manag. Rev. 34(3), 401–422 (2009)
46. Lui, A., Lamb, G.W.: Artificial intelligence and augmented intelligence collaboration: regaining trust and confidence in the financial sector. Inf. Commun. Technol. Law 27(3), 267–283 (2018)
47. Hoffman, R.R., Johnson, M., Bradshaw, J.M., Underbrink, A.: Trust in automation. IEEE Intell. Syst. 28(1), 84–88 (2013)
48. Lee, M., Frank, L., IJsselsteijn, W.: Brokerbot: A cryptocurrency chatbot in the social-technical gap of trust. Comput. Supp. Cooper. Work 30(1), 79–117 (2021)
49. Nickel, P.J., Franssen, M., Kroes, P.: Can we make sense of the notion of trustworthy technology? Knowl. Technol. Policy 23(3), 429–444 (2010)
50. Hasselbring, W., Reussner, R.: Toward trustworthy software systems. Computer 39(4), 91–92 (2006)
51. Lee, J.D., See, K.A.: Trust in automation: designing for appropriate reliance. Hum. Fact. 46(1), 50–80 (2004)
52. Hamon, R., Junklewitz, H., Sanchez, I.: Robustness and Explainability of Artificial Intelligence. Publications Office of the European Union (2020)
53. Bird, S., et al.: Fairlearn: A toolkit for assessing and improving fairness in AI. Microsoft, Tech. Rep. MSR-TR-2020-32 (2021)
54. Thiebes, S., Lins, S., Sunyaev, A.: Trustworthy artificial intelligence. Electron. Mark. 31(2), 447–464 (2020). https://doi.org/10.1007/s12525-020-00441-4
55. Smuha, N.: The EU approach to ethics guidelines for trustworthy artificial intelligence. Comput. Law Rev. Internat. 20(4), 97–106 (2019). https://doi.org/10.9785/cri-2019-200402
56. UK House of Lords. AI in the UK: ready, willing and able? (2017). https://publications.par liament.uk/pa/ld201719/ ldselect/ldai/100/10002.htm
57. OECD Recommendation of the Council on Artificial Intelligence, OECD/LEGAL/0449 (2019). https://legalinstruments.oecd.org/en/instruments/OECD-LEGAL-0449
58. Vought, R.T.: Guidance for Regulation of Artificial Intelligence Applications (2019). https:// www.whitehouse.gov/wp-content/uploads/2020/01/Draft-OMB-Memo-on-Regulation-of-AI-1-7-19.pdf
59. Nielsen, J.: Enhancing the explanatory power of usability heuristics. In: Proceedings of the SIGCHI Conference on Human Factors in Computing Systems, pp. 152–158 (1994)
60. Gol Mohammadi, N., et al.: Trustworthiness Attributes and metrics for engineering trusted internet-based software systems. In: Helfert, M., Desprez, F., Ferguson, D., Leymann, F. (eds.) Cloud Computing and Services Science. CLOSER 2013. Communications in Computer and Information Science, vol. 453, pp. 19–35 Springer, Cham (2013, May). https://doi.org/10. 1007/978-3-319-11561-0_2

61. Nielsen, J.: Trust or bust: communicating trustworthiness in web design (1999, March 6)
62. Shneiderman, B.: Designing trust into online experiences. Commun. ACM **43**(12), 57–59 (2000)
63. Borg, M., et al.: Exploring the assessment list for trustworthy AI in the context of advanced driver-assistance systems (2021). *arXiv [cs.CY]*. arXiv. http://arxiv.org/abs/2103.09051
64. Siau, K., Wang, W.: Building trust in artificial intelligence, machine learning, and robotics. Cutter Bus Technol. J. **31**(2), 47–53 (2018)
65. Schlicker, N., Langer, M.: Towards warranted trust: a model on the relation between actual and perceived system trustworthiness. Proc. Mensch Und Comput. **2021**, 325–329 (2021)
66. Oulasvirta, A., Hornbæk, K.: HCI research as problem-solving. In: Proceedings of the 2016 CHI Conference on Human Factors in Computing Systems. CHI 2016: CHI Conference on Human Factors in Computing Systems, San Jose, California, USA (2016, May 7). https://doi.org/10.1145/2858036.2858283
67. Yaffe-Bellany, D.: Sam Bankman-Fried Blames "Huge Management Failures" for FTX Collapse. The New York Times (2022, November 30). https://www.nytimes.com/2022/11/30/business/sam-bankman-fried-ftx-collapse.html
68. Zhang, D.C., Highhouse, S., Nye, C.D.: Development and validation of the general risk propensity scale (GRiPS). J. Behav. Decis. Mak. **32**(2), 152–167 (2019)
69. Rosson, M.B., Carroll, J.M.: Scenario based design. Chapter 53 in Jacko, J., Sears, A. (eds.), The Human-Computer Interaction Handbook: Fundamentals, Evolving Technologies and Emerging Applications. Lawrence Erlbaum Associates, 2009, pp. 1032–1050 (2009)
70. Tavakol, M., Dennick, R.: Making sense of Cronbach's alpha. Int. J. Med. Educ. **2**, 53 (2011)
71. Cooper, A., Reimann, R., Cronin, D., Noessel, C.: About Face: the Essentials of Interaction Design. Wiley (2014)
72. Liu, X., Wang, G.A., Johri, A., Zhou, M., Fan, W.: Harnessing global expertise: a comparative study of expertise profiling methods for online communities. Inf. Syst. Front. **16**(4), 715–727 (2012). https://doi.org/10.1007/s10796-012-9385-6
73. Bevan, N., Carter, J., Harker, S.: ISO 9241-11 revised: What have we learnt about usability since 1998? In: Kurosu, M. (ed.) HCI 2015. LNCS, vol. 9169, pp. 143–151. Springer, Cham (2015). https://doi.org/10.1007/978-3-319-20901-2_13
74. Casare, A.R., Da Silva, C.G., Basso, T., Moraes, R.: Towards usability interface trustworthiness in e-commerce systems. In: International Conferences Interfaces and Human Computer Interaction (2021)
75. Brooke, J.: SUS: a 'quick and dirty' usability. Usability evaluation in industry, Redhatch Consulting Ltd (2021). 189. https://hell.meiert.org/core/pdf/sus.pdf. Accessed June 2021
76. Tseng, S., Fogg, B.J.: Credibility and computing technology. Commun. ACM **42**(5), 39–44 (1999)
77. Sbaffi, L., Rowley, J.: Trust and credibility in web-based health information: a review and agenda for future research. J. Med. Internet Res. **19**(6), e7579 (2017)
78. Binance. Topping up SAFU to $1B, Binance Blog (9 November 2022). https://www.binance.com/en/blog/community/topping-up-safu-to-$1b-8460049926432191856
79. Atoum, I., Bong, C.H., Kulathuramaiyer, N.: Towards resolving software quality-in-use measurement challenges (2015). *arXiv preprint* arXiv:1501.07676
80. Miguel, J.P., Mauricio, D., Rodríguez, G.: A review of software quality models for the evaluation of software products (2014). *arXiv preprint* arXiv:1412.2977
81. Kim, C. Y., Lee, K.: Risk management to cryptocurrency exchange and investors guidelines to prevent potential threats. In: 2018 International Conference on Platform Technology and Service (PlatCon). JEJU (2018, January). https://doi.org/10.1109/platcon.2018.8472760

Am I Like Me? Avatar Self-similarity and Satisfaction in a Professional Training Environment

Monika Pröbster[1]([⊠]) [iD], Ronja-Debora Tomaske-Graff[2] [iD], Doris Herget[2],
Martina Lucht[2] [iD], and Nicola Marsden[1] [iD]

[1] Heilbronn University, Max-Planck-Street 39, 74081 Heilbronn, Germany
monika.proebster@gmail.com
[2] WBS Gruppe, Lorenzweg 5, 12099 Berlin, Germany

Abstract. In virtual environments, avatars are used to represent users. Previous research focusing on video games has found that similarity of self and avatar leads to higher satisfaction with one's avatar. We extend the existing research by examining avatar use in a real-world professional training setting. We asked 472 participants in a full-time online training program about their avatars in their 3D learning environment, i.e., about their satisfaction with their avatars, how similar their avatar was to them, reasons for avatar choice and switching, modifications, and suggestions for improvements. We found that higher self-similarity with one's avatar leads to greater satisfaction with the avatar and that this effect was partly related to participant gender, with women considering avatar self-similarity as more important than men. Moreover, we found differential patterns for avatar use for female and male participants. Based on our findings, we argue that avatars should represent the diversity that exists in the users to allow for greater identification and for the resulting benefits, since having an avatar that is similar to oneself might improve the experience for all users and help to close a gender fairness-gap that exists regarding a positive learning environment.

Keywords: Avatars · Stereotypes · Online training · Empirical study

1 Introduction

Professional training is increasingly taking place online. To heighten learner engagement, some learning platforms are highly immersive, offering a 3D environment in which the learners are represented by avatars. Avatars are considered to serve as extensions of the self, thus, users can identify with them and allow them to navigate a virtual world, as well as interact with their environment and other users [1]. The rising popularity of online platforms, games and digital activities has spurred a wave of research on avatars and their uses, identifying various effects that different avatars have on their users as well as other factors that influence avatar perception, customization and use itself (for a review see [2]). A considerable number of studies focuses on users' relation to their own avatars and their identification with their avatars. Several studies found that a higher self-similarity with one's avatar can increase one's identification with the avatar [4, 13–15]. Higher identification with one's avatar can also positively affect learning [15].

P. Zaphiris and A. Ioannou (Eds.): HCII 2023, LNCS 14040, pp. 384–400, 2023.
https://doi.org/10.1007/978-3-031-34411-4_26

Although these effects, especially regarding learning, seem to be highly relevant in educational settings, previous studies mainly focused on (online) gaming and related fields such as *Second Life*. There is little research on avatar perception in professional education settings and the existing research usually does not focus on avatar perception and identification [16]. Studies on avatars in online-gaming also often concentrated problematic and addictive behaviors in relation to avatars (see Green et al. for a review [17]).

As avatars also integrate and reflect social values and social norms [18, 19], different types of avatars may deemed appropriate in professional training or work-related contexts as compared to recreational settings [18]. Furthermore, a lot of studies have been done with a younger demographic (e.g., university students), whereas the age range of the participants in further education is usually much broader and people are also older on average. However, the representation of older and middle-aged people with avatars has its special challenges, including the avoidance of stereotypical representations, as well as considering different perspectives and needs of these user's groups regarding their avatars [20]. Additionally, effects observed in online games and related settings may differ from those relevant in professional education, as the contexts, incentives and motivations of the users are different. To close this research gap, we examined the perception of avatars in an immersive educational platform used by a major provider of professional training in Germany.

2 Related Work

2.1 Avatar Perception

Virtual worlds can be defined as immersive 3D environments that enable users to interact with one another via the internet and are usually either game-based or social based worlds. They are increasingly used in professional training settings [21]. Avatars serve as a means to navigate and interact with these virtual worlds. Users can experience the activities via manipulating, crafting, and personalizing these avatars [22, 23]. They may vary highly in terms of looks and functionalities, however, they are usually used as a representation of the self. People can identify with them i.e., merging temporarily their avatar's identities with their own self-perception [1]. This way, users understand and attach themselves to their avatar as a second self, representing one's role in virtual environment and as a means to communicate and interact with other users, thus also serving social functions [23, 24].

Identification is one of the reasons why experiencing media is enjoyable [25], e.g., in literature or television, where people adopt the protagonists emotions, experiences, and objectives and feel with the characters [25, 26]. However, one main difference between characters in these media and avatars in virtual worlds, e.g., gaming, is that the users have direct control over the behavior and actions of their "character" and the distance between players and their avatars diminishes [1].

Professional training in virtual worlds often happens in social settings, e.g., groups of people participate in the same course and/or work together on assignments. As identification is one of the key elements of avatar perception, social identity theory [27] can provide further insights on avatar perception and user-avatar relation. Basically, people categorize themselves and others based on individual and social categories [28]. They establish personal identity based on individual attributes and qualities. Social identity is based on similarities with others. Besides referring to the memberships in specific groups, such as sports teams, these similarities can be derived from broader categories such as gender, ethnicity, age—depending on how relevant a person deems this category for her- or himself [29]. Customizing one's avatar in line with categories that seem relevant to oneself thus allows for more identification and can serve as a means to express one's group membership.

2.2 Avatar Self-similarity and Identification

The similarity of an avatar to the player—a factor users can usually influence by customizing their avatar—has been found to be one of the main factors contributing to identification with one's avatar [8]. Especially if the similarity of the avatar to oneself is high, players feel more connected with their avatar [1]. Moreover, people have been shown to be more empathic towards avatars which they customized themselves compared to generic ones [30].

Avatar self-similarity has been shown to be positively related to identification with the avatar in a range of studies. Trepte [4] found a connection between avatar self-similarity and identification with the avatar, which enhanced the enjoyment experience of a game. It needs to be noted that the correlation of self-similarity and identification was stronger for avatars used in non-competitive games than in competitive games. Furthermore, Birk et al. [5] replicated these findings and found that customizing avatars lead to higher identification and, likewise, customizing an avatar resulted in significantly less attrition and more sustained engagement in a digital self-improvement program. Further studies found that players often prefer avatars that are similar to them with regard to gender role, outward appearance and biological sex [31–33]. Self-similarity was positively related to game enjoyment, too [31]. Research related to the virtual interaction platform *Second Life* also shows that users prefer same sex avatars, as 82% chose an avatar with their real gender and only 4% of women users chose a male avatar and 14% of men chose a female avatar [32]. Analogously, in a study on avatars in social VR by Freeman et al., participants expressed a strong desire for "being myself" via their avatars [3]. Soutter et al. [34] found that avatar self-similarity increased identification with the avatar—which in turn was strongly related to experiencing a flow state, i.e., a state of deep immersion full of enjoyment in the process of the activity [35]. Positive effects of self-similarity are not limited to visual likeness of one's avatar, but can also stem from voice similarity, which lead to an increase in performance, time spent, similarity identification, competence, relatedness, and immersion [36]. In another study on game performance, avatar self-identification promoted player experience, intrinsic motivation, and self-efficacy, as well as performance [9].

Generally speaking, identification with media characters can be differentiated between "similarity identification" and "wishful identification" [37]. Regarding avatar identification, three subcomponents can be differentiated: self-similarity, wishful identification and embodied presence [38]. Identification via self-similarity assumes that similarity with the self leads to higher self-relevance of the avatar, while wishful identification offers players the possibility to present themselves more like they would like to

be [38]. A convergence between the characteristics of an avatar and the ideal characteristics of the player, their ideal self [39], has been discovered to be beneficial, as it creates
higher levels of immersion, motivation, and positive affect during game play. However,
wishful avatar identification has also been associated with higher levels of aggression
[40] and addiction to online-gaming [41].

Vasalou et al. [42] found that users regularly adapt their avatars to their own appearance: These avatars with high self-similarity increase self-focused attention and thus
may increase positive attitudes that influence virtual behaviors. A study by Rahill and
Sebrechts [11] focused on how an avatar's similarity to the user through customization
(similar vs. dissimilar) and its designer (constructed by self vs. by others) contribute to
presence and performance in a game. Her results support the importance of both avatar
similarity and player construction of avatars for game performance, as well as virtual
presence, perception of performance, and perception of control. Moreover, the gains in
performance due to self-similarity could also be observed in teams: Teams using "mor-
phed team avatars", which combined both a similarity between the team members and
member–avatar similarity in their appearances, performed better and showed greater
social attraction than teams using avatars with less similarities [43].

Findings by Koulouris et al. [10] also suggest that the specific customization style
influences avatar perception. Avatar customization in a self-competitive VR exergame
initially suggested that customization significantly increased identification and intrinsic
motivation, as well as physical performance. In a second study, the authors found that
idealized avatars increased wishful identification but decreased exergame performance
compared to realistic avatars. However, their third study indicated that, 'enhancing' realistic avatars with idealized characteristics increases wishful identification but does not
have any adverse effects. Comparing the effect of wishful identifications vs. self-similar
identification, a recent study on learning (in a university context) suggests that self-
similarity may even be more beneficial for learning outcomes than wishful identification
[44].

Still, in some cases, users might prefer dissimilar avatars for identity play, e.g., via
gender-swapping [45]. Besides, sometimes game characteristics—especially in competitive games—drive the choice of avatars in such a way that attributes that seem relevant
to successful gameplay and winning are more important than similarity to the player
[4, 46]. Besides, strategic avatar choices can also play a role, e.g., in the context of
marketing. Abrahams and colleagues [47] showed that on online market platforms, the
presence of truthful avatars of sellers increases the trustworthiness of sellers. Yet in an
experimental study, they could show that this effect is overruled by strategic choices:
Because female avatars are more trusted, men were more likely to represent themselves
with a female avatar.

2.3 Benefits of Avatar Identification

A greater identification with one's avatar as the virtual representation of the person has
been associated with a considerable number of benefits. First and foremost, a stronger
avatar identification is linked to an increased motivation in games [8]. All three kinds of
avatar identification outlined above—similarity identification, embodied identification,

and wishful identification— can increase a number of factors like autonomy, immersion, invested effort, enjoyment, and positive affect [7]. A systematic review of health interventions through avatars showed that identifying with one's avatar played a role in eliciting healthy behaviors [48].

A positive effect of avatar identification on enjoyment was also found in a range of studies. Birk et al. [14] found that enjoyment and effort in gameplay decreased faster for participants who identified less with their avatars. A study by Ng et al. [15] showed strong effects for creating a custom avatar on feelings of engagement and presence, and modest effects on measures of learning.

Long-term effects could also be observed, e.g., a higher avatar identification is positively related to participation in gaming communities and social presence, which in turn is positively related to online gamer loyalty, i.e., gamers' continued intention to play [49]. An increased identification with and sense of responsibility for one's character were both associated with increased appreciation of a game [50].

The effects of avatar identification do not only stem from having chosen or customized an avatar according to one's own characteristics. Once a person starts using an avatar, the identificatory leap in this virtual representation has an effect that directly influences the user's behavior: Users conform to their avatars' characteristics and expected behaviors, an occurrence known as the Proteus effect [51]. In a meta-analysis, the Proteus effect was shown to be a reliable phenomenon with a large effect size compared to other digital media effects [52]. Examples of the Proteus effect include higher confidence in participants that were assigned a taller avatar [51] or reduced implicit racial bias against dark-skinned people when light-skinned participants received a dark-skinned virtual body [53]. In the use of avatars, perceived self-similarity and the Proteus effect come together, as a study by De Rooij et al. suggests [54]: They showed that embodying a non-creative avatar diminishes creativity, but also that similarity in appearance between the user and its avatar positively moderated the ability to generate creative ideas and therefore, self-similarity may impact creativity.

2.4 Research Questions

Extending previous studies, this research aims to replicate previous findings on the self-similarity of avatars, while also exploring the avatar use in a real-world setting on a professional training platform. We are testing four hypotheses and further explore the data.

Based on the research outlined above showing that perceived self-similarity with one's avatar leads to higher satisfaction with one's avatar we hypothesize:

H1: Perceived self-similarity is related to higher satisfaction with one's avatar, i.e. participants, who experience a higher self-similarity with their avatar, report higher levels of satisfaction with their avatar.

We further test whether the importance of avatar self-similarity differs for women and men. Female participants may value options for modification and self-similarity higher than males because, socially, women are more judged by their appearances and also put more effort into it [55]. It can be assumed that it is more important for women than for men to be able to reference their real appearance and carry it over into the virtual world, leading to the next hypothesis:

H2: Self-similarity of their avatar is more important to female participants than to male participants.

We are examining a professional training platform in use by a training provider. In this real-world setting we encounter circumstances that are given facts in this situation. One of these circumstances in the professional training platform we are studying is that female avatars are lower in number and less diverse in their physical appearances. Based on the existing research on customization and self-similarity outlined above we thus expect women to express lower self-similarity and lower satisfaction with their avatar than male participants. We thus hypothesize:

H3.1 Female participants experience less self-similarity with their avatars compared to male participants.

H3.2. Female participants are less satisfied with their avatars than male participants.

Beyond these hypotheses, we explore the choice of avatars: The role of similarities regarding gender, age, hair style/color, and clothing style as well as other potential reasons for the choice of avatars are examined and the role of participant gender is taken into consideration. Furthermore, we scrutinize the reasons for switching to another avatar.

The virtual learning environment that is being used by the company only allows certain modifications regarding the avatars: Hats (for female/male avatars), hairbands with bows (only female avatars), color of clothes (depending on the specific avatar, only certain items can be changed, but if so, it is possible to use all RGB-colors). We explore how avatars are modified and which reasons are given for the modifications, look at the importance of self-similarity and having options for modifications of one's avatar and possible differences related to gender. Finally, we study which attributes of the avatars are considered as positive and beneficial and which improvements or changes to the avatars are suggested by the participants.

3   Method

The study examines the avatars used in the real-world training environment Learnspace 3D". It is a platform custom made for one of the largest professional training providers in Germany [56]. The virtual environment where all classes are conducted, consists of different buildings, rooms, and landscape elements that can be accessed via (desktop) computers. The participants are represented by avatars that they use to navigate the environment and to interact with the other participants. Participants select an avatar before they first enter Learnspace 3D and can go back to modify their avatar at any time. There are 19 female and 21 male avatars to choose from and there were no avatars that were read as non-binary by the researchers. The avatars offer limited options for modifications (i.e., adding glasses, hats, or hairbands, and changing the color of one's clothes), see Fig. 1. Hairstyles, hair color, height, clothing items themselves, or body types cannot be modified.

Participants. There was a total of 472 participants (56.6% female, 39.2% male, 0.6% diverse, and 3.6% missing; age ranged from 20 to 77; M = 46.3, SD = 11.52; 40 participants did not include their age). Participants were enrolled full-time in an educational program (N = 302) or worked as trainers in the programs (N = 164), 6 participants

Fig. 1. Example of four avatars

did not indicate their role, yielding a total of 466 participants (from the 472 that started filling out the questionnaire 6 did not fill out any questions and thus were omitted). Of these participants, 11.2% had used the education platform for less than a month, 24.7% indicated a time between one and three months, 17.6% between four and six months, and 45.3% for more than six months (1.2% missing).

Materials and Procedure. Participants were recruited either via their trainers in their respective courses or via e-mail by the company of the education platform. The study was conducted in German using the Keyingress 6.01 as a survey tool for the online questionnaire. The survey was in the field from September 15th to September 26th, 2022, i.e., for 11 days.

In the questionnaire, we first gathered basic information regarding the use of the Learnspace 3D itself via multiple-choice questions: Role of the user (trainer/participant), duration of use (ranging from "less than a month" to "more than 6 months") gender of the avatar (female/male) and their currently selected avatar. The avatars were presented via pictures of the 19 female and 21 male avatars on different pages, plus the option "I don't remember."

Next, we asked how satisfied participants were with their current avatar using a 5-point Likert scale ranging from 1 (not satisfied) to 5 (satisfied) and how self-similar they considered their avatar to be (from 1 (not similar) to 5 (similar)). Multiple-choice questions regarding the reasons for choosing an avatar and on modifications that the participant had made followed. Two open questions (What do you like/dislike about your avatar?) and another multiple-choice question regarding possible improvements or changes followed, featuring several options (more options regarding clothes and accessories; a higher number of avatars; a lower number of avatars; a higher range of different ethnic backgrounds; stars, shapes or symbols instead of human representations; more gender options; more older avatars; other (please specify). Moreover, participants were asked how important self-similarity with their avatars and how important having options for modification was to them, both questions using 5-point Likert scales. Additionally, participants could indicate (dis)similarities with their avatars using multiple-choice options. One question inquired whether participants had changed their avatar, potentially repeatedly, and a subsequent multiple-choice question examined the reasons (trying something different, others had the same avatar, fitting better into the group, a more elegant style, a more casual style, looking more alike, looking different from real life) plus free-text options. Moreover, participants stated whether they were more satisfied with their new avatars on a 5-point-likert scale and if they felt that others treated them differently embodying their new avatars. The participants further rated their personal (technical) navigation experience in the Learnspace 3D on a 5-point Likert scale. In the end, demographical data regarding age, gender, migration background, and education was gathered.

4 Results

4.1 Hypothesis

The testing of the hypotheses yielded the following results:

H1: Perceived self-similarity is related to higher satisfaction with One's avatar.
Regarding overall satisfaction with their avatar, 4.4% participants reported being dissatisfied, 8.6% were rather dissatisfied, 34.1% were undecided, 29.7% were rather satisfied and 23.1% were satisfied. A regression analysis (method: enter) showed that self-similarity predicted satisfaction with one's avatar, $F(1;461) = 189.23$, $p < .001$, explaining 29.0% of the variance. Therefore, H1 was confirmed.

H2: Self-similarity of their avatar is more important to women than to men
The ANOVA ($N = 443$) showed that self-similarity was more important to women ($M = 3.42$; $SD = 1.01$) than to men ($M = 3.11$, $SD = 1.15$, $F(1;442) = 9.16$, $p < .003$). Along the same lines, being able to modify their avatars was also more important to women ($M = 3.84$, $SD = 1.05$) than to men, ($M = 3.60$; $SD = 1.18$, $F(1;442) = 4.76$, $p < .03$). So, while both men and women considered similarity to their avatars to be important, there was a significant difference between men and women and H2 was confirmed.

H3.1 female participants experience less self-similarity with their avatars compared to male participants.
The ANOVA ($N = 450$) of the variable "self-similarity" and the between-subject variable "participant gender" showed the effect of gender on self-similarity was not significant, $F(1;450) = 3.45$, $p < .064$, and female participants ($M = 2.91$, $SD = 1.08$) and male

participants (M = 3.01, SD = 1.12) indicated comparable levels of similarity with their avatars. Therefore, H3.1 was not confirmed.

H3.2 Female participants are less satisfied with their avatars than male participants
The ANOVA (N = 450) with the between-subject-variable "participant gender" did not yield any significant effects regarding the satisfaction with one's avatar, $F(1;450) = .588$, p > .444., with both female participants (M = 3.51, SD = 1.05) and male participants (M = 3.69, SD = 1.10) being mostly undecided or rather satisfied with their avatars. Thus, while female participants reported a slight tendency for a lower self-similarity with their avatars, they did not report less satisfaction with their avatars. Therefore, H3.2 was not confirmed.

4.2 Exploration

Avatar Choices.
Different patterns of avatar choice were observed between men and women. There were two avatars that were selected by females in over 40% of the cases (25.0% female participants chose the same avatar and 16.8 % another one). Male participants' choices were distributed more evenly across the 21 male avatars, 13.0 % chose the same avatar, followed by 9.2% for another avatar and remaining avatars were chosen with frequencies between 0.5% and 6.8%. Almost all participants chose an avatar of the gender they identified with. Three participants, i.e., 0.6% indicated "diverse" for their own gender. One participant reported actively choosing an incongruent gender for their avatar.

Asked about the reasons for choosing their avatar in a multiple-choice question, about half gave similar gender as a reason (52.7%), next up was a similar way of dressing (41.8%). About one third of the men, but only one fifth of the women gave similar age as a reason to choose the avatar (for 31.9% of men, but only for 18.7% of women, X^2 (1) = 10.35, p < .001).

There were 6.0% of women and 13,5% of men who indicated they chose their avatar because it does not look like themselves.

Reasons for Switching One's Avatar.
Female and male participants did not differ regarding the frequency to switch avatars, X^2 (3) = 3.038, p < .386, n = 446. Approximately half of the participants never changed their avatars (55.2%), 20.4% changed their avatars once, 8.3% changed twice, and 16.1% changed three or more times. The motives given -among those how changed their avatars- in the multiple choice fields 55.6% were "just trying something new", 28.5 wanted "a more similar avatar", 22.2% reported that others had the same avatar, 24.2% wished for "a more casual style", 16.4% looked for "a more elegant style", 6.3% wished to look different than in real life and 4.8% wanted "to fit better into the group".

The wish to embody an avatar different from one's real time appearance was reported as a reason for switching one's avatar more among men (11,4%) than women (3,3%, $X^2(1) = 5.14$, p < .023, N = 200).

Avatar Modifications. The platform offers the possibility to change the colors of the avatar's clothes, which 74.6% of the participants reported they did. Moreover, 47.5%

added glasses, 11.4% added hats, 7.8% added hairbands (the latter is only possible for female avatars). A few participants (1.1%) also stated, they did not remember their adaptions exactly and 15.0% did not do modify their avatars at all.

Feedback on Positive and Negative Attributes of the Avatars and Suggestions. *Multiple Choice*: Regarding the multiple-choice questions, participants wished for a higher range of different ethnical backgrounds to choose from (21.5%), more avatar options for an older age (20.1%), and for diverse gender options (9.0 %). Stars or other shapes as alternatives to human avatars were named by 6.0% of the participants and 2.3% suggested "fewer options". Concerning the clothing of the avatars, 79.4% of female participants and 67.0% of male participants opted for "more clothing options", X^2 (1) = 8.771, p < .003, n = 452.

Free-text Questions: The participants criticized the selection of slender avatars and asking for more diversity in body types (n = 32). Moreover, participants expressed the wishes for headscarfes/hijabs (n = 3) and options for beards (n = 9), modifiable hairstyle and color (n = 95), and especially featuring more options for grey/white hair avatars as well and as older avatars in general (n = 20).

Additionally, the clothing options were also criticized frequently (n = 95). There were statements that bemoaned the lack of options and individualizations in general, but also specific criticism regarding necklines that were too low and underwear that was visible in some of the female avatars. Further, the limited facial expressions and gestures were commented on (n = 40), the former sometimes referred to as "unfriendly", "rigid" or "creepy", and the latter as "very limited". Also, the reduced possibilities of moving and interacting with avatars were criticized (n = 23). There were also more general comments pointing to a lack in self-similarity (n = 24) as a negative aspect about one's avatar.

On the positive side, people mentioned their "(approximate) likeness with the avatar" (n = 45), the (elegant/business/formal) dressing style of the avatar (n = 60), the options for changing the colors of the clothes (n = 31) and the avatar's hair (n = 34). Being in good physical shape (n = 14) was also mentioned as favorable aspect.

Pre-experience with Virtual Worlds. Female participants reported less experience with virtual worlds as used in games or simulations, χ^2 (2) = 33.140, p < .001, n = 450; 18.4% of females reported frequent experiences with virtual worlds, 15.0% reported occasionally usage, and 66.5% indicated no previous experiences. Male participants reported frequent experiences (38.8% of male participants), and experiences on occasion (22.3%) and no previous experience (39.7%). Moreover, pre-experience with virtual worlds was related negatively to satisfaction with one's avatar, as shown in the ANOVA (n = 458) of the variable "satisfaction with one's avatar" with the between-subjects variable "pre-experience with virtual worlds", F (2;455) =10.77, p < .001. Participants with frequent pre-experience with virtual worlds (M = 3.22, SD = 1.12) were less satisfied with their avatars than participants who had only occasional experiences (M = 3.57, SD = 1.08, t (205) = 2.25, p<.025) and also less satisfied than those who had no previous experiences (M = 3.75, SD = .99, t (372) = −4.68, p < .001). Previously unexperienced and users with occasional experiences did not differ, t <-1.42, p > .157.

5 Discussion

Our first hypothesis, i.e., perceived self-similarity being related to higher satisfaction with one's avatar, was confirmed: We found that similarity of the chosen avatar to oneself predicted a large share of the satisfaction with one's avatar. The link between self-similarity and avatar satisfaction is in line with previous studies, which found a positive connection of avatar self-similarity and identification [3–5]. The present study extents these findings since previous studies examined games and affiliated measures: The positive effect of avatar self-similarity does not only exist in gaming but holds up in a professional education context. Avatars therefore offer a starting point to improve satisfaction and identification in online learning environments, since learners who have the possibility to have an avatar that they perceive as similar to themselves have a more positive experience within the learning process.

In line with our second hypothesis, female participants generally considered avatar self-similarity as more important than male participants. Moreover, female participants also stressed the importance of the availability of modifications for the avatars more than male participants did. These findings can be interpreted in terms of gender stereotypes: The way gender is constructed in our society, physical appearance is more salient for women than for men [57] and outer appearance thus is more important for women than for men [55]. Women are judged more by their outer appearance than men and experience more pressure to be attractive [58], thus they put more effort into their appearance [59] Having put more effort into their appearance, it might come as no surprise that it is more important for women than for men to be able to reference their real appearance in a virtual setting. However, finding these gendered societal constructions playing a role in women's user experience on a learning platform can offer an unexpected chance to improve gender equality in this professional setting: If a training platform wants to be gender-sensitive, fair, and inclusive, it needs to ensure the offer the same experience to all genders. Our results show that being able to have an avatar that is similar to oneself might help to close a gender fairness-gap that exists regarding a positive learning environment.

Our third hypothesis could not be confirmed. We could not find that female participants experienced less self-similarity with their avatars compared to male participants or that they were less satisfied with their avatars than male participants. While the results pointed in the hypothesized direction, they were not statistically significant. We have two interpretations of this result: For one, this might change if the participants actually have a larger variety of avatars that they are satisfied with and that they feel they can identify with. On the learning platform we examined, we found that most of the participants did not perceive the avatars as having a high similarity to themselves. Also, the satisfaction with the avatars was not particularly high with most participants being "undecided" or only "rather satisfied" with their avatars. Another interpretation is the different gaming behavior of men and women: Women play more casual games, typically for shorter periods compared with men [60] and thus are slightly less experienced with simulations or games where avatars are used—an occurrence we also found in our study. Moreover, a higher experience with virtual worlds was related to less satisfaction with one's avatar in our data. The assumption that participants compare the Learnspace 3D avatars to those of other software and systems is also backed up by the free-text answers, in which participants mentioned avatars of the SIMS and *Second Life* and stated that, compared to the avatars in other simulations, the avatars in the Learnspace 3D were of lower quality. The avatars' facial expressions were also criticized frequently and referred to as "creepy", which suggests that the level of realism of the avatars is, at least to some participants, in the uncanny valley [61].

Regarding the exploratory analysis, we found interesting patterns of avatar use for female and male participants: While male participants chose from a large variety of different avatars in an evenly distributed way, a considerable share of females chose between only two avatars. The avatar chosen by almost a quarter of the female participants a blond avatar, young, and slender female avatar is dressed in inconspicuous clothes and has a common hairstyle (ponytail). Second up was a white young female avatar with long dark hair and casual clothes. This concentration on a very limited number of avatars could be explained with a number of possible reasons. First of all, the number of females is slightly lower than for males, and there are fewer women with business attire. The options for older female avatars are extremely low and those that exist were criticized as "very old-fashioned/granny-like" in terms of clothing and/or hairstyle and having unfriendly, even "bitter" facial expressions. Two of the other female avatars have visible underwear. Thus, several avatars are considered inappropriate by some users. Besides the fewer options for the expression of one's individuality in general, this concentration on a small set of avatars is linked to problems in the learning groups, since there is a high probability that several female participants are represented by the same avatar—expressed by the participants in the open answers as "the women look almost all the same". Especially female trainers mentioned that they see a problem in looking like the participants of their courses.

Regarding the reason for choosing an avatar, a similar gender and dressing styles were named most frequently, followed by a similar age. Our results do not seem to support previous studies, where females supposedly preferred an idealized thinner body for their avatars [62]. Men mentioned the similar age more frequently than women. This reflects that there were fewer choices for older avatars for women compared to those for men. Deliberately choosing an avatar that looked different from oneself was rare, but it is notable that this reason was mentioned twice as often by men than by women. Still, this is consistent with the finding regarding the higher importance of avatar self-similarity for women than for men.

About half of the participants never changed their avatars and men and women did not differ in their reasons to switch avatars. A small number of participants reported that they switched their avatars very often, sometimes daily. The reasons they gave was that they simply want to and to try out another avatar or switch to another gender. These findings are in line with previous studies that referred to the use of avatars as a means of experimenting with different or new identities [45].

Overall, the free-text answers profusely reflected the wish to assimilate the avatar's looks to one's looks in real life, they pointed to similarities as positive aspects, and expressed the frustration with the lack of options.

5.1 Limitations

The fact that we were examining a virtual environment in real use by learners in a professional training setting heightens the ecological validity of our results compared to a simulation or an experimental setup. At the same time, this real-world setting comes with limitations, since we could only examine the choices of avatars that the company was actually offering. And as with all technical artifacts, the choices of avatars given here are the result of development and selection processes that reflect societal biases and stereotypes [63], which once again becomes clear in our findings, showing that the avatars represent a lack of diversity and heteronormative beauty norms.

There were some potentially relevant factors that could not been considered in the statistical analysis, foremost different migration backgrounds, as there were too few people in the respective groups. However, several diversity issues were found via the open answers and included in the sections on feedback.

We concentrated on self-similarity and avatar identification and their effects on satisfaction with one's avatar. While previous studies suggest that these factors also influence motivation and learning in a positive way, our study did not check or aim to replicate these assumptions. Further studies would allow more insights into the possible effects on learning outcomes in professional education.

5.2 Further Implications

Though we did not explicitly focus on the goals and needs in terms of sociability, credibility, the wish to present a professional image or indicate competence, the participants addressed these aspects repeatedly in the free-text answers, often naming a formal/business attire as a prerequisite for their online appearance or criticizing the limited options in these regards. Yet it needs to be considered that an expressed wish for a certain feature does not necessarily mean that an avatar with this feature will be chosen.

Future studies could further explore the special requirements in professional and educational contexts and how avatars should be designed to cater to the goals and needs. Moreover, the level of abstractions and photorealism is also a potentially influential factor.

Additionally, social group identity and social group dynamics in a course may be influenced by the choice of avatars and the options and constraints to express group membership. Since stereotypical avatars can reaffirm stereotypes [64], our results seem especially troublesome in the context of further professional education, where, unlike in the voluntary and recreational use of games, participants (as well as trainers) *have to* use the provided systems. Referring to various previous studies on the Proteus effect, female avatars that are considered rather sexualized thus may also result in certain self-stereotypization and self-objectivation [65]. Furthermore, having a high number of identical avatars, can reduce identifiability [66] and may increase anonymity within a group, which may reduce interpersonal trust. Looking at our own results as well as on the vast body of previous studies regarding the positive effects of avatar self-similarity and increased identification on learning, engagement, and motivation, offering numerous options for individual avatar customization to increase self-similarity and identification seem especially crucial in online educational programs.

6 Conclusion

The results from our study with participants who use an immersive learning environment on a daily basis indicate that avatars' self-similarity plays an important role. These findings can be used as a starting point for designing a more positive experience within the learning process in learning environments that use avatars. Our results show that gendered societal constructions play a role in women's user experience on a learning platform in the sense that female participants generally considered avatar self-similarity as more important than male participants. Making sure that all genders can have an avatar that is similar to oneself can thus help making learning environments more gender-sensitive, fair, and inclusive. Based on our findings, we argue that avatars should represent the diversity that exists in the users to allow for greater identification and for the resulting benefits.

References

1. Klimmt, C., Hefner, D., Vorderer, P.: The video game experience as "true" identification: a theory of enjoyable alterations of players' self-perception. Commun. Theory **19**(4), 351–373 (2009)
2. Nowak, K.L., Fox, J.: Avatars and computer-mediated communication: a review of the definitions, uses, and effects of digital representations. Rev. Commun. Res. **6**, 30–53 (2018)
3. Freeman, G., Zamanifard, S., Maloney, D., Adkins, A.: My body, my avatar: how people perceive their avatars in social virtual reality. In: Book My Body, My Avatar: How People Perceive Their Avatars in Social Virtual Reality' (2020, edn.), pp. 1–8 (2020)
4. Trepte, S., Reinecke, L.: Avatar creation and video game enjoyment: effects of life-satisfaction, game competitiveness, and identification with the avatar. J. Media Psychol. Theor Methods Appl. **22**(4), 71 (2010)
5. Birk, M.V., Mandryk, R.L.: Combating attrition in digital self-improvement programs using avatar customization. In: Combating Attrition in Digital Self-Improvement Programs Using Avatar Customization' (2018, edn.), pp. 1–15 (2018)
6. Lee, K.M.: Presence, explicated. Commun. Theory **14**(1), 27–50 (2004)
7. Birk, M.V., Atkins, C., Bowey, J.T., Mandryk, R.L.: Fostering intrinsic motivation through avatar identification in digital games. In: Fostering intrinsic Motivation Through Avatar Identification in Digital Games' (2016, edn.), pp. 2982–2995 (2016)
8. Turkay, S., Kinzer, C.K.: The relationship between avatar-based customization, player identification, and motivation: In: Transforming Gaming and Computer Simulation Technologies Across Industries, pp. 48–79. IGI Global (2017)
9. Kao, D., Harrell, D.F.: The effects of badges and avatar identification on play and making in educational games. In: The Effects of Badges and Avatar Identification on Play and Making in Educational Games (2018, edn.), pp. 1–19 (2018)
10. Koulouris, J., Jeffery, Z., Best, J., O'neill, E., Lutteroth, C.: Me vs. super (wo) man: effects of customization and identification in a VR Exergame. In: Me vs. Super (wo) man: Effects of Customization and Identification in a VR Exergame (2020, edn.), pp. 1–17 (2018)
11. Rahill, K.M., Sebrechts, M.M.: Effects of Avatar player-similarity and player-construction on gaming performance. Comput. Hum. Behav. Rep. **4**, 100131 (2021)
12. Kim, C., Lee, S.-G., Kang, M.: I became an attractive person in the virtual world: users' identification with virtual communities and avatars. Comput. Hum. Behav. **28**(5), 1663–1669 (2012)

13. Li, B.J., Lwin, M.O.: Player see, player do: Testing an exergame motivation model based on the influence of the self avatar. Comput. Hum. Behav. **59**, 350–357 (2016)
14. Birk, M.V., Mandryk, R.L., Atkins, C.: The motivational push of games: the interplay of intrinsic motivation and external rewards in games for training. In: The Motivational Push of Games: The Interplay of Intrinsic Motivation and External Rewards in Games for Training (2016, edn.), pp. 291–303 (2016)
15. Ng, R., Lindgren, R.: Examining the effects of avatar customization and narrative on engagement and learning in video games. In: Examining the Effects of Avatar Customization and Narrative on Engagement and Learning in Video Games (2013, edn.), pp. 87–90. IEEE (2013)
16. Bosch, C., Ellis, T.: Using avatars to address teacher self-efficacy. J. Glob. Educ, Res. **5**(1), 15–35 (2021)
17. Green, R., Delfabbro, P.H., King, D.L.: Avatar-and self-related processes and problematic gaming: a systematic review. Addict. Behav. **108**, 106461 (2020)
18. Inkpen, K.M., Sedlins, M.: Me and my avatar: exploring users' comfort with avatars for workplace communication. In: Book Me and My Avatar: Exploring Users' Comfort with Avatars for Workplace Communication' (2011, edn.), pp. 383–386 (2011)
19. Manninen, T., Kujanpää, T.: The value of virtual assets: the role of game characters in MMOGs. Int, J. Bus. Sci. Appl. Manag. **2**(1), 21–33 (2007)
20. Carrasco, R., Baker, S., Waycott, J., Vetere, F.: Negotiating stereotypes of older adults through avatars. In: Negotiating Stereotypes of Older Adults Through Avatars (2017, edn.), pp. 218–227 (2017)
21. Lucht, M., Larbi, M.B., Angerhöfer, S.: Lernen für die Arbeitswelt von heute. Digitalisierung am Übergang Schule Beruf, p. 81 (2021)
22. Ducheneaut, N., Wen, M.-H., Yee, N., Wadley, G.: Body and mind: a study of avatar personalization in three virtual worlds. In: Body and Mind: A Study of Avatar Personalization in Three Virtual Worlds' (2009, edn.), pp. 1151–1160 (2009)
23. Schroeder, R.: The Social Life of Avatars: Presence and Interaction in Shared Virtual Environments. Springer, London (2001). https://doi.org/10.1007/978-1-4471-0277-9
24. Friedl, M.: Online game interactivity theory with cdrom. Charles River Media. In: Online Game Interactivity Theory with CDROM. Charles River Media Inc. (2002, edn.) (2002)
25. Cohen, J.: Defining identification: a theoretical look at the identification of audiences with media characters. Mass Commun. Soc. **4**(3), 245–264 (2001)
26. Oatley, K.: Meetings of minds: dialogue, sympathy, and identification, in reading fiction. Poetics **26**(5–6), 439–454 (1999)
27. Tajfel, H.: Social categorization, social identity, and social comparisons. In: Tajfel, H. (ed.) Differentiation Between Social Groups: Studies in the Social Psychology of Intergroup Relations, pp. 61–76. Academic Press, London (1978)
28. Hogg, M.A., Terry, D.I.: Social identity and self-categorization processes in organizational contexts. Acad. Manag. Rev. **25**(1), 121–140 (2000)
29. Ashmore, R.D., Deaux, K., McLaughlin-Volpe, T.: An organizing framework for collective identity: articulation and significance of multidimensionality. Psychol. Bull. **130**(1), 80–114 (2004)
30. You, S., Sundar, S.S.: I feel for my avatar: embodied perception in VEs. In: I Feel For My Avatar: Embodied Perception in VEs (2013, edn.), pp. 3135–3138 (2013)
31. Hsu, S.H., Lee, F.-L., Wu, M.-C.: Designing action games for appealing to buyers. Cyberpsychol. Behav. **8**(6), 585–591 (2005)
32. Rymaszewski, M., Au, W.J., Wallace, M., Winters, C., Ondrejka, C., Batstone-Cunningham, B.: Second Life: The Official Guide, Wiley (2007)
33. Trepte, S., Reinecke, L., Behr, K.-M.: Creating virtual alter egos or superheroines? Gamers' strategies of avatar creation in terms of gender and sex. Int. J. Gam. Comput. Mediat. Simulat. **1**(2), 52–76 (2009)

34. Soutter, A.R.B., Hitchens, M.: The relationship between character identification and flow state within video games. Comput. Hum. Behav. **55**, 1030–1038 (2016)
35. Csikszentmihalyi, M., Csikzentmihaly, M.: Flow: The Psychology of Optimal Experience. Harper & Row, New York (1990)
36. Kao, D., Ratan, R., Mousas, C., Magana, A.J.: The effects of a self-similar avatar voice in educational games. In: Proceedings of the ACM on Human-Computer Interaction, 2021, vol. 5, (CHI PLAY), pp. 1–28 (2021)
37. Feilitzen, C., Linné, O.: Identifying with television characters. J. Commun. **25**, 51–55 (1975)
38. Looy, J., Courtois, C., Vocht, M., Marez, L.D.: Player identification in online games: validation of a scale for measuring identification in MMORPGs. Media Psychol. **15**(2), 197–221 (2012)
39. Przybylski, A.K., Weinstein, N., Murayama, K., Lynch, M.F., Ryan, R.M.: The ideal self at play: the appeal of video games that let you be all you can be. Psychol. Sci. **23**(1), 69–76 (2012)
40. Konijn, E.A., Nije Bijvank, M., Bushman, B.J.: I wish I were a warrior: the role of wishful identification in the effects of violent video games on aggression in adolescent boys. Dev. Psychol. **43**(4), 1038 (2007)
41. Smahel, D., Blinka, L., Ledabyl, O.: Playing MMORPGs: connections between addiction and identifying with a character. Cyberpsychol. Behav. **11**(6), 715–718 (2008)
42. Vasalou, A., Joinson, A.N., Pitt, J.: Constructing my online self: avatars that increase self-focused attention. In: Constructing My Online Self: Avatars That Increase Self-focused Attention (2007, edn.), pp. 445–448 (2007)
43. Van Der Land, S.F., Schouten, A.P., Feldberg, F., Huysman, M., van den Hooff, B.: Does avatar appearance matter? How team visual similarity and member–avatar similarity influence virtual team performance. Hum. Commun. Res. **41**(1), 128–153 (2015)
44. Ratan, R., Klein, M.S., Ucha, C.R., Cherchiglia, L.L.: Avatar customization orientation and undergraduate-course outcomes: actual-self avatars are better than ideal-self and future-self avatars. Comput. Educ. **191**, 104643 (2022)
45. Hussain, Z., Griffiths, M.D.: Gender swapping and socializing in cyberspace: an exploratory study. Cyberpsychol. Behav. **11**(1), 47–53 (2008)
46. Vasalou, A., Joinson, A.N.: Me, myself and I: the role of interactional context on self-presentation through avatars. Comput. Hum. Behav. **25**(2), 510–520 (2009)
47. Abraham, D., Greiner, B., Stephanides, M.: On the Internet you can be anyone: an experiment on strategic avatar choice in online marketplaces. In: On the Internet you can be anyone: an experiment on strategic avatar choice in online marketplaces (MUNI ECON Working Paper, 2021, edn.) (2021)
48. Rheu, M., Jang, Y., Peng, W.: Enhancing healthy behaviors through virtual self: a systematic review of health interventions using avatars. Games Health J. **9**(2), 85–94 (2020)
49. Teng, C.-I.: Impact of avatar identification on online gamer loyalty: perspectives of social identity and social capital theories. Int. J. Inf. Manage. **37**(6), 601–610 (2017)
50. Bowman, N.D., Oliver, M.B., Rogers, R., Sherrick, B., Woolley, J., Chung, M.-Y.: In control or in their shoes? How character attachment differentially influences video game enjoyment and appreciation. J. Gaming Virtual Worlds **8**(1), 83–99 (2016)
51. Yee, N., Bailenson, J.: The Proteus effect: the effect of transformed self-representation on behavior. Hum. Commun. Res. **33**(3), 271–290 (2007)
52. Ratan, R., Beyea, D., Li, B.J., Graciano, L.: Avatar characteristics induce users' behavioral conformity with small-to-medium effect sizes: a meta-analysis of the proteus effect. Media Psychol. **23**(5), 651–675 (2020)
53. Peck, T.C., Seinfeld, S., Aglioti, S.M., Slater, M.: Putting yourself in the skin of a black avatar reduces implicit racial bias. Conscious. Cogn. **22**(3), 779–787 (2013)

54. De Rooij, A., Van Der Land, S., Van Erp, S.: The creative Proteus effect: how self-similarity, embodiment, and priming of creative stereotypes with avatars influences creative ideation. In: The Creative Proteus Effect: How Self-similarity, Embodiment, and Priming of Creative Stereotypes with Avatars Influences Creative Ideation (2017, edn.), pp. 232–236 (2017)

55. Quittkat, H.L., Hartmann, A.S., Düsing, R., Buhlmann, U., Vocks, S.: Body dissatisfaction, importance of appearance, and body appreciation in men and women over the lifespan. Front. Psych. **10**, 864 (2019)

56. TriCAT: Best Practice WBS Training AG (2018)

57. Grogan, S.: Body image: Understanding Body Dissatisfaction in Men, Women, and Children. Routledge (2021)

58. Stuart, A., Donaghue, N.: Choosing to conform: the discursive complexities of choice in relation to feminine beauty practices. Fem. Psychol. **22**(1), 98–121 (2012)

59. England, D.E., Descartes, L., Collier-Meek, M.A.: Gender role portrayal and the Disney princesses. Sex Roles **64**(7), 555–567 (2011)

60. Lopez-Fernandez, O., Williams, A.J., Kuss, D.J.: Measuring female gaming: Gamer profile, predictors, prevalence, and characteristics from psychological and gender perspectives. Front. Psychol. **10**, 898 (2019)

61. Geller, T.: Overcoming the uncanny valley. IEEE Comput. Graphics Appl. **28**(4), 11–17 (2008)

62. Thaler, A., et al.: Visual perception and evaluation of photo-realistic self-avatars from 3D body scans in males and females. Front. ICT **5**, 18 (2018)

63. Raudonat, K., Pröbster, M., Schmieder, K., Martinetz, S., Marsden, N.: Where bias can creep in-Gendersensibilität beim Einsatz von KI-Technologien im Kontext beruflicher Weiterbildung im Forschungsprojekt KIRA', INFORMATIK 2022 (2022)

64. Pröbster, M., Soto, M.V., Connolly, C., Marsden, N.: Avatar-based virtual reality and the associated gender stereotypes in a university environment. Eur. J. Open Dist. E-Learn. **24**(1), 11–24 (2022)

65. Fox, J., Bailenson, J.N., Tricase, L.: The embodiment of sexualized virtual selves: The Proteus effect and experiences of self-objectification via avatars. Comput. Hum. Behav. **29**(3), 930–938 (2013)

66. Midha, V., Nandedkar, A.: Impact of similarity between avatar and their users on their perceived identifiability: evidence from virtual teams in second life platform. Comput. Hum. Behav. **28**(3), 929–932 (2012)

Mapping the Factors Affecting Online Education During the Pandemic in Greece: Understanding the Importance of Designing Experiences Through Different Cultural and Philosophical Approaches

Angeliki Tevekeli[1]([✉]) [iD] and Vasiliki Mylonopoulou[2] [iD]

[1] KTH - Royal Institute of Technology, Stockholm, Sweden
tevekeli@kth.se
[2] University of Gothenburg, Forskningsgången 6, 417 56 Gothenburg, Sweden
vasiliki.mylonopoulou@ait.gu.se

Abstract. Due to the Covid-19 pandemic, education in many countries transferred abruptly online. Students, teachers, and parents - who were also working from home - had to adjust to the new reality. To understand this new reality and the experiences of the students, teachers, and parents about online education we conducted a qualitative study using interviews and contextual inquiry. The data collected were thematically analyzed and discussed based on the different perspectives. The article presents a conceptual mapping of the online education experience of students, teachers, and parents in Greece and proposes a conceptual design framework as well as a set of guiding questions to support the design process for a better user experience of cross-cultural online educational platforms in similar contexts.

Keywords: Online student experience · online learning · COVID-19 pandemic · user experience design · user interface design · UI · UX · UCD · Greek philosophy · HCI · intercultural interaction design

1 Introduction

Lock down during the COVID-19 pandemic forced students worldwide to follow school lessons online. A decision applied in most of the European countries for certain periods of time depending on the registered cases and country's population. This paper investigates and analyzes the online learning and teaching experience in the digital classroom and proposes a conceptual design framework for online learning platforms based on how the Greek students, teachers and parents experienced online education during the pandemic. It proposes new viewpoints of thinking while designing intercultural online educational applications by digging deeper into what UI/UX designers should examine and take into consideration in the design process in order to offer more effective learning and teaching experiences.

P. Zaphiris and A. Ioannou (Eds.): HCII 2023, LNCS 14040, pp. 401–419, 2023.
https://doi.org/10.1007/978-3-031-34411-4_27

The culture in which individuals are raised exposes them to what the members of their culture consider appropriate and credible behavior in various contexts [16]. According to Hall [17] in certain cultures, individuals are able to make relatively few assumptions concerning: a) how much others knew about the purpose for interacting in a particular context and b) how they were expected to behave (roles) in relation to achieving that purpose. By discussing with the Greek students, parents and teachers and at the same time by evaluating the platforms used for the online education, the authors realized that the notions known should be reconsidered. We focus on different philosophical and cultural approaches in regards to both the user and the designer as "members of a culture generally have a preferred set of responses to the world" [18].

Interface design is globally applied using the same methods which progress as users constantly adjust to the fast pace of technological evolvement. While user needs change user generations evolve and give new criteria for design thinking. The designer's cultural background affects decisions and practices in the interface, and therefore user experience, and should also be taken into consideration when designing for global use along with the different cultural patterns (beliefs, values, norms and social practices) of both the user and designer "as those address the manner in which a culture orients itself to activities, social relations, the self, the world and the passage of time" [19]. During the briefing and user research phase a combination of empathy, knowledge, and understanding in multidimensional aspects influence final decisions of the design and development of an application. It's a complex procedure that depends on explicit and tacit knowledge.

To understand how to design effective online learning platforms, we first need to understand the differences between physical and digital classrooms, as well as to deeply understand and know how the user feels [23]. In this study, by user we refer to students and teachers. In addition, we involve students' parents as we they are daily engaged with their children education and they are concerned about their pedagogical progress.

2   Background

Research shows that the Covid-19 pandemic forced a number of changes in teaching and learning and impacted students, teachers and parents in various aspects. Several challenges, including the use of digital platforms and digital competence emerged [33, 37]. 19% of the teachers in secondary education in Greece, teaching online during lockdown in the Covid-19 pandemic, evaluated their teaching experience as negative whereas 29.7% remained neutral and 51.1% were satisfied. 46,6% were dissatisfied with the support provided and 21,6% evaluated the applications used as dissatisfying [32]. The effectiveness of the platforms used during the confinement has been globally questioned for all levels of education [34, 35].

One of the most important skills an experienced UI/UX designer cultivates through the years is empathy [38]. To be able to perceive the internal frame of reference of another with accuracy and with the emotional components and meanings which pertain thereto as if one were the person [4, 5]. Empathy is a series of actions in the design process. It involves research, immersion and detachment [39]. Therefore, interacting with users is not only about asking the right questions but actively listening to the answers, understand their feelings and emotions, and interpret all these to user experience.

3 Methodology

This is a qualitative interpretivist study that took place from March 2020 to February 2021. The participants were a convenience sample and they were divided into three groups: Students (16–18 years old), their parents (44–55 years old), and their educators (42–59 years old).

3.1 Context of Research

On the 11th of March 2020, the Greek government instructed the Secondary Education to be transferred fully online due to the increase of the Covid-19 registered cases. This was the first time the physical schools closed and the students had to follow their courses through synchronous and asynchronous online means. Schools opened for physical attendance in May 2020. However, in November 2020 the courses were transferred again online and they continued as such until April 2021.

During these two periods of online attendance (March 2020–May 2020, November 2020–April 2021), students in upper Secondary Education used a commercial video conference tool - Cisco Webex (https://www.webex.com/) - for synchronous online lessons and a web platform from the Panhellenic School Network (www.sch.gr) for asynchronous communication. Each student has their own credentials for logging in the platform. The platform supports the students and teaching staff communication with an e-mail service and an e-class service. The e-class service allowed document exchange, sharing of information related to modules, and relevant notifications to students.

3.2 Positionality

"The concept of positionality is referenced in terms of the researcher's insider or outsider relationship to the community engaged in the inquiry [30]". By positionality in this article, we refer to the creation of knowledge partially based on the researchers' background. This study involves interpretation and collection of qualitative data. By presenting our background we aim to add in the transparency of the methodological approach we used. Kathryn Herr and Gary Anderson in their book on action research dissertations [31] define this type of researcher as an insider, one who studies their own practice.

The first author collected and analysed the data and discussed the results. She has 25 years of work experience in design and actively works as a UI/UX designer and researcher in the industry. Her empirical knowledge extends from the role of a designer to the role of an educator and a parent. As a parent of a student who studies in Greece, she encountered the above mentioned platforms in her personal time as well. She has also worked using CANVAS, BLACKBOARD and MOODLE LMS platforms for more than four years both as an educator and as a student herself.

The second author supported on the data analysis and interpretation as well as on the structure and presentation of the paper's methodology and results. She has seven years of experience in interpretivist studies and similar experience with the Human-Computer Interaction research field. The past four years has personal experience with the educational platform CANVAS (https://www.instructure.com/canvas).

3.3 Data Collection

The data collected from the three groups were qualitative in nature. In the students' group a Likert scale was used additionally to record their level of lecture satisfaction. The qualitative data were recorded through notes taken by the observer/interviewer. In this section we will further describe how the data collected from each group of participants.

Students. To better understand the student's perspective, a combination of focus group discussions, contextual inquiry method, and Likert scale diaries were utilized [25]. Five data collection sessions with students were conducted in a familiar to them environment. The participants were 20 students, divided in groups of four. The students' sessions began with a focus group discussion about the pros and cons of the physical and digital classroom. Then the sessions continued with the platform usability and user experience evaluation through contextual inquiry - utilizing semi-structured interviews and observations as described by [25].

For understanding the usability issues that could contribute to the user experience a contextual inquiry method was used [25]. This was essential for the identification of the students' perception in regards to usability and therefore the effectiveness of the application used. The students were observed in real time as they followed their lectures. To understand better the students' interaction with the interface, the students were interviewed based on their usage of the platform also in real time.

In addition to the five sessions, students filled in a Likert scale diary to express how they felt about each teaching hour. The diary used emoticons to represent different levels of satisfaction. The students made a record in their diary every hour for a week. A days sample is shown in Table 1 below.

Table 1. Likert Scale Day Diary Sample - Starting from the left, the first choice represented "very dissatisfied", the second "dissatisfied", the third/middle one "indifferent", the next one "satisfied", and the last one "very satisfied".

	Monday
1st hour	😠😞😐🙂😄
2nd hour	😠😞😐🙂😄
3rd hour	😠😞😐🙂😄
4rth hour	😠😞😐🙂😄
5th hour	😠😞😐🙂😄
6th hour	😠😞😐🙂😄
7th hour	😠😞😐🙂😄

Parents. Semi-structured interviews with the 19 parents of the students participating in the study were conducted. The interviews were designed to collect data about the parents' experience with their children during their daily online lessons, their thoughts, worries and related problems. The interviews were conducted via Skype, zoom and phone due to lock down restrictions.

Educators. Contextual inquiry was conducted with four educators in their work setting - utilizing semi-structured interviews and observations as described by [25]. In the case of the educators the interviews followed the observations of their lectures in order not to interrupt the flow of the lecture. Apart from questions related to the platform usability, the educators answered questions related to their students' participation, and their experience both as users and as pedagogists.

3.4 Data Analysis

The aim of the contextual inquiries, focus groups, and diary was threefold. First, they were used to explore the pros and cons of the digital and physical classroom. Second, they gave an idea about the usability and user experience issues of the systems in use. Third, they were used to illustrate the experience of online learning/teaching from the perspective of students, educators, and parents. The qualitative data from the contextual inquires and focus discussions were thematically analysed. The students' experience was complimented with the quantitative data collected from the Likert-scale diaries. The data from the Likert-scale diaries were descriptively analysed with the use of IBM SPSS. In Vivo analysis has also been applied for highlighting the participants' words [40].

4 Results

20 students between the ages of 16–18 years old, 19 of the students' parents between the ages 44–55 years old and 4 of the students' educators between the ages of 42–59 years old participated in this study.

4.1 Likert Scale

The Likert scale shows that the students are generally indifferent or dissatisfied with the online teaching sessions' experience. 20 students filled and handed in their diaries. Each student created 35 entries (five days, seven hours per day). Most entries showed that the students were indifferent (51%) or dissatisfied (42%) with the lectures. Few students were very dissatisfied (3%) or satisfied (3,2%), while only 0.8% entries recorded that the students were very satisfied. Figure 1 presents the results visually.

3%   42%   51%   3,2%   0,8%

Fig. 1. Diary analytics

4.2 Discussions

All the groups (students, parents, and educators) had similar concerns. From the thematic analysis 6 categories were created:

- *Infrastructure* including both the physical infostructure such as classrooms and access to internet or computers and the systemic infostructure such as administrative related issues.
- *Health* including issues related to health and wellbeing of students.
- *Social interactions*, which related to the interactions between students, as well as, students and teachers.
- *Pedagogy* and inclusivity related to the learning and teaching aspects including matters related to students' diversity in learning.
- *Embodied experiences* related to mental, behavioural, emotional and sensual affect.
- *Parenting* (only parents) includes parental worries related to conflicts and the relationship between parents and their children.

Infrastructure. Issues related to infrastructure were prevalent in all participating groups. Students were the ones who were not completely satisfied with the physical classroom/school due to crowded classrooms and lack of or badly maintained facilities. However, they did mention that during the confinement they missed the access to these facilities even though they were poor. For example, the library, labs, or other activity rooms. A positive side effect students mentioned the reduction on absences. The students could participate even when they were unable to leave home due to sickness or they could be digitally present without really following the course. There is a limit of absences per student in the Greek secondary education. If this limit is reached, the student cannot be promoted to the next class.

Infostructure issues were mentioned also related to the online classroom. The most prevalent was the technical problems with the digital tools such as usability issues (see next section) and the lack of technical support. The lack of hardware (individual computers for each student, microphones, cameras etc.) was also an important issue together with the poor internet connection. These issues are mentioned by all the participating groups. Similarly, the unwanted visual and auditory noise was mentioned by students and teachers equally, *"We don't want to turn the camera and microphone on because our parents work remotely from home during the lock down. During most of the school hours we are located in the same room. Sometimes we have to sit on the same desk or table as there is no other place available in the house. They speak loud either over the phone or in a video call with their colleagues or clients"*.

Students often felt that some teachers had low digital literacy skills which influenced their education. On the same hand some teachers mentioned that they felt incompetent in relation to their use of digital tools, hindering their performance as teachers.

Teachers mentioned as issue the heavy workload they had in the beginning of the confinement when the school was transferred online. They had to digitalise and transfer their material online and use a plethora of tools to communicate as the unified digital tools came later into the picture. Even after the tools came into place some courses needed resources which were out of reach e.g., books from the library. Moreover, in the start of the transition to online classroom, the communication between teachers and students were impractical, inefficient, and involved the support of the parents as the materials were not interactive and they needed to be printed, filled in, scanned and sent. Some teachers believed that using videos would increase the motivation of students to study however; the students interviewed have different opinion as they often disregarded the teacher's video recommendations.

A teacher mentioned the noisy surroundings both visually and auditorily as she was a mother of seven and three of her children were under the age of 4. She mentioned circumstances were her children appeared in the camera or made too much noise while she was holding a class. She had to stop teaching in order to calm them down. Noise was a more general concern as some teachers lived in noisy environments mostly because the whole family was in the house and their children were also taking classes online.

A few parents also mentioned their lack of autonomy as they did not have a choice on what platforms their children will use. However, they mentioned that they were familiar with these platforms as they were using them for their work (working from distance).

In families with more than one child there was a lack of hardware, as parents were also working remotely occupying hardware. In these cases, the students had to use their mobile devices to follow their lessons.

Health. Students were concerned about their level of physical activity, as they believed they moved and exercised less during the confinement period. They mentioned that they spent many hours in the same room, which could have an impact on their mental health as well. Similar concerns regarding the students' physical and mental health were raised by parents and educators. A parent who is a paediatrician referred that the American Academy of Paediatrics advices 2 h screen time per day for surfing and playing online games whereas the screen time for learning activities doesn't count as harmful [6]. Screen time and its effects on students' health were also perceived as important health issues from all research participants.

Social Interactions. Students lacked interacting with their peers and educators as they did in the physical school, e.g., during breaks, *"taking classes online through a grey and boring screen from their room is not natural"*. They felt that the engagement in discussions is limited in the digital classroom. Students missed flirting and socializing with their co-students during breaks and they also missed bonding. While in digital classroom they felt they don't belong in a social group and they did not feel any variations in the different schooldays. In the same line, parents and educators mentioned they were worried about the lack of student socialization with their peers.

Students mentioned that phenomena like bullying, homophobia, drugs, racism among them were eliminated during the confinement. They believe the reduction of these phenomena is due to lack of physical contact and communication between students. *"The camera off option makes it easier for me to be who I am"*, one of the students mentioned. He confined that being a homosexual at the age of 16 in Greece is a reason for bullying at school. He felt more calm in the online classroom as students didn't offend or bully him due to the camera off option.

Pedagogy and Inclusivity. Educators mentioned that they felt as if the pedagogical methods applied in the physical classroom are not adequate for the digital one. 2 of them, aged 40+ cannot handle technology efficiently and they find it difficult to adopt.

They are very annoyed about the turned off cameras and the constant technical problems in regards to internet connection and speed. They believe that students use this as an excuse to skip class. They also mentioned that they feel as if there is no *"character"* and *"identity"* in the lectures in regards to their fields.

They reported they faced difficulties addressing the particularities of each student in the online classroom. For example they observed that students with ADHD (Attention Deficit Hyperactivity Disorder) as well as introvert characters had difficulties in participating online. Two of the educators mentioned the following in our discussion: *"We constantly need to remind ourselves that these students need a different approach online. Not being able to see them as the cameras are off is a problem. In the physical classroom we know exactly how to help them engage and participate but during the first online sessions, in the beginning of the confinement, it was difficult to understand this phenomenon as we were looking at grey squares with a name on. We didn't know how to handle this neurodiversity through the platform we used. We haven't being trained on how to do deal with it. Calling out their names and asking them to participate while we couldn't see them was certainly not the solution. We tried this many times and it didn't work. It was complete silence and a sense that we were making them feel uncomfortable. So we stopped asking them to engage and participate this way. We started communicating in written with them, either through e-mail or through the chat in a private mode. We still need to understand how this can be handled. We need training on this or better tools that facilitate our communication with our students"*.

The four educators of the same 20 students participating in the study described their students as follows:

- About 13 out of 20 students (65%) would have stayed silent hadn't the educator addressed a question directly to them. These students had a similar low profile in the physical classroom. However, the teachers mentioned that students being online and silent are not the same as being physically present and silent. The teachers felt that their students in the online sessions are not visible.
- 5 out of 20 students (25%) participated when the educator addresses a question that is not targeted directly to them.
- 2 out of 20 students (10%) prefer to write in the chat or communicate via e-mail. These two students have reported technical issues e.g. that they don't own a camera or a microphone. Educators confined they believe this is an excuse and not an actual technical problem. The school has offered to contribute with a microphone or a camera to help but the students have not accepted the help. In an online classroom of 20 students, students find it difficult to participate actively when discussion and interaction with the teacher is required.

Students, in the same line, reported they are less motivated to participate in the e-classroom, particularly the students who perceived themselves as introverts or timid. These students reported that in the online classroom they stay silent for hours as no-one interacts with them while in the physical classroom teachers find a way to help them engage. Students reported that: *"It's as if we are not visible in the online lessons"*. The students underlined that the silence in the physical classroom is a different kind of silence than in the online lessons, a digital silence.

The communication between the teacher and the students was also influenced. In particular, the students felt that there is a wall between them and the teacher. In the discussion with students the following were reported: *"It's as if there is a wall between us and the teacher. A hidden layer that is not seen but is there. This could be the software we use or the screen. In fact it feels as if there's more than one wall or layer creating a distance between us and the teacher. Whereas, in the physical classroom there are no walls. We are all connected and placed in the same space or area. Nothing separates us from the teacher"*. The students explained in more detail these layers and walls: The 1st wall is their PC screen, 2nd wall is the software or platform, and 3rd wall is the teacher's screen. The students also mentioned that these *"walls"* affect the way knowledge is transferred. *"It's as if knowledge hits on these walls and is not transferred clearly to us. It is as if the walls absorb part of the knowledge and it* [the knowledge] *reaches us* [the students] *with less information than when the teacher expressed it"*.

They felt like they don't use their imagination, they miss experimentation and observation of phenomena. Most of the students mentioned that they miss experiments in lectures like Physics, Chemistry and Biology. One of the students said *"If we don't experiment then we can't imagine how things work or what the application of certain theories is in real life"*. They lack familiarity with the school environment, space, and place. Students mentioned that taking courses online is a totally different experience than being at school. School has a variety of dimensions whereas online lessons are boring, flat and that the space they use is monotonous. *"School space is full of life, online space is dead"*. *"This type of learning doesn't remind us of school"*, *"We miss positive vibes and enthusiasm"*. Some students commented also on the assessment and assessment methods. For example, they felt that they get better grades than usual because there are no tests. They speculated that there are no tests because the teachers could not control if the students cheat or not.

Parents were concerned that these months in confinement will have an effect in their children's academic future. Particularly, they were worried about their children's level of learning and efficiency in learning. For example, parents of children with high performance in the years before the pandemic were worried about their children's grades due to their limited participation in the online classroom. They also comment on the appropriateness of the platforms for education: *"how can a platform that we use for work can possibly be suitable for our children's education?"*. A small number of parents felt that some teachers spoke unstoppably and did not give the opportunity to students to ask questions or participate. Parents of neurodiverse children (children with Dyslexia, Attention deficit hyperactivity disorder, dyscalculia etc.) were worried that the online learning environment couldn't support their children, as it was currently constructed.

Embodied Experiences. Students missed certain embodied experiences, feelings, and sensations during the digital lessons. For example, they missed smells from the lunch break and sounds from the physical surroundings. They also missed school break noises, the bell ringing (in Greece bell sounds indicate the end and start of the break), the sound of laughter, loud discussions. These experiences made their bodily senses to explode and made them feel alive and happy.

On the other hand, some students enjoyed the comfort of their home. They did not waking up early in the morning to prepare for school. They found convenient to wake up and get into classroom in their pyjamas.

Students noticed that while in the digital classroom, the teachers' voices sounded all the same *"If you turn your head opposite to the screen and you just listen, without looking at the screen, you realise that all teacher's voices are the same."*. The students perceived no difference in the colour of the voice. In the same line, the students mentioned that during the online sessions they missed the passion that teachers show in the physical classroom. One of the students mentioned: *"There are no goose bumps, no felt emotions in our bodies in the digital classroom"* while she was caressing her arm to show the sense of feeling. Finally, students mentioned that digital classroom doesn't support the creation of anamnesis in the sense of recollections. *"Every day in the online sessions is the same with the previous one, every hour feels the same. Teaching sounds the same even if the person is different"*. They reported that *"taking classes online through a grey and boring screen from your room is not natural"*.

During their physical presence in school their experiences are so intense that *"they create anamnesis that will last for a lifetime, whereas in the digital classroom this is not happening"*. When the students were asked to describe how they experience the online learning platform they use during the pandemic in three words, the most prevalent words were: <u>Vioma</u> (lived experience including physical sensations/embodiment), <u>Diadrasis</u> (Interaction with the platform and the other participants in the classroom) and <u>Apodosis</u> (Effectiveness in relation to learning).

Parenting. Some parents reported that there was added tension between them and their children. They felt that teenagers are challenging to handle, in general, and the confinement period of pandemic made it worse. Many parents (12/19) argued with their teenage children because they believed that their children didn't participate in the lessons adequately. *"Our teenage children seem as if they don't care about the lessons"*.

4.3 Usability Evaluation

During the periods in which school was transferred online, the students used two platforms: Webex by Cisco (https://www.webex.com/), a virtual conferencing tool, for attending the live (synchronous) online lessons each day and the Panhellenic School Network platform under the domain http://www.sch.gr for all the official communication with the teachers and school administration, including the exchange of assignments in an asynchronous way. However, these platforms came with usability problems that hinder or made complicated the communication between teachers and students. These issues contributed to the "walls" the students have described in their communication with the teachers.

Due to the complicated functionality of the e-mail platform and the uncertainty of the delivery of the mails sent, three out of four teachers also used social media such as Facebook messenger to communicate with individual students or group of students or other additional software depending on their course needs e.g. The educator teaching chemistry shared course material, book lists and references via Facebook messenger. She had created a group which included all students of the classroom. She mentioned that "as students spent most of their time using social media platforms and chat it was more effective to share my course material through this channel".

The platforms were (as described and observed) complicated, hard to use and navigate and they failed to foster communication. In addition, the user experience and education were influenced by technical issues as overloading and failure of the platforms (i.e., when all the students of a country tried to get online at the same time) and the lack of ad-hoc technical support when needed.

WEBEX (https://www.webex.com/).

- Lack of live technical support.
- Screen sharing disappears when a student speaks in focus mode.
- Lack of interface personalization.
- Raising hand option requires three clicks in the mobile interface.
- It is described as boring and tiresome interface.

www.sch.gr

- Login difficulties a) due to the user credentials which were difficult to remember and impossible to change. The credentials were arranged and delivered to each student by the school administration. This caused frustration to most of the students as they had no control over it. b) Very often, during the first hour of the school day, when all students were trying to log in, the platform would crash. c) Multiple clicks to reach the login page.
- Hard to navigate menu and submenus. There is a variety of menus in the pages. Users find this confusing and hard to understand.
- Students find it hard to visit their e-class if not bookmarked. Each teacher has a different e-class url address, so students need to login and log out each hour. This means six-seven different url addresses each day.
- Notifications are not available, so they miss important deadlines for task assignments and tests. Students found it difficult to understand that in order to view assignment and test deadlines and dates they had to visit the calendar. As students mentioned they are not accustomed to receive information through a digital calendar whereas educators found this option very helpful.
- E-mail communication was problematic as the e-mails often got lost and the students had to check out their emails in three different locations. Students could send an email to their teachers in two ways, (a) by the message option in each student's e-class (Fig. 2) and (b) through the webmail platform https://webmail.sch.gr/ (Fig. 3). Often, messages were not received, and students weren't notified if their message was delivered. Webmail was frequently inaccessible as the platform crashed and users could not login, therefore teachers used their personal e-mail accounts or the messaging function of social media platforms to communicate assignments and deadlines.

Fig. 2. Message option in each student's e-class

Fig. 3. Webmail platform in https://webmail.sch.gr/

5 Discussion: Designing a Digital Learning Environment from a Culturally Different Percpective

The results of this study gave us a series of important notions we can use in order to create the conceptual design framework for UI/UX designers participating in the design process of intercultural online learning platforms. This section discusses these notions and the reason why they should be considered when designing. The notions are analysed through a different cultural angle based on Greek philosophy as the route and basis of their meaning. We mention certain philosophical sections referring to these notions and their connection in order to show the connection of the notions from the past to today and the link between their meaning and the users' perspectives as we retrieved it in this study. We find deep meaning, understanding and correlation between the results we retrieved and Greek philosophy. As it is proven by research [32–35, 37], users are dissatisfied with their online learning experience we find it important to investigate the meaning and the routes of notions in an effort to understand better why this dissatisfaction exists. We believe that part of this dissatisfaction stems from the fact that we haven't registered and understood the needs of all the stakeholders involved. There is a great need for rebuilding the platforms used for education and this should be done by starting from understanding what is important for the users involved. Since we refer to applications/platforms that are globally used we need to understand this notions and meanings from a cultural perspective as people coming from different cultural backgrounds perceive notions differently.

The notions referred to the conceptual design framework (Fig. 4) are of great importance for the success and efficiency of an intercultural educational platform as designers transform notions into experiences. We start by analysing the three prevalent notions as these were the reported from students: Vioma (Life experience), Diadrasis (Interaction) and Apodosis (Effectiveness).

5.1 Vioma (Life Experience)

As reported in the results section, the notion 'Vioma' [Βίωμα = Life experience] was mentioned in various points of this study. It was mentioned when students reported they can't create recollections through the online sessions and also when they were asked to describe, by using only three words, the notion 'experience' as they felt it during their online lessons.

If one translates the word 'Vioma' from Greek to English they will most definitely get "Experience" as a result but in Greek these are two different words. 'Vioma' means "deep immediate experience that one acquires by living something personally". 'Vioma' forms a humans' character and gives a special meaning in their lives. The etymology comes from the verb 'Live' [Βιώ = Ζω (Live)] whereas experience in Greek actually means "knowledge gained by seeing or doing something, from practical rather than theoretical engagement" (www.lexigram.gr).

According to the results of this study "vioma" is connected to recollections (anamnesis), memories, anaphora (reference), logic and aesthesis.

Anamnesis (Recollections)

As reported in the results section, students can't create recollections through online sessions. In Greek 'recollections' is translated to 'anamnesis'.

Memories are Build Through the 'Aesthesis'

"'Εκ μὲν οὖν αἰσθήσεως γίνεται μνήμη, ὥσπερ λέγομεν, ἐκ δὲ μνήμης πολλάκις τοῦ αὐτοῦ γινομένης ἐμπειρία· αἱ γὰρ πολλαὶ μνῆμαι τῷ ἀριθμῷ ἐμπειρία μία ἐστίν" – Aristotle, Posterior Analytics B.19, 100a.1, 100a.5

Translation: "out of sense-perception comes to be what we call memory, and out of frequently repeated memories of the same thing develops experience." [10].

Mneme (Memory)

Aristotle in his book Metaphysics [1, 2] refers to mneme in regards to experience with the following:

"γίγνεται δ' ἐκ τῆς μνήμης ἐμπειρία τοῖς ἀνθρώποις· αἱ γὰρ πολλαὶ μνῆμαι τοῦ αὐτοῦ πράγμα -981a.1 τος μιᾶς ἐμπειρίας δύναμιν ἀποτελοῦσιν" [1, 2].

Translation: "It is from recollections that humans acquire experience, because the numerous mnemes of the same thing eventually produce the effect of a single experience."

Physiological

Students used the word "Physiological". This is a synthetic word in Greek. It comes from 'physis' and 'logic' it means against the logic of nature.

Logic

According to Aristotle in Rhetorica, 1355a.10 a syllogism is a product of logic and this is what the students expressed when they said that there is no logic behind taking lessons online during the pandemic. The whole philosophy of this kind of education has no logic to their teenage minds. Staying in a room all day studying though a grey screen is irrational to them.

"οὗτος καὶ ἐνθυμηματικὸς ἂν εἴη μάλιστα, προσλαβὼν περὶ ποῖά τέ ἐστι τὸ ἐνθύμημα καὶ τίνας ἔχει διαφορὰς πρὸς τοὺς λογικοὺς συλλογισμούς. τό τε γὰρ ἀληθὲς καὶ τὸ ὅμοιον τῷ ἀληθεῖ"

Translation: "he who is best able to see how and from what elements a syllogism is produced will also be best skilled in the enthymeme, when he has further learnt what its subject-matter is and in what respects it differs from the syllogism of strict logic. The true and the approximately true are apprehended by the same faculty; it may also be noted that men have a sufficient natural instinct for what is true, and usually do arrive at the truth. Hence the man who makes a good guess at truth is likely to make a good guess at probabilities." [9].

Students also reported they lack 'anaphora' (reference) to what they so far know as school. They need interfaces that are designed to give them the 'aesthesis' (sensation, feeling, emotion) of the physical school in order to create life lasting experiences 'viomata'.

5.2 Diadrasis (Interaction)

Students understand usability differently than we do. When asked about it they referred to 'diadrasis' (interaction). Usability as we know it must be reconsidered for 'digital natives' [36] as technology is embedded in their lives, while their skills are not uniform [7]. They were born using apps whereas we 'digital immigrants' learned how to use them. They connect diadrasis to aesthesis, prosvasis, semiotics and ergonomy,

5.3 Apodosis (Effectiveness)

From the information collected though the discussions and interviews it is reported that students, educators and parents consider an online learning platform as effective when it produces results in regards to the pedagogy used and the gnosis or noesis acquired.

Gnosis (Knowledge)

There is no connection to education if Gnosi (Knowledge) is not present.

"ὁμολογοῦνται δ' οὐσίαι εἶναι τῶν αἰσθητῶν τινές, ὥστε ἐν ταύταις ζητητέον πρῶτον. πρὸ ἔργου γὰρ τὸ μεταβαίνειν εἰς τὸ γνωριμώτερον. ἡ γὰρ μάθησις οὕτω γίγνεται πᾶσι διὰ τῶν ἧττον γνωρίμων φύσει εἰς τὰ γνώριμα μᾶλλον· καὶ τοῦτο ἔργον ἐστίν, ὥσπερ ἐν ταῖς πράξεσι τὸ ποιῆσαι ἐκ τῶν ἑκάστῳ ἀγαθῶν τὰ ὅλως ἀγαθὰ ἑκάστῳ ἀγαθά, οὕτως ἐκ τῶν αὐτῷ γνωριμωτέρων τὰ τῇ φύσει γνώριμα αὐτῷ γνώριμα. τὰ δ' ἑκάστοις γνώριμα καὶ πρῶτα πολλάκις ἠρέμα ἐστὶ γνώριμα, καὶ μικρὸν ἢ οὐθὲν ἔχει τοῦ ὄντος· ἀλλ' ὅμως ἐκ τῶν φαύλως μὲν γνωστῶν αὐτῷ δὲ γνωστῶν τὰ ὅλως γνωστὰ γνῶναι πειρατέον, μεταβαίνοντας, ὥσπερ εἴρηται, διὰ τούτων αὐτῶν. Aristotle, Metaphysics, 1029a.30, 1029b.3, 1029b.5, 1029b.10.

Translation: "Now it is agreed that some sensible things are substances, and so we should begin our inquiry in connection with these. It is convenient to advance to the more intelligible; for learning is always acquired in this way, by advancing through what is less intelligible by nature to what is more so. And just as in actions it is our task to start from the good of the individual and make absolute good for the individual, so it is our task to start from what is more intelligible to oneself and make what is by nature intelligible to oneself." [12, 13].

5.4 Energeia (Energy)

According to students, positive energy keeps their interest in studying high both in the physical and in the online classroom. They want to feel positive 'energeia' (energy) in order to build their 'anamnesis' (recollections) and 'diadrasis' (interaction) through aesthetically interesting and personalized interfaces. They need to feel enthusiasm, euthymia and euphoria while learning online.

"ἐπεὶ καὶ ἡδονὴ ἡ ἐνέργεια τούτου (καὶ διὰ τοῦτο ἐγρήγορσις αἴσθησις νόησις ἥδιστον, ἐλπίδες δὲ καὶ μνῆμαι διὰ ταῦτα)." – Aristotle, Metaphysics, 1072b.15.

Translation: "actuality is also pleasure (and for this reason waking, sensation and thinking are most pleasant, and hopes and memories are pleasant because of them)." [11].

6 The Conceptual Design Framework

The results of this study are visualized in the Conceptual Design Framework in Fig. 4 as a different cultural approach and proposal for UI/UX Designers.

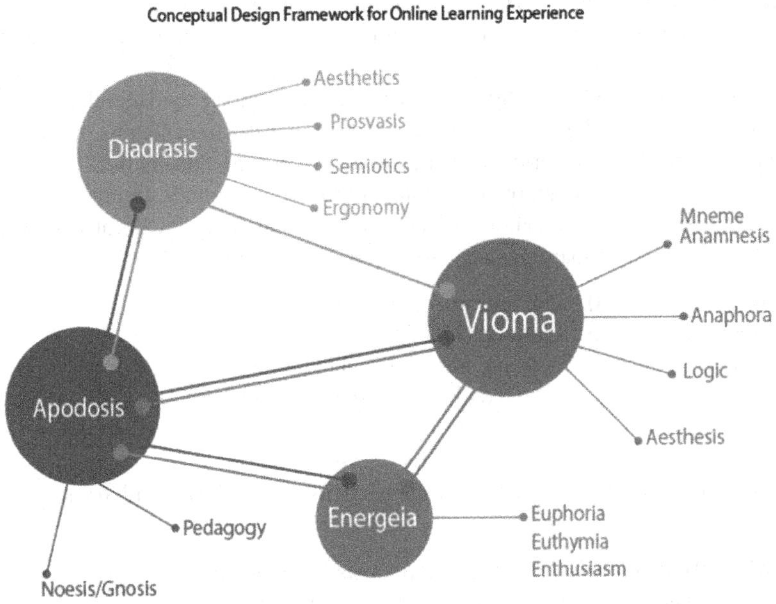

Fig. 4. Conceptual Design Framework for Online Learning Experience

6.1 How to Use the Conceptual Design Framework

Each circle is the result of the main notions discussed in this research in regards to experience. These notions are the results retrieved from the results of this research. There are three main circles: Diadrasis (Interaction), Vioma (Lived Experience), Apodosis (Effectiveness) and a secondary one named Energeia (Energy). These circles are connected to each other with lines showing the relation and importance of interconnectivity between them. In order to keep the balance and therefore better learning and teaching experience through the online learning platform designed, the UI/UX design team should take into consideration and work on concepts and ideas for all the notions included.

6.2 Questions to Support the UX Design Process

The conceptual framework can't support the design process without a series of questions per main notion area. These questions work as the basis for brainstorming and discussion among the design team and as a result for the creation of concepts and ideas to support the design and development of features who will offer a better learning and teaching experience through the online learning platform developed. Although the main question that each UI/UX designer should examine is: "How do we design and build effective, personalised and adoptive learning and teaching experiences through interactive features?" the following questions will help the creation of concepts and ideas per notion and will enhance the effectiveness of the online learning platform.

Vioma (Lived Experience). The notion vioma is connected to:
Mneme/Anamnesis (memory/recollection), Anaphora (reference), Logic and Aesthesis
Questions: How can UX design enhance students' memories and recollections? What kind of features need to be designed and developed in order to make this possible? How can this be applicable in a variety of educational systems and diversities?
Proposal: Through metaphors in virtual environments, sounds, interaction in online classrooms besides the session hours that remind students of the breaks at school, virtual excursions and games (board games, chess), virtual libraries and labs.

Diadrasis (Interaction). The notion Diadrasis is connected to:
Aesthetics, Prosvasis, Semiotics and Ergonomy.
Questions: How do we design interfaces and experiences for all?
Proposal: By giving personalisation and adaptation features per user, by providing online tech support, by giving accessibility features, by educating teachers through online courses through the learning platforms, by building platforms which facilitate communication without the need of other software or platforms to interact with the stakeholders involved.

Apodosis (Effectiveness). The notion Apodosis is connected to:
Pedagogy and Gnosis/Noesis (knowledge/understanding).
Questions: How do we design effective learning and teaching experiences for all? How do we design platforms that facilitate the transfer of knowledge? How do we design platforms which support the teachers' pedagogical role and practice?
Proposal: By understanding and registering needs from all stakeholders involved, by providing personalisation per user, by designing all the necessary tools per field taught area (e.g. in order for a mathematician to teach there is need for an interactive whiteboard, geometrical instruments, scientific calculator).

7   Identifying the User Profile Types of the Online Student

Identifying different profiles in a physical classroom is easy for an experienced educator. There are pedagogical approaches for the engagement of the variety of student idiosyncrasies but what is happening in a digital classroom when cameras and microphones are off? How do we recognize different personalities and characteristics?

By identifying students profiles the UI/UX Designer will be able to propose features that will help the engagement [14, 15] of all and possibly propose the design and development of a diagnostic performance tool that will analyze on the spot performances and actions in order to help the educator identify online characteristics for student's activity.

From the student participation percentage reported in the results section we ended up in the following user profile types. This will be the basis for future research as the online learning applications and platforms change and so do the user profiles:

Type 1: Students who participate when the educator addresses a question directly to them.
Type 2: Students who participate when the educator addresses a question to all.
Type 3: Students who never participate verbally by any means. They either write in the chat or communicate via e-mail.

All students had their cameras off throughout the sessions. From an educators' point of view this is a dreadful experience. There is a tremendous difference of the student profiles between the physical and the digital classroom. Even students of high performance rate in the physical classroom don't participate actively. According to the teachers there is a reduction of up to 70% in each individual's performance and this varies depending on the grade. Those in the final grades of secondary education have lost all interest in participating actively.

8   Conclusion

Focusing on other cultures, different meanings of notions, as well as philosophies gives a completely different understanding and approach of user experience and user centred design. A proof for this need is the fact that Greek students used a different notion while expressing 'experience' because as they mentioned 'experience' isn't enough.

We need to redefine usability for young children, teenagers and young adults. What UI/UX designers follow until now from the International Standards (ISO 9241-11:2018) to methodologies, protocols and the global bibliography should be reconsidered as these generations experience usability in completely different ways than we who design applications for them do. The Digital Natives (born > 1998) [7] have been brought up using the internet from their early years, they don't know life without it, and they use interfaces, platforms, applications, systems differently. Digital systems are in their gins. They are the future of the world. If we train them with cold and insensitive tools they will do the same in their lives and work. Bring pedagogy into e-class not technology into pedagogy. Making decisions based on the technological concerns - without considering the essential mission of education in schools – undermines the ethical dimensions of preparing students for the adult world [8]. Let's give students life lasting experiences through our interfaces in the online learning environments. We live in the era of artificial intelligence and a pandemic proves that our tools are not ready for a human to human interaction through them. Last but not least the need for a uniform platform that includes all tools is essential in order to avoid the use of multiple applications that create confusion on all sides.

During conducting this study many areas of research have risen. Pedagogical HCI (digital or hybrid pedagogy) needs to be applied in the design and development of online learning e-learning platforms and applications taking into consideration the differences of student cultural profiles in order to empower learning through technology. Understanding the importance of designing experiences through different cultural and philosophical approaches gives a whole new meaning to the user experience design process.

Acknowledgments. We would like to thank all the participants, students, parents, educators, who helped us conduct this study for their time and the wonderful discussions we had.

References

1. Kalfas, B.: Anthology of texts and translations by Aristotle. In: Kalfas, B. (ed.) The Philosophy of Aristotle. Association of Greek Academic Libraries, Athens (2015). http://hdl.handle.net/11419/682. Accessed 25 Feb 2021
2. Kalfas, B.: The Philosophy of Aristotle. Association of Greek Academic Libraries, Athens (2015). http://hdl.handle.net/11419/683. Accessed 25 Feb 2021
3. http://data.perseus.org/citations/urn:cts:greekLit:tlg0086.tlg025.perseus-grc1:1.980b. Accessed 25 Feb 2021
4. Rogers, C.R.: Empathic: an unappreciated way of being. Counselling Psychol. **5**(2), 2–10 (1975)
5. Rogers, C.R.: A theory of therapy, personality and interpersonal relationships, as developed in the client-centered framework. In: Koch, S. (ed.) Psychology: A Study of Science, pp. 210–211. McGraw Hill, New York (1959)
6. American Academy of Pediatrics: Bright Futures for Heath Supervision of Infants, Children and Adolescents, pp. 539–557 (2008)
7. Bennett, S., Maton, K., Kervin, L.: The 'digital natives' debate: a critical review of the evidence. Br. J. Edu. Technol. **39**(5), 775–786 (2008)
8. Kilfoye, C.: A voice from the past calls for classroom technology. The Phi Delta Kappan **94**(7), 53–56 (2013). JSTOR. www.jstor.org/stable/23611702. Accessed 25 Feb 2021
9. http://classics.mit.edu/Aristotle/rhetoric.1.i.html. Accessed 25 Feb 2021
10. http://classics.mit.edu/Aristotle/posterior.2.ii.html. Accessed 25 Feb 2021
11. http://data.perseus.org/citations/urn:cts:greekLit:tlg0086.tlg025.perseus-grc1:12.1072b. Accessed 25 Feb 2021
12. http://data.perseus.org/citations/urn:cts:greekLit:tlg0086.tlg025.perseus-grc1:7.1029a. Accessed 25 Feb 2021
13. http://data.perseus.org/citations/urn:cts:greekLit:tlg0086.tlg025.perseus-grc1:7.1029b. Accessed 25 Feb 2021
14. O'Brien, H.L., Toms, E.G.: What is user engagement? A conceptual framework for defining user engagement with technology. J. Am. Soc. Inf. Sci. Technol. **59**(6), 938–955 (2008)
15. Bryson, C. (ed.): Understanding and Developing Student Engagement (2014)
16. Berry, J.W., Berry, J.W., Poortinga, Y.H., Segall, M.H., Dasen, P.R.: Cross-Cultural Psychology: Research and Applications. Cambridge University Press, Cambridge (2002)

17. Hall, E.T.: The Hidden Dimension, vol. 609. Doubleday, Garden City (1966)

18. Lustig, M.W., Koester, J.: Intercultural Competence – Interpersonal Communication Across Cultures, p. 85, 7th edn. Pearson (2013)

19. Kluckhohn, F.R., Strodtbeck, F.L.: Variations in value orientations (1961)

20. Beyer, H., Holtzblatt, K.: Contextual design. Interactions 6(1), 32–42 (1999)

21. Hall, L., Hume, C., Tazzyman, S.: Five degrees of happiness: effective smiley face Likert scales for evaluating with children. In: Proceedings of the 15th International Conference on Interaction Design and Children, pp. 311–321, June 2016

22. Ramsay, M., Nielsen, J.: WAP usability deja vu: 1994 all over again. Nielsen Norman Group (2000)

23. Norman, D.A.: Human-centered design considered harmful. Interactions 12(4), 14–19 (2005)

24. Chin, J.P., Diehl, V.A., Norman, K.L.: Development of an instrument measuring user satisfaction of the human-computer interface. In: Proceedings of the SIGCHI Conference on Human Factors in Computing Systems, pp. 213–218, May 1988

25. Lazar, J., Feng, J.H., Hochheiser, H.: Research Methods in Human-Computer Interaction. Morgan Kaufmann (2017)

26. Boone, H.N., Boone, D.A.: Analyzing Likert data. J. Extension 50(2), 1–5 (2012)

27. Holtzblatt, K., Beyer, H.: Contextual design: evolved. In: Synthesis Lectures on Human-Centered Informatics, vol. 7, no. 4, pp. 1–91 (2014)

28. Blume, H.: Atlantic (1998). https://www.theatlantic.com/magazine/archive/1998/09/neurod iversity/305909/. Accessed 25 Mar 2021

29. Beyer, H., Holtzblatt, K.: Contextual Design: Defining Customer-Centered Systems. Morgan Kaufmann, San Francisco (1998)

30. Coghlan, D., Brydon-Miller, M.: The SAGE Encyclopedia of Action Research, vols. 1–2. SAGE Publications Ltd. London (2014). https://doi.org/10.4135/9781446294406

31. Herr, K., Anderson, G.: The Action Research Dissertation. Sage, Thousand Oaks (2005)

32. Nikiforos, S., Tzanavaris, S., Kermanidis, K.L.: Post-pandemic pedagogy: distance education in Greece during COVID-19 pandemic through the eyes of the teachers. Eur. J. Eng. Technol. Res. (2020)

33. Siakalli, M., Mousoulidou, M., Christodoulou, A., Savvidou, A., Kouppa, K.: Secondary education and COVID-19. Encyclopedia 2(1), 409–427 (2022). MDPI AG. https://doi.org/10.3390/encyclopedia2010025

34. Progga, F.T., Shahria, M.D.T., Ahmed, N.: The effectiveness and acceptance of collaborative E-learning in the context of Bangladesh. In: 2020 IEEE International Conference on Teaching, Assessment, and Learning for Engineering (TALE). 2020 IEEE International Conference on Teaching, Assessment, and Learning for Engineering (TALE), pp. 554–558 (2020). https://doi.org/10.1109/TALE48869.2020.9368445

35. Ali, W.: Online and remote learning in higher education institutes: a necessity in light of COVID-19 pandemic. High. Educ. Stud. 10(3), 16 (2020). https://doi.org/10.5539/hes.v10 n3p16

36. Prensky, M.: Digital natives, digital immigrants part 2: do they really think differently? On the Horiz. 9, 1–6 (2001). https://doi.org/10.1108/10748120110424843

37. Maphosa, V.: Factors influencing student's perceptions towards E-learning adoption during COVID-19 pandemic: a developing country context. Eur. J. Interact. Multimed. Educ. 2(2), e02109 (2021). https://doi.org/10.30935/ejimed/11000

38. Wright, P., McCarthy, J.: Empathy and experience in HCI. In: Proceedings of the SIGCHI Conference on Human Factors in Computing Systems, pp. 637–646, April 2008

39. Kouprie, M., Visser, F.S.: A framework for empathy in design: stepping into and out of the user's life. J. Eng. Des. 20(5), 437–448 (2009)

40. Saldaña, J.: The Coding Manual for Qualitative Researchers. SAGE Publications Ltd. (2021)

Usability Study of a Pilot Database Interface for Consulting Open Educational Resources in the Context of the ENCORE Project

Andrea Vázquez-Ingelmo[1]([⊠]), Alicia García-Holgado[1],
Francisco José García-Peñalvo[1], and Filippo Chiarello[2]

[1] Grupo de Investigación GRIAL, Departamento de Informática y Automática, Instituto Universitario de Ciencias de la Educación, Universidad de Salamanca, Salamanca, Spain
{andreavazquez,aliciagh,fgarcia}@usal.es
[2] School of Engineering, Department of Energy, Systems, Land and Construction Engineering, University of Pisa, Pisa, Italy
filippo.chiarello@unipi.it
https://ror.org/02f40zc51

Abstract. Open educational resources (OER) are materials such as textbooks, lessons, and other teaching and learning tools that are freely accessible for use. OER are gaining popularity as a means for educators to give their students access to high-quality, economical educational materials. OER can encourage sharing information and resources throughout the educational community while also helping lower the cost of education for both students and teachers. In this context, the ENCORE project seeks, among other goals, to assist students and workers in acquiring the skills necessary to deal with economic, ecological, and technological challenges as well as to address the skills gap between the supply of educational institutions and the demand of employers and assist educators in staying abreast of the constantly changing landscape of skills. One of the first steps to reach the project's goals is to build a robust database that contains quality OERs linked to green, digital, and entrepreneurial (GDE) skills. A graphical interface has been developed to retrieve and display information about the OERs, and, in turn, to make these resources available for any stakeholder. However, due to the significant quantity of information, it is important to develop an interface that enhances user experience. This work presents a usability study of the ENCORE project's OER database interface carried out through a System Usability Scale (SUS) questionnaire, as well as future interface improvements based on the results.

Keywords: Data management · Open Educational Resources · GDE skills · Usability · SUS

1 Introduction

Open educational resources (OER) are increasing their popularity due to their free accessibility and their high availability for teachers and students. Open textbooks, lessons, and any freely accessible learning tool can foster information sharing through educational

P. Zaphiris and A. Ioannou (Eds.): HCII 2023, LNCS 14040, pp. 420–429, 2023.
https://doi.org/10.1007/978-3-031-34411-4_28

communities while helping to overcome the cost of education, enriching the learning experience.

However, it is important to keep improving the means to access OERs. to leverage them, continue extending their use, and develop new quality resources.

In this context, the ENCORE project (ref. 101055893 - ERASMUS-EDU-2021-PI-ALL-INNO) aims to assist students and workers in acquiring the skills necessary to deal with economic, ecological, and technological challenges as well as to address the skills gap between the supply of educational institutions and the demand of employers and assist educators in staying abreast of the constantly changing landscape of skills.

To do so, one of the first steps to reach the project's goals is to build a robust database that contains quality OERs linked to green, digital, and entrepreneurial (GDE) skills.

The ENCORE database seeks to offer quality OERs through a simple and interoperable interface that allows users to search, filter, examine, and access quality educational resources.

This work presents the initial version of the ENCORE database interface and the results obtained from a preliminary usability study through the System Usability Scale (SUS) evaluation. The results of this initial evaluation are promising and have been vastly useful in supporting the introduction of new improvements and features for subsequent versions of the database management system.

The rest of this paper is organized as follows. Section 2 describes the methodology followed to develop the database, as well as the usability study protocol. Section 3 outlines the evaluated version of the database interface. Section 4 presents the quantitative and qualitative results obtained from the SUS evaluation. Finally, Sect. 5 discusses the results and Sect. 6 presents the conclusions of the work.

2 Methodology

2.1 Database Conceptualization

The main goal of the ENCORE database is to unify OERs and make them available and searchable by different parameters. To unify and characterize these resources, it is crucial to work under a well-defined and general schema.

Following this idea, the ENCORE database schema is based on the Dublin Core Metadata Element Set (DCMES) [1, 2]. This open-standard metadata provides different attributes to define educational resources. Furthermore, since DCMES's objectives center on "simplicity of creation and maintenance, commonly recognized semantics, worldwide scope, and extensibility," they are in line with the specifications of the ENCORE database [1, 2].

Considering this schema, each OER is characterized by the following DC metadata attributes (Fig. 1):

- Title. An OER should have a title describing its content.
- Description. The description is crucial in the context of the ENCORE project. OERs must be clearly described to extract the GDE skills from their content.
- Subject. The subject of the OER depicts the field addressed by the resource, and it is also crucial to identify the skills addressed through the content.

- Creator. The author or authors of the OER.
- Contributor. Entity or entities that contributed to the OER content.
- Publisher. Entity or entities in charge of making the resource available.
- Publication date. The date in which the OER was published.
- Type. Category of the resource (image, dataset, text, etc.).
- Format. Technical format of the resource (application/pdf, image/gif, etc.).
- Source. Reference to other resources from which the OER was derived.
- Language. The language of the OER.
- Coverage. The applicability of the resource.
- Rights. Information related to the OER's rights.
- Relation. This attribute is represented to the "related to" relationship in the domain model and depicts related resources to a certain OER.

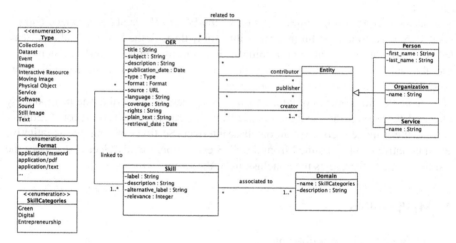

Fig. 1. Domain model of the ENCORE database.

2.2 Database Development

Selecting the proper technologies is crucial to provide an efficient, flexible, and robust database. In this sense, different database technologies were analyzed to identify their main features and potential caveats in the project's context. After the analysis, PostgreSQL was selected as the base technology for the ENCORE database.

PostgreSQL is a robust object-relational database system that is completely free and open source. Due to its many features, including native partitioning, parallel query, support for foreign data wrappers, robust JSON features, streaming and logical replication, and the availability of numerous open-source tools for high availability (HA), backups, and monitoring, PostgreSQL aligns with the ENCORE database requirements.

Moreover, the possibility of handling queries using either SQL or NoSQL syntax provides great flexibility, as well as scalability, as the database schema could be modified to fit new requirements or necessities without consuming significant resources.

The database is complemented with a custom graphical interface developed with the Django (https://www.djangoproject.com/) web framework.

2.3 Usability Study

The System Usability Scale was selected as the instrument to assess the platform's usability (SUS). The SUS questionnaire offers a practical, reliable, and valid [3, 4] method for rating a system's usability. Given that there are only 10 things in the test, it is also a useful tool that can be used with a variety of systems [5].

The items of the questionnaires are positive and negative alternated statements rated on a 1 to 5 Likert scale (from "strongly disagree" to "strongly agree", respectively) [6].

The simplicity and reliability that the SUS test provides fit the goals of the preliminary usability study of the ENCORE database management system interface.

The instrument was implemented using a customized version of LimeSurvey (https://www.limesurvey.org), an Open-Source on-line survey web application.

The data collected by the instrument were downloaded to obtain a structured dataset with all the answers. Although the score calculation is relatively simple [6], the analysis of the responses has been made through the Python Pandas [7] library to keep track of the data transformations.

The interpretation of the results is based on previous System Usability Scale studies and benchmarks [8, 9] which allow SUS score comparisons and provide insights about the perceived usability of the system.

The participants of this study were reached out through the ENCORE project's consortium. For this initial evaluation, they were asked to try and navigate through the platform and fill out the SUS questionnaire with their opinions and suggestions for improvements.

3   Platform Overview

The ENCORE database management system's first version consists of a single-page web application. The application's homepage shows the OER database through a data table containing the main attributes of each OER (Fig. 2); title, subject, publication date, retrieval date, resource format, level (of the contents), and related GDE skills.

Also, a set of data visualizations summarize the contents of the database, including the total number of OERs, unique creators, the number of different OER formats, and the top GDE skills covered by the OERs.

More details regarding each record are displayed in the interface when clicking on the information icon, including the description, creators, publishers, etc.

The system also allows users to filter the results displayed on the screen. Every attribute present in the database is available for filtering (Fig. 3).

Finally, it is important to remark that in the evaluated first version of the platform, the database was populated with automatically generated (synthetic) data.

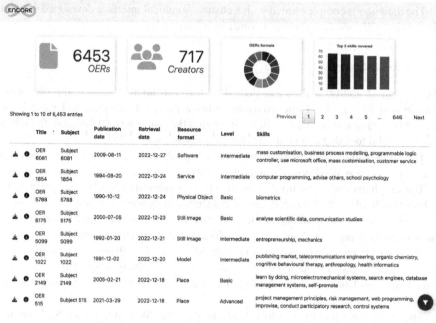

Fig. 2. Homepage of the ENCORE database system.

Fig. 3. Filtering capabilities of the ENCORE database.

4 Results

Ten users from the ENCORE project's consortium participated in the survey, which, although small, is a reliable sample for the SUS questionnaire [4].

The guidelines from [6] were followed to compute the SUS score. In this case, the score contributions from each item were added. Given that each item's score must range from 0 to 4, the positive items of the questionnaire were subtracted 1 point, while the negative items' scores were subtracted from 5, to normalize the sample. The sum of the scores is finally multiplied by 2.5 to obtain the overall value of the SUS between 0 to 100.

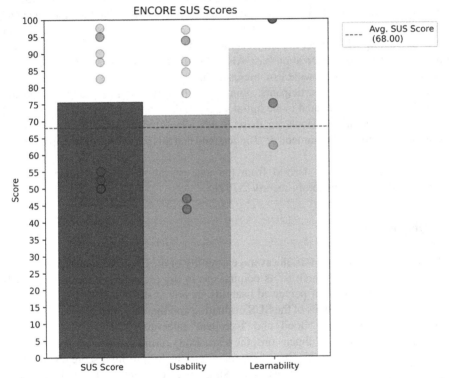

Fig. 4. Visual representation of the SUS questionnaire results. Individual points represent the individual responses.

The SUS score was calculated following the scoring instructions [6] for every participant's responses. Additionally, the learnability score (from items 4 and 10) and usability score (from items 1, 2, 3, 5, 6, 7, 8, and 9) were also calculated and transformed to fit a scale from 0 to 100. These calculations yielded the following results (Fig. 4):

- The average perceived usability of the ENCORE database is **75.5**, which is considered a good SUS score (interpretation based on the studies done in [8, 9]).

- On the other hand, the perceived learnability is significantly higher (**91.25**) than the usability (**71.56**), both also being good scores.

Some useful comments were also retrieved from the participants. The main concerns are related to using synthetic data for the first version of the database, and the filters. For example, Participant #1 pointed out that "Having a code in the subject section does not orient well." This issue is only related to the use of synthetic data, as the subjects were not meaningful yet.

Regarding the filter panel, participant #2 highlighted that the position of the filter is not intuitive, participant #3 suggested switching the position of the OER list, and participant #5 remarked that the position did not seem right.

Participant #9 also mentioned interesting usage scenarios: "Since the OER loaded are 'fake,' it was difficult for me to evaluate most dimensions. I liked the interface and the visualizations. But as a teacher, the first thing I would do is to try and search for some interesting OER about my subjects taught. Then I would analyze the quality and how informative the visualizations are. Also, I would consider how efficient the search engine is in leading me to what I'm interested in."

Finally, most of the participants, pointed out that the sorting capabilities did not work. This problem is related to the initial stages of development and will be addressed in subsequent iterations. However, these issues were known by the participants. For example, participant #7 commented: "I understand that this is a test it will be implemented in the future."

The complete results derived from the analysis and related comments can be consulted at https://zenodo.org/record/7576915.

5   Discussion

After carrying out the analysis, the average usability of the ENCORE database interface for 10 users was 75.5, which is, as pointed out in the previous section, a good SUS score above the average of perceived usability in web systems (68.00) [5]. Following the interpretation guidelines of the SUS evaluation and the SUS adjective rating [8], the obtained score falls in the "Good" and "Excellent" intervals.

Regarding the derived dimensions, the learnability of the system obtained excellent results with a score of 91.25. One of the main reasons for this high score could be the system's simplicity, as it only consists of a single page containing a table of OERs and a set of filters. In this sense, users did not perceive any problems in learning how to use the system from scratch.

On the other hand, the usability dimension scored the lowest result in this analysis, with a 71.56 rating. This result is also good following the SUS analysis interpretation, however, the open comment section of the questionnaire shed light on the usability issues present in the system.

For example, the main issues were related to the filters, as users indicated that their location on the screen was not intuitive or practical. Also, the navigation of the OER table was also complex, as several important attributes needed to be displayed in a limited screen space.

Following the user evaluation results and comments, a new version of the ENCORE database interface is being designed to tackle the mentioned issues. One of the goals of the new interface is related to the OER attributes arrangement to improve the readability of the records (Fig. 5).

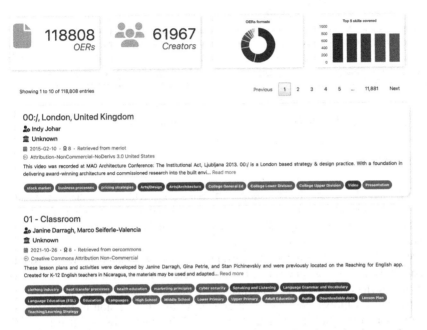

Fig. 5. Improvements made on the interface following the evaluation results.

In this sense, the original OER table has been broken down into individual "cards" that hold the same amount of information in a newer, more readable format. As displayed in Fig. 6, each OER record holds (in order of appearance) the title, the creator(s), the publisher(s), the date of publication, the quality score given by the ENCORE OER quality guidelines (out of the scope of this paper), the ROER from which it was retrieved, the copyright, the description, and a set of pills that depict the related skills (pink), the subject (blue), the audience (light blue), the format (purple), and the media type (light purple).

Further improvements will involve the modification of the filters section to address the issues related to the intuitiveness and usability of this crucial feature.

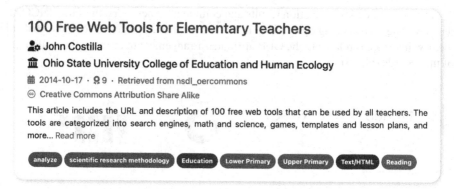

Fig. 6. Detail of a record in the new interface.

6   Conclusions

The ENCORE database is a software component that aims to centralize, characterize, and make Open Educational Resources available for teachers and students. This database will be employed to link OERs to GDE skills, create conceptual maps of the OER contents, and develop learning paths, among other uses.

However, it is crucial to provide a powerful user interface to enable users to leverage the valuable information contained in the ENCORE database. For these reasons, a custom interface has been developed to ease navigation among thousands of OERs.

The System Usability Score has been applied to the first version of the database interface to obtain insights about its usability. It is important to remark that the SUS is not diagnostic, but it gives an overview of the usability of a system. The database interface obtained an average score of 75.50, which is a score above the average (68.00) and is considered a good result.

However, the SUS questionnaire was complemented with an open field to gather comments and opinions about the system. This information gave hints about the improvements to be made to increase the system's usability, which is being addressed following the suggestions.

Future works will be focused on solving the usability issues related to the filtering feature of the system, as well as continuing to test the platform with end users.

Acknowledgments. This project was undertaken with the support of the Erasmus+ Programme of the European Union: "Partnerships for Innovation: Alliances." (ERASMUS-EDU-2021-PI-ALL-INNO). Project ENriching Circular use of OeR for Education (ENCORE) (Reference number 101055893). Views and opinions expressed are those of the author(s) only and do not necessarily reflect those of the European Union or the European Education and Culture Executive Agency (EACEA). Neither the European Union nor EACEA can be held responsible for them.

References

1. Kunze, J., Baker, T.: The Dublin core metadata element set (2007)
2. Weibel, S., Kunze, J., Lagoze, C., Wolf, M.: Dublin core metadata for resource discovery (1998)
3. Brooke, J.: SUS: a retrospective. J. Usability Stud. **8**, 29–40 (2013)
4. Tullis, T.S., Stetson, J.N.: A comparison of questionnaires for assessing website usability. In: Usability Professional Association Conference, pp. 1–12
5. Bangor, A., Kortum, P.T., Miller, J.T.: An empirical evaluation of the system usability scale. Intl. J. Hum.-Comput. Interact. **24**, 574–594 (2008)
6. Brooke, J.: SUS-A quick and dirty usability scale. Usability Eval. Ind. **189**, 4–7 (1996)
7. McKinney, W.: pandas: a foundational Python library for data analysis and statistics. Python High Perform. Sci. Comput. **14**(9), 1–9 (2011)
8. Bangor, A., Kortum, P., Miller, J.: Determining what individual SUS scores mean: adding an adjective rating scale. J. Usability Stud. **4**, 114–123 (2009)
9. Sauro, J.: A practical guide to the system usability scale: Background, benchmarks & best practices. Createspace Independent Pub, Scotts Valley, CA, US (2011)

Technology-Supported Teaching

Digital Skills During Emergency Remote Teaching, for VUCA Environments

Carmen Graciela Arbulú Pérez Vargas(✉) ⓘ, Moreno Muro Juan Pablo ⓘ,
Lourdes Gisella Palacios Ladines ⓘ, Cristian Augusto Jurado Fernández ⓘ,
and Pérez Delgado José Willams ⓘ

César Vallejo University, Lambayeque, Perú
{carbulu,mmurojp,jfernandezca,pdelgadoj}@ucvvirtual.edu.pe,
lpalacios@ucv.edu.pe

Abstract. The confinement caused by COVID-19, led to the physical closure of Peruvian universities, without interruption of the educational service, the research corresponds to a private university licensed by the National Superintendence of Higher University Education, The objective was to analyze digital skills during the exercise of emergency remote teaching, in situations of Volatility, Uncertainty, Complexity and Ambiguity, (identified by the acronym VUCA) by undergraduate and graduate teachers from a private Peruvian university. Using quantitative methodology, a questionnaire was applied that shows Digital skills at the basic level decreased from 36% to 6%, while the advanced level went from 12% to 36%. Sensory (visual, auditory) and intellectual or learning adaptations were developed by teachers during virtual tutoring, listening, reading, answering questions also predominated, time dedication and use of space and time in virtual environments increased. of learning, the digital technologies that have facilitated distance learning have been 100% synchronous videoconferences, 85% use of collaborative tools, digital resources, platform and Internet connection. Digital skills the basic level decreased from 36% to 6%, the advanced level went from 12% to 36%. The sensory (visual, auditory) and intellectual or learning adaptations were developed by the teachers during the virtual tutorial, listening, reading, answering questions predominated, time dedication and use of space increased, time in the virtual environments of learning, the digital technologies that have facilitated distance learning have been 100% synchronous videoconferences, 85% collaborative tools, digital resources and the Internet.

Keywords: First Keyword · Second Keyword · Third Keyword

1 Introduction

1.1 Emergency Remote Teaching (ERE)

The educational model during the health emergency due to the COVID-19 pandemic, was assumed in Peru by private and public licensed universities with a guarantee of responsibility, given that they had basic conditions for quality service (CBC). One of

P. Zaphiris and A. Ioannou (Eds.): HCII 2023, LNCS 14040, pp. 433–443, 2023.
https://doi.org/10.1007/978-3-031-34411-4_29

the indicators of these conditions is the Infrastructure and adequate equipment for the fulfillment of their functions, which was essential for the universities to have the capacity to implement emergency remote education against COVID-19. This is because, among other variables, the availability of internet was established as a requirement in each university location, with sufficient bandwidth for university higher education (Minedu 2021).

In this context of educational disruption, it led universities to face in a very complex way in terms of technological infrastructure, connectivity, remote pedagogy and other aspects, new learning ecosystems with virtual interaction between the subjects of the teacher-student pairing (Minedu 2021).

In the midst of uncertain, complex and ambiguous volatile conditions that disturb and impact the linearity of universities, these factors led to managing and rethinking learning, adapted to challenges and opportunities, that technologies provide: "emergency remote education (ERE) was the temporary shift of instruction to an alternative mode due to crisis circumstances" In which it was not about recreating a robust educational ecosystem, but rather providing temporary access to instruction and educational supports in a way that is quickly established and is reliably available during an emergency or crisis (Hodges et al. 2020).

On the other hand, to achieve student satisfaction regarding the new modality of education and academic performance, due to the facilities of the built environment and the health, safety, comfort, impact of the experience on the professional future, and how it would affect it. Were current concerns during remote distance learning (ERE) (Tleuken et al. 2022; Ni, Fitzmaurice 2021) taking these aspects into account, the challenge for universities was greater.

1.2   VUCA Environments in Emergency Remote Teaching

The investigations show that this acronym was stamped by the US Army War College at the end of 1990, it can be said that its fabric covers all fields of human activity, the social, economic and geopolitical fields associated with digitization and a change in the technological structure, which begin to have a broader impact, including the educational system, which exerts its influence in terms of quantity and quality of information, making turbulent transitions in a globalized and digitized world (Zainab and Abd 2022). (Taskan et al. 2022).

For this reason, since the COVID-19 pandemic, the conceptual essence of its meaning has served to make a series of reflections for a greater understanding in the educational field, showing concern for the pedagogical risks that teachers must face and new ways of teacher leadership that adapts to a VUCA context (Taskan et al. 2022; Panthalookaran 2022; Salakhova et al. 2021). VUCA is a transdisciplinary concept whose definitions vary, depending on the disciplines and situations in which it is used, other ideas refer to the overlapping of the VUCA components, there is no clear distinction between the constructs, along the same lines beyond establishing a by definition, VUCA conditions make any effort to understand the future and plan responses futile (Gaultier Le Bris S. et al. 2019; Taskan et al. 2022; Bennett and Lemoine 2014).

1.3 Digital Competence and Learning Ecosystems

Teaching practice in recent years has resulted from the breaking of the classic canons of use of space and time in virtual learning environments, with the integration of multiformats with some characteristics of the new learning ecologies (Leal-urueña and Rojas-mesa 2018), the COVID-19 pandemic being a trigger that has accelerated the adoption of interactive learning ecosystems, simulations of objects in virtual environments that raise the possibility of generating an interface that is increasingly accessible to the user, diversifying the number of common devices, virtual equipment, smartphones or tablets, from which it is accessed, expanding their number and developing specific standards that are responsive (Rubio-Tamayo, J; Guimarães 2018).

It is undeniable then, the importance of usability as a key factor in the external cognitive load, in the performance of a particular task imposed on the cognitive system of the learner, the instruction should not overload the working memory which would impede learning (Paas et al. 2003, p.64; Andrade-Lotero 2012). The biggest challenge, of virtual teachers, goes beyond being a content digitizer that is reduced to the change of format, but mediation, which achieves so that various contents are translated into all forms of learning, with many resources that favors technology and the internet (Suárez 2019).

Thus, some precedents place the digital teaching competence as transversal in their practice related to other great competences such as: knowing how to do, knowing how to be with others and knowing how to be (Nieto and Callejas 2017, p. 17) and their feasible evaluation through of rubrics, when dimensions such as didactics, planning, organization, personal and professional ethics, scenarios or context where the teacher acts are considered, with levels of digital competence such as: beginners, medium, expert and transformative (Lázaro-Cantabrana et al. 2019).

However, in light of the ERE, if one takes into account the ecological metaphor applied to the media, which considers two interpretations: the media as generators of environments that "affect the subjects who use them" and the media "as species that live in the same ecosystem and establish relationships with each other" (Scolari 2013), would imply a new perspective of promoting and evaluating digital skills, because the indicators from pre-pandemic planning would not be adjusted to the ERE.

Focusing the reflection on the educational field, specifically on teaching praxis, the so-called Digital Teaching Competence (CDD) emerges, with a tendency towards instrumental aspects, however, it is still conceived as a line of research under construction; with aspects that the teacher must master (Cabero 2020, p. 2). The systemic approach favors the way of approaching the development of digital skills in all those involved to assume a different way of understanding quality learning (Andrade-Arenas et al. 2022), necessary to face volatile, uncertain, complex and ambiguous.

It is then a priority to consider the importance of developing digital competence in teachers. More than a decade ago UNESCO considered:

«Digital competence implies the critical and safe use of Information Society Technologies for work, free time and communication. Relying on basic ICT skills: use of computers to retrieve, evaluate, store, produce, present and exchange information,

and to communicate and participate in collaborative networks via the Internet»
(European Parliament and the Council, 2006).

It is clear that the university campuses face dimensions of the VUCA environment
during the health crisis, with technology being part of the solution and at the same time
part of the problem, hence the idea that.

"Technology at the University is not the end, but it is the essential means to develop
in a society that is already digital. Just as the University must evolve and break with
some anchors of the past, its technology must accompany it in this process of change"
(García Peñalvo; F, 2018).

*Technological ecosystems are a general framework for developing any type of
technological solution in which data and information are the center of the problem
(García-Holgado & GarcíaPeñalvo; García-Holgado et al., 2015).*

The present investigation, which initially formed part of a collaboration with the
Autonomous University of Barcelona, in the collection of information from both teachers
and students on Stress and digital skills during emergency remote teaching (Peru-Spain),
which provided a first reflection on the results and allowed the researchers to approach
the investigation from another angle.

How were digital skills adapted during the exercise of emergency remote teaching, for
VUCA environments, in undergraduate and postgraduate teachers of a private Peruvian
university?

The general objective of analyzing digital skills during the exercise of emergency
remote teaching, for VUCA environments, in undergraduate and postgraduate teachers
of a private Peruvian university was raised.

As well as, Determine the level of digital skills that were developed during remote
teaching under volatile uncertain, complex and ambiguous conditions (VUCA) in a
Peruvian university.

- Identifies the adaptations, actions and dedication of teachers during emergency remote
  teaching in VUCA contexts.
- Specify the technologies that facilitated remote teaching during the health crisis in a
  Peruvian university.

2 Methodology

Digital skills during emergency remote teaching, for VUCA environment is a research
developed taking into account the nature of descriptive studies, because they provide
data to describe the state of phenomena or the relationships between phenomena at a
fixed point in time. Considered as a "snapshot" of the frequency and characteristics of a
phenomenon in a population at a given time. The inclusion criteria were undergraduate
teachers of the education and postgraduate careers of the master's and doctorates in Education, the exclusion criteria were belonging to other careers and postgraduate programs
(Cabezas et al. 2018; Hernández, et al. 2014). The sample consisted of 50 Peruvian
teachers from the same university, of which five were male and 45 were female. The
ages fluctuated between 38, 47 and 59 years. On the other hand, we sought to give some

qualitative interpretations from the feelings of the teachers. The sample of the population consisted of a total of 50 teachers.

3 Results and Discussion

The results showed that family conformation increased during the pandemic with respect to parents and decreased with respect to brothers/sisters, which would indicate that parents were under the care of their children during the pandemic. Regarding the years of university teaching experience, it is in the range of 20 to 22 years, undergraduate and postgraduate, of which 72% belong to the initial education school, and 28% to postgraduate.

40% connect to the internet through their own account, 46% do so from a family internet account, 4% from someone else's internet account, 8% with cell phone data and 2% do not have internet (Table 1).

Table 1. Special accommodation during remote teaching

Alternatives	Answers	%
I don't require it	10	20.0%
Yes, sensory (visual, auditory)	15	30.0%
Yes, intellectual or learning	17	34.0%
yes, physics	3	6.0%
yes, neurological	0	0.0%
I prefer not to say	5	10.0%
Total	50	100.0%

Note: Questionnaire on digital skills during emergency remote teaching applied to teachers.

As identified, there are two adaptations made for remote teaching, the sensory (visual, auditory) with 30% of responses and the intellectual or learning with 34%, of affirmations and do not require them 20%, although these adaptations are given in the most personal sphere, supports the statements of Leal-urueña and Rojas-mesa (2018),

Regarding the characteristics of the new learning ecologies, the complexity of information must be analyzed as a whole, as argued by Gaultier Le Bris, et al. (2019) (Table 2).

The results on the hours of the week dedicated to remote teaching (ERE), have decreased in the ranges of 12 h; 13–25 h; going from 40% to 30%, 26% to 14%, respectively. However, the increase in hours from 36 to 45; and more than 46 h have gone from 22% to 30% and 4% to 16%, respectively, this means that for the rest of the teachers the hours dedicated to teaching increased and that the use of space and time in virtual environments of learning, would refute the idea of having specific standards that are adaptable (Rubio-Tamayo, J; Guimarães, 2018), because in the context of uncertainty due to volatility, it encompasses the constant change of the world (Taskan et al. 2022) (Figs. 1 and 2).

Table 2. Hours per week dedicated to teaching before and during the state of emergency

Alternatives	before	%	during	%
< 12 h	20	40.0%	15	30%
13–25 h	13	26.0%	7	14.0%
26–35 h	4	8%	5	10%
36–45 h	11	22%	15	30%
> 46 and over	2	4%	8	16%
Total	50	100	50	100

Note: Questionnaire on digital skills during emergency remote teaching applied to teachers

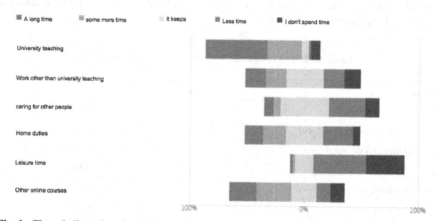

Fig. 1. Time dedicated to the activity during the emergency period
Note: Questionnaire on digital skills during emergency remote teaching applied to teachers

University teaching is the activity that demanded a lot of time during the emergency period 80%, work other than teaching is maintained, caring for other people is the one that dedicates less time 10%, housework does not dedicate time, 5%, leisure time does not dedicate time to it, the answers are given in 25%

The device through which you connect to the internet is 90% of your own cell phone, 70% of your own laptop, 65% of your own computer (Fig. 3).

The technology that has facilitated teaching in 98% has been the Learning Platform used by the university, followed by 90% the Internet connection, 85% the time available for learning for students, the availability of the Internet financed by the university to teachers who lacked this service, a platform financed with the necessary conditions for an optimal educational service, as required by the licensing indicators for universities, as well as sufficient bandwidth for university higher education (Minedu 2021). In addition, for the assurance and use of the platform, there are user manuals for each educational actor, such as the user manual for the blackboard learn ultra-teacher/virtual tutor platform, this as a result of planning and permanent adaptations. to meet the expectations of

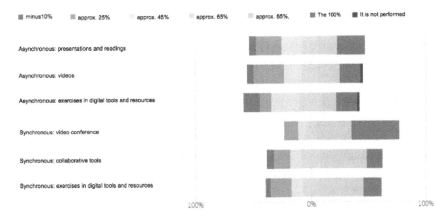

Fig. 2. Frequency of use of electronic devices for emergency remote teaching.
Note: Questionnaire on digital skills during emergency remote teaching applied to teachers

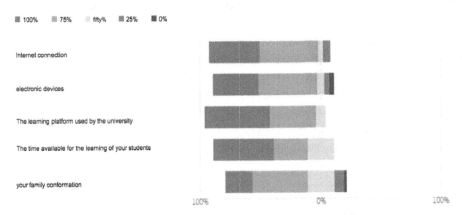

Fig. 3. Digital technologies that have facilitated emergency remote teaching
Note: Questionnaire on digital skills during emergency remote teaching applied to teachers

students about professional training (Tleuken et al. 2022; Ni, Fitzmaurice 2021) (Taskan et al. 2022) (Figs. 4 and 5).

It is evident that 100% of teachers during the state of emergency developed the synchronous modality: videoconference; 85% synchronous collaborative tools and the same percentage for synchronous: exercises and digital resources, this confirms that despite the pedagogical risks that teachers face, they developed new forms of leadership to adapt to a VUCA (Taskan et al. 2022; Panthalookaran 2022; Salakhova et al. 2021).

The activities that have been carried out in the highest percentage during the state of emergency were 85% listening and reading, answering questions orally and presenting, 65% interacting with multimedia resources, working collaboratively with colleagues 65% and using communication channels, ideas de García Peñalvo (2018), are evident in this reality, when he argues that technology in the University is not the end, but it is the essential means to develop in a society that is already digital (Table 3).

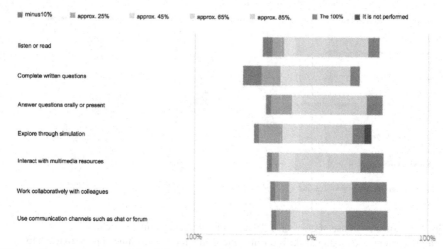

Fig. 4. Percentage of use of the following teaching modalities during ERE

Note: Questionnaire on digital skills during emergency remote teaching applied to teachers

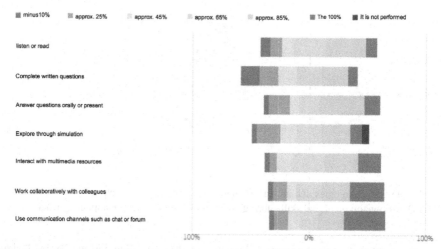

Fig. 5. Percentage of activities that have been carried out during the ERE

Note: Questionnaire on digital skills during emergency remote teaching applied to teachers

Digital skills during remote teaching, finding teachers in VUCA environments managed to develop them, at the basic level the existing 36% decreased to 6%, the intermediate level rose slightly from 52% to 58%, the advanced level showed a considerable increase, going from 12% to 36%, this happened because the university has two virtual platforms, and had been promoting the development of digital skills, teachers were familiar with them, but interaction with students was added, through audio and video in real time by zoom, these adaptations were strengthened with access to instruction and educational supports that were reliably available during the emergency or crisis corroborating the Hodges (2020) claims.

Table 3. Level of digital skills before and during the state of emergency

Alternatives	before	%	after	%
Essential	18	36%	3	6%
Intermediate	26	52%	29	58%
Advanced	6	12%	18	36%
Specialist	0	0.0%	0	0.0%
	50	100%	50	100%

Note: Questionnaire on digital skills during emergency remote teaching applied to teachers

4   Conclusions

- The digital competences of teachers, undergraduate and postgraduate during remote teaching, developed despite the existence of volatile uncertain, complex and ambiguous conditions (VUCA) that disturbed the homeostasis of the university, at the basic level it decreased from 36% to 6%, the advanced level increased from 12% to 36%, this response was due to the condition of a licensed university, which met the basic quality conditions and indicators that guaranteed the educational service through its learning ecosystems interactive, developed on its virtual platforms.
- The sensory (visual, auditory) and intellectual or learning adaptations were developed by the students during the virtual tutoring, listening, reading, answering questions also predominated, during emergency remote teaching, the time dedication increased as well as the use of space and time in virtual learning environments.
- Due to the nature of the pedagogical activity, the digital technologies that have facilitated remote teaching were 100% synchronous videoconferences and 85% use of collaborative tools and digital resources, platform, Internet connection.

References

Andrade-Arenas, L., Alva, R.Y., Vargas, G.V., Somoza, Y.P.: Remote supervision in times of pandemic at the university level under the systemic approach. Int. J. Emerg. Technol. Learn. **17**(6), 73 (2022). https://doi.org/10.3991/ijet.v17i06.27941

Andrade-Lotero, L.A.: Teoría de la carga cognitiva, diseño multimedia y aprendizaje: un estado del arte. magis, Revista Internacional de Investigación en Educación **5**(10), 75–92 (2012)

Bennett, N., Lemoine, G.J.: What a difference a word makes: understanding threats to performance in a VUCA world. Bus. Horiz. **57**(3), 311–317 (2014). https://doi.org/10.1016/j.bushor.2014.01.001

Binti Ali, Z., Abd Latif, S.: Competency development of teacher leaders: a panacea for a vuca world? J. Pharm. Negative Results, 5541–5550 (2022). https://doi.org/10.47750/pnr.2022.13.S09.676

Cabero-Almenara, J., Barroso-Osuna, J., Palacios Rodríguez, A., Llorente-Cejudo, C.: Digital competence frameworks for university teachers: their evaluation through the expert competence coefficient. Interuniversity Electron. J. Teach. Training **23**(2), 1–18 (2020). https://doi.org/10.6018/reifop.413601

García-Holgado, A, García-Peñalvo, F.J.: Validation of the learning ecosystem metamodel using transformation rules. Future Gener. Comput. Syst. (2018). https://doi.org/10.1016/j.future.2018.09.011

Garcia Penalvo, F.: University Technological Ecosystems, pp. 164–170 (2018).http://tic.crue.org/publications/

García-Holgado, A., Vázquez-Ingelmo,A., García-Peñalvo, F.J., Conde, M.R.: Improvement of learning outcomes in software engineering: active methodologies supported through the virtual campus. In: IEEE Revista Iberoamericana de Tecnologias del Aprendizaje, vol. 16, no. 2, pp. 143–153 (2021). https://doi.org/10.1109/RITA.2021.3089926

García-Holgado, A., García-Peñalvo, F.J.: Validation of the learning ecosystem metamodel using transformation rules. Future Gener. Comput. Syst. **91**, 300–310 (2019). https://doi.org/10.1016/j.future.2018.09.011. ISSN 0167-739X

Gaultier Le Bris, S., Rouvrais, S., Waldeck, R.: Learning methodology for VUCA situations. Methods Interdisciplinarity **1**, 117–148 (2019). https://doi.org/10.1002/9781119681519.ch6

Hodges, C., Moore, S., Lockee, B., Trust, T., Bond, A.: The difference between "Emergency Remote Teaching" (ERDE) and "Online Learning" (AEL) | The Flipped Classroom. EDUCASE Rev. **17** (2020). https://er.educause.edu/articles/2020/3/the-difference-between-emergency-remote-teaching-and-online-learning

Lázaro-Cantabrana, J.L., Usart-Rodríguez, M., Gisbert-Cervera, M.: Assessing teacher digital competence: the construction of an instrument for measuring the knowledge of pre-service teachers. J. New Approaches Educ. Res. **8**(1), 73–78 (2019). https://doi.org/10.7821/naer.2019.1.370

Leal-Urueña, L.A., Rojas-Mesa, J.E.: Ecology for initial teacher training based on ICT affordances. Techne Episteme Didaxis: TED, (44), 15–31 (2018). https://doi.org/10.17227/ted.num44-8986

Ministerio de Educación de Perú: The university system against COVID-19 during 2020 and 2021 (2021). Minedu. https://www.minedu.gob.pe/conectados/pdf/universidad-publica-covid-19-minedu.pdf

Ni Fhloinn, E., Fitzmaurice, O.: Challenges and opportunities: experiences of mathematics lecturers engaged in emergency remote teaching during the COVID-19 pandemic. Mathematics **9**, 2303 (2021). https://doi.org/10.3390/math9182303

Nieto, E., Pech, S., Callejas, A.: Assessment of teaching digital competence. ICT and language teaching. In: Sumozas, R., Nieto, E. (eds.). Assessment of Digital Teaching Competence, pp. 17–33 (2017)

Paas, F., Tuovinen, J.E., Tabbers, H., Van Gerven, P.W.M.: Cognitive load measurement as a means to advance cognitive load theory. Educ. Psychol. **38**(1), 63–71 (2003). https://doi.org/10.1207/S15326985EP3801_8

Panthalookaran, V.: Education in a VUCA-driven world: salient features of an entrepreneurial pedagogy. High. Educ. Future **9**(2), 234–249 (2022). https://doi.org/10.1177/2347631122111 08808

Ruiz-Cabezas, A., Medina, M.C., Pérez, E., Medina, A.: University teachers' training: The Digital Competence. [Formación del profesorado Universitario en la Competencia Digital]. Pixel-Bit. Revista de Medios y Educación **58**, 181–215 (2020). https://doi.org/10.12795/pixelbit.74676

Salakhova, V.B., Masalimova, A.R., Belyakova, N.V, Morozova, N.S., Osipova, N.V, Prokopyev, A.I.: Competitive teacher for higher education: risk-based models of its development. Eurasia J. Math. Sci. Technol. Educ. **17**(10), em2021 (2021). https://doi.org/10.29333/ejmste/11187

Suárez Urquijo, S.L., Flórez Álvarez, J., Peláez, A.M.: Las competencias digitales docentes y su importancia en ambientes virtuales de aprendizaje. Revista Reflexiones Y Saberes (10), 33–41 (2019). Recuperado a partir de https://revistavirtual.ucn.edu.co/index.php/RevistaRyS/article/view/1069

Taskan, B., Junça-Silva, A., Caetano, A.: Clarifying the conceptual map of VUCA: a systematic review. Int. J. Organ. Anal. **30**(7), 196–217 (2022). https://doi.org/10.1108/IJOA-02-2022-3136

Tleuken, A., et al.: Which qualities should build environments possess to ensure satisfaction of higher-education students with remote education during pandemics? Build. Environ. **207**(PB), 108567 (2022). https://doi.org/10.1016/j.buildenv.2021.108567

Waldeck, R., Gaultier Le Bris, S., Rouvrais, S.: Interdisciplinarity and VUCA. Methods interdisciplinarity **1**, 99–116 (2019)

Definition of a Learning Analytics Ecosystem for the ILEDA Project Piloting

Miguel Á. Conde[1]([✉]) [iD], Atanas Georgiev[2] [iD], Sonsoles López-Pernas[3] [iD],
Jovana Jovic[4] [iD], Ignacio Crespo-Martínez[1] [iD], Miroslava Raspopovic Milic[4] [iD],
Mohammed Saqr[3] [iD], and Katina Pancheva[2] [iD]

[1] Robotics Research Group, Engineering School, University of León, 24071 León, Spain
{mcong,icrem}@unileon.es
[2] Faculty of Mathematics and Informatics, Sofia University, Sofia, Bulgaria
{atanas,katina}@fmi.uni-sofia.bg
[3] School of Computing, University of Eastern Finland, Joensuu Campus, Joensuu, Finland
{sonsoles.lopez,mohammed.saqr}@uef.fi
[4] Faculty of Information Technology, Belgrade Metropolitan University, Tadeuša Košćuška 63,
11000 Belgrade, Serbia
{jovana.jovic,miroslava.raspopovic}@metropolitan.ac.rs

Abstract. Understanding how students progress in their learning is an important step towards achieving the success of the educational process. One way of understanding student progress is by using learning analytics methods on different student data. The ILEDA project aims to improve online and blended learning by using educational data analytics. For this purpose, the project involves four universities from four different countries and develops several activities. One of these activities. That aims to facilitate the analysis of student progress, is the definition of a Learning Analytics Ecosystem. The aim of defining the ecosystem is to generate solutions that will benefit all institutions and that will allow to look for possible patterns and common issues needing addressing. This paper describes the development of such an ecosystem and its future implementations.

Keywords: Learning Analytics · Interoperability · Ecosystems · Evidences · Dashboards

1 Introduction

The evolution of technology and its impact on our society have been very relevant in the last 30 years. In the field of education, the popularization of Internet and virtual learning environments meant an important change, especially with the rise of what is known as e-learning and its modalities such as blended learning [1]. In 2020 and 2021, the COVID-19 pandemic situation made the utilization of these modalities essential for most educational institutions [2–6], opening new challenges that need to be addressed, new problems to deal with and possible solutions [7].

In this situation, no matter which modalities of teaching and learning are used, the ultimate goal is to improve study. Improving students' learning is very complex

P. Zaphiris and A. Ioannou (Eds.): HCII 2023, LNCS 14040, pp. 444–453, 2023.
https://doi.org/10.1007/978-3-031-34411-4_30

having in mind that each student has their own learning pace, needs and prior knowledge [8]; and it is even more complex in online and blended learning, as students develop their educational activities in a different context and not necessarily the institutional one [9]. With different contexts and educational activities, it is essential to look for innovative tools to support effective teaching and learning by offering flexibility for different solutions and including a mix of digital solutions for different pedagogies, approaches, and technological platforms. This is the main objective of the ILEDA project, which aims to solve several problems in participation in online and blended courses and to provide support for learning environments that are in use at the participating educational institutions. The support for learning environments is planned through the design and implementation of an open Learning Analytics (LA) software tool that can be integrated in any learning environment and used to actively monitor student performance [10]. The project involves Belgrade Metropolitan University– Serbia (BMU), the University of León – Spain (ULE) and the University of Eastern Finland (UEF) and it is led by Sofia University St. Kliment Ohridski – Bulgaria (SU).

One of the specific objectives of the project is to compile and adopt existing software tools that can accomplish the collection and analysis of learners' data. The ILEDA project addresses such objective by: (i) designing and developing a software tool that collects and provides analyses of students' activities using online platforms, (ii) compiling and adopting existing software tools for the collection and analysis of student activities using online platforms, (iii) integration of the designed LA tool with the learning management systems (LMS) at each partner university, and (iv) collection of feedback and system usage satisfaction from teachers and students. These objectives are addressed through different activities and this paper is focused on one of them: the development of a software LA tool that can be used by all participants and will be shared as open-source software for the wider audience.

One may pose the question: why to define a new LA solution when there are already different available LA tools? The reason is that existing LA tools use to be focused in a specific metric, context or topic and do not cover all of the LA needed when introducing and adopting new instructional methods, so adaptations and development of a new LA tool would be necessary. Three of the institutions, US, ULE and UEF are using Moodle as their institutional Learning Management System (LMS). For Moodle, there are already some LA tools available, but they do not utilize all the necessary data collection and analyses needed. On the other hand, LA tools for LAMS (the system used by BMU) are rather limited, or rather non-existent. Therefore, there is a need to develop a tool that is compatible with the LMSs of all the participating institutions, so it can later be validated during a pilot phase and the results of the application of new tools and methodologies in all the partnership institutions can be compared. This is an LA ecosystem that will integrate data from all the partner institutions.

The rest of the paper is structured as follows. Section 2 presents the analysis of the software solution. Section 3 shows the design of the solution and Sect. 4 includes how the tool is implemented. Finally, Sect. 5 poses some conclusions.

2 Analysis of the LA Solution

In order to understand how to develop the new LA tool, it is necessary to first consider how the involved institutions apply LA within their courses, consider their technical, pedagogical, and legal constraints. Once this is considered, the LA solution can be designed.

2.1 Understanding LA in Each Institution

Before beginning with the development of an LA solution, it was necessary to understand the LA landscape in the higher education institutions involved in the ILEDA project. To do so, each partner completed a survey in which each institution described their context regarding LA. The topics of the survey were defined based on [11] and on a previously defined project framework for LA. They were:

- Technological systems employed: Referred to the LMSs, educational tools, and communication tools that are available to both the teachers and the students.
- LA tools currently available: It is very important to know what is and what is not integrated into the technical ecosystem or if the LA tools are external.
- Institutional LA policies: Whether the institution has defined a protocol to track students' progress, teachers' activities, used content, etc.
- Data access policy: It is necessary to know the data protection law that is going to be applied, what part of the students' and teachers' activities data can be stored and how much of that data will be accessible for further analysis, and if some data must be analyzed in an anonymous way or not.
- Application scope: It is necessary to know at what level the tool is going to be applied, i.e., at the institutional level the LA aims could be different than at the course or activity levels.
- Ethical policy: If some of the data cannot be used for ethical reasons, this should be considered, especially at the beginning of the application of LA. In most cases ethical policies can be defined at an institutional level following regional, national or European recommendations and guidelines.
- Expert support: Whether there is a technical team that can support the teacher in accessing the data, generating reports, or installing LA tools.

Several findings were extracted from the feedback collected: 1) three of the partners are using Moodle (US, ULE and UEF) and one of the partners is using LAMS (BMU); 2) most of the partners only use the LA tools provided by the LMS and also one of them (ULE) has developed a tool to measure a specific competence; 3) regarding data privacy, most of the partners follow EU-GDPR; 4) course data is accessible on institutional computers only for the teachers who in charge of teaching it; 5) the partner institutions do not have a specifically designed LA policy; 6) for piloting, and as a first step in the development, the LA tool application scope will be at the course level; and 6) expert/technical support is not always available.

Once the context of each institution and the application level for the piloting were defined, it was necessary to establish the metrics to be used during the piloting. The partnership decided that each institution would develop two courses, one following a Project Based Learning approach [12, 13] and the other one following a Flipped Classroom approach [14, 15]. Taking this into account, the chosen indicators were as follows:

- Grades

  - Final grade of the course.
  - Checkpoints (to measure the percentage of progress considering the active methodology applied in each subject).

- Use of resources (video, documents, activities, reading material, etc.)

  - Clicks
  - Time spent
  - Quiz attempts (if some of the questionnaires allow several attempts, something common in checkpoint tests).

- Other

  - Students' login (time of access, login)
  - Session time.

With this information about the contexts and metrics, the LA solution requires the use of open solutions or standards to deal with the integration complexity and guarantee the future scalability of the system.

2.2 Analysis

When dealing with the LA tool analysis, it is necessary to consider the partners' contextual information, but we should not forget other important constraints related with technical issues about the LMS:

1) The university LMSs are closed to tests of new tools, especially because they are being used by many teachers and students and a tool failure would have an important impact on the integrity of the system. This implies the need to replicate institutional environments on a testing server and upload copies of the courses so that the analysis could not affect the currently running institutional servers.
2) In the case of BMU, where LAMS is used, additional development is needed in order to achieve the solution that can be properly integrated in the defined LA ecosystem.

Taking these technical issues into account, it is necessary to understand the main stakeholders involved in the process and how this process works. These stakeholders are:

- The lecturer will oversee the pilot course in each institutional LMS and should carry out periodic backups.
- The technician that should restore the course's backup in an LMS instance (that we named as ILEDA LMS) defined for the project.

- The decision maker will have a system in which the information can be explored to make decisions for the local institution or related to the information of the institutional members.

How these actors interact with the system can be seen in Fig. 1. The LA tool should be able to gather the information from the ILEDA LMS in each institution and send it to a common repository that will provide visualizations of the data to be checked by the decision maker.

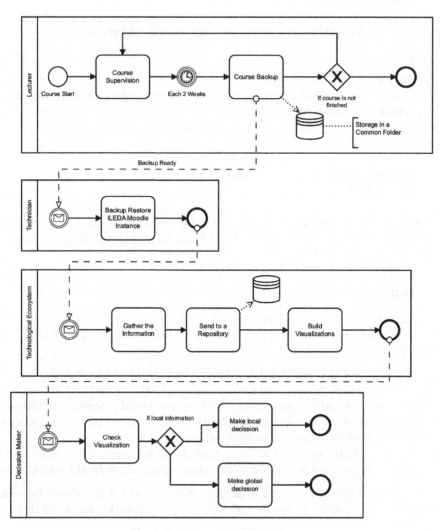

Fig. 1. LA Ecosystem BPMN diagram

3 Solution Design

The first issue to consider for designing the tool is the necessity to use a specification or standard that allows integrating the different partners' LMSs. This constraint requires making a technological decision that will affect the tool design. In order to do so, the possible implementation needs to use a specification that can be applied to different LMSs and could be, as far as possible, independent of the institutional technology. An open and standard solution in this case would be a technical implementation based on xAPI.

The Experience API (or xAPI) is a relatively new specification for learning technology that makes it possible to collect data about a wide range of learning experiences a person has (online and offline). This API captures data in a consistent format about a person or group's activities from many technologies. Very different systems can securely communicate by capturing and sharing this stream of activities using xAPI's simple vocabulary [16]. This technology allows the definition of a tool that can collect information from the LMS but also from other data sources, so using it in LA guarantees an open solution, not only in the sense of open-source software but also in the sense of including new technologies or data sources. Implementing xAPI requires sending students' data to a Learning Record Store (LRS), "a server (i.e. system capable of receiving and processing web requests) that is responsible for receiving, storing and providing access to Learning Records" [17]. In this case, we will consider a local LRS with the data of each institution and a global LRS with the data of all the partners.

Figure 2 describes how the solution is designed for each partner. In that figure, it is possible to see that each institution will have an LMS testing instance that includes the data of the courses involved in the piloting. Such data will be sent to a local instance of an LRS, where the information will be accessed, exploited and represented. The data in the LRS will be accessed through a dashboard that will provide a specific representation of the metrics to each partner. During the piloting, the LRS local instances will send the data to a global LRS that will compile the information of each local instance so the results among each partner courses can be compared. This data should be previously anonymized, so no personal information is associated with the learning evidence outside the local educational institution. The global LRS will include a dashboard that will allow decision-makers to explore, compare, and present the data from the different institutions. We should point out that this scheme is similar for all the institutions except for BMU, who will need to wrap LAMS information and EMS grades following xAPI specification before sending it to the LRS.

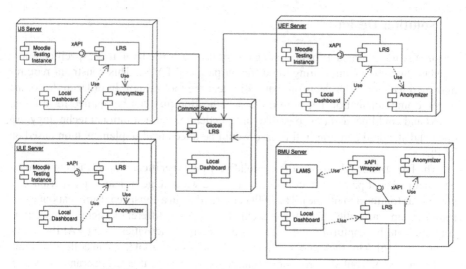

Fig. 2. Deployment diagram for ILEDA project LA tool

4 LA Ecosystem Implementation

Once the solution was defined and the decision to use the xAPI specification was made, it was necessary to address the LA ecosystem development, which must be open source and public once the project is finished. This development implies several decisions such as: the way in which xAPI is integrated with the LMS, the LRS to use, and the dashboards to use.

In order to make these three decisions, the ILEDA partnership conducted a study about the different possible ways to implement the LA ecosystem. Regarding the integration of xAPI, it is necessary to consider that three of the partners use Moodle and other LAMS LMS. For the former, it was necessary to take into account whether to develop an ad hoc plugin or to use one available in the Moodle plugin repository. The partners decided to use an existing one that met the specification: to be open source and to be compatible with the LRS. BMU required the definition of an xAPI Wrapper that could extract information from LAMS and other academic systems in order to build the xAPI statements and send them to LRS.

For the LRS choice, the criteria were similar than for the xAPI integration system, that is, an open-source system, that follows the xAPI specification, and given our design, it should be built as a standalone solution. With these features, 26 options were studied, and the final decision was choosing Learning Locker as it fits with the project's requirements, has a well-maintained Moodle Plugin, and is easy to modify.

The LRS was updated to facilitate the use of a more upgraded database version, to include new features, to facilitate the generation of aggregated data (session time based on statements) and to anonymize the information forwarded from a local LRS to the global one. The Moodle plugin also needed some adaption in order to send to the LRS only the new statements, since originally, when restoring Moodle courses (see Fig. 1), the logs were replicated and therefore the same statements were sent again.

The way in which the different components interact can be seen in Fig. 3. It shows that the Moodle plugin installed in the ILEDA Moodle instance of the partners pre-processes students' data by removing duplicates; it builds the xAPI statements and sends them to the local instance of the LRS. The local LRS stores the statements, anonymizes them before forwarding them to the global LRS, and provides local visualizations to be accessed by the institutional decision makers. Finally, the global LRS receives the statements from each partner's local LRS, stores them, and provides visualizations with the aggregated and anonymized data so as to compare the results from students from the different socio-economic environments.

It is necessary to point out that the type of visualizations depends on the metrics selected, but for the first release they are simple graphs with 2 or 3 variables. They are provided by the Learning Locker LRS and will be improved in future releases of the LA Ecosystem. A sample of the local dashboard, integrated into the LRS, with some visualizations can be seen in Fig. 4.

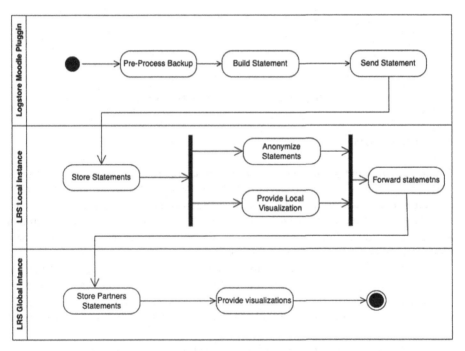

Fig. 3. Activity diagram about the components interaction

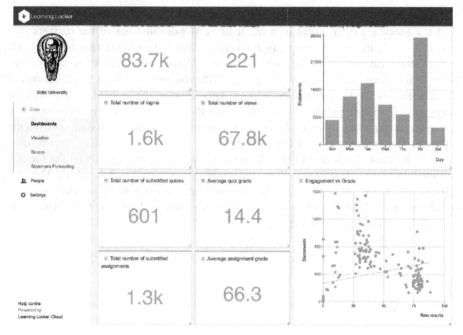

Fig. 4. Sofia University LRS Dashboard

5 Conclusions

The work carried out during the ILEDA project has required an important effort from different perspectives and especially from the technological point of view. LA could be used independently in each of the participating institutions, but it is necessary to be able to define a common infrastructure that facilitates making decisions not only from a local but from a global perspective, i.e., not only considering what happens at a single institution but in the rest of the partners' courses.

This effort has required the definition of an LA ecosystem, that integrates data from different sources and even from different LMSs. This implies an interoperability effort that meant to use specifications such as xAPI. In this paper, we have described why we used this ecosystem and how it was developed, showing the process and difficulty of integrating LA systems.

The next step on this research is the validation of the LA ecosystem that is going to be completed in the next semester with 8 courses and more than 500 students. It is expected that the ecosystem will require adaptations and probably new dashboards to represent new relevant information based on students' data.

Acknowledgements. Research presented in this paper is supported by the project "Improving online and blended learning with educational data analytics" ILEDA - 2021–1-BG01-KA220-HED-000031121.

References

1. Valtonen, T., López-Pernas, S., Saqr, M., Vartiainen, H., Sointu, E.T., Tedre, M.: The nature and building blocks of educational technology research. Comput. Hum. Behav. **128**, 107123 (2022)
2. García-Peñalvo, F.J., Corell, A., Abella-García, V., Grande, M.: Online assessment in higher education in the time of COVID-19. Educ. Knowl. Soc. **21**(12) (2020)
3. García-Peñalvo, F.J., Corell, A., Rivero-Ortega, R., Rodríguez-Conde, M.J., Rodríguez-García, N.: Impact of the COVID-19 on higher education: an experience-based approach. In: García-Peñalvo, F.J. (ed.) Information Technology Trends for a Global and Interdisciplinary Research Community, pp. 1–18. IGI Global, Hershey, PA, USA (2021)
4. Aristovnik, A., Keržič, D., Ravšelj, D., Tomaževič, N., Umek, L.: Impacts of the COVID-19 pandemic on life of higher education students: a global perspective. Sustainability **12**, 8438 (2020)
5. Carrillo, C., Flores, M.A.: COVID-19 and teacher education: a literature review of online teaching and learning practices. Eur. J. Teach. Educ. **43**, 466–487 (2020)
6. Adedoyin, O.B., Soykan, E.: Covid-19 pandemic and online learning: the challenges and opportunities. Interact. Learn. Environ. **31**(2), 863–875 (2020)
7. Saqr, M., Raspopovic-Milic, M., Pancheva, K., Jovic, J., Peltekova, E., Conde, M.Á.: A multimethod synthesis of Covid-19 education research: the tight rope between covidization and meaningfulness. Univ. Access Inf. Soc. (In press)
8. Attwell, G.: The personal learning environments - the future of eLearning? eLearning Pap. **2**, 1–8 (2007)
9. Conde, M.Á., García, F.J., Rodríguez-Conde, M.J., Alier, M., Casany, M.J., Piguillem, J.: An evolving learning management system for new educational environments using 2.0 tools. Interact. Learn. Environ. **22**, 188–204 (2014)
10. Conde, M.Á., López-Pernas, S., Peltekova, E., Pancheva, K., Milic, M.R., Saqr, M.: Multi-stakeholder perspective on the gap between existing realities and new requirements for online and blended learning: an exploratory study. In: 10th edition of the Technological Ecosystems for Enhancing Multiculturality (TEEM 2022), 19–21 October 2022. Springer, Salamanca (In press)
11. Conde, M.Á.: Going beyond the LMS logs. The complexity of analyzing learning evidences. In: 13th International Conference on e-Learning 2022 - eLearning Conference, 29–30 September 2022, Belgrade, Serbia (In press)
12. Blumenfeld, P.C., Soloway, E., Marx, R.W., Krajcik, J.S., Guzdial, M., Palincsar, A.: Motivating project-based learning: sustaining the doing supporting the learning. Educ. Psychol. **26**, 369–398 (1991)
13. Thomas, J.W.: A review of research on project-based learning. Autodesk Foundation, San Rafael, California (2000)
14. Lage, M.J., Platt, G.J., Treglia, M.: Inverting the classroom: a gateway to creating an inclusive learning environment. J. Econ. Educ. **31**, 30–43 (2000)
15. Sein-Echaluce, M.L., Fidalgo-Blanco, Á., Balbín, A.M., García-Peñalvo, F.J.: Flipped learning 4.0. an extended flipped classroom model with education 4.0 and organisational learning processes. Univ. Access Inf. Soc. (2022)
16. xAPI solved and explained. https://xapi.com/. Accesed 09 Feb 2023
17. Experience API. https://github.com/adlnet/xAPI-Spec/blob/master/xAPI-About.md#par tone. Accessed 09 Feb 2023

Scenarios, Methods, and Didactics in Teaching Using Video-Conferencing Systems and Interactive Tools: Empirical Investigation on Problems and Good Practices

Md. Saifuddin Khalid(✉) ⓘ, Tobias Alexander Bang Tretow-Fishⓘ, and Mahmuda Parveenⓘ

Department of Applied Mathematics and Computer Science, Technical University of Denmark, Lyngby, Denmark
skhalid@dtu.dk

Abstract. The restrictions during COVID-19 pandemic resulted in gaining more experience on video conferencing systems (VCS) and continued adoption during post-pandemic teaching scenarios. Designing and installing video conferencing systems in various classroom scenarios are expensive, increase complexity, and reduce interaction opportunities unless the designs for learning activities are well-defined and well-executed. For improving the quality of contact hours, the EdViCon Erasmus + project's aim is to explore the existing diversity of scenarios of video conferencing systems' use, various methods, and didactics applied for engaging students using various software and VCS features and define and develop two portable VCS toolkits and training. This paper reports the empirical case of Technical University of Denmark by applying phonomyography [1] as the methodology for exploring the VCS use scenarios, methods, and didactics for exploring problems and good practices. Despite increased adoption and number of papers on VCS, the insights on the diversity of the scenarios of use during contact hours has not been sufficiently reported from the viewpoint of HCI researchers. This study applies Shuman's [2] concept of signature pedagogies as the theoretical viewpoint for defining scenarios of the use of VCS in teaching and David Benyon's [3] PACT (people, activities, context, technologies) framework for analysing functionalities, methods, and didactics. The causes and effects of problems with VCS-mediated contact-hour activities were grouped into seven and 12 categories respectively. Seven types of teaching environments, three types of video-conferencing systems (fixed, on-wheels, and mobile), and the various tools used for engaging students were identified.

Keywords: Video conferencing · higher education · student engagement

1 Introduction

During the COVID-19 pandemic many institutions decided to use video conferencing systems (VCs) as a teaching tool instead of face-to-face teaching. To some educators and students, teaching through a video conferencing system is the future of teaching,

© The Author(s), under exclusive license to Springer Nature Switzerland AG 2023
P. Zaphiris and A. Ioannou (Eds.): HCII 2023, LNCS 14040, pp. 454–474, 2023.
https://doi.org/10.1007/978-3-031-34411-4_31

to some it is essential for desired learning experience in today's classrooms, and to some it is a technostress. Typically, the video conferencing system that are used in the classrooms require expensive setup and various hardware components (for example, loudspeaker, wireless microphone, wireless or fixed mics for audiences, control panel for controlling the lights, curtains, projectors, screens, computers, cameras, etc.) Installing the hardware in the various types of classrooms and engaging students during the various types of teaching activities are highly resource intensive. Furthermore, a mapping of the diversity of classroom designs, course activity designs, and the use of digital learning technologies for engaging students during the contact hours cannot be identified in the existing literature. Amidst the pandemic, this study began with the intention of mapping the different scenarios of VCS use during the *contact hours* (when teachers and students are in live interaction), problems and good practices of using VCS technologies and didactical designs, and digital tools for engaging students. The outcomes of this empirical study is expected to contribute with technological and pedagogical aspects for the improvement of teaching-learning activities during contact hours.

As part of the Erasmus + KA2 project "Portable Video Conferencing Toolkits and Online Applications for Engaging Learning Experience Design in Higher Education Classroom" (EdViCon)[1], this paper reports the empirical investigation conducted at the Technical University of Denmark (DTU). So, the elements of innovation and academic novelty of this paper are:

1. A collection of existing problems and scenarios of using video conferencing systems, which are communicated with graphical and tabular methods. The novelty is the diversity of scenarios and both technological and pedagogical concerns in the uses of video conferencing systems and student engagement.
2. A collection of existing best practices of the methods and didactics for video conferencing-mediated teaching including and student-engagement technologies, which are collected in the form of surveys, interviews, observations, and other methods and communicated visually. The innovation is the explored diversity of best practices in specific scenarios of VCS use integrated with the various online tools for engaging students.

The underlying objective is to find the heterogeneity in the activities of the contact hours, the challenges faced in the process of adopting video conferencing systems, and engaging students. The findings are expected to provide cases of good practices and digital technologies for improving synchronous online and blended teaching.

2 Related Works

Existing literature reviewed the use and the comparison of the features of various video conferencing software, which include but not limited to Zoom, Microsoft Teams, Google Meet, WebEx, AdobeConnect, ClickMeeting, and BigBlueButton [4]. The diverse scenarios of the contact hours are not synthesized in the review and not emphasized in the empirical papers included in the review.

---

[1] https://edvicon.compute.dtu.dk/.

The study [5] reports that the first-year pharmacy students were taught the fundamentals in Pharmaceutical Chemistry at the Faculty of Pharmacy, University Technology MARA applying Community of Inquiry approach by participating in online activities through remote video-based laboratories.

In [6], 200 first to fourth year engineering undergraduate students and 30 faculty members from two Engineering institutions in Chennai city and Andhra Pradesh (urban and rural) were asked to share the efficacy of the existing infrastructure facilities for providing online collaborative learning in VC. In [7], 16 graduate students and their instructor participated in a course on discourse and conversation analysis at a public university in the south-eastern United States. The course was conducted in a blended format of physical teaching and online teaching through WebEx. The study tried to analyse turn-taking in single and dual channels of sound and chat as well as repair sequences of turn-taking through the system.

In [8], 49 third-year medical students from 10 different institutions in New Jersey and Pennsylvania participated in a non-credited virtual course. The study examined the conversion of an in-person workshop for orthopaedic trauma basics to a virtual course during emergency teaching due to COVID-19. The virtual course had weekly lectures and virtual interactive small group sessions conducted through WebEx. In a later stage of the study, they assessed the students' perceived value of the class.

In [9], 70 students enrolled at the Computer Science and Cybersecurity course of St. John's University's Division of Computer Science, Math and Science was posed rubrics on learning curve, asynchronous scheduling availability, system response time, student engagement, and overall quality of course delivery experience. The intention was to circumvent the difficulties during COVID-19 restrictions by showcasing the educational journey of engaging in group work through Video conference systems while doing hands-on lab work.

The related work on VCS in the existing literature reports comparison of various VCS software features, cases of various methods (e.g., turn-taking), scenarios (e.g., computer science hands-on lab), and addressed various problems. This paper intends to contribute a holistic overview from one higher educational institution for supporting decision-making and further innovation in making portable video-conferencing toolkits for resource-constraint higher education institutions.

3   Context, Methodology, and Methods

3.1   Context

The context of the study is the Technical University of Denmark (DTU), which is one of the top 2–200 universities, as ranked by various systems. There are about 11200 students and 6000 employees. DTU has four campuses: Lyngby, Ballerup, Risø (which are 10–40 km from Copenhagen), and Sisimiut campus in Greenland. In 2021, DTU had 18 BEng programs (3976 students), 19 BSc Eng. Programmes (4065 students), 33 MSc Eng. Programs (5373 students), and 17 PhD schools (1527 students)[2]. Students are from

---

[2] https://www.dtu.dk/english/about/facts-and-figures, DTU Facts and Figures 2022, https://issuu.com/dtudk/docs/dtu-facts-and-figures-22?fr=sNDI5MzQ5MzI1MjI.

114 countries with 32% enrolled students are women. 54% of faculty are below 50 years of age, 38% of total staff are woman, and with 91 nationalities 12% have an international background. This study covers the teaching facilities in Lyngby campus, which covers a 106-hectare site. All the activities associated with teaching-learning, including but not limited to, the use of video conferencing systems (VCs), classroom environment, use of tools in engaging during the contact hours, are subject to the institutional and national higher education culture of Denmark.

3.2 Methodology and Methods

This sub-section includes the participants, the methods applied for data collection, and the methods for data analysis.

The participants or sources include three target groups (TG): (1) academics and administrative personnel, (2) E-learning consultants, IT support, and Teacher trainers, and (3) Students.

This study conducts the empathize and define activities of the design thinking process [10] by applying Phenomenography [1] as the methodology. Phenomenography [1] covers 'what' and 'how' questions in the phenomenon, where video conferencing mediated interactive contact hours is being investigated.

Data collection includes four methods: in-situ interviews, problem-tree analysis [11, 12] workshops, classroom observation, and one questionnaire survey.

1. In-situ depth interviews [13] are conducted with three audio-visual support roles from the central IT unit, three e-learning (pedagogical) support professionals, and five course instructors from the computer science department (but different signature pedagogies and roles). A semi-structured questionnaire was developed, and analysis of the interviews were conducted by using the PACT (People, Activities, Context, and Technologies) framework [3].
2. Two focus-group discussions are conducted by using problem-tree analysis [12], which shows the causes, effects and a central problem associated with the use of video-conferencing systems and students' engagement during online or hybrid contact hours. During the first workshop, 17 research and administrative personnel from one of the research sections from the computer science department participated in three groups. In the second workshop, 21 graduate students enrolled in an elective course on digital learning technology and entrepreneurship participated in their respected course project groups. The students also grouped their courses according to similarities of contact hours and the summarized the use of online tools for engagement or collaborative learning. Applying the concept of signature pedagogies [2], the teaching environments were considered for further observation.
3. Observations of three classrooms, two galleries, two laboratories, and two meeting (supervision and oral exam) rooms are conducted by taking pictures and notes on the use of video conferencing systems. Seven scenarios of contact-hour environments are selected based on the list of all the courses offered by the department of applied mathematics and computer science according to the second focus-group discussion, where the rooms for the enlisted courses are identified and selected the rooms based on the diversity in the courses' signature pedagogies [2].

4. Survey responses from 42 academics regarding their use of digital learning technologies and software they would recommend to their colleagues provide insights on engaging students during contact hours. Although the responses are analysed from the perspective of engaging students during VCS mediated contact hours, but applicable for face-to-face teaching as well.

In the following, the context, the source or participants, and the methods for the data collection and analysis are presented.

3.3 Instruments and Protocol

In-Depth Interview Protocol. The in-depth interview [13] instrument is inspired by the PACT framework [3]. From this framing, the researchers applied an investigative and explorative approach [14] (Adams, 2015, p. 492–505) to understand the PACT dimensions from the different perspectives of the interview participants. The interviews consisted of two steps:

1. The participant describes how they use VCs from their perspective (either as students, IT-support, or as a teacher). As the participant describes their use of VCs the researchers make the participant elaborate their responses from a PACT framework inspired interview protocol.
2. The participant describes good practice scenarios of using VCs. This is done by putting emphasis on the activities associated with teaching with VCs and if students like them.

The interview protocol includes the following questions (P: People, A: Activities, C: Context, T:Technologies). The survey instrument and data complements the findings from the interviews.

P: What are the roles of the people who you work with? Example: For a teacher it's students and other teachers, teaching assistants, etc. Example: for an e-learning consultant, it's teachers and IT support etc.

A: What are the names of activities that you do in the "contact hours"? What works well and what does not? Example: Lecture, monitoring, meetings, guidance. What didactics and methods do you use? Example: Groupwork in Zoom breakout rooms.

C: 1. How would you define the contact-hour context of your VC experience? 2. What are the core tasks of the unit you work at (e.g., for academic departments, these are usually teaching and research; for IT-support units, these can be supporting personal computers or other infrastructure)? 3. What are the organizational guidelines that you follow? Example: for teachers, course name, study program, if the students are at home or in the class, what kind of class/lab/studio etc.

T: 1. How various technological features and tools are used during a VC-mediated contact session? 2. What tools do you use for engagement and how? 3. What works well that you would recommend to others? 4. What are some of the main concerns that you would ask other roles/colleagues to address?

Survey. The IT-support team of the university's central IT services has a sub-group responsible for the integration and adoption of digital learning technologies. The team requested for responses from the faculty members of all departments though an online survey questionnaire. The questionnaire includes the following questions: (1) Name of the department, (2) Language (Danish/English), (3) Which digital learning tools have you used in your teaching? (Name as many as possible), (4) Which tool would you recommend to a colleague? (5) What forms of teaching have these tools supported? (Select all that apply) (6) May we contact you regarding your experience with these tools?

Observation. During and after the interviews, the contexts and technologies mentioned by the interviewees are observed while pictures and notes are taken. The observation of experimental setups for VC-mediated teaching are excluded.

Focus-Group Discussion: Problem-Tree Analysis. Problem-tree analysis (PTA) [11, 12, 15] is a flow diagramming technique that enables the researcher to assess stated problems' or later identified problems' causes and effects from the perspective of the participants. By applying this method researchers can illuminate the negative aspects of a situation and represent 'cause-and-effect' relationships between e.g. multiple problems [11]. In this study, the protocol for conducting the problem-tree analysis consists of 7 steps. (1) Participants are divided into groups and are asked to reflect on their experience with VCs. Next, they were asked individually to define, in their perspective, the main problem regarding VCs. Afterwards, the individual problems are brought into the group where they suggest different problems, negotiate, and discuss with each other to produce a single general "problem statement". (2) Each group sits face-to-face (or online) around a table and receives a mind map template with a depiction of a tree. The tree has three major empty spaces to write down: (a) One major problem statement (in the middle of the tree), (b) Multiple causes of the problem (the roots of the tree), (c) Multiple effects of the problem (the branches of the tree). 3. The participants are asked "What causes your problem?" and write as many post-it or notes they could on the tree, each note containing one cause. This was done as an individual task where participants did not need to negotiate or discuss their actions. 4. The participants were then asked, "What are the effects of your problem?" and write as many post-it or notes as possible, each note containing one effect (positive or negative). This is also done as an individual task like step 3. (5) After the individual notes were placed, the participants were asked to present the causes and effects of the problem to each other in a very brief manner. (6) After the presentations, the participants worked together in grouping similar and related causes and effects together. (7) Next, the participants are asked to draw connecting lines between multiple causes, causes and effects, and multiple effects - this is to highlight their relationship. From these 7 steps a problem-tree analysis is produced, and the researchers collected the physical (or digital) sketches which formed the basis of the data. The authors of the paper facilitated the workshops, further categorized the causes and effects, and excluded the general problem statement as participants had difficulty in agreeing on generalized statement.

The students participated in a second discussion after the PTA. They were asked to think about the video conferencing experience during home-based classes amidst COVID-19 restriction and the subsequent hybrid classroom experience where some students participated from home and others attended face-to-face at the university. The participants were introduced to the concepts of signature pedagogies, teaching styles, learning preferences, and were asked the following: (1) Considering signature pedagogies, what are the different structures of course activities you have? (2) Group the different courses with similar structure and write the structure down in brief terms. (3) Write down which digital tools were used for engaging you during the contact hours of the teaching while considering your experience during the COVID-19 restrictions and later. The participants were facilitated to reflect on the good practices in VC-mediated and other digital tool supported activities during the contact hours.

4 Analysis and Findings

The findings from the mixed-method study are presented in two sub-sections, which separately unfold the two problem statements and underlying research questions.

4.1 Existing Problems and Scenarios of VCS-Mediated Teaching Context

Only one of the groups (students' group four) could agree on a problem statement for the problem-tree analysis: "*The professors are not able to read the room online and need to prepare better for the class and use of technologies*". The participants discussed that if the professor cannot see and/or understand the experience of the students, then both pedagogical and technological preparation is required. The participants discussed that the "read the room" refers to observing facial cues, interactions, feedback, etc. which can be restricted by technology, perception, or pedagogical preferences.

Causes and Effects of Problems with Videoconference-Mediated Teaching. The authors grouped the causes stated in the PTAs made by the students as categories numbered SC1–4 and the employees (teachers and staff) in categories numbered TC1–4 as shown in Table 1.

The similarities between the categories of causes perceived by students and teachers are: 'SC1: Interpersonal and social issues' & TC2: Pedagogical-behavioural. Students focused on the problems and limitations of interacting with each other and only in a limited way interacting with the teacher. The teachers emphasized on the behavioural factors in the phenomenon and the pedagogical implications. Students and teachers shared the category of 'SC3& TC1: technical issues' as they engage with the technical aspects from different perspectives. Students focus on issues related to communicating through and with technology whereas teachers focus on lack of features and connectivity.

Unique for the students' category is 'SC2: Issues related to learning' touching upon the experienced problems of engaging with the software, support issues, and problematic organisational and physical circumstances participating in VC teaching. A unique category for teachers is the 'TC3: lack of resources' where resources is understood as time, training, quality of LMS e.g., Lastly, both students and teachers have an 'SC4&TC4: unsorted' category containing elements of lack of access to different tools, limitations of participation, functionalities of the VC, critique of the system, and organisational issues related to the application of the VC.

Table 1. Causes identified through problem-tree analysis.

Category	Causes/Groups	S1	S2	S3	S4	S5	E1	E2	E3
SC1: Inter-personal and social interaction issues	Experiencing difficulties with intrinsic motivation			X					
	No opportunities for socialising	X	X	X		X			
	A lack of and a need for physical presence	X	X						
	Non-anonymous chat/questioning requirements by some professors				X				
	Lack of familiarity with the VCs (fx. Muted and un-muted complications)			X	X				
SC2: Issues related to students' perception & preferences	VCs teaching is not engaging or motivating	X		X					
	Difficult to get help or support over VCs from teacher or fellow students (fx. Coding)	X		X					
	Changed structuring of lectures causes problems (fx. No breaks or few of them, long talks without interaction)					X			
	The surroundings of my home does not engage me in teaching			X		X			
SC3: Technological troubles	Communication barriers due to technical circumstances of VCs (fx. One way of communication, lack of body language)		X						

(*continued*)

Table 1. (*continued*)

Category	Causes/Groups	S1	S2	S3	S4	S5	E1	E2	E3
	Technical issues regarding VCs interrupts the flow of communication (fx. Late/long response time while speaking, updating software issues, network and bandwidth issues, video and audio issues)		X		X	X			
	VCs technology needs improvement (fx. Digitalizing of "reading the room" skill)				X				
	VCs has limitations on time and participants				X				
SC4: Unsorted	Access to different tools				X				
	VCs enables multitasking					X			
	Lack of interaction while editing online board		X						
	Can't participate all the time		X						
TC1: Technical issues	Lack of features in VC (no tool for zooming, indication for student questions, not intelligent enough, blackboard alternatives, limitations of VC etc.)						X	X	X
	Technical issues related to VC (Connection, audio, and video problems, etc.)						X	X	
TC2: Pedagogical-behavioural	Online students are de-prioritized in teaching context (inattention, turning off webcam, lack of a connection with students etc.)						X	X	
	Two different modes of teaching simultaneously (guidelines for teachers' actions, attention, different context, etc.)						X	X	X

(*continued*)

Table 1. (*continued*)

Category	Causes/Groups	S1	S2	S3	S4	S5	E1	E2	E3
TC3: Resources	Lack of resources (time, training, quality LMS etc.)						X	X	X
TC4: Unsorted	Question answer sessions not equal						X		
	The system isn't ready for teachers, technicians, or students. Everyone needs to be better prepared						X		
	Independent training by teachers						X		
	Large numbers of students								X

The authors also grouped the *effects* stated in the PTAs made by the students as categories numbered SE1–6 and the employees (teachers and staff) in categories numbered TE1–6 as shown in Table 2.

The following similarities between students' and teachers' effect categories were shared. Students' 'SE1: Improving teaching' and teachers' 'TE1: improvement of teaching context' were teachers focus on the positive effects of VC being flexibility and customization for teachers and students. Students also emphasises customization as well as technological features of the VC. Another similar category is students' 'SE2: worsening teaching' and teachers' 'TE4: worsening of teachers' conditions' and 'TE5: worsening of teaching context'. Students focus on the exact opposite of students' improving teaching category whereas teachers mention less motivation with teaching VC, lower quality of teaching quality, less collaboration, less opportunity for feedback, and less activity from students. Last of the categories sharing similarities is students' and teachers' 'SE5&TE6: technicalities. Students appreciate the new learning materials whereas teachers experience issues with IT support as well as VC features.

Students and teachers also have uniquely represented categories such as students' category of 'SE3: interpersonal and socially related'. In this category students describe the lack of motivation and socialization they experience. Another unique category for students is 'SE4: rules and behaviour' which deals with how to navigate the online environment. Lastly, students have an 'SE6: unsorted' category emphasising the benefits of working from home, problems of engaging with other students, and how easy it is to skip classes. Teachers' unique categories are 'TE2: differences between physical and online students' underlining differences between online and physical students related to attentiveness and students' academic levels. The final unique category for teachers is the 'TE5: organisational benefits' related to the possibility of increased student capacity in classes.

Table 2. Effects identified through problem-tree analysis.

Category	Effects/Groups	S1	S2	S3	S4	S5	E1	E2	E3
SE1: Improving teaching	Improvement to teaching reasons being VC features (Microphone, Blackboard access, etc.)	X		X					
	Improvement to learning preferences (Own pace learning etc.)			X					
SE2: Worsening teaching	Worsening to learning preferences (Slower understanding, less personalized, group work difficult, difficult to engage in class, fear of asking questions etc.)	X	X		X				
	Worsening to teaching reasons being VC features (Can't hear other students' questions and answers etc.)			X					
SE3: Interpersonal and socially related	Lack intrinsic motivation (feeling ignored, distracted, annoyed, loneliness etc.)	X			X	X			
	Difficult to socialize over VCs with teacher or students (Asking questions, getting help or support, no interactions etc.)		X			X			
SE4: Rules and behaviour	Online learning norms (web camera on, muting when not on etc.)			X					
SE5: Technicalities	Online Learning materials (Reading improvement, etc.)	X							
SE6: Unsorted	Working from home autonomy (Rest opportunities, food etc.)			X					
	Harder to event to invite student participation			X		X			
	Easy to skip class					X			

(*continued*)

Table 2. (*continued*)

Category	Effects/Groups	S1	S2	S3	S4	S5	E1	E2	E3
TE1: Improvement of teaching context	Opportunities for students to choose their learning preferences							X	
	Improved flexibility for teachers and students							X	X
TE2: Differences between physical and online students	Difference in attentiveness (online versus physical students.)						X	X	
	Larger difference between good and bad students (Learning, independence)							X	
TE3: Worsening of teachers' conditions	VC teaching is a less satisfying way of teaching							X	
	VC teaching results in lower quality of the course and heavier workload								X
TE4: Worsening of teaching context	Less opportunity for collaboration							X	
	Lack of feedback in interactions between students and teacher						X	X	X
	Lack of familiarity of students' knowledge, skills, and competences from online activity							X	X
	Decrease in student activity in lecture and with content						X		
TE5: Organizational benefits	Increased capacity of courses								X
TE6: Technicalities	Issues with IT support							X	
	Problems with VC features (cumbersome to navigate)						X		X

While some of the technological issues can be supported by the IT roles (SC3, TC1, TC4, and TE6), a lot of the issues can be addressed by pedagogical strategies and practices by the teachers or small organizational changes (elements of SC1, SC2, TC1, TC2, TC3, TC4, SE2, SE3, SE4, SE6, TE2, TE3, and TE4.) Other issues are conditional to the signature pedagogy of VC-mediated teaching (elements of SC2, SC3, TC1, TC2, SE3, SE4, TE2, TE3). This implication of signature pedagogies in the contact hours and learning process need to be communicated to students and teachers by introducing the *concepts of surface, implicit and deep structure of the profession* [2] influencing teaching style.

Analysis of Interviews and Observations of Videoconferencing Setups and Toolkits. The activities conducted during the contact hours with the professors are typically defined and stated as: 1) lecture 2) supervision 3) exam. For each of the three activities in contact hours, the scenarios of the VCS use differ due to further differences in people and context. For example, the context differs when lectures are given in auditorium, design studio, laboratory, and home or office space. People differences can be, for example, supervision or oral exam of students individually or in group. Moreover, the technologies (VCS and other resources) in the location of the activities influence the scenarios. For example, a lecture in an auditorium is streamed to one or more auditoriums or online, may involve writing on a touchscreen or pen tablet or through Remarkable2™.

From observations and from the interviews three broad categories of VCS have been identified: (1) fixed installations in the rooms, (2) mobile setup on tables/wheels, and (3) portable bags containing equipment.

The teaching contexts of a teacher using the three types of VCS have seven different types of contexts, which have different surface structures from the perspective of signature pedagogies. (a) *Galleries/auditorium*, elevated seats facing towards the teacher with a high capacity of students (Fig. 1). The camera is placed in the back of the room capturing the teachers' movement at the blackboards and at the desk. This enables the teacher to move around in the room and use multiple blackboards and/or whiteboards. Camera and screen-sharing are streamed to digital and physical attending students. (b) *Studio* for group-wise seating, tables arranged around the room with a possibility for rearranging the setup and to move around the room (Fig. 2). Screen-sharing is streamed to digital and physical attending students. (c) *Traditional classroom*: Teacher-faced rows with less capacity than the auditorium (Fig. 3). Screen-sharing is streamed to physical attending students (d-e) *Laboratories* with hardware installed or tables where hardware can be installed to work on it individually or in groups. Cameras installed at the tables can showcase teacher experiment activity as well as screen-sharing is streamed to physical attending students (Fig. 5 & 6) (f) *Supervision:* Teachers' table for online lecture or supervision involving laptop camera, external webcam, mobile stand & camera, pen tablet & remarkable, and a white board behind or beside the seat (Fig. 4). (g) *Meeting rooms* of three types but mainly for supervisions and thesis defence (fixed, mobile, and portable versions of setup), which are shown in Fig. 7 & 8.

The mobile version of VCS is similar to the hardware components of fixed installations and some of the components are fixed, for example, projector, automated screen, wall-mounted configuration buttons etc. There are two different versions of the portable VCS bags, where the bags are expensive as those are designed to be borrowed from the IT unit, audio-visual unit, or library. The Portable bags were designed and assembled by the audio-visual team of the university. Two portable VCS setups contained the following items presented in Fig. 9–14 showcasing the five items of the portable kit and the portable kit itself. Each of the bags contain single-page instructions for setup, which is laminated and securely tried inside the bag.

Fig. 1. Auditorium - signature pedagogy (a)

Fig. 2. Studio - signature pedagogy of (b)

Fig. 3. Traditional class - signature pedagogy (c)

Fig. 4. VCS-mediated *supervision* & can simulate signature pedagogies (a, b, c & f)

Fig. 5. Laboratory cum traditional classroom - Signature pedagogy (d)

Fig. 6. Dedicated Laboratory - Signature pedagogy (e)

Fig. 7. VC system setup for a meeting room at DTU corresponding to the signature pedagogy of (g) for a mobile or portable setup.

Fig. 8. VC system setup for a meeting room at DTU corresponding to the signature pedagogy of (g) with a fixed setup.

Fig. 9. Owl Labs Meeting Owl 3: Camera, microphone, and speaker system in portable kit

Fig. 10. Jabra 750: Microphone and speaker system in portable kit

Fig. 11. Camera tripod in portable kit

Fig. 12. USB charger in portable kit

Fig. 13. USB extension cable in portable kit

Fig. 14. An example of the portable kit.

4.2 Existing Methods, Didactics, and Practices for Engaging Teaching

This section includes the findings from the second workshop with students, survey responses from teachers, and interviews with the teachers and other roles.

Student Engagement Tools: Faculty Survey Responses. From the survey distributed to teaching staff at DTU (n = 42), employees were asked which tools they adopted in their teaching, which of these tools they would recommend to their colleagues, and which teaching forms of teaching the tools support. Analysing the text of the survey responses, the frequency distribution of the tools mentioned more than once are shown in Fig. 15. The video conferencing software mentioned in the survey are Zoom, Teams, and Adobe Connect. The software used for streaming recorded videos is video.dtu.dk which is now replaced by Panopto.

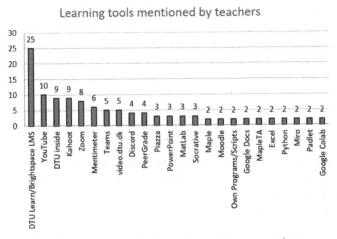

Fig. 15. Software used by the teachers during contact hours.

The tools adopted for engaging students during contact hours, whether VC-mediated teaching or face-to-face are Kahoot, Socrative, Polleverywhere, Mentimeter, Piazza, Miro, Padlet, Wooclap, and Google collab. For facilitating discussion during and beyond the contact hours, the adopted tools are Discord, Piazza, Zoom channel, and Microsoft Teams. Although Teams, Zoom channel, Slack, and Discord were mentioned by the teachers, they did not recommend those for supporting engagement during contact hours.

The responses include scenarios of good practices of tools, which include videoconference mediated teaching using customized setup designed by the teachers for laboratory context:

"PowerPoint presentation on PC where I need at least 2 for the YouTube videos. A camera on three leg-stand connected to the PC to show off the experimental setups as a lot of students needs to see it. Camera + PC + Zoom enables the experimental setups projected onto the screen and to students' PCs." was a survey comment from a teacher. The comment shows that the teacher considers online and physical students in the planning of teaching a typically lab experiment.

Another teacher presents how teaching is conducted through podcasts and video as well as how this is applied in teaching:

"Podcasts - Video-recorded lectures, including the option to start recordings yourself in the auditorium (permanent installation with audio/clip microphones). Video-recorded lectures from walk-in study at DTU Library (a help yourself system, but it was fine). Electronic whiteboard (rarely works though/I can't figure it out with the limited time I've invested in it). Electronic projector. One that has a white plate on the catheter, which (live) photographs the plate so that it can be projected onto the wall behind. There was one like that in one of the auditoriums, but it disappeared, and Kahoot." as a teacher describe the teaching practice using digital tools for VCS-mediation, recording, and student engagement.

These comments showcase that teachers at the university uses a variety of different tools and have a reflective practice as they engage students during the contact hours and conduct VC-mediated teaching. The scenarios of good practices mentioned by the teachers can also be validated by the scenarios documented during the focus-group discussions with the students.

One constructive criticism of digital learning technologies stated by a teacher: *"Becoming Europe's best engineering education does not come through using digital learning tools - Menti, for example, is as much entertainment as it is a functional tool - but through being able to engage and motivate the students, whose everyday lives are already largely distanced by digital tools. Reflection and independent thinking do not come from using digital learning tools, any more than you get good architecture from using a nail gun instead of a hammer."*

Didactics and Methods of VCS-mediate Teaching: FGD with Students. At workshop two with the students, scenarios on the different teaching and learning practices were shared by the students (see Table 3). The different categories of VC systems use and the use of various tools for engaging teaching during contact hours are grouped into multiple themes.

"Online individual work - Learning through the screen"

Students shared which tools were used to support the work during lectures, exercises, group work, and hand-ins etc. These tools were either used synchronously or in parallel with the VC lecture (e.g., note taking in OneNote), to support the VC lecture (e.g., Quizzes with Kahoot), or to conduct the VC lecture with (e.g., Zoom). Other tools were used to facilitate exercise work when the VC lecture was completed such as Miro, Overleaf, Google drive and Colab etc.

In synthesizing the students' responses three specific scenarios were identified.
Scenario 1: Video lectures and student collaborative work on online documents,

Scenario 2: Synchronous video lectures and laboratory work or physical group work,

Scenario 3: Pre-recorded video lectures, exercises, TA support, and hand-in of reports.

These three scenarios share similarities with the categories of "Traditional classes - Learning by listening" and "Theory framed group work - Learning through exercises" while not having a lot in common with either "Project- and group-work - Learning through deliveries" or "One to one teaching or supervision - Learning through relation".

5 Discussion and Conclusion

Learning experience during the contact hours is influenced by the video conferencing systems (VCS), other digital and non-digital resources associated with the learning activities. This study involved students, teachers, and IT roles from the Computer Science department of the Technical University of Denmark in exploring the problems underlying the VCS use, the use contexts or pedagogical scenarios of contact hours, and the technological and pedagogical good practices in engaging students during the contact hours. Despite the national, institutional, and individual level of technological competencies, some of the participants agreed on the problem statement: *"The professors are not able to read the room online and need to prepare better for the class and use of technologies"*. The authors interpret that the challenges are not technological but rather pedagogical and technological-pedagogical [16, 17]. Every class is a multi-channel user experience (UX) context, where the professor's physical movement, the slides and its content, the writings on a board or tablet, and use of other tools like Kahoot (including audio) provide the desired interaction experience. The interaction experience through these multiple channels is, however, only part of the learning experience. The live interaction, whether face-to-face or VCS-mediated involves the art of theatrical engagement, coming from the profession and involving the resources in the teaching context. The causes of the problem are grouped into different categories from students' viewpoints and teachers' and staffs' perspective. The lack of inter-personal, social interaction and behavioural aspects of the contact hours are some of the central causes that are not associated with the individual differences in teaching or learning preferences. The negative effects of the VCS-mediated teaching can be focused on the social and engagement dimensions.

Applying the concept of signature pedagogies and PACT analysis, seven contexts of contact-hour environments are identified: auditorium, studio, traditional classroom, laboratories (fixed installation and portable equipment), teacher's table, and meeting or group rooms.

Five best practice scenarios were identified for teaching, and of these five three scenarios were associated with VCS-mediated teaching: (1) video lectures and student collaborative work on online documents, (2) synchronous video lectures and laboratory work or physical group work, and (3) pre-recorded video lectures, exercises, TA support, and hand-in of reports. Furthermore, Piazza is recently institutionally adopted and the tool allows anonymous questions addressing fear factor. Kahoot and Socrative allows gamified quizzes, which have become popular engagement tools for increased social interaction. Panopto is adopted for allowing video recording and flipped-teaching approach. From the students' perspective, motivating the students to engage through fun and reflection using Menti improves the learning experience.

Table 3. Analysis of Scenarios found in the student workshop 2.

Scenarios	Tools	Individual activities/Tags	Groups					
			1	2	3	4	5	6
Traditional classes - Learning by listening	Traditional blackboard, Mobius, Piazza, PowerPoint, Discord, Tandem, Coursera, Google Classroom, Zoom, Moodle, Teams, Slack, GitHub, Codejudge, Peergrade, OneNote, Theme cords, Ankyl flashcards, DTU Media lab, Facebook, Overleaf, Brightspace LMS, Zotero, Discord	Students only listen to a lecture in auditoriums or smaller classes		X		X		X
		Students listen & invited to ask questions. Teacher initiates discussions and issues breaks	X	X	X	X	X	
		Teacher presents theory and provides exercise examples. After the presentation students are meant to do calculation exercises and laboratory work. To get help from TAs students raise their hands	X	X	X	X	X	
		Hand-ins on a daily, weekly, monthly basis is in focus of the lectures & exercises		X		X	X	
Online individual work - Learning through the screen	Zoom, Slack, Miro, Overleaf, Google docs, Kahoot, Pollev, Google colab, recorded lecture, OneNote, Theme cords, Ankyl flashcards, Colab, Deep note, IDE´s/coding environment, GitHub, DTU learn (Forum), Google drive	Video lectures and collaborative work on online documents such as Deep learning coding in an online auditorium setting	X	X		X	X	X
		Synchronous video lectures and laboratory work or physical group work	X	X			X	X
		Pre-recorded video lectures, exercises, TA support, and hand-in of reports	X		X			
Theory framed group work - Learning through exercises	Piazza, Slack, GitHub, Miro, Figma, Google drive	Some theory from a teacher but with the intention of working on simulation of practical application such as laboratory work, programming, or soldering circuit boards. Teacher shows a method, and we apply it to our case right away in a back-and-forth method	X	X	X			X
		Lectures from people from industry presenting topics or tools to situate exercises				X		

(*continued*)

Table 3. (*continued*)

Scenarios	Tools	Individual activities/Tags	Groups					
			1	2	3	4	5	6
Project- and group-work - Learning through deliveries	Miro, Figma, Google drive, Overleaf, Cloud based servers, Peergrade, Metaverse VR, Trello, Zoom, Overleaf, Grammarly, Google translate, ResearchGate, DTU find-it (Library search), DTU Learn Forum (Brightspace LMS), Microsoft Teams, GitHub, Canva	Identifying a problem and investigating it to solve it. e.g., through staging co-creation workshops, interviews			X	X		X
		Hands On experience from internship with accompanying field work			X		X	
		Supervision structure for the project work with presentation of work to other students			X		X	
		Hand-in as the basis of the project work such as bachelor thesis				X		
		Group Work presentation as the delivery and group activities as the method such as discussions, project development process				X		
One to one teaching or supervision - Learning through relation		Supervision sections with teachers		X				

The portable video conferencing tools and the student engagement tools adopted and recommended by the students and professors is expected improve the learning experience for VCS-mediated or supported classrooms.

Future case studies can inform specific signature pedagogies of different professions with particular scenarios involving the VCS, engagement tools, and the multi-channel interaction including their evaluations. Considering each of the scenarios (associated with signature pedagogies), the VCS problems identified, and engagement tools recommended by professors, the two video conferencing toolkits and student engagement tools will be further ideated and tested.

References

1. Åkerlind, G.S.: Variation and commonality in phenomenographic research methods. High. Educ. Res. Dev. **31**, 115–127 (2012). https://doi.org/10.1080/07294360.2011.642845
2. Shulman, L.S.: Signature pedagogies in the professions. Daedalus **134**, 52–59 (2005). https://doi.org/10.1162/0011526054622015
3. Benyon, D.: Chapter 2. PACT: a framework for designing UX. In: Designing user experience: a guide to HCI, UX and interaction design, pp. 27–48. Addison Wesley, Harlow (2019)
4. Cavus, N., Sekyere-Asiedu, D.: A comparison of online video conference platforms: their contributions to education during COVID-19 pandemic. WJET **13**, 1180–1191 (2021). https://doi.org/10.18844/wjet.v13i4.6329

5. Abdul Rahim, A.S.: Mirror mirror on the wall: escape a remote virtual stereochemistry lab together. J. Chem. Educ. **99**, 2160–2167 (2022). https://doi.org/10.1021/acs.jchemed.2c00050

6. Akkara, S., Mallampalli, M.S.: Online teaching and learning in india during lockdown and its impact on teaching practices. In: Auer, M.E., Centea, D. (eds.) ICBL 2020. AISC, vol. 1314, pp. 151–158. Springer, Cham (2021). https://doi.org/10.1007/978-3-030-67209-6_17

7. Earnshaw, Y.: Navigating turn-taking and conversational repair in an online synchronous course. OLJ **21** (2017). https://doi.org/10.24059/olj.v21i4.1029

8. Morley, M., et al.: A Virtual Curriculum to Prepare Medical Students to Achieve Accreditation Council for Graduate Medical Education Level-1 Milestones in Orthopaedic Surgery. JBJS Open Access **6** (2021). https://doi.org/10.2106/JBJS.OA.20.00117

9. Troja, E., DeBello, J.E., Roman, N.: Teaching efficient computer science and cybersecurity courses amidst the COVID-19 Pandemic. In: 2021 IEEE Global Engineering Education Conference (EDUCON), pp. 510–520. IEEE, Vienna (2021). https://doi.org/10.1109/EDUCON46332.2021.9454150

10. Gibbons, S.: Design Thinking 101. https://www.nngroup.com/articles/design-thinking/. Accessed 11 Mar 2018

11. Khalid, M., Nyvang, T.: Application of participatory learning and action methods in educational technology research a rural bangladeshi case. In: Georgsen, M., Zander, P.-O.M. (eds.) Changing education through ICT in developing countries, pp. 107–130. Aalborg University Press, Aalborg (2013)

12. Narayanasamy, N.: Participatory rural appraisal: principles, methods and application. SAGE Publications, Los Angeles (2009)

13. Polaine, A., Løvlie, L., Reason, B.: Service design: from insight to implementation. Rosenfeld Media, Brooklyn (2013)

14. Adams, W.C.: Conducting semi-structured interviews. In: Handbook of Practical Program Evaluation, pp. 492–505. John Wiley & Sons, Ltd (2015). https://doi.org/10.1002/9781119171386.ch19

15. Khalid, M., Nyvang, T.: A change agent's facilitation process for overcoming the barriers of ICT adoption for educational administration – a case of rural-bangladesh vocational institution. AJET **30**, 547–561 (2014)

16. Ling Koh, J.H., Chai, C.S., Tay, L.Y.: TPACK-in-action: unpacking the contextual influences of teachers' construction of technological pedagogical content knowledge (TPACK). Comput. Educ. **78**, 20–29 (2014). https://doi.org/10.1016/j.compedu.2014.04.022

17. Koehler, M.J., Mishra, P.: What is TPACK. Contemp. Issues Technol. Teacher Educ. **9**, 60–70 (2009)

Will ChatGPT Get You Caught? Rethinking of Plagiarism Detection

Mohammad Khalil[1]([⊠]) and Erkan Er[2]

[1] Centre for the Science of Learning and Technology (SLATE), University of Bergen, Bergen,
Norway
mohammad.khalil@uib.no
[2] Middle East Technical University, Ankara, Turkey

Abstract. The rise of Artificial Intelligence (AI) technology and its impact on education has been a topic of growing concern in recent years. The new generation AI systems such as chatbots have become more accessible on the Internet and stronger in terms of capabilities. The use of chatbots, particularly ChatGPT, for generating academic essays at schools and colleges has sparked fears among scholars. This study aims to explore the originality of contents produced by one of the most popular AI chatbots, ChatGPT. To this end, two popular plagiarism detection tools were used to evaluate the originality of 50 essays generated by ChatGPT on various topics. Our results manifest that ChatGPT has a great potential to generate sophisticated text outputs without being well caught by the plagiarism check software. In other words, ChatGPT can create content on many topics with high originality as if they were written by someone. These findings align with the recent concerns about students using chatbots for an easy shortcut to success with minimal or no effort. Moreover, ChatGPT was asked to verify if the essays were generated by itself, as an additional measure of plagiarism check, and it showed superior performance compared to the traditional plagiarism-detection tools. The paper discusses the need for institutions to consider appropriate measures to mitigate potential plagiarism issues and advise on the ongoing debate surrounding the impact of AI technology on education. Further implications are discussed in the paper.

Keywords: Education · Chatbots · AI · ChatGPT · Plagiarism · Essays · Cheating

1 Introduction

Chatbots are usually referred to as programs that can be integrated into various platforms, such as messaging apps, websites, and virtual assistants, to simulate human-like conversations. Functioned by natural language processing and machine learning techniques, chatbots try to understand and respond to user input in a conversational manner [9]. Artificial Intelligence (AI) chatbots are increasingly being used in a variety of contexts, including customer service, online shopping, entertainment, and education. These intelligent chatbots can help automate certain tasks, provide information, and improve user experience and productivity.

© The Author(s), under exclusive license to Springer Nature Switzerland AG 2023
P. Zaphiris and A. Ioannou (Eds.): HCII 2023, LNCS 14040, pp. 475–487, 2023.
https://doi.org/10.1007/978-3-031-34411-4_32

Recently, there have been numerous debates captivating the new AI chatbot, Chat-GPT by OpenAI. ChatGPT stands for Chat Generative Pre-trained Transformer and becomes a new concept of a revolutionary AI chatbot grounded in deep learning algorithms that is designed to simulate conversation with human users over the Internet. According to recent blogs over the internet, this chatbot took the internet by storm via part of the community claiming that it will be the new Google search engine.

This powerful and easily accessible technology has recently led to concerns about plagiarism in educational settings. A recent blog article by Stephen Marche "The College Essay Is Dead" raises concerns on the usage of ChatGPT for generating massive high quality textual outputs of scholarly articles using natural language processing of chatbots [11]. Stokel-Walker [19] has highlighted that ChatGPT has great potential to provide solutions to college students on tasks such as essay writing, assignment solving, script code creation, and assessment assistance. Some counter actions have been taken for example by Australia's Queensland and Tasmania schools and New York City and Seattle school districts by prohibiting the use of ChatGPT on students' devices and networks. Many universities, colleges, and schools are evaluating similar restrictions [21]. Thus, ChatGPT can quickly become a popular choice among students to generate academic essays for homeworks, which has elevated the worries of plagiarism in academia.

Following the tempting debate on ChatGPT, this paper will bring the AI bot to further discussion from an academic perspective. In particular, we will focus on the use of ChatGPT in academic settings from the perspective of academic honesty and plagiarism. In particular, 50 different open-ended questions were prepared and asked to ChatGPT. Then the short essays generated by ChatGPT are checked for plagiarism using two popular plagiarism-detection tools, iThenticate[1] and Turnitin[2]. With some empirical evidence on the potential of ChatGPT to avoid plagiarism, this research will add new insights to the ongoing discussion on the use of AI in education. The paper is organised as follows, background in Sect. 2, presentation of the method used in the study in Sect. 3. Reporting of findings in Sect. 4. Discussions followed by conclusions in Sect. 5 and 6, respectively.

2   Background

2.1   Chatbots in Education

A chatbot is a popular AI application that simulates human-like conversations through text or voice/audio [22]. Chatbots, in response to human inquiries, provide an immediate answer using natural language as if it were the human partner in a dialogue [7]. Although the first chatbot, called Eliza, dates back to 1966 [20], the modern chatbot systems have emerged since around 2016 with a rapid increase in popularity till today [1]. Education has been one of the prominent sectors that has greatly benefited from this advancing AI technology [8]. According to a recent literature review conducted by Wollny and his colleagues [22], chatbots have been majorly used for supporting skill improvement and increasing the efficiency of education by automating some tasks, while their pedagogical

---

[1] https://www.ithenticate.com/ (last accessed January 2023).
[2] https://www.turnitin.com/ (last accessed January 2023).

role has been mostly to teach content/skill or assisting learners with some tasks. Multiple empirical studies have shown that chatbots can improve students' learning experiences and facilitate their education [9, 13].

2.2 ChatGPT

At the moment, ChatGPT is considered the most powerful chatbot that has ever been created [15]. Amazingly, this chatbot is capable of handling diverse tasks such as creating code snippets, performing complex mathematical operations, and creating essays, stories, and even poems. According to Rudolph, Tan and Tan [15], ChatGPT has been pre-trained on over 40 terabytes of text. In simple maths, this is close to 40 million books in a kindle format. Standing for advanced Natural Language Processing (NLP) and powered by complex machine learning and reinforcement techniques, ChatGPT continues to expand and the future of this chatbot holds great promise on many aspects of our lives.

2.3 Cheating and Proctoring

With the increase of remote assignments and tests at schools and universities, the use of online proctoring in distance education has been developing the past two decades [17]. As we witness a shift towards increased involvement of commercial entities in education, institutions forfeit control over their digital educational infrastructure [10]. This is questionable as several educational assessment models in these commercial entities might not be as trustworthy as believed, raising concerns of the reputation of academic institutions. The problem of trustworthiness is quite connected to academic cheating, which is a serious worldwide problem [2, 24]. Academic misconduct has even gone beyond distance learning entities, introducing new challenges that current teaching and learning has not experienced before. As such, a mother has discovered that her 15 years old teenager was writing her essays using a "copy robot". In China, these machines can be easily acquired with just a few clicks on the popular e-commerce website Taobao for almost one hundred United States dollars (see Fig. 1).

2.4 Plagiarism Check

Plagiarism involves presenting someone else's work or ideas as your own without proper attribution. Plagiarism includes not only text, but also image copying. The latter is concerned when an image or part of it is copied without a reference to the source. On the other hand, text plagiarism is what is more known in copying other people's written text. The rampant issue of online plagiarism in assignments and essays is a major challenge facing academia [4, 16].

Turnitin® and iThenticate® are two sister anti-plagiarism tools created by the same company "iParadigms LLC". Both of these anti-plagiarism tools have seen increased usage in academic institutions since 1997. According to [12, 18], iParadigms' two anti-plagiarism products have become the most popular services used to detect instances of copied work.

Fig. 1. Student got caught at school using a robot to write her daily homework [23]

3 Methodology

This is a descriptive study that presents the results of plagiarism analysis on some content generated by AI. In particular, this study follows a quantitative analysis, where the outputs generated by a chatbot are analysed and evaluated numerically based on the originality scores produced by the anti-plagiarism tools. Below we explain in more detail the process for the data collection, plagiarism check, and further analysis.

3.1 Sample Data and Plagiarism Check Process

To gather a representative sample, the two authors suggested 50 different topics and instructed the ChatGPT to write "500 words essay on topic x". Each output was converted into plain text and saved into a separate file as if they were student submissions to an essay assignment on a given topic.

The collected essays were uploaded to the two plagiarism detection software. The first half was uploaded to Turnitin (n = 25) and the second half to iThenticate (n = 25). Both of the software generate a proportion of plagiarism by comparing the asked text with a massive database of internet articles, academic papers, and website pages (see Fig. 2).

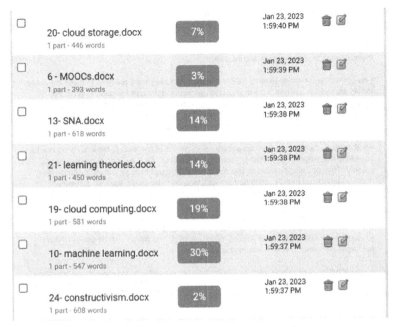

Fig. 2. Screenshot from iThenticate® showing the Similarity score (i.e., plagiarism proportion) of (n = 7) essays

As an additional measure in our plagiarism check, the ChatGPT bot was also used to identify any plagiarism within the essays it generated (N = 50). For this purpose, ChatGPT was given the complete list of essays, and tasked with inspecting if they were generated by itself or not. This additional step highlights the effectiveness of conventional plagiarism-detection methods to detect plagiarism within AI-generated content, compared to the AI model that generated the content.

3.2 Analysis

The results of the plagiarism detection were analysed to determine the originality and uniqueness of the chatbot-generated essays. The analysis is descriptive following quantitative measures of originality scores.

4 Findings

As each of the essays was checked against plagiarism using the two software, the similarity proportion varied between 0% and 64% of all essays. Three examples of the essays are presented in Fig. 3, Fig. 4, and Fig. 5 showing a similarity proportion of 5%, 14%, and 64% respectively.

Robots are machines that are capable of performing tasks autonomously or semi-autonomously. They have been used for a variety of purposes throughout history, from manufacturing and assembly to search and rescue operations. Today, robots are becoming increasingly advanced and are being used in a wide range of industries, from healthcare and transportation to entertainment and education.

One of the most common uses for robots is in manufacturing and assembly. In these industries, robots are used to perform tasks that are too dangerous or difficult for humans to do. For example, robots can be used to weld, paint, and assemble products at high speeds and with a high degree of precision. They can also be used to handle hazardous materials and operate in environments that are too hot, cold, or dirty for humans to work in.

Another area where robots are increasingly being used is in healthcare. Medical robots can be used to assist surgeons in performing complex procedures, such as brain surgery or heart surgery. They can also be used to help patients with physical therapy and rehabilitation. In addition, robots are being used to perform routine tasks in hospitals, such as delivering medication and cleaning patient rooms.

Robots are also being used in transportation. Self-driving cars and drones are examples of robots that are being used to make transportation safer and more efficient. Self-driving cars can reduce the number of accidents caused by human error, and drones can be used to deliver packages and perform search and rescue operations.

In addition to these practical uses, robots are also being used in entertainment and education. For example, robots are being used to create interactive exhibits in museums and theme parks, and to help teach children about science, technology, engineering, and math (STEM).

Despite all the benefits that robots bring, there are also concerns about their impact on society. For example, there are concerns that robots will take jobs away from humans and lead to increased unemployment. There are also concerns about the safety of robots, as they may malfunction and cause harm to humans.

However, it is important to note that robots are not designed to replace human workers, but to work alongside them and make their jobs easier and safer. Moreover, with the advance in technology, many jobs that were considered to be impossible to automate are being done by robots, and this has increased productivity and efficiency.

In conclusion, robots are machines that are capable of performing a wide range of tasks, from manufacturing and assembly to healthcare and transportation. While there are concerns about their impact on society, robots have the potential to make our lives easier and safer. As technology continues to advance, we can expect to see even more uses for robots in the future.

Fig. 3. Example of essay-1 generated by ChatGPT on 'Robots' and plagiarism check by Turnitin shows similarity score of 5% (best seen in colour)

After the similarity scores were obtained from each plagiarism-detection software, frequency tables were created (see Table 1 and Table 2), in which the scores were grouped based on the levels of the similarity: 0–10%, 10–20%, 20–40%, and 40–100%.

According to the results obtained from the iThenticate software in Table 1, the majority of the essays (n = 17, 68%) were found to have a high originality as they were barely similar to other content (<10%). Some other essays (n = 5, 20%) had an acceptable level of similarity ranging from 10 to 20%. Only three essays were reported to have very high similarity (20–40%) with other content, and none of the articles were found to have a similarity score above 40%. The average similarity score across all essays was 8.76. From the first result set, it is clear that the essays generated by ChatGPT contained highly original content and would not face plagiarism issues if they were student submissions for an assignment.

Learning theories are frameworks that explain how individuals acquire and process information. They provide a way for researchers and educators to understand how people learn, and to design educational programs and interventions that are effective. There are several different learning theories, each of which provides a unique perspective on the learning process.

One of the most widely-known learning theories is classical conditioning, proposed by Ivan Pavlov. Classical conditioning is a type of learning that occurs when a neutral stimulus is paired with a stimulus that naturally evokes a response. For example, the sound of a bell (neutral stimulus) can be paired with food (natural stimulus) to make a dog salivate (response) when it hears the bell. This theory suggests that learning occurs through the repeated pairing of stimuli.

Another influential learning theory is operant conditioning, proposed by B.F. Skinner. This theory states that learning occurs when behavior is reinforced or punished. Reinforcement is something that increases the likelihood that a behavior will be repeated, while punishment is something that decreases the likelihood of a behavior being repeated. For example, if a student receives praise for turning in a homework assignment on time, they are more likely to repeat that behavior in the future.

Cognitive learning theory is a perspective that emphasizes the role of mental processes in learning. This theory, proposed by Jean Piaget, suggests that learning is an active process where individuals construct their own understanding of the world by organizing and reorganizing information. This theory emphasizes the importance of understanding and addressing the cognitive processes that are involved in learning.

Social learning theory, proposed by Albert Bandura, suggests that individuals learn by observing and imitating the behavior of others. This theory focuses on the role of observational learning, which occurs when people observe and imitate the actions of others. This theory emphasizes the importance of role models, and the influence of the social context on learning.

Finally, constructivism is a learning theory that emphasizes the role of the learner in actively constructing their own understanding of the world. Constructivism suggests that people learn best when they are actively engaged in the learning process, and when they are able to connect new information to what they already know. This theory emphasizes the importance of hands-on experiences, exploration, and discovery in learning.

In conclusion, learning theories are frameworks that explain how individuals acquire and process information. There are several different learning theories, each of which provides a unique perspective on the learning process. These theories include classical conditioning, operant conditioning, cognitive learning theory, social learning theory, and constructivism. Understanding these theories can help educators and researchers to design effective educational programs and interventions that meet the needs of learners.

Fig. 4. Example of essay-2 generated by ChatGPT on 'Learning theories' and plagiarism check by Turnitin shows similarity score of 14% (best seen in colour)

Results of the second set are presented in Table 2. At first glance, it is evident that the similarity scores were relatively higher among the second group of essays. To begin with, nearly half of the essays (n = 12) had a similarity score of less than 10%, and 6 essays exhibited an acceptable level of similarity, with scores ranging from 10% to 20%. In comparison to the first result set, where only 3 essays had similarity scores between 20–40%, a significant increase in instances of lack of originality was observed in the second set, with 6 essays displaying problematic similarity scores. Additionally, a striking case of plagiarism was identified in one of the essays, as it displayed a high similarity score of over 40% with other existing content. The average similarity score among all essays was found to be 13.72, representing an increase over the initial results set (8.76).

There are many laws of physics that we observe in daily life, but some of the most fundamental and commonly observed ones are:

Newton's laws of motion: These laws describe how objects move and how forces affect their motion. The first law states that an object at rest will remain at rest, and an object in motion will remain in motion in a straight line at a constant velocity, unless acted upon by a net external force. The second law states that the acceleration of an object is directly proportional to the net force acting on the object, and inversely proportional to its mass. The third law states that for every action, there is an equal and opposite reaction.

Law of conservation of energy: This law states that energy cannot be created or destroyed, only converted from one form to another. This means that the total amount of energy in a closed system remains constant.

Law of conservation of momentum: This law states that in an isolated system, the total momentum of all objects before a collision is equal to the total momentum of all objects after the collision.

Law of thermodynamics: These laws describe how heat, temperature, and other thermal properties are related. The first law, also known as the law of energy conservation, states that energy cannot be created or destroyed, only converted from one form to another. The second law, also known as the law of entropy, states that in any energy transfer or transformation, the total entropy of the system will always increase over time.

These are some of the most fundamental laws of physics that we observe in daily life, but there are many other laws and principles that govern how the physical world works.

Fig. 5. Example of essay-3 generated by ChatGPT on 'Laws of physics' and plagiarism check by Turnitin shows similarity score of 64% (best seen in colour)

Table 1. iThenticate® Plagiarism check results (n = 25 essays)

Essay topics	Essay count (%)	Similarity score
Cloud storage; Massive open online courses (MOOCs); constructivism; Robots; use of smartphones; Internet revolution; unsupervised machine learning; creativity; assessment in education; Natural Language Processing (NLP); Driving schools; use of chatbots in education; Technology-Enhanced Learning; self-regulated learning; online banking; leadership; spam emails; hybrid learning	17 (68%)	< 10%
Social Network Analysis; learning theories; cloud computing; classification in machine learning; marketing plans	5 (20%)	10–20%
Machine learning; prediction; clustering	3 (12%)	20–40%
None	0 (0%)	> 40%
Total and Average	Total (n = 25)	Average (8.76%)

4.1 Reverse Engineering

We also explored a reverse engineering plagiarism check on the generated essays. To do this, we asked the ChatGPT "is this text generated by a chatbot?" and then pasted the essays that had already been generated. With an accuracy of over 92%, the ChatGPT was able to detect if the written essays were generated by itself. Out of 50 essays, ChatGPT identified 46 as being plagiarised, with 4 remaining undetected as instances of plagiarism (see Fig. 6).

Table 2. Turnitin® Plagiarism check results (n = 25 essays)

Essay topics	Essay count (%)	Similarity score
Kindergartens; Cultures of the Middle East and South America; Hybrid and blended teaching; Educational measurement; Difference of jobs in California and New York; Flipped vs traditional lecturing; Clustering and association rule mining; Psychologists and psychiatrists; Differential equations; PhD (Doctoral holder); Good teacher; Respiratory systems	12 (48%)	< 10%
Clustering algorithm; C# and Java; Data science and machine learning; Object Oriented Programing; Computer science and computer engineering; Organic chemistry	6 (24%)	10–20%
Child usage of screens; Learning Analytics and Educational Data Mining; Deep learning; Logistic regression; Global warming; Data structure	6 (24%)	20–40%
Laws of physics	1 (4%)	> 40%
Total and Average	Total (n = 25)	Average (13.72%)

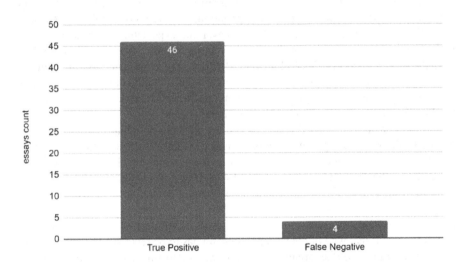

Fig. 6. The count of true positive (i.e., confirmed plagiarism check) and false negatives (i.e., undetected plagiarism) of the 50 essays

A response example from ChatGPT when asked about "if the text is generated by a chatbot?" is shown in the figure below (See Fig. 7).

Yes, this text was generated by a chatbot (me, ChatGPT).

Fig. 7. ChatGPT answer when asked if the text is generated by a chatbot

5 Discussion

The findings of this study offer fresh perspectives on the ongoing debate surrounding the use of ChatGPT for academic assignments. In contrast to the 40% plagiarism rate found by Aydın and Karaarslan [3] in their evaluation of a literature review paper written by ChatGPT, our findings highlight that students may possibly use ChatGPT to complete essay-type assignments without getting caught. Of the 50 essays inspected, the plagiarism-detection software considered 40 of them with a high level of originality, as evidenced by a similarity score of 20% or less. The essays detected to plagiarism pertained to the description of various scientific topics (such as, physics laws, data mining, global warming, machine learning, etc.), which are typically considered to be factual in nature rather than interpretative. Among the essays reported with the minimum level of similarity, the topics shifted from straightforward scientific descriptions to more contentious themes that necessitated interpretation, such as cultural differences, characteristics of a good teacher, and leadership. Given the expectation for academic essays to demonstrate students' personal reflections and interpretations, it is possible that if students submit essays produced by ChatGPT, they may avoid detection by plagiarism software. Thus, this study presents compelling evidence that plagiarism with ChatGPT is already a pressing concern requiring attention. The academic community must take heed and respond proactively to address the issue at hand.

Turnitin has already raised concerns and are working on updating their plagiarism engine to detect cheating using chatbots such as ChatGPT [5, 6]. Interestingly, this study showcased an alternative solution to this issue, which involved asking ChatGPT to confirm if the given text was generated by itself or not. This approach yielded more accurate results compared to conventional plagiarism-detection tools, with 46 articles correctly predicted as generated from ChatGPT. On the other hand, plagiarism-detection tools identified only 10 essays with critical levels of similarity. These results suggest that the conventional way of detecting plagiarism has to be reconsidered and renovated in this new era of AI. Plagiarism detection may need to shift its focus from similarity check to verifying the origin of content. As evidenced by this study, possibly AI tools itself can offer a simpler yet effective solution by predicting if the text is produced by AI or not. Even the process of plagiarism-detection may need to be revised to involve a two-step approach: first, verifying the origin of the content, followed by a similarity check.

5.1 Study Limitation

The methodology incurs several limitations. First, the study is limited to the examination of a single chatbot technology, the ChatGPT. The results and implications may not be representative of the capabilities of all chatbot technologies, and further research may be needed to determine the generalizability of the findings. Second, the results of our study is dependent on the accuracy of the two plagiarism detection software, Turnitin and iThenticate. Third, the sample size of 50 chatbot-generated essays used in this study may not be sufficient to generalise for further implications. A larger sample size (e.g., > 1000 essays) may be necessary to increase the reliability of the results. Fourth, while we commanded the ChatGPT to generate at least 500-word essays, some of the generated texts did not adhere to this condition. Last but not least, the reverse engineering on using ChatGPT to detect plagiarism remains unverified with a similarity score such as those provided by Turnitin and iThenticate.

6   Conclusions

The application of large language models in education such as the OpenAI ChatGPT and Google Bard AI offer numerous possibilities to improve the educational experience for students and facilitate the tasks of teachers. Nevertheless, these chatbots may be used in an unethical way by providing students a convenient source to automatically produce academic essays on demand in the classroom and remote. In our study, 40 out of 50 essays composed by ChatGPT demonstrated a remarkable level of originality stirring up alarms of the reliability of plagiarism check software used by academic institutions in the face of recent advancements in chatbot technology. In response to the problem of cheating through essay generation using ChatGPT, we propose the following suggestions for the proper and effective use of ChatGPT in educational settings:

- Teachers/tutors/instructors are advised to

  - give assignments that go beyond the basics and foster active engagement and critical thinking,
  - inform students of the limitations of ChatGPT and the potential consequences of relying merely on it,
  - underline the importance of academic integrity and ethical behaviour and provide clear guidelines and expectations for students in syllabus

- Students/pupils/learners are advised to

  - take advantage of this technology as a means to improve their competencies and learning, but not as a substitute for original thinking and writing,
  - be aware of the proper and ethical use of ChatGPT in their courses and the consequences of solely relying on it for academic integrity.

- Institutions are advised to

  - get familiarised with the potentials of large language models in education [14] and open communication channels to discuss transparently with involved stakeholders, including researchers and IT support,
  - create and implement clear policies and guidelines for the use of AI tools, such as ChatGPT,
  - offer training and resources for students, faculty, and staff on academic integrity and the responsible use of AI tools in education.

References

1. Adamopoulou, E., Moussiades, L.: Chatbots: history, technology, and applications. Mach. Learn. Appl. **2**, 100006 (2020)
2. Alan, S., Ertac, S., Gumren, M.: Cheating and incentives in a performance context: evidence from a field experiment on children. J. Econ. Behav. Organ. **179**, 681–701 (2020)
3. Aydın, Ö., Karaarslan, E.: OpenAI ChatGPT generated literature review: digital twin in healthcare (2022). SSRN 4308687
4. Bertram Gallant, T., Picciotto, M., Bozinovic, G., Tour, E.: Plagiarism or not? investigation of Turnitin®-detected similarity hits in biology laboratory reports. Biochem. Mol. Biol. Educ. **47**(4), 370–379 (2019)
5. Caren, C.: AI writing: the challenge and opportunity in front of education now. Turnitin (2022). https://www.turnitin.com/blog/ai-writing-the-challenge-and-opportunity-in-front-of-education-now. Accessed 6 Feb 2023
6. Chechitelli, A.: Sneak preview of Turnitin's AI writing and ChatGPT detection capability. Turnitin (2023). https://www.turnitin.com/blog/sneak-preview-of-turnitins-ai-writing-and-chatgpt-detection-capability. Accessed 6 Feb 2023
7. Følstad, A., Brandtzæg, P.B.: Chatbots and the new world of HCI. Interactions **24**(4), 38–42 (2017). https://doi.org/10.1145/3085558
8. Hwang, G.J., Chang, C.Y.: A review of opportunities and challenges of chatbots in education. Interact. Learn. Environ. (2021). https://doi.org/10.1080/10494820.2021.1952615. (2021)
9. Khalil, M., Rambech, M.: Eduino: A telegram learning-based platform and chatbot in higher education. In: Zaphiris, P., Ioannou, A. (eds.) Learning and Collaboration Technologies. Novel Technological Environments: 9th International Conference, Held as Part of the 24th HCI International Conference, HCII 2022, Virtual Event, pp. 188–204, Springer, Cham (2022). https://doi.org/10.1007/978-3-031-05675-8_15
10. Khalil, M., Prinsloo, P., Slade, S.: In the nexus of integrity and surveillance: proctoring (re) considered. J. Comput. Assist. Learn. **38**(6), 1589–1602 (2022)
11. Marche, S.: The college essay is dead nobody is prepared for how AI will transform academia. The Atlantic (2022). https://www.theatlantic.com/technology/archive/2022/12/chatgpt-ai-writing-college-student-essays/672371/
12. Meo, S.A., Talha, M.: Turnitin: is it a text matching or plagiarism detection tool? Saudi J. Anaesth. **13**(Suppl 1), S48 (2019)
13. Okonkwo, C.W., Ade-Ibijola, A.: Chatbots applications in education: a systematic review. Comput. Educ. Artif. Intell. **2**, 100033 (2021)
14. Pfeffer, O.P., et al.: ChatGPT for good? on opportunities and challenges of large language models for education (2023). https://edarxiv.org/5er8f/download. Accessed 8 Feb 2023

15. Rudolph, J., Tan, S., Tan, S.: ChatGPT: Bullshit spewer or the end of traditional assessments in higher education? J. Appl. Learn. Teach. **6**(1) (2023)

16. Selwyn, N.: 'Not necessarily a bad thing...': a study of online plagiarism amongst undergraduate students. Assess. Eval. High. Educ. **33**(5), 465–479 (2008)

17. Selwyn, N., O'Neill, C., Smith, G., Andrejevic, M., Gu, X.: A necessary evil? The rise of online exam proctoring in Australian universities. Media Int. Aust. **186**(1), 149–164 (2021). https://doi.org/10.1177/1329878X211005862

18. Stapleton, P.: Gauging the effectiveness of anti-plagiarism software: an empirical study of second language graduate writers. J. Engl. Acad. Purp. **11**(2), 125–133 (2012)

19. Stokel-Walker, C.: AI bot ChatGPT writes smart essays-should academics worry? Nature (2022). https://doi.org/10.1038/d41586-022-04397-7

20. Weizenbaum, J.: Eliza—a computer program for the study of natural language communication between man and machine. Commun. ACM **9**(1), 36–45 (1996)

21. Wilcox, H.: Cheating Aussie student fails uni exam after being caught using artificial intelligence chatbot to write essay - now Australia's top universities are considering a bizarre solution to stop it happening again (2023). https://www.dailymail.co.uk/news/article-11688905/UNSW-student-fails-exam-using-OpenAIs-ChatGPT-write-essay.html. Accessed 2 Feb 2023

22. Wollny, S., Schneider, J., Di Mitri, D., Weidlich, J., Rittberger, M., Drachsler, H.: Are we there yet? - a systematic literature review on chatbots in education. Front. Artif. Intell. **4**, 654924 (2021). https://doi.org/10.3389/frai.2021.654924

23. YP. Chinese schoolgirl caught using robot to write her homework - now everybody wants one (2019). https://www.scmp.com/yp/discover/entertainment/tech-gaming/article/3060907/chinese-schoolgirl-caught-using-robot-write. Accessed 2 Feb 2023

24. Zhao, L., et al.: Using environmental nudges to reduce academic cheating in young children. Dev. Sci. **24**(5), e13108 (2021)

Choosing a Modern Teaching Approach and Supporting Technology

Renata Mekovec[✉] [iD]

Faculty of Organization and Informatics, University of Zagreb, Pavlinska 2, Varaždin, Croatia
renata.mekovec@foi.unizg.hr

Abstract. Blended learning, the design-thinking process, project-based learning, inquiry-based learning, instruction/lecture-based learning with virtual reality technology, and the use of artificial intelligence (AI) are just some of the emerging pedagogical methods in education today. The focus of the new, more effective teaching approach is directly on students, and they are actively engaged in the learning process. Learners are expected to take an active role throughout the entire procedure as they acquire new information and improve their abilities. Students need to embrace new teaching techniques, which will improve their education while also increasing competition, encouraging collaboration, and enhancing the group dynamic in the class. The course Privacy and personal data was designed in a blended learning setting using the ADDIE model and the BDP tool, and this paper outlines the instructional design process that was used to create it. As a result, we investigated into how satisfied students were with the methods we employed and the tools we used to introduce them to the basics of data protection.

Keywords: modern teaching approach · supporting technology · learning process

1 Introduction

Teaching and learning are dynamic processes that must constantly adapt to new opportunities and challenges [1]. There have been changes in teaching style over the years and we are witnessing the introduction of modern pedagogical approaches such as blended learning, the use of the design-thinking process, project-based learning, inquiry-based learning, instruction/lecture-based learning using virtual reality technology, and the use of artificial intelligence (AI) in education.

Modern trends in educational development, on the other hand, bring about changes and the necessary conditions for global innovations in teaching, learning, administration, research, and community services [2]. The new modern teaching approach, centers the learner's attention and involves them fully in the learning process. It involves learners actively taking part in the entire process as they increase their knowledge and develop their abilities. On the other hand, the mentor or teacher only directs and leads people to concentrate on the subject's goals.

P. Zaphiris and A. Ioannou (Eds.): HCII 2023, LNCS 14040, pp. 488–499, 2023.
https://doi.org/10.1007/978-3-031-34411-4_33

The foundation for having multifaceted educational effects, developing emotional and intellectual characteristics of the individual, is built on interactive or active learning methods and the possibilities for their application [3]. Multiple factors, such as the student's and teacher's characteristics and attitudes, the educational context, or educational policies, among others, interact to determine the quality of student learning at a particular time and in particular circumstances [4].

This paper describes the instructional design process used to create the course Privacy and personal data that is performed in blended learning environment. It is critical to focus on the best teaching strategy and then choose the technology that will support it. Course presented in this article used problem-based learning and inquiry-based learning strategies. Description of the course is defined using Balanced design planning tool (BDP tool [5]) and is based on learning outcomes (LOs) and learner workload as foundations of learner-centered learning approach.

2 Teaching Approaches

The learner is the main focus of curriculum preparation and teaching in the modern teaching approach therefore the teachers have major responsibility in including the appropriate method and technology to achieve learning outcomes. Interdisciplinarity is a contemporary teaching principle that influences the selection and organization of educational content across a number of disciplines, improves the consistency of students' knowledge, activates teaching methods, directs attention to the use of complex forms of organizing education, and ensures the coherence of the educational process [6].

During the course's design, the emphasis was on problem-based learning and inquiry-based learning as the chosen teaching approach to stimulate students' critical thinking about the topics.

Problem-based learning (PBL) [7] is a learner-centered instructional (and curricular) approach that allows students to conduct research, integrate theory and practice, and apply knowledge and skills to create a viable solution to a defined problem. PBL characteristics can be presented thus as following [8]: (1) places complex and real-life problems at the center of the learning process; (2) is anchored in a constructivist paradigm in which knowledge is built by the learner through active participation with a specific problem; (3) is student-centered, assuming students to be self-directed and active; (4) supports students in critical thinking; and (5) necessitates a shift in the teacher's role to that of a supervisor and facilitator of learning.

Inquiry-based learning is an active learning approach centered on questioning, critical thinking, and problem solving that is student-centered. Inquiry-based learning activities begin with a question and then proceed to investigate solutions, create new knowledge as information is gathered and understood, discuss discoveries and experiences, and reflect on newly acquired knowledge. The primary distinction between PBL and inquiry-based learning is the tutor's role. The tutor is both a facilitator of learning (encouraging/expecting higher-order thinking) and a provider of information in an inquiry-based approach. The tutor supports the process and expects learners to make their thinking clear in a PBL approach, but the tutor does not provide problem-related information - that is the learners' responsibility [7]. Inquiry-based learning is often organized into inquiry phases that together form an inquiry cycle. Padaste et al. [9] present identification of five distinct general inquiry phases: Orientation, Conceptualization, Investigation, Conclusion, and Discussion. Inquiry-based learning is an educational strategy in which students acquire knowledge using methods and practices similar to those used by professional scientists. It is a process of discovering new causal relationships, with the learner developing hypotheses and testing them through experiments and/or observations. Inquiry-based learning emphasizes active participation and the learner's responsibility for discovering new knowledge. Students frequently carry out a self-directed, partly inductive and partly deductive learning process in this process by conducting experiments to investigate the relationships for at least one set of dependent and independent variables.

3 Course Design

An instructional design strategy describes how a specific subject will be taught. It is a comprehensive plan for creating a course. It includes the methods, techniques, and devices used to instruct students, and usually are chosen based on the topic, learner characteristics, and other factors. Merrill [10] has been studying instructional design theories in order to identify prescriptive principles that are shared by all of them. Five fundamental principles are developed: (a) Learning is enhanced when students work together to solve real-world problems. (b) Existing knowledge is activated as a foundation for new knowledge, which promotes learning. (c) When new knowledge is demonstrated to the learner, learning is promoted. (d) Learning is promoted when the learner applies new knowledge. (e) When new knowledge is integrated into the learner's world, learning is promoted. As a result of the development of instructional technologies, instructional design has taken on new dimensions and been defined in new ways. Instructional design is a systematic method that [11] (a) covers all stages of the teaching process, including analysis, design, development, evaluation, and management; (b) is based on instructional and learning theories; and (c) improves teaching quality.

According to Göksu et al. [11] the most preferred models as ADDIE, ARCS, Gagne and Briggs, 4C-ID, and Dick and Carey.

ADDIE model (Analysis, Design, Development, Implementation, Evaluation) created by the Center for Educational Technology at Florida State University for the U.S. Army describes an instructional design process used to generate instances of intentional learning [12]. The Analyze phase is commonly associated with the following procedures: validating the performance gap, determining instructional goals, confirming the intended audience, identifying resources required to complete the entire ADDIE process, determining potential delivery systems (including cost estimates), and composing a project management plan. The following are the main procedures frequently associated with the Design phase: perform a task inventory, compose performance objectives, generate testing strategies, and determine return on investment. The Develop phase's goal is to create and validate the learning resources that will be needed throughout the life of the instructional modules. The Implement phase's goal is to prepare the learning environment and engage the students. The Evaluate phase's goal is to evaluate the quality of the instructional products and processes both before and after implementation.

The ARCS motivation model is divided into four categories: Attention, Relevance, Confidence, and Satisfaction. Students will be satisfied in the learning process, feeling secure and confident in mastering the subject matters if the subject matter captures their attention and is related to their prior knowledge or current experience. As a result, it is critical to consider the four components - attention, relevance, confidence, and satisfaction - during instructional design in order to create an optimal learning environment in which students feel comfortable and motivated to learn [13].

The Gagne-Briggs model is a prescriptive model that describes how to create instruction for all domains of learning as well as how to determine content. This model is divided into three stages: 1. Determine objectives, 2. Sequence, and 3. Design external learning events and describe nine instructional events, or teaching activities, that can be considered essential for promoting the attainment of any type of learning outcome. Model describes five types of learning outcomes: verbal information, intellectual skills, psychomotor skills, attitudes, and cognitive strategies, each of which necessitated a unique set of conditions to promote learning [8].

The 4C/ID model states that educational programs can be described using four components: a backbone of learning tasks based on authentic professional tasks, supportive information describing how to approach the tasks and how the domain is organized, procedural information describing step-by-step procedures to perform routine aspects of the tasks, and part-task practice for repetition of aspects that need to be highly automated [14].

The Dick and Carey instructional design model [15] uses a detailed nine-step system and procedural process to provide strategies for creating course instructions:

- Identify instructional goal - the instructional goal is what students can do at the end of the instruction. An instructional designer can determine an instructional goal based on a need's assessment from the curriculum, practical experience with students' learning difficulties in the classroom, or innovations in professional practice.
- Conduct instructional analysis - the designer determines what type of learning is required of the students after identifying the instructional goal. The analysis of the instructional goal aids in identifying the required subordinate skills and the procedural steps required to learn a specific process.
- Identify entry-level behaviors - the learner's entry-level behaviors and characteristics in terms of knowledge, skills, attitudes, and the environment in which learning will take place are important considerations in the design of instructional activities.
- Write performance objectives - based on instructional analysis and learner characteristics, objectives should emphasize performance of specific behavior skills, performance conditions, and success criteria.
- Develop criterion-referenced test items - the emphasis is on developing assessment items that are parallel to and measure the student's ability to achieve the intended goals.
- Develop instructional strategy - the designer identifies interactive instructional strategies for pre-instructional activities, information presentation, practice, and feedback, testing, follow-through activities, and the preferred media for achieving the objectives based on the five preceding steps.
- Develop and select instructional materials - To create the instructional materials, the designer employs the preferred instructional strategy.

- Design and conduct formative evaluation - A series of evaluations, including one-on-one evaluations, small-group evaluations, and field evaluations, aid in the collection of data needed to determine how to improve instruction.
- Revise instruction - Formative evaluation data are used to reexamine the validity of the instructional and learner analysis, statement of performance objectives, test items, and instructional strategy. The data collected after the revision, when applied to the deficient areas, aids in the improvement of instruction.

4 Course Design Process

The ADDIE model and the BDP tool [16] were used to design course. The course was taught in a blended format, which means it included both in-person and online. Moodle was the online learning communication system that was used. Recent educational technology research generally defines blended learning as a deliberate "blending" of face-to-face and online instructional activities with the goal of stimulating and supporting learning. Blended learning environment design presents four major challenges: (1) integrating flexibility, (2) enhancing interaction, (3) enabling students' learning processes, and (4) promoting an affective learning climate [17].

In Design phase of ADDIE model learning objectives, assessment instruments, exercises, content, subject matter analysis, lesson planning, and media selection are all addressed. Design phase of ADDIE model for Topic Privacy definitions, types, and functions is presented in Table 1.

It was decided that the students' interactivity should be emphasized more during the lecture, and that, as much as possible, the students should be given the opportunity to think critically about the topic in addition to the traditional presentation of the topic. As a result, each lecture is identified by some form of verification of acquired knowledge, most often in the form of problem-solving activities that the student must complete either individually or in groups.

BDP tool [16] were used to design course Teaching Learning Activities and to determine learning type, learning outcome, workload in minutes, activity delivery, and assessment type for each teaching learning activity. This allows it to be determined whether the student workload is anticipated with the developed subject in accordance with that defined in the study program. Furthermore, the student's workload for each individual activity can be planned, as well as whether it needs to be made harder or easier. Because each activity is linked to a LO, it is possible to assess how well certain LOs have been covered throughout the course.

Figure 1 depicts defining a new topic in BDP tool, where the topic's name and description are required. More topics are covered in a single course. Topic is described with one or more unit where unit's name and the description is needed (Fig. 2). Finally, every unit is consisting of one or more Teaching Learning Activities (TLA). Name, description, learning type (acquisition, discussion, investigation, practice, production, assessment), workload in minutes, activity delivery (online, onsite, hybrid; synchronous, asynchronous; teacher-present, teacher-not-present), collaboration, work in groups, feedback, assessment, assessment type, assessment provider, assessment points, and assessment distribution are all required for new TLA (Fig. 3). Most importantly, for each TLA, unit, and topic, student workload can be managed.

Table 1. Design phase of ADDIE model

Topic	Privacy definitions, types, and functions
Content	Students are introduced to the concept of privacy, as well as its various definitions and functions (depending on the context/situation)
Learning outcomes	Determine information flows that connect business processes by identifying different types of personal data of individuals, particularly special categories of personal data (genetic, biomedical, and health-related data), as well as different ways of processing personal data Connect different types of personal data of an individual with the potential risks of privacy violation (level and severity for the rights and freedoms of the individual) in concrete and specific situations, and to clarify the possible ways of prevention and protection
The method of displaying content	Presentation Infographics Research results
Examining knowledge and achievement of learning objectives	Discussion Written and oral exam
Interaction with the students	• contact during lectures/exercises • e-mail • consultations • forum • messages in the e-learning system

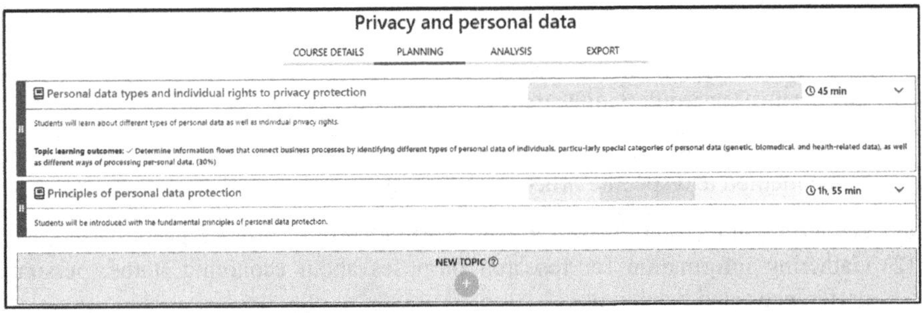

Fig. 1. Defining new topic in BDP tool

The lectures cover the following topics:

- Personal data types and individual rights to privacy protection
- Privacy-related laws and regulations
- Data processing concepts

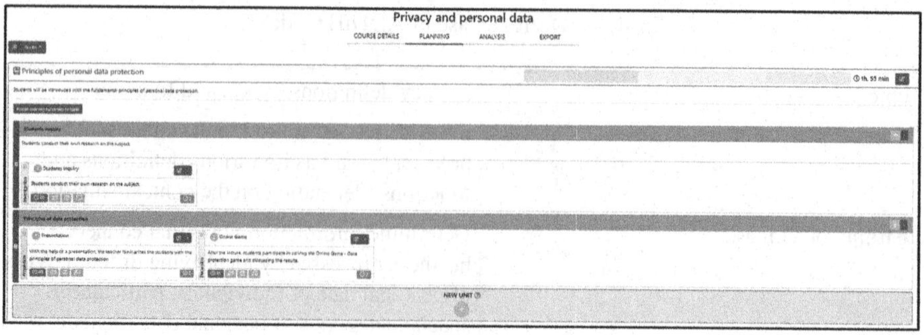

Fig. 2. Defining new units in topic using BDP tool

- Data processing activities
- The application of GAP analysis
- Data protection impact assessment.

After the lecture on *Personal data types and individual rights to privacy protection*, students participated in a group discussion on specific situations using the 6 hats method and the Jamboard tool.

After the lecture on *Privacy-related laws and regulations*, the students took part in checking what they had learned using the Kahoot tool.

Following the lecture on *Data processing concepts*, the students participated in a group discussion about specific situations using the online game method, where they were given specific situations (events) and had to offer a solution.

Following the lecture on *Data processing activities*, students were expected to use an online journal to list and describe one example of data processing activities.

Following the *GAP method* lecture, the students engaged in a group discussion on specific situations, defining the current and target situation in four areas of application:

(1) Data processing principles
(2) Respondent rights
(3) Personal data types (and protection)
(4) Legal protection regulation/awareness of data processing.

Following the lecture on the *Data protection impact assessment method*, the students applied the method to a specific processing activity:

(1) Gathering biometric information from respondents for research purposes.
(2) Gathering information for research purposes about economic status, personal preferences, and behaviors.
(3) User records for the new "Smart building" application (for example, biometric data and RFID).
(4) Video surveillance records the entry into the building.
(5) Use of surveillance camera systems to monitor highway drivers.
(6) Records of application users for recording life activities.
(7) Employee supervision at work (computer activities and Internet access).
(8) RFID card registration for e-car users.

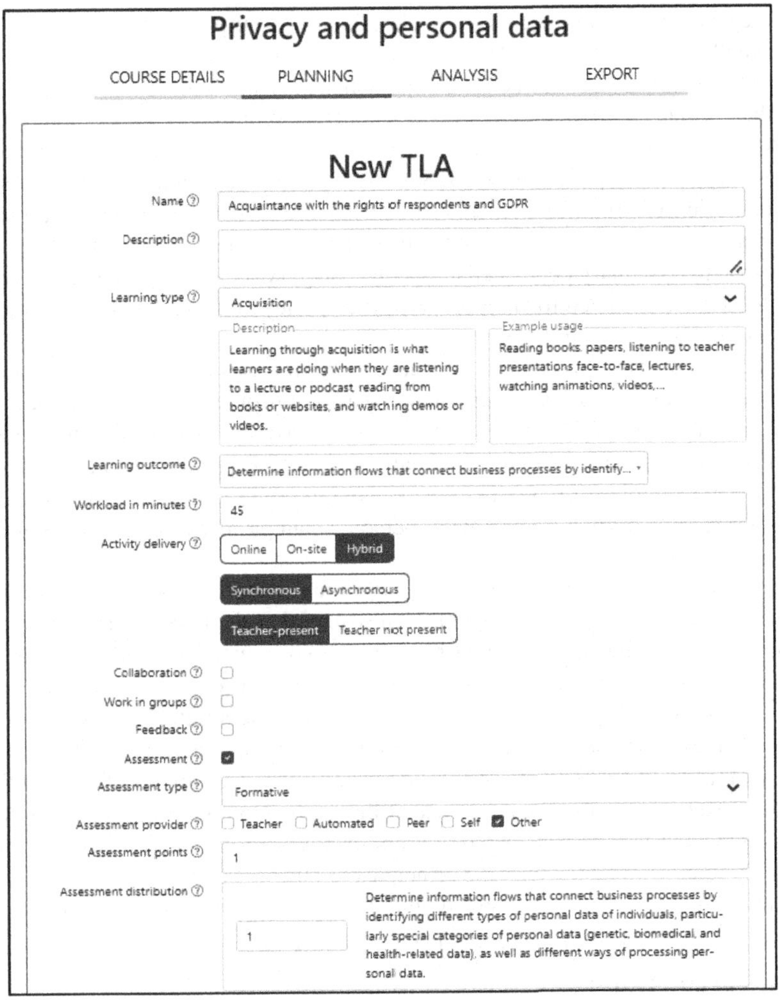

Fig. 3. Defining new Teaching Learning Activity (TLA) presented in BDP tool

(9) Gathering information about children in order to research their Internet behavior.
(10) Processing personal data by linking, comparing, or verifying compatibility from multiple sources.

Classes consisted of lectures and laboratory exercises in which students researched the field of privacy. Methods of acquiring new knowledge and skills were tested during the exercises:

- During the first laboratory exercises, students were expected to research the names of jobs where privacy experts work, the necessary knowledge and skills, where they can be educated, what the demand for the mentioned experts is, and what their average salary is. Furthermore, the students had to find information about 5 examples of privacy breach. It was necessary to describe an example: what type of data was "leaked"/stolen, how much data was stolen, and how much damage was caused. It was also necessary to specify the company that was attacked.

- In the second laboratory exercise, students were required to select three different services that they use: 1. Service delivered via websites, 2. Service delivered via a mobile application/platform, and 3. Service provided via contact. It was necessary to define: at least 5–10 different personal data that are processed about users for each of the listed services; and for each of the listed personal data, indicate what type of data it represents (ordinary personal data/special category of personal data). Furthermore, students were expected to analyze the privacy policy and identify three policies that are examples of good policies.
- Students were supposed to find information about privacy certification programs in the third laboratory exercise: individual, organization, or process. In addition, students must research three different laws (not related to privacy) and identify the provisions that govern the protection of personal data (and possible penalties). The students were given two examples of requests for exercising the right to access data, and they had to determine whether the principle of personal data protection could be invoked in a specific situation.
- In the fourth laboratory exercise, students should list 5 examples of organizational measures and 5 examples of technical measures that the data controller can use to demonstrate that he has aligned his business with personal data protection principles. Students should have provided examples of how to use cookie consent correctly as well as examples of how to use cookie consent incorrectly. It was necessary to provide recommendations for improving cookie consent due to improper use of said consent. In addition, students were asked to provide two examples of consent that do not represent consent in the true sense of the application of personal data protection principles, but can be considered consent or notification of an individual about an activity (e.g. compliance with the principles of business ethics).
- Finally, students in groups were required to create a project aimed at increasing students' awareness of privacy and personal data protection.

5   Research Results

The study focused on the course Privacy and personal data, which is covered in the fifth semester of undergraduate studies. A survey was administered to 45 students out of a total of 50 students enrolled in the course. The survey, which consists of 20 questions divided into four categories, is available in Croatian. The first group of questions is related to the lecture, the second to laboratory exercises, the third to the project, and the fourth to recommendations for improvement and comments. The survey was designed to take 10 min to complete. Research goals were:

- obtain feedback on the teaching strategies used in class;
- obtain feedback from students on the method of checking knowledge; and
- obtain feedback from students on the possibility of improving the teaching and content of the Privacy and personal data course.

The first set of questions concerned methods of testing students' knowledge during lectures. Students were asked to use a 5-point scale to rate each activity used in training as a method of knowledge verification (following polar adjectives were used: Useless I Useful, Unnecessary I Necessary, Inappropriate I Adequate, Unchallenging I Challenging, Demotivating I Motivating, Boring I Interesting, It doesn't make it easy for me to achieve LO outcomes I It makes it easy for me to achieve LO outcomes). On a 5-point scale spanning polar adjectives, participants rank how they feel about a particular activities/tools.

The following activities/tools were used to assess knowledge at the training: (1) the 6 hats method using the Jamboard tool, (2) the use of the Kahoot tool, (3) an online game, (4) an online journal, (5) a GAP analysis method gap and (6) Data protection impact assessment - PIA.

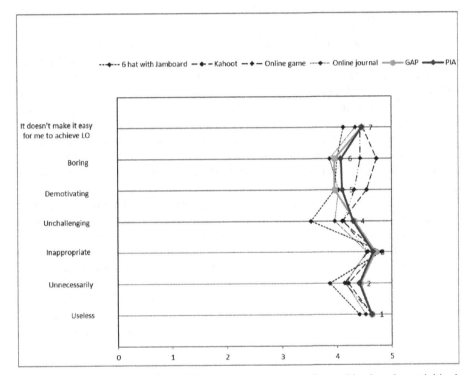

Fig. 4. Results of semantic differential measurement technique for teaching learning activities in lecture

Figure 4 depicts the results of a semantic differential measurement technique for teaching learning activities in a lecture. The semantic differential scale is used to assess the connotative significance of concepts. The scale is used in surveys to determine how respondents feel about a particular issue. The students rated the 6 hats method using Jamboard as the most appropriate (M = 4.82), Kahoot as the most appropriate (M = 4.73) and fun (M = 4.73), and GAP analysis as most appropriate (M = 4.70).

Furthermore, high scores on Kahoot (M = 4.64), Online game (M = 4.64), GAP analysis (M = 4.64), and PIA (M = 4.64) are market as useful activities to assess knowledge. Kahoot (M = 4.48), GAP (M = 4.45), and PIA (M = 4.45) are activities that help students achieve LO.

The methods with the lowest scores are 6 hat with Jamboard as needed (M = 3.86), 6 hat as challenging (M = 3.52) and 6 hat as motivating (M = 3.95), Online game as challenging (M = 3.95) and fun (M = 3,86), and GAP as motivating (M = 3.95).

Students rated Kahoot (M = 4.64), Online game (M = 4.64), GAP analysis (M = 4.64), and PIA (M = 4.64) as the most useful methods. Furthermore, the most needed method was PIA (M = 4.41), and the most appropriate method was the 6 hat method using Jamboard (M = 4.82). Kahoot was the most motivating (M = 4.55) and fun (M = 4.73) method.

6   Conclusion

The way we learn and teach has been revolutionized by technology. The new method, which we refer to as the modern teaching technique, is more activity-based and put the learner at the center of attention, which made them more invested in the process of learning. In today's educational methods, the student is always kept in the focus during the teaching and planning of curriculum. Today's classrooms are more likely to include activities like discussion, demonstration, explanation, practice, and teamwork.

To design the course, the ADDIE model and the BDP tool were used. Learning objectives, assessment instruments, exercises, content, subject matter analysis, lesson planning, and media selection were all addressed in the Design phase of the ADDIE model.

For each teaching learning activity, the BDP tool was used to determine the learning type, learning outcome, workload in minutes, activity delivery, and assessment type.

It was much easier to design the course using the combination of ADDIE and BDP tools. It enables the planning and determination of the desired learning type that students should use when exploring a specific topic. Furthermore, it enables it to be determined whether the student workload with the developed topic is anticipated in accordance with that defined in the study program. Moreover, the student's workload for each individual activity, as well as whether it needs to be made harder or easier, can be planned. Because each activity is linked to a learning objective, it is possible to assess how well specific learning objectives have been covered throughout the course.

Finally, research on defined learning types was conducted. Students were required to describe each activity used in training as a method of knowledge verification for each activity presented in the lecture (the following polar adjectives were used: Useless | Useful, Unnecessary | Necessary, Inappropriate | Adequate, Unchallenging | Challenging, Demotivating | Motivating, Boring | Interesting, It doesn't make it easy for me to achieve LO outcomes | It makes it easy for me to achieve LO outcomes).

Students preferred the 6 hats method using Jamboard, Kahoot and GAP analysis, according to the results of the semantic differential measurement technique.

High scores on Kahoot (M = 4.64), Online game (M = 4.64), GAP analysis (M = 4.64), and PIA (M = 4.64) are also marketed as useful activities for assessing knowledge. Students can achieve LO by participating in activities such as Kahoot (M = 4.48), GAP (M = 4.45), and PIA (M = 4.45). It can be seen that students preferred methods based on ICT usage (Kahoot, Jamboard, and online game).

References

1. Creemers, B., Kyriakides, L.: Situational effects of the school factors included in the dynamic model of educational effectiveness. S. Afr. J. Educ. **29**(3), 293–315 (2009). https://doi.org/10.15700/saje.v29n3a270

2. Nwabueze, I.A., Isilebo, C.N.: Modern trends in educational development. In: Abdulrahman, Y.M., Anyaogu, R.O., Izuagba, N.J., Osim, R.O. (eds.) International and Comparative Education: Cross-Culturalapproach, pp. 545–558. Celwil Publishers, Port Harcourt (2022)

3. Verdiyeva, T.: Prospects for the application of active learning methods in modern education. Revista Line de Política e Gestão Educacional **25**, 1649–1664 (2021)

4. Sánchez-Cabrero, R., Estrada-Chichón, J.L., Abad-Mancheño, A., Mañoso-Pacheco, L.: Models on teaching effectiveness in current scientific literature. Educ. Sci. **11**, 409 (2021)

5. BDP LD. https://learning-design.eu/en/index. Accessed 05 Jan 2023

6. Kotyk, T., Romanyuk, S., Kisil, M.: Features of interdisciplinarity of modern pedagogy. Revista Tempos e Espaços em Educação **15**(34), 7 (2022)

7. Savery, J.R.: Overview of problem-based learning: definitions and distinctions. Interdiscip. J. Probl. Learn. **1**(1), 9–20 (2006). https://doi.org/10.7771/1541-5015.1002

8. Reiser, R.A.: A history of instructional design and technology: part II: a history of instructional design. Educ. Technol. Res. Dev. **49**(2), 57–67 (2001). https://doi.org/10.1007/BF02504928

9. Pedaste, M., et al.: Phases of inquiry-based learning: definitions and the inquiry cycle. Educ. Res. Rev. **14**, 47–61 (2015). https://doi.org/10.1016/J.EDUREV.2015.02.003

10. Merrill, M.D.: First principles of instruction. Educ. Technol. Res. Dev. **50**(3), 43–59 (2002). https://doi.org/10.1007/BF02505024

11. Göksu, I., Özcan, K.V., Cakir, R., Göktas, Y.: Content analysis of research trends in instructional design models: 1999–2014. J. Learn. Des. **10**(2), 85–109 (2017)

12. Branch, R.M.: Instructional Design: The ADDIE Approach, vol. 53, no. 9, pp. 1–198. Department of Educational Psychology and Instructional Technology University of Georgia (2009)

13. Liao, H.-C., Wang, Y.: Applying the ARCS motivation model in technological and vocational education. Contemp. Issues Educ. Res. **1**(2), 53 (2011). https://doi.org/10.19030/CIER.V1I2.1202

14. Frerejean, J., van Geel, M., Keuning, T., Dolmans, D., van Merriënboer, J.J.G., Visscher, A.J.: Ten steps to 4C/ID: training differentiation skills in a professional development program for teachers. Instr. Sci. **49**(3), 395–418 (2021). https://doi.org/10.1007/S11251-021-09540-X/TABLES/4

15. Obizoba, C.: Instructional design models-framework for innovative teaching and learning methodologies. Int. J. High. Educ. Manag. **2** (2015). www.ijhem.abrmr.com. Accessed 19 Feb 2023

16. Divjak, B., Grabar, D., Svetec, B., Vondra, P.: Balanced learning design planning: concept and tool. J. Inf. Organ. Sci. **46**(2), 361–375 (2022). https://doi.org/10.31341/jios.46.2.6

17. Boelens, R., De Wever, B., Voet, M.: Four key challenges to the design of blended learning: a systematic literature review. Educ. Res. Rev. **22**, 1–18 (2017)

Lesson-Planning Groupware for Teachers: Situated Participatory Design

Leandro Queiros[1] , Alex Sandro Gomes[1] , Rosane Alencar[1] , Aluísio Pereira[1] ,
and Fernando Moreira[2]([⊠])

[1] Federal University of Pernambuco, Recife, Brazil
{flmq,asg,rmas3,ajp3}@cin.ufpe.br
[2] REMIT, IJP, Universidade Portucalense, Porto & IEETA, Universidade de Aveiro, Aveiro, Portugal
fmoreira@upt.pt

Abstract. Collaboration allows teachers to interact with regularity, specificity, and depth in order to create new dynamics and understandings on teaching. Teachers orchestrate the central elements surrounding the goals that need to be achieved in the classroom performance, the objectives, and the purpose of the lesson plan. Thus, the aim of this study is to investigate the perceptions of teachers regarding the prototype of a collaborative system to support the sharing of knowledge and educational materials and interpersonal learning experiences. The current study uses design prototyping procedures and techniques to augment the manner in which these professionals approach lesson planning. Dialectically, this in-depth understanding, using multiple methods of participatory design, has guided us to evolve the design of a computational device to support professional lesson planning and to speculate future digital possibilities for this practice. Situated participatory design has made it possible for teachers to visualize themselves in possible future scenarios, using groupware as a tool that is able to support their collaborative classroom preparation practices.

Keywords: Teacher collaboration · learning experience · situated actions · collaborative lesson planning

1 Introduction

Groupware tools are recommended to support group work, such as learning design tools [1] and online collaborative lesson planning (CLP) [2]. Collaborative software enables team members to perform a common task through computer networks, even if they are in geographically distinct locations [3]. Thus, CLP has become a relevant inquiry topic in Technology Enhanced Learning [4–7]. Teachers prefer to work collectively with other educators rather than performing individual activities [8]. However, teachers face several barriers in adopting these tools in lesson planning practices, including the usability of the tools and a low perception of space in order to share ideas, needs, or solutions to problems [9, 10]. Situated approaches may explore some of these needs in the early stages of the groupware tool development process [2].

P. Zaphiris and A. Ioannou (Eds.): HCII 2023, LNCS 14040, pp. 500–516, 2023.
https://doi.org/10.1007/978-3-031-34411-4_34

Thus, the present study has used design prototyping procedures and techniques to augment our knowledge on how these professionals approach lesson planning Dialectically this in-depth understanding, using multiple methods of participatory design, has guided us to evolve the design of a computational device to support professional lesson planning and to speculate on future digital possibilities for this practice. The participatory design approach uses prototyping to construct knowledge and to make sense of practices for users through participatory design practices. Thus, this article presents the creation of a participatory design for groupware that mediates the practice of collaborative lesson planning, guided by the following research questions: 1) "What are the expressed needs of teachers when they co-create groupware sketches for lesson planning?"; 2) "Do the teachers perceive that their needs have been met by the co-created groupware prototypes?".

The article consists of three other sections. Section 2 presents work related to Learning Design practices and tools. Section 3 describes the method, with the approach, collection, and data analysis procedures. Section 4 presents the results and discussions. Lastly, Sect. 5 includes the final considerations, limitations, and implications for groupware design.

2 Collaborative Lesson Planning Groupware Design

This section presents a literature review on collaborative teaching practices, participatory design of groupware, and related work on groupware as a mediator of collaborative lesson planning.

2.1 Lesson Planning Practices

Lesson planning is probably the most important activity undertaken by teachers in the proactive teaching phase [11]. Thus, the collaboration of an educator is essential for teaching, since it provides teachers with mutual dependence, collective responsibilities, reciprocal openness, and emotional security [12, 13].

Teachers must plan, create or reuse various educational resources, which have different levels and complexities regarding their manipulation. Mastering these resources is of paramount importance in order to orchestrate them when executing the pedagogical activity. Depending on the granularity of the learning object, the teacher must arrange more than a dozen artifacts. The outline of a lesson does not need to be an exhaustive, complex document. Milkova [14] reports that an effective lesson plan should provide "a general outline of your teaching objectives, learning objectives and the means to achieve them." The main objective is for students and teachers to learn from each other (Ibid.).

Teachers orchestrate the central elements surrounding the goals that need to be achieved by the classroom performance, the objectives, and the purpose of the lesson plan. With each choice made, fundamental aspects of planning emerge, and attached to each, is a series of nodes that subdivide the key aspects [15, 16].

The core elements and "nodes" of lesson planning may be adapted or developed according to the context in which it will be applied. Not all naturalistic decision-making is the same, and no unitary process can fit into all situations. The granularity of devising the plan may vary according to the theoretical/practical choices and learning scenarios applied by each teacher. Thus, this article adopts the concept of the learning experience as an umbrella term for a lesson plan and the curation of organizing resources for a lesson.

Although the origin of the primary model adopted for lesson plans is in the last century, it is still currently adopted by teachers of basic education. However, "it is still not clear whether and how knowledge co-construction projects are related to the use of a lesson plan and the main learning regulation activities" [17]. The most common lesson plan model adopted by teachers and curriculum consultants was proposed by Tyler in 1949 [18] and has maintained the same structure until the present moment.

Despite the formalization of the lesson plan as being a form to be filled out, teachers have adopted it over the years in their school routines, either due to school demands or a lack of knowledge of other practices.

2.2 Lesson Planning Practices

The main features of the tools to support lesson planning activities include guidance, representation, and sharing. Guidance features are functionalities that enable teachers to understand, adjust, reuse, and adopt new effective teaching methods [15]. These are designed to help teachers reflect on their teaching and learning decisions [19]. Representational aspects are how teachers may represent teaching and learning activities a priori. Learning design (LD) develops a widely accepted framework for designing teaching and learning activities. Some functions cover the sharing functionalities, thereby enabling the propagation of pedagogical plans among peers [20].

Implementation corresponds to tools and resources needed during the act of teaching. Tools are software (discussion forums, wikis, quiz systems) and physical tools (whiteboard, flipchart, pens, articles). It should be noted that LD software needs to be configured by a teacher, learning designer, or others who are accountable for managing, configuring, and applying it [20].

Lastly, student responses are able to capture various types of information regarding student learning, such as outcomes, competencies, skills, and understanding. Feedback corresponds to student reactions in real-time to teaching, which may be identified by the teacher and used as information to improve teaching [20, 21].

The appraisal of teaching, such as course surveys, can also play a vital role in future improvements in the teaching practice. In assessment, the literature on formative and summative assessment relates to the textbook, since it presents several ways to assess learning. Learning analytics enables a more profitable use of data for educational research, in which LD software systems provide an opportunity for tracking student activity more deeply, since the progress of each student is recorded as a by-product of using technology to manage the sequence of such activities [20, 22, 23].

2.3 Related Work: Collaborative Lesson Planning Groupware Design

Several studies have contributed to the development of this research. The article "ILDE: community environment for conceptualizing, authoring and deploying learning activities" [24] aimed to develop and integrate several collaborative systems to promote the adoption of LD, providing support to mentors throughout the design and implementation processes. The work asserted that teachers cooperate in the co-creation and sharing of digital educational resources. The article does not use data related to understanding the context nor related to lesson planning activities. The work proposes the use of at least five tools to mediate lesson planning. Furthermore, the article does not explore how the transfer of resources and knowledge among teachers will take place.

The work by [25], "Reconstrução de um Repositório de Objetos de Aprendizagem para Matemática," [The Reconstruction of a Repository of Learning Objects for Mathematics] redesigns the web repository of Learning Objects for Mathematics (OBAMA), developed as a platform that offers access to basic education teachers. The system has space for the production, assessment, and sharing of lesson plans, which use learning objects found in the repository itself. In other words, teachers cannot create their own learning objects and use them in their lesson plans. The method is an evolution of a repository of learning purposes. Obama evolved into a mediating tool for activities and class planning. However, the work presents no evidence on how developing a new visual identity and improving aspects are related to its usability, nor how the design and reprogramming of the interface were conceived.

The article [9], "Une analyse de l'activité de planification des enseignants: vers la conception d'instruments," [An analysis of the teacher's planning activity: towards the design of instruments], presents, as a result of analyzing the instrumental system of the planning activity, the real need to support teachers in the creation of educational resources, given that there is a gap in the teacher training process. The study reports that the planning tools do not meet the real needs of teachers and that they are difficult to use. Ten years after using them, teachers still require assistance with the proper use of the tools that help with lesson planning. The study itself ultimately asked why no system meets the needs of teachers in short-, medium- and long-term planning.

Some studies have been developed that center on the design of information systems aimed at planning educational learning units. There is a lack of studies that investigate the conception, development, testing, and assessment of this type of system and, within this context, create challenges for the development of this work. At the same time, this also raises the opportunity and justification for the development of this research.

In this regard, we have adopted a situated approach [26] to prototyping in order to broaden our understanding of what is vital in the practice of collaborative lesson planning. This will guide the development of a future system, especially considering that knowledge in the literature is limited.

3   Collaborative Lesson Planning Groupware Design

This article assumes a projective, situated research paradigm while co-conceiving collaborative lesson-planning solutions with teachers. We adopted a situated prototyping practice in the present tense, which helps to build knowledge and to guide the continuous design of future versions. It inspires reflections and knowledge building with regard to the meaning and usage of the current version and speculations for the various future transformations on incremental prototypes [27]. The continually evolving material hypothesis regards the emerging version of the prototype for a collaborative system created to support lesson planning for basic education teachers. The material hypothesis manipulation in participatory design practices continually constructs new knowledge and a new version and converges into a meaningful design solution proposal [28].

3.1 Participants

For the study, the following inclusion criteria were: (a) teachers with three or more years of teaching experience in a high school; (b) in-service teachers in public high schools; and (c) teachers who were voluntarily willing to participate in the research.

The following exclusion criteria were established: (a) participants who remained unwilling or refused to sign the consent form; (b) respondents who either deliberately provided false answers or who responded to less than half of the survey items. We also asked fellow researchers if they knew any of the teachers who met the inclusion and exclusion requirements in the sampling process.

The teachers had different backgrounds, time of teaching experience, and ages. Participants 1 through 8 co-created in the participatory workshop, and 9 through 12 participated in the low-fidelity prototype situated manipulation. All names below have been changed so that participants may remain unrecognized and unidentified.

3.2 Situated Participatory Design

The participatory design process began by holding a stakeholder's workshop [29] with basic education teachers. During the sessions, we collected narrative interviews, created a menu of ideas, prototyped artifact versions, and reflected on the proposals presented.

Creative Workshop. First, we held three creative workshop sessions, two with 2 teachers and the third with 4 teachers in the same gathering, totaling 8 teachers. The theme was the registration unit for content analysis, which includes the coding and creation of categories [30]. Based on themes, we categorized data and created a low-fidelity prototype of groupware to mediate lesson planning activities. Narrative interviews realized during the sessions enabled us to obtain evidence that corroborated findings in the literature and the reported situations experienced by the participants.

Preparation: Initially, the objective of the virtual event was presented to the participants. During each co-creative session, teachers were asked to answer the following questions individually from the episodic interview: (i) Going back in time, when did you ever prepare your class at home or at school? (ii) Could you give me an account of this experience? (iii) How do you link artifacts/people/emotions with regard to lesson planning? (iv) In the near future, what do you hope to improve regarding your lesson planning? (v) How do you usually share your experience and digital educational resources with other teachers?

The group activities strived to stimulate creativity and collaboration, fostering the creation of innovative solutions.

Ideation: In the ideation session, the participants received a link to Google Presentations, where they saw the technique guidelines in the Menu of Ideas. After prototyping, each participant took a photo of their design and uploaded it onto the slide. Participants were invited to comment on their designs and freely discuss designs created by other teachers. Producing a Menu of Ideas enabled us to generate ideas for the project under study.

After this, the participants were guided to participate in the composition of the solution, creating and sharing alternatives for the design presented through prototyping by producing sketches.

Prototyping: The researchers evolved the design solution with the data collected from the focus groups through data triangulation (participatory workshop + previous research + researcher contributions) to match the perception of the participants through the generated ideas. Prototyping enables us to obtain the representation of a story visually through static frames produced through drawings.

In the second section, teachers performed a free exploration using the low-fidelity prototype and thinking aloud. After this, they performed three situated acts: (i) they created a traditional learning experience, invited a teacher to collaborate, and added an attached file, (ii) they created a dynamic learning experience by inviting a teacher to collaborate, (iii) they researched a French Revolution learning experience and began the encounter.

Lastly, a narrative interview was conducted using the following questions (a) With regard to unstructured and non-sequential dynamic planning, could you comment on its use in future scenarios? What is the purpose of this interaction, of exchanging experiences and digital educational resources with other teachers? (b) How do you think the program could help record experiences and resources over time? (c) How do you think the platform can help you in your daily life? (d) Do you think the platform can encourage creativity and innovation in your teaching work? (e) There are several unforeseen events at school. Do you believe that the platform could help you to mediate or anticipate this type of event? (f) How did you feel when testing the prototype? (g) What did you like or dislike? Why? (h) Is there anything I have not asked about the subject that you would like to add?

All audio and video data were transcribed using the oTranscribe [https://otranscribe. com/] transcription tool and analyzed using the ATLAS.ti [https://atlasti.com/] tool. The project results were developed in a navigable prototype format, available in the Figma [https://figma.com/] tool.

They made their inquiries via WhatsApp® messages. They asked their colleagues whether they would like to collaborate in the research, with answers to a semi-structured interview, an agreed day, and at a time that best suited the interviewee. These interviews were conducted online, via Google Meet, for between 1 and 2 h. The collection period took place between April 5 and August 26, 2021. The sessions were recorded so that the researchers could carry out data analysis retrospectively. A researcher was the mediator of the groups.

3.3 Data Analysis

Lave [19] defines the unit of analysis for situated action as "the activity of persons acting in a setting", and the length of analysis is the relationship between the person and the setting. A setting is delimited as "a relation between acting persons and the arenas in relation with which they act." Considering that we intend to project a future solution with and for teachers, we need to pay attention to the flux of ongoing action to unfold actual activity in a natural setting (Ibid.).

Audio and video data collected during the co-design sessions were analyzed using [26] to examine the manner in which the participant interactions and the software were composed. Lastly, teachers were invited to arrange another time to manipulate the results consolidated in a low-fidelity prototype version.

The categories were created by the researchers who authored this study and reflect the desire of the participants for facilities. These emerged from the analysis and reflections carried out from the collected data [31]. Therefore, the following methodological criteria were acknowledged during data analysis [30]. The categories of facilities and their respective number of features were: collaborative space (9), digital notebook (9), digital calendar (7), digital library (7), educational news blog (3), teacher community (8), questions database, learning experience and notes (3). This data was synthesized in order to consolidate it and verify any overlap of data and its relationship with the object of study.

Data categorization made it possible to associate functionalities with the soft goals of a collaborative system that mediates classroom planning activities [32]. The soft goals were: (SG1) Unstructured and non-sequential collaborations, (SG2) Experience and Time, (SG3) Incentive for Creativity and Innovation, (SG4) Support for Unpredictability.

- (SG1) Collaborative systems must allow for unstructured and non-hierarchical collaboration, supporting unpredictability, experiences, and time management, encouraging creativity and innovation. Moreover, together with other people, cooperation may promote collaborative creativity, brought about by multiple experiences and inclinations towards different themes;
- (SG2) Collaborative systems should allow the capture of lived experience over time so that educators may record and collect resources, memories, ideas, and reports of practices. In addition, it should allow for the insertion of what should be done soon, including collaborative outlooks;
- (SG3) Collaborative systems must present content and data that inspire teachers and, consequently, enable them to generate positive results and recognize their professional growth and, consequently, the growth of their students. Personalization may be permitted, as it is a motivating element of pedagogical practice. However, innovation must be promoted to impact the physical and digital structure, the relationships with teaching-learning, and interpersonal communication.
- (SG4) Should collaborative systems support the teacher and anticipate teaching situations, or how may one type of system support planning with contingencies that cannot be foreseen? We can imagine the requirements for dealing with unknown events in this soft-goals category, relating feelings and emotions to digital technologies and the school environment. Lastly, problems must be moderated through a resolution that does not depend upon the school.

The concluding part of this data analysis was to conduct a free, open survey of tools that offered inspiring technologies for the low-fidelity prototyping of the collaborative system. Prototyping was based on the Lesson Plan Information System [33]. We also performed a benchmark analysis using the free exploration of educational tools that have correlated functionalities to the purpose of this study, such as Reddit, Facebook,

Notion, Teacher Portal, Stack Overflow, Miro, Teacherly, Google Drive, Chalk, Proedu, and Teacher Pay Teacher. The tools were explored through the prior knowledge of the researchers.

4 Results and Discussion

In the following sections, we present the main results from the participatory design and analysis of situated co-creation and collaborative lesson planning and situated knowledge sharing and the reuse of digital educational resources.

4.1 Ideating and Sketching with Teachers and the Evolution of the Model

During the co-creation section, teachers were invited to handle, criticize and advance ideas related to possible future solutions. The debates were stimulated with a low-fidelity prototype, in which they were able to experiment to identify its characteristics and offer fresh insights. The ideas proposed by the teachers were large and generic. For example, one solution that some of them suggested was a kind of social network of teachers where they could share experiences and digital educational resources. This kind of contribution indicates a kind of platform. Notwithstanding, in terms of functionalities and the mapping between essential needs and functionalities, they did not clarify what was to be designed. The same occurred when teachers suggested something in order to reduce the bureaucracy of the teacher's work and to participate in maintaining educational events for teachers.

At this moment of the ideation section, all participants commented and reflected on what they had written. Ideas such as these are interesting for engaging participants in the proposal to compose, but are not informative or productive regarding value and functionality.

Sketching with and for teachers proved to be significant. Producing illustrations allows what has been written in the previous step to be complimented. In addition, it allows teachers to externalize what was not yet possible to be easily expressed through words. Thus, teachers elaborated groupware proposals that would allow them to carry out activities related to the preparation of collaborative classes.

Participant Jessica described the meanings present in the drawing she had created. She stated that "Overall, this would be an environment into which it would be possible for a teacher to put this content and its resources. So that there is no need to search other sites and other places." The teacher discussed the importance of the system in a future work scenario with both the participants and the researcher. The teachers agreed that the device allows for searching, finding, and using content created by the teacher. Moreover, the tool enables access to content from other repositories in the same environment.

Teachers use ordinary terms to represent the intentions of the system. Each of the seven planets corresponded to a set of features. For example, Planet 4, corresponded to a space for writing and exchanging experimental practices. Planet 2 represents an environment where it is possible to have a database of questions, which would help them to practice exam preparation and diagnostic and x-ray activities. In Fig. 1, the illustrated teacher designed a collaborative universe of lesson planning.

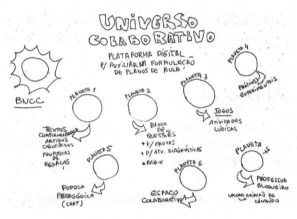

Fig. 1. Sketch of a collaborative system.

The spaces represent the situated environments of a common teacher. The daily necessities are evidenced in the teacher's sketches, such as Planet 6, which is a collaborative space for teachers, where it is possible to share knowledge, and digital educational resources and promote individual and group professional growth. Teachers argued that they have a real necessity for professional development.

4.2   The Iterative Prototype Evolution

This section presents how teachers and researchers created many ongoing circles of interactions to evolve the conceptual model. We built low-fidelity prototypes of the Collaborative Space, Digital Notebook, Digital Agenda, Digital Library, Educational News Blog, Teacher Community, Question Bank, Learning Experience, and Reports categories based on the participatory design by teachers. We discussed how future digital possibilities could emerge from such a design practice. In addition, we correlated the functionalities with the soft goals of a collaborative system that mediates classroom planning activities [32]: (SG1) Unstructured and non-sequential collaborations (SG2) Experience and Time, (SG3) Incentive to Creativity and Innovation, (SG4) Support for unpredictability. The following are short descriptions of the prototype features. Below is the summary of data triangulation, describing the relationship between the categories created with features, evidence, and soft goals.

The user journey starts on the Home page, where the initial concept and functionalities of the collaborative system are exhibited. It is possible to contact previews with learning experiences and read how the user may optimize time using the solution. This is the page for registering a new user or entering the platform.

We proposed facilities so that each teacher has to have both a private and public profile for the community. In the private profile, the teacher may have resources that other teachers cannot see. In the public profile, all other teacher users can see the resources that have this open-access setting.

Each teacher has a personal page where his/her public resources are displayed. In addition, all teachers may enter professional information or any other information they consider to be pertinent. If it is of interest, this information and resources may be considered as a professional portfolio.

Teacher participation created appropriate dynamics for the discussion and construction of knowledge and the development of the conceptual model of the solution. Initially, we proposed a design based on the needs discovered in a deep participatory phase. We intend to evolve the conceptual model from the participatory study. We used an initial conceptual model as an artifact to create and design with participants.

4.3 The Iterative Prototype Evolution

Creating a lesson plan is one of the numerous activities that is necessary for class preparation. As discussed in the recent literature, for various reasons, this activity often occurs solely for bureaucratic purposes.

In the second section, teachers performed a free exploration using the low-fidelity prototype and thinking aloud. As plausible future teacher scenarios, they: (i) Created a traditional learning experience, invited a teacher to collaborate, and added an attached file, (ii) Created a dynamic learning experience by inviting a teacher to collaborate. There are different features to support these two pursuits, as will be described below.

Thus, a virtual environment was prototyped that attempted to reproduce an adequate space for creating a learning experience, which is possible to develop according to the interests and teaching approaches desired by the teachers.

Creating a 'traditional learning experience' is able to support teachers in creating lesson plans in a more familiar, conventional format, where users may invite other teachers to co-build, in addition to digital media such as images, videos, and links from outside environments (see Fig. 2).

Fig. 2. Feature created traditional learning experience.

Teacher Felipe manipulated the prototype, simulating a possible future scenario. He said, "Title of the experiment, introduction to the database. Conceptual database, relational database, this one is cool. Level of education, technical high school, integrated high school, or subsequent. Database, introduction to the database, the competence of BNCC, there... Now. Skill, knowledge in database, co-creating with one more person. Yes, I could share it with another teacher who has this discipline and this class. That would be great, that would be great, to do that with another teacher. This would be excellent. I would put Henrique here, and it will be there in the future."

Such perception was optimistic with regard to using the system in a collaborative environment with a teacher who teaches the same subject [8]. The two can co-create a lesson plan, reuse educational resources, and thereby eliminate lonely and isolated practices. Hence, it becomes a moment of digital presence [34].

Creating a 'dynamic learning experience' corresponds to an environment in which teachers are free to develop their lesson preparation with the necessary granularity and accessible representation according to their educational objective. This facility is represented as a whiteboard with almost infinite borders. The functions permit and support innumerable future scenarios to co-create learning practices, projects, and activity performance. Teacher Gilberto envisions a future scenario for using the dynamic learning experience "For example, we work with planning, workshops, working with dynamics, working with educational excursions. You need to do multidisciplinary work, such as geography, history, sociology, and visiting, for example, the Catimbau Valley. So, you will study the geographic, historical, sociological, and anthropological questions of that community there so many years ago, you see! So, it is certainly essential to have a platform that addresses this need."

The authors themselves believe that such space may be used for countless educational scenarios. It is possible to create lesson plans in an accessible format to meet the necessities of teachers. It is possible to make video calls between teachers registered in the groupware, insert images, create a mind map, and post notes, among other digital resources that support class preparation activities. The anticipated space is almost the contrary to traditional creation, which, as we have seen, is created for formal specifications of the educational system, having minimal use and meaning for the actual practice of class preparation.

The 'My school' facility is an appropriate space and permits organizing, collaborative (or not) creation, and classifying documents into notebooks by educational institutions. It also has an organizing calendar that classifies the monthly events, where users may add more events and manage them. In this area, users may share learning experiences, notes, and other documents through QR-code, a feature designed to reduce the impact of unpredictability and bring dynamism to the teacher's experience. Teacher Ana mentioned the importance of digital notes in the present and future: "Regarding the use of notebooks for teachers, we already have to do as many things as possible digitally... so for those who are usually taking notes, notaries, etc., it may be helpful when you are going to make a lesson script for example."

Teachers may organize their files as they wish. However, we understand that the system can support the teacher with organizational suggestions, whether through schools, archives, or any other element of basic education.

The 'Digital Educational Resources Library' is a kind of storage place for digital educational resources. Resources are created by the community of teachers, in addition to those that are indexed from platforms that provide open educational resources. It is possible to reuse and share the results via user experience and with other teachers. The search allows results to be filtered by grade level, file type, and peer review rating.

The 'Question Database' is the storage environment for evaluation sources, such as questions, quizzes, tests, simulations, and essay topics. It is possible to filter the available questions by discipline, content, and topic. There is also an option of adding this evaluative content to new learning experiences created on the platform, making the preparation of tests more candid.

4.4 Knowledge Sharing and Reusing Digital Educational Resource Facilities

One constant challenge lies in seeking and selecting digital educational resources that may be applied to their school contexts. This arrangement may be supported by an environment where teachers are able to receive peer assistance.

This second theme is related to question (iii) Research a French Revolution learning experience and opens the experience. There are several ways to research an educational resource, such as reuse, conducting a search in the teacher community, or knowledge sharing in dialogue with another teacher by text, video, or audio message. Research in the library of digital educational resources makes it possible to find sources stored in different repositories of open learning objects and academic texts.

The 'Teacher Community' is the environment for teachers enrolled in the collaborative system, where their learning experiences and resources may be shared. This space is intended to provide an opportunity for kinship between peers. Such connections may be initiated via the teacher profile, learning experience, and peer review verification on their learning experiences [35]. When taking the prototype test, teacher Felipe mentioned the teacher community, stating that "Yes, if they are part of my community, I can, I can start a subject, I can put in a subject, it's a form of communication, communication will always be positive. And here the tool gives conditions, here look, here, message, search for people, so these people may not necessarily be doing this planning, but they may be consulted." The teacher realized the value of being able to collaborate in a community with different goals. This is a space where it is possible to exchange experiences, reflect on other people's practices and imagine future scenarios.

From the navigation, it is possible to start collaboration, message exchange, reuse, and favor a specific teacher so that users may follow new interactions selected for the topic of interest to both. This search allows results to be filtered by grade level, file type, and peer review rating (see Fig. 3). The teacher said, "Yes, it has a positive impact. It impacts positively. I can look for it there. I can use something that I have already created before. It's good, it's good, it's always good. It's something we always do. Searching on these platforms, you can reuse something and edit a few tweaks, which is something not to do from scratch. He saves it, but it seems for the most part he doesn't want the guy to reuse it. It seems that people like to slaughter, see you do it from scratch. This is good. Sharing and reuse are good. I liked it." Teacher Felipe highlighted the significance of reusing digital educational resources. Having a search system and reusing material from another teacher will undoubtedly impact his class preparation work.

Fig. 3. A teacher's profile page, with experiences rated by other teachers.

When carrying out the prototyping, the collaborative space was remodeled and designed to enable users to clarify doubts and answer questions that users share on the platform. Teacher Gilberto gave his perception of this environment for exchanging information and experience, "It's cool, man. You can talk to people, and see answers. You can talk a lot. You can get a lot of information here. Staff suggestions. Excellent!" Users themselves may choose which answer is most suitable for a question, and receive more comprehensive answers using the related questions.

To present the essential contents, the answers to the questions may be classified to illustrate a contribution or no contribution. Only those that were positive would indicate the number of interactions that had been performed.

Direct messages and Informs are spaces designed for exchanging experiences and resources synchronously and asynchronously. Exchanges may be made via text, audio, or video, privately. When performing a communication, a notification of interaction in the system is generated, creating an alert for the user related to the issue. The collaborative system may dynamically generate new messages and notifications.

The 'Educational' Blog features news created and shared by the platform teachers [36]. It is also possible to share such news in private messages. Asked about his perception of an 'Educational Blog', Teacher Gilberto stated that "I think it's cool. I understand that it's a blog that will have information for my daily school life. To help prepare classes. To gain information about news around education." The blog writers curate the collaborative system and help bring relevant information from the universe of education.

In the final section, we argue the research questions: how do basic education teachers perceive sketching low-fidelity prototype co-created groupware. We also discuss how interactions through the low-fidelity prototype reveal new insights on the collaboration among them and guide the design of the groupware tool intended to mediate class preparation and knowledge and the interchange of digital educational resources.

5   Conclusions

The main objective of this study was to investigate the situated participatory design of low-fidelity prototype co-created groupware and reveal new insights on the collaboration among them and guide the design of the groupware tool. In this article, we have presented a study whereby a prototype was co-designed to concretize how groupware may be part of collaborative class development activities.

A participatory design study with a qualitative approach was conducted. Data were generated from a creative workshop, from which it was possible to propose nine categories of data analysis. These data were triangulated (participatory workshop, literature, and researchers' contributions). A prototype situated manipulation was conducted on a collaborative system co-created with basic education teachers, unlike those who had engaged in the participatory workshop. Hence, this situated manipulation presented results that corroborate the data generated in the participatory phase, the suggested data categories, and soft-goal validity for collaborative systems measuring classroom planning practices.

The idea has provided teachers with a basis for prototyping the possible solutions, such as digital solutions [37], better school infrastructure, continuing education, internet access, etc. At the same time, the interactive prototype has provided them with possibilities to visualize themselves in the future using groupware as an artifact that is able to support their classroom preparation practices.

The foundation for the prototype was knowledge and experience regarding the collaborative lesson plan. The prototype aimed to clarify how teachers could create, reuse and share knowledge and information with teachers in an isolated context, limited by a lack of training and inadequate infrastructure, with co-designed groupware.

The prototype simulated a possible future device so that teachers could collaborate and use it as a mediating artifact for preparing their lesson plans in their future work. The paper has demonstrated that the features co-created and simulated in prototypes may be used in collaborative lesson plan practices.

We have demonstrated that the situated prototype manipulation and the participatory design approach are new to teachers. We consider that the seaworthy prototype navigation was limited in terms of situated experiences. The artifacts need to be more interactive in order to give a more realistic experience of preparation for a collaborative educational experience, or software developed with the basic features essential to the study.

The study also examined the situated actions of teachers regarding the collaborative system that supports the sharing of knowledge and educational materials. The research outcomes have addressed how the qualitative approach to participatory design may promote solutions for future collaborative systems to work on collaborative classroom planning.

The study introduces new opportunities to confirm, assess and gain new insights into using the features in groupware, which may contribute greatly to understanding how solutions co-designed with the teachers may be assertive and illustrate their fundamental necessities. In this sense, we ask ourselves how the teacher perceives interchangeable knowledge and planning practices mediated by adopting groupware.

514   L. Queiros et al.

Acknowledgements. This work was supported by the FCT – Fundação para a Ciência e a Tecnologia, I.P. [Project UIDB/05105/2020].

References

1. Koper, R.: An Introduction to Learning Design. In: Koper, R., Tattersall, C. (eds.) Learning Design: A Handbook on Modelling and Delivering Networked Education and Training, pp. 3–20. Springer, Berlin-Heidelberg (2005)
2. da Silva, J.B., Bilessimo, S.M.S., da Silva, I.N.: Collaborative virtual community to share class plans for STEAM education. In: 2020 IEEE Global Engineering Education Conference (EDUCON), pp. 158–163. IEEE (2020, April). https://doi.org/10.1109/ICALT.2013.87
3. Candotti, C.T., Hoppen, N.: Reunião virtual e o uso de groupware-uma nova possibilidade de realizar trabalho em grupo. Anais do Encontro Nacional da Associação Nacional de Pós-Graduação e Pesquisa em Administração (1999)
4. Nguyen, G.N., Bower, M.: Novice teacher technology-enhanced learning design practices: the case of the silent pedagogy. Br. J. Edu. Technol. **49**(6), 1027–1043 (2018)
5. Fonseca, D., García-Peñalvo, F.J., Camba, J.D.: New methods and technologies for enhancing usability and accessibility of educational data. Univ. Access Inf. Soc. **20**(3), 421–427 (2021)
6. Moreira, F., Ferreira, M.J., Pereira, C.S., Gomes, A.S., Collazos, C., Escudero, D.F.: ECLECTIC as a learning ecosystem for higher education disruption. Univ. Access Inf. Soc. **18**(3), 615–631 (2019). https://doi.org/10.1007/s10209-019-00682-x
7. Moreira, F., Ferreira, M.J., Pereira, C.S., Escudero, D.F., Collazos, C., Gomes, A.: Higher education teachers training (HET2) Model: active learning in higher education environment. In: Rocha, Á., Adeli, H., Dzemyda, G., Moreira, F., Ramalho Correia, A.M. (eds.) WorldCIST 2021. AISC, vol. 1367, pp. 103–112. Springer, Cham (2021). https://doi.org/10.1007/978-3-030-72660-7_11
8. Patton, K., Parker, M.: Teacher education communities of practice: more than a culture of collaboration. Teach. Teach. Educ. **67**, 351–360 (2017). https://doi.org/10.1016/j.tate.2017.06.013
9. Body, G., Munoz, G., Bourmaud, G." Une analyse de l'activité de planification des enseignants: vers la conception d'instruments. In 3ème colloque international de Didactique professionnelle «Conception et Formation» (2014, October)
10. Vázquez-Ingelmo, A., García-Peñalvo, F.J., Therón, R., Amo Filva, D., Fonseca, D.: Connecting domain-specific features to source code: towards the automatization of dashboard generation. Clust. Comput. **23**(3), 1803–1816 (2019)
11. Clark, C.M., Yinger, R.J.: Research on teacher thinking. Curric. Inq. **7**(4), 279–304 (1977)
12. Nias, J.: Why teachers need their colleagues: a developmental perspective. In: Hopkins, D. (ed.) The Practice and Theory of School Improvement, Springer, pp. 1257–1271. Dordrecht (1998). https://doi.org/10.1007/1-4020-4452-6_12
13. Lau, S.M.C., Stille, S.: Participatory research with teachers: toward a pragmatic and dynamic view of equity and parity in research relationships. Eur. J. Teach. Educ. **37**(2), 156–170 (2014). https://doi.org/10.1080/02619768.2014.882313
14. Milkova, S.: Strategies for effective lesson planning. Cent. Res. Learn. Teach. **1**(1), 1–29 (2012)
15. Vu, T.M.H., Tchounikine, P.: Supporting teacher scripting with an ontological model of task-technique content knowledge. Comput. Educ. **163**, 104098 (2021)
16. John, P.D.: Lesson planning and the student teacher: re-thinking the dominant model. J. Curric. Stud. **38**(4), 483–498 (2006). https://doi.org/10.1080/00220270500363620

17. Vuopala, E., Näykki, P., Isohätälä, J., Järvelä, S.: Knowledge co-construction activities and task-related monitoring in scripted collaborative learning. Learn. Cult. Soc. Interact. 21, 234–249 (2019). https://doi.org/10.1016/j.lcsi.2019.03.011
18. Tyler, R.W.: Basic Principles of Curriculum and Instruction. University of Chicago Press, Chicago (1949)
19. Zalavra, E., Papanikolaou, K., Dimitriadis, Y., Sgouropoulou, C.: Exploring teachers' needs for guidance while designing for technology-enhanced learning with digital tools. In: De Laet, T., Klemke, R., Alario-Hoyos, C., Hilliger, I., Ortega-Arranz, A. (eds.) EC-TEL 2021. LNCS, vol. 12884, pp. 358–362. Springer, Cham (2021). https://doi.org/10.1007/978-3-030-86436-1_35
20. Dalziel, J., et al.: The Larnaca declaration on learning design—2013. In: Learning Design, pp. 13–53. Routledge (2015)
21. Sanchez-Sepulveda, M.V., et al.: Evaluation of an interactive educational system in urban knowledge acquisition and representation based on students' profiles. Expert. Syst. 37(5), e12570 (2020)
22. Filvà, D.A., García-Peñalvo, F.J., Forment, M.A., Fonseca. D., Casañ, M.J.: Privacy and identity management in learning analytics processes with blockchain. In: Proceedings of the Sixth International Conference on Technological Ecosystems for Enhancing Multiculturality (acm.org), pp. 997–1003 (2015). https://doi.org/10.1145/3284179.3284354
23. Forment, M.A., Filvà, D.A., García-Peñalvo, F.J., Fonseca. D., Casañ, M.J.: Learning Analytics' privacy on the blockchain. In: Proceedings of the Sixth International Conference on Technological Ecosystems for Enhancing Multiculturality (acm.org), pp. 294–298 (2018). https://doi.org/10.1145/3284179.3284231
24. Hernández-Leo, D., Asensio-Pérez, J.I., Derntl, M., Prieto, L.P., Chacón, J.: ILDE: community environment for conceptualizing, authoring and deploying learning activities. In: Rensing, C., de Freitas, S., Ley, T., Muñoz-Merino, P.J. (eds.) EC-TEL 2014. LNCS, vol. 8719, pp. 490–493. Springer, Cham (2014). https://doi.org/10.1007/978-3-319-11200-8_48
25. Batista, S.D., Brito, D., Melo, E., Oliveira, A., Oliveira, N., Maia, D.: Reconstrução de um repositório de objetos de aprendizagem para Matemática. In: Congresso sobre Tecnologias na Educação (Ctrl + E) (2017)
26. Lave, J.: Cognition in Practice: Mind, Mathematics and Culture in Everyday Life. Cambridge University Press (1988)
27. Hevner, A., Chatterjee, S.: Design science research in information systems. In: Design Research in Information Systems. Integrated Series in Information Systems, vol. 22, pp. 9–22. Springer, Boston (2010). https://doi.org/10.1007/978-1-4419-5653-8_2
28. Koskinen, I., Zimmerman, J., Binder, T., Redstrom, J., Wensveen, S.: Design Research Through Practice: From the Lab, Field, and Showroom. Elsevier (2011). https://doi.org/10.1016/C2010-0-65896-2
29. Kaplan, K.: Facilitating an Effective Design Studio Workshop, 2p. Nielsen Norman Group (2017)
30. Bardin, L.: Análise de conteúdo. São Paulo: Edições 70. Brasil.(2014a). Manual de enfrentamento à violência contra a pessoa idosa. Brasília: Secretaria de Direitos Humanos da Presidência da República (2011)
31. Merriam, S.B., Tisdell, E.J.: Qualitative Research: A Guide to Design and Implementation. Wiley (2015)
32. Anonymization for peer review. Unpredictability in unstructured and non-sequential Teachers' classes preparations activities: unveiling groupware soft-goals, Anonymization for peer review. No prelo (2021)

33. Queiros, L.M., Jofilsan, N.C., Campos Filho, A.S., Gomes, A.S., de Oliveira, F.K., da Silva, C.J.P.: Usability testing for teachers' lesson planning services. In: 2018 IEEE Frontiers in Education Conference (FIE), pp. 1–8. IEEE (2018). https://doi.org/10.1109/FIE.2018.865 8583
34. Pink, S., Horst, H., Postill, J., Hjorth, L., Lewis, T., Tacchi, J.: Digital Ethnography: Principles and Practice. Sage (2015)
35. Eshchar-Netz, L., Vedder-Weiss, D.: Teacher learning in communities of practice: the affordances of co-planning for novice and veteran teachers' learning. J. Res. Sci. Teach. **58**(3), 366–391 (2021)
36. Onyango, G., Gitonga, R., Rugar, T.: Technology integrated lesson plan based on experiential learning. In: Proceedings of the 2017 International Conference on Education and E-Learning, pp. 34–40 (2017)
37. Pink, S.: Digital futures anthropology. In: Digital Anthropology, pp. 307–324. Routledge (2021)

Main Gaps in the Training and Assessment of Teamwork Competency in the University Context

María Luisa Sein-Echaluce[1]([✉]) [iD], Ángel Fidalgo-Blanco[2] [iD],
and Francisco José García-Peñalvo[3] [iD]

[1] Departamento de Matemática Aplicada, Escuela de Ingeniería y Arquitectura, Universidad de Zaragoza, Zaragoza, Spain
mlsein@unizar.es
[2] LITI Laboratorio, Universidad Politécnica de Madrid, Madrid, Spain
angel.fidalgo@upm.es
[3] Grupo de Investigación GRIAL, Departamento de Informática y Automática, Instituto, Universitario de Ciencias de la Educación, Universidad de Salamanca, Salamanca, Spain
fgarcia@usal.es

Abstract. Individual competencies associated with teamwork are highly demanded in all productive and scientific sectors. International accreditation agencies have defined a set of indicators to identify the individual competencies associated with teamwork competence. Practically all universities address the challenge for graduates to acquire teamwork skills in groups and individually. In this context, it is essential to know whether students have acquired teamwork skills before entering the university and what training method they have followed to acquire them. In this research work, a tool has been developed to determine if they have followed procedures that generate evidence of these individual competencies throughout the development of teamwork, as well as the evaluation method used by the teachers who have trained them in this competency. The study was carried out on 171 students from two different subjects, degrees, and universities. The results confirm the central hypothesis of the work that the training method used before entering the university is of the "black box" type, where the faculty does not follow the evidence continuously and evaluates only the final result of the work.

Keywords: assessment · shared leadership · teamwork competence · university

1 Introduction

Teamwork is a highly demanded skill in all fields of knowledge since any work, service, or product requires collaborative actions between people. International organizations [1] have focused on the importance of teamwork for decades, and this interest has only grown.

In the academic field, great attention is paid to training in teamwork skills, not only because of its high demand in society. This Teamwork Competence (TC) enhances learning, creativity, social skills, and communication among students [2, 3]. Likewise, it favors another set of competencies, called soft skills, which significantly impact the new Industry 4.0 [4].

Most students already perform teamwork during their pre-university academic training, and it is assumed that they have acquired the TC by the time they reach university. Nevertheless, in many cases, this supposed acquisition affects the training and evaluation of TC at the university.

The main hypothesis of this work is that most of the students have carried out the teamwork under a "black box" model. That is, teachers do not intervene or act during the development of teamwork and only evaluate the final product, giving the same grade to all members of the same team. This method makes it difficult for teachers to obtain evidence to assess both group (acquired by the team) and individual (acquired by its members) acquisition of TC.

The present work has the following objectives:

- To identify students' level of acquisition of TC when they begin their studies at the university.
- To know the degree of knowledge of techniques and tools for developing teamwork.
- To know the evaluation process of the TC, together with the evidence used by the teaching staff to evaluate it.

Based on the teamwork model of the International Project Management Association (IPMA) [5–7], one of the most important in project management accreditation, a survey has been developed to find out if the students have received training on teamwork tools and processes and if they have used them. The survey identifies the perception of the main problems that the students have with teamwork, the processes used by the students during their development, the technological tools used, and the method of evaluation of the processes and evidence used by the teachers.

The study was carried out in two Spanish universities: University of Zaragoza and Technical University of Madrid, in the first year of two different Engineering degrees, with a sample of 171 students. The results show, for example, that the main problem with teamwork, as perceived by the students, is the unequal workload among team members.

Regarding the training received, processes in which the students have received a high level of training are identified, such as the presentation of the final work, and other processes with very little training, such as the creation of evidences for the follow-up of the work. There is a significant lack of knowledge and use concerning the use of technological tools in the different processes. This work confirms the hypothesis that teamwork is carried out through a "black box" model, since the evaluation is mostly carried out at the end of the teamwork and not during its development. This makes it difficult for teachers to detect deficiencies in the individual formation of this competence and, therefore, to solve them during its development.

In the following sections, the teamwork model applied during the experience will be presented, followed by the context, the tools, and the results which support the research hypothesis and the conclusions of this work.

2   Teamwork Model

The realization of teamwork involves a set of processes and phases that are planned to achieve both a good result of the work and adequate development of the work. This set of phases and processes is called the teamwork model. One of the most widely used models in the realization of academic teamwork is the Tuckman model [8], which establishes four phases before the final delivery of the work: Forming, Storming, Norming, and Performing.

This model was extended from various contexts, for example, in the university context by MIT [9] and in the professional field by IPMA, and, in both cases, a fifth phase called "Delivering& Documentation" was added [5].

Subsequently, in 2018 IPMA [7] added a set of individual competencies, competencies that participants in teamwork should develop to acquire TC.

The first column of Table 1 shows the competence indicators of successful teamwork competencies in the TC, which are included in IPMA. The second column of Table 1 includes some of the measures which describe highly detailed performance points within each competence indicator, which can be observed in the teams' development of the current work.

Table 1. Indicators and measures for individual competencies of teamwork (IPMA, 2018) [7]

Indicator	Measure
I-1-Facilitates the selection and building of the team	- Clarifies outcomes and creates a common vision Facilitates the team to develop norms and rules
I-2-Promote cooperation and networking between team members	-Promotes cooperation with people both within and outside the team - Uses tool for collaboration
I-3-Support, facilitate and review the development of the team and its members	-Promotes continuous Learning and knowledge sharing -Plans and promotes "lessons learned" events
I-4-Empower teams to determine tasks and responsibilities	-Challenges the team to distribute all the tasks - Stimulates transparency about performance
I-5-Recognise opportunities to facilitate learning and inspires form continuous improvement	-Uses effects of errors as opportunities to learn - Analyses and discusses mistakes to determine improvement in processes

From the teamwork phases mentioned above (Forming, Forming, Storming, Norming, Performing, and Delivering& Documentation), evidence is obtained to evaluate group competencies, and through the indicators in Table 1, individual competencies can be assessed.

In this work, and based on these individual competencies, a tool (survey) was developed to measure the acquisition of TC before entering university. In the section defining the survey questions, the relationship of the question to the indicator expressed in column 1 of Table 1 is indicated next to the group of questions or a specific question.

To train and evaluate this teamwork model, the authors defined the Comprehensive Training Model of the Teamwork Competence (CTMTC) method [10, 11] that allows obtaining individual and group evidence to train, follow and evaluate the group and individual competencies defined in IPMA. The CTMTC method makes intensive use of information and communication technologies through technological ecosystems [12], making it possible to obtain evidence continuously. The analysis of this evidence in real-time makes it possible to observe the evolution and possible deficiencies in individual and group competencies.

Groups have conducted research from several universities [13–16] using the CTMTC method with excellent results and characteristics typical of agile organizations, such as process transparency [17]. Likewise, this method uses shared leadership, exercised by several team members [18], which improves the team's performance [19] since it allows a wide variety of behaviors [20].

Regardless of the teamwork model applied, the evaluation can be carried out in two ways: after the teamwork is completed (black box) and during the teamwork (white box).

The teamwork model defined here as a "black box" represents a method where the teacher does not observe the evolution of teamwork in real-time. That is to say, the evaluation in the acquisition of TC is performed once the teamwork is finished, together with the final result of the teamwork.

In this process, there may be initial training on TC, as well as the different roles of the team members. However, there is usually no follow-up, which makes it impossible to check the evolution of teamwork or to verify the acquisition of individual competencies.

The model referred to in this paper as the "white box" is one in which the teacher can see the evolution of teamwork in real-time In this method, the teacher can evaluate the competence continuously without waiting for the work's final result. This model also allows for a continuous training process, detecting critical situations and being able to correct them.

The following is a description of the context in which the study was conducted.

3   Context

The present study is based on the elaboration of a survey that was filled out by the students of two subjects in the first year (first semester) in two different universities:

- Subject "Mathematics II" of the Chemical Engineering degree of the University of Zaragoza, with 105 enrolled students, of which 85 participated in the survey (17 work teams with an average of 5 students per team).
- Subject "Fundamentals of Programming" of the Biotechnology degree at the Polytechnic University of Madrid, with 109 enrolled students, of which 86 participated in the survey (18 work teams with an average of 6 students per team).

At the beginning of the course, and before starting the training on the CTMTC teamwork method applied in each subject, the students filled out the survey included in the next section, followed by the results and the conclusions of this study.

4 Tool (Survey)

1. Identification: write the first letter of your first surname followed by the last three numerical digits of your ID (or equivalent) (e.g., P123).
2. Gender

    Answers: •Female •Male •I prefer not to answer

3. Age
4. Indicate your overall grade, out of 14. (e.g., 10.5 separated by a comma)
5. When did you start your university studies?

    Answers: •This year: 2022-2023 • Previous year: 2021-2022 •Year before 2021

6. How much academic teamwork have you completed during your high school or vocational module studies? Select a range: •None •Between 1 and 5 •Between 6 and 10 •More than 10
7. Have you been trained in the following aspects of teamwork? (1-never, 5-always).
    NOTE: It corresponds to the indicators I-1, I-2, I-3, and I-4 of Table 1.
    • Explanation of teamwork characteristics
    • Approach to work in terms of the work objectives
    • Planning, assignment of tasks, milestones, and timeline
    • Table of individual responsibilities
    • How to follow up on the work
    • Parts of the final report
    • How to present and defend the work
8. Answer between 1 and 5 (1 never, 5 always) the following questions about how you have carried out the previous teamwork

    NOTE: It corresponds to the indicators I-3, I-4, and I-5 of the Table 1.

8.1 - A portion of the work was assigned to each team member, and a completion date was set.
8.2 - A follow-up mechanism was established to check how each team member's work was progressing.
8.3 - The steps that should be taken to carry out the teamwork was identified before the tasks were distributed.
8.4 - A calendar of activities was drawn up, including the result to be obtained in each activity.
9. Indicate what you liked least about the teamwork you have done in the past.

    NOTE: It corresponds to indicator I-2 of Table 1.

– The different workload among members
– The "freeloader"
– The little learning of teamwork skills
– All members getting the same grade
– Other

– If you checked "Other" in the previous question, please briefly indicate which one it would be.

The following questions (11 to 32) refer to your experience with teamwork during your high school or vocational module studies. In some of them you will be asked how often certain behaviors have been given. The values mean: 1 (never), 5(always).

NOTE: It corresponds to the indicators I-1, I-2, I-3, I-4, and I-5 of Table 1.

11. Detail technological tools (specific software) that you have used to develop teamwork
12. Did the faculty score planning (execution of work, significant tasks, coordination, etc.) as part of the teamwork grade?
13. A.1. If in A you marked 1(never), do not answer this question. What information did the teacher use to score such planning?
14. A.2. If in A you marked 1 (never), do not answer this question. When did the teacher evaluate this planning?

Answers: • Before finishing the work •After finishing the work • No answer

15. B. Have you made a map of responsibilities (the document that reflects the tasks and responsibilities of each component and is visible to the whole team)?
16. B.1 Did the faculty member rate the mapping of responsibilities?
17. B.2 If in B.1. You marked 1(never), do not answer this question. What information did the teacher use to score this responsibility map?
18. B.3 If in B.1 you marked 1 (never), do not answer this question. When did the teacher evaluate the map of responsibilities? •Before finishing the work •After finishing the work •No answer
19. C. Did you help your colleagues in any work team (solve doubts, provide useful information, help with more complicated tasks, ideas for improvement, etc.)?
20. C.1 Did the faculty member score that helps?
21. C.2 If in C.1 you marked 1(never), do not answer this question. What information did the teacher use to rate the help provided?
22. C.3 If in C.1 you marked 1 (never), do not answer this question. When did the teacher carry out the evaluation related to this help? •Before finishing the work •After finishing the work •No answer
23. D. When you have carried out a teamwork, have you tried to make it useful, original, understandable, and with a sufficient scientific level?
24. D.1 What aspect did the faculty value the most?
   • Understandable
   • With a sufficient scientific level
   • Original
   • Useful
25. E. Did the team have any mechanism for its members to know, at all times, how the work was progressing?
26. E.1. If in E you answered "1(never)", do not answer this question. What was that mechanism?
27. E.2 Did the faculty punctuate the use of such a mechanism?

28. E.3 If in E.2 you marked 1 (never), do not answer this question. When did the teacher evaluate the use of this mechanism? • Before finishing the work. • After finishing the work. • No answer
29. F. In the team, were decisions made through discussions?
30. F.1 Did the faculty grade your participation in such discussions?
31. F.2 If in F.1 you marked 1(never) do not answer this question. What information did the teacher use to score your participation in the discussions?
32. F.3 If in F.1 you marked 1 (never), do not answer this question. When did the teacher evaluate your participation in the discussions? •Before finishing the work. •After finishing the work. •No answer

5   Results

Students enrolled in both subjects totaled 214, of whom 171 participated in the research, representing a participation rate of 79.91% of the total number of students enrolled.

To check that the sample can be formed by the sum of students from both universities (Technical University of Madrid- UPM and University of Zaragoza-UZ), questions Q6 and Q8 will be used to check that there are no significant differences between both groups of students. Question Q6 is about the number of academic teamwork the students have completed before starting at the university, and question Q8 is composed by 4 subquestions about how you have carried out the previous teamwork.

Table 2 shows the mean and standard deviation Mean and Sd for each of the questions used as contrast variables for each of the university (UPM and UZ).

Table 2. Questions Q6 and Q8 for both universities

Variable	Mean UZ	Sd UZ	Mean UPM	Sd UPM
Q6	2.788235	0.8604279	2.965116	0.8602007
Q8.1	3.823529	1.0255831	4.104651	0.8681159
Q8.2	2.529412	1.1400526	2.500000	0.9911372
Q8.3	3.164706	1.111060	3.453488	1.080925
Q8.4	2.352941	1.120224	2.000000	1.017494

To check that the samples (of the two universities) are equivalent, the Shapiro-Wilk test is applied to analyze whether the distribution is non-normal. Subsequently, the Wilcoxon test is applied, considering two paired samples. Table 3 shows the p-values of each test. Therefore, it can be concluded that the samples are not parametric and that there are no significant differences between them. Thus, the entire set of samples will be considered in the following analyses.

Once it has been demonstrated that the research can be done with the total number of participating students, the means and standard deviation for each subquestion in section Q8 are included in Table 4.

Table 3. Tests to show that the samples are equivalent

Variable	p-value Shapiro Wilk	p-value Wilcoxon
Q6	0.000000004208	0.2007
Q8.1	0.00000001267	0.0853
Q8.2	0.0000005548	0.9413
Q8.3	0.00001027	0.1224
Q8.4	0.000000008269	0.03714

Table 4. Total mean and standard deviation for the items in question Q8.

Variable	Mean	Sd
Q8.1	3.964912	0.9572924
Q8.2	2.51462	1.064711
Q8.3	3.309942	1.102332
Q8.4	2.175439	1.081222

Table 4 shows that the most common teamwork characteristic is the one reflected in option 8.1, "Part of the work was assigned to each team member, and a completion date was set," and the least used is 8.4, "A calendar of activities was drawn up, including the result to be obtained in each activity."

Next, the analysis of both characteristics ("assignment of work" 8.1 and "planning" 8.4) will be carried out to determine the processes used in the previous teamwork and the evaluation method used by the teachers.

Regarding the most used teamwork characteristic, "assignment of work" (8.1), it corresponds to the "Norming," one phase of the CTMTC method, where the different responsibilities are defined. The survey asked about the procedure used to make the team aware of the distribution of tasks (Q15), whether the teacher evaluated this procedure (Q16), and when the evaluation was carried out (Q18).

In Figs. 1 and 2, the y-axis represents the number of students who responded to the response (x-axis) answers from 1-never to 5-always, on a Likert scale.

Figure 1 (Q15) shows the number of students who used a document to specify tasks (planning- 8.4) and, therefore, to know the workload of each team member. It can be seen that 63.15% have never or rarely used it. At the same time, 36.85% recognize that they have used it some time, almost always, or permanently.

Figure 2 (Q16) analyzes that 36.85% of the students whether the teacher considered such work in the evaluation of teamwork. 84.79% of participants recognized that it was never or seldom evaluated. In turn, out of the 15,21% who indicated that it was evaluated at least once, 64% recognized that it was done before the end of the teamwork, as shown in Fig. 3 (Q18).

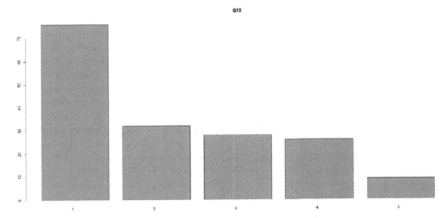

Fig. 1. Question Q15, Frequency distribution for each value of Likert scale: 1 (44.44%), 2 (18.71%), 3 (16.37%), 4 (15.22%) and 5 (5.26%).

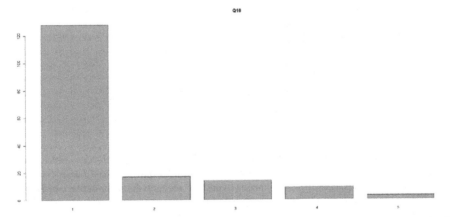

Fig. 2. Question Q16. Frequency distribution for each value of Likert scale: 1 (74.85%), 2 (9.94%), 3 (8.20%), 4 (5.26%) and 5 (1.75%).

As this habit is the most used by the students, the survey also clearly reflects the reason. If question Q9 is analyzed, the issue that most concerns the students is the unequal workload distribution. Figure 4 shows in a visual way how the variables "freeloader" and "unequal distribution of the workload" stand out.

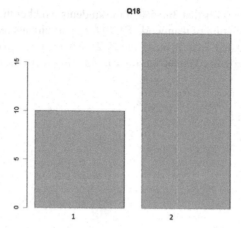

Fig. 3. Question Q18. Frequency distribution for each answer: 1-After (35.71%) and 2- Before (64.29%).

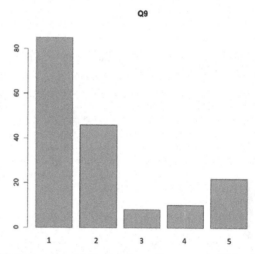

Fig. 4. Question Q09. Frequency distribution for each response: "1-freeloader" (49.71%), "2-different workload" (26.90%), "3-little learning" (8.20%), "4-other" (5.85%) and "5-the same grade" (12.86%). Thus, concern about unequal workload accounts for a per-centage of 76.61%.

Regarding the least used characteristic, "planning," this corresponds to the execution phase in the development of teamwork, where the most used tool is the chronogram. Question Q12 analyzes whether the teacher evaluated the planning, and question Q14 when this evaluation was made.

Figure 5 shows the number of answers on the Likert scale (1-Never to 5-Always) 34.5% recognize that the teacher did not evaluate the planning as opposed to 8.77% who indicate that the planning was always evaluated. However, a high percentage of the students, 54.97%, recognize that at least once they had completed the evaluation.

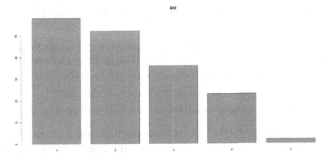

Fig. 5. Question Q12. Frequency distribution for each value of the Likert scale: 1 (34.5%), 2 (10.53%), 3 (22.22%), 4 (23.98%) and 5 (8.77%).

Figure 6 shows the responses to question Q14, which indicates the time the teachers did the evaluation (1- After, 2-Before) and shows that the planning evaluation was mainly carried out at the end of the teamwork.

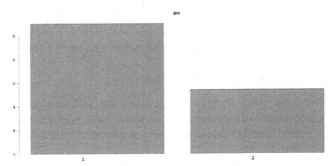

Fig. 6. Question Q14. Frequency distribution for each answer: After (67.07%) and Before (32.93%).

6 Conclusions

To determine whether the teamwork method used by the sample of students before starting university is a "white box" or "black box" model, the students' teamwork habits have been identified, and two habits have been analyzed: the most used and the least used.

The habit most used by the students when performing previous teamwork, the "assignment of tasks to each team member," is of great concern to the students, mainly because of the unequal distribution of work, which produces members with a significantly lower workload than the rest.

A detailed analysis has been carried out for this feature, and the diagnosis is as follows:

- No mechanisms are used to reflect student workload in a shared manner. Figure 1 shows that 64% have never or rarely used any mechanism. This means that no evidence is left that can be used by both faculty and team members to check, evaluate and make decisions about this aspect.

- Teachers do not usually evaluate this characteristic. Figure 2 shows that teachers do not usually evaluate the workload distribution, with 75% acknowledging that it has never been done and 10% indicating that it has seldom been done.
- Likewise, of the small percentage that indicates that they have been evaluated, 36% recognize that they are evaluated afterward and 64% before (Fig. 3).

For the feature least used by the work teams, planning, with a mean of 2,17, the results show that there is a significant difference between those who always used mechanisms to leave evidence of what they were doing during teamwork (9%) and those who never used them (35%).

Therefore, although in a less significant way than the most applied characteristic (the distribution of tasks), mechanisms for leaving evidence are not usually used. However, if we analyze the percentage of students who at least once use mechanisms to leave evidence, 56% of students are in that case.

Although the teachers have used a mechanism to assess the ongoing development of teamwork, the evaluation is done only at the end of the teamwork process.

Thus, two analyses with different results lead to the same conclusion:

- Students do not usually use mechanisms that reflect evidence of teamwork development.
- Teachers do not usually evaluate such evidence.

On the other hand, when there is such a follow-up, although not significantly, a percentage of close to 50% of participants say that they have produced evidence and that the teacher evaluated them, but this evaluation was carried out after the teamwork was completed.

Thus, it is possible to confirm the hypothesis that teamwork, carried out before entering university, has followed a "black-box" method, where it is tremendously challenging to train this competency.

The IPMA model shows the need for training in individual competencies; however, this study demonstrates that acquiring these competencies is challenging due to the "black box" model used for the most part. This model does not offer the possibility of continuous monitoring of students to determine whether they are acquiring the competencies. On the other hand, students do not usually carry out processes that leave evidence of the individual competencies expressed in IPMA, making training in these competencies even more difficult.

Students are not accustomed to using tools that leave evidence to evaluate this competency, and when teachers perform this evaluation, it is done at the end of the work, when it is no longer possible to make decisions to improve the learning of this competency.

It should be noted in this study that the aspect of teamwork that students like the least is the unequal workload of each person in the team.

One of the aspects to be improved is the provision of mechanisms to ensure that the work team has a homogeneous workload and that there are no people who take advantage of the work of the rest of the team.

It is essential to carry out training on teamwork competencies under "white box" methods and generate processes that generate evidence showing the degree of acquisition of individual competencies. It is necessary to identify those educational environments and contexts where teamwork is being carried out under the "black box" method and to identify whether the team uses processes that generate evidence. Therefore, the research will continue using the same measurement tool in different courses and grades in different universities.

Acknowledgements. This research was partially funded by the Spanish Government Ministry of Economy and Competitiveness through the AVisSA project grant number (PID2020-118345RBI00) and the Educational Innovation Project of the Technical University of Madrid IE23.0606. The authors would like to thank the research groups EtnoEdu of the University of Zaragoza, GRIAL of the University of Salamanca, and LITI of the Technical University of Madrid for their support.

References

1. Scott, C.L.: The Futures of learning 2: what kind of learning for the 21st century? In: ERF Working Papers Series, No. 14. p. 14. UNESCO Education Research and Foresight, Paris, France (2015)
2. Belanger, E., Moller, J., She, J.: Challenges to engineering design teamwork in a remote learning environment. Educ. Sci. **12**, 741 (2022). https://doi.org/10.3390/educsci12110741
3. James, M., et al.: Collaborative case-based learning with programmatic team-based assessment: a novel methodology for developing advanced skills in early-years medical students. BMC Med. Educ. **22**, 1–12 (2022). https://doi.org/10.1186/S12909-022-03111-5
4. Sein-Echaluce, M.L., Fidalgo-Blanco, Á., Balbín, A.M., García-Peñalvo, F.J.: Flipped Learning 4.0. An extended flipped classroom model with Education 4.0 and organisational learning processes. Univers Access Inf Soc. 1, 1–13 (2022). https://doi.org/10.1007/s10209-022-009 45-0
5. IPMA: ICB -IPMA Competence Baseline Version 3.0. International Project Management Association, Nijkerk (NL) (2006)
6. Sedlmayer, M.: Individual Competence Baseline for Project Management. , 4th ed. Zurich (2015)
7. IPMA: IPMA Reference Guide ICB4 in an Agile World. International Project Management Association, Zurich (2018)
8. Tuckman, B.W., Ann, M., Jensen, C.: Stages of small-group development revisited. Group Organ. Stud. **2**, 419–427 (1977). https://doi.org/10.1177/105960117700200404
9. Stein, J.: Using the Stages of Team Development | MIT Human Resources, https://hr.mit.edu/learning-topics/teams/articles/stages-development, last accessed 2022/08/29
10. Fidalgo-Blanco, Á., Leris, D., Sein-Echaluce, M.L., García-Peñalvo, F.J.: Monitoring Indicators for CTMTC: comprehensive training model of the teamwork competence in engineering domain. Int. J. Eng. Educ. **31**, 829–838 (2015)
11. Sein-Echaluce, M.L., Fidalgo-Blanco, Á., García-Peñalvo, F.J.: Agile CTMTC: Adapting Stages for a Shorter Application of the Teamwork Method. In: Zaphiris, P., Ioannou, A. (ed.) Learning and Collaboration Technologies. Novel Technological Environments. HCII 2022. Lecture Notes in Computer Science, vol 13329. pp. 274–286. Springer, Cham (2022). https://doi.org/10.1007/978-3-031-05675-8_21

12. Sein-Echaluce, M.L., Fidalgo-Blanco, Á., Esteban-Escaño, J.: Technological ecosystems and ontologies for an educational model based on Web 3.0. Univ. Access Inf. Soc. **18**(3), 645–658 (2019). https://doi.org/10.1007/s10209-019-00684-9

13. Barreiro García, J., Martínez Pellitero, S., González Alonso, M.I.: Aplicación de la metodología CTMTC para evaluación formativa del trabajo grupal en ingeniería de fabricación. Revista Infancia, Educación y Aprendizaje. 3, 499–504 (2017). https://doi.org/10.22370/IEYA.2017.3.2.770

14. González, M.Á.C., et al.: Evaluación cuantitativa de la adquisición de la competencia de trabajo en equipo mediante la metodología CTMTC. Premios a la innovación en la enseñanza. **16**, 73–107 (2017)

15. Conde, M.Á., Hernández-García, Á., García-Peñalvo, F.J., Fidalgo-Blanco, Á., Sein-Echaluce, M.: Evaluation of the CTMTC Methodology for Assessment of Teamwork Competence Development and Acquisition in Higher Education. In: Zaphiris, P., Ioannou, A. (eds.) LCT 2016. LNCS, vol. 9753, pp. 201–212. Springer, Cham (2016). https://doi.org/10.1007/978-3-319-39483-1_19

16. Fidalgo-Blanco, Á., Lerís, D., Sein-Echaluce, M.L., García-Peñalvo, F.J.: Indicadores para el seguimiento y evaluación de la competencia de trabajo en equipo a través del método CTMTC, pp. 280–285. Aprendizaje, Innovación y Competitividad (2013)

17. Fidalgo-Blanco, Á., Sein-Echaluce, M.L., García-Peñalvo, F.J.: Education 4.0-based Method to Improve Learning: Lessons Learned from COVID-19. RIED-Revista Iberoamericana de Educación a Distancia. 25, (2022). https://doi.org/10.5944/RIED.25.2.32320

18. Lyndon, S., Pandey, A., Navare, A.: Emergence and outcomes of shared leadership: unraveling the role of transactive memory system and team mindfulness using mixed-methods approach. Leadership and Organization Development Journal. 43, (2022). https://doi.org/10.1108/LODJ-05-2021-0202

19. Shoukat, M.H., Elgammal, I., Shah, S.A., Shaukat, H.: Nexus between shared leadership, workplace bullying, team learning, job insecurity and team performance in health care. Team Performance Management. 28, (2022). https://doi.org/10.1108/TPM-04-2021-0034

20. Sweeney, A.: Looking within: a longitudinal qualitative analysis of shared leadership behaviours in organisational teams. Team Perform. Manag. **28**, 441–460 (2022). https://doi.org/10.1108/TPM-02-2022-0013

Prototyping the Learning Analytics Dashboards of an Adaptive Learning Platform: Faculty Perceptions Versus Designers' Intentions

Tobias Alexander Bang Tretow-Fish[✉][iD], Md. Saifuddin Khalid[iD], and Victor Anton Charles Leweke

Department of Applied Mathematics and Computer Science, Technical University of Denmark, Kongens Lyngby, Denmark
compute@compute.dtu.dk
https://www.compute.dtu.dk/english

Abstract. This study contributes with a case study on redesigning three Learning Analytics Dashboards (LADs) of the adaptive learning platform Rhapsode™ with instructions for pedagogical actions. Applying self determination theory's elements of competence and relatedness and mental models in a design thinking process, the differences among the teachers perceptions and the designers intentions are highlighted through several methods to answer the questions of: How might we improve the learning analytics dashboards by prioritizing course instructors' perceived competence and relatedness? and How might we redesign learning analytics dashboards by including course instructors' purpose, insights, and recommending actions?

These questions are answered first by developing three Role-based Personas of Alina Action, Niels Novice, and Paul Privacy along with scenarios and user stories. Second, prototypes of interfaces are designed and tested in three iterations showing insights, recommended actions, and explanation of mechanics. Feedback from the tests on the prototypes receives positive feedback from all teacher personas. The teacher persona of Niels Novice also supplies a criticism of the insights and recommended actions on the basis of creating undesired interpretation, potential bias, taking away freedom of interpretation, and authoritative system that "instructs/orders" action. Additionally, the scope of the study cannot meet the persona of Paul Privacy's reservations on students' possible experience of surveillance.

Keywords: Actionable Learning Analytics Dashboard · Adaptive Learning Platform · Mental model · Motivation theory · Design Thinking

1 Introduction

The learning analytics dashboards (LADs) of digital learning platforms provide the students with feedback to guide their learning and the teachers gain insights

P. Zaphiris and A. Ioannou (Eds.): HCII 2023, LNCS 14040, pp. 531–545, 2023.
https://doi.org/10.1007/978-3-031-34411-4_36

on content and students' activities to prepare their teaching [21]. Despite the advancement of the fields of user experience design, data science, and didactic design and their impact on the digital learning systems, the studies on LADs or Learning Analytics (LA) have not reported any case of implementing or redesigning dashboard for supporting faculty preparation based on the analytics on students' learning [13,21]. In higher education, the focus of the empirical studies on LA had been on increasing students success [1,6], improving retention by identifying students at risk (based on click-stream or engagement on the platform) [12,22], self-awareness of under-performing peers [9]. In this study, the adaptive learning platform Rhapsode™ was implemented in a Danish Nursing education program's course as a pilot during Fall 2021. The course instructors were expected to consider the LADs on the Rhapsode Educator platform as part of their preparation for their lectures.

The design of the LADs and the use of insights from the Rhapsode™ Educator platform depend on the course instructors' motivation, knowledge, and mental model [3,16]. The same factors influence the designers, who differ in their roles and thereby the expectations. Based on course instructors' perceived usefulness and to comply with GDPR regulations, the screenshots of three LADs were selected from the Rhapsode™ platform for redesigning interface mockups. Considering mental model and self-determination theory [17] as the theoretical framework for designing and evaluating LADs, the differences in the users and designers resulted in devising the following research questions. The questions were not defined at the beginning but were outcome of *how might we?* method ideation method applied as part the user-centred design thinking process.

1. How might we improve the learning analytics dashboards by prioritizing course instructors' perceived competence and relatedness?
2. How might we redesign learning analytics dashboards by including course instructors' purpose, insights, and recommending actions?

The questions are unfolded in the following sections, which report a three-iteration prototyping process as part of the implementation of design thinking framework [18].

2   Related Work and Concepts

This section includes (1) a short review of related empirical studies on the development and evaluation of LADs focused on actionable insights, (2) the "mental models" [3,16] that shapes the design of interactive systems, and (3) motivation theories - selected from the web-based learning theories [5,17].

In relation to empirical studies on LADs focused on actionable insights [20] approached three challenges faced during their deployment of LADs in educational contexts. The challenges are (1) representation and actions, (2) ethics, and (3) agility. The paper reviews existing strengths and weaknesses of LADs, and attempts to address the reviewed issues by developing descriptive, predictive and data-driven prescriptive analytics into one display. The analytics presented on their LADs are statistical inferences on students' activities resulting predictions on performance rather than pedagogical support for teachers and students for instructions, guidance, or overview of the data. In other words, the actionability of the LAD is lacking. A study by [8] also informs on LADs focused on actionable insights by investigating an Introductory Coding course conducted with the pedagogical method of Flipped Learning. The outcome was actionable LADs for students encompassing (1) feedback to instructors, (2) percentile rank chart of grades, (3) a homework activity chart, and (4) a video activity chart. The LADs showed good results in improving students' self-regulated learning skills, course performance, learning behaviour, and emotions showing that actionable LADs make a difference when applied with a pedagogical intent.

The study by [7] states that *"it is still unclear how can LA be designed to position teachers as designers of effective interventions and orchestration actions."* The chapter argues actionable LA and proposes three HCD principles for LA solutions: (1) positioning of teachers and other stakeholders with agency, (2) integration of the learning design cycle and the LA design process, and (3) reliance on educational theories to guide the LA solution design and implementation."

The *self-determination theory* [17] states that there are three different needs for optimal self-motivation: autonomy, competence, and relatedness. *Autonomy* refers to independence. *Competence* is defined as the "the need to control the outcome and feel that you can accomplice a task", and *relatedness* is the feeling of connection and to experience care for others. This study applies the three principles proposed by [7]: (1) from the viewpoint of interviewed course instructors and designers, the competence and relatedness dimension of SDT is given the priority for redesigning three selected LADs, (2) applied DT as the learning cycle, and (3) considering learning theories for web-based instructional design, the motivation theory is selected and applied. Furthermore, the concept of mental model [3,16] is applied to define and discuss the differing perceptions of various users and designers (i.e. the authors in the case of this paper). Mental models are associated with the self-determination and motivation [17] of users and designers.

3   Methodology and Methods

Figure 1 shows the methodology applied for the iterative design process [18] but excluding the Agile sprint. Table 1 summarizes the methods including three iterations of prototyping and testing.

The interview protocol (Appendix A) consists of six themes with three to six questions for each of the themes. Both notes and transcription of audio recording were created, and translated from Danish to English.

Table 1. Table of methods applied

Process	Methods	Participant	Activities and Purpose
Empathize	Interview and Rich picture [14]	Teacher	Four interviews following the interview protocol (Appendix A). The interviews followed three themes of (1) Which LADs and LA the teacher used when she assessed students' work, (2) Which actions the teacher took based on information from the LADs and LA, and (3) The teachers' current thoughts on the platform. The results from the interview were put into the rich picture format to structure and analyse.
Define	Role-Based Persona [15]	Authors	Based on the interview data, three teacher personas were constructed to better understand pains and needs.
Ideate	How might we (HMW)? [11]	Authors	Two point-of-view statements were shortlisted based on the pain points identified from the interviews. Authors made multiple HMW questions, selected two through dot-voting, and these are included as the design questions for this paper
	Scenarios [19]	Designers	Scenarios were used to identify teacher interactions with the platform. They would then describe a certain situation or interaction with the current prototype.
	User stories [4]	Interview	User stories were produced to describe features from the teachers point of view. They enabled us to identify the teachers' needs and goals related to the platform.
Prototype and Test	Interface Design: Information Design and Visualization [2]	Authors	Three iterations of interface redesign of three LADs of Rhapsode™ Educators by third author. Included short introduction, categorizing students' performance, and suggesting the course instructors' actions on giving feedback to students
	Cognitive walk-through [2]	Authors	Two authors role-played as teachers requiring guidance on how to used existing LADs for taking preparation for engaging students during lectures on whether the LADs are (1) understandable, (2) insightful, and (3) actionable
	Think aloud commentaries [2]	Authors	Two authors role-played using concurrent think-aloud protocol answering questions (1) what do you "understand"? (2) what are the insights or takeaways about students? (3) What and how will you take actions as part of subsequent preparation? (4) How should the interfaces be improved?
	Co-discovery [2]	Teachers, faculty staff, and authors	Two authors conducted tests with three pairs of teachers - tested the revised interfaces using the same questions as above

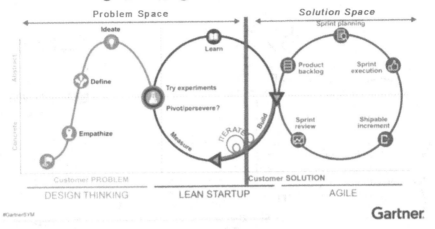

Combine Design Thinking, Lean Startup and Agile

Fig. 1. Methodology Combining Design Thinking, Lean Startup and Agile for Supporting Digital Innovation Efforts [10]

4   Results

In the Design Thinking process' step of empathizing, four interviews at four different times of the course was conducted with a course teacher, who used the Rhapsode™ platform for their first time in their teaching. The interviews were conducted alongside the teacher exploring how the platform could be used to prepare the lectures. From the interview data three personas, three scenarios along with the selection and use of three LADs from the Rhapsode™ Educator platform, and three user stories were created. This laid the groundwork for the development of the first prototype which was a click-through prototype. Review on mental model and motivation theory contributed to revise the *how might we* questions. In the subsequent two iterations, the LADs were redesigned and tested. The central outcomes from the methods applied in the design process are presented below.

4.1   Empathize

The interviews were conducted through four separate sessions with a teacher exploring how to interact with Rhapsode as they prepared their lecture upon the data. Each interview session followed an identical guide (Table 2) the information collected during each session is compiled in a rich picture (Fig. 2) representation to empathize the results from the interviews.

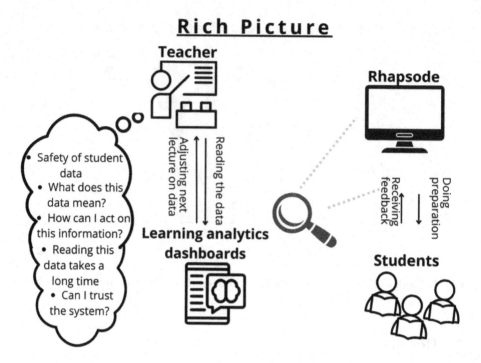

Fig. 2. The representation of results from the four sessions of interview.

4.2   Define

Define identified the SD Theory elements [17] to build our personas on from the interview sessions.

Role-Based Personas: Three teacher personas were made to understand the pains and needs based on the interviews regarding former experience on LADs. Establishing the personas from interview data and SD theory, competence was an element shared among Alina Action and Niels Novice. Alina Action focuses on taking explicit pedagogical action such as sending reminding email to students while Niels Novice wants data he can assess based on his pedagogical knowledge and experience. The concept of relatedness was shared among Paul Privacy and Niels Novice. Paul Privacy focus on students' data privacy while Niels Novice focus on students' experience of difficulty.

Paul Privacy: A young teacher who has already used online platforms during own studies although the adaptive aspect is new. The teacher found it quite easy navigating the platform but values students' privacy and worries that they might feel spied on.

Alina Action: The teacher dislikes spending much time looking at summary tables and figures that may have too many interpretation possibilities. Alina appreciates concise dashboards that display actionable insights and gives examples of specific interactions or information to be shared with students as extrinsic motivation. The teacher likes to save time required to think about pedagogical actions based on summary tables and figures only. Then, spend the saved time with students who may encounter difficulties with the course material or activities.

Niels Novice: The teacher has been teaching for many years but relatively new in the utilization LADs as part of the pedagogical process. Niels would like to see LA as summary of class progress and the topics students are feeling challenged. He finds explicit instructions by the analytics as a barrier for pedagogical development and excessive transfer of agency to the system from people.

4.3 Ideate

Ideation took the point-of-departure from multiple point-of-view [11] statements, which were the inputs for a brainstorming session resulting in two How Might We (HMW) questions.

How Might We? The how might we questions are the research questions for this study.

- How might we improve the learning analytics dashboards by prioritizing course instructors' perceived competence and relatedness?
- How might we redesign learning analytics dashboards by including their purpose, insights, and recommending actions for course instructors?

Envisioned Scenarios: For answering the HMW questions, descriptions of the envisioned scenarios of dashboards' design and use were made from the viewpoint of the personas (by authors, based on interviews with teachers).

Scenario (1): Alina Action goes onto the platform and focuses on a dashboard displaying individual performances of students for each learning goal. She notices that a few students have never engaged with the material on the platform, and she wants to let the students know without pressuring them. She also notices the recommended action, which suggests to send an automated message reminding the students to engage with the material. She can look at the email, edit it, and upon inspection, if she likes the format, send the reminder.

Scenario (2): Paul Privacy looks at the dashboard that ranks the most difficult learning goals according to different filters. The mechanics that defines a learning goal as "most difficult" is clear and he can clearly identify which questions he wants to tackle during the next lecture.

Scenario (3): Niels Novice logs onto the platform and spends some time looking at the heatmap showing the scores of each student for each learning goal. He appreciates the color coding of each element, but he is not able to discern which learning goals are most problematic, from just looking at the dashboard. After inspection of the insight and recommended action, he is provided with a few learning goals that should be discussed during the next lecture.

User Stories. To fulfill the scenarios, the following user stories were made for redesigning the interfaces of three LADs.

1. As a teacher, I want each of the dashboards to contain a feature to give students feedback via email on their progress on Rhapsode so that I can provide feedback to students based on easy understandable insights and recommend actions presented on the dashboards.
2. As a teacher, I want to make sure the students feel accompanied during the learning process, so that students don't have the impression of being constantly under surveillance.
3. As a teacher, I want to be presented with descriptions of the mechanics of each dashboard as well as filters so that I can get the opportunities for displaying data differently.

The scope of this study is to improve the LADs for teacher interpretation opportunity to follow up on GDPR issues is not within this scope and we will not continue with 2nd scenario.

4.4   Prototype and Test

Based on the user stories, the interfaces of the three selected LADs were redesigned in three iterations but only the outcomes of the third iteration is presented here. The before and after versions of the LADs are shown in the Figs. 3a&b, 4a&b, and 5a&b.

In the first iteration, cognitive walk-through of the first two authors suggested: reducing the amount of information in the LADs. In the second iteration, first two authors role-played persona Alina Action and suggested: Clearer defined mechanics, better alignment of recommended actions and their paired insight, a categorization of in-class and online recommended actions, addition of visual assistance such as highlighting of learning goals mentioned in the insight section, and coherent layout.

In the third iteration, co-discovery of pairs of teachers gave following feedback: Further relating insight to the presented data, re-wording of recommended actions to reduce teacher work and providing discretion to students, rephrasing sentences such as "fail" to "low score", and minor design changes such as an addition of a background image and changing of the color palette for visual comfort.

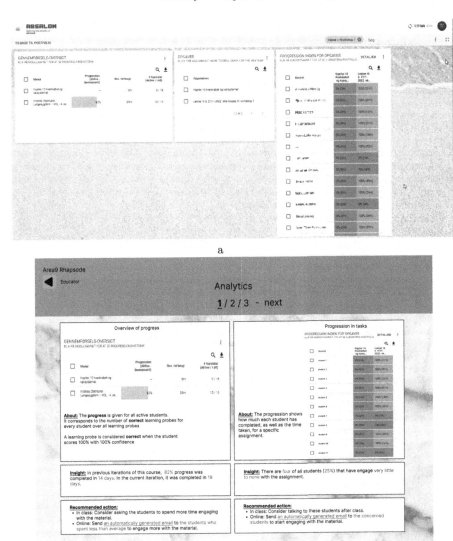

Fig. 3. The 1st LADs design process. From top to bottom: Fig. 3 a) depict the original LAD of *Overview of progress* and *Progression in tasks*, Fig. 3 b) depicts the prototype of the same LADs in their 3rd iteration with a reduction of content and an addition of an about, insight, and recommended action section.

Additionally from the third iteration teachers criticized the insights and recommended actions for removing autonomy from teachers by producing potentially biased interpretations of students' learning processes and making an authoritative system that orders teachers to take specific actions. This critic we closely connect with the persona of Niels Novice.

a

b

Fig. 4. The 2nd LAD's design process. From top to bottom: Fig. 4 a) depicts the original LAD of *most difficulty learning goals*, Fig. 4 b) depicts the prototype of the same LAD in its 3rd iteration with a reduction of content and an addition of an about, insight, and recommended action section.

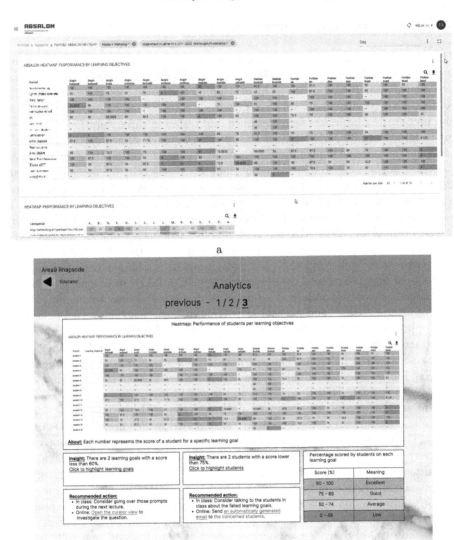

a

b

Fig. 5. The 3rd LAD's design process. From top to bottom: Fig. 5 a) depicts the original LAD of *Heatmap: Performance of students per learning objectives*, Fig. 5 b) depicts the prototype of the same LAD in its 3rd iteration with a reduction of content and an addition of an about, insight, and recommended action section, as well as a color legend.

5   Discussion and Conclusion

The objectives of this study were to answer *(1) How might we improve the learning analytics dashboards by prioritizing course instructors' perceived competence and relatedness?* It was answered by developing the Role-based Personas of Alina Action, Niels Novice, and Paul Privacy with accompanying envisioned scenarios and user stories, interfaces were designed and tested in three iterations for showing insights, recommended actions to support the teachers pedagogic actions in-class and online, and explanation of the mechanics. Answering the second HMW *(2) How might we redesign learning analytics dashboards by including course instructors' purpose, insights, and recommending actions?* The developed prototype of LADs were refined through three iterations focusing on SD theory's competence and relatedness. In third iteration of the prototype the inclusion of the purpose on the LADs received positive feedback from all teacher personas but the insights and recommended actions were strongly criticized by the teacher persona Niels Novice. Niels's many years of teaching experience and the new role of integrating and coordinating the use of LADs in teaching considers the change as creating undesired interpretation, potential bias, taking away freedom of interpretation, and authoritative system that "instructs/orders" action. The opposing statements about the change in the LADs are due to the perceived reduction of autonomy. Furthermore, the scope of the study cannot meet the persona of Paul Privacy's concerns regarding students' possible experience of being looked over the shoulders since it is not within the scope of this study to evaluate possible GDPR concerns on the platform.

The mental models of designers and users shape the requirements for the design and evaluation of the interactive systems [2], which are the LADs in this study. The mental models are shaped by the learning process, where motivation and purpose of LAD use (reflected in envisioned scenarios) play the central role. The designers' intention was to redesign the LADs based on course instructors' perceived competence and relatedness for communicating purpose, insights, and recommending action. The underlying factors shaping mental model shaping the desired design and use of LADs require investigations involving teachers from diverse cultural and academic backgrounds. Such studies will hopefully enable establishing success criteria for the design and development of LADs that impact pedagogical practice.

A   Appendix

Table 2. Interview protocol of themes and questions.

Theme	Questions
1. Planning and preparation with Rhapsode	• Would you like to start by describing how you have prepared your teaching? (e.g. with colleagues, before the holidays, yesterday, after reading the Rhapsode report, after reading a book)
	• How much time do you spend on preparation? When do you spend the time?
	• What role does Rhapsode play in your preparation?
2. Comments on the teaching in general	• Would you like to describe the content areas and activities/methods of today's teaching?
	• Did it go the way you expected/what was different?
	• Had the students prepared as you had imagined?
3. Comments on the didactical changes	• How do you think it is to teach with this method?
	• What do you think the students think about this method of teaching?
	• Do they learn more or something different now compared to a traditional lecturing approach, do you assess?
	• Is it easy to get all students to participate in the lecturers?
4. Comments on Rhapsode and the students' preparation	• How do you assess students preparation in Rhapsode? Have they gotten used to that way of working?
	• Do they all get through the whole preparation? 70/80%?
	• Remember how they prepared for Rhapsode? Is it different now?
5. Assessment of learning outcomes	• Do you find that you have to repeat material that Rhapsode also instructs in?
	• Do you believe that students can use the knowledge they acquire in Rhapsode?
	• What do you have to do to bring that knowledge into play?
	• Do you experience changed learning outcomes after the implementation of the didactical changed teaching and Rhapsode?
6. Rhapsode (Improvement/ Changes/ Ideas)	• Do you think there is something that's missing/could be improved in Rhapsode?
	• What is the hardest part about having to let students prepare in Rhapsode?
	• And the best/biggest advantage?
	• What's the most difficult thing about working with the changed didactics and what is the best?
	• If you had to give some advice to a new colleague about Rhapsode and didactical changes in the teaching, what would the advice be about?

References

1. Arnold, K.E., Pistilli, M.D.: Course signals at purdue: using learning analytics to increase student success. In: Proceedings of the 2nd International Conference on Learning Analytics and Knowledge, pp. 267–270 (2012)
2. Benyon, D.: Designing User Experience. Pearson UK, London (2019)

3. Carroll, J.M., Olson, J.R.: Mental models. In: Helander, M. (ed.) Handbook of Human-Computer Interaction, pp. 45–65. North-Holland, Amsterdam (1988). https://doi.org/10.1016/B978-0-444-70536-5.50007-5. https://www.sciencedirect.com/science/article/pii/B9780444705365500075

4. Cohn, M.: User Stories Applied: For Agile Software Development. Addison-Wesley Professional, Boston (2004)

5. Davidson-Shivers, G.V., Rasmussen, K.L., Lowenthal, P.R.: Foundations of online learning and instructional design. In: Davidson-Shivers, G.V., Rasmussen, K.L., Lowenthal, P.R (eds.) Web-Based Learning, pp. 43–79. Springer, Cham (2018). https://doi.org/10.1007/978-3-319-67840-5_2

6. Dietz-Uhler, B., Hurn, J.E.: Using learning analytics to predict (and improve) student success: a faculty perspective. J. Interact. Online Learn. 12(1), 17–26 (2013)

7. Dimitriadis, Y., Martínez-Maldonado, R., Wiley, K.: Human-centered design principles for actionable learning analytics. In: Tsiatsos, T., Demetriadis, S., Mikropoulos, A., Dagdilelis, V. (eds.) Research on E-Learning and ICT in Education, pp. 277–296. Springer, Cham (2021). https://doi.org/10.1007/978-3-030-64363-8_15

8. Duan, X., Wang, C., Rouamba, G.: Designing a learning analytics dashboard to provide students with actionable feedback and evaluating its impacts. In: Cukurova, M., Rummel, N., Gillet, D., McLaren, B., Uhomoibhi, J. (eds.) CSEDU: Proceedings of the 14th International Conference on Computer Supported Education, vol. 2, pp. 117–127. INSTICC (2022). https://doi.org/10.5220/0011116400003182. 14th International Conference on Computer Supported Education (CSEDU), Electr Network, Apr 22-24, 2022

9. Fritz, J.: Classroom walls that talk: using online course activity data of successful students to raise self-awareness of underperforming peers. Internet High. Educ. 14(2), 89–97 (2011)

10. Gartner Research: Combine design thinking, lean startup and agile (2019). https://www.gartner.com/en/documents/3941917. Accessed 11 Jan 2022

11. IDEO: "how might we" questions. https://dschool.stanford.edu/resources/how-might-we-questions

12. Larrabee Sønderlund, A., Hughes, E., Smith, J.: The efficacy of learning analytics interventions in higher education: a systematic review. Br. J. Edu. Technol. 50(5), 2594–2618 (2019)

13. Leitner, P., Khalil, M., Ebner, M.: Learning analytics in higher education-a literature review. In: Learning Analytics: Fundaments, Applications, and Trends, pp. 1–23 (2017)

14. Monk, A., Howard, S.: Methods & tools: the rich picture: a tool for reasoning about work context. Interactions 5(2), 21–30 (1998). https://doi.org/10.1145/274430.274434

15. Nielsen, L.: Personas - User Focused Design. Springer, London (2013). https://doi.org/10.1007/978-1-4471-4084-9

16. Rasmuss, J.: Mental Models and the Control of Actions in Complex Environments. Risø National Library, Roskilde (1987). https://backend.orbit.dtu.dk/ws/portalfiles/portal/137296640/RM2656.PDF. invited Paper for the Austrian Computer Society, 6th Workshop on Informatics and Psychology: "Mental Models and Human Computer-Interaction" Schaerding, Austria, June 1987

17. Ryan, R.M., Deci, E.L.: Intrinsic and extrinsic motivations: classic definitions and new directions. Contemp. Educ. Psychol. 25(1), 54–67 (2000)

18. Sari, E., Tedjasaputra, A.: Design thinking 101 for education. In: Proceedings of the 4th International Conference on Human-Computer Interaction and User Experience in Indonesia, CHIuXiD 2018, pp. 119–122 (2018)

19. Sharp, H., Preece, J., Rogers, Y.: Interaction Design: Beyond Human-Computer Interaction. Wiley, Hoboken (2015)
20. Susnjak, T., Ramaswami, G.S., Mathrani, A.: Learning analytics dashboard: a tool for providing actionable insights to learners. Int. J. Educ. Technol. High. Educ. **19**(12), 1–23 (2022)
21. Tretow-Fish, T.A.B., Khalid, M.: Evaluating learning analytics of adaptive learning systems: a work in progress systematic review. In: Brooks, E., Sjöberg, J., Møller, A.K. (eds.) International Conference on Design, Learning, and Innovation, pp. 37–52. Springer, Cham (2022). https://doi.org/10.1007/978-3-031-06675-7_3
22. Wolff, A., Zdrahal, Z., Nikolov, A., Pantucek, M.: Improving retention: predicting at-risk students by analysing clicking behaviour in a virtual learning environment. In: Proceedings of the Third International Conference on Learning Analytics and Knowledge, pp. 145–149 (2013)

Operationalising Transparency as an Integral Value of Learning Analytics Systems – From Ethical and Data Protection to Technical Design Requirements

Hristina Veljanova[1]([✉]) [iD], Carla Barreiros[2,3] [iD], Nicole Gosch[1] [iD], Elisabeth Staudegger[1] [iD], Martin Ebner[4] [iD], and Stefanie Lindstaedt[2,3] [iD]

[1] Institute of the Foundations of Law, University of Graz, Graz, Austria
{hristina.veljanova,nicole.gosch,
elisabeth.staudegger}@uni-graz.at
[2] Institute Interactive Systems and Data Science, Graz University of Technology, Graz, Austria
{carla.soutabarreiros,lindstaedt}@tugraz.at
[3] Department of Educational Technology, Graz University of Technology, Graz, Austria
[4] Know-Center GmbH, Graz, Austria
martin.ebner@tugraz.at

Abstract. With the rising complexity of technology and its introduction into educational settings, the question of trusting and designing trustworthy learning analytics (LA) systems has gained importance. Transparency is one of the values that can contribute to enhancing an LA system's trustworthiness. It has been included and discussed as a separate core value or principle in many ethical frameworks for LA. Even though these frameworks provide valuable contributions, they are mostly limited to the conceptual level. Defining what transparency entails in the context of LA is an important aspect, nevertheless, the translation and operationalisation of such abstract concepts into technology should be equally considered.

In this paper, we focus on the question of how transparency can be translated into concrete design requirements in order to enhance the trustworthiness of LA systems. We present a normative framework in the form of an interdisciplinary Criteria Catalogue for trustworthy LA, which consists of seven core areas, including transparency. Second, we demonstrate how transparency can be translated and operationalised into more specific and low-level elements by using an example of the Learners' Corner LA dashboard developed within the project "Learning Analytics – Students in Focus". Third, we share the results of a study conducted to better understand students' information needs in relation to LA tools and evaluate our design choices for the introduction of three quick information buttons within the Learners' Corner.

Keywords: Learning analytics · transparency · trustworthy LA systems · human-centred LA

P. Zaphiris and A. Ioannou (Eds.): HCII 2023, LNCS 14040, pp. 546–562, 2023.
https://doi.org/10.1007/978-3-031-34411-4_37

1 Introduction

Since information technology (IT) systems are not "natural" entities but mere artefacts, it is our responsibility to decide how we want to design them. As such, we can consciously or unconsciously design technology that supports or diminishes certain values.

The value "transparency" constitutes an integral part of building a trustworthy learning analytics (LA) system. Moreover, it represents an instrumental value, which enables the realisation of other values, such as privacy, autonomy, respect, or non-discrimination. Many scholars in the LA community have recognised its relevance and role in LA. A literature review shows that most ethical frameworks for LA include transparency as their core value or principle [7, 8, 10–12]. While very significant, these frameworks provide mostly a conceptual understanding of transparency. Understanding what transparency entails in an LA setting is an important aspect. Translating and operationalising such intangible and abstract concepts directly into technology is another issue, which even though complex and challenging, deserves equal attention.

In this paper, we propose an approach that acts as a bridge between ethicists, data protection experts, pedagogy experts, and computer scientists, facilitating the translation of values into technical systems. First, we give a brief overview of how transparency is understood and defined in the LA literature. Second, we present a normative framework in the form of an interdisciplinary Criteria Catalogue for trustworthy LA systems. The Criteria Catalogue consists of seven abstract values, or as we call them core areas, that should be considered in the design, development, and implementation of LA tools. Transparency is one of these core values. In the next step, we demonstrate how transparency can be translated and operationalised into more specific and low-level elements by using an example of the Learners' Corner LA dashboard developed within the project "Learning Analytics – Students in Focus". In its current version, the Learners' Corner dashboard includes three tools: a planner tool, an activity tool, and a learning diary tool, which all aim to support the learning process and contribute to the understanding and improvement of students' ability to self-regulate their learning process. Furthermore, we adopt an LA human-centred design approach and involve students and teachers already in the creation and evaluation phases of the LA tools.

In addition, we present the results of a study that had a two-fold goal i) to understand students' information needs in relation to these LA tools and discover what information mostly enhances an LA tool's trustworthiness; ii) to evaluate our design choices for the introduction of three quick information buttons within the Learners' Corner. Lastly, we discuss how operationalising transparency as an integral value of LA systems can enhance trustworthiness and enable higher education learners to make more data-informed decisions.

2 Transparent Learning Analytics

The great relevance and role of transparency in LA have also been recognised by many scholars in the LA community. A literature review shows that a great share of the ethical frameworks for LA includes transparency as their value or principle. For instance, within their ethical framework for LA Slade and Prinsloo mention transparency in relation to data [11]. They state that higher education institutions (HEIs) should be transparent about the purposes for which they will use the data, the parties that will have access to it as well as how an individual's identity will be protected. Slade and Tait talk about transparency as a core issue that should be considered when using LA [12]. They refer to institutional transparency or being transparent towards students (and other stakeholders) regarding the purposes of learning analytics as well as the collection, analysis, and use of their data. This includes questions such as what type of data is (not) collected, how the data is used, and whether students can access it. Khalil and Ebner introduce transparency in their eight-dimensional LA constraints framework [7]. They emphasise the need to have transparent LA methods that could also be easily described to staff and students. One way to ensure transparency is to provide information about the collection, use and involvement of third parties when analysing students' information. This would enable students to better understand the methods that are used to track their performance as well as how the evaluation and interventions are processed. Pardo and Siemens discuss transparency as one of the principles of LA deployment [8]. According to them, transparency is about ensuring that students, instructors, and administrative staff have access to the description of the analytics process as well as are acquainted with the type of information that is collected, how it is collected, stored, and processed. The way data management procedures are presented also constitutes an important aspect of transparency. In this regard, the question of how historic data is handled once the students leave the institution becomes relevant for building trust. As part of their "Code of practice for learning analytics" Sclater and Bailey identify transparency and consent together as one important requirement [10]. Acting according to this requirement would mean that institutions clearly explain to staff and students what the objectives of LA are, what data is considered necessary to achieve those objectives, and what does not fall into that scope. Moreover, the data sources, the purposes of the analytics, those who have access to it, the metrics, the scope, and the data interpretation should be made explicit and clear. This also includes greater transparency of the processes that are used to produce the analytics or greater transparency of the algorithms.

3 Interdisciplinary Criteria Catalogue for Trustworthy LA Applications: Idea and Methodology

In this section, we present a normative framework in the form of an interdisciplinary Criteria Catalogue for trustworthy LA applications. The Criteria Catalogue is characterised by the following few ideas. First, it is student-centred and places students and their interests in the main focus. Second, the Criteria Catalogue is a user-friendly tool that could support students to assess the trustworthiness of LA applications that they use or would like to use. In this way, it gives more power in the hands of students in relation to their data. Third, even though ethical and data protection considerations are the pillars, the Criteria Catalogue is an output of four disciplines, including also pedagogy and computer science. Fourth, data protection is considered an integral part of the normative framework, nevertheless, the goal of the Criteria Catalogue is not to provide a mere translation of existing legal requirements but rather to go beyond the compliance level and investigate what more could be done in the design, implementation and use of

LA applications. When dealing with questions of trust and trustworthiness, complying with the bare legal minimum should be seen as just the first step. We cannot expect that legislation can cover all possible situations and can provide straightforward answers to all questions. As a result, ethics and ethical considerations can fill in this gap [3]. Last but not least, in the development of the Criteria Catalogue we are guided by the well-known approach "value sensitive design", which states that moral and societal values should be considered in all phases of a product, that is, in the design, implementation and deployment. Value sensitive design rests upon a three-partite methodology consisting of conceptual, empirical and technical investigation [4].

The Criteria Catalogue has a hierarchical structure. It consists of three levels as depicted in Fig. 1. On the first level are the core areas, which represent values that should be considered in the design, development, and implementation of LA tools. The core areas are very abstract, as a result, on the second level they are broken down into criteria. The criteria are more concrete, however, they are still not defined in such a manner that they can be easily measured. On the third level, the criteria are broken down into corresponding indicators.

Fig. 1. The hierarchical structure of the Criteria Catalogue.

The identification of the core areas was the result of an extensive literature review as well as interdisciplinary work. Following the identification of prominent ethical frameworks in the literature, e.g., Slade and Prinsloo [11], Drachsler and Greller [1], Slade and Tait [12], Khalil and Ebner [7], Kay, Korn and Oppenheim [6], The Open University [13], we created a matrix with the principles and terms that dominate these frameworks. This approach served the purpose to identify any potential gaps in the frameworks. This was followed by an in-depth ethical analysis of the most relevant ethical issues and challenges regarding the design and use of LA applications. All this led to the identification of seven core areas (transparency, privacy and good data governance, autonomy, non-discrimination, respect, responsibility and accountability, and protection). The core areas were defined from the perspective of each participating discipline of the project, i.e., ethics, law, pedagogy, computer science, and educational technology and in a next step merged into one interdisciplinary understanding [15].

4   Transparency as an Integral Value of LA Systems

Transparency is an instrumental value, which means it supports the realisation of other values such as privacy, responsibility or autonomy and is therefore connected to all core areas from the Criteria Catalogue. For instance, transparency enhances the protection of privacy in LA systems by making it clear what kind of data is being collected, how it is being used, and who has access to it. Furthermore, transparency fosters autonomy by enabling individuals to exert control over their personal data and its usage by LA systems. When an LA system is transparent, it is possible to understand how it works and how decisions are made, which allows for the identification of potential biases, errors, and unethical behaviour. This information can then be used to hold those responsible accountable for ensuring that the LA system is aligned with ethical, legal, and societal norms.

To set the ground for the translation and operationalisation process of transparency, in what follows, we will present the four disciplinary understandings of transparency and how they led to the interdisciplinary understanding of transparency that was used throughout the project. Once we have established the basis, we will demonstrate a few examples of criteria and indicators derived from the value "transparency".

From an ethical perspective, transparency stands for openness and communication regarding actions that others have legitimate expectations to be informed about. In the digital environment of relevance is information transparency, which implies that any information provided to others should be meaningful, veridical, comprehensible, accessible, and useful [14]. In the context of LA, transparency would demand openness regarding the goal of the LA tools, HEIs' activities with students' data, students' rights in relation to their data, measures that are taken to safeguard students' data, the roles and responsibilities of involved parties, and LA-based (algorithmic) decision-making processes.

From a legal perspective, the right and obligation to transparency often correlates with the legally enshrined right and obligation to information. In the context of LA, legal duties to provide information are anchored in higher education law at the national level as well as in data protection law at the EU level. Article 5(1)(a) of the General Data Protection Regulation (GDPR) [2] ensures the principle of transparency in that personal data must be processed in a way that is comprehensible to the data subject. For this purpose, a right to transparent information is generally established in Article 12, 13 and 14 of the GDPR.

From a pedagogy perspective, transparency in teaching-learning arrangements means transparency and comprehensibility of teaching/learning goals, processes, and results. This type of transparency helps students to understand what is expected of them and what they can expect to learn and achieve, thus contributing to a more effective and efficient educational experience [16]. Additionally, by promoting transparency in the teaching and learning process, educators can increase trust and accountability, fostering a more positive learning environment.

From a technical perspective, the concept of transparency concerns the procedures and processes used in technology and therefore in particular the question of how technology can be made transparent. This aspect of transparency is crucial in ensuring that the inner workings of technology, including algorithms and decision-making processes, are transparent and can be audited and reviewed. Additionally, technical transparency can also enhance users' understanding of and trust in technology, enabling informed and responsible usage. Transparency also revolves around the disclosure of and easy accessibility to information regarding data processing.

Table 1. depicts the four disciplinary understandings of transparency in LA and how they were merged into an interdisciplinary understanding.

Table 1. From disciplinary to interdisciplinary understanding of transparency

TRANSPARENCY	DISCIPLINARY UNDERSTANDING			
	Ethics	**Law**	**Pedagogy**	**Computer science**
	o Goals of LA tools o HEI's activities with students' data o Students' rights in relation to their data o Measures to safeguard students' data o Roles and responsibilities of involved parties o (Algorithmic) decision-making	o Right to transparent information o Obligation to information o Processing of personal data	o Teaching/ learning goals o Teaching/ learning processes o Teaching/ learning results o Expectations	o Technology procedures o Technology processes o Algorithms and decision-making processes o Data processing
	INTERDISCIPLINARY UNDERSTANDING			
	Learning analytics tools should be provided in line with HEIs's information obligations for the purpose of achieving greater information transparency. This includes communicating information to all relevant stakeholders that is meaningful, comprehensible, useful, user-friendly and easily accessible." [15]			

Based on both the disciplinary and interdisciplinary inputs, we developed corresponding criteria. These include for example:

✓	Clear information representation
✓	Clear instructions and explanations for using and understanding the LA tool
✓	Clearly specified processing of personal data
✓	Clear allocation of roles and duties
✓	GDPR compliance and strong privacy commitment
✓	Strong commitment to legal compliance
✓	Feedback, evaluation and complaint management

We then derived from these criteria even more detailed user-friendly indicators. These include:

> **Clear information representation**

(1) Clearly visible "Information-button" on the start page of the LA dashboard with all relevant information related to the technical, ethical, legal, and other aspects of the LA system

(2) Notified relevant stakeholders such as instructors, staff, institutes, centres or the dean's office about the use of LA

(3) Information understandable to students from all age groups as well as students with disabilities

(4) No "dark patterns" within LA

> **Clear instructions and explanations for using and understanding the LA tool**

(1) Provided "Instruction and explanation material" section within the "Information-button" containing information about the functionality of the tool

(2) Provided instruction and explanation material about the functionality of the tool, the delivered feedback and contact points

(3) Provided instruction and explanation material in several languages and formats

(4) Provided contact place for technical issues

(5) Timely, clearly and understandably communicated changes of the functionalities of the tool in the "Instruction and explanation material" section as well as via students' emails

(6) Accessible information material about the LA tool prior to the first use of the tool and outside of the tool dashboard

> **Clear allocation of roles and duties**

(1) Clear distribution of data protection, ethical, didactic and technical roles and responsibilities for the LA application

(2) Clear distribution of technical roles for the design, development, rollout and update processes of deployed LA systems

(3) Provided information about the obligations arising from the use of the LA application to other stakeholders including information about any changes to their obligations

(4) Easily accessible and well-illustrated responsibility matrix with information about the HEI's data protection, ethical, didactic and technical responsibilities

(5) Reminder for students about self-responsibility for their learning success

Feedback, evaluation and complaint management

(1) Information for students about consideration of their feedback

(2) Adequate mechanisms for handling complaints and problem solving that go beyond law enforcement and official judicial mechanisms offered in a three-step procedure, e.g.: a) FAQ, b) chat-bot, chat, contact person or centre, c) alternative dispute resolution (ADR).

In the following, we will show how some of these transparency-enhancing indicators can be embedded in the design and development of an LA system.

5 Learners' Corner – Learning Analytics Dashboard Prototype

The Learners' Corner is the learning analytics dashboard at course level developed by Graz University of Technology (TU Graz) within the "Learning Analytics – Students in Focus" project. The Learners' Corner dashboard includes tools to support students in regulating their learning process. Self-regulated students are proven to be effective learners that can set goals, plan, monitor their progress, reflect, and define strategies for the future [5, 9, 17–19]. Currently, the Learners' Corner dashboard includes several learning analytics tools, which aim to contribute to the understanding and improvement of students' ability to self-regulate their learning process. Even though our project focuses on students' needs and students' view of the dashboard, we also investigate the teachers' view to facilitate and support the teaching process and monitor the students' learning process.

The Learners' Corner LA dashboard is a prototype composed of three visual tools that aim to support students in acquiring or developing self-regulated learning (SRL) skills such as setting goals, planning, managing time, monitoring performance, comparing performance with peers, and reflecting. The three tools included in the students' interface are the planner, the activity, and the learning diary. The tools are designed with and evaluated by the experts of the interdisciplinary project team, the students, the teachers, and other educational stakeholders.

We follow a human-centred learning analytics (HCLA) approach, bringing to the forefront the needs of the users and the will to include them in the co-creation process to design the Learners' Corner dashboard. The involvement of several stakeholders ensures that users' needs are addressed and contributes to increasing transparency during the entire process. Also, as previously mentioned, our design is greatly affected by the Criteria Catalogue, e.g., the Learners' Corner dashboard will include an "information button" as described in Sect. 4. In addition, we will also include three quick information buttons for each tool to provide visual and contextualised information according to the guidelines provided by the Criteria Catalogue. These three quick information buttons provide i) general information about the tool and the data that is collected, ii) information about privacy, i.e., private (the individual-level data is private), aggregated (the individual-level data is combined with others generating high-level data which is shared), anonymised (the individual-level data is sanitised, meaning that first all personally identifiable information is removed and only then shared), shared (the individual-level data is shared), iii) information about the processing methods, i.e., statistics, artificial intelligence (AI).

Figure 2 depicts the Learners' Corner dashboard, highlighting the planned quick information buttons available for each of the learning analytics tools. In the example presented on the right, a student observing the buttons' icons should be able to immediately know that there is information available about the tool, that the data collected by the tool is shared, and that the data is processed using AI methods. The student can then click each button to access detailed information.

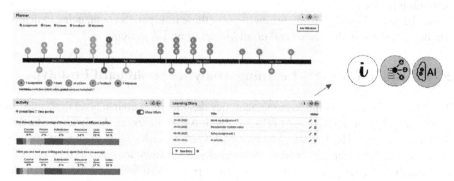

Fig. 2. Learners' Corner dashboard (left) composed of three learning analytics tools, i.e., the planner, the activity, and the learning diary. Highlighted the quick information buttons available for each of the tools (right).

Figure 3 presents the icons used for the quick information buttons, which are intended to provide visual information to the student. In the top row, one can see the icon for the general information quick button. In the middle row, there are four distinct icons, which represent the different data privacy status of the tool (private, aggregated, anonymised and shared). In the bottom row, there are two icons, which represent the different data processing methods. Note that we also decided to use different colour mode to support the user in distinguishing between the buttons and the different states.

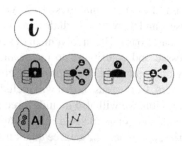

Fig. 3. Icons used in the three quick information buttons: general information about the tool (top row), information about data privacy (middle row), and information about the data processing methods (bottom row)

6 Study

Next, we present a study that had a two-fold goal i) to understand students' needs for information about these LA tools and discover which information was most valuable; ii) to evaluate our design choices regarding the quick information buttons within the Learners' Corner.

6.1 Research Methodology

For the purposes of our study, we conducted an online survey, which was developed using Google Forms and consisted of four sections. The first section informed the participants about the goals of the study, described the Learners' Corner dashboard and tools and included a textual description of the quick information buttons and images of the icons. The images were acquired using the prototype. The second section contained questions regarding the participants' demographics, e.g., gender, age-range, and study program. The third section contained questions about information needs and questions with regard to learning analytics tools. The fourth section contained questions about the quick information buttons and the icons' understandability. All questions were accompanied by a text and an image.

6.2 Participants

Twenty participants (7 male, 10 female, 2 diverse, 1 prefer not to answer) completed the online survey, six aged between 18 and 20, four aged between 21 and 23, three aged between 24 and 27, one aged between 27 and 30, five aged between 31 and 40, and one aged more than 41. The participants' attended different higher education institutions from two different countries and the study program varied, e.g., architecture, computer science, education, psychology, economics, veterinary, and history. Also, the participants attended distinct levels of study, i.e., bachelor, master, and PhD. Three of the students belong to the students' union. All participants in the study were volunteers and were recruited through an invitation email.

6.3 Procedure

Each participant accessed the online survey using the link they were provided with. The survey was available for two weeks, and it took between 10–15 min to answer it. After reading all the information about the study in section one, the participants were able to continue with the survey. In section two, the participants answered demographic questions. Next, the participants were presented with sections three and four which contained questions about information needs and the understandability of the quick information buttons. Before concluding the survey, the participants had the chance to write comments.

6.4   Results

In this section we present the findings of our study about the students' information needs and the design of the quick information buttons.

Information Needs Characterisation. We characterise students' information needs with regard to the use of educational digital tools and learning analytics.

Sources of information. The terms and conditions agreement outlines the terms that users must agree to if they want to interact with the digital tool. Typically reading this statement is the first contact with the system. We asked about the participants' level of agreement with the statement "I read the "terms and conditions" statement before I start using a new educational digital tool, app, or system". Nine participants (45%) stated that they read the "terms and conditions" statement before using an educational digital tool, app, or system. One participant (5%) neither agrees nor disagrees, and ten participants (50%) do not read the information (Strongly disagree - 6p, Disagree - 4). These results are worrisome as more than half of the participants do not read relevant information.

Information Seeking Behaviour. We wanted to investigate if the students seek information about privacy and ethical policies. Therefore, we asked the participants to convey their level of agreement with the following sentence "I always look for additional information about data privacy compliance and ethical policies when I use an educational tool, app, or system." Only five participants (25%) stated that they seek additional information about data privacy compliance and ethical policies. Six participants (30%) neither disagree nor agree, and nine participants (45%) stated that they do not seek additional information (strongly disagree – 5p, disagree – 4p). These results suggest that providing easy access to information may not be enough.

Valued Information. We asked the participants what type of information they consider important to have explicitly available in a learning analytics educational digital tool, app or system. The participants were able to select more than one answer and had the possibility to add new information needs. The three types of information that the participants valued the most are: information on how to correctly use the tools (10p), information on how the data is being processed (9p), and information about who can access the data (8p). See Fig. 4.

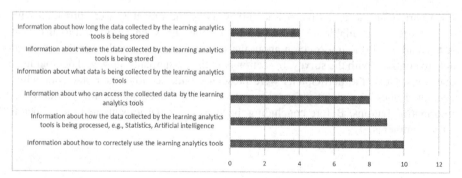

Fig. 4. The bar chart shows the type of information that the participants consider important to have explicitly available (participants could select more than one option).

Next, we asked the participants to indicate which of these types of information is the most important one. The three most voted types of information were: information on how to correctly use the tools (6p), information on how the data is being processed (4p), and information about where the data is being stored. See Fig. 5.

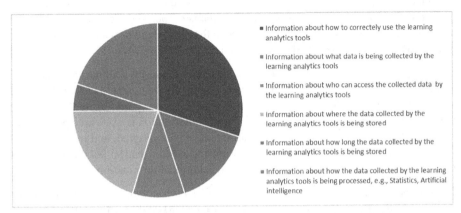

Fig. 5. The pie chart presents the information types considered the most important (participants could only select one option).

About the Quick Information Buttons. Next, we present findings related to the quick information buttons and the icons used for the buttons.

Perceived Usefulness. We asked about the participants' level of agreement with the statement "I find the three quick information buttons useful". Twelve participants (60%) consider that the presence of quick information buttons is useful, six participants (30%) neither agree nor disagree, one participant disagrees (5%), and one strongly disagrees (5%). These results validate the design choice of combining the visual information (icons) and the easy access to information via the quick information buttons.

Function of the Three Quick Information Buttons. We presented an image of the three quick information buttons (random icons were used for each button) and asked the participants what kind of information they would expect to be provided with when clicking each of the buttons. Fourteen participants (70%) identified correctly the first button as the one that provides access to general information about the tool. Twelve participants (60%) correctly identified the second button as the one that provides information about data privacy. Thirteen participants (65%) correctly identified the third button as the one that provides information about the data processing methods. These results are very promising because the participants did not receive information about the function of the buttons and were still able to intuitively recognise their function.

About the Icons Used for the Quick Information Buttons. The icons are an essential part of many interfaces, as they are visual symbols that represent objects and actions. By using icons as means of visual communication, we need to ensure that the users are able to decode their meaning in an easy and quick manner. Therefore, we were interested to know how the icons would be perceived. Recall that we did not provide any explanation of the icons' meaning prior to the questionnaire.

Perceived Understanding of the Icons. We presented an image of all the icons used and asked about the participants' level of agreement with the statement "I can easily understand the meaning of the quick information icons". Eleven participants (55%) stated that they can understand the meaning of the quick information icons. Three participants (15%) neither agree nor disagree, five participants (5%) disagree, and one participant (5%) strongly disagrees. These results are promising as more than half of the participants think they understand all the icons without any additional information.

Understanding the Icon Used for the General Quick Information Button. We presented an image of the general quick information button and asked the participants to identify its meaning. Twenty students (100%) were able to correctly identify the icon's meaning, which suggests that no alterations are required. This result is not surprising as we used a well-known icon to represent information. The understanding of an icon depends on previous experience and therefore the use of familiar icons is advised.

Understanding the Four Icons Used in the Data Privacy Button. We presented an image of all the data privacy icons and asked the participants to identify their meanings. Fifteen participants (75%) correctly identified the icon indicating that the data is private. Ten participants (50%) correctly identified the icon indicating that the data is aggregated. Fifteen participants (75%) correctly identified the icon indicating that the data is anonymised, and ten participants (45%) correctly identified the icon indicating that the data is shared. The participants had to consider four different icons and concepts (i.e., private, aggregated, anonymized, and shared) without any previous information or training, which may explain why the participants' performance decreased. Also, these results show that the icons representing the state aggregated and the state shared may need to be improved and complemented with text labels to overcome ambiguity and inform the meaning of the icon in the context.

Understanding the Two Icons Used in the Data Processing Methods Button. Eighteen participants (90%) correctly identified the icon indicating that statistic methods were used, and eighteen participants (90%) were able to identify that AI methods were used. These results confirm that the data processing methods icons are correctly understood.

Learnability and Effort. We asked about the participants' level of agreement with the statement "I think I need to make an effort to understand the meaning of the quick information icons". Eight participants (40%, strongly agree – 2p, agree – 6p) consider that they would need to make an effort to understand the meaning of the icons. Six participants (30%) neither agree nor disagree, and six participants (30%, strongly disagree – 2p, agree – 4p) disagree that understanding the icons would be an effort.

Aesthetic. We asked about the participants' level of agreement with the statement "I find the quick information icons aesthetically pleasing". Thirteen participants (65%, 2 strongly agree – 2p, agree – 11p) considered the icons used in the quick information buttons aesthetically pleasant. Five participants (25%) neither agree nor disagree, one participant (5%) disagrees, and one participant (5%) strongly disagrees. It is known that users are more likely to interact with icons that are aesthetically pleasing, therefore, we may consider making another iteration to improve the icons.

7   Discussion

The findings demonstrated in this work suggest that important information is not reaching out to all students. Students may avoid reading the information before starting to use the tools, and many also admit not to seek information at a later stage. As a consequence, many students are poorly informed about relevant issues, e.g., data privacy. It was not our goal to identify the reasons why, however, we can postulate that students' attitudes and behaviour may be related to reasons, such as: 1) the complexity of the language used in the documentation (e.g., formal, legal terms); 2) the extensive amount of time required to read the information as these statements tend to be long; 3) the timing when the information is offered, typically reading the information is just an obstacle before starting to use the tool, so one just answers "yes" to overcome the block; 4) and the relevance of the information in the context.

The inclusion of quick information buttons in the Learners' Corner design may reach out to some of these students. The quick information buttons' goal is to convey the most important information in a visual and contextualised manner. The use of icons and the possibility of clicking for detail was considered useful and aesthetically pleasing. We believe that students will be able to recognise the privacy status and the data processing method at a glance, once they are acquainted with the icons. We will improve the icons and add text labels to facilitate their understanding. Additionally, we are considering including a step-by-step guide about how to access and use the different information buttons. In future works, we may consider the inclusion of other types of visual representations, such as pictures or memes.

Other key findings are related to the information needs of the students. Students would like to have easily available information about how to use the tools, information about the privacy status, and information about the processing methods. These results agree well with our initial criteria for the content provided in the quick information buttons.

Overall, the study results reinforce the belief that the inclusion of the quick information buttons approach is a promising alternative to the single information button. Moreover, in order to enhance trust and trustworthiness, the inclusion of such information buttons should always be accompanied by content that is clear, understandable and user-friendly.

8 Conclusion

In this paper, we focused on transparency as an integral value of trustworthy LA systems. After providing four disciplinary (ethical, legal, didactical, and technical) and an interdisciplinary understanding of transparency in the context of LA, we tackled the question of how transparency can be translated and operationalised into more concrete technical design requirements. We presented the results of a study, which had the goal of better understanding students' information needs in relation to LA tools, as well as evaluating the design of quick information buttons within our Learners' Corner LA dashboard. This is just one example of a value translation. The literature on LA abounds in frameworks consisting of various core values or principles. While defining such frameworks is an important step in understanding what values or principles matter and hence should be promoted in the design and implementation of LA tools, nevertheless, this is just a first step. More efforts should be made to translate and operationalise those values and principles and bring them to the level of design requirements that can be easily implemented in LA tools.

Acknowledgements. The developed work presented here was co-funded by the Federal Ministry of Education, Science and Research, Austria, as part of the 2019 call for proposals for digital and social transformation in higher education for the project "Learning Analytics" (2021–2024, partner organizations: the Graz University of Technology, the University of Vienna, and the University of Graz).

References

1. Drachsler, H., Greller, W.: Privacy and analytics - it's a DELICATE issue. A checklist for trusted learning analytics. In: Proceedings of the Sixth International Conference on Learning Analytics & Knowledge. Association for Computing Machinery, pp. 89–98. New York, NY, USA (2016). https://doi.org/10.1145/2883851.2883893

2. European Union. Consolidated text: Regulation (EU) 2016/679 of the European Parliament and of the Council of 27 April 2016 on the protection of natural persons with regard to the processing of personal data and on the free movement of such data, and repealing Directive 95/46/EC (General Data Protection Regulation) (Text with EEA relevance). RL 2016/679/EU (2016)
3. Floridi, L.: Soft ethics and the governance of the digital. Philos. Technol. **31**(1), 1–8 (2018). https://doi.org/10.1007/s13347-018-0303-9
4. Friedman, B., Kahn, P.H., Borning, A., Huldtgren, A.: Value sensitive design and information systems. In: Doorn, N., Schuurbiers, D., van de Poel, I., Gorman, M.E. (eds.) Early engagement and new technologies: Opening up the laboratory. PET, vol. 16, pp. 55–95. Springer, Dordrecht (2013). https://doi.org/10.1007/978-94-007-7844-3_4
5. Harris, K.R., Graham, S.: Programmatic intervention research: illustrations from the evolution of self-regulated strategy development. Learn. Disabil. Q. **22**(4), 251–262 (1999). https://doi.org/10.2307/1511259
6. Kay, D., Korn, N., Oppenheim, C.: Legal, Risk and Ethical Aspects of Analytics in Higher Education. CETIS (2012)
7. Khalil, M., Ebner, M.: Learning analytics: principles and constraints. In Proceedings of World Conference on Educational Multimedia, Hypermedia and Telecommunications 2015, pp. 1326–1336. AACE, Chesapeake, VA (2015)
8. Pardo, A., Siemens, G.: Ethical and privacy principles for learning analytics. Br. J. Edu. Technol. **45**(3), 438–450 (2014)
9. Pintrich, P.R.: Chapter 14—The role of goal orientation in self-regulated learning. In: Boekaerts, M., Pintrich, P.R., Zeidner, M. (eds.) Handbook of Self-Regulation, pp. 451–502. Academic Press (2000). https://doi.org/10.1016/B978-012109890-2/50043-3
10. Sclater, N., Bailey, P.: Code of Practice for Learning Analytics (2018)
11. Slade, S., Prinsloo, P.: Learning analytics - ethical issues and dilemmas. Am. Behav. Sci. **57**, 1509–1528 (2013). https://doi.org/10.1177/0002764213479366
12. Slade, S., Tait, A.: Global Guidelines: Ethics in Learning Analytics (2019)
13. The Open University. Policy on Ethical Use of Student Data for Learning Analytics (September 2014). https://help.open.ac.uk/documents/policies/ethical-use-of-student-data/files/22/ethical-use-of-student-data-policy.pdf. Accessed 10 Feb 2023
14. Turilli, M., Floridi, L.: The ethics of information transparency. Ethics Inf. Technol. **11**, 105–112 (2009)
15. Veljanova, H., Barreiros, C., Gosch, N., Staudegger, E., Ebner, M., Lindstaedt, S.: Towards trustworthy learning analytics applications: an interdisciplinary approach using the example of learning diaries. In: HCI International 2022 Posters: 24th International Conference on Human-Computer Interaction, HCII 2022, Virtual Event, June 26–July 1, 2022, Proceedings, Part III, 138–145. Cham: Springer International Publishing (2022). https://doi.org/10.1007/978-3-031-06391-6_19
16. Winkelmes, M.-A.: Transparency in teaching: faculty share data and improve students' learning. Lib. Educ. **99** (2013)
17. Zimmerman, B.J.: Self-regulated learning and academic achievement: an overview. Educ. Psychol. **25**, 3–17 (1990). https://doi.org/10.1207/s15326985ep2501_2

18. Zimmerman, B., Schunk, D.: Self-Regulated Learning and Academic Achievement: Theoretical Perspectives. Lawrence Erlbaum Associates, Mahwah, NJ (2001)
19. Zimmerman, B.J.: Self-regulated learning: theories, measures, and outcomes. In: Wright, J.D. (ed.) International Encyclopedia of the Social & Behavioral Sciences (Second Edition). pp. 541–546. Elsevier, Oxford (2015). https://doi.org/10.1016/B978-0-08-097086-8.26060-1

Towards Personalized Instruction: Co-designing a Teacher-Centered Dashboard for Learning Engagement Analysis in Blended Learning Environments

Han Zhang[1,2] ⓘ, Xu Sun[1,3](✉) ⓘ, Yanhui Zhang[1], Qingfeng Wang[1], and Cheng Yao[2,4]

[1] University of Nottingham Ningbo, China, 199 Taikang East Road, Ningbo 315100, China
{hvxhz2,xu.sun,yanhui.zhang}@nottingham.edu.cn
[2] Ningbo Research Institute, Zhejiang University, 1 Qianhu South Road, Ningbo 315100, China
yaoch@zju.edu.cn
[3] Nottingham Ningbo China Beacons of Excellence Research and Innovation Institute, 211 Xingguang Road, Ningbo 315100, China
[4] Zhejiang University, 866 Yuhangtang Road, Hangzhou 310058, China

Abstract. Learning engagement is an important factor in academic success and instructional quality. In authentic settings, analyzing learner engagement status can be challenging due to the complexity of its multidimensional construct. It requires constant monitoring of multimodal engagement indicators (cognitive-level indicators, e.g., effort, emotional-level indicators, e.g., positive/negative emotions) and individualized pacing of learners, identifying when and who needs assistance, as well as making pedagogical strategy that matches the needs of the learners (or group of learners). This study combines user requirements with computational techniques to construct a multimodal learning engagement analysis framework in the blended setting. In addition, a teacher-faced dashboard prototype is developed to statistically summarize and visualize multimodal indicators in a way that enables teachers to deploy personalized instruction schemes. The teachers' perspectives discussed in this study portray the great potential of introducing Artificial Intelligent (AI)-augmented models and visual analytics techniques aimed at deploying personalized instructions in the blended learning environment.

Keywords: Learning Engagement · Multimodal Data · Human-centered Design · Dashboard · Visualization

1 Introduction

Research has shown that learning engagement, defined as the involvement of the student's cognitive and emotional energy to accomplish learning tasks, is correlated with desired learning outcomes [1, 8, 21]. While early research has concentrated on linking engagement with drop-out rates, now engagement is understood more as a "process", calling for a deeper comprehension of trajectories of engagement status and its relationship to learning gain. However, effective measurement of engagement during the

© The Author(s), under exclusive license to Springer Nature Switzerland AG 2023
P. Zaphiris and A. Ioannou (Eds.): HCII 2023, LNCS 14040, pp. 563–574, 2023.
https://doi.org/10.1007/978-3-031-34411-4_38

learning process can be complex, especially in blended learning [8]. Blended learning is the thoughtful integration of face-to-face and online instruction, combining the humanness and spontaneous nature of face-to-face activities with the diversified learning pathways of online learning, which might more fully engage learners [8, 13].

Based on the conceptual framework proposed by Harverson and Graham [8], learner engagement in blended learning environments is a multidimensional construct, with various types of indicators. Traditionally, learning engagement is commonly investigated through self-reporting, teacher scoring, observational checklist, and interviews represented by several empirical surveys, such as National Student Engagement Survey, Classroom Survey of Student Engagement [8, 13]. Though these measurements have shown the personal and contextual factors of learning engagement, they have validity issues including (1) response biases of self-report, (2) high time-costing, (3) subjective judgment of teacher scoring and observation, (4) insufficient contextual information and (5) limited application in larger courses [3, 8, 13, 14]. Recently, with the growing emergence of computational methods and sensing technology, data-driven, objective measurements of learning engagement are preferred by researchers. For example, many studies have measured engagement in learning by collecting learning log data [1, 8, 20]. Goldberg et al. used an eye-tracking system to distinguish whether learners were attentive or not [7] while video data can tell us about learners' emotional engagement [8]. Compared to unimodal analysis, multimodal learning analytics can portray complex learning experiences by using a broad set of complementary metrics [8]. Research from Krithika and Priya used eye movements and head rotation to infer levels of engagement in the online environment [12]. Abnormal head rotation or long-time inability to capture facial information and eye movements indicate that the learner is not interested and bored with the content. In the work of Goldberg et al. [7], they developed a machine learning algorithm combining head posture, gaze features, and facial expressions to estimate real-time engagement. The outcomes of the proposed algorithm achieved moderate to high correlations with students' self-ratings. This finding has proved that multimodal learning data analysis can reduce the burden entailed by manual data gathering and empower teachers to monitor and identify at-risk learners in multi-task teaching scenarios.

Learning Analytic (LA) dashboard is defined as "a single display that aggregates different indicators about learners, learning processes, and learning contexts into one or multiple visualizations" [18]. LA dashboards and AI models that provide actionable analytics based on rich process data, show the potential to support teachers in multidimensional decision-making, timely feedback, and personalized instruction [1, 3, 5]. To date, several tools (e.g., an affective report card and a dashboard [1, 2, 4, 11]) were designed to learn about learners' level of engagement. However, despite of these efforts, teachers often do not adopt these tools due to little consistency or specificity, and insufficient inclusion of behavioral indicators for engagement status analysis [10]. In addition, these tools either do not fit class reality or are not suitable for the teachers' pedagogical preferences and habits, resulting in a high attrition rate [22]. Therefore, participatory or co-design processes that involve teachers throughout the development process may be a reliable approach for designing user-centered LA tools that can meaningfully enhance teachers' interpretability of multimodal indicators and gain their trust [2, 17].

To achieve this, it is critical to combine AI-enabled techniques with the emotional and cognitive indicators of learning engagement analysis, the teachers' practical needs, and understand how the design of the dashboard can be aligned with teachers' pedagogical intentions. Our research followed a co-design methodology with teachers to develop a learning analytics dashboard that will enhance their ability to explore learning engagement from multimodal indicators that are tailored to their personalized pedagogical strategies. The study sought to answer the following research questions:

- **RQ1:** What types of learning indicators can assist teachers in analyzing engagement status and how to collect these indicators in the blended learning setting?
- **RQ2:** How can these indicators defined in RQ1 be visualized on a dashboard so that personalized instruction can be effectively integrated into their teaching practices?

Therefore, we proposed an AI-augmented framework for integrating multimodal indicators of learning engagement in the blended learning setting based on the domain and user inquiry from 11 teachers. We also co-designed a teacher-centered dashboard specifically for learning engagement analysis, which presents multimodal learning behavioral data from both cognitive and emotional levels. With this learning analytics dashboard, teachers can adaptively adjust instruction strategies that are tailored to learners' engagement status based on multimodal, multi-dimensional analysis.

2 Co-design Methodology

To target the research questions, we employed a broad range of design research approaches to achieve teacher-centered design throughout this study. At a high level, our design process followed the LATUX workflow for designing and deploying awareness tools in technology-enhanced learning tools [9, 15]. As described in the following sections, choices of methods at each phase of our iterative design process were made adaptively, based on the research/design goal at a given stage of the process. A brief overview of the overall design process, illustrating major design phases and examples of methods used at each phase, is presented below.

(1) **Initial domain and user inquiry:** We delivered semi-structured interviews and re-enactment interviews with teachers, and field observations in authentic blended learning environments to explore design alternatives.
(2) **Data collection and preparation:** With the help of computational models such as computer vision algorithms and deep learning models, we developed an AI-augmented framework to capture real-time multimodal learning data in blended learning settings. Then, we deployed the framework in a mock-up experiment with several researchers and teachers for usability feedback.
(3) **Iterative dashboard prototyping:** We gradually increased the fidelity of prototypes through several informal discussions with teachers, using methods including participatory sketching, concept mapping and functionality testing.
(4) **Pilot implementation and evaluation:** We conducted semi-structured interviews and surveys of teachers' experience/perception of the dashboard, as well as field observations of student learning performances.

3 Domain and User Inquiry

The first step of our research focused on two main issues: investigating the problem domain and understanding targeted users' needs. The approach to inform our design was user- and domain-centric, focusing on identifying learning behavioral indicators critical to students' learning engagement status. Our initial semi-structured interviews were based on the theoretical frameworks proposed by Halverson and Graham [8] which consider learning engagement as being composed of two dimensions: emotional and cognitive. We first conducted preliminary semi-structured interviews with 11 CS peer tutors, focusing on their practical challenges and expectations regarding to learning engagement monitoring in blended learning settings. In particular, we collected their perspectives on the integration of multimodal indicators in their process-oriented educational activities. To help them better understand the technical details, we presented the automated learning behavior-tracking applications offered by eye-trackers and computer vision models. We then carried out a re-enactment interview, where a specific use case was designed to bring interviewees into an authentic AI-augmented teaching scenario. Both interviews were conducted by the first author between March to April, 2022, in the school building of Xinxiang Vocational and Technical College. We analyzed the audio and video recordings using NVivo 12 with inductive open coding, which aimed to determine the common needs in supporting teachers. After revising the results, we summarized the generated requirements in three aspects.

Learning Engagement Monitoring: Teachers characterize learners' cognitive and emotional engagement in learning activities as demonstrated through actions, expressions, language, physical changes, psychological changes, and self-reports. They stressed the importance of multi-source, multimodal learning behavior analysis for monitoring learning engagement. Several of them mentioned a lack of information (i.e., only head pose or self-report) preventing them from identifying accurately students that have faced difficulties in focusing on learning activities. Moreover, teachers reported that the inner relations between cognitive and emotional indicators, as well as the relations between learning engagement and learning gain, are 'hidden' in direct observation, which might be difficult for them to grasp in sophisticated teaching tasks.

Personalized Instruction: Teachers often use instructions to congratulate, encourage, remind, or alert learners in class. They highlighted the complexity of using the existing online learning platforms to keep track of learner engagement and to pinpoint at-risk learners, which hindered effective feedback and personalized instruction with learners [16]. Also, teachers illustrated different granularities (i.e., topic-level, concept-level, or temporal-level) of learning activities that should be considered in learning engagement monitoring. Specifically, teachers expressed interest in knowing which topics or activities did not engage students, or which proved to be the most boring to focus on, in order to adjust their pedagogical strategies in learning activities design.

Context of Use: We identified distinctive technological features of AI-augmented blended learning settings: data-driven teaching decision-making, instantaneous engagement evaluation, and interactive visualization of multimodal indicators. For multimodal data collection, teachers highlighted that non-invasive, easy-to-use approaches are preferred. In this way, different learning indicators and sensing techniques should be considered for application according to the nature of online and traditional learning.

Based on the factors derived from the interviews, we proposed a multimodal learning engagement analysis model in the blended learning environment:

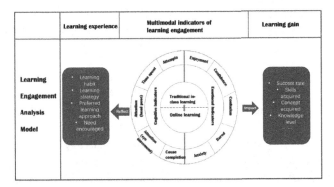

Fig. 1. AI-augmented framework for multimodal learning engagement analysis

4   Multimodal Data Structure

The second effort is AI-augmented multimodal data collection in blended learning settings. According to the framework (Fig. 1), we propose the following indicators to describe learner engagement (Table 1):

Log Data: The dashboard collected student performance through various types of log data involving attempts, time on tasks, course completion, success rate, and misconception. All log data are generated from the online java learning system, *JavaProgrammingPractice*, which teachers have already integrated into their teaching routines.

Facial Data: The proposed AI-augmented framework captured students' facial expressions (enjoyment, confidence, confusion, boredom, and anxiety), which highlight students' emotional engagement, using a deep learning model for facial expression detection [4]. To be specific, in the online learning system, the integrated webcams were adopted as a probe for capturing facial emotional data while in traditional class settings, the Kinect sensors were set in front of desks to support facial emotion detection.

Head Pose Data: The head pose data were only collected in traditional face-to-face learning situations. Depth cameras embedded in the Kinect sensors were used to estimate head pose (i.e., head-up, head-down, and head-tilted) during the live sessions [24]. Attention time is calculated by the proportion of head-up time to total activity time.

Eye-Tracking Data: The eye movements were tracked to determine gaze points and gaze duration in online sessions, so that to determine students' status as focused or

Table 1. Summary of multimodal learning data collection

Type of use	Indicators	Description	Data type
Cognitive indicators of learning engagement	Attempts	Total count of the submission times of specific learning activities	Log data
	Time spent	Total amount of time spent on specific learning activities	Log data
	Course completion	Activity-level measures of persistence	Log data
	Attention time (online)	Real-time trajectory of eye location	Eye-tracking data
	Attention time (in-class)	Real-time trajectory of head pose	Head pose data
Emotional indicators of learning engagement	Emotion state	Real-time detection of facial emotions	Facial expression category
Learning gain	Success rate	Overall success rate of specific learning activities	Log data
	Estimated knowledge level	Self-reported personal knowledge, skills, and attitude toward specific learning activities	Self-reported data

distracted. For example, if the students' gaze points were fixed on the screen, he/she was classified as attentive to the lecture whilst if the eye points were looking elsewhere (i.e., the student was looking at the blank area of the screen), the student was categorized as distracted. Therefore, the attention time in the online session is calculated by the proportion of attentive gaze duration to total session time. The real-time eye movement trajectories are collected through a portable eye tracker (Tobbi Eye Tracker 5), which can be easily equipped on personal computer devices.

Self-reported Data: Self-reported survey was delivered after each learning activity, aiming to gather estimated knowledge gain, attention level, and attitude toward learning procedures and teaching strategies.

5   Iterative Prototyping

Following the co-design methodology, we derived the following design goals from the initial user studies and architecture of the dashboard.

DG1: Offer at-a-glance indicators to facilitate monitoring of learner engagement over time. This dashboard is designed to support teachers to understand what is going on, juxtaposing the state of learning gain and corresponding engagement indicators of students.

DG2: Allow teachers to adjust the granularity of the visualized indicators according to their pedagogical strategies, i.e., concept-level, and topic-level.

DG3: Incorporate indicators based on learning engagement status and desired to learn outcomes, i.e., overall success rate. Teachers emphasized the need for close monitoring of specific learners or groups of learners in order to understand what they should focus their instructions on.

Aligning with the teacher requirements and design goals, the following figure shows the data architecture of the dashboard (Fig. 2).

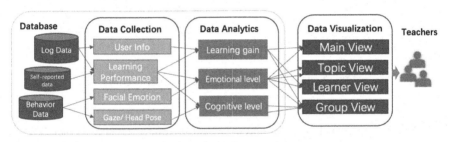

Fig. 2. An overview of the architecture of the dashboard

A major challenge in designing the dashboard was to condense all the information required into a small visual space so that teachers could receive clear and direct information about learners' engagement status from an emotional and cognitive viewpoint, as well as their corresponding learning performances [6, 19]. Following the "overview first, zoom and filter, then details on-demand" [5], the iterative prototyping process involved 5 teachers defining the structure of the information in four different views, allowing teachers to drill down for detailed information as needed. With the help of computational models and visual analytics techniques, we presented multimodal indicators and statistical learning features in the teacher-centered dashboard.

Figure 3 portrays the overview of the proposed prototype of the dashboard. We combined textual, visual, and color encoding when visualizing the indicators to facilitate glanceable exploring of the types and relationships between different views, learning groups, and indicators. The dashboard aggregates the real-time information at two levels of granularity: per week and per topic as well as two dimensions of engagement indicators: cognitive-level and emotional-level indicators. Different groups of students are clustered based on the pre-defined instruction scheme, which allows teachers to adjust the indicators within the clustering model. A radar graph is adopted to display multi-dimensional data so that instructors can understand the weaknesses and strengths of specific students and the whole class on average. In the header of the dashboard, we designed a teacher-controlled panel that consists of several dropdown boxes to facilitate filtering and navigating specific learners or groups of learners.

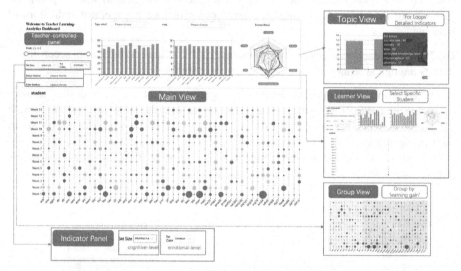

Fig. 3. The overview of the dashboard user interface.

Main View: This view (Fig. 3) presents overall information to monitor learners' engagement status at the class level during a semester (**DG1**). Each column represents one specific student while each row shows the engagement indicators in a specific week. To show how multi-variables affect learning engagement jointly, the dashboard uses size and color in the dot matrix to show different indicators. The indicator panel enables teachers to explore cognitive- and emotional-level indicators of learning engagement. Given the nature of continuous data type, we select "size" to display cognitive-level indicators, number of attempts, time on tasks, course completion, and attention time. For example, if teachers select the size as attention time, the larger the circle, the more attention time learners have spent on each learning activity. Meanwhile, different colors are designed to show different emotion categories, enjoyment (blue), confidence (light blue), confusion (yellow), boredom (orange), and anxiety (red). As we can see from the main view, learners are easily feeling anxiety in the first week of the semester.

Topic View: This view statistically visualizes the learning gain and engagement status from a different granularity, topic level (**DG2**). Since in most cases, the teachers arrange each teaching week as a unit module, sometimes the boundaries throughout the term get diffused. According to our survey, more than half of teachers hope to check the learners' learning situation in a certain learning unit (such as if-else, while loops, arrays, etc.). In the topic panel, bar charts are adopted to present the learning gain (overall success rate and estimated knowledge level) while the radar graph aims to show detailed information about average engagement indicators of selected topics. By using the topic-level information, teachers can infer which topics may have a higher attrition rate and which topics can be easily mastered by most learners, leading to the data-driven teaching decision-make.

Learner View: To let teachers identify specific students quickly, especially in a very large class, the learner view allows users to select a learner from a drop-down list (**DG3**). Then, teachers can easily see the evolution of specific students during the whole academic term by examining the indicators along the different rows (**DG1**), in a similar way to the Main view. The topic view will adaptively summarize the strengths and weaknesses at the topic level and concept level of the chosen learner (**DG2**).

Group View: Our clustering method is aimed to divide learners into homogeneous groups based on the pre-defined instruction scheme, learning gain. This view displays the cluster of learners as the high learning gain group, medium learning gain group and low learning gain group (**DG3**). The indicators within each group can provide rich information about relationships between cognitive- and emotional-level engagement status and learning gain, altering their pedagogical strategies in a personalized way.

6 Pilot Study and Evaluation

We conducted a four-month field study with 11 teachers to capture teachers' experience and perception of the dashboard, and how it may assist them in informing their personalized instructions. Meanwhile, we organized a workshop with teachers to define a personalized instruction scheme that explains each cluster in a way that is both pedagogically meaningful and can be generated automatically. Then, we tested the functionalities of the prototype by using data from a 13-week programming college class taken by 55 undergrad students. All students are required to use the online java practicing system (*JavaProgrammingPractice*) integrated with an AI-augmented engagement (real-time facial emotion and attention) detection framework using live videos of students, which assesses the engagement status using both behavioral data, log data, and self-reported data. This study has passed the ethical assessment at Xinxiang Vocational and Technical College.

To evaluate the effectiveness of the visualization interface, we conducted another run of interviews with 5 teachers, who had not participated in the design process. Teachers expressed their views on different teaching tasks by using the proposed dashboard (Fig. 4).

To sum up, most teachers reported that this dashboard can serve as a powerful scaffold of understanding learners' states of engagement. By monitoring and capturing learning indicators, the dashboard can support teachers to realize whether their pedagogical designs are helping students to get involved with the course.

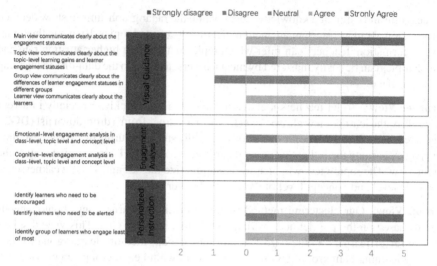

Fig. 4. Diverging bar chart of usability ratings of the proposed dashboard

7 Conclusion

In conclusion, we have exemplified the way to involve non-technical stakeholders in AI-augmented learning analytics dashboard design. Following the co-design methodology, we collected requirements from teachers, which enables us to establish a multimodal learning engagement analysis framework in blended learning settings. Based on the framework, we proposed a learning analytics dashboard, which integrates multimodal cognitive and emotional indicators in the learning behavior analysis, presenting a more holistic understanding of how learning engagement may impact the overall learning performances. In addition, this dashboard enables the multimodal learning indicators to be visualized in a way that combines the strength of computational models and teacher-controlled visual analysis based on their pedagogical strategy. According to our evaluation results, this dashboard can serve as an assessment tool to evaluate how the multimodal engagement indicators from both cognitive and emotional aspects, correlate with overall learning gain in the blended learning environments. In this way, this tool may shed light on the design of pedagogical intervention toward learning engagement and on how teacher-centered dashboard could better bridge online and in-class learning.

Acknowledgement. This work was supported by the first Batch of 2021 MOE of PRC Industry-University Collaborative Education Program (Program No. 202101042006, Kingfar-CES "Human Factors and Ergonomics" Program).

References

1. Carrillo, R., Renaud, C., Prié, Y., Lavoué, É.: Dashboard for monitoring student engagement in mind mapping activities. In: 2017 IEEE 17th International Conference on Advanced Learning Technologies (ICALT), pp. 433–437 (2017). https://doi.org/10.1109/ICALT.2017.100

2. Dourado, R.A., Rodrigues, R.L., Ferreira, N., Mello, R. F., Gomes, A. S., Verbert, K.: A teacher-facing learning analytics dashboard for process-oriented feedback in online learning. In: LAK21: 11th International Learning Analytics and Knowledge Conference, pp. 482–489 (2021)
3. Ez-Zaouia, M.: Teacher-centered dashboards design process. In: 2nd International Workshop on EXplainable Learning Analytics, Companion Proceedings of the 10th International Conference on Learning Analytics & Knowledge LAK20 (2020, March)
4. Ez-zaouia, M., Lavoué, E.: EMODA: A tutor oriented multimodal and contextual emotional dashboard. In: Proceedings of the Seventh International Learning Analytics & Knowledge Conference, pp. 429–438 (2017). https://doi.org/10.1145/3027385.3027434
5. Ez-zaouia, M., Tabard, A., Lavoué, E.: PROGDASH: lessons learned from a learning dashboard In-the-wild: In: Proceedings of the 12th International Conference on Computer Supported Education, pp. 105–117 (2020). https://doi.org/10.5220/0009424801050117
6. Fernandez Nieto, G.M., Kitto, K., Buckingham Shum, S., Martinez-Maldonado, R.: Beyond the learning analytics dashboard: alternative ways to communicate student data insights combining visualisation, narrative and storytelling. In: LAK22: 12th International Learning Analytics and Knowledge Conference, pp. 219–229 (2022). https://doi.org/10.1145/3506860.350 6895
7. Goldberg, P., et al.: Attentive or Not? Toward a machine learning approach to assessing students' visible engagement in classroom instruction. Educ. Psychol. Rev. **33**(1), 27–49 (2019). https://doi.org/10.1007/s10648-019-09514-z
8. Halverson, L.R., Graham, C.R.: Learner engagement in blended learning environments: a conceptual framework. Online Learn. **23**(2) (2019). https://doi.org/10.24059/olj.v23i2.148
9. Hillaire, G.E., Schlichtmann, G., Ducharme, K.: Prototyping visual learning analytics guided by an educational theory informed goal. J. Learn. Anal. **3**(3), 115–142 (2016). https://doi.org/10.18608/jla.2016.33.7
10. Holstein, K., Hong, G., Tegene, M., McLaren, B. M., Aleven, V.: The classroom as a dashboard: Co-designing wearable cognitive augmentation for K-12 teachers. In: Proceedings of the 8th International Conference on Learning Analytics and Knowledge, pp. 79–88 (2018). https://doi.org/10.1145/3170358.3170377
11. Johnson, J., Conderman, G., Van Laarhoven, T., Liberty, L.: Wearable technologies: a new way to address student anxiety. Kappa Delta Pi Record **58**(3), 124–129 (2022). https://doi.org/10.1080/00228958.2022.2076531
12. Krithika, L.B., Priya, G.L.: Student emotion recognition system (SERS) for E-learning improvement based on learner concentration metric. Procedia Comput. Sci. **85**, 767–776 (2016)
13. Lechuga, C.G., Doroudi, S.: Three algorithms for grouping students: a bridge between personalized tutoring system data and classroom pedagogy. Int. J. Artif. Intell. Educ (2022). https://doi.org/10.1007/s40593-022-00309-y
14. Li, H., Ding, W., Liu, Z.: Identifying At-Risk K-12 students in multimodal online environments: a machine learning approach (arXiv:2003.09670). arXiv. http://arxiv.org/abs/2003.09670 (2020)
15. Martinez-Maldonado, R., Pardo, A., Mirriahi, N., Yacef, K., Kay, J., Clayphan, A.: The LATUX workflow: designing and deploying awareness tools in technology-enabled learning settings. In: Proceedings of the Fifth International Conference on Learning Analytics and Knowledge, pp. 1–10. https://doi.org/10.1145/2723576.2723583
16. Nazaretsky, T., Hershkovitz, S., Alexandron, G. Kappa learning: a new item-similarity method for clustering educational items from response data, **10p** (2019)
17. Pozdniakov, S., et al.: The question-driven dashboard: how can we design analytics interfaces aligned to teachers' inquiry? In: LAK22: 12th International Learning Analytics and Knowledge Conference, pp. 175–185 (2022). https://doi.org/10.1145/3506860.3506885

18. Schwendimann, B.A., et al.: Perceiving learning at a glance: a systematic literature review of learning dashboard research. IEEE Trans. Learn. Technol. **10**(1), 30–41 (2017). https://doi.org/10.1109/TLT.2016.2599522

19. Sellier, N., & An, P.: How peripheral interactive systems can support teachers with differentiated instruction: using fireflies as a probe. In: Proceedings of the 2020 ACM Designing Interactive Systems Conference, 1117–1129 (2020). https://doi.org/10.1145/3357236.3395497

20. Shankar, S.K., Prieto, L.P., Rodríguez-Triana, M. J., Ruiz-Calleja, A.: A review of multimodal learning analytics architectures. In: 2018 IEEE 18th International Conference on Advanced Learning Technologies (ICALT), pp. 212–214 (2018). https://doi.org/10.1109/ICALT.2018.00057

21. Sharma, K., Giannakos, M.: Multimodal data capabilities for learning: what can multimodal data tell us about learning? Br. J. Edu. Technol. **51**(5), 1450–1484 (2020). https://doi.org/10.1111/bjet.12993

22. Vieira, C., Parsons, P., Byrd, V.: Visual learning analytics of educational data: a systematic literature review and research agenda. Comput. Educ. **122**, 119–135 (2018). https://doi.org/10.1016/j.compedu.2018.03.018

23. Zamecnik, A., et al.: Team interactions with learning analytics dashboards. Comput. Educ. **185**, 104514 (2022). https://doi.org/10.1016/j.compedu.2022.104514

24. Zhao, L., et al.: Modelling co-located team communication from voice detection and positioning data in healthcare simulation. In: LAK22: 12th International Learning Analytics and Knowledge Conference, pp. 370–380 (2022). https://doi.org/10.1145/3506860.3506935

Supporting Creativity in Learning

Preliminary Study on Students' Experiences in Design-Based Interdisciplinary Learning

Wenzhi Chen[1,2]([✉]) [iD], Dong Xu[1] [iD], and Ying-Shung Lee[3] [iD]

[1] Chang Gung University, Taoyuan 33302, Taiwan (R.O.C.)
wenzhi@mail.cgu.edu.tw
[2] Ming Chi University of Technology, New Taipei City 243303, Taiwan (R.O.C.)
[3] National Taiwan University of Science and Technology, Taipei City 106335, Taiwan (R.O.C.)

Abstract. Design is a crucial component of enterprise innovation. Due to rapid changes in society, the economy, and science and technology, design problems are becoming increasingly complex, making it necessary to integrate professional knowledge and technology of different domains into design education. Hence, the primary purpose of this study was to investigate learning problems in design-based interdisciplinary education, examine the learning resources used by students to overcome learning problems, and identify the causes of those problems. In this study, 24 students participating in design-based interdisciplinary courses/activities engaged in focus group discussions. The data were transcribed, and we used Atlas.ti qualitative analysis software to conduct open coding and clustering according to grounded theory and to construct a model of interdisciplinary learning problems. This paper provides new insights into the learning process for multidisciplinary design. Moreover, it offers a reference to enable design teachers to plan interdisciplinary design courses and students to participate in interdisciplinary learning, thus improving teaching effectiveness in interdisciplinary design education and establishing a foundation for future related research.

Keywords: Interdisciplinary · Learning Experience · Learning Problems

1 Introduction

Due to developments in society, the economy, and technology, the world is experiencing many complex problems, making it necessary to integrate knowledge from diverse domains into problem-solving [1, 2]. However, most students focus on problems relating to a single major or knowledge domain and find it difficult to deal with complex cross-disciplinary problems. Therefore, in recent years, higher education has emphasized interdisciplinary teaching approaches [2–4]. In the face of increasingly complex design issues, such interdisciplinary approaches to teaching design have become increasingly critical in design education [5, 6].

Teaching across disciplines requires multiple resources and the participation of experts across many disciplines [2, 7]. Interdisciplinary education research has mostly focused on the planning and implementation of interdisciplinary teaching, with few studies examining the setting and evaluation of educational goals and learning outcomes. Regarding design-based interdisciplinary teaching, which often requires cooperation among teachers and students from different domains, research reports have often depended on teaching planning and implementation case studies. Therefore, there is a great need to assess students' learning goals, experiences, problems, and outcomes in interdisciplinary courses.

2 Literature Review

2.1 The Challenge of Interdisciplinary Education

Interdisciplinary education can provide students with the knowledge and skills to view the world through multiple perspectives, synthesize diverse disciplines to better understand phenomena, understand the interdependencies between disciplines or subjects, and locate disciplines within an complex system [8]. Interdisciplinary learning environments can help students learn to think critically; evaluate and synthesize knowledge across various disciplines; engage in problem-solving, creativity, and innovation; and develop collaboration and communication skills [9–11]. Students taking interdisciplinary courses can learn from interdisciplinary teaching methods and approaches, including lifelong learning and exploration [11]. Embedding interdisciplinary courses into higher education curricula enables students to develop the ability to synthesize and apply knowledge and skills from multiple disciplines and find solutions to problems that are impossible to identify using only a single disciplinary lens [3].

Teaching in an interdisciplinary manner requires pedagogical support [12], since no single pedagogical approach can meet interdisciplinary teaching and learning needs. Moreover, students' prior preparation and previous learning experiences affect their interdisciplinary learning [3]. Richards [13] pointed out that team-taught courses often fail to achieve their objectives because individual members of the teaching team fail to understand their shared concerns and priorities in a way that is truly interdisciplinary. An excellent interdisciplinary learning experience requires close team cooperation, good planning, and instructors drawn from different fields to provide opportunities to integrate various teaching techniques [14].

Many instructors and students from different domains participate in interdisciplinary design projects, but diverse domain-specific knowledge, skills, and teaching/learning approaches may cause problems for both design and learning performance.

2.2 Learning Problems in Design-Based Interdisciplinary Courses

The learning process impacts the effectiveness of learning. The learning problems students often encounter in design majors can affect design and learning processes and outcomes [15]. Learning problems are complex and involve many factors, such as curriculum organization and planning, the topics and subjects studied, teaching styles and methods, and learning styles [16].

Interdisciplinary education varies according to the disciplines of the participants. Design-based interdisciplinary learning differs from domain-specific learning because of the uniqueness of the design field and education. Self, Evans, Jun and Southee [2] explored potential drivers of and barriers to interdisciplinary design education from a student-learning perspective. They conducted an in-depth student interview study at two interdisciplinary design schools in South Korea and the United Kingdom and found that interdisciplinary perspectives were shared across both schools. However, interdisciplinary ability depends heavily on the attitudes and interests of students and has little to do with the planning of courses themselves. At the school level, teacher bias and potential integration issues were identified as challenges for interdisciplinary studies. The findings also showed that application is crucial for capturing and synthesizing perspectives across disciplines. The study also found that design students had good responses to interdisciplinary learning courses, indicating that they could apply design expertise to interdisciplinary work projects [2].

Self and Baek [6] surveyed students' experiences with cross-disciplinary teaching in design education. They found that students evaluated instruction provided by a single professional teacher positively and achieved better learning quality and outcomes, but multiple teachers forming a teaching team seemed to cause problems. The researchers pointed out that cross-disciplinary teaching teams can provide knowledge and perspectives from different disciplines, giving students more opportunities to understand the relationships between disciplines and course topics. However, the effectiveness of interdisciplinary teaching strategies is worth exploring.

3 Methods

In this research, we explored students' experiences and learning problems in design-based interdisciplinary learning. The main research questions were as follows:

1. What challenges do students face in design-based interdisciplinary projects?
2. What learning problems do those students experience?
3. What factors or issues cause learning problems?
4. What learning resources do students use to overcome interdisciplinary learning problems?

3.1 Research Framework

This study was based on the design learning problem framework proposed by Chen [15] but included interdisciplinary-related factors to form a research framework, as shown in Fig. 1. Many procedures and tasks are used in design-based interdisciplinary courses and activities to help students solve interdisciplinary design problems. When students apply these interdisciplinary design procedures or undertake related assignments, learning problems can arise for several reasons. In such courses, because the combinations of teachers and students and the learning environments differ from those of general design learning, the learning problems are also more complicated than those encountered in a general design major. Students must seek additional learning resources to solve the learning problems they encounter, and they must then overcome those problems to carry out design processes, complete their design programs, and propose final design solutions.

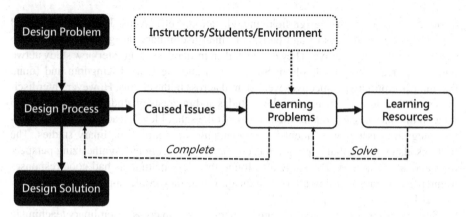

Fig. 1. The research framework.

3.2 Subjects

The subjects of this research were undergraduate students who had experience in design-based interdisciplinary courses and activities in relevant university departments. We conducted focus groups with 24 participants, divided into 8 groups with 2–4 people per group. Of these, four groups of students were drawn from private universities of science and technology, three from private general universities, and one from a public university. Twelve interviewees were female, and twelve were male.

3.3 Data Collection and Analysis

The process and materials for the focus groups met the requirements of the Research Ethics Review Committee of National Taiwan University. During the focus groups, the moderator first explained the purpose of the research, the related procedures, and the relevant rights and obligations, as stated in the informed consent form. The focus groups started after the participants fully understood the content and norms of the research and signed informed consent forms.

All the focus groups were audio recorded and then transcribed, and the transcripts were checked to ensure they were correct and complete. All the data were analyzed based on grounded theory and using Atlas.ti qualitative analysis software. Three design experts helped analyze the data. First, relevant concepts and issues extract from the transcripts through open coding, which resulted in 878 codes. The codes are then categorized and organized according to the research questions. Finally, we constructed a structural model of the learning problems identified in a design-based interdisciplinary project.

4 Results

4.1 The Challenges of Design-Based Interdisciplinary Learning

The challenges of the design-based interdisciplinary project that the students mentioned were as follows: 1) problem exploration and definition, 2) concept and idea development, 3) design integration and execution problems, 4) design thinking problems, and 5) team and professional integration problems. Of these, the first three problems were mainly related to the design process, whereas the last two were related to overall implementation issues. The most challenging design problems were problems 1, 2, and 3.

Problem Exploration and Definition. Because teachers and students from different domains participate in interdisciplinary learning projects, differences in defining design problems may arise due to different professional perspectives or experiences. People from different domains often consider design issues from their domain-specific professional perspectives, and their inability to understand others' domain-specific knowledge and/or inability to empathize with different perspectives may lead to a lack of mutual understanding regarding design issues.

In turn, domain-specific thinking can affect the recognition and definition of the design problem, making it difficult to complete the project. In addition, because professional viewpoints differ, the directions of exploration may also differ. Therefore, in the early stages of design project, members may collect and analyze data relating to their own domains. This may undermine communication, making it difficult to know which professional domain to focus on and how to deal with the overall design problems.

Concept and Idea Development. Due to the lack of a standardized viewpoint and standardized definitions of design concepts and solutions, students often do not know where to focus their efforts, which adversely affects concept development. Team members from different domains often think about problems in terms of their own professional perspectives, and their lack of knowledge and experience in other domains means that they are unable to understand or judge the views and opinions put forward by those other domains. Therefore, because they are often unable to clearly and effectively formulate design specifications, they may adjust the learning direction and goals and thus affect the development of the design concept.

Design Integration and Execution. In a high-performing interdisciplinary team, people from various domains contribute their professional knowledge and technologies and integrate them to propose better design concepts and solutions. Nevertheless, in the focus groups, some students stated that they could not understand the opinions of other domain members because they lacked the essential knowledge and skills of those do-mains. Integrating different domain-specific views and experiences is often challenging, resulting in friction and conflict and making it almost impossible to achieve effective design integration and implementation. If a particular team member dominates the design integration, the design may be compromised, resulting in a less-than-optimal design solution.

Issues of Design Thinking. Diverse design methods and procedures are often introduced and used in interdisciplinary design learning projects. In the focus groups, some participants claimed that participants from non-design fields did not understand and were not familiar with design thinking. Therefore, during the implementation of design projects, participants from the design field often felt that they wasted time explaining concepts to them or teaching and guiding them on related procedures. Some non-design participants found it difficult to familiarize themselves with the methods and spirit of design thinking and to use design thinking methods effectively, which caused problems for the team and affected the progress and results of the design projects.

Team and Professional Integration. During the focus groups, it became clear that the interdisciplinary design project teams were unfamiliar with the knowledge and skills of different domains. They found it difficult to learn and accept other knowledge and viewpoints, which, coupled with personal learning motivation, attitude, personality, and other differences, often led to failure to effectively integrate knowledge and skills from different domains. This failure to effectively use and integrate the characteristics of different domains could lead to conflicts and compromises, meaning that the design concept and solution did not best solve the design problem or only represented the perspective of a single field.

4.2 Caused Issues, Learning Problems, and Learning Resources

Caused Issues for Learning Problems. The caused issues of learning problems in design-based interdisciplinary learning projects are summarized as follows: 1) curriculum planning and execution, 2) pilot course, 3) team break-in, and 4) personal motivation and attitude.

Curriculum Planning and Execution. Good curriculum planning is essential for underpinning learning projects. During the focus groups, it became clear that some factors affected students' learning processes, including project implementation procedures, resources, support, participating teachers, and time management. Factors such as the choice of professional field can impact the progress and effectiveness of interdisciplinary learning projects. For example, teachers in the appropriate domains should be chosen according to the nature of the project, but due to departmental resource limitations, there may be no suitable teachers or students available, which affects the overall project progress.

In addition, different professional domains have different ways of thinking and problem-solving. Sometimes, when planning the implementation of a project, if the differences and needs of different domains are not considered, it inevitably causes problems. Although people from different domains can share their professional knowledge and skills with each other, they may fail to select suitable professionals and resources ac-cording to design themes and problems, provide suitable interactive communication methods and environments, or provide sufficient and suitable support. Thus, they can directly influence design project processes and outcomes.

Pilot Course. Some participants mentioned that they participated in interdisciplinary design projects but lacked foundational knowledge of other domains. This meant that they sometimes did not understand the methods used in the project, such as design thinking methods, and this was especially the case for students from non-design departments, who often encountered process problems. The need to stop teaching and first explain methods to these students affected the progress of the project.

Some participants suggested that it would be useful to provide pilot courses or pre-course preparation activities to help students understand the related domain knowledge and design methods. Helping students develop skills and attitudes for interacting and communicating with people from other domains would make project execution much smoother.

Team Break-In. Good teamwork has a specific impact on the execution of a project. Some participants mentioned that students from different departments and domains often had different personalities and work attitudes. The lack of a suitable icebreaking procedure or breaking-in process often affected the project work.

In addition, the personalities, professional knowledge, and abilities of team members could affect project progress. Some participants felt that if different personalities and professional abilities were not integrated before the project began, they could waste time communicating and adjusting during the design process. They mentioned a need for additional resources and support, such as providing appropriate icebreaking activities and explaining to all team members how to achieve the goals.

Personal Motivation and Attitude. One of the purposes of interdisciplinary design learning projects is to help students understand the characteristics of different domains and to learn to cooperate and communicate with people from different domains. However, some students reported interaction and communication problems in the focus groups that related not only to the domain but also to personal motivation and ability to learn, which could affect the progress of the entire project.

Some students said that because some interdisciplinary courses were compulsory, they had no choice about participating, which weakened their learning motivation. Some students did not understand the objectives of learning and cultivating skills by participating in interdisciplinary learning projects. They did not realize the advantages of participating in such courses, which also affected their learning motivation and attitudes.

The Learning Problems. The learning problems students faced in design-based interdisciplinary learning projects are summarized as follows: 1) cross-disciplinary integration, 2) professional techniques, 3) resources, 4) team interaction and communication, and 5) personal learning methods and motivations.

Difficulties in Integrating Across Domains. The participants encountered many problems dealing with different professional domains. For example, instructors could introduce so much domain-specific knowledge that it was difficult to absorb in a short time without a relevant foundation. Participants from different domains were also troubled by professional egoism. Different domains had different interpretations of design problems, viewpoints, and methods of thinking and proposing solutions, which led to difficulties in defining problems, directing the team's exploration, and avoiding inconsistent methods of data collection and analysis. When students did not openly discuss the thinking angles of different domains, it often affected the work content and progress of the project.

In addition, because team members could not communicate effectively on domain-specific issues, they tended to rely on members with specific domain knowledge to complete the work, which limited the participation of others. Ultimately, this caused problems in dividing and effectively integrating the work, which also affected the students' learning processes and effectiveness.

In addition, because team members could not communicate effectively on domain-specific issues, they tended to rely on members with specific domain knowledge to complete the work, which limited the participation of others. Ultimately, this caused problems in dividing and effectively integrating the work, which also affected the students' learning processes and effectiveness.

Professional Techniques and Issues. Complex design problems require the integration of different professional techniques for dealing with them. However, since some domain-specific knowledge and techniques cannot be learned and understood quickly, this may limit solution-oriented thinking.

In addition, an insufficient foundation for using certain techniques can sometimes make it impossible to communicate with domain-specific professionals, which also affects design conceptualization and solutions. Insufficient knowledge and experience of some advanced technologies, engineering materials, and processing methods, as well as markets and costs, can undermine the development of design concepts and decisions.

Resource Problem. Although interdisciplinary design projects integrate professionals from different domains and their domain-specific knowledge and technologies, they can cause resource problems relating to funding, cost, time, and space.

Interdisciplinary projects often require the integration of many disciplines for concept trials, which require experimental and operational materials and sufficient space and time to complete related tests. For some projects, if specific experimental equipment and space are needed, they must be borrowed from relevant units or acquired individually, which consumes resources and necessitates additional support.

Interaction and Communication. The participants particularly mentioned problems in team interaction and communication, including members' personalities, working styles, fair distribution of work, leadership, learning styles, attitudes, and ways of relating to each other.

Many participants said that, in addition to professional differences, team members' personalities, working styles, and attitudes often caused problems in teamwork, to the extent of affecting the progress and quality of work.

There were also leadership problems due to leaders' different ways of working, leadership styles, and sense of responsibility. Some leaders could be arbitrary in assigning work or not considering team members' abilities. Others could be weak and irresponsible, with a laissez-faire management style that reduced the team's efficiency in completing work on schedule and undermined project outcomes and quality.

Due to differences in the personalities and working methods of team members, tensions and conflicts could also occur, which, if not dealt with effectively by the team leader or members, could affect the team atmosphere and the progress of the entire project. Therefore, team members' interactions and communication directly affected individual learning and the outcomes of projects.

Personal Learning Style and Motivation. According to the data, the motivations for participating in interdisciplinary activities differed. Some students said that they thought that interdisciplinary design courses and activities provided good learning opportunities, enabling them to meet and interact with people from different domains. These students actively participated in courses and activities, and they felt able to deal with problems positively and openly.

However, some participants only participated in interdisciplinary courses and activities because they were compulsory, and they tended to adopt harmful strategies or procrastination to deal with this negative experience, which affected the progress and effectiveness of the team and the entire project.

In addition, there could be differences in individual learning styles and methods. When facing mutual problems, the students sometimes found it challenging to synchronize their styles and methods. In addition, many of the students preferred to work alone and found it difficult to accept and adapt to teamwork.

The Learning Resources. The various resources mentioned by the participants could be divided into several categories, many of which were related to human resources, including teachers and practitioners, peers (from the same discipline or different disciplines), family and friends, professionals, and manufacturers. Other, physical resources included the Internet, time, money, space, and equipment. Students indicated that they also sought various forms of assistance when facing problems, needing additional resources and support, or experiencing severe conflicts among team members, such as expressing their emotions to others or asking them for assistance.

5 Conclusion

Design problems are becoming increasingly complex, and their solutions require cross-disciplinary cooperation. Design education has thus introduced interdisciplinary approaches to teaching, meaning that educators must cultivate students' abilities to cooperate with people from different disciplines to solve complex problems. The primary purpose of this study was to explore the learning problems students encounter when participating in design-based interdisciplinary design courses and activities.

According to the data, most of the students' learning problems in interdisciplinary design projects resulted from the involvement of diverse professional fields and the influence of students' personalities, characteristics, and different fields of study. Self and Baek [6] explored students' interdisciplinary experiences in design education and found that students taught by a single instructor had more positive overall opinions of course quality and experienced significantly more encouragement to participate than team-taught students. However, they also found that team teaching increased the students' experiences of balanced contributions from different disciplinary perspectives. Moreover, the team-teaching approach was significantly more effective in providing students with opportunities to understand the relevance of different disciplines to the course subject. Likewise, the students in this study experienced problems communicating and cooperating with teammates due to unfamiliarity with their domain-specific knowledge and techniques. However, team teaching also helped students learn how to work with people from different disciplines. Self, Evans, Jun and Southee [2] found that successful interdisciplinary projects depend heavily on individual students' attitudes and interests. The results of the focus groups also provided evidence that students' motivations, learning styles, personalities, and attitudes can affect the processes and performance of design-based interdisciplinary courses and activities.

In this study, we explored students' challenges and learning problems in design-based interdisciplinary courses and activities from the students' perspectives. Focus groups were conducted to collect qualitative data and formulate the model of learning problems on design-based interdisciplinary education.

These preliminary results can provide a reference for future research on interdisciplinary teaching and learning, and we intend to design a questionnaire based on this study's results to collect quantitative data, verify the results, and propose a final model.

Acknowledgments. This research was funded by the National Science and Technology Council of Taiwan under grant numbers MOST 109-2410-H-182-001 and MOST 110-2410-H-182-020. Thanks are extended to all participants and research assistants for their contributions to these projects. The data collection was conducted according to the ethical review approval process of the Research Ethics Committee of National Taiwan University (NTU-REC No: 202005ES126).

References

1. Palmer, C.L.: Work at the boundaries of science: Information and the interdisciplinary research process. Springer Science & Business Media, Dordrecht, Netherlands (2001)
2. Self, J.A., Evans, M., Jun, T., Southee, D.: Interdisciplinary: challenges and opportunities for design education. Int. J. Technol. Des. Educ. **29**(4), 843–876 (2018). https://doi.org/10.1007/s10798-018-9460-5
3. Ashby, I., Exter, M.: Designing for interdisciplinarity in higher education: considerations for instructional designers. Tech Trends **63**(2), 202–208 (2018)
4. Wright, N., Wrigley, C.: Broadening design-led education horizons: conceptual insights and future research directions. Int. J. Technol. Des. Educ. **29**(1), 1–23 (2017). https://doi.org/10.1007/s10798-017-9429-9
5. Linked. https://www.linkedin.com/pulse/20140325102438-12181762-state-of-design-how-design-education-must-change/. Accessed 12 Dec 2019
6. Self, J.A., Baek, J.S.: Interdisciplinarity in design education: understanding the undergraduate student experience. Int. J. Technol. Des. Educ. **27**(3), 459–480 (2016). https://doi.org/10.1007/s10798-016-9355-2
7. Holley, K.: Interdisciplinary Curriculum and Learning in Higher Education. Oxford University Press (2017)
8. Fortuin, K.P.J., Koppen, C.V., Kroeze, C.: The contribution of systems analysis to training students in cognitive interdisciplinary skills in environmental science education. J. Environ. Stud. Sci. **3**(2), 139–152 (2013)
9. Cowden, C.D., Santiago, M.F.: Interdisciplinary explorations: promoting critical thinking via problem-based learning in an advanced biochemistry class. J. Chem. Educ. **93**(3), 464–469 (2015)
10. Mobley, C., Lee, C., Morse, C., Allen, I., Murphy, C.: Learning about sustainability: an interdisciplinary graduate seminar in biocomplexity. Int. J. Sustain. Higher Educ. **15**(1), 16–33 (2014)
11. Styron, R.: Interdisciplinary education: a reflection of the real world. Syst. Cybernet. Inf. **11**(9), 47–52 (2013)
12. Augsburg, T., et al.: Insights on Interdisciplinary Teaching and Learning. Michigan State University, East Lansing (2013)
13. Richards, D.G.: The meaning and relevance of "synthesis" in interdisciplinary studies. J. Gen. Educ. **45**(2), 114–128 (1996)

14. Lefeber, D., Mireles, M., Ye, F., Ostwald, S.: Facilitating a paradigm shift in geriatric care: an innovative educational and training model for interdisciplinary teamwork. Am. Acupunct. **63**, 32–41 (2013)
15. Chen, W.: Exploring the learning problems and resource usage of undergraduate industrial design students in design studio courses. Int. J. Technol. Des. Educ. **26**(3), 461–487 (2015). https://doi.org/10.1007/s10798-015-9315-2
16. Chang, P.-F., Hsiau, S.-S., Yeh, T.-L., Wu, J.-C.: The development and implementation of the technological creativity course: an interdisciplinary approach. In: International Conference on Engineering Education ICEE-2000, Taipei, Taiwan (2000)

Supporting Collaboration in Challenge-Based Learning by Integrating Digital Technologies: Insights from a Design-Based Research Study

Caterina Hauser[✉]

University of Graz, Universitätsplatz 3, 8010 Graz, Austria
caterina.hauser@uni-graz.at

Abstract. The complexities of 21st century challenges and crises necessitate a multi-disciplinary, holistic, and multi-perspective approach to find effective solutions. To fulfill their mission of providing quality education suited to the 21st century, higher education institutions need to equip students with the competences, experiences and knowledge necessary to tackle complex issues. Challenge-based learning (CBL) is an innovative method of teaching and learning that has the potential to achieve this goal. It is an active, interdisciplinary, collaborative approach to teaching and learning, in which learning revolves around collaborative efforts to solve authentic, complex and open-ended challenges. Although increasingly recognized for its potential, CBL is in its infancy. Research on CBL has yet to shed light on the instructional design underlying the approach, as well as the integration of digital technologies into CBL practice. The present paper contributes to bridging these research gaps with a focus on one central characteristic of CBL, collaboration, to provide insights into design elements for supporting collaboration in digitally-enhanced CBL based on the implementation of CBL into a university course on artificial intelligence as part of a design-based research study.

Keywords: Collaboration · Challenge-Based Learning · Educational Design Principles · New Approach to Teaching and Learning · Digitally-Enhanced Teaching and Learning · Higher Education Teaching and Learning

1 Introduction

The challenges and crises of the 21st century – such as AI legislation or the climate crisis – are characterized by a complexity that require a holistic, multi-perspectival, interdisciplinary approach for developing effective solutions. To fulfill their mission of providing quality education suited to the 21st century, higher educational institutions need to furnish students with the essential competencies and experience needed to collaborate on complex problems in their future careers. One novel approach to teaching and learning which has the potential to satisfy this mission is challenge-based learning (CBL). CBL is an active approach to teaching and learning which revolves around students collaborating in interdisciplinary teams to solve an authentic, open-ended challenge to deepen their knowledge and develop transversal and transdisciplinary competences.

P. Zaphiris and A. Ioannou (Eds.): HCII 2023, LNCS 14040, pp. 588–600, 2023.
https://doi.org/10.1007/978-3-031-34411-4_40

While CBL has increasingly been receiving attention in the context of HEIs, in particular in technical subjects (e.g. Leijon et al. 2021; Sukackė et al. 2022; Vilalta-Perdomo et al. 2022), Gallagher and Savage (2020) point out that the approach is still in its infancy. Despite recent endeavours to study the pedagogical underpinnings of CBL (see, for example, Doulougeri et al. 2022), research on CBL has yet to shed light on the instructional design underlying the approach, as well as the integration of digital technologies into CBL practice. The present paper contributes to bridging these research gaps with a focus on one central characteristic of CBL, collaboration, to provide insights into design elements for supporting collaboration in digitally-enhanced CBL. Design principles for enabling effective student collaboration and how they are integrated with learning technologies will be discussed and refined using the case of a blended-learning introductory university course on artificial intelligence (see Fig. 1). Thus, the research question "How can design principles for collaboration as part of a digitally-enhanced challenge-based learning design be improved based on classroom data?" will be answered.

2 Background

Challenge-based learning is novel approach to teaching and learning which originates from the Apple project Apple Classroom of Tomorrow Today (ACOT^2) in 2008 (Nichols and Cator 2008), which aimed to prevent drop-out rates in secondary education. The approach has since been integrated into higher education teaching and learning and especially in the last decade increased in popularity in this setting. University consortia and alliances such as the European Consortium of Innovative Universities (ECIU) (Eraña-Rojas et al. 2019), the CHARM-EU university alliance (Griffin et al. 2022) and the Arqus University Alliance (Stefani and Han 2022) can be considered drivers in research and practice of CBL in tertiary settings. STEM subjects are the most common context of CBL endeavours (Gallagher and Savage 2022), with engineering education in particular being one field in which CBL is flourishing (Doulougeri et al. 2022). Despite research addressing aspects of the learning design and digital enhancement (e.g. Griffin et al. 2022; Nguyen et al. 2023), more research on digitally-enhanced CBL with a focus on learning design is needed to fill the research gap and promote the maturity of CBL (Gallagher and Savage 2020).

CBL is defined as an active approach which centers around interdisciplinary teams of students collaborating, often together with stakeholders, to select, define and work on an authentic, relevant, open-ended challenge connected to the sustainable development goals or the grand challenges, to deepen their understanding and acquire key 21st century competences, such as collaboration (Conde et al. 2019; Gallagher and Savage 2020; Leijon et al. 2021; Malmqvist et al. 2015; Sukackė et al. 2022; Vilalta-Perdomo et al. 2022). With roots in both constructivist and experiential learning theories, learning in CBL results from individual and collective action and critical reflexivity in facing authentic, complex problems (Vilalta-Perdomo et al. 2022).

Collaboration therefore is a central characteristic of CBL, intricately interwoven with other characteristics, such as the teacher role, the learning process, and the intended learning outcomes. This key role of collaboration in CBL can be further split into two functions in the learning approach: (1) as a practice, it is a key characteristic of the learning design and thus as a means trough which learning is to be achieved, and (2) as a competence, it is an intended learning outcome. Collaboration as a practice in today's world (and perhaps more so in one affected by Covid-19) cannot be separated from digital practice and competence e (European Commission 2022). Therefore, digital competences are also inter-related with collaborative competences.

3 Design Principles for Collaboration in Digitally-Enhanced Challenge-Based Learning

Design principles, in a broad understanding, are guidelines for design decisions intended to explain connections between theory and practice, which showcase a broad scope in conceptual realization (van den Akker 2013). Doulougeri et al. (2022), for example, formulate "develop learning activities that foster collaborative learning" (p. 46) as a design principle for collaboration in CBL, and "make use of the learning technologies to foster teaching and learning" (p. 47) for the use of learning technology in CBL. Combining Doulougeri et al.'s (2022) two broad principles, the following uses the course *Understanding Artificial Intelligence and Facing its Challenges* (see the methodology section for more information about the course) to describe how elements of the digitally-enhanced course were designed with support of collaboration in mind.

The course *Understanding Artificial Intelligence and Facing its Challenges* was organized in an active blended learning format (Armellini and Padilla Rodriguez 2021), integrating a pre-MOOC-design (Braun et al. 2020) and an inverted classroom design (Handke and Sperl 2012) in the first part of the course (see Fig. 1). In this phase, the students completed the Massive Open Online Course (MOOC) *Elements of AI* as a means of acquiring basic knowledge in AI and as a means for providing common ground through a common knowledge base for collaboration. Activities for individual reflection and asynchronous group discussions on the LMS Moodle as well as virtual mid- and end-of-MOOC meetings supported understanding and critical reflection of the topic. This MOOC-phase lasted the first six weeks of the course (eight weeks if the study-free two weeks of Easter Break are counted) was followed by the challenge-phase, which consisted of two 2-day in-person sessions spread over the last two months of the semester and rounded off by a final in-person session. Students were required to bring their own digital devices as all the activities, tools and processes in the challenge-phase were mapped and conducted on the Moodle. In the first blocked session, students were informed of the team distribution, completed a succession of teambuilding tasks and underwent a guided brainstorming process for brainstorming potential challenges, choosing, defining and crafting a proposal for working on it in teams. The aim of this block was for students to have an approved challenge proposal, describing the challenge, their plan for working on it and showing their solution and understanding. Student teams were to continue working on their challenge by researching individual tasks and checking in with their team members. The second block was intended for teams to check in with each other and the teacher (process and progress) and particularly to synthesize findings, solve problems encountered, and negotiate how to continue. In the final sessions, students held short presentations to show their findings and the artefact they created to show their understanding and challenge outcome. A short research synthesis and reflection on the learning experience constituted the final deliverable to be created as a team. Each of the in-person blocks, including the final session, included a group reflective and individual reflective task (see Methodology Section) focused on aspects related to collaboration and the learning experience in CBL.

This condensed description contains several considerations of design for collaborative processes in the digital design. First of all, the overall design follows Gilly Salmon (2013) Five Stage Model for E-Learning, which not only support online learning but collaborative (online) learning. This way, the MOOC phase created a basis for collaboration through increased familiarity with the digital environment (becoming familiar with the LMS and its tools) and building an inter-personal base (getting to know the class, exchanging and discussing ideas, creating small-scale shared meaning, common ground). The latter aspect is further eased by the online environment as it allows students and the teacher to go back to e.g. fora to re-read introductions, discussion contributions or shared resources.

In the in-person sessions, a collaborative space for each team was provided in which all activities for collaboration support were provided. This space was also intended for teams to continue using outside class. The tasks for teambuilding included an activity for negotiating rules for working in a team, which were documented. Together with the discursive group reflective tasks, this document provides scaffolding for reflecting on how the team works together and wants to progress (both in terms of interpersonal aspects and goals for the collaboration). These activities as well as the guided brainstorming process simultaneously collaborative processes supported through the tools used. Thus, one function of them was to help students build actional knowledge later transferable to outside the classroom where teams might not be able to meet.

Course Architecture

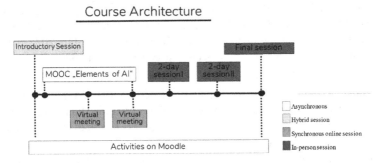

Fig. 1. Course Architecture for the Course Understanding Artificial Intelligence and Facing its Challenges, Course Architecture by Caterina Hauser, CC BY 4.0

4   Methodology

4.1   Aims of the Study and Research Question

The present study is part of a larger project which investigates CBL as a learning design in order to develop, implement and refine a digitally-enhanced CBL design for higher education. This study focuses on one central characteristic of CBL, collaboration, and aims to investigate the design elements for supporting collaboration in a digitally-enhanced CBL design. The following research question is addressed:

"How can design principles for collaboration as part of a digitally-enhanced challenge-based learning design be improved based on classroom data?"

To answer this research question, I analysed classroom data of the 13 students, their 3 teams and my own reflections as their teacher which were collected as during the implementation of the learning design in the university course "Understanding Artificial Intelligence and Facing its Challenges".

4.2 Research Paradigm: Design-Based Research

The present using a design-based research (DBR) approach. Having emerged out of a dissatisfaction with the gap between education research on the one hand and education in action in its complex and various ecological systems on the other hand, DBR has the joint design, development and advancement of theory and practice as its goal (Barab 2014, pp. 151–152; The Design-Based Research Collective 2003, p. 5). In DBR, researchers draw on theory to iteratively design and re-design an intervention for and implement it in a specific context, which serves to simultaneously gain insight into theory on teaching and learning and contribute to its development. This research approach was chosen to due to the suitability of the dual goal of DBR for the present research goal, namely developing design and theory simultaneously through theory-based design and design-based theory contributions.

4.3 Research Context

The context for the present study was the course *Understanding Artificial Intelligence and Facing its Challenges* held at the University of Graz, Austria in summer semester 2022 and designed part of a larger research project. This course is a one-semester course which lasted from the beginning of March until the beginning of July 2022. The course is credited with 5 ECTS and as a free elective was open to up to 30 students registered at the University of Graz.

Participants. All students who participated in the course (n = 13; female = 8, male = 5) volunteered to take part in the study. The students comprised a heterogenous group in terms of (1) fields of studies and (2) academic age (i.e. length of study). The majority pursed a field of studies in the humanities (53%), followed by natural sciences (27%), a teaching degree (with the subjects pertaining to the humanities and natural sciences respectively) and Environmental Sciences (7%). Of each specific degree programmes, English and American Studies is the one with the highest enrolment rate of the study participants with 33%, followed by German Language and Literature and Environmental Systems Sciences: Natural Sciences-Technology with 13% each. 73% of the degree programmes pursued by the participants were Bachelor's and 27% Master's Degrees. The invitation to participate in the research was extended in the first lession of the course, announced on the learning management system in use in the course and sent via email to students who were absent in the first session.

Ethical Considerations. I carefully considered ethical guidelines for the present study and context (British Educational Research Association 2018; Dörnyei 2012; Ferguson et al.). I designed an informed consent form for participation in the study which included information about the study, the data to be collected, the right to withdraw and how the student's anonymity would be ensured. I discussed this form in class and pro-vided explanations to absent students via email. I especially reflected on my dual role as teacher-researcher (Ferguson et al. 2004), the power relations associated with it, and designed the research instruments to allow for anonymity. The present research was submitted to and approved by the Ethics Committee of the University of Graz prior to the beginning of the study.

4.4 Methods of Data Collection

Qualitative and quantitative methods were combined in the present study to study the students' and teacher's perceptions of their experiences with CBL in the university course. Three instruments were used to collect data in the present study: To study the student experience, a combination of a qualitative and a quantitative instrument (which also includes a qualitative component) was chosen. A questionnaire with 27 closed-ended items and two open-ended questions was used as part of the larger study to investigate individual learners' experience in the CBL environment. The two open-ended question ((1) "Do you feel any aspects of the course design could be improved? If yes, how?" and (2) "Please use this space for any feedback you want to give on this class or your learning experience so far.") and three of the items, which formed multi-item scale for the construct collaboration, were analysed in the present study. These were: (1) "Working in my team helps me to see different perspectives of an issue." (2) "Everyone in my team has been contributing to our work." (3) "My team discusses different options before taking a decision."

I designed reflective tasks as a qualitative tool to gain insight into the collective experience of student teams. These tasks consisted of four sections with guiding questions about characteristics of CBL (the challenge process, collaboration, participatory character and the learning experience more generally). Data related to all sections was included in the analysis of the present study.

Both research instruments were designed to function not only as a research instrument but also as an activity meaningfully embedded into the learning design: both foster individual or group reflection on learning, learning strategies and collaboration (which are inherent parts of CBL). The qualitative instrument of a reflective teacher diary was chosen as a means to provide a rich description of my insider experience (Lopera Medina 2013; Sá 2002).

4.5 Procedure

I administered both the questionnaire and the group reflective task three times during the course in class time: after the first in-person block, the second one and at the end of the final session of the course (see Fig. 1). The questionnaire was administered through the survey tool Limesurvey (the version hosted and provided by the University of Graz for all staff and students was used: https://survey.uni-graz.at/). The group reflective task was administered through a digital collaborative writing tool (an etherpad on uniCLOUD (https://cloud.uni-graz.at/landing/), hosted by the University of Graz for use by both students and staff. Students accessed the guided questions via this tool, discussed them in their teams and synchronously documented.

I kept the teacher reflective diary (as a word document) form the beginning of the course until I finished grading all students. I used both pre-defined prompts, my classroom experience and the student data to reflect on my experience as a teacher in and outside the classroom.

4.6 Data Analysis

All qualitative data (teacher reflections, group reflective tasks, and open-ended survey items) were analyzed using reflexive thematic analysis (Braun and Clarke 2022) and the analytic tool MAXQDA. I chose this approach as it proposes the centrality of the researcher's reflexivity in the analysis, which is necessary for a tripartite role as a teacher-researcher-designer – my insider perspective as designer of the learning design and environment as well as active participant within it have an effect on my analysis and point of view.

The quantitative data was analyzed using descriptive statistics in SPSS. Multi-item scales were combined using the mean of the total score divided by the number of items and treated as interval data.

5 Findings

The quantitative data reveal that across all three administrations of the survey all students perceived collaboration to be part of their learning experience: The analysis shows that the calculated scale scores fall within the categories of "agreement" and "strong agreement" (see Table 1). Disagreement, which was evident in response to single items is absent in the calculation for the construct "collaboration" in all three iterations. Regarding the responses to item (2) separately, it is evident that three students disagreed with it in the first administration after the first in-person session. In consideration of the context, it can be deduced that these responses are grounded in the inability of some team members to contribute to the work due to their absence from class. No other item response expressed disagreement.

The results further show that over the course of the challenge-phase, students perceived their collaborative experience to be represented by the questionnaire items to a higher degree. Strong agreement across the scale increased from seven to all but one student, i.e. 12 students, in the second iteration. In the final iteration, one student's score no longer represents strong agreement on the scale. Comparing the frequencies for item (1) between the second and third iteration, an increase in the number of "strong agreement" by two students is evident. In contrast, for both items (2) and (3), one student changed their response from "strongly agree" to "agree".

These findings indicate that students overall perceived their team to collaborate effectively in terms of a participatory approach, with shared and distributed perspectives, workload and decision-making. However, this data on its own does not provide insights into the actioned realization of the collaborative elements abstracted in the items. The thematic analysis of the qualitative student and teacher data provides depth through additional perspectives.

Table 1. Comparison of Scores for Collaboration of the First to Third Administration of the Survey

Administration	1st		2nd		3rd	
	Frequency	Percent	Frequency	Percent	Frequency	Percent
"agree"	5	38.5	1	7.7	2	15.4
"strongly agree"	7	53.8	12	92.3	11	86.6
Total	12	92.3	13	100	13	100
Missing	1	7.7	0	0	0	0
Total	13	100	13	100	13	100

In the qualitative data, two themes were evident from my analysis. The first theme is *sharing is caring*. Sharing in collaboration has different facets: collaboration means sharing in an experience, collective thinking, exchange of resources, skills and perspectives, which can be summarized as sharing as a collective process. Caring is intertwined with and enables these processes, as caring for the process and their participants. Sharing, however, is also present in the sharing of the work(load), i.e. sharing as dividing. Distributing tasks and responsibilities is caring if it accommodates different needs and resources. While both meaning levels are equally important for collaboration, their blending is one basis for fruitful collaboration. Dividing the workload in a first exchange and combining each individual's contribution in a final step is a nascent version of collaboration, common in university education. It is the collective experience which leads to learning, personal and professional development as well as quality output.

The notion of sharing as a way of caring in these two manifestations was prevalent in both the students' (individually and as a team) descriptions of collaborating and my observations about these processes as a teacher. Distributed assignments amongst the members of teams, or sharing the work, was connected to accommodation of different needs, interests and time resources, as for example noted by team Beavers: "Because we splitted up the parts that each of us wants to go deeper into there was also a huge possibility to push the learning material into a direction of each others personal preferences." (group reflective task, 3rd administration).

However, one team in particular realized the potential of collective process for both the sake of the collective and individual experience: "Through communication we could determine future steps/strategies and topics that are relevant for our challenge while respecting our own interests so nobody is stuck with a topic that one doesn't enjoy." (group reflective task, 2nd administration, team Ants). My own reflections also highlight the difference between this collaborative process in comparison with the other two:

"Team Ants is the one that discusses and negotiates constantly in the in-person sessions. They wrote parts of their blog posts individually, but then together discuss each written part together, giving each other feedback on clarification, language, structure.

Team Bees has also a very strong focus on distributed responsibilities, collective decision making, and exchange. Team Beavers does not use class time as effectively. However, teams 2 and 3 repeatedly face student absence, which I believe was especially hindering for collective exchange in team Beavers, and also hindered me in providing assistance." (teacher reflective diary, reflection after 2nd in-person session).

Connections between sharing and caring and presence vs absence could also be made. Presence was one fundamental means by which students could share in the experience, with absence equaled with being denied the experience. Some students and teams reported a desire for "more sessions to get together and talk about our project" (survey, 3rd administration, participant 10). Team Beavers, which faced the highest degree of team member absence in the in-person sessions, connected more opportunity for synchronous collaboration with a fuller realization of this collective process:

"Hindering was that we are not employees that are working together in the same room all day. That of course would bring another dynamic into working on the challenge. It would be beneficial to more often work and learn in the same accommodation because the barrier of talking with each other is a lot lower." (group reflective task, 3rd administration).

However, it was team Bees who expressed their frustration over disruption caused by team-member absence: "not everybody is here EVER" (group reflective task, 2nd administration, team Bees) after having realized the potential for collective experience in these spaces in the previous session: "The lectures [i.e. scheduled sessions] are to be seen as opportunities to work together in person, exchanging new ideas bringing up points etc." (Group reflective task, first administration, team Bees).

Students who perceived sharing of the workload as the main collaborative form did not recognize nor experience the potential of the collective process: "I'm not sure how necessary it is to have the second in person session in this course as by now the roles should be distributed." (Survey, 2nd administration, participant 13). Sharing as dividing work seen as the main collaboration weakens the connection to caring, and the potential is not recognized: "So sitting next to each other and silently reading documents and papers without interacting with each other is something that could also be done at home, for example. I sometimes felt that we were just killing time." (Survey, 3rd administration, participant 13).

The theme of *sharing is caring* helps illustrate the different majority of collaborative processes achieved in the implementation. The different degree to which a collective process was achieved by each team puts into perspective the students' collaborative experience as approached with the quantitative instrument. This highlights the tension between what students perceive as collaboration and the potential for even a more mutually beneficial experience.

A second theme evident in the data on collaboration is *the collaborative atmosphere*. This theme is expressed in several ways in the data – that the collaborative atmosphere is conceptualized as team chemistry, a desire for interaction, and the learning environment through its design. Students and teams relate that they "have a good team chemistry and nobody wants to let the team down" (group reflective task, 2nd administration, team Ants), that "communication felt rather natural" (group reflective task, 1st administration, team Bees), having "my luck with the group members" (survey, 3rd administration, participant 5) or sharing "interpersonal compatibility" (group group reflective task, 2nd administration, team Beavers). These manifestations of the collaborative atmosphere can be subsumed under the term "team chemistry" as factors which are independent from the course design.

The analysis also showed the combination of both team chemistry and design elements together creating the collaborative atmosphere. Participant 5's reflection as one aspect being luck continues by identifying the design as an additional factor for facilitating collaboration: "but partly also because the course design facilitated a good team work through forcing us to reflect on how we should and want to work together" (survey, 3rd iteration, participant 5). One team draws an explicit comparison not just to other experiences but university education as a whole:

"In university, you normally get assigned to a group and work on something and that's it. In this course, we get a jump-start by reflecting on what it means to work together as a group. We are supposed to set up rules, define goals and choose a very specific topic that we want to work on." (group reflective task, 1st administration, team Bees).

These explicit statements refer to the teambuilding activities as part of the design as one basis for working together in their teams. Student and team reflections further mentioned or more implicitly referred to design elements and the design of the course leading up to the teamwork as resulting in the atmosphere. The online socialization phase part of the blended learning design and its design elements (e.g. introduction in the forum, forum discussion, ice-breakers in synchronous online meetings) provided the fundament for the basis further added by the teambuilding and brainstorming processes in the challenge-phase. The blended learning-design itself can also be connected to an increased desire or need for interaction which students reported and which I also observed especially in the second half of the MOOC and actualized in the first in-person session. My diary reflections further contain my perception of both the MOOC-phase and the activities in the challenge-phases as succeeding in aiding teams build a social ground for collaboration. In addition, I reflected on how the team division process I had carefully planned based on my analysis of students' work in the MOOC-phase at least partly may account for what the students referred to as "luck", or "chemistry".

The theme of *the collaborative atmosphere* further contributes to a more nuanced picture of the experience of students with collaboration in the implementation context. While the quantitative data may lead to concluding successful and full realization of collaboration as a collective process, the analysis of the qualitative student and teacher data reveals three levels of maturity in collaboration achieved by the three teams. In addition, the two identified themes reveal the subtler sense-making mechanisms the students possess in relation to collaboration: the basis for efficient collaboration is (partly) seen in elements beyond the students' or teacher's influence ("luck") as evident in the collaborative atmosphere, and the conceptualization of the essence of collaboration being division of the workload part of the theme *sharing is caring*. As a collective, these findings have implications and show scope for refinement of the digitally-enhanced challenge-based learning design.

6 Discussion

The current study investigates the design and re-design for a digitally-enhanced challenge-based learning design for higher education. In this paper, I aimed to study selected design elements of this design from the focal lens of collaboration, to refine the design based on classroom data.

The proposed digitally-enhanced challenge-based learning design and its implementation in the course "Understanding Artificial Intelligence and Facing its Challenges" was successful to some degree in the creation of a collaborative learning environment surrounding the solution of an authentic, relevant challenge. The blended-learning design in combination with a pre-MOOC-design and the online socialization have contributed to forming a basis and common ground for the challenge-phase. The team division, teambuilding activities and brainstorming process for selecting, defining and working on a challenge provided a scaffolding for collaboration. However, the analysis shows that aspects of these design need to be refined in order to enable all students and teams to mature their collaborative processes and competences.

The analysis reveals that the design principle for scaffolding collaboration needs to be refined in order to (1) support students' development of an understanding of what collaboration entails, (2) support students in applying this understanding to achieve effective collaboration or enhance collaborative processes. One way to do this is by adapting the MOOC-phase to integrate online socialization and more targeted collaboration preparation. As collective sharing of ideas and knowledge was achieved only in one team, a re-design of both synchronous and asynchronous discussion activities to scaffold this process can help develop students' understanding of collaboration through experience. At the same time, as a form of online socialization, carefully designed activities can help foster online practices for virtual collaboration. The perception of presence being the enabler for sharing in collaboration while absence is a preventer as shown in the theme *sharing is caring* is one manifestation of a lack of competence with virtual collaboration that needs to be actively dismantled.

The present study is a small-scale study based on the first implementation of larger digitally-enhanced challenge-based learning design. It provides insights into design elements at work in a specific context and uses classroom data to refine these elements to support collaborative processes in CBL. These initial results indicate the importance of design principles for building effective teams using digital technologies in an effective way in a challenge-based learning environment and will be enriched with further results to refine and present design principles for collaboration in digitally enhanced CBL.

This study is limited by time-restrictions imposed on the larger study it is part of. It presents design elements in an early stage which need to be tested and refined in multiple-design cycles in different contexts. However, the insights gained can nonetheless provide practitioners with an orientation point for their own practice and investigation.

A further limitation concerns the context of the research design and its implementation. University policies on data protection and privacy as well as the General Data Protection Regulation (GDPR) constrained the repertoire of digital tools whose use was allowed in the present study. Thus, the study is restricted to a design surrounding these tools. Nevertheless, the pedagogical constructs underlying the use of digital tools is independent of the tool used.

Acknowledgements. This work is part of the project "Teaching Digital Thinking" funded by the Austrian Federal Ministry of Education, Science and Research.

References

Armellini, A., Padilla Rodriguez, B.C.: Active Blended Learning. In: Padilla Rodriguez, B.C., Armellini, A.: (eds.) Premier Reference Source. Cases on Active Blended Learning in Higher Education, pp. 1–22. IGI Global (2021). https://doi.org/10.4018/978-1-7998-7856-8.ch001

Barab, S.: Design-based research: a methodological toolkit for engineering change. In: Sawyer, R.K., Sawyer, R.K. (eds.) The Cambridge Handbook of the Learning Sciences, pp. 151–170. Cambridge University Press (2014). https://doi.org/10.1017/CBO9781139519526.011

Braun, C., Fickert, L., Schön, S., Ebner, M.: Der Online-Kurs als Vorkurs einer LehrveranstaltungUmsetzung und Evaluation des Pre-MOOC-Konzepts in einem technischen Studiengang. In: Müller Werder, C., Erlemann, J. (eds.) Seamless Learning – lebenslanges, durchgängiges Lernen ermöglichen, pp. 39–47. Waxmann Verlag GmbH (2020)

Braun, V., Clarke, V.: Thematic Analysis: A Practical Guide. Sage (2022)

British Educational Research Association. Ethical Guidelines for Educational Research (2018)

Conde, M.Á., et al.: RoboSTEAM - a challenge based learning approach for integrating STEAM and develop computational thinking. In: González (ed.) Proceedings of the Seventh International Conference on Technological Ecosystems for Enhancing Multiculturality, pp. 24–30. ACM/Association for Computing Machinery (2019). https://doi.org/10.1145/3362789.3362893

The Design-Based Research Collective: Design-based research: an emerging paradigm for educational inquiry. Educ. Res. 32(1), 5–8 (2003). https://doi.org/10.3102/0013189X032001005

Dörnyei, Z.: Research Methods in Applied Linguistics: Quantitative, Qualitative, and Mixed Methodologies [Nachdr.]. Oxford Applied Linguistics. Oxford Univ. Press (2012)

Doulougeri, K., van den Beemt, A., Vermunt, J.D., Bots, M., Bombaerts, G.: Challenge-based learning in engineering education: towards mapping the landscape and guiding educational practice. In: Vilalta-Perdomo, E., Membrillo-Hernández, J., Michel-Villarreal, R., Lakshmi, G., Martínez-Acosta, M. (eds.) Emerald Handbook of Challenge Based Learning, pp. 35–68. EMERALD GROUP PUBL (2022)

Eraña-Rojas, I.E., López Cabrera, M.V., Ríos Barrientos, E., Membrillo-Hernández, J.: A challenge based learning experience in forensic medicine. J. Forensic Leg. Med. **68**, 1–5 (2019). https://doi.org/10.1016/j.jflm.2019.101873

European Commission. Digcomp 2.2, The Digital Competence framework for citizens: With new examples of knowledge, skills and attitudes. Publications Office (2022). https://doi.org/10.2760/115376

Ferguson, L.M., Yonge, O., Myrick, F.: Students' involvement in faculty research: ethical and methodological issues. Int. J. Qual. Methods 3(4), 56–68 (2004). https://doi.org/10.1177/160940690400300405

Gallagher, S. E., & Savage, T.: Challenge-based learning in higher education: an exploratory literature review. In: Teaching in Higher Education, pp. 1–23 (2020). https://doi.org/10.1080/13562517.2020.1863354

Gallagher, S.E., Savage, T.: Challenge based learning: recommendations for the future of higher education. In: Vilalta-Perdomo, E., Membrillo-Hernández, J., Michel-Villarreal, R., Lakshmi, G., Martínez-Acosta, M. (eds.) Emerald Handbook of Challenge Based Learning, pp. 391–411. EMERALD GROUP PUBL (2022)

Gilly Salmon. (n.d.). E-moderating. https://www.gillysalmon.com/e-moderating.html. Accessed 29 May 2021

Griffin, D., et al.: Best Practices for sustainable inter-institutional hybrid learning at CHARM European University. Educ. Sci. **12**(11), 797 (2022). https://doi.org/10.3390/educsci12110797

Handke, J., Sperl, A.: Das inverted classroom model: Begleitband zur ersten deutschen ICM-Konferenz. Oldenbourg Verlag (2012). https://doi.org/10.1515/9783486716641

Leijon, M., Gudmundsson, P., Staaf, P., Christersson, C.: Challenge based learning in higher education– a systematic literature review. Innov. Educ. Teach. Int. **59**, 1–10 (2021). https://doi.org/10.1080/14703297.2021.1892503

Lopera Medina, S.: Diary Insights of an EFL reading teacher. Profile **15**(2), 115–126 (2013). https://www.researchgate.net/publication/262435674_Diary_Insights_of_an_EFL_Reading_Teacher

Malmqvist, J., Kohn Rådberg, K., Lundqvist, U.: Comparative analysis of challenge-based learning experiences. In: Proceedings of the 11th International CDIO Conference, Chengdu, China. https://research.chalmers.se/en/publication/218615

Nguyen, H., Gijlers, H., Pisoni, G.: Identifying struggling teams in online challenge-based learning. Advance online publication, Higher Education, Skills and Work-Based Learning (2023). https://doi.org/10.1108/HESWBL-06-2022-0131

Nichols, M., Cator, K.: Challenge Based Learning White Paper. Apple Inc., California (2008)

Sá, J.: Diary writing: an interpretative research method of teaching and learning. Educ. Res. Eval. **8**(2), 149–168 (2002). https://doi.org/10.1076/edre.8.2.149.3858

Stefani, P. de, Han, L.: An Inter-university CBL course and its reception by the student body: reflections and lessons learned (in Times of COVID-19). Front. Educ. **7**, 853699, 321 (2022). https://doi.org/10.3389/feduc.2022.853699

Sukackė, V., et al.: Towards active evidence-based learning in engineering education: a systematic literature review of PBL, PjBL, and CBL. Sustainability **14**(21), 13955 (2022). https://doi.org/10.3390/su142113955

Vilalta-Perdomo, E., Membrillo-Hernández, J., Michel-Villarreal, R., Lakshmi, G., Martínez-Acosta, M.: (eds.): Emerald Handbook of Challenge Based Learning. Emerald Group Publication (2022)

Evaluating the Development of Soft Skills Through the Integration of Digital Making Activities in Undergraduate Computing Courses

Dora Konstantinou(✉) 📵, Antigoni Parmaxi 📵, and Panayiotis Zaphiris 📵

Cyprus University of Technology, 30 Archbishop Kyprianos Street, 3036 Limassol, Cyprus
dok.konstantinou@edu.cut.ac.cy, {antigoni.parmaxi, panayiotis.zaphiris}@cut.ac.cy

Abstract. The purpose of this exploratory study was the integration of Digital Making activities in the curriculum of a computing course aiming to examine the guidelines for integrating Digital Making activities in the curriculum of a computing course as well as to explore the development of participants' soft skills. This exploratory study was performed during the Spring 2021 semester in an Introductory Programming course at a higher education institution in the Mediterranean in which ten (10) undergraduate students from various nationalities were enrolled. Students were working in randomly generated groups in a self-directed learning environment in which web resources along with manuals of the provided equipment were accessible by each participant. Each group had to work in a self-regulated learning environment to innovate, design and implement two (2) 'Smart Artefacts' which can solve real-life problems, using Microbit programmable boards and reusable materials within an unstructured Digital Making Curriculum. Data was collected from students, peers and the instructor using a mixed methodology that included self and peer assessment questionnaires along with observation and diary recordings. Existing assessment tools from the ATS2020 project were adopted for the evaluation of soft skills development. The analysis of the collected data was performed in two phases: a) The quantitative data were analyzed using paired t-test analysis, b) The qualitative data were analyzed and discussed with a group of experts. The preliminary results of the particular exploratory study, demonstrate the development of students' soft skills through Digital Making with emphasis on the skills of Collaboration, Creativity, Critical Thinking and Communication. However, there were unclear outcomes for Cultural Respect and Connectivity skills. Implications for practitioners and researchers regarding the Instructional Design and Assessment Methodology framing the integration of Digital Making activities in the wider HCI (Human-Computer-Interaction) context in computing courses are also provided.

Keywords: Higher Education · Human-Computer Interaction (HCI) · Digital Making · Soft Skills Development · Makerspaces · 6Cs

1 Introduction

The notion of "Soft Skills" was initially coined in 1972 in a US Army training manual [1] and since then, the research area in discussion still attracts interest due to its exploration difficulty. Soft Skills are referring to personal competences such as social and communication skills, as well as friendliness, collaboration skills and generally all personality traits which can characterize relationships between people [2]. Soft Skills are traditionally considered complementary of Hard Skills, which are the abilities to perform a certain type of task or activity. Emotional intelligence is the basis of what we commonly call soft skills, transferable skills or transversal skills and although for some these skills are innate, for others they can be developed and sharpened over time [3].

Success at work depends to a great extent on the acquisition of soft skills, since hard skills, as well as academic qualifications, are no longer sufficient to secure a successful career path [4–8]. Hard skills contribute only 15% to an individual's success and 85% of success is owned by soft skills [7]; nevertheless, soft skills are hard to acquire [9]. Career success hinges on critical soft skills along with digital mindset abilities under the RISC framework: Resiliency, Inner strength, Strategic thinking, and Collaborative spirit [10]. Accordingly, employers are now looking for prospective employees with flexibility, critical thinking, problem-solving, teamwork and other soft skills [11], since these skills can give their organization a competitive advantage in the worldwide market [12]. All these changes in the labour market reveal a gap between school and college graduates and the essential soft skills required for employment [11]. The academic community now faces the challenge of having to respond to the current needs of an employer, while curricula need to be reassessed to prepare students for the demands of the workplace [12].

Through a systematic literature review performed in the area of Educational Makerspace, it has been noted that both students and adults who are involved in Making activities, demonstrated significant improvement in particular soft skills. Nevertheless, making activities were mainly performed as extracurricular while most of the studies were examining the development of a maximum of two skills and not the development of a set of soft skills [13].

The particular study emphasizes the exploration of soft skills development through Digital Making activities which is situated under the wider area of Human-Computer-Interaction (HCI). Sufficient research findings are proving that Digital Making and HCI have overlapping research areas, such as the role of technology in the community and in supporting wellbeing [14]. Moreover, the process of making artefacts inside a Makerspace is aiming to the design and development of artefacts which are interacting with humans, likewise in HCI [15].

The purpose of this exploratory study is to deliver the Instructional Design for the integration of Digital Making activities within the formal curriculum of computing courses with the aim to examine the development of 6Cs (Creativity, Collaboration, Communication, Critical Thinking, Connectivity and Cultural Respect) which are falling under the umbrella of the 21st Century Skills. The 4Cs (Communication, Critical thinking, Collaboration, and Creativity) are considered as the essential skills of the 21st Century [16]. However, education experts came up with additional 2Cs: the skills of

Connectivity and Citizenship coined by Miller in 2015 [17] and the skills Character Education and Culture Respect coined by Fullan and Scott in 2015 [18].

For this exploratory study, Digital Making activities have been designed grounded on learning theories that enforce the development of 21st Century Skills. These activities were conducted within an Introductory Programming course, which was offered to undergraduate computing students of a Higher Education Institution in Cyprus during the Spring 2021 semester. The particular study aims to answer the following research questions:

1. What are the guidelines for integrating Digital Making activities in the curriculum of a computing course?
2. Can Digital Making develop students' soft skills?
   a. Which set of soft skills seems to be mainly developed through Digital Making?
   b. Which set of soft skills seems to be least developed through Digital Making?

2 Theoretical Framework

2.1 Making - Digital Making – HCI

Making can happen in a variety of places, in so-called "makerspaces" as well as in classrooms, museums, libraries, studios, homes, or garages, where learning through Making appeals both in formal (in-school) and informal (after-school) education. Makerspaces, particularly those that exist in a university or other formal educational settings, also provide an opportunity to bridge formal with informal learning of HCI or instill human-centered values [19]. Makerspaces are built on a holistic constructivist ideology [20] since Making activities are grounded on constructivist and constructionism learning theories. Both constructivism and constructionist encourage students to active learning instead of imposing knowledge on a teacher or an expert. The Piagetian theory of constructivism visions the learner as an active constructor of knowledge while Papert's constructionism theory emphasizes learning by making public artefacts by utilizing digital media and computer-based technologies [21]. In further analysis, constructionism is based on the process of "learning by doing" or "learning by making" [22]; these methods have been frequently applied in STEAM education, over the years. A few years later, the term "distributed constructionism" arose by Resnick, which focused on situations whereby more than one person is involved in the design and construction activities, claiming that "distributed cognition" is developed through interactions of a person with the surrounding environment [23, 24]. Through Resnick's studies, it has been concluded that students cannot only share ideas but also improve their collaboration and intelligence while working together in real time on the development of an artefact or a project by utilizing computers and generally computer networks [23].

Digital Making is the term used to describe the action of creating or making an artefact using digital technology. Digital Making can be situated within the broader maker movement and includes a wide range of digital tools, such as coding environments and newer digital technologies such as electronic kits, e-textiles, robotics and 3D Printers, where digital artefacts are programmed to interact with users and the environment [25]. Along the same lines, Making and especially Digital Making can be situated under the wider umbrella of HCI since Makers intend to create artefacts similar to HCI commercial products, likewise IoT home device and other devices that can improve users quality of life [15]. With regard to soft skills development, research findings indicate improvement of Creativity, Innovation, Entrepreneurship, Critical Thinking Collaboration and Communication skills through making, mainly in non-formal education [13]. Nevertheless, the area of Makerspaces and Making is under-researched and, therefore, further findings are required to prove their learning sufficiency in formal education.

2.2 Learning Theories for Developing the 21st Century Skills

It has been demonstrated over the years, that Student-Centered Learning (SCL) approaches can develop 21st Century Skills [26]. In a SCL environment, students are in the center of the educational enterprise, and their intellectual and emotional learning experiences should determine all decisions taken regarding what is done in the class and how [27]. The SCL approach is grounded on learning theories such as problem-based learning, project-based learning, constructivism/constructionism as well as self-directed learning theories [28]. Project-Based Learning is interlaced with Problem-Based Learning since participants have to act in a collaborative or cooperative learning environment to deliver a project [29]. Both Problem Based and Self-Directed learning are strongly recommended for the development of the 21st Century Skills and Competencies [30].

Additionally, research findings are highlighting the importance of Self-Directed Learning (SDL) in a Problem-Based Learning Environment. SDL is essential when students are confronted by completing goals [31]. At the same time, the role of the instructor in a SDL environment is stressed as interaction with students is required as well as guidance and encouragement for help-seeking and promotion of reflection [32]. Self-Regulated Learning (SRL) or Self-Directed Learning (SDL) is mainly recommended for college/university students, since it gives to students the freedom to manage their time, their study environment and their learning resources [33].

2.3 Soft Skills Definition and Assessment Methods

Soft skills is a term directly connected with emotional intelligence [3] and can be a) Intrapersonal and b) Interpersonal [2]. The first category refers to self-developed skills while the second category refers to skills that can be developed when interacting with other people [2]. The classification of soft skills is becoming more complex when an effort is put into defining this extensive range of skills, as well as identifying which skill sets are essential in each context [34]. For example, in the context of ICT (Information Communication Technology) in which our research interest is focused, research findings are indicating that, among the 23 professions (e.g. Designers, Developers, Technicians etc.) included in this context, there is a different set of soft skills required for each profession [35]. In order to illustrate the wide range of soft skills required in the 21st century, a comparison of six frameworks (P21, EnGauge, EU, OECD, ATCS, NETS/ISTE) that aimed to examine the development of such skills during the last two decades constructed by Voogt and Roblin is elaborated in Table 1 [36].

Overall, throughout the above analysis, a general set of skills assessed by frameworks has been outlined and it is evident that 6Cs [17, 18] which includes 1) critical thinking and real-world problem solving 2) communication, 3) collaboration, 4) cultural respect,

Table 1. Similarities and differences between frameworks examining the 21st century skills [36]

Mentioned in all Frameworks	Mentioned in Most Frameworks	Mentioned in few Frameworks	Mentioned only in one Framework
1. Collaboration 2. Communication 3. ICT Literacy 4. Social and/or cultural skills; citizenship	1. Creativity 2. Critical Thinking 3. Problem Solving 4. Develop quality products/Productivity (except ATCS)	1. Learning to learn (ATCS, EU) 2. Self-direction (P21, En Gauge, OECD) 3. Planning (En Gauge, OECD) 4. Flexibility and Adaptability (P21,En Gauge) 5. Core Subjects: 6. Mathematics; communication in mother tongue; science (EU, P21, ATCS); 7. History and Arts (P21 and ATCS)	1. Risk Taking (En Gauge) 2. Manage and Solve conflicts (OECD) 3. Sense of initiative and entrepreneurship (EU) 4. Interdisciplinary themes (P21) 5. Core subjects: Economics; Geography; Government and Civics (P21)

5) creativity and 6) connectivity of knowledge together with Digital Literacy skills can be noted as the significant skills required for the 21st Century.

The absence of standard procedures in evaluating the success rate of soft skills, especially in education, is undeniable [37]. Accordingly, the main research concern in the area of soft skills is the assessment tools available and whether they are fit for purpose. Few research aiming to develop assessment tools on soft skills including self-assessment tools, rubrics and many other qualitative data collection methods such as interviews, observations and experts' assessments [2, 4, 11]. Nevertheless, the lack of quantitative assessment tools remains a challenge for future research [11]. Moreover, a formative type rather than a summative type of assessment is considered suitable for assessing the development of soft skills [38]. Few frameworks aiming at the development and the assessment of 21st Century skills exist in the literature as already presented in Table 1. Since our research interest is focusing on the development of 6Cs, this results in concentrating on the frameworks of P21 (Partnership for 21st Century Learning) and ATCS (Assessment and Teaching of 21st century skills). Further research was employed in the literature concerning P21 and ATCS frameworks and came to our attention that their assessment methodology was adapted by several projects pointing to the development of students' skills in various contexts as well as at various educational levels. However, our focus remains in the context of ICT, and we were able to find out two projects: GRASS [39] and ATS2020 [40], which we have examined in detail prior to designing the methodology of this study. The GRASS project was in the concept of awarding Open Budges to participants in regard to the skills of self-regulation, leadership, collaboration, skilled communication, problem solving and innovation. Similarly, the ATS2020 is a project which utilizes self-assessment, teacher-assessment and portfolio assessment in formal education. The assessment tools delivered from this project have been validated and they asses collaboration, communication, creativity & innovation, information literacy and autonomous learning skills.

3 Methodology

The methodological design of the particular exploratory study is constituted of two parts a) the instructional design which describes the setup of the experiment and b) the assessment methodology used for assessing the development of soft skills, as illustrated in Fig. 1.

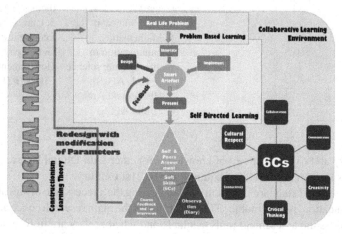

Fig. 1. Instructional Design & Assessment Methodology

3.1 Instructional Design

The instructional design of the particular study is based on a Student-Centred Learning (SCL) approach grounded on learning theories whose effectiveness in the development of the 21st Century Skills has been described previously in this paper. These theories are Problem Based Learning (PBL) in a Self-Directed Learning (SDL) Environment.

Digital Making activities were included in an Introductory Programming course which was offered during the Spring 2021 semester (beginning of March 2021 towards the end of May 2021), to ten (10) first-year computing students of a multinational Higher Tertiary Educational Institution in the Mediterranean European zone. Specifically, students had to work in groups for constructing digital smart artefacts to solve real-life problems, using MicroBit and at the same time, they were able to put into practice the knowledge gained during the Introductory Programming course.

A consent form for participating in the study was provided to all students. Fourteen (14) out of seventeen (17) expressed interest in participating in this research, three (3) of whom were females and eleven (11) males. Due to the COVID-19 pandemic, several precautionary measures were imposed when entering the class and during the course. As a result, four (4) male students withdrew from the study, leading the number of participants to ten (10). Three multinational groups (A, B and C) of three (3), four (4) and four (4) students respectively were formed as presented in Table 2, aiming to get them exposed to a collaborative environment and demonstrate their skills. The three female participants were each assigned to a different group, while male participants were assigned to the groups randomly. The sample of participants was relatively small, although the collection of data was in-depth since the duration of the intervention lasted seven (7) weeks and the collection of data utilized self and peer assessment as well as observation.

Table 2. Groups Demographic Characteristics

Group Name	Number of Participants	Demographic Characteristics
A	3	Gender: (1) female, (2) male Nationalities: (2) Asian, (1) European Average Age: 26
B	3	Gender: (1) female, (2) male Nationalities: (2) European, (1) African Average Age: 20.3
C	4	Gender: (1) female, (3) male Nationalities: (1) Asian, (1) European, (2) African Average Age: 20.75

Groups were tasked to work on their own in a problem-based learning environment in which they had to identify two real-life problems, innovate a solution, and design and implement a Smart artefact to solve each problem. Reusable materials along with MicroBit programmable boards in addition to a MicroBit Smart Home Kit and a MicroBit IOT kit were provided to each group in a self-regulated learning environment.

Seven (7) intervention sessions with a duration of one hundred and ten (110) minutes each, were performed during the semester as presented in Table 3. During the first intervention session, the three groups used the equipment that was available while the second and third intervention sessions were dedicated to brainstorming ideas with their partners on how to utilize equipment, design and develop a SMART artefact that can solve a real-life problem. Self-Directed Learning was implemented since participants had the opportunity to utilize internet resources for exploring how to set up and program the MicroBit boards and the Smart Home and IoT kits. During the fourth intervention session, the participants presented their artefacts to the other groups and then carried out self and peer evaluations. In the fifth, sixth and seventh intervention sessions, the participants went through the same process; brainstorming ideas on how to utilize the equipment and develop a second SMART artefact, which they could also use in a real-life situation. This was followed by a presentation and the second round of self and peer evaluations. During the presentations, the members of each group had to explain the novelty of their artefact, its implementation process, its functionality and its limitations.

Members of other groups were able to ask questions for clarification or make comments and suggestions for improvements.

Table 3. Task design for Digital Making activities

Intervention sessions (110 min each)	Processes and Tasks
1st	Consent Form for participation in the study Explore the equipment and its functionality
2nd 3rd	Innovate/Design/Implement a Smart Artifact to solve a real-life problem Construct a solution for a Real Life Problem in a Self-Directed Learning Environment
4th	Present the novelty and the functionality of their Smart Artefact Perform self and peer assessment
5th 6th	Innovate/Design/Implement a Smart Artifact to solve a Real-life problem Construct a solution for a Real Life Problem Real Life Problem in a Self-Directed Learning Environment
7th	Present the novelty and the functionality of their Smart Artefact Perform self, peer assessment and course feedback

3.2 Assessment Methodology

The assessment methodology employed for this study is based on assessment methods used by other similar projects that aimed to examine the development of soft skills in the context of ICT such as ATS2020 and GRASS projects. After analyzing the areas of competencies and skills of ATS2020, it was determined that the skills under examination fall under the umbrella of 6Cs which are defined in the literature as Communication, Creativity, Critical Thinking, Collaboration, Cultural Respect and Connectivity skills [18]. Therefore, the assessment tools used for this study were adopted by ATS2020 which follows a formative assessment method. Nevertheless, a certain limitation regarding ATS2020 assessment method has been identified since this project utilizes only self-assessment, teacher assessment and portfolio assessment. On the contrary, GRASS [41] is utilizing the peers-assessment method. Besides that, there are also research findings proving that giving and receiving feedback can improve a range of social and communication skills such as criticism, negotiation and communication skills [42] and therefore peers assessment was implicated in this study.

All the participants had to perform a self-assessment and peer-assessments for each member of their group, on completion of each project. Two (2) sessions of self and peer assessments were performed, during the 4th and 7th intervention sessions. The self-assessment questionnaire (SAQ) and peer-assessment questionnaire (PAQ) used a Likert scale which was adopted from the ATS2020 project.

Although the number of participants in this study is considered low, the number of collected self and peers assessments can be considered as adequate for performing statistical analysis. Specifically, the total number of collected self and peer assessments is sixty-two (62) as presented in Table 4. Additionally, the instructor/researcher was constantly observing and recording the whole process in a diary.

Table 4. Number of Self and Peer Assessments

	Self-Assessments	Peer Assessments	Total
Group A (Participants N = 3)	6 (2 × 3)	12 (2 × 2 × 3)	18
Group B (Participants N = 3)	6 (2 × 3)	12 (2 × 2 × 3)	18
Group C (Participants N = 4)	8 (2 × 4)	18 (2 × 3 × 3)	26
Total (Participants N = 10)	20	42	62

4 Analysis of the Findings

The analysis of data collected through self and peer assessment was performed using statistical analysis software (SPSS). For each skill under evaluation, the mean value of the first assessment (4th intervention session) was compared to the mean value of the second assessment (7th intervention session). All data were converted into a percentage format to verify: a) whether there is a significant improvement towards skills development and b) which set of skills are mainly improved through Digital Making activities. The quantitative results collected through self and peer assessment were compared with the qualitative results collected during the observation to verify that driven conclusions and outcomes had converged. The preliminary research findings showed improvement of participants' soft skills through Digital Making activities, although the driven outcomes from quantitative and qualitative data were contradictory for some of the skills.

4.1 Soft Skills Overall Development: Statistical Analysis

A paired t-test analysis was performed on the collected data aiming to identify whether there is a significant difference between the two mean values [43] as presented in Table 5.

The results indicate that all six skills experienced some degree of development, although further analysis is required to verify whether the development is statistically significant. To reject the Null Hypothesis "there is no significant difference between

Table 5. Paired T-test Analysis

	Mean (1st Assessment)	Mean (2nd Assessment)	Mean Difference	t Stat	P-value
COLLABORATION	83.87	93.95	10.08	−2.92626	0.016859
COMMUNICATION	79.78	90.65	10.87	−3.32465	0.008874
CREATIVITY	77.70	88.58	10.88	−2.81624	0.020171
CRITICAL THINKING	77.83	89.25	11.42	−2.40351	0.039669
CULTURAL RESPECT	91.78	98.67	6.89	−2.81818	0.020107
CONNECTIVITY	86.83	91.46	4.63	−1.84068	0.098805

the two means", the following two factors should be examined: A) The value of $P < = .05$ and B) the absolute value of t-stat $> = $ t Critical [43]. Concerning the skills of Collaboration, Communication, Creativity, Critical Thinking and Cultural Respect, sufficient statistical findings are demonstrating that the Null Hypothesis can be rejected and therefore their development is characterized as statistically significant. In contrast, for the skill of connectivity, neither the P nor the T values were able to meet the set criteria; therefore, the Null Hypothesis couldn't be rejected in this case.

4.2 Soft Skills Development: Observation Report

The researcher was constantly observing the groups while working in a self-directed learning environment for developing a Smart Artefact. Students' interactions in every intervention session and when skills of collaboration, communication, creativity, critical thinking, connectivity and cultural respect skills were demonstrated, these were recorded in a diary. The collected data aimed at triangulating and therefore compared with self and peers reported results. The data collected were also discussed with a group of experts and the following outcomes were generated: 1) Although the participants' communication skills were generally moderate at the beginning since students were not much talkative, these showed clear improvement by the time the course ended. Some of the students who were more passive at the beginning soon grew in confidence and became more active and talkative within their groups. One noticeable exception was Group A, in which a few problems with communication existed. Due to these incidents, negative environment developed within the particular group and this may have caused the negative evaluation among the peers of the group and also students were not able to demonstrate skills like collaboration and communication. 2) Similarly, all the participants demonstrated essential improvement in their collaborative skills. However, not all students exhibited the same degree of collaboration during the design, implementation and presentation of the first project but this could be due to a lack of programming skills.

However, during the design, implementation and presentation of the second project, students with low programming skills were more involved by searching the web for solutions and/or preparing the presentation of the smart-artefact. 3) The results for the skill of creativity, although positive, did not always show the linear increase of the other skills. For example, the level of creativity which was based on the criteria of "idea innovation" demonstrated by Group A was higher in the first project than in the second. In contrast, creativity for Groups B and C was higher in the second project than in the first one. 4) Moreover, participants were able to solve problems and think critically. All six projects were completed, nevertheless, only four of these successfully adhered to the main idea and the two of these showed some divergence, as described in Table 6. These two projects were coming from two groups who had experienced some problems in their implementation and they decided to redesign and implement a different artefact. Specifically, the second project of Group A had a different functionality to that of the main idea, although the concept had an environmentally friendly approach comparable to the main idea.

Similarly, the second project of Group C had a different functionality than the main idea, although both had the same purpose, which was the monitoring of an area. 5) Students showed the ability to make use of the knowledge gained during their first projects in their second projects. Two Groups used the same sensors for their first and second projects, claiming that they feel much more confident reusing the same sensors since they knew how to programing them. Students who demonstrated strong programming skills during the course and were able to write up and execute code on the provided equipment from the second session intervention, were more comfortable and actively involved in Digital Making activities and project implementation. Therefore, it can be concluded that previously gained knowledge can be applied in Digital Making activities and the knowledge gained from a previous project can be embedded into another Digital Making project. 6) Generally, throughout the course, all students were very polite to their classmates from the beginning towards the end of the course. The fact that students were already coming from a multinational environment the skill of cultural respect may had limited space for improvement.

All six projects delivered by three groups, are presented in Table 6 which contains the initial idea as defined by each group, the materials used for the implementation along with pictures of the final artefact/deliverable as presented in the class

Table 6. Comparison of Initial Idea with the Deliverable Artefact

Group	Preliminary Idea	Deliverable Artefact	Intervention 2 – 4 (Project #1)
A	**Title:** "Happy Puppy" **Functionality:** An automated system that throws treats to dogs when barking is recognized	**Title:** "Happy Puppy" **Functionality:** An automated system that throws treats to dogs when barking is recognized. **Materials Used:** Trash bin, paper box, straws, tape, MicroBit controller, servo motor and noise sensor. **Comments:** The deliverable artefact was identical to the initial idea and excellent functioning. Optimizations for filling in the basket and a base for holding the artefact were included.	
B	**Title:** "Fridge Door Controller" **Functionality:** An automation that is attached to a door and is activated when the door opens a led lamp is switched on and alarm drills.	**Title:** "Fridge Door Controller" **Functionality:** An automation attached to a door that is activated when the door opens, a led lamp is switched on and alarm drills. **Materials Used:** Paper Box, Tape, MicroBit Controller, Crash Sensor, Rainbow Led. **Comments:** The artefact is attached to a box that was set on vertical orientation for the demonstration. The artefact was identical to the initial idea and well-functioning.	

(continued)

Table 6. (*continued*)

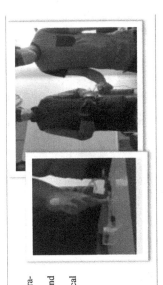

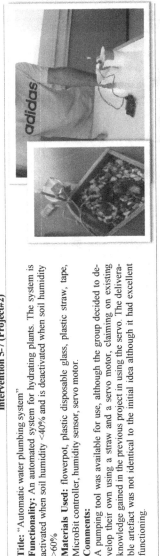

C Title: "Smart Air Fan" Functionality: Smart air fan is automatically switched on when temperature >25 Celsius.	Title: "Smart Air Fan" Functionality: Smart air fan is automatically switched on when temperature >25 Celsius. Materials Used: MicroBit, Motor with Fun, Temperature Sensor and OLED Screen. Comments: Artefact wasn't autonomous (not placed on a base). Identical with the initial idea and well-functioning.

Intervention 5-7 (Project#2)

A Title: "Smart Home Cooling System" Functionality: Automated system being next to the control of a home air-cooler and switches on when room temperature > 27 Celsius and switches off when temperature < 24 Celsius	Title: "Automatic water plumbing system" Functionality: An automated system for hydrating plants. The system is activated when soil humidity <40% and is deactivated when soil humidity >60% Materials Used: flowerpot, plastic disposable glass, plastic straw, tape, MicroBit controller, humidity sensor, servo motor. Comments: A pumping tool was available for use, although the group decided to develop their own using a straw and a servo motor, claiming on existing knowledge gained in the previous project in using the servo. The deliverable artefact was not identical to the initial idea although it had excellent functioning.

(*continued*)

Table 6. (*continued*)

B

Title: "Smart Hat"
Functionality: Wearable hat used for hydration by providing an amount of liquid on demand, directly from a plastic cap attached to the hat.

Title: "Smart Hat"
Functionality: Wearable hat used for hydration by providing an amount of liquid on demand, directly from a plastic cap attached to the hat.
Materials Used: Paper box, fabric hat, disposable plastic cap, MicroBit Controller, crash sensor, submersible pump.
Comments: The wearable artefact was identical to the initial idea and excellent functioning.

C

Title: "Motion Monitor and Photographing system"
Functionality: Security system which is connected on a mobile phone and captures a photo when motion is detected.

Title: "COVID-19 Entrance Controller"
Functionality: The artifact can be placed at the entrance of a shop and counts people entering the shop and the number of people entering is presented on a LED Screen.
Materials Used: MicroBit Controller, PIR Sensor, OLED Display.
Comments: The deliverable artefact was not identical with the initial idea and its functioning was not fully compliant with its purpose. Specifically, the artefact was counting the number of people entering without counting the number of people existing to give an accurate number of visitors inside the building.

5 Discussion

The preliminary research findings through the collected data from self and peer assessment indicated that five out of six soft skills under evaluation demonstrated significant improvement during the particular study. These skills are Critical Thinking, Creativity, Communication, Collaboration and Cultural Respect. Further analysis of the collected data was performed, aiming to rank the level of development of each skill. According to the findings driven by quantitative and qualitative collected data, it can be concluded that the skills of Creativity, Communication, Collaboration and Critical Thinking are proportionally developed at a higher rate than the skill of Cultural Respect which is moderately developed.

Conversely, the skill of Connectivity was self-reported and also through the observation it has been noted that the majority of students demonstrated strong capabilities in applying existing knowledge and/or reapplying knowledge within projects during the interventions. However, peers were not able to recognize its development and this was reflected in their assessment. Consequently, due to the contradictive outcomes concerning the skill of Connectivity, its development was characterized as non-significant by the t-test analysis. On the contrary, the low development of the skill of cultural respect required an in-depth analysis of the collected data, which revealed that this skill had been evaluated highly at the beginning of the course and perhaps this left limited space for improvement during the second evaluation. The fact that the participants were already coming from a multicultural environment may have also influenced the initial high evaluations of this skill.

5.1 Theoretical Implications

The particular study can equally contribute with productive insights both for academics and practitioners in the wider area of HCI. An indicative instructional design manual for integrating Digital Making activities in computing courses aiming at the development of soft skills is presented in this paper. The setup presented in the instructional design can also be considered useful by practitioners for organizing hackathons or other events in which participants can innovate, porotype or design and implement Smart Technological Artefacts that can interact with humans and/or the general environment for solving real-life problems.

6 Limitations and Future Research

This research is an exploratory study and it was performed with a small number of participants during the COVID-19 pandemic. The indicative research questions can be answered through the driven outcomes, although a larger sample of participants is required to enhance the findings of this study. Interviews with participants on the completion of the course could allow researchers to collect more data on the contradictory data and generate more solid outcomes for these skills. Furthermore, the design of a rubric for evaluating the deliverable artefacts is also considered valuable for this study, since Digital Making activities will be included in the formal course curriculum.

Changes may also be valuable on the Instructional Design aiming to examine further the contradictive results and to overcome any communication or collaboration difficulties within groups that led to negative assessments.

Contradictive outcomes were mainly focused on the skill of Connectivity and therefore emphasis should be given during the next studies in the investigation of its development. According to the literature, connectivity skills are also referred to as Metacognitive skills, which help students manage their learning and/or problem-solving skills [45]. Moreover, research findings have demonstrated that metacognitive skills efficiency has a proportional relationship with the level of difficulty of a particular problem, especially in the context of programming [46]. Consequently, the role of the instructor during the activities should be re-defined, since research findings indicate that when participants are provided with further guidance they enhance their monitoring and controlling thinking process [46]. The instructor should assume the role of coordinator by gradually setting up a higher level of difficulty between the projects. For instance, the number of sensors used in the second project should be higher than the number of sensors used in the first one or else provide the Smart Home Kit to start with and then the IoT Kit for their second project since the second one is more complex in use.

Through an overview of the collected peer-assessment, a connection between communication issues and negative assessments was noticeable. In detail, the members of Group A performed a negative evaluation of their peers after miscommunication issues within the team. Perhaps, this could have been avoided by re-forming the problematic group [47], since this method is considered a good strategy for overcoming problems and at the same time it can advance learning. Additionally, the involvement of participants from non-multicultural backgrounds can be valuable and provide further opportunities in examining the development of Cultural Respect skills in the future.

References

1. Newman, K.: Chutes and Ladders (2008)
2. Cimatti, B.: Definition, development, assessment of soft skills and their role for the quality of organizations and enterprises. Int. J. Qual. Res. **10**, 97–130 (2016). https://doi.org/10.18421/IJQR10.01-05
3. Wheeler, R.: Soft skills - the importance of cultivating emotional intelligence. AALL Spectrum **20**, 28 (2016)
4. Beard, D., Schwieger, D., Surendran, K.: Integrating soft skills assessment through university, college, and programmatic efforts at an AACSB accredited institution. J. Inf. Syst. Educ. **19**, 229–240 (2008)
5. Duncan, G.J., Dunifon, R.: "Soft-Skills" and Long-run labor market success. In: Polachek, S.W., Tatsiramos, K. (eds.) 35th Anniversary Retrospective, pp. 313–339. Emerald Group Publishing Limited (2012)
6. Gibson, L.A., Sodeman, W.A.: Millennials and Technology: Addressing the Communication Gap in Education and Practice. 14 (2014)
7. John, J.: Study on the Nature of Impact of Soft Skills Training Programme on the Soft Skills Development of Management Students. Social Science Research Network, Rochester (2009)
8. Schulz, B.: The importance of soft skills: Education beyond academic knowledge (2008)
9. Seth, G.: Your soft skills inventory. https://seths.blog/2017/12/your-soft-skills-inventory/

10. Morman, L.: How do we prepare the next generation for a career in our digital era? Computer **52**, 72–74 (2019). https://doi.org/10.1109/MC.2019.2903328
11. AbuJbara, N.K., Worley, J.A.: Leading toward new horizons with soft skills. On Horizon **26**, 247–259 (2018). https://doi.org/10.1108/OTH-10-2017-0085
12. Ritter, B., Small, E., Mortimer, J., Doll, J.: Designing management curriculum for workplace readiness: developing students' soft skills. J. Manag. Educ. **42**, 105256291770367 (2017). https://doi.org/10.1177/1052562917703679
13. Konstantinou, D., Parmaxi, A., Zaphiris, P.: Mapping research directions on makerspaces in education. Educational Media International (2021). https://doi.org/10.1080/09523987.2021.1976826
14. Taylor, N., Hurley, U., Connolly, P.: Making community: the wider role of makerspaces in public life. In: Proceedings of the 2016 CHI Conference on Human Factors in Computing Systems, pp. 1415–1425. Association for Computing Machinery, New York (2016)
15. Lindtner, S., Hertz, G.D., Dourish, P.: Emerging sites of HCI innovation: hackerspaces, hardware startups & incubators. In: Proceedings of the SIGCHI Conference on Human Factors in Computing Systems, pp. 439–448. Association for Computing Machinery, New York (2014)
16. Chiruguru, D., Chiruguru, S.: The Essential Skills of 21st Century Classroom (4Cs) (2020)
17. Miller, B.S.: The 6 C's Squared Version of Education in the 21st Century (2015). https://www.bamradionetwork.com/the-6-c-s-squared-version-of-education-in-the-21st-century/
18. Fullan, M., Scott, G.: New Pedagogies for Deep Learning Whitepaper: 9 (2014)
19. Okerlund, J., Latulipe, C., Wilson, D.: Considering HCI mindsets and practices in the making phenomenon: a value-based approach. In: Proceedings of the 2nd Annual Symposium on HCI Education, p. 7 (2020)
20. González-González, C.S., Arias, L.G.A.: Maker movement in education: maker mindset and makerspaces, 5 (2018)
21. Papert, S.: A Word for Learning: Constructionism in Practice (1996)
22. Papert, S., Harel, I.: Constructionism. Ablex (1991)
23. Resnick, M.: Distributed Constructionism. MIT Media Lab (1996)
24. Salomon, G.: Distributed Cognitions: Psychological and Educational Considerations. Cambridge University Press, Cambridge (1997)
25. Hughes, J., Gadanidis, G., Yiu, C.: Digital making in elementary mathematics education. Digit. Exp. Math. Educ. **3**(2), 139–153 (2016). https://doi.org/10.1007/s40751-016-0020-x
26. Overby, K.: Student-Centered Learning. 9, 5 (2011)
27. Wright, G.B.: Student-centered learning in higher education. Int. J. Teach. Learn. High. Educ. **23**, 92–97 (2011)
28. O'Neill, G., McMahon, T.: Student–centred learning: what does it mean for students and lecturers? 10 (2005)
29. Guo, P., Saab, N., Post, L.S., Admiraal, W.: A review of project-based learning in higher education: student outcomes and measures. Int. J. Educ. Res. **102**, 101586 (2020). https://doi.org/10.1016/j.ijer.2020.101586
30. Griffin, P., Care, E., Bui, M., Zoanetti, N.: Development of the Assessment Design and Delivery of Collaborative Problem Solving in the Assessment and Teaching of 21st Century Skills Project. https://www.igi-global.com/chapter/development-assessment-design-delivery-collaborative/www.igi-global.com/chapter/development-assessment-design-delivery-collaborative/74972
31. Randi, J., Corno, L.: Teacher innovations in self-regulated learning. In: Boekaerts, M., Pintrich, P.R., Zeidner, M. (eds.) Handbook of Self-Regulation, pp. 651–685. Academic Press, San Diego (2000)
32. English, M., Kitsantas, A.: Supporting student self-regulated learning in problem- and project-based learning. Interdisc. J. Probl.-Based Learn. **7** (2013). https://doi.org/10.7771/1541-5015.1339

33. Pintrich, P.R.: Understanding self-regulated learning. New Dir. Teach. Learn. **1995**, 3–12 (1995). https://doi.org/10.1002/tl.37219956304
34. Economou, A.: Research Report on Transversal Skills Frameworks: ATS2020 - Assesemnt of Transversal Skills 2020 (2014)
35. Valavosiki, V.-A., Stiakakis, E., Chatzigeorgiou, A.: Development of a framework for the assessment of soft skills in the ICT sector. In: Sifaleras, A., Petridis, K. (eds.) Operational Research in the Digital Era — ICT Challenges. SPBE, pp. 105–123. Springer, Cham (2019). https://doi.org/10.1007/978-3-319-95666-4_8
36. Voogt, J., Roblin, N.P.: A comparative analysis of international frameworks for 21st century competences: implications for national curriculum policies. J. Curriculum Studies **44**, 299–321 (2012)
37. Surjoseputro, S.: Passion and Problem Solving Skills. Jurnal Pendidikan Dan Tejada (2014)
38. Torres, M.F., Sousa, A.J., Torres, R.T.: Pedagogical and technological replanning: a successful case study on integration and transversal skills for engineering freshmen. Int. J. Technol. Des. Educ. **28**(2), 573–591 (2017). https://doi.org/10.1007/s10798-017-9399-y
39. Čubrić, G., Salopek Čubrić, I.: Technology – based assessment of soft skills in higher education. ENTRENOVA - ENTerprise REsearch InNOVAtion **2**, 208–213 (2016)
40. Konstantinou, C., Polydorou, N., Nicolaou, C.T., Karagiorgi, Y.: ATS2020 Developing and assessing transversal skills in primary and lower secondary education. Presented at the 10th Annual International Conference of Education, Research and Innovation, Seville, Spain November (2017)
41. Devedzic, V., et al.: Metrics for students' soft skills. Appl. Measur. Educ. **31**, 283–296 (2018). https://doi.org/10.1080/08957347.2018.1495212
42. Topping, K.J., Smith, E.F., Swanson, I., Elliot, A.: Formative peer assessment of academic writing between postgraduate students. Assess. Eval. High. Educ. **25**, 149–169 (2000). https://doi.org/10.1080/713611428
43. Boslaugh, S.: Statistics in a Nutshell (2012)
44. Schraw, G.: Promoting general metacognitive awareness. In: Hartman, H.J. (ed.) Metacognition in Learning and Instruction: Theory, Research and Practice, pp. 3–16. Springer, Netherlands, Dordrecht (2001)
45. Havenga, M.: Metacognitive and problem-solving skills to promote self-directed learning in computer programming: teachers' experiences, vol. 10, p. 14 (2013)
46. Oakley, B., Brent, R., Felder, R.M., Elhajj, I.: Turning student groups into effective teams. New Forums Press, vol. 2, (2004)

AgroEdu Through Co-crafting: Incorporating Minecraft into Co-design Activities for Agricultural Education

Xinliu Li and Baosheng Wang[✉]

School of Design, Hunan University, HN 731, Changsha, China
lixl@hnu.edu.cn, walterwang840217@gmail.com

Abstract. Although agriculture is no longer a main source of income and employment in modern society, it is still a key factor for sustainable development. With the development of urbanization, people, especially the younger generation, have largely lost their bonds to agriculture. Agricultural education is getting more and more attention. The exploration of agricultural teaching models and tools will be of great help to the popularization and development of agricultural education for children. There are some mature agricultural education frameworks abroad, but few cases and studies in China. The educational system referenced in this study is based on the localization and revision of the existing system. This paper documents a case of applying co-design activities to an agricultural education class, and proposes merging the game platform and game elements of a crafting game into a set of co-design toolbox, which is used to aid in the design process for inspiring, exploring, generating and prototyping. A quasi-experimental non-equivalent control group design was used to collect data by a mixed method. The results of pre and post test in two experimental environments were analyzed, and they showed that this form of teaching is better than the traditional teaching mode in terms of learning effect and learning experience. This paper provides a new method for how to incorporate games into design activities in agricultural teaching environment, and explains how the game-based toolbox is used, when, and for what purpose in the context of this study.

Keywords: Agricultural education · Minecraft · co-design with children · participatory design · toolboxes · agricultural literacy

1 Introduction

Agriculture has been a topical issue in recent years for its importance of tying to issues such as food safety, agricultural sustainability and mode of life. Many developed countries have formed relatively complete agricultural education systems. It is meaningful to develop a localized agricultural education framework and explore innovative ways of teaching.

In previous studies, the participation designers in co-design activities have expanded to people of different ages and living conditions, from children to the elderly to various

© The Author(s), under exclusive license to Springer Nature Switzerland AG 2023
P. Zaphiris and A. Ioannou (Eds.): HCII 2023, LNCS 14040, pp. 619–630, 2023.
https://doi.org/10.1007/978-3-031-34411-4_42

communities. In this paper, we mainly focus on using co-design methods in teaching environment with children. When we looked at co-design activities planning, we often find that a collaborative design dialogue can be explored and presented through a variety of tools and techniques. Therefore, when designing a project, it is necessary to decide which design approaches, methods, tools and techniques to use in a particular project.

The use of games in educational Settings is nothing new. According to research, nearly 75% of teachers use some kind of digital game to assist their curriculum (Jaclyn, 2021). Among them, crafting game can bring more space for teaching with its great ability of openness, extensibility and reality reflection. In addition, as children's agricultural education is oriented towards quality education, it does not have high requirements for the adaptation and expression of terms and formulas like professional disciplines, so there is a lot of room for the integration and play of games in agricultural education. However, in the current researches on game-based agricultural learning, either students are simply required to learn and interact in games, or gamified course design, or students are guided to participate in the design activities in the early stage of game generation. These forms are either partial to the application of games, or it is difficult to guarantee the effect for the high requirements on students' ability. This paper attempts to propose a method for incorporating game elements into a co-design toolbox for using in teaching activities. And it will answer the questions of how the toolbox is used, when, and for what purpose in subsequent sections.

2 Related Work

2.1 Agricultural Literacy and Agricultural Education

Agriculture is so relevant to our lives and its significance to our sustainable future is unparalleled. However, the non-agricultural population know almost nothing about how complex it is to maintain a viable agricultural system. Agricultural literacy is rarely mentioned and valued by people outside the agricultural disciplines. With the development of urbanization and the trend of industrial diversification, fewer people come into contact with and understand agriculture, especially the younger generation, whose cognition and attitude towards agriculture tend to be one-sided. Improving agricultural literacy is essential for local children to grow into more responsible consumers and even better local producers and local agricultural decision makers in the future.

Across the globe, American agricultural literacy and agricultural education system is one of the relatively comprehensive models. USDA officially established agricultural in the Classroom (AITC) in 1981. The National Research Council's Committee on Secondary Agricultural Education recommended that "all students should receive some systematic agricultural education from kindergarten through grade 12" (National Research Council, 1988, p. 2).

Since then, a variety of researchers have tried to define agricultural literacy. Frick (1990) reported the first conclusive definition of agricultural literacy: "Agricultural literacy can be defined as having knowledge and understanding of our food and fibre systems... Individuals with this knowledge will be able to synthesize, analyse and exchange basic information about agriculture" (p. 52). Leising and Zilbert (1994) explored agricultural literacy from the same perspective and developed a systematic curriculum framework that identified what students should know or be able to do.

There have been some frameworks in Agricultural Literacy Education since then.Food and Fiber Systems Literacy Framework (FFSL) since 1998 has been used by teachers, state agricultural education leaders, curriculum directors and others in more than 30 states (University of Minnesota, 2012). Project Food, Land & People, Inc. (FLP) is also a conceptual framework encompassing six integrated concepts from agricultural awareness to responsible decision-making for food, land and people today and in the future (Project Food, Land and People, 2012). The National Agricultural Literacy Outcomes (NALOs), which combines influential research and The above Agricultural Literacy framework, has developed five key subject areas that focus on The newer definition of Agricultural Literacy: "Understand and be able to communicate The sources and values of agriculture, Because it affects the quality of life" (National Agricultural Literacy Outcomes, 2014).

China's agricultural education started late and did not form a systematic content. Due to industrial structure change and curriculum revision, the proportion of agricultural content in the current curriculum has also decreased, and students' learning opportunities are limited. Especially in urban schools, pupils have little experience of agriculture and know little about where food comes from and the transition from farm to table. Developing a localized agricultural education system in China and exploring teaching methods and tools for agriculture in the classroom are meaningful and important. Table 1 shows the agricultural education framework after localization and revision of the existing framework according to local conditions.

Table 1. Revised agricultural education framework

Theme	Description
I. The Food and Fiber System: Understanding Agriculture	The relationship between agriculture and the environment; the importance and stewardship of natural resources in sustainably delivering high quality food, fiber, and energy while at the same time maintaining a quality environment
II. Culture, Society, Economy & Geography	The historical and cultural origin of the development of agriculture in the local area; the operation mode of agricultural products trading; and its significance to the local area
III. Food, Health & Lifestyle	The relationship between food production, storage, preparation, consumption, and health
IV. Science, Technology, Engineering & Mathematics	Understanding the science, engineering, technology, and mathematics of agriculture, food, and natural resources is crucial for the future of all humanity

2.2 Using Minecraft in Education

The rapid growth of the Internet has brought games to a wider audience. Many researchers agree that game is an ideal medium for learning (Gee, 2007; Prensky, 2005; Squire, 2011).

Minecraft (MC) is a sandbox video game, also called crafting game. Due to the rich mechanism, extensive resources and flexible editability, MC has been widely used in the teaching activities of many subjects. Examples include social skills (Petrov, 2014), computer science (Garcia Martinez, 2014), language and literacy (Hanghoj et al., 2014), informatics (Wagner, 2014), chemistry (Hancl, 2013), etc.

But the use cases for agricultural education are still limited, even though there are sufficient simulations of the natural world in the game. In MC, children can be exposed to various elements related to agriculture (Lane & Yi, 2017), for example, exploring and investigating the different biomes and climates that match the Earth, including grasslands, jungles, deserts, forests, and coniferous forests; navigating through different types of terrain, such as hills, mountains, caves, and oceans; interacting with a variety of animals, including farmed animals (e.g. cattle, sheep, pigs, chickens, horses, fish, etc.) and a variety of wildlife; engaging in agricultural production, planting and harvesting food crops (wheat, corn, etc.), melons, fruits and vegetables, etc.; conducting simple food cooking and commodity resource trading.

Therefore, this study believes that MC has great application potential in agricultural education. Using digital games, like MC in agricultural classroom has many advantages. Compared with traditional education model, it can improve students' learning interest and motivation (Hidi & Renninger, 2006; Rotgans & Schmidt, 2011). Compared with field teaching mode, it is more flexible and convenient for indoor organization and management.

2.3 Tools and Techniques to Engage Children in Co-design

Sanders and Stappers (2008) describe co-design as an approach to extend participatory design and co-creation. Wenger (1998) argues that the process of participating in a co-design practice is like a 'complex process that combines doing, talking, thinking, feeling, and belonging. It involves our whole person including our bodies, minds, emotions, and social relations.'

We believe that design practice projects in any environment are explored and presented in a collaborative design dialogue through a variety of tools and techniques. They can actually be combined, adapted, and extended, To form a new Co-design toolboxes (Simonsen et al., 2012).Therefore, when designing a project, it is necessary to decide which design approaches, methods, tools and techniques to use in a particular project. Over the years, many studies have been conducted on how tools and techniques are used in participatory design practices. Among them, Sanders et al. (2012) proposed a framework for organizing the tools and techniques of participatory design, describing how engagement practices occur in an iterative cycle of making, telling, and enacting. Making means making tangible things including 2-D collages, 2-D mappings and 3-D mock-ups. Talking can be telling and explaining through diaries/daily logs and cards. And the forms of enacting can vary from game boards and game pieces and rules for playing to acting out, skits and play acting.

When collaborative design takes place in the learning environment, the design and use of Tools and Techniques should be in line with the cognitive level and behavioral ability of children in the corresponding age group. This study seeks to integrate a video game and its elements into the development of the design toolbox, and attempts to answer the questions of which tools and techniques are used, when, and for what purpose in the context of this study.

3   Case Study

3.1   Participant

This project involved a class of students aged 9–12 in grade 5 of the primary school in Baoding City, China. Before the workshop, we discussed the time and frequency of the whole design activity with the teacher, so as to ensure that the children have the corresponding rest time and the initiative to participate in each activity. In order to prevent children from forgetting or affecting their main lessons because of a long interval between workshops, there are 4 workshops in the whole game design process. The whole class is divided into groups with the help of teachers. At the same time, ensure that members of each group in creativity, painting ability, expression and organization ability have certain complementary advantages. In addition, two other design professionals and two teachers, participated in the activity and were responsible for guiding, observing, recording, photographing and maintaining the scene order. There were fifteen students participated in the complete co-design learning workshop as the experimental group, while another fifteen served as the control group to receive agricultural content teaching in the traditional mode.

3.2   Data Collection

A quasi-experimental non-equivalent control group design was adopted and mixed-method approaches were used to collect data. Qualitative research methods involved multiple data collection sources, including interviews with students and faculty, 12 on-site diaries (completed by designers after each activity), design reflection list (completed by students after design activity), observation notes, audio and video information, and workshop outputs (e.g., post-it notes, pic collages, drawn chart, prototypes, etc.). Quantitative research mainly evaluates the learning effect and learning experience. Learning effect mainly assesses the change of students' agricultural literacy before and after taking the course. It consists of 12 multiple choice questions to test agricultural knowledge and 10 Likert scales to measure agricultural attitudes. Learning experience focuses on assessing students' desire, enjoyment and participation in classroom activities. It consists of 15 scale questions. The test contents were selected from existing mature evaluation systems (Sara et al., 2020; Igo et al., 1999; Reeve and Tseng, 2011), some of which were adjusted according to the practical application situation.

3.3 The Co-crafting Design Process

In this article, co-crafting refers to the form of co-design which we make full use of crafting game itself and its properties and elements, and incorporate them into design activities, as well as setting the final design goal like building a land-scape/object/comprehensive scene together in the game.

In this campaign, the final design goal was defined as "building a miniature agricultural landscape in MC based on local geomorphic features". The whole activity includes four sessions, as shown in Fig. 1. From the design stage, it can be summarized as inspiring, exploring, generating and prototyping. Each two sessions will experience diverging and converging of thinking and focus scope. Among these, the inspiring and exploring sessions are in the define stage to figure out what can usually be included in the "agricultural landscape" of the design task. The generating and prototyping sessions belong to the execute stage, which will convert the knowledge accumulated from previous exploration into the ideas needed to complete the design task and put them into practice.

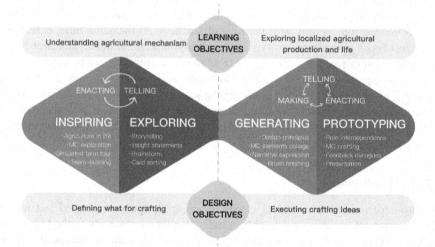

Fig. 1. Overview of the co-crafting design process

Defining What for Crafting. This phase mainly includes the inspiring and exploring sessions. The inspiring session mainly led children to have a preliminary understanding of agriculture (see Fig. 2a). Through multimedia teaching, children are inspired to focus on how agriculture is relevant to all aspects of our lives. After the introduction of the game platform, we let children enter the game from a unified player's perspective after a preliminary introduction to the game, and experience how different creatures will be generated in different biological communities under specific terrain and climate characteristics. After that, they visit the FARM LIFE world developed by pixelheads in MC and experience the preset farm life in the game. Because we expect children to learn more about local agriculture, the teaching content is also directed towards the agricultural attributes of the school area. After announcing the design tasks to be completed in the following sessions, we divided the children into three groups according to the three main local terrains: plain, mountain and lake, and they were respectively responsible for exploring the agricultural development mode corresponding to the terrains in the following sessions. Each group included a two-person group and a three-person group.

The children are required to accumulate agricultural knowledge materials corresponding to the terrain they are responsible for by communicating with their families, conducting field research and searching by themselves after class. In the second session, the children brought the fragments of knowledge collected after class to share with everyone. Figure 2b shows the children reading the printed materials after class on the stage. In addition, students living near the corresponding terrain also shared their experiences of local farming. Finally, after some discussions and brainstorm, a lot of local agricultural production and life related contents were accumulated in each terrain. Through the card sort, the children further collate the content.

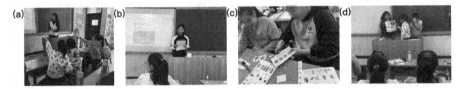

Fig. 2. Photos of children participating in different stages of design process

Executing Crafting Ideas. After the preparation of the first two sessions, the children have already had a preliminary idea of the implementation of the design task. Through the introduction of design principles, it is convenient for children to have a better understanding of the rules, limitations and main objectives of design activities. Then each group was given several pieces of game material for collage, for which the children built their initial ideas on paper (see Fig. 2c). Of course, the material is far from completely covering the children's ideas, so they are also allowed to assist the design and expression of the scene through the brush. Figure 2d shows that the children can't wait to share the scenes and stories in their collage when they finish their first version.

In the final class, children are encouraged to put the content of the paper prototype to the online gaming platform. After the initial exploration of the game in the first session, and seeing various game elements interspersed in the later sessions, the children can quickly pick up the game. In the game, there are objects and scenes preset by the research team. Groups in charge of different terrain will be given kits containing different objects. The contents of the kits refer to the idea expressed by the children on the paper prototype in last session. After completion, each group shared their own group's scene construction through screen casting, listened to others' opinions and views on the design results they were responsible for, and carried out further iteration and improvement. In Fig. 3, three screenshots were extracted respectively of the teams responsible for agricultural landscapes with different terrains when they were crafting in the game.

Fig. 3. Screenshots of three theme groups crafting in MC

4 Results

A descriptive analysis of learning effect and learning experience was conducted by SPSS software. In addition, in order to control the initial differences between the experimental group and the control group in terms of participation motivation and agricultural literacy, ANCOVA test was used to make the comparison between the two groups more fair and objective, and enhance credibility.

The assessment of learning effect consists of two parts: the multiple choice question of agricultural knowledge assessment and the five-level scale of agricultural attitude assessment, with the total score between 0–60 and 0–50. Learning experience is assessed primarily on a five-level participation scale, with scores ranging from 0 to 75.

Descriptive analysis showed that the average scores of the experimental group on learning effect in knowledge and attitude increased from 28.73 (SD = 8.87) and 31.27 (SD = 7.23) in the pretest to 45.67 (SD = 7.41) and 48.87 (SD = 1.68) in the post-test. The average score of learning experience increased from 38.93 (SD = 10.73) in the pretest to 63.07 (SD = 9.28) in the post-test, which was larger than that in the control group.

At the same time, the results of ANCOVA test are shown in Table 2 and Table 3. Learners in the two groups have significant differences in learning effect (F = 17.685, p < 0.01) and learning experience (F = 46.134, p < 0.01), which means that the experimental group has obtained better results in learning activities than the control group.

Table 2. Analysis of covariance for Learning Effect post-test scores by group

Source	SS	df	MS	F	Sig
Pretest	327.666	1	327.666	4.196	.050
Groups	1381.009	1	1381.009	17.685	.000
Error	2108.467	27	78.091		
Total	232965.000	30			

Table 3. Analysis of covariance for Learning Experience post-test scores by group

Source	SS	df	MS	F	Sig
Pretest	387.882	1	387.882	6.414	.017
Groups	2789.880	1	2789.880	46.134	.000
Error	1632.785	27	60.474		
Total	89245.000	30			

5 Discussion

The whole design activity is divided into four sessions. By integrating game elements into the co-design toolbox, the whole design activity is integrated by unified elements and design tasks, which is more coherent than the workshops with piecemeal tools and activity forms. Compared with the traditional education mode, this form is innovative and interesting. And the experimental results show that it can obtain better teaching effect.

But there is no denying that the use of games in educational classrooms itself has some limitations, such as children tend to get caught up in irrelevant elements of a game other than the main task, making them unable to stay focused on the design goal. In addition, although the game has largely simulated the environments and objects of the real world, the game elements and functional mechanics are still limited.

6 Conclusion

The case study in this paper show that incorporating games into agricultural education classrooms is an interesting and effective teaching model. Different from other game-based learning, this paper does not simply bring game platforms into class for students to learn and interact with games, nor does it guide children to design a new game from scratch, but sets the final designing task as completing the crafting game. With the great openness, extensibility and reality simulating capabilities of crafting game, children can discover many things while generating ideas, and have a lot of freedom in it. The results showed that the co-design toolbox combined with game elements played a role in moving the entire design process, and the experimental group obtained better learning effects than the traditional teaching mode.

Of course, each game platform has its own visual style and unique mechanics that not all children will enjoy and adapt to. Also the application of participatory design in education is still being explored. Although this form in the study has achieved better learning effect than the traditional one, it has certain implementation threshold and design cost, and its extensibility also needs to be improved. The follow-up research will continue to focus on the direction of localized agricultural education and give further consideration to the above problems.

Acknowledgments. Throughout the writing I have received a great deal of support and assistance. I would first like to thank my supervisor, whose expertise was invaluable in formulating the research questions and methodology. His insightful feedback pushed me to sharpen my thinking and brought my work to a higher level. Also I would like to thank my parents and friends for their wise counsel and sympathetic ear.

This research is supported by Hunan Science and Technology Key Research Project (No. 2022GK2070), and Hunan Social Science Foundation (No. 19YBA085).

References

National Research Council: Understanding Agriculture-New Directions for Education. Council Committee on Agricultural Education in Secondary Schools, Board of Agriculture. National Academy Press, Washington (1988)

Frick, M.J., Kahler, A.A., Miller, W.W.: The subject areas and concepts of agricultural literacy. In: 17th Annual National Agricultural Education Research Meeting, Cincinnati (1990)

Leising, J.G., Zilbert, E.E.: Validation of the California agriculture literacy framework. In: Proceedings of the National Agricultural Education Research Meeting, USA, vol. 21, pp. 112–119 (1994)

University of Minnesota: Reinventing the Food and Fiber Systems (Agricultural) Literacy Curriculum Framework (2012). http://www.reeis.usda.gov/web/crisprojectpages/0223482-reinve nting-the-food-andfiber-systems-agricultural-literacy-curriculum-framework.html. Accessed 11 Nov 2015, from USDA Research, Education and Economics Information Systems

Project Food, Land & People (2012). http://www.foodlandpeople.org/. Accessed 22 Aug 2015, from Food, Land & People

National Agricultural Literacy Outcomes (2014). Accessed from National Agriculture in the Classroom

Druin, A.: Cooperative inquiry: developing new technologies for children with children. In: Proceedings of the SIGCHI Conference on Human Factors in Computing Systems, CHI 1999, pp. 592–599. ACM, New York (1999). https://doi.org/10.1145/302979.303166

Druin, A.: The role of children in the design of new technology. Behav. Inf. Technol. 21, 1–25 (2002)

Druin, A., Weeks, A., Massey, S., Bederson, B.B.: Children's interests and concerns when using the international children's digital library: a four-country case study. In: Proceedings of the 7th ACM/IEEE-CS Joint Conference on Digital Libraries, JCDL 2007, pp. 167–176. ACM, New York (2007). https://doi.org/10.1145/1255175.1255207

Guha, M., Druin, A., Fails, J.: Cooperative inquiry revisited: reflections of the past and guidelines for the future of intergenerational co-design. Int. J. Child-Comput. Interact. 1, 14–23 (2013)

Schuler, D., Namioka, A.: Participatory Design: Principles and Practices. The United States of America: Library of Congress (1993)

Klapwijk, R.M., Gielen, M.A., Schut, A., van Mechelen, M.P.P.: Guidebook—your turn for the teacher: guidebook to develop real-life design lessons for use with 8–14 years old pupils. Technische Universiteit Delft (2021)

Van Mechelen, M., Laenen, A., Zaman, B., Willems, B., Abeele, V.V.: Collaborative Design Thinking (CoDeT): a co-design approach for high child-to-adult ratios. Int. J. Hum. Comput. Stud. 130, 179–195 (2019). https://doi.org/10.1016/j.ijhcs.2019.06.013

Gielen, M.A.: Exploring the child's mind – contextmapping research with children. Digit. Creativity 19(3), 174–184 (2008). https://doi.org/10.1080/14626260802312640

Van Mechelen, M., Derboven, J., Laenen, A., Willems, B., Geerts, D., Vanden Abeele, V.: The GLID method: moving from design features to underlying values in co-design. Int. J. Hum. Comput. Stud. 97, 116–128 (2017). https://doi.org/10.1016/j.ijhcs.2016.09.005

de Vries, E.: Students' construction of external representations in design-based learning situations. Learn. Instr. **16**, 213–227 (2006)

Doppelt, Y., Mehalik, M.M., Schunn, C.D., Silk, E., Krysinski, D.: Engagement and achievements: a case study of design-based learning in a science context. J. Technol. Educ. **19**(2), 22–39 (2008)

Fortus, D., Dershimet, R.C., Krajcik, J., Marx, R.W., Mamlok-Naaman, R.: Design-based science and student learning. J. Res. Sci. Teach. **41**(10), 1081–1110 (2004)

Ke, F.: An implementation of design-based learning through creating educational computer games: a case study on mathematics learning during design and computing. Comput. Educ. **73**, 26–39 (2014)

Chen, C.H., Chiu, C.H.: Employing intergroup competition in multitouch design-based learning to foster student engagement, learning achievement, and creativity. Comput. Educ. **103**, 99–113 (2016)

Fortus, D., Krajcik, J., Dershimer, R.C., Marx, R.W., Mamlok-Naamand, R.: Design-based science and real world problem-solving. Int. J. Sci. Educ. **27**(7), 855–879 (2005)

Lewin, C., Cranmer, S., McNicol, S.: Developing digital pedagogy through learning design: an activity theory perspective: developing digital pedagogy through learning design. Br. J. Edu. Technol. **49**(6), 1131–1144 (2018). https://doi.org/10.1111/bjet.12705

Bennett, A.G., Cassim, F.: How design education can use generative play to innovate for social change: a case study on the design of South African children's health education toolkits **11**(2), 16 (2017)

Engeström, Y.: Expansive learning at work: toward an activity theoretical reconceptualization. J. Educ. Work. **14**(1), 133–156 (2001). https://doi.org/10.1080/13639080020028747

Sangiorgi, D.: Building up a framework for service design research. Paper Presented at the 8th EAD (European Academy of Desgin) Conference 'Connexity', Aberdeen, Scotland (2009)

Callaghan, M., McShane, N., Eguíluz, A.G., Savin-Baden, M.: Extending the activity theory based model for serious games design in engineering to integrate analytics. Int. J. Eng. Pedagogy (IJEP) **8**(1), 109 (2018). https://doi.org/10.3991/ijep.v8i1.8087

Law, E.L.-C., Sun, X.: Evaluating user experience of adaptive digital educational games with Activity Theory. Int. J. Hum. Comput. Stud. **70**(7), 478–497 (2012). https://doi.org/10.1016/j.ijhcs.2012.01.007

Zahedi, M., Tessier, V., Hawey, D.: Understanding collaborative design through activity theory. Des. J. **20**(sup1), S4611–S4620 (2017). https://doi.org/10.1080/14606925.2017.1352958

Zahedi, M., Tessier, V.: Designerly activity theory: toward a new ontology for design research. In: Design Research Society Conference 2018, 28 June 2018. https://doi.org/10.21606/drs.2018.197

Zheng, X., Kim, H., Lai, W., Hwang, G.: Cognitive regulations in ICT-supported flipped classroom interactions: an activity theory perspective. Br. J. Edu. Technol. **51**(1), 103–130 (2020). https://doi.org/10.1111/bjet.12763

Drain, A., Shekar, A., Grigg, N.: Insights, Solutions and Empowerment: a framework for evaluating participatory design. CoDesign **17**(1), 1–21 (2021). https://doi.org/10.1080/15710882.2018.1540641

Iivari, N., Kinnula, M., Kuure, L.: With best intentions: a Foucauldian examination on children's genuine participation in ICT design. Inf. Technol. People **28**(2), 246–280 (2015). https://doi.org/10.1108/ITP-12-2013-0223

Klapwijk, R.M.: Formative assessment of creativity. In: de Vries, M. (ed.) Handbook of technology education, pp. 765–784. Springer, Cham (2018). https://doi.org/10.1007/978-3-319-44687-5_55

Campbell, D., Stanley, J.: Experimental and Quasi-Experimental Designs for Research. Rand-McNally, Chicago (1963)

Lane, H.C., Yi, S.: Playing with virtual blocks: minecraft as a learning environment for practice and research. In: Cognitive Development in Digital Contexts, pp. 145–166. Elsevier (2017). https://doi.org/10.1016/B978-0-12-809481-5.00007-9

Sanders, E.B., Stappers, P.J.: Co-creation and the new landscapes of design. CoDesign: Int. J. CoCreation Des. Arts **4**(1), 5–18 (2008)

Wenger, E.: Communities of Practice:Learning: Meaning and Identity. Cambridge University Press, Cambridge (1998)

Simonsen, J., Robertson, T.: Tools and techniques: ways to engage telling, making and enacting. In: Routledge International Handbook of Participatory Design, pp. 165–201. Routledge (2012). https://doi.org/10.4324/9780203108543-14

Development and validation of a children's agricultural literacy instrument for local food. J. Agric. Educ. **61**(3) (2020). https://doi.org/10.5032/jae.2020.0300233

Reeve, J., Tseng, C.-M.: Agency as a fourth aspect of students' engagement during learning activities. Contemp. Educ. Psychol. **36**(4), 257–267 (2011). https://doi.org/10.1016/j.cedpsych.2011.05.002

Design and Assessment of a Tool for Improving Creativity and Imagination in School Children

Pawan Pagaria(⊠), Abhijeet Kujur, and Jyoti Kumar

Indian Institute of Technology, Delhi, India
alwayspawan@gmail.com

Abstract. Education is the backbone of every society, and its core goal is to internalize the maximum potential of every child. With the advent of technologies like AI, Machine Learning, Robotics, Automation, the landscape of the future is witnessing a major shift. The skills required in future are also different from what is being taught in the current school education. Creativity has been reported to be among the top three required skills in the next decade with complex problem solving and critical thinking acquiring the top two positions. For creativity to work, imagination is needed as a fuel. This paper reports about the development of imagination and creativity in kids using a new pedagogical tool called 'platos'. The pedagogical tool was developed using platonic solids as props for intervention. The tool was further assessed using neurophysiological instruments like EEG and GSR. These neurophysiological instruments are capable of sensing electrical movements in humans. The neurophysiological responses of the frontal and parietal part of the brain were filtered and then the results were analysed. Furthermore, the changes in sweat gland or galvanic skin response (aka EDA) activity were captured. GSR is a direct indication for emotional state changes also known as emotional arousal/anxiety. Combining Skin conductance with valence, moments of key engagements can be understood, and their significance can be established. The idea was to check the neurophysiological responses of the students while they undergo any hands-on creative activity. The findings indicated that in order for youngsters to acquire innovative and creative perceptions of geometrical forms and spatial comprehension, a creative visual intervention is necessary to enhance their creativity.

Keywords: Imagination · Creativity · Platonic Solids · EEG · GSR · HRV

1 Introduction

Imagination is more important than knowledge. - Albert Einstein.

The ability to imagine is something which separates us from the rest of the species. It is also the first step to create. The innate ability to recognise patterns, combine existing data points in unique ways, use analogies to create new solutions, all requires imagination. As per Burke [1], imagination is the core of our survival and acts as an advanced component of human identity. Imagination is a kind of experience which is both deep

P. Zaphiris and A. Ioannou (Eds.): HCII 2023, LNCS 14040, pp. 631–641, 2023.
https://doi.org/10.1007/978-3-031-34411-4_43

and intuitive and is present at a level beneath verbal and speech articulation. Imagination helps in understanding various abstract relationships in life, for example imagining one's relation with the tree outside the window helps in making sense of the exchange of oxygen between the tree and human [2]. Gündoğan [3] posits that imagination is the act of creating something which one has never experienced before or being told about.

Creativity and imagination are intertwined, however the later precedes the former. Imagination is required for creativity to flourish. Creation of new and unfamiliar images using existing knowledge is creative imagination [4]. As per Duffy [5], learning and experience aid to the development of imagination & creativity. The quality of imagination varies with age of an individual. Due to the difference in maturity, imagination of children differs compared to adults. Imagination in a child is simple, elementary and poor whereas in adults it is more subtler, complex and diverse [6]. Though children produce imagination in lower quality than adults yet they appear more fanciful because their emotions are less controlled and their reliability is high [7].

According to Silva, "It is a world in which comfort with ideas and abstractions is the passport to a good job, in which creativity and innovation are the key to the good life, in which high levels of education—a very different kind of education than most of us have had—are going to be the only security there is" [8]. As per Ribot [9], every invention, whether large or small, before being implemented, embodied, was held together by the imagination alone. It was a structure erected in the mind through the agency of new combinations and relationships. Creativity is a skill which can be nurtured and harnessed, however the current school education system provides a limited scope for it. A rejig in pedagogical approaches in school education might pave the way for creativity to flourish. Introduction of play-based activities have proven to be the fertile ground for creative thinking to develop [10]. Though all play is not creative, yet play is necessary to be creative [11].

Platonic solids are regular polyhedral and range from basic tetrahedron to complex dodecahedron. Laser cut nets of platonic solids were created in paper and precise half cuts were created at the folding area. The laser cut nets along with ring magnets acted as objects of exploration and education. The tool used geometry as an aid to titillate imagination, as geometry is already part of the school curriculum, and it has the potential to immediately connect with existing curricular structure. The completed paper polyhedrons act as props for students to create imaginary objects. The whole exercise was designed for exploration in three dimensions and to create objects which a child is free to propose. Electroencephalogram (EEG) detects electrical activity in our brain using small, metal discs (electrodes) attached to your scalp. The output shows wavy lines on an EEG recording. The frontal lobe plays an important role in creative thought, reflection, emotional response, writing etc.

2   Literature Review

2.1   Geometry and Its Relationship with Creativity

There is a strong perception that creativity is related to art class rather than a mathematics classroom. Though creative thinking is equally related to mathematics yet mathematics is more about rational, critical and sequential thinking [12]. Creativity in mathematics is based on one's knowledge base rather than academic achievement [13]. If a student is able to create something to facilitate his learning abilities in a mathematics classroom, it is assumed that it's a display of creative ability [14]. However as per Fisher [15], creativity is not only related to the context of learning but also to widen the horizon beyond subject learning [16]. One more aspect of mathematics is geometry. In geometry learning classroom, the main focus is on knowing the mathematical terms and properties of basic shapes like square, rectangle, triangle, cylinder etc. [17]. Apart from understanding the physical world through geometry, it also helps in development of spatial reasoning. This additionally helps in development of skills like cognitive, generalization, analytical and comparison skills, which are helpful in enhancing one's creative thinking ability [18].

Hands-on exploration plays a major role in learning of geometry and at the same time helps in development of creativity and originality in students [19]. Use of physical intervention such as tangram, Lego, Frobel's blocks is highly recommended for learning and will provide better learning opportunities and help in self exploration of spatial relationships [20]. Many studies have established the use of tangrams as an effective tool to learn geometric concepts and developing imagination, creativity, and shape analysis [21–23]. However, there is a dearth of studies which uses platonic solids as a tool for titillating imagination and creativity in children.

2.2 Human Perception of Platonic Solids: Cognitive and Affective Aspects

Platonic solids are convex regular polyhedral. In the classic treatise, Euclid proved that there are only five regular polyhedral- the tetrahedron, cube, octahedron, icosahedron and dodecahedron [24]. In one of Plato's dialogues *Timaeus* ca. 350 BC, platonic solids are described and each of the platonic solids are equated to the basic components of nature. The tetrahedron with fire, octahedron with air, cube with earth, icosahedron with water and dodecahedron with which the constellations and heavens are comprised of. Consciously or subconsciously, platonic solids are part of our daily life, be it toddler playing with wooden cubes, the tetrahedral structure of methane, the icosahedral form of the viruses or the occurrence of such solids in art, architecture and molecular biology [25]. Various exploration and experimentation has been done using platonic solids. Archimedes (ca 212 BC) integrated platonic solids and came up with semi-regular convex polyhedra as Archimedean solids. From Leonardo Da Vinci (1452–1519), Johannes Kepler (1571–1630) to Buckminster Fuller (1895–1983) many eminent thinkers have explored polyhedrons in many ways ranging from relation of polyhedrons with solar system to its application in architecture. Hence, it may be concluded that the human creativity is intertwined with the daily life perception and visualisation of platonic solids.

2.3 Neurophysiological Measures of Creative Ideation

Creativity is gaining popularity not just in the realm of popular culture, but also in a wide range of scientific areas. Two important mental processes combine to create a creative output- Cognition & Emotion. Creativity or the process of creative ideation has also been studied in cognitive sciences, psychology, and neurosciences [26, 27]. Using electroencephalography (EEG) and GSR, neuroscientific investigations on creative ideation may provide light on the many ways in which creative thinking arises in the brains of school going children. Neuroimaging studies examined brain activity during a variety of creativity-related activities, from divergent thinking to insightful problem solving to artistic or musical innovation [27, 28].

EEG activity may be measured in a variety of ways, and several approaches have previously proven fruitful in the study of creativity [28]. Among these approaches are the evaluation of variations in spectral power in different EEG frequency bands, the method of event-related potentials (ERP), and the examination of functional connectivity (or functional coupling) between brain regions. This study focuses on the investigation of task- or event-related EEG frequency power variations. EEG spectral analysis may be performed to calculate the band-specific frequency power for particular time intervals. Moreover, task- or event-related power changes may be assessed by comparing the power in a particular frequency band during a cognitive activity (e.g., a creativity challenge) to the power in the prior reference period. Research indicates that EEG alpha wave activity is responsive to varying creativity-related task demands [29].

3   Methodology and Materials

3.1   Stimuli

The experiment was designed to assess the change in imagination & creativity when children were asked to interact with 'Platos' tool kit. 'Platos' tool kit consists of laser cut paper nets of all the platonic solids. The kit also consists of an instruction manual, and a packet of glue drops for sticking the paper solids together. The basic idea of this tool kit is that the children make the solids using the laser cut nets (which are also provided with half cut for easy folding). In this experiment, the children were provided with pre-formed paper solids using the nets (Fig. 1a). The only task assigned to children was to combine the solids using glue drops provided. This was done to test the core functionality of the kit. A small video of different formations using the solids was made as an intervention to see the change in the level of creativity and imagination of the children, post its introduction (Fig. 1b). An entire stimulus was created as a self-paced presentation as per Fig. 2. The entire stimuli were displayed on a 52 inch dell monitor, which was place approximately one feet away from the participants. The snapshots of the stimuli can be seen in the figure below.

(a)   (b)

Fig. 1. (a) Platonic Solids (Paper Solids), (b) Visual Intervention (1:07 min video clip)

3.2 Participants

This study was conducted on 8 participants (4 Male,4 Female; Mean Age $= 12.18$ years, SD $= 2.207$ years). All the participants were school students. All the participants were residents of urban areas and none of them were under any medication. They were all familiar with computers and were able to follow the instructions on screen without any external help.

3.3 Procedure

In the study, participants were instructed to wear a Emotiv Epoc EEG-headset (14 channels), a galvanic skin response (GSR) sensor Empatica wristwatch. They were then exposed to the stimuli as the sequence in Fig. 2. Prior to the experiment, participants were briefed about the overall stimuli and were asked if they understood the entire activity to be performed. They were instructed to be relaxed and have less body and head movement during the activity. They were asked to perform the task as per instructions on the screen.

The first slide was on 'welcoming' the participant, second was on narrating the hypothetical scenario, third was on giving them basic instruction on precaution to follow, fourth was to make them aware that the experiment is going to start, and they can take a deep breath. On the fifth slide, instruction was to close their eyes and relax for three minutes. The participants here were also instructed that they will hear a tap on the door when the relaxation period is over. On the sixth slide they were asked to create as many objects they can imagine using the paper platonic solids in front of them. The participants were also told to note all the ideas on a sheet of paper provided. This activity lasted for ten minutes, followed by a rest of one min with open eyes as the next instruction. On the eighth slide, it was instructed that a small video on different formations of platonic solid will be shown. A video, the duration of which was one minute seven seconds was played and it automatically led to the ninth slide. Instructions on this slide were similar on the sixth slide, where they were again asked to create objects using platonic solids for ten minutes. The tenth slide, the final slide again asked the participants to do relaxation with closed eyes for three minutes.

After the experiment was over, the participants were then interviewed for eight to ten minutes to share their experiences on the activity. Questions like - What they liked most and disliked about the activity? How engaging was the activity? Were the solids helpful in conceiving new ideas?

While the entire activity was being carried out, the data from the EEG Headset and GSR was being captured and recorded on the connected computer. Figure 3. Presents an overview of the setup with participants performing the task with platonic solids.

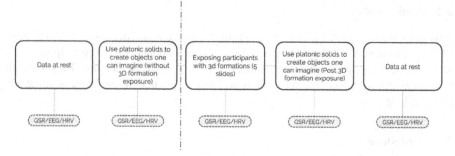

Fig. 2. Overall Flow of the stimuli

Fig. 3. Participants activity during the experiment

4   Analysis and Results

This research collected data using two primary methods. The first method involves the evaluation of EEG frequency band power. During kinaesthetic engagement with platonic solids, participants described their creativity in terms of cognition, emotion, and experience. The frequency domain analysis of EEG power is reported to reflect the affective and cognitive aspects in a particular experimental context [30]. The second source of information was gathered as the psychogalvanic reflexes from the GSR device. The GSR wristwatch recorded the data while the participants were trying to create different objects by combining different platonic solids. Finally, the two types of data were evaluated and analysed as mentioned in this section.

4.1   EEG Response During the Use of Platonic Solids

Using an EEG headband sensor, the participants' affective and cognitive levels were mapped while they engaged with the platonic solids before and after the visual intervention. The visual intervention displayed the animated illustration of probable objects that can be created through platonic solids. The link between EEG frequency power of various channels and the two experimental conditions are well established in this section. EEG is classified into five frequency bands based on brain functions: delta (1–3 Hz), theta (4–7 Hz), alpha (8–13 Hz), beta (14–30 Hz) and gamma (31–50 Hz) [31] [32]. Typically, delta and theta brain waves are present during sleep or a calm state of mind. Alpha is mostly produced during moments of low mental activity, while beta and gamma are produced during more complicated cognitive processes. However, there is a dearth of EEG based study while there is an interaction with platonic solids. Nonetheless, EEG measures of emotional states have been reported on several occasions [33–35]. Additionally, EEG has been used to evaluate cognitive function. Lower EEG frequency bands, such as Alpha, remain synchronised throughout the resting state and become more synchronised with increasing task difficulty [31]. When cognitive stress increases, the power of higher frequency bands like beta and gamma increases. Due to the fact that EEG-based evaluation of use of platonic solids encompasses both the cognitive and emotional states of the user, EEG is an effective approach for assessing the components that contribute to creative thought and imagination in brain activity. The frequency band power of EEG data was used as a property in this study to examine the association between brain activity and thoughts created during the activity with platonic solids. The graph below depicts the EEG frequency band power of subjects using platonic solids before and after the visual intervention. The EEG data is displayed in 4 parts: (i) Closed-eye resting EEG response of the participants before and after the visual intervention, (ii) EEG power bands generated while the participants were using platonic solids, (iii) Alpha power during creative ideation in the frontal region, and (iv) Alpha power during creative ideation in the parietal region.

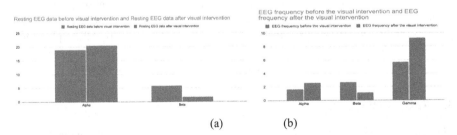

(a)   (b)

Fig. 4. (a)Closed-eye resting EEG response of the participants before and after the visual intervention (b)EEG power bands generated while the participants were using platonic solids

The EEG data was filtered, sorted and other artifacts like electrical noise, movement related noise were removed. In the light of the acquired data, it can be inferred that the visual intervention in the case of platonic solids or 3D geometrical solids is statistically beneficial for enhancing the creative thinking among school children. The Bonferroni

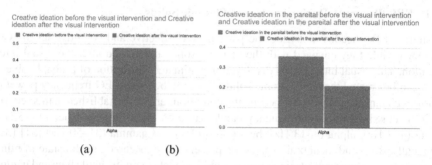

Fig. 5. (a) Alpha power during creative ideation in the frontal region (b) Alpha power during creative ideation in the parietal region

adjustment for multiple comparisons changed the significance level to 0.05 to account for the number of segments before and after the visual intervention. Figure 4(a) demonstrates that alpha, which is a marker of low mental activity, is slightly less before the visual intervention. At the same time beta is the marker of a higher cognitive activity and is seen a bit higher in the beginning before the intervention. This implies that the stress level of the participants decreased during the experiment as they got engaged with the process of creative ideation that included exposure to a visual intervention. Figure 4(b) illustrates the EEG responses of the participants before and after the intervention. Higher relaxed state of the brain via alpha band is observed after the visual intervention. Similarly, higher cognitive activity is seen before the participants were exposed to the intervention. Neuroscientific research on creativity has shown mixed results. Despite recent studies' discouraging findings on creativity's neurobiology, EEG alpha power seems to be highly responsive to numerous creativity-related demands involved in creative ideation. Alpha power increases after creative treatments and depends on creativity-related task demands and idea originality. Right hemisphere of the frontal and parietal region of the brain are associated with the creative ideation. Figure 5(a) shows that alpha power at the right hemisphere of the frontal region is increased after the intervention justifying the creativity-related task demands. Figure 5(b) elaborates the alpha power of the right parietal region. The graph shows that before the creativity intervention the alpha is high due to the less ideation processes. Consequently, the information processing increased in the right parietal region after the intervention, and thus alpha decreased.

4.2   GSR Findings

The Galvanic skin response is used to measure the skin's electrical conductivity. As the Asymptomatic Nervous System (ANS) controls sweat gland activity, it varies with time [36]. Previous research has shown that skin conductivity rises synchronously with emotional arousal [37]. A commercial GSR sensor (Empatica E4 wristwatch sensor) was employed for psychogalvanic reflexes measurement. The sensor was fixed on the wrist of the participant. In order to define the variability of the GSR signal, data were evaluated and analysed in the temporal domain. Using techniques of normalisation, data was filtered. The following formula was used to produce normalised data: Experimental

GSR minus GSR at baseline = GSR normalised. The graph below depicts the rate of change of arousal under two distinct stimulus settings.

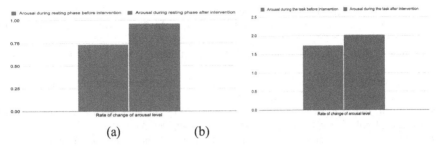

(a)   (b)

Fig. 6. (a) Comparison of arousal level during resting stage, (b) Comparison of arousal level during the hands-on activity.

The Fig. 6 (b) above depict the increase in the rate of emotional arousal as measured by the GSR sensor during the usage of platonic solids. With the introduction of the visual intervention, which consists of animated video clips demonstrating how to employ platonic solids, the rate of change of emotional arousal changes considerably. After an appreciable delay [38], the mean degree of arousal across all participants peaked. The amount of skin conductance rises in proportion to the length of contact with platonic solids. The GSR data shows that the arousal level is increasing between the two resting phases and hands-on activity before and after the visual intervention. This increase in arousal may be due to the creative ideation that happened after the exposure of visual cues. This concludes that the visual creative cues are helpful in enhancing the perception level of 3D geometrical shapes in children.

5   Discussion and Conclusions

Therefore, based on the experiment conducted to evaluate the interaction between platonic solids and schoolchildren's creative ideation processes regarding geometrical shapes, it can be concluded that a visual prompt as a form of intervention may increase the conditions in which creativity and imagination flourish. Similarly, the use of neurophysiological instruments such as EEG and GSR gives a greater understanding when analyzing the interplay between hand-held equipment designed to increase schoolchildren's 3D geometrical inventiveness. Throughout the experience mapping process, GSR, EEG, and other neurophysiological techniques can better monitor the pain locations, stress levels, and present emotional states of children. There is a need to include these neurophysiological assessment methods to increase user engagement with creativity-enhancing hands-on tools.

References

1. Burkez, P.A.: The healing power of the imagination. Int. J. Children's Spirituality **4**, 9–17 (1999)

2. Mountain, V.: Educational contexts for the development of children's spirituality: exploring the use of imagination. Int J Child S Spiritual **12**, 191–205 (2007)
3. Gündoğan, A.: The test of creative imagination: making the test suitable to the age group of 5–6 years. Early Child Dev Care **189**, 1219–1227 (2019)
4. Lindqvist, G.: Vygotsky's theory of creativity. Creat Res J **15**, 245–251 (2003)
5. Duffy, B.: Supporting Creativity And Imagination In The Early Years. McGraw-Hill Education (UK) (2006)
6. Tsai, K.C.: Play, imagination, and creativity: A brief literature review. J Educ Learn **1**, 15–20 (2012)
7. Gajdamaschko, N.: Vygotsky on imagination: Why an understanding of the imagination is an important issue for schoolteachers. Teach. Educ. **16**, 13–22 (2005)
8. Kaufman, K.J.: 21 Ways to 21st Century Skills: Why Students Need Them and Ideas for Practical Implementation. Kappa Delta Pi Record **49**, 78–83 (2013)
9. Sawyer, K.: A call to action: the challenges of creative teaching and learning. Teach Coll Rec **117**, 1–34 (2015)
10. Saracho, O.: Young Children's Creativity and Pretend Play. Early Child Dev Care **172**, 431–438 (2002)
11. Craft, A.: Creative thinking in the early years of education. Early Years **23**, 143–154 (2003)
12. Siew, N.M., Chong, C.L.: Fostering students' creativity through van hiele's 5 phase-based tangram activities. J Educ Learn **3**, 66–80 (2014)
13. Hong, E., Aqui, Y.: Cognitive and motivational characteristics of adolescents gifted in mathematics: comparisons among students with different types of giftedness. Gift Child Q **48**, 191–201 (2004)
14. Haylock, D.W.: A framework for assessing mathematical creativity in school chilren. Educational studies in mathematics. https://doi.org/10.1007/BF00367914
15. Fisher, R.: Expanding minds: developing creative thinking in young learners. CATS: The IATEFL Young Learners SIG Journal
16. Britain, G.: Department for Education and Employment 2000. Developing a Global Dimension in the School
17. Zanzali, N.A.A.: Designing the mathematics curriculum in Malaysia: Making mathematics more meaningful. Universiti Teknologi Malaysia (2000)
18. Erdoğan, T., Akkaya, S.Ç.: The effect of the Van Hiele model based instruction on the creative thinking levels of 6th grade primary school students. Adv Health Sci Educ Theory Pract **9**, 181–194 (2009)
19. Abdullah, A.H., Zakaria, E.: The activities based on Van Hiele's phase-based learning: Experts' and pre-service teachers' views. J. Math. Stat. Allied Fields
20. Copley, J.V.: Geometry and spatial sense in the early childhood curriculum. The young child and mathematics
21. Lin, C.-P., Shao, Y.-J., Wong, L.-H., Li, Y.-J., Niramitranon, J.: The impact of using synchronous collaborative virtual tangram in children's geometric. Turk Online J Educ Technol **10**, 250–258 (2011)
22. Singh, M.: Modern teaching of Mathematics. Anmol Publications PVT, LTD (2005)
23. Tchoshanov, M.: Building students' mathematical proficiency: connecting mathematical ideas using the Tangram. Learning and Teaching Mathematics **2011**, 16–23 (2011)
24. Steinhaus, H.: Mathematical Snapshots. Courier Corporation (1999)
25. Ashman, T.: A playful geometry workshop: Creating 3D polyhedral structures from innovative 2D self-assembling paper folding units. In: Proceedings of Bridges 2014: Mathematics, Music, Art, Architecture, Culture, pp. 485–492 (2014)
26. Smith, S.M., Ward, T.B., Finke, R.A.: The Creative Cognition Approach. MIT Press (1995)
27. Arden, R., Chavez, R.S., Grazioplene, R., Jung, R.E.: Neuroimaging creativity: a psychometric view. Behav Brain Res **214**, 143–156 (2010)

28. Dietrich, A., Kanso, R.: A review of EEG, ERP, and neuroimaging studies of creativity and insight. Psychol Bull **136**, 822–848 (2010)
29. Jauk, E., Benedek, M., Neubauer, A.C.: Tackling creativity at its roots: evidence for different patterns of EEG alpha activity related to convergent and divergent modes of task processing. Int J Psychophysiol **84**, 219–225 (2012)
30. Kumar, J., Kumar, J.: Affective Modelling of Users in HCI Using EEG. Procedia Comput Sci **84**, 107–114 (2016)
31. Antonenko, P., Paas, F., Grabner, R., van Gog, T.: Using electroencephalography to measure cognitive load. Educ Psychol Rev **22**, 425–438 (2010)
32. Zarjam, P., Epps, J., Chen, F.: Spectral EEG featuresfor evaluating cognitive load. In: 2011 Annual International Conference of the IEEE Engineering in Medicine and Biology Society, pp. 3841–3844 (2011)
33. Koelstra, S., et al.: Single Trial Classification of EEG and Peripheral Physiological Signals for Recognition of Emotions Induced by Music Videos. In: Yao, Y., Sun, R., Poggio, T., Liu, J., Zhong, N., Huang, J. (eds.) BI 2010. LNCS (LNAI), vol. 6334, pp. 89–100. Springer, Heidelberg (2010). https://doi.org/10.1007/978-3-642-15314-3_9
34. Lee, Y.-Y., Hsieh, S.: Classifying different emotional states by means of EEG-based functional connectivity patterns. PLoS ONE **9**, e95415 (2014)
35. Chen, J., Hu, B., Moore, P., Zhang, X., Ma, X.: Electroencephalogram-based emotion assessment system using ontology and data mining techniques. Appl Soft Comput **30**, 663–674 (2015)
36. Collet, C., Vernet-Maury, E., Delhomme, G., Dittmar, A.: Autonomic nervous system response patterns specificity to basic emotions. J Auton Nerv Syst **62**, 45–57 (1997)
37. Leiner, D., Fahr, A., Früh, H.: EDA positive change: a simple algorithm for electrodermal activity to measure general audience arousal during media exposure. Commun Methods Meas **6**, 237–250 (2012)
38. Alexander, D.M., Trengove, C., Johnston, P., Cooper, T., August, J.P., Gordon, E.: Separating individual skin conductance responses in a short interstimulus-interval paradigm. J Neurosci Methods **146**, 116–123 (2005)

Digital Fabrication in Arts and Crafts Education: A Critical Review

Susanne Stigberg$^{(\boxtimes)}$ ⓘ, Fahad Faisal Said ⓘ, and Daniela Blauhut

Department of Computer Science and Communication, Høgskolen i Østfold,
Halden, Norway
{susannks,fahad.f.said,daniela.blauhut}@hiof.no

Abstract. This article presents a critical review of research on digital fabrication in K-12 arts and crafts education. We provide an overview of the research field from two perspectives: 1) digital fabrication technologies and classroom practices, and 2) applied theoretical frameworks and research methodologies. Results show that robotics, e-textiles and 3D are the most common digital fabrication themes in arts and crafts education. In the typical DF research project, a qualitative paradigm is chosen, and learning is described from a constructionist perspective. We conclude the article with two specific opportunities for consolidating research on digital fabrication for arts and crafts education.

Keywords: Digital fabrication · arts & crafts education · critical review

1 Introduction

Digital fabrication (DF) is "the process of translating a digital design developed on a computer into a physical object" [8]. DF technologies such as 3D-printers, embroidery machines, laser cutters or vinyl cutters, have become affordable and can be found at Makerspaces and FabLabs around the world. These tools enable people to create professionally looking items rapidly and at a relatively low cost. Blickstein [9] argues that DF and making can play a major role in education, "bringing powerful ideas, literacies, and expressive tools to children". In recent years, there have been efforts to introduce programming and digital technologies into arts and crafts (A&C) curricula [22]. Teachers have started to implement DF in A&C education in order to introduce programming, making and design thinking to students [1]. We see a plethora of possibilities for DF in A&C education including accessibility, versatility, collaboration, customization, automation and innovation. Digital fabrication can offer a different approach to making, enable students to experiment with new materials and techniques, facilitate alternative forms of collaboration among students and inspire students to pursue innovative approaches to arts and crafts, using technology to push boundaries of traditional crafting techniques. In this paper, we review previous research on DF in K-12 A&C education to understand what DF technologies have been utilized so far and how DF has been incorporated in A&C education.

P. Zaphiris and A. Ioannou (Eds.): HCII 2023, LNCS 14040, pp. 642–657, 2023.
https://doi.org/10.1007/978-3-031-34411-4_44

2   Method

We carried out a systematic literature review (SLR) with the objective to synthesize existing studies on DF in K-12 A&C education. The review follows the Preferred Reporting Items for Systematic Reviews and Meta-Analysis (PRISMA 2020) guidelines [42], a well-established standard for documenting reviews. Before conducting the SLR, we assessed its novelty. There exists a number of literature reviews on DF in education. In their study, Iivari et al. [24] conduct a critical analysis of current research on DF and making with children. The aim of their analysis was to determine the potential for DF and making to empower children as future digital innovators. Stigberg [48] presents a critical review on digital fabrication for creating teaching material for mathematics education and Hansen et al. [19] systematically review literature on 3D-printing for biological education. DF is strongly related to STEAM education. Conde et al. [12] review how STEAM can be integrated into curricula through the use of robotics and mechatronics and challenge-based learning, to aid the acquisition of digital literacy and 21st-century skills. However, to the best of our knowledge, an SLR that focuses on DF studies in K-12 A&C education does not exist. To guide our SLR, we formulated two research questions (RQi) as follows:

RQ1: What has been reported on DF in K-12 A&C education focusing on DF technologies and classroom activities?

RQ2: What characterizes research on DF in K-12 A&C education?

2.1   Information Sources and Search

Our research objective is covered by an interdisciplinary research field with a research community in computer science and HCI as well as educational sciences. To take into account this diversity, we decided to search in three databases: ACM Digital Library, IEEE Xplore and Ebsco. ACM Digital Library host relevant conferences such as FabLearn and Child-Computer-Interaction, IEEE Xplore includes journals and conferences on STEM education and Ebsco is a well-known educational research database.

Time Frame: DF and making in education is a growing research area. The first FabLearn conference was held in 2011 in Standford, USA [2]. In 2013, Blinkstein wrote his manifest on "Digital fabrication and 'making' in education: The democratization of invention" [9]. Accordingly, we included studies from the last ten years to explore state of the art of DF in A&C education.
`"filter": {"publicationYear":{ "gte":2013 }}`

Search Query: We searched for publications with keywords connected to digital fabrication in title, abstract or keywords. We included *digital fabrication*; *3d,3D* and *laser cutter* as most common digital fabrication tools; as well as *programming* to extent our search. Furthermore publications should report on K-12 educational studies. We added the keywords *school* and *education*. Finally,

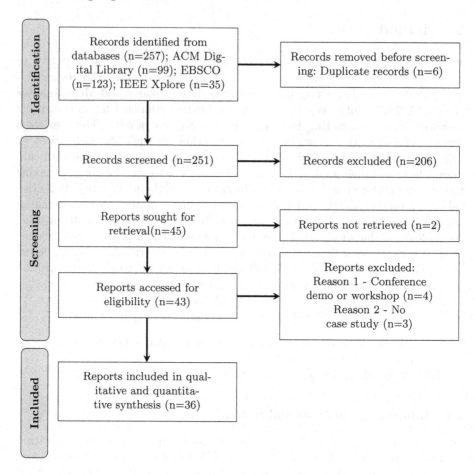

Fig. 1. PRISMA flow diagram of research paper selection process

we are interested in arts and crafts education, including keywords *arts*, *crafts* and *STEAM* to the search query. STEAM stands for Science, Technology, Engineering, Arts and Mathematics and is an educational approach that integrates these subjects in a interdisciplinary and applied learning approach (e.g. [21]). To exclude education on university level as well as informal education we added three exclusion keywords *university*, *informal* and *extracurricular*.

The final search query used in the ACM digital library:

```
("digital fabrication" OR 3D OR 3d OR programming OR "laser
cutter") AND (arts OR crafts OR STEAM) AND (education OR school)
AND NOT university AND NOT (informal OR extracurricular)
```

The search queries for the other two databases are formulated accordingly.

2.2 Eligibility Criteria

A publication is eligible for review if it fits the following inclusion criteria:

- The publication is a peer-reviewed article, report, white paper, thesis, or book.
- The publication describes a study in K-12 education
- The publication describes a digital fabrication tool or techniques.
- The publication focuses on arts & crafts education.

A publication is excluded if:

- The full text version is not accessible.
- It is not written in English.
- It does not report from a field study or intervention.

2.3 Study Selection and Data Collection Process

The study selection process is represented by means of the PRISMA 2020 flow diagram (see Fig. 1). A total of 257 publications were identified during the initial search. Six publications were excluded because of duplication. 206 publications were excluded as a result of assessing the abstract against inclusion criteria. 45 full-text articles were accessed for eligibility. Two publications were excluded because there was no full-text available. Furthermore, seven publications were excluded as they were presenting a workshop or demonstration at conferences, or did not report from a field study or intervention. Finally, the remaining 36 publications were included in the review synthesis. The included publications can be found in Table 1. The complete search can be found at shorturl.at/glABZ.

Table 1. Overview of included reports

Ref.	Year	Author(s)	Title
[25]	2013	Cross et al.	A visual robot-programming environment for multidisciplinary education
[30]	2014	Kafai et al.	A Crafts-Oriented Approach to Computing in High School: Introducing Computational Concepts, Practices, and Perspectives with Electronic Textiles
[46]	2014	Searle et al.	Diversifying High School Students' Views about Computing with Electronic Textiles
[43]	2014	Tillinghast et al.	Integrating three dimensional visualization and additive manufacturing into K-12 classrooms
[32]	2015	Kafai & Vasudevan	Hi-Lo Tech Games: Crafting, Coding and Collaboration of Augmented Board Games by High School Youth
[31]	2015	Kafai & Vasudavan	Constructionist Gaming Beyond the Screen: Middle School Students' Crafting and Computing of Touchpads, Board Games, and Controllers

(continued)

Table 1. (*continued*)

Ref.	Year	Author(s)	Title
[47]	2015	Searle & Kafai	Boys' Needlework: Understanding Gendered and Indigenous Perspectives on Computing and Crafting with Electronic Textiles
[4]	2015	Baek et al.	Application of Intelligent Product Design on STEAM Education
[26]	2015	Cross et al.	Arts & Bots: Application and outcomes of a secondary school robotics program
[28]	2016	Jeon et al.	Making Live Theatre with Multiple Robots as Actors: Bringing Robots to Rural Schools to Promote STEAM Education for Underserved Students
[17]	2016	Gross & Gross	Transformation: Constructivism, Design Thinking, and Elementary STEAM
[13]	2016	Hamner et al.	Training teachers to integrate engineering into non-technical middle school curriculum
[14]	2016	Fields et a.l.	Deconstruction Kits for Learning: Students' Collaborative Debugging of Electronic Textile Designs
[27]	2016	Kennedy et al.	STEAM approach by integrating the arts and STEM through origami in K-12
[41]	2017	Ngamka-jornwiwat et al.	Understanding the role of arts and humanities in social robotics design: An experiment for STEAM enrichment program in Thailand
[23]	2017	Hughes	Digital making with "At-Risk" youth.
[33]	2017	Kekelis et al.	Making and Mentors: What It Takes to Make Them Better Together
[6]	2017	Barnes et al.	Child-Robot Theater: STEAM Education in an Afterschool Program
[37]	2017	Litts et al.	Understanding High School Students' Reading, Remixing, and Writing Codeable Circuits for Electronic Textiles
[5]	2018	Baker & Alexander	A Major Making Undertaking: A New Librarian Transforms A Middle School Library into a Makerspace Aligned to High School Career Endorsements
[49]	2018	Sullivan & Bers	Dancing Robots: Integrating Art, Music, and Robotics in Singapore's Early Childhood Centers
[45]	2018	Pandian	Playful STEAM Learning Using Robots
[11]	2018	Chien & Chu	The Different Learning Outcomes of High School and College Students on a 3D-Printing STEAM Engineering Design Curriculum.
[39]	2019	Milara et al.	The STEAM Path: Building a Community of Practice for Local Schools around STEAM and Digital Fabrication
[40]	2019	Montero	Fostering Creativity Self-Perception in Formal Learning through Digital Fabrication and Making

(*continued*)

Table 1. (*continued*)

Ref.	Year	Author(s)	Title
[29]	2019	Kafai et al.	Stitching the Loop with Electronic Textiles: Promoting Equity in High School Students' Competencies and Perceptions of Computer Science
[7]	2019	Barnes et al.	Informal STEAM Education Case Study: Child-Robot Musical Theater
[35]	2020	Ko et al.	Robot-Theater Programs for Different Age Groups to Promote STEAM Education and Robotics Research
[36]	2021	Lemonica Rosa	Social Necklace Project: A Student-Made Gadget to Help People during the COVID19 Pandemic
[44]	2021	Misthou et al.	Coding Club: a K-12 good practice for a STEM learning community
[15]	2021	Grasselli	Digital Sculptors
[18]	2021	Guridi	Arpilleras Parlantes: Designing Educational Material for the Creation of Interactive Textile Art Based on a Traditional Chilean Craft.
[38]	2021	Martinéz Moreno et al.	Maker Education in Primary Education: Changes in Students' Maker-Mindset and Gender Differences
[3]	2021	Alves Oliveira et al.	Robotics-Based Interventions for Children's Creativity
[50]	2022	Tenhovirta et al.	Cross-age peer tutoring in a technology-enhanced STEAM project at a lower secondary school
[10]	2022	Buxton et al.	Developing a Makerspace Learning and Assessment Framework

2.4   Data Extraction and Synthesis

We used Zotero to extract attributes from the selected publications in an automatic fashion, such as title, author(s) name(s), publication year, publication source and keywords. In addition, all three authors extracted data regarding classroom practices including school level, DF technologies, and teaching activities (RQ1), as well as research characteristics such as theoretical framework and methodology including data collection and analysis (RQ2). Previous literature has introduced two data synthesis approaches: descriptive/narrative and quantitative data synthesis [34]. This study adopts a mixed synthesis approach to encompass a quantitative description of previous work as well as a qualitative approach identifying themes to answer our research questions.

Table 2. Reports screened by inclusion criteria

Journal	Screened	DF	K-12	A&C	Retrieval	Included
IEEE	35	15	18	10	8	8
EBSCO	123	15	66	36	10	8
ACM	99	38	44	37	27	20
Total	257	68	128	83	45	36

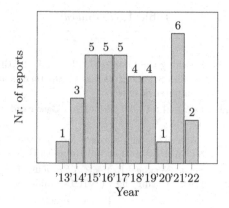

Fig. 2. Reports grouped by year

3 Results

There is limited research on DF in A&C education (36) scattered across a range
of research fields e.g. human computer interaction focusing on robots and children, educational technology, computer science education and digital fabrication.
We found an average of 3,6 publications per year, with a maximum of 6 publications in 2021 and a minimum of 1 publication in 2013 and 2020 (see Fig. 2).
A vast majority of the initially selected publications (257) present research on
STEAM or programming and do not mention DF technologies (189) or A&C
education (174) specifically in the abstract. Frequently, studies present interdisciplinary projects that aim to enhance students' computational thinking and
innovation skills. 129 publications were excluded, as they dealt with research on
university-level or lifelong learning interventions. Table 2 provides an overview
of screened and retrieved records by inclusion criteria. Lastly, two records were
excluded due to missing full text and seven records did not present a field study
or intervention. We have analysed the remaining 36 publications from two perspectives: Firstly, focusing on applied DF technologies and classroom practices.
Secondly, focusing on theoretical frameworks and research methodologies.

3.1 What Has Been Reported on DF in K-12 A&C Education
Focusing on DF Technologies and Classroom Practices?

We found three programs related to DF in A&C education: robotics (12), e-
textiles (7) and 3D (5). We defined a DF program as an emerging theme in the
review with more than three associated publications.

Robotics are used as an approach to integrate STEAM and computing in
A&C education. We found examples of playing with ready-made robots, pseudo
coding and block programming in K-5 education [3,6,7,28,35,49] and building robots using electronics, sensors, actuators and programming (e.g. Arduino)

aimed at middle and high school students [4, 13, 25, 26, 41, 45]. Robots are used to play theatre [6, 7, 28, 35], design social interactions such as dancing [49] or expressing emotions [41], and for creating interactive installations [13, 25, 26] and applications [4].

E-textiles research explores crafts-oriented approaches to programming and computing [14, 18, 30, 37] and investigates if these approaches facilitate more inclusive computer science education focusing on diversity and equity [29, 46, 47].

3D research investigates how 3D modelling and printing can be utilized in A&C education, not focusing on programming. Grasselli [15] explores new forms of sculpturing experimenting with different sculpting materials such as clay, 3D pen, digital manipulation, and 3D printing. Tillinghast et al. [43] discuss different approaches to include 3D modelling and printing in K-12 classroom. Chien and Chu [11] investigate high school students skills in 3d modelling and printing to materialize design ideas. Kennedy et al. [27] propose an origami based curriculum focusing on 3d modelling and printing to integrate arts with mathematics and engineering topics.

Two publications present the design of board games as a way to introduce DF and computing in A&C education [31, 32]. Other DF technologies, found in the review, are MakeyMakey [38], microbit [36], and paper electronics [23]. Seven publications discuss aspects of DF and making in A&C education without mentioning specific technologies [5, 10, 17, 33, 39, 44, 50]. Figure 3 presents an overview of publications grouped by DF themes and K-12 level. DF and making is mainly introduced to students in middle or high school (30). However, we found two publications that focus on kindergarten level [10, 49]. Sullivan and Bers [49] present a case study on how pre-schoolers can learn about coding by integrating art, music, and robotics. Buxton [10] proposes a makerspace learning and assessment framework for younger children. Nine studies investigate DF for elementary school students up to 10 years using predominately robotics (e.g., [3, 6, 7, 28, 35]). Studies on

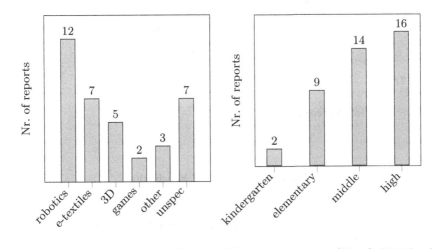

Fig. 3. Reports grouped by (Left):Digital Fabrication themes, (Right): K-12 level

e-textiles were aimed exclusively at high school students [14,18,29,30,37,46,47]. Research on DF in A&C education focuses on hands-on activities in workshops and project work in groups as teaching approaches. Teaching periods varied between publications from short-term (e.g. 1–3 weeks [47]) to long-term projects (e.g. [23,28]).

3.2 What Characterizes Research on DF in K-12 A&C Education?

Research on DF in A&C education is scattered over several research communities. We could find three research clusters in our review, focusing on robotics (see Fig. 4) and e-textiles (see Fig. 5). We used VOSViewer [51] to search for research clusters by mapping researchers' co-authorship from the bibliometric data. We draw a link between authors if they have co-authored a minimum of two publications. The complete network map can be found at https://tinyurl.com/22ma9cbx. We found two research communities, situated in the United States, investigating robotics in A&C education. Jeon, Barnes, Vasey, Duford, Fakhrhosseini and Ryan explored how robotics can be utilized to implement STEAM projects in elementary education (K-5) using theatre play [6,7,28,35]. Cross, Hamner, Bartley, Nourbakhsh inquired how robotics and programming can be utilized in different subjects by creating interactive installations in their Arts and Bots project for middle school students [13,25,26]. E-textile research is dominated by one research cluster from the United States. Kafai, Fields, Lui, Searle, Vasudevan, and Walker explore the use of e-textiles as crafts-oriented approach to computer science to diversify students' perception of computing [14,29,30,37,46,47]. Kafai and Vasudevan have also collaborated on publications exploring board games to promote computational thinking in our review [31,32].

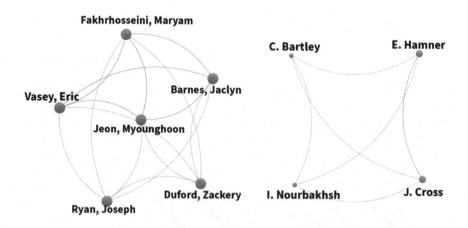

Fig. 4. Researcher clusters in robotics

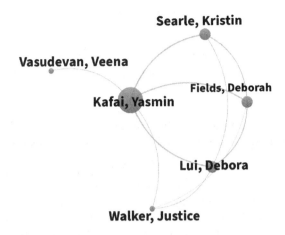

Fig. 5. Reseacher cluster in e-textiles

Methodology. The included studies typically take place within a classroom environment and show a significant range in student participation, with an average of 50 participants. The smallest number of participants is 4 [25], while the largest number is 239 [38]. Our review identified 20 qualitative studies [5,7,10,13–15,17,18,23,25,30–33,35,39,46,47,49,50] that utilized interviews, observations, video logs, or diaries as their data sources. The most common method of analysis was thematic analysis, used to identify and understand different perspectives, and to uncover the underlying patterns and themes in the data. Most studies used multiple data sources to provide a rich and diverse set of insights into their research questions. Furthermore, we found 13 quantitative studies [3,4,6,11,26,27,29,36–38,40,41,44] that employed pre/post surveys, self-assessment questionnaires, or assessment tasks as data sources. The most commonly used method of analysis was Analysis of Variance (ANOVA) to determine the impact of the DF interventions. Three publications do not state data collection and analysis methods [28,43,45].

Theoretical Framework. Constructionism was the most frequently cited theoretical framework in our review [15,17,28,31,32,36,41,44,49,50], followed by STEAM [3,4,6,7,11,27,38], computational thinking [25,30,31], and various social-cultural learning theories such as Zone of Proximal Development [17,50], crafts-oriented theories [30,46], Community of Practice [5,39]. Other less frequently mentioned frameworks include theories on identity work [47] or creativity [40]. Constructionism is a learning theory that emphasizes the importance of hands-on and experiential learning [20]. According to this theory, students are more likely to understand and retain new information when they actively construct their own understanding through practical activities and real-world experiences. This perspective has been used to support the idea of DF and programming as well as to argue for hands-on activities and project-based teaching.

4   Discussion

Critical reflecting on the review findings, we put forward two opportunities for the research community to enhance and expand the field of research on DF in K-12 A&C education.

4.1   Opportunity: Exploring the Interplay of Artistic Expression, Crafting Techniques and Diverse DF Technologies

The major motivations for including DF in A&C education in this review were to introduce STEAM (e.g., [11,27,39,41]) and computational thinking (e.g., [25,32, 37]) for K-12 students. A significant number of publications suggest that students enjoy computing-oriented activities and that DF approaches make programming more accessible, creative and diverse. Multiple articles argue that it is necessary to include programming and computing not only in STEM courses, but also in arts education to support students diversity and equity (e.g. [11,31,32,38]). Our review revealed three major themes presented in this articles: robotics, e-textiles and 3D. We did not find articles presenting DF technologies such as embroidery machines, laser cutter, or vinyl cutter. It is necessary to explore diverse DF technologies and investigate how these can change or extend traditional crafting techniques such as sewing, manual shaping or modelling with clay. Material selection and material combination play an important role in A&C education. Considering the possibilities of DF technologies, it is important to explore these alternative material experiences with DF technologies. Grasselli [15] inquired into new forms of sculpturing experimenting with different sculpting materials such as clay, 3D pen, digital manipulation, and 3D printing. We see an opportunity for more in-depth exploration of the impact of DF technologies and materials on crafting techniques, material exploration and artistic expressions in A&C education.

4.2   Opportunity: Exploring Alternative Theoretical Perspectives on DF in A&C Education

The reviewed publications present intervention-based studies evaluating DF approaches against pre-defined research objectives. We did not find purely field studies that describe how teachers use DF in A&C education. Moreover, there is a lack of design cases and exemplars that showcase DF in A&C education, sharing teaching practices and strengthening the DF research community. Most publications frame their studies using theories of STEAM, computational thinking or constructionism. We found sporadic examples of alternative theoretical frameworks, e.g., creativity [40] or identity work [47]. There is an opportunity to re-frame DF research using theories related to A&C education e.g., aesthetics education [16], design theories, material culture studies, or artistic perspectives.

5 Conclusion

This paper presents a SLR on DF in K-12 A&C education. We identified 257 records from three databases and selected 36 publications for the synthesis. We analysed publications from two perspectives: 1) digital fabrication technologies and classroom practices, and 2) applied theoretical frameworks and research methodologies. Results show that robotics, e-textiles and 3D are the most common DF themes in A&C education and that STEAM projects and programming skills are predominantly motivations for including DF in A&C education. We believe that there is an opportunity to explore diverse DF technologies and investigate how DF can change or extend traditional crafting techniques and artistic expressions. In the typical DF research project, a qualitative paradigm is chosen, and learning is described from a constructionist perspective. We advocate for expanding the theoretical foundation of DF research to encompass artistic theories such as aesthetics education [16], design theories, material culture studies, or artistic perspectives.

References

1. Eva bryter traditionerna med slöjd och programmering. https://skolvarlden.se/artiklar/eva-bryter-traditionerna-med-slojd-och-programmering
2. FabLearn Conferences. https://fablearn.org/conferences/
3. Alves-Oliveira, P., Arriaga, P., Nogueira, S.I., Paiva, A.: Robotics-based interventions for children's creativity. In: Creativity and Cognition. C&C 2021. Association for Computing Machinery, New York (2021). https://doi.org/10.1145/3450741.3465267
4. Baek, C., Choi, J.J., Han, J., Kwak, S.: Application of intelligent product design on STEAM education. In: Proceedings of the 3rd International Conference on Human-Agent Interaction, HAI 2015, pp. 249–250. Association for Computing Machinery, New York (2015). https://doi.org/10.1145/2814940.2814988
5. Baker, S., Alexander, B.: A major making undertaking: a new librarian transforms a middle school library into a makerspace aligned to high school career endorsements. Knowl. Quest **46**(5), 64–69 (2018)
6. Barnes, J., FakhrHosseini, M., Vasey, E., Duford, Z., Ryan, J., Jeon, M.: Child-robot theater: STEAM education in an afterschool program. In: Proceedings of the Companion of the 2017 ACM/IEEE International Conference on Human-Robot Interaction, HRI 2017, p. 404. Association for Computing Machinery, New York (2017). https://doi.org/10.1145/3029798.3036643
7. Barnes, J., FakhrHosseini, M., Vasey, E., Park, C.H., Jeon, M.: Informal STEAM education case study: child-robot musical theater. In: Extended Abstracts of the 2019 CHI Conference on Human Factors in Computing Systems, CHI EA 2019, pp. 1–6. Association for Computing Machinery, New York (2019). https://doi.org/10.1145/3290607.3312890
8. Berry, R.Q., Bull, G., Browning, C., Thomas, C.D., Starkweather, G., Aylor, J.: Use of digital fabrication to incorporate engineering design principles in elementary mathematics education. Contemp. Issues Technol. Teach. Educ. **10**(2), 167–172 (2010)

9. Blikstein, P.: Digital fabrication and 'making' in education: the democratization of invention. In: FabLabs: Of Machines, Makers and Inventors, vol. 4, no. 1, pp. 1–21 (2013)
10. Buxton, A., Kay, L., Nutbrown, B.: Developing a makerspace learning and assessment framework. In: 6th FabLearn Europe/MakeEd Conference 2022. FabLearn Europe/MakeEd 2022. Association for Computing Machinery, New York (2022). https://doi.org/10.1145/3535227.3535232
11. Chien, Y.H., Chu, P.Y.: The different learning outcomes of high school and college students on a 3D-printing STEAM engineering design curriculum. Int. J. Sci. Math. Educ. 16(6), 1047–1064 (2018)
12. Conde, M., Rodríguez-Sedano, F.J., Fernández-Llamas, C., Gonçalves, J., Lima, J., García-Peñalvo, F.J.: Fostering STEAM through challenge-based learning, robotics, and physical devices: a systematic mapping literature review. Comput. Appl. Eng. Educ. 29(1), 46–65 (2021). https://doi.org/10.1002/cae.22354
13. Hamner, E., Cross, J., Zito, L., Bernstein, D., Mutch-Jones, K.: Training teachers to integrate engineering into non-technical middle school curriculum. In: 2016 IEEE Frontiers in Education Conference (FIE), pp. 1–9 (2016). https://doi.org/10.1109/FIE.2016.7757528
14. Fields, D., Searle, K., Kafai, Y.: Deconstruction kits for learning: students' collaborative debugging of electronic textile designs. In: Proceedings of the 6th Annual Conference on Creativity and Fabrication in Education, FabLearn 2016, pp. 82–85. Association for Computing Machinery, New York (2016). https://doi.org/10.1145/3003397.3003410
15. Grasselli, M.G.: Digital Sculptors. J. E-Learn. Knowl. Soc. 17(3), 18–23 (2021)
16. Greene, M.: The spaces of aesthetic education. J. Aesthetic Educ. 20(4), 56–62 (1986). https://doi.org/10.2307/3332600
17. Gross, K., Gross, S.: Transformation: constructivism, design thinking, and elementary STEAM. Art Educ. 69(6), 36–43 (2016)
18. Guridi, S., Vicencio, T., Gajardo, R.: Arpilleras parlantes: designing educational material for the creation of interactive textile art based on a traditional chilean craft. In: Proceedings of the Fifteenth International Conference on Tangible, Embedded, and Embodied Interaction, TEI 2021. Association for Computing Machinery, New York (2021). https://doi.org/10.1145/3430524.3440657
19. Hansen, A.K., Langdon, T.R., Mendrin, L.W., Peters, K., Ramos, J., Lent, D.D.: Exploring the potential of 3D-printing in biological education: a review of the literature. Integr. Comp. Biol. 60(4), 896–905 (2020)
20. Harel, I.E., Papert, S.E.: Constructionism. Ablex Publishing (1991)
21. Hasti, H., Amo-Filva, D., Fonseca, D., Verdugo-Castro, S., García-Holgado, A., García-Peñalvo, F.J.: Towards closing STEAM diversity gaps: a grey review of existing initiatives. Appl. Sci. 12(24), 12666 (2022). https://doi.org/10.3390/app122412666
22. Hoebeke, S., Strand, I., Haakonsen, P.: Programming as a new creative material in art and design education. Techne serien - Forskning i slöjdpedagogik och slöjdvetenskap 28(2), 233–240 (2021)
23. Hughes, J.M.: Digital making with "At-Risk" youth. Int. J. Inf. Learn. Technol. 34(2), 102–113 (2017)
24. Iivari, N., Molin-Juustila, T., Kinnula, M.: The future digital innovators: empowering the young generation with digital fabrication and making (2016)

25. Cross, J., Bartley, C., Hamner, E., Nourbakhsh, I.: A visual robot-programming environment for multidisciplinary education. In: 2013 IEEE International Conference on Robotics and Automation, pp. 445–452 (2013). https://doi.org/10.1109/ICRA.2013.6630613

26. Cross, J., Hamner, E., Bartley, C., Nourbakhsh, I.: Arts & bots: application and outcomes of a secondary school robotics program. In: 2015 IEEE Frontiers in Education Conference (FIE), pp. 1–9 (2015). https://doi.org/10.1109/FIE.2015.7344375

27. Kennedy, J., Lee, E., Fontecchio, A.: STEAM approach by integrating the arts and STEM through origami in K-12. In: 2016 IEEE Frontiers in Education Conference (FIE), pp. 1–5 (2016). https://doi.org/10.1109/FIE.2016.7757415

28. Jeon, M., et al.: Making live theatre with multiple robots as actors: bringing robots to rural schools to promote STEAM education for underserved students. In: The Eleventh ACM/IEEE International Conference on Human Robot Interaction, HRI 2016, pp. 445–446. IEEE Press (2016)

29. Kafai, Y., et al.: Stitching the loop with electronic textiles: promoting equity in high school students' competencies and perceptions of computer science. In: Proceedings of the 50th ACM Technical Symposium on Computer Science Education, SIGCSE 2019, pp. 1176–1182. Association for Computing Machinery, New York (2019). https://doi.org/10.1145/3287324.3287426

30. Kafai, Y., Lee, E., Searle, K., Fields, D., Kaplan, E., Lui, D.: A crafts-oriented approach to computing in high school: introducing computational concepts, practices, and perspectives with electronic textiles. ACM Trans. Comput. Educ. 14(1) (2014). https://doi.org/10.1145/2576874

31. Kafai, Y., Vasudevan, V.: Constructionist gaming beyond the screen: middle school students' crafting and computing of touchpads, board games, and controllers. In: Proceedings of the Workshop in Primary and Secondary Computing Education, WiPSCE 2015, pp. 49–54. Association for Computing Machinery, New York (2015). https://doi.org/10.1145/2818314.2818334

32. Kafai, Y., Vasudevan, V.: Hi-Lo tech games: crafting, coding and collaboration of augmented board games by high school youth. In: Proceedings of the 14th International Conference on Interaction Design and Children, IDC 2015, pp. 130–139. Association for Computing Machinery, New York (2015). https://doi.org/10.1145/2771839.2771853

33. Kekelis, L., Ryoo, J.J., McLeod, E.: Making and mentors: what it takes to make them better together. Afterschool Matters 26, 8–17 (2017)

34. Kitchenham, B.A., Charters, S.: Guidelines for performing systematic literature reviews in software engineering. Technical report, EBSE 2007-001, Keele University (2007)

35. Ko, S., Swaim, H., Sanghavi, H., Dong, J., Nadri, C., Jeon, M.: Robot-theater programs for different age groups to promote STEAM education and robotics research. In: Companion of the 2020 ACM/IEEE International Conference on Human-Robot Interaction, HRI 2020, pp. 299–301. Association for Computing Machinery, New York (2020). https://doi.org/10.1145/3371382.3378353

36. Lemonica Rosa, R.: Social necklace project: a student-made gadget to help people during the COVID19 pandemic. In: FabLearn Europe/MakeEd 2021 - An International Conference on Computing, Design and Making in Education. FabLearn Europe/MakeEd 2021. Association for Computing Machinery, New York (2021). https://doi.org/10.1145/3466725.3466737

37. Litts, B., Kafai, Y., Lui, D., Walker, J., Widman, S.: Understanding high school students' reading, remixing, and writing codeable circuits for electronic textiles. In: Proceedings of the 2017 ACM SIGCSE Technical Symposium on Computer Science Education, SIGCSE 2017, pp. 381–386. Association for Computing Machinery, New York (2017). https://doi.org/10.1145/3017680.3017740

38. Martínez Moreno, J., Santos, P., Hernandez-Leo, D.: Maker education in primary education: changes in students' maker-mindset and gender differences. In: Ninth International Conference on Technological Ecosystems for Enhancing Multiculturality (TEEM 2021), TEEM 2021, pp. 120–125. Association for Computing Machinery, New York (2021). https://doi.org/10.1145/3486011.3486431

39. Milara, I.S., Pitkänen, K., Niva, A., Iwata, M., Laru, J., Riekki, J.: The STEAM path: building a community of practice for local schools around STEAM and digital fabrication. In: Proceedings of the FabLearn Europe 2019 Conference. FabLearn Europe 2019. Association for Computing Machinery, New York (2019). https://doi.org/10.1145/3335055.3335072

40. Montero, C.S.: Fostering creativity self-perception in formal learning through digital fabrication and making. In: Proceedings of the 19th Koli Calling International Conference on Computing Education Research. Koli Calling 2019. Association for Computing Machinery, New York (2019). https://doi.org/10.1145/3364510.3366153

41. Ngamkajornwiwat, P., Pataranutaporn, P., Surareungchai, W., Ngamarunchot, B., Suwinyattichaiporn, T.: Understanding the role of arts and humanities in social robotics design: an experiment for STEAM enrichment program in Thailand. In: 2017 IEEE 6th International Conference on Teaching, Assessment, and Learning for Engineering (TALE), pp. 457–460 (2017). https://doi.org/10.1109/TALE.2017.8252378

42. Page, M.J., et al.: The PRISMA 2020 statement: an updated guideline for reporting systematic reviews. BMJ **372**, n71 (2021). https://doi.org/10.1136/bmj.n71

43. Tillinghast, R.C., et al.: Integrating three dimensional visualization and additive manufacturing into K-12 classrooms. In: 2014 IEEE Integrated STEM Education Conference, pp. 1–7 (2014). https://doi.org/10.1109/ISECon.2014.6891051

44. Misthou, S., Moumoutzis, N., Loukatos, D.: Coding club: a K-12 good practice for a STEM learning community. In: 2021 IEEE Global Engineering Education Conference (EDUCON), pp. 955–963 (2021). https://doi.org/10.1109/EDUCON46332.2021.9454039

45. Pandian, S.R.: Playful STEAM learning using robots. In: 2018 IEEE International Conference on Teaching, Assessment, and Learning for Engineering (TALE), pp. 279–285 (2018). https://doi.org/10.1109/TALE.2018.8615299

46. Searle, K., Fields, D., Lui, D., Kafai, Y.: Diversifying high school students' views about computing with electronic textiles. In: Proceedings of the Tenth Annual Conference on International Computing Education Research, ICER 2014, pp. 75–82. Association for Computing Machinery, New York (2014). https://doi.org/10.1145/2632320.2632352

47. Searle, K., Kafai, Y.: Boys' needlework: understanding gendered and indigenous perspectives on computing and crafting with electronic textiles. In: Proceedings of the Eleventh Annual International Conference on International Computing Education Research, ICER 2015, pp. 31–39. Association for Computing Machinery, New York (2015). https://doi.org/10.1145/2787622.2787724

48. Stigberg, H.: Digital fabrication for mathematics education: a critical review of the field. In: Twelfth Congress of the European Society for Research in Mathematics Education (CERME 2012). Twelfth Congress of the European Society for Research in Mathematics Education (CERME12), vol. TWG22, no 14, Bozen-Bolzano, Italy (2022). https://hal.archives-ouvertes.fr/hal-03753504
49. Sullivan, A., Bers, M.U.: Dancing robots: integrating art, music, and robotics in Singapore's early childhood centers. Int. J. Technol. Des. Educ. **28**(2), 325–346 (2018)
50. Tenhovirta, S., Korhonen, T., Seitamaa-Hakkarainen, P., Hakkarainen, K.: Cross-age peer tutoring in a technology-enhanced STEAM project at a lower secondary school. Int. J. Technol. Des. Educ. **32**(3), 1701–1723 (2022)
51. Waltman, L., van Eck, N.J., Noyons, E.C.M.: A unified approach to mapping and clustering of bibliometric networks. J. Informet. **4**, 629–635 (2010). https://doi.org/10.1016/j.joi.2010.07.002

Correction to: Investigating the Critical Nature of HE Emergency Remote Learning Networks During the COVID-19 Pandemic

Allaa Barefah, Elspeth McKay, and Walaa Barefah

Correction to:
Chapter "Investigating the Critical Nature of HE Emergency Remote Learning Networks During the COVID-19 Pandemic" in: P. Zaphiris and A. Ioannou (Eds.): *Learning and Collaboration Technologies*, **LNCS 14040, https://doi.org/10.1007/978-3-031-34411-4_17**

The original published version of this paper was inadvertently published with the word "Title" at the beginning of the chapter title. The chapter and the book has been updated with the changes.

The updated original version of this chapter can be found at
https://doi.org/10.1007/978-3-031-34411-4_17

Correction to: Discovering Best Practices for Educational Video Conferencing Systems

Tord Talmo and Mikhail Fominykh

Correction to:
Chapter 14 in: P. Zaphiris and A. Ioannou (Eds.):
Learning and Collaboration Technologies, **LNCS 14040,**
https://doi.org/10.1007/978-3-031-34411-4_14

In an older version of this paper, there was error in the author name, "Mikhail Forminykh" was incorrect. This has been corrected to "Mikhail Fominykh".

The updated version of this chapter can be found at
https://doi.org/10.1007/978-3-031-34411-4_14

© The Author(s), under exclusive license to Springer Nature Switzerland AG 2023
P. Zaphiris and A. Ioannou (Eds.): HCII 2023, LNCS 14040, p. C2, 2023.
https://doi.org/10.1007/978-3-031-34411-4_46

Author Index

P. Zaphiris and A. Ioannou (Eds.): HCII 2023, LNCS 14040, pp. 659–662, 2023.
https://doi.org/10.1007/978-3-031-34411-4

Printed in the United States
by Baker & Taylor Publisher Services